The Distributional Aspects
of Social Security and
Social Security Reform

**A National Bureau
of Economic Research
Conference Report**

The Distributional Aspects
of Social Security and
Social Security Reform

Edited by **Martin Feldstein and Jeffrey B. Liebman**

The University of Chicago Press

Chicago and London

MARTIN FELDSTEIN is the George F. Baker Professor of Economics, Harvard University, and president of the National Bureau of Economic Research. JEFFREY B. LIEBMAN is associate professor of public policy at the John F. Kennedy School of Government, Harvard University, and a faculty research fellow of the National Bureau of Economic Research.

The University of Chicago Press, Chicago 60637
The University of Chicago Press, Ltd., London
© 2002 by the National Bureau of Economic Research
All rights reserved. Published 2002
Printed in the United States of America
11 10 09 08 07 06 05 04 03 02   1 2 3 4 5
ISBN: 0-226-24106-8 (cloth)

Library of Congress Cataloging-in-Publication Data

The distributional aspects of social security and social security
    reform / edited by Martin Feldstein and Jeffrey B. Liebman.
        p. cm. — (National Bureau of Economic Research conference
    report)
    Papers presented at a conference held in October of 1999.
    Includes bibliographical references and index.
    ISBN 0-226-24106-8 (cloth : alk. paper)
        1. Social security—United States—Congresses.   2. Social
    security—United States—Finance—Congresses.   3. Pension
    trusts—Investments—United States—Congresses.
    4. Privatization—United States—Congresses.   I. Feldstein,
    Martin S.   II. Leibman, Jeffrey B.   III. Series

    HD7125 .D574 2002
    368.4'3'00973—dc21   2002016568

Contents

Preface

The effects of Social Security reform on the distribution of retirement income is one of the most contentious issues in the policy debate about the future of Social Security in the United States. Opponents of shifting from the existing pay-as-you-go (PAYGO) system to one with an investment-based component worry that the ability of the current program to transfer income to the aged poor, or to those who would otherwise be poor in old age, might be lost in such a change.

There is no doubt that the current U.S. Social Security system has substantially reduced poverty among the aged. Although some of the improved incomes of the aged would have occurred nonetheless, through increased private pensions or individual saving, the official Social Security program and the expansion of the companion means-tested Supplemental Security Insurance program have undoubtedly contributed to that improvement.

There is, however, much confusion about the effect of the existing programs on the distribution of income of the aged and about the way that alternative programs would alter that distribution. The current National Bureau of Economic Research (NBER) project was organized to assess various aspects of the impact of Social Security on the distribution of income and wealth and, more explicitly, to measure the way that a shift to a mixed system with a significant investment-based component would affect those distributions.

This project is part of an integrated series of studies that the NBER has undertaken during the past several years to analyze the feasibility and potential consequences of such a reform. We began this work with a general analysis, in *Privatizing Social Security* (edited by Martin Feldstein, 1998) of the issues that arise in the transition from a pure PAYGO system (such as we have in the United States) to one that includes individual investment-based accounts. That volume contains analytic studies of some aspects of the transition as it might occur in the United States as well as studies of the actual transitions that have occurred in a variety of countries around the world.

John Shoven organized an NBER project on the administrative costs of an investment-based social security system (*Administrative Cost Aspects of Social Security Reform,* 2000), while John Campbell and Martin Feldstein led an NBER project that looked at various risk aspects of the existing Social Security system and of shifting Social Security to investment-based accounts or to mixed systems that include both PAYGO and investment-based portions (*Risk Aspects of Investment-Based Social Security Reform,* 2000). An additional volume, *Social Security Pension Reform in Europe,* will report the results of a project managed by Martin Feldstein and Horst Siebert on the recent European experience and the changes that have been made in most of the countries of western and central Europe.

A large number of NBER researchers, as well as others who are not affiliated with the NBER, have participated in these studies. Preliminary results have been presented and discussed extensively at summer institute sessions and at meetings of the public economics and the aging programs.

The papers in the present volume were presented at a conference in Woodstock, Vermont, in October 1999. Joshua Pollet prepared the summary of the discussion that is included in this volume.

We are grateful to the Ford Foundation for the financial support that made this project possible. We also want to thank the individual members of the NBER staff for their help with the many aspects of the planning and execution of the research, the conference, and the volume. In addition to the researchers and the research assistants named in the individual papers, we want to thank Kirsten Foss Davis, Helena Fitz-Patrick, and Norma MacKenzie for logistical support of the meetings and assistance in the preparation of this volume.

Martin Feldstein
Jeffrey Liebman

Introduction

Martin Feldstein and Jeffrey B. Liebman

Social Security is the largest and probably the most popular program of the federal government. It reduces the number of the aged in poverty and transfers more than 4 percent of gross domestic product (GDP) to retired workers, disabled workers, and their dependents. These benefits are larger than the defense budget and nearly twice as large as the transfers provided by all of the other means-tested programs (including Medicaid, food stamps, et.) combined. For a retiree who has always had the average level of earnings, Social Security benefits equal 42 percent of earnings in the year before retirement. An average-earning retiree with a spouse can receive up to 63 percent of preretirement earnings, depending on the spouse's previous earnings. After benefits begin, they are fully indexed for inflation so that their real value never declines.

It will be difficult but not impossible to maintain this level of generosity in the future, when the increasing life expectancy of the population in general and of retirees in particular will make it substantially more expensive to provide such benefits. Instead of the ratio of three workers per retiree that prevails today, the demographic trend will cause the ratio to fall to two workers per retiree, implying that a 50 percent rise in the payroll tax rate would be needed to maintain the current rules linking benefits to preretirement earnings. The Social Security actuaries estimate that the payroll tax for the Old-Age, Survivors, and Disability Insurance (OASDI) program will eventually have to rise from the present 12.4 percent to 19.0

Martin Feldstein is the George F. Baker Professor of Economics, Harvard University, and president of the National Bureau of Economic Research. Jeffrey B. Liebman is associate professor of public policy at the John F. Kennedy School of Government, Harvard University, and a faculty research fellow of the National Bureau of Economic Research.

percent. The retirement of the employees born in the baby boom years after World War II will accelerate this process, but the problem of rising costs is not the baby boom wave of retirees but the longer-term increase in longevity (and decline in fertility), and therefore the increase in the relative number of retirees.

The projected cost increases have led to a variety of alternative proposals to close the gap between the projected tax receipts and benefits: slowing the growth of future benefits, raising tax revenue, investing the OASDI trust fund in private financial assets, and shifting from a pure pay-as-you-go (PAYGO) system to one with investment-based personal retirement accounts. As the papers in this volume show, the distributional consequences of these different proposals vary substantially.

Researchers at the National Bureau of Economic Research (NBER) have been engaged for several years in studying alternative Social Security reforms, particularly reforms that would involve using investment-based personal retirement accounts to augment the benefits from PAYGO taxes. These analyses have focused on the aggregate national effects of such reforms and on the potential experience of a typical middle-income employee. The studies in the present volume go beyond the previous work by looking at how the current system and alternative reforms would affect a variety of groups, particularly those groups who now depend on Social Security to avoid poverty in old age: women (especially those who are widowed or divorced at a relatively early age), workers with low education or low earnings, and others who are less likely than average to have additional private saving or pension incomes and more likely to have irregular employment histories.

Previous NBER Studies of Social Security Reform

Before discussing these distributional aspects of Social Security and Social Security reform, it is helpful to put the current studies into the context of the broader analysis of Social Security reform in earlier NBER studies. Our research began with an investigation of the economic feasibility of a transition from the current PAYGO system to one with either a pure investment-based system or a mixture of PAYGO and investment-based accounts, while providing the benefits to current and future retirees that are promised in current law. This research included studies of the experience in a number of other countries that had successfully made such a transition as well as detailed calculations of what would be required in the United States. A basic conclusion of this research was that such a transition is feasible: Contributing a small additional fraction of payroll earnings to personal retirement accounts that are invested in portfolios of stocks and bonds would permit a gradual reduction in future PAYGO benefits, while maintaining a combined benefit from the two sources that is at least as large as the benefits promised by current law. The ability of a large number of countries in different parts of the world to achieve such a transition suggested that it would be possible in practice as well as in our computations. The results of these studies are presented in Feldstein (1998). Subsequent studies, including Feldstein and Samwick (1997, 1998), provide more detailed and realistic calculations of the transition process.

This first set of studies did not deal explicitly with the risks involved in either the existing PAYGO system or the alternative systems that rely, at least in part, on investment in stocks and bonds. The PAYGO system is subject to the uncertainty created by possible fluctuations in growth rates of productivity and labor force that alter the implicit return on Social Security PAYGO taxes. A PAYGO system is also subject to the political uncertainty of whether future generations of taxpayers will be willing to pay the higher taxes necessary to finance benefits at a time when the rate of return is less than that available in private pensions.[1] The NBER project presented in Campbell and Feldstein (2001) analyzed these PAYGO risks and the risks inherent in a variety of investment-based systems. Separate studies considered the risks if the investments were held in a single government investment account, as well as the risks involved in individual personal retirement accounts. Based on the stochastic distribution of returns on stocks and bonds over the past fifty years, a mixed system that combines PAYGO and investment-based components could be designed in a way that would involve very little risk that retirees would receive less than the benefits projected under current law. Such a system could nevertheless have a substantially smaller long-run total cost to future employees than would be required in a pure PAYGO system.[2]

Finally, John Shoven organized a project to examine the issues involved in administering an investment-based system and the costs of doing so (Shoven 2000). Those studies show that the costs of managing the funds are small relative to the potential costs involved in collecting funds from individuals, maintaining records of individual accounts, mailing regular account statements to investors, and answering phone calls from investors. Goldberg and Graetz (1999) described a low-cost system of individual accounts in which funds are collected from employers as part of the Social

---

1. This political uncertainty appears to be the reason that the Roosevelt administration originally proposed a funded system. Treasury Secretary Henry Morgenthau testified in 1935 to the Ways and Means Committee that "There are some who believe that we can meet this problem as we go by borrowing from the future to pay the costs. . . . They would place all confidence in the taxing power of the future to meet the needs as they arise. We do not share this view. We cannot safely expect future generations to continue to divert such large sums to the support of the aged unless we lighten the burden upon the future in other directions. . . . We desire to establish this system on such sound foundations that it can be continued indefinitely in the future" (Costa 1999, 173).

2. During the transition period, the total of account contributions and PAYGO taxes would be more than under the pure PAYGO approach.

Security tax but invested in privately managed individual accounts by firms designated by employees.

Distributional Aspects: Some Key Conclusions

The present volume looks at the effects of alternative Social Security reforms on a variety of population groups and examines the distributional effects of the current Social Security system. Six findings in these studies strike us as particularly important.

First, despite the very substantial current spending of the Social Security program, there are significant gaps in the protection provided to the existing elderly. Some 10.5 percent of those over age sixty-five are officially classified as poor. Among elderly women who are widowed, divorced, or never married, 19 percent have incomes below the poverty line. Average benefits for a retired worker are only $9,360 a year (the official poverty line for an elderly individual is $7,818 and is $9,863 for an elderly couple).

Second, the various means of cutting benefits that have been proposed in the political debate as alternatives to higher taxes (reducing the cost-of-living adjustment, altering the benefit formula, increasing the number of years used in calculating average lifetime earnings, raising the retirement age, etc.) would distribute their cuts differently, but all would have a significant adverse effect on the standard of living of future retires.

Third, the existing system is not nearly as redistributive as the benefit formula would imply. The formula that specifies higher annual benefits per dollar of contribution for those with low-average earnings is substantially offset by the higher mortality rates among individuals with low levels of income and education. The higher mortality rates mean that such individuals are less likely to receive any benefits, and that those who do begin to receive benefits will do so for a shorter period of time. The lack of bequests in the PAYGO program substantially reduces the rate of return for these high-mortality groups. The higher benefits provided to the spouses of high-income workers also reduces the progressivity of the system.

Fourth, continuing the current pure PAYGO system would mean a 7.0 percentage point increase in the current 12.4 percent payroll tax rate. This tax places a particularly high burden on low- and middle-income employees, for whom it is typically larger than the income tax (because the payroll tax has no personal exemptions or deductions). A rise in the payroll tax rate would imply a significant increase in the share of the overall tax burden borne by low- and middle-income employees and a proportionately larger decline in their standard of living.

Fifth, adding an investment-based system of personal retirement accounts with deposits of 3 percent of payroll would increase the long-run benefits of every major demographic group, including women, blacks, and individuals with low education. Although this system would require extra funds in the transition years, the 3 percent additional contributions would in the long run be less than half of the payroll tax rise required in the pure PAYGO system.

Sixth, an investment-based system would increase the amount of capital per worker in the economy, raising real wages and, to a lesser extent, depressing the real rate of return on capital. These changes in wages and capital returns would benefit low- and middle-income employees relative to other groups.

Indirect Effects of Social Security on the Distribution of Income

Before presenting a brief summary of each of the individual studies, we consider here the more general ways in which the current Social Security system affects the distribution of incomes. It is common in discussions of Social Security—including most of the analyses in this volume—to assume that an additional dollar of Social Security benefits raises the retiree's income and consumption by a dollar. There are four major reasons that this direct effect is an incomplete picture of the distributional effect of the Social Security program.

First, Social Security taxes and the expectation of future Social Security benefits reduce personal saving, including employer-financed pension saving, and therefore reduce the amount of such personal income from this source that individuals have in retirement. If each dollar of Social Security wealth (i.e., the present actuarial value of future Social Security benefits) reduces personal saving by approximately fifty cents, a dollar of benefits raises retirement consumption by only fifty cents. We know of no studies of how this saving-offset effect varies among demographic groups.

Second, the Social Security program induces individuals to retire earlier than they otherwise would (see, e.g., Gruber and Wise 1999). This reduces the earnings of older individuals and thus offsets some of effect of the benefits on disposable income.

Third, the changes in saving and in the labor supply of individuals (both at retirement and at earlier working ages) that are induced by Social Security have general equilibrium effects on the rate of interest and on the level of real wages. Because the reduction in the capital stock is likely to be proportionally greater than the reduction in the labor supply, the net effect is to reduce wages and to increase the return to capital. The study by Kotlikoff, Smetters, and Walliser in this volume analyzes this effect.

Finally, Social Security is to some extent a substitute for intrafamily transfers. To the extent that Social Security benefits are offset by lower transfers from working children to their retired parents, the benefits raise the consumption of the children rather than of the retirees.

These indirect effects must be kept in mind when considering the effects of the Social Security program and of alternative reforms.

Individual Studies

Four of the individual studies in this volume deal with the distributional aspects of the current system, two deal with reforms within the context of the pay-as-you-go system, and four deal with the distributional aspects of a shift to a system that includes investment-based individual retirement accounts. The ten studies are organized in this manner in the volume as well as in this summary.

Jeffrey B. Liebman considers redistribution in the current Social Security system. He emphasizes that spouse benefits and differential mortality offset a substantial share of the redistribution provided by the progressive benefit formula, and that families with identical lifetime earnings can receive very different returns from Social Security. He also suggests that the system is likely to become more progressive in the future, as cohorts in which women had higher labor force participation rates reach retirement.

Kathleen McGarry focuses on the Supplemental Security Income (SSI) program, which provides means-tested benefits for the elderly poor. She notes that many of those who appear to be eligible for SSI benefits do not apply for them. She studies the factors that discourage eligibility and applies her analysis to estimate the effects of program changes on participation and poverty. Her analysis shows that relatively small expenditures ($12 billion per year in 1993 dollars) could raise SSI benefits to the poverty level, although incomplete take-up would still leave some of the elderly in poverty.

Although most of the studies in this volume deal with the distribution of income, two of the chapters deal with different aspects of the distribution problem. Jagadeesh Gokhale and Laurence J. Kotlikoff deal with the distribution of wealth. They show that by depressing saving and therefore leaving most Americans with little or no bequeathable wealth, the Social Security program reduces wealth—particularly among lower- and middle-income households. The authors also note that in depressing wealth accumulation, Social Security increases the overall wealth inequality in the country.

Angus Deaton, Pierre-Olivier Gourinchas, and Christina Paxson study the way that the inequality of consumption behaves in a life-cycle model without bequests. Social Security, by substituting PAYGO benefits for actual accumulation, reduces the inequality of wealth that results from variations in lifetime earnings and therefore of retirement consumption that would occur if there were greater reliance on individual saving. The contrast with the Gokhale-Kotlikoff paper shows the important role that bequests can play in determining long-run wealth inequality.

Julia Lynn Coronado, Don Fullerton, and Thomas Glass use the Panel Study of Income Dynamics to generate estimates of lifetime incomes for a large sample of individuals, and then calculate the present value of taxes and benefits for each person. The degree of progressivity as measured by the net present value of benefits minus taxes depends on how incomes are measured. The current system is slightly progressive on a lifetime basis when individuals are classified by the present value of lifetime incomes, but becomes less so when incomes are defined to include the value of the leisure. The authors then use this framework to assess the effects of various pay-as-you-go reforms on the overall progressivity of the system.

Jagadeesh Gokhale and Laurence J. Kotlikoff use an extensive simulation model to generate lifetime incomes of current and future employees, and use those simulated incomes to assess the effects of alternative reforms on the implicit rates of return that individuals in different income and demographic groups receive on their Social Security taxes. They find that if current rules and tax rates were feasible in the future, individuals would get an implicit real return of slightly less than 2 percent. Because benefits must be cut or taxes raised to maintain the solvency of the system, the actual future rates of return must be even lower. Gokhale and Kotlikoff examine the effects of a variety of different proposals on these rates of return for different demographic and economic groups.

Martin Feldstein and Jeffrey B. Liebman use actual Social Security lifetime earning and benefit records matched to government survey data on a cohort of retirees to study the distributional impact of a change from the existing PAYGO Social Security system to one that combines both PAYGO and investment-based components. These data have an advantage in that the households in the sample reflect the full range of life experiences, including irregular work histories, unusual marriage and divorce patterns, and premature deaths. The study analyzes a system that combines the benefits that can be financed by the existing payroll tax with the annuity that could be financed by personal retirement accounts based on contributions equal to 3 percent of payroll. Although the mixed system would temporarily cost more than the pure PAYGO system, in the long run it would be substantially less expensive. More specifically, the increase in the cost of such a mixed system relative to current PAYGO taxes would be less than half of the rise in taxes required to maintain current benefit rules in a pure PAYGO system. Despite its lower cost, the mixed system would give most individuals in virtually all demographic groups higher average benefits than they would receive under the current system. The mixed system would also result in a smaller share of individuals in every category with benefits below the poverty level. These basic conclusions remain true even if the future rate of return in the investment-based component of the mixed system were substantially less than past experience implies. Moreover, by funding the personal retirement accounts in a redistributive manner, it is possible to have benefits for all income groups rise by a similar percentage.

Laurence J. Kotlikoff, Kent Smetters, and Jan Walliser use a computable general equilibrium model to analyze how the shift to an investment-based system would change wages and interest rates. They conclude that an investment-based system would help the poor both because of the higher return on investment-based accounts and because of the increased capital per worker in the economy.

Martin Feldstein and Elena Ranguelova examine the potential magnitudes of the bequests that might result in an investment-based plan under different rules about bequests. Permitting employees who die before retirement to bequeath the assets in their personal retirement accounts would reduce the funds available at age sixty-seven by about one-sixth, implying that (for example) the same level of annuity could be achieved with a 3.6 percent PRA saving rate and preretirement bequests, or with a 3.0 percent PRA with no bequest. The paper also studies a variety of possible post-retirement bequest rules. By taking into account the uncertain nature of the return on the PRAs, the authors study the distribution of bequest sizes as well as their mean levels.

Jeffrey R. Brown analyzes the financial redistribution that would occur under various annuity and bequest options in an individual accounts program. A key part of his analysis is applying mortality rates differentiated by gender, race, ethnicity, and education level to calculate the transfers that would take place between different groups under different assumptions about the structure of the annuity program. Mandating a single life annuity could result in much larger transfers from high-mortality groups (such as black males) to low-mortality groups (such as white females) than would occur if joint life annuities or bequest options were allowed.

The current U.S. Social Security system has large impacts on poverty and on the distribution of income and wealth. The studies in this volume highlight the importance of focusing on the distributional aspects of reform plans, because the distributional implications of the plans can vary greatly depending on plan details. In addition, the studies show that with appropriate attention to low-income groups and others at high risk of poverty in old age, reforms can both reduce the long-run burden of the aging society on future taxpayers and reduce poverty rates among the elderly.

References

Campbell, John Y., and Martin Feldstein, eds. 2001. *Risk aspects of investment-based Social Security reform.* Chicago: University of Chicago Press.
Costa, Dora. 1999. *The evolution of retirement.* Chicago: University of Chicago Press.
Feldstein, Martin, ed. 1998. *Privatizing Social Security.* Chicago: University of Chicago Press.

Feldstein, Martin, and Andrew Samwick. 1997. The economics of prefunding Social Security and Medicare benefits. In *NBER Macroeconomics Annual 1997,* ed. Ben S. Bernanke and Julio Rotemberg, chap. 3. Cambridge: MIT Press.

———. 1998. The transition path in privatizing Social Security. In *Privatizing Social Security,* ed. Martin Feldstein, 215–60. Chicago: University of Chicago Press.

Goldberg, Fred T., Jr., and Michael J. Graetz. 2000. Reforming Social Security: A practical and workable system of personal retirement accounts. In *Administrative aspects of investment-based Social Security reform,* ed. John B. Shoven, 9–37. Chicago: University of Chicago Press.

Gruber, John, and David A. Wise, eds. 1999. *Social security programs and retirement around the world.* Chicago: University of Chicago Press.

Shoven, John, ed. 2000. *Administrative aspects of investment-based Social Security reform.* Chicago: University of Chicago Press.

1

Redistribution in the Current U.S. Social Security System

Jeffrey B. Liebman

Social Security is the largest income-transfer program in the United States. In 2001 the program is expected to bring in $532 billion in (noninterest) revenue, mostly from payroll taxation of current workers, and to pay out $439 billion, mostly in benefit checks to retirees.[1] Because its benefit formula replaces a greater fraction of the lifetime earnings of lower earners than of higher earners, Social Security is generally thought to be progressive, providing a better deal to low earners in a cohort than to high earners in the same cohort. In addition, the program is considered to be particularly important in preventing poverty among the lowest-income elderly.[2]

Jeffrey B. Liebman is an associate professor of public policy at the John F. Kennedy School of Government, Harvard University, and a faculty research fellow of the National Bureau of Economic Research.

The author is grateful to Jeffrey R. Brown, Don Fullerton, Stephen C. Goss, David Pattison, Andrew A. Samwick, and Stephen Zeldes for discussions about this research; to Joshua Pollet, Peter Spiegler, Elisabeth Welty, and Ying Qian for excellent research assistance; to Henry Aaron, Gary Burtless, Peter Diamond, Martin Feldstein, and conference participants for comments on an earlier draft; and to Hugh Richards for providing tabulations from the National Longitudinal Mortality Survey. This research was conducted while the author was also a Bureau of the Census research associate at the Boston Research Data Center; research results and conclusions expressed are those of the author and do not necessarily indicate concurrence by the Bureau of the Census. This paper has been screened by a Bureau of the Census employee to insure that no confidential data are revealed. This research was funded by a grant from the Russell Sage Foundation and by a First Award from the National Institute on Aging.

1. These numbers are for the entire Old-Age, Survivors, and Disability Insurance program (OASDI). The nondisability portion of the program (OASI) that is the focus of this paper is projected to have (noninterest) income of $455 billion and expenditures of $378 billion.

2. Social Security Administration (2000) calculates (ignoring behavioral effects) that without Social Security elderly poverty would rise from 9 percent to 48 percent. Burtless (1994) argues that social insurance programs such as Social Security are more important than means-tested transfers in lifting families out of poverty.

A number of proposed Social Security reforms would increase the link between a worker's Social Security contributions and retirement income, replacing or supplementing the current system with a system of defined contribution personal retirement accounts funded proportionally to earnings.[3] These proposals have led to concern that the amount of redistribution and poverty alleviation accomplished through Social Security would decline if a system based on individual accounts were established.

However, much of the intracohort redistribution in the U.S. Social Security system is related to factors other than income. Social Security transfers income from individuals with low life expectancies to those with high life expectancies, from single workers and from married couples with substantial earnings by the secondary earner to married one-earner couples, and from individuals who have worked for more than thirty-five years to those who have concentrated their earnings in thirty-five or fewer years. Since high-income households tend to have higher life expectancies and receive larger spouse benefits, some of the progressivity of the basic benefit formula is offset. Understanding the redistribution that occurs through the current U.S. Social Security system is important for assessing the potential costs of moving to a mixed Social Security system that incorporates both pay-as-you-go and individual-account components, and for designing modifications to the traditional system that could complement other reforms.

The main results in this paper come from a microsimulation model of the retirement portion of Social Security and use a data set that matches the 1990 and 1991 Surveys of Income and Program Participation (SIPP) to Social Security administrative earnings and benefit records. The model simulates the distribution of internal rates of return, net transfers, and lifetime net tax rates that would have been received from Social Security by members of the 1925 to 1929 birth cohorts if they had lived under current Social Security rules for their entire lives, and finds that Social Security provides within-cohort transfers of 13 percent of Social Security benefits when discounted at the overall cohort rate of return of 1.29 percent.[4] However, much of the redistribution that occurs through Social Security is not related to income, and thus income-related transfers are only 5 to 9 percent of Social Security benefits paid (or $19 to 34 billion), at

---

3. There is no reason why the individual accounts must be funded proportionally to earnings. Feldstein and Liebman (this volume) show that by funding personal retirement accounts with a combination of flat per-worker contributions and proportional contributions, an investment-based defined contribution system can accomplish as much redistribution as the current system, or more.

4. More specifically, within-cohort transfers are measured as the present discounted value of Social Security benefits received minus taxes paid, all discounted at the cohort rate of return. Therefore, someone whose rate of return is greater than the cohort rate of return receives a positive transfer, and someone whose rate of return is lower than the cohort return receives a negative transfer. Total transfers can be calculated by summing either the positive or negative transfers (which each sum to the same quantity).

2001 aggregate benefit levels.[5] At higher discount rates, Social Security appears more redistributive by some measures and less redistributive by others.

The paper begins in section 1.1 by presenting basic data on the *annual* redistribution that occurs through Social Security, then reviews, in section 1.2, the reasons for preferring a *lifetime* measure of redistribution and the sources of lifetime redistribution in the U.S. Social Security system. Section 1.3 discusses the simulation model, and section 1.4 explains the methodology used for measuring lifetime redistribution. Section 1.5 provides the results on redistribution in the current system, and section 1.6 compares my results to those in recent studies by Caldwell et al. (1999), Coronado, Fullerton, and Glass (2000), and Gustman and Steinmeier (2001), and discusses implications of the results for Social Security reform. Section 1.7 concludes.

1.1 Annual Redistribution from Social Security

Each year, Social Security raises tax revenue from workers and pays out benefits to retirees and other beneficiaries. Table 1.1 presents estimates from the 1998 Current Population Survey (CPS) for calendar year 1998 that describe these annual flows of taxes and benefits for different demographic groups.[6]

The first row of the table shows that in 1998, overall, Social Security paid out $375 billion in benefit payments and raised $430 billion in payroll taxes. The ratio of benefits to taxes was therefore 0.87. Dividing the −$55 billion difference between benefits and taxes by the entire U.S. population of 272 million produces a per capita difference of −$203.

As would be expected, the gap between benefits received and taxes paid differs substantially across demographic groups. Individuals who are under the age of eighteen receive twice as much in benefits as they pay in taxes, because few children have labor income, whereas some receive benefits if their parents are disabled or deceased. In contrast, individuals in the prime working years of thirty to forty-nine years of age receive benefits that are only 8 percent of the taxes they pay. Individuals aged sixty-five and above receive thirty times as much in benefits as they pay in taxes.

Forty-six percent of Social Security benefits go to people in families whose non–Social Security income is below the poverty line. This result is

---

5. As will be explained in detail later, income-related transfers are calculated by assigning each individual a transfer that is the average for the individual's level of income.

6. The CPS measures total OASDI benefits and does not distinguish between retirement and disability benefits. I assume that the full incidence of the OASDI payroll tax is on the worker and estimate OASDI payroll taxes as 12.4 percent of earnings for individuals with a positive value in the CPS FICA variable (individuals with positive earnings and a zero value in the FICA variable are in sectors of the economy not covered by Social Security). I multiply each individual's Social Security benefit by 1.17 and tax payments by 0.984 so that aggregate OASDI benefits and taxes match the levels reported for calendar year 1998 in Board of Trustees of the Federal Old-Age, Survivors, and Disability Insurance Trust Funds (2001).

Table 1.1   Annual Redistribution from the U.S. Social Security System for 1998

	OASDI Benefits ($ billions)	OASDI Payroll Taxes ($ billions)	Ratio of Benefits to Taxes	Per Capita Difference ($)
All	375	430	0.87	−203
Age				
Under 18	3	1	2.00	18
18–29	4	74	0.05	−1,575
30–49	19	248	0.08	−2,736
50–64	49	97	0.50	−1,231
65+	301	10	29.63	8,981
Family income excluding Social Security benefits relative to poverty threshold				
Less than 50%	125	−1	89.64	3,930
50–100%	48	6	7.49	1,837
100–200%	71	31	2.28	882
200–300%	43	52	0.82	−218
More than 300%	88	339	0.26	−1,933
Sex				
Male	184	272	0.68	−660
Female	191	158	1.20	233
Region				
Northeast	77	87	0.89	−187
Midwest	90	105	0.86	−233
South	137	140	0.98	−30
West	70	98	0.71	−451
Race				
White	334	372	0.90	−168
Black	33	38	0.87	−147
Asian and other	8	20	0.38	−935
Hispanic status				
Non-Hispanic	357	397	0.90	−166
Hispanic	18	33	0.53	−487
Education				
Less than high school	108	30	3.57	1,616
High school	134	119	1.13	172
More than high school	132	281	0.47	−1,093

Sources: Author's calculations from the March 1999 Current Population Survey. OASDI benefits and taxes are scaled to match aggregate levels for 1998 as reported in Board of Trustees (2001). OASDI taxes include both employer and employee share. For children under 18, the family head's education level is used for the tabulation by education.

not surprising, because Social Security represents 90 percent or more of income for 30 percent of elderly families and 50 percent or more for 63 percent of elderly families (Social Security Administration 2000). Total Social Security benefits for females are slightly greater than those for males, because the greater longevity for women outweighs their lower average benefit levels. Due to their higher average level of earnings, men pay substantially more in Social Security taxes than do women. Thus, annual Social Security benefits for men are only 68 percent of taxes paid, whereas benefits for women are 120 percent of taxes paid.

The ratio of benefits to taxes paid is highest in the South, with its disproportionate share of retirees, and lowest in the West, with its large share of younger workers (including recent immigrants). Similarly, although whites and blacks each receive benefits that are roughly 90 percent of taxes paid, demographic groups such as Asians and Hispanics (which include many recent immigrants and relatively few elderly) pay out two to three times as much in taxes as they receive in benefits each year. Finally, individuals in low-education groups receive on average substantially more in Social Security benefits than they pay in taxes, whereas the reverse is true for individuals in high-education groups. This primarily reflects the increase in education levels over time in the United States (i.e., elderly Social Security beneficiaries come from cohorts with lower average education levels than do current workers).

1.2   Sources of Intracohort Lifetime Redistribution in the United States

The results on annual redistribution are interesting because they describe large annual transfers of resources among different demographic groups—transfers that depend mostly on the ratio of beneficiaries to earners within each group. Over a lifetime, however, most individuals transition from earning income and paying Old-Age, Survivors, and Disability Insurance (OASDI) taxes to receiving Social Security benefits. Therefore, taking a lifetime perspective provides a better measure of how the U.S. Social Security system treats different types of individuals.

How a person fares under the Social Security system depends both on how well he or she is treated relative to other people in his or her birth cohort, and on how well the birth cohort is treated as a whole. Although this paper focuses on intracohort redistribution, it is important to note that there are interactions between intercohort and intracohort redistribution. In particular, the early cohorts of Social Security beneficiaries received windfalls because they were the initial generations in a pay-as-you-go (PAYGO) system, and received substantial benefits even though they had paid relatively little in taxes. Because Social Security benefits rise with income, the largest dollar windfalls went to upper-income beneficiaries in these early cohorts. As later cohorts with lower rates of return have retired, the system has become more progressive because the increased payroll tax rates have resulted in higher-income individuals' paying substantially more taxes in present-value terms than they receive in benefits.[7]

7. Burkhauser and Warlick (1981), Hurd and Shoven (1985), Duggan, Gillingham, and Greenlees (1993), and Steuerle and Bakija (1994) show that the higher rates of return earned by early cohorts of Social Security beneficiaries led to net transfers for the system that were often greater for high-income individuals.

The fundamental source of intracohort redistribution from Social Security is its progressive benefit formula. Although OASDI payroll taxes are proportional to earnings up to a cap that is currently $80,400, the benefit formula replaces a higher fraction of lifetime earnings for low earners than high earners. Benefits are calculated by indexing earnings to average wage growth (through the year the worker turns sixty), summing the highest thirty-five years of earnings, and then dividing by 420 (35×12) to produce a worker's Average Indexed Monthly Earnings (AIME). The worker's Primary Insurance Amount (PIA)—the monthly benefit the worker will receive if he or she retires at the full-benefit age—is currently calculated as 90 percent of the first $561 of AIME, plus 32 percent of AIME between $561 and $3,381, and 15 percent of any AIME above $3,381.

This basic relationship between AIME and benefit levels is altered by two major factors. First, higher-income individuals tend to live longer (Kitagawa and Hauser 1973; Rogot, Sorlie, and Johnson 1992; Pappas et al. 1993) and therefore receive benefits for more years.[8] Second, the aged spouse of a retired worker is entitled to a spouse benefit equal to 50 percent of the worker's benefit while the worker is alive, and to a survivor benefit equal to the worker's full benefit after the worker dies. These benefits for spouses and survivors imply that Social Security redistributes from single workers to married couples and from men to women. As will be shown later, by some measures they also offset some of the progressivity of the retired worker benefit because spouses of high earners receive higher spouse benefits than spouses of low earners.[9]

Additional redistribution occurs to individuals with short spells in covered work, such as immigrants and government workers, whose AIMEs can substantially understate lifetime income.[10] In contrast, workers with substantial earnings in years outside their thirty-five highest years are not rewarded by Social Security for that work. Finally, to the extent that the rate of wage growth used to index earnings differs from the benchmark interest rate used to calculate redistribution, the timing of earnings throughout

8. Aaron (1977), Steuerle and Bakija (1994), and Garrett (1995) present illustrative calculations for hypothetical workers that suggest that this effect can be large. Panis and Lillard (1996) show using microdata that income transfers from whites to blacks and high-income to low-income workers are much smaller once differential mortality is considered. In contrast, Duggan, Gillingham, and Greenlees (1995) analyze mortality patterns in the Continuous Work History Survey and conclude that differential mortality does little to offset the progressivity of Social Security. For comparable research on Medicare, see McClellan and Skinner (1997).
9. Boskin, Kotlikoff, Puffert, and Shoven (1987) present results showing how marital status affects the rates of return from Social Security.
10. See Gustman and Steinmeier (2000) for a discussion of Social Security's treatment of immigrants. In theory, the government pension offset and windfall elimination provisions reduce the extent to which workers in noncovered employment receive windfalls from Social Security. In practice, it is often difficult for the Social Security Administration to apply these provisions, because workers do not always report their government pension income to the Social Security Administration.

the lifetime can affect the amount of redistribution a worker receives from the system.[11]

1.3 Data

This paper uses a microsimulation model based on a match of individuals in the 1990 and 1991 panels of the SIPP to Social Security administrative earnings and benefit records for those same individuals. I select SIPP sample members who were born between 1925 and 1929, and construct lifetime earnings and marital histories from age twenty-one through age sixty-four using the administrative records and the SIPP topical module on marriage. I then simulate the sample members' Social Security payroll taxes and benefit levels under current Social Security rules (rather than under the ones they actually experienced).

The strength of the simulation model is that it reflects the full range of experience of a historical cohort. Because the data contain forty-three years of actual covered earnings for each sample member as well as complete marital histories, the results give a comprehensive view of the outcomes that would have occurred for this cohort if it had experienced these alternative Social Security rules.[12] Compared with other microsimulation models used to study the distributional effects of Social Security, this historical cohort model relies little on projected or imputed data. Because I am particularly concerned with the lower tail of the benefit distribution, my ability to observe extreme cases and to reflect the complicated cross-correlations among marital status, earnings, retirement, and mortality is important.[13]

The simulation model requires two types of imputations. First, I construct earning histories for spouses who were absent at the time of the 1990–91 SIPP (due to death or divorce). Second, I impute earnings for individuals located at the taxable maximum for years in which the taxable maximum was at a lower level relative to average wages than it is currently. Further details of the matching and imputation methods are described in the data appendix that appears at the end of Feldstein and Liebman (chap. 7 in this volume).

Once complete earnings and marital histories have been constructed, it is possible to calculate Social Security benefit streams for each individual

11. Social Security benefits are partially taxable for some upper-income taxpayers. I interpret this feature as part of the personal income tax system rather than the Social Security system and do not study it here.
12. The model ignores behavioral responses to these alternative Social Security rules.
13. The drawback of analyzing a historical cohort is that future cohorts will differ along key dimensions from the 1925–1929 cohort. In particular, women will have much greater earnings, and a larger share of individuals in later cohorts will be divorced or never married. In section 1.6, I discuss the likely impact of these factors on the distributional impact of Social Security.

at ages 60 through 100. I assume that sample members claim benefits at their actual retirement ages (obtained from the Social Security benefit records), and then calculate Social Security benefits at each age from 60 through 100.[14] For married and divorced sample members, the model calculates separate benefit streams corresponding to the benefits the sample member would receive if his or her spouse were still alive and if the spouse were dead (assuming that the sample member is still alive). Expected lifetime benefits can then be calculated by weighting each potential benefit-year by the probability that the sample member is alive in that year. For married and divorced individuals, the weights on each of the two benefit streams account additionally for the probability that the spouse is alive. To account for socioeconomic differences in mortality, I use for each race-by-sex-by-education group separate mortality tables that were constructed using a nonlinear least squares regression to fit a standard actuarial function (the Gompertz-Makeham formula) to nonparametric, age-specific mortality rates from the National Longitudinal Mortality Study.[15]

1.4 Methodology for Measuring Redistribution

This paper focuses on the redistribution in the *retirement* portion of Social Security. Contributions and benefits related to disability and pre-retirement survivors are not studied.[16] Including these benefits would increase the measured amount of redistribution to lower socioeconomic groups; however, many Social Security reform plans would preserve disability benefits at current-law levels.[17] Therefore, it is the redistribution in the retirement portion of Social Security that would most likely be affected by Social Security reform.

---

14. Benefits vary by age because they can depend on whether the sample member's spouse has started receiving benefits and on whether the spouse is still alive.

15. These mortality estimates were developed in joint work with Jeffrey Brown and Joshua Pollet (see Brown, Liebman, and Pollet in the appendix to this volume), and are the same as those used in Brown and in Feldstein and Liebman (chapters 10 and 7, respectively, in this volume). We thank Hugh Richards for providing us with tabulations from the NLMS. We produced separate mortality tables by Hispanic status as well. However, because the data were much thinner and because the demography literature suggests that there is considerable heterogeneity in life expectancies across Hispanic groups, I decided not to differentiate by ethnicity in this paper. For evidence on Hispanic mortality, see Sorlie et al. (1993) and Hummer et al. (1999).

16. Individuals receiving disability benefits according to the data from the Social Security Master Beneficiary Record are excluded from the sample. Thus, OASI benefits paid to formerly disabled beneficiaries after the age-sixty-five conversion of disability benefits to retirement benefits are not modeled.

17. Elmendorf, Liebman, and Wilcox (2001) report that the individual account–based Social Security reform plans studied by the Clinton administration would have shielded Disability Insurance (DI) benefits from cuts. The NCRP plan is a notable exception that applied benefit cuts to disability benefits.

In a social insurance program such as Social Security, the insurance and redistribution functions are closely related. Viewed from a point in time before an individual knows his or her socioeconomic status (and therefore the distribution from which his or her lifetime earnings, marriage, and mortality experience will be drawn), all of the features of Social Security that result in some workers' receiving higher returns on their contributions than others can be interpreted as insurance—insurance against living too long, against having low wages, and against marrying a nonworking spouse. From behind this veil of ignorance, all workers have the same ex ante expected return from Social Security, and different outcomes that occur ex post are simply the payoffs from the social insurance; there is no redistribution. Alternatively, one could view the program from the standpoint of a worker who has just entered the workforce for the first time, say, at age twenty-five. Based on education level, sex, and family background, this worker has an expected distribution of future earnings, marriage, and mortality experience. One could interpret differences in expected net benefits from Social Security across groups defined by characteristics predetermined by age twenty-five (such as race, education, and sex) as redistribution, and within-group variation as ex post payoffs from the insurance.[18]

In this paper, I take a third approach and interpret Social Security as providing insurance solely against longevity risk, and attribute other differences in payoffs from Social Security to redistribution. In particular, differences in payoffs to Social Security due to different lifetime earnings and marriage patterns are considered to be redistribution. Differences due to *expected* mortality (from age twenty-one on), defined within sex-by-race-by-education groups, are also interpreted as redistribution.[19] Differences in payoffs due to differences in the ex post mortality experienced by individuals within the sex-by-race-by-education groups are not considered redistribution and are integrated out by averaging over the possible dates of death with appropriate probability weights.

To implement this concept, I use three measures of redistribution. The first is the internal rate of return, r, that equalizes the present discounted value of Social Security contributions and benefits:

$$0 = \sum_{age=21}^{age=100} \frac{S_{age}(B_{age} - T_{age})}{(1 + r)^{age-21}},$$

18. Some of the results in Feldstein and Liebman (this volume) can be interpreted in this way. A complete accounting of the benefits expected from Social Security at age twenty-five would also incorporate the disability and young survivors' benefits that are omitted from my analysis.

19. This portion of the redistribution through Social Security is common to any system that requires everyone to annuitize at a single price. Brown (this volume) discusses the redistribution that would occur in an individual account–based system that required everyone to annuitize at a single price.

where B represents Social Security benefits, T represents Social Security taxes, and S represents the probability of surviving to a given age.

The second is the net transfer received from Social Security, a dollar measure of the difference between an individual's lifetime benefits and lifetime taxes:

$$\text{NetTransfer} = \sum_{age=21}^{age=100} \frac{S_{age}(B_{age} - T_{age})}{(1 + r_d)^{age-65}}.$$

Specifically, the net transfer is the present discounted value of the individual's lifetime Social Security benefits minus the present value of the individual's lifetime taxes, discounted at a rate r_d and measured as of age sixty-five. In order to focus on within-cohort redistribution, the main results in this paper discount at the cohort rate of return, which for this cohort under the assumptions described below turns out to be 1.29 percent. Therefore, an individual who receives exactly the cohort rate of return on his or her Social Security taxes will have a net transfer of zero, whereas someone with a rate of return higher than that of the cohort will receive a positive transfer, and someone with a lower rate of return will receive a negative transfer. I also show results for real discount rates of 3 and 5 percent.

The third measure of redistribution is the lifetime net tax rate from Social Security. This is simply the net transfer divided by the present discounted value of lifetime earnings.

Three details about the contribution and benefit streams affect the results. First, because only individuals who survive to the age at which they are interviewed in the SIPP are in the sample, I scale up the Social Security contributions of sample members to reflect the probability that a person in his or her sex-by-race-by-education group would not live to each age. Therefore, group averages on rates of return or transfers can be interpreted as the expected return for all individuals in that group who were alive as of age twenty-one (to facilitate comparisons with previous studies, all of the present discounted values that I present are accumulated forward to age sixty-five).

Second, in order that the results reflect the U.S. Social Security system in a steady state rather than one in which the rates of return earned by different cohorts are changing, and that the results be comparable to studies that focus on Social Security reforms that would be implemented over the coming century, I calibrate the life expectancies and payroll tax rates to reflect conditions in 2075 (the endpoint of the Social Security actuaries' seventy-five-year horizon). In particular, I scale my estimated sex-by-race-by-education mortality tables to be consistent with the Social Security Administration's projections for individuals born in 1990, and I assume a payroll tax rate of 15.4 percent, which is roughly the payroll tax rate that would be necessary to support the portion of OASI benefits modeled in this paper.[20] Under these assumptions, the overall internal rate of return from Social Security for my simulation cohort is 1.29 percent.[21]

Third, because my unit of observation is the individual, I must allocate the payroll taxes and Social Security benefits of married couples across the two spouses. In years during which a married couple is married, I split the total payroll tax paid by the two spouses equally. Similarly, during retirement years in which both spouses are alive, the total Social Security benefits received by the couple are split equally into the benefit streams of each spouse. However, during years before the couple was married, the entire contribution of each spouse stays in the contribution stream of the spouse making the contribution, and Social Security benefits received after one spouse is dead are credited only to the surviving spouse. This approach implies that (except for differential earnings before marriage) the entire difference in rates of return and transfers between two spouses comes from the longer life expectancy of the wife.[22]

One last methodological issue needs attention. In examining the relationship between redistribution from Social Security and lifetime income, the particular definition of income used to classify individuals can have a large impact on the results. I use two different lifetime income measures based on earnings histories. The first is the AIME of the higher earner in the household. The AIME is the measure of income used by the Social Security benefit formula and is calculated by summing the highest thirty-five years of earnings (wage-indexed and including zeros, if any) for the worker and dividing by 420 (35 × 12). I use only the higher earner's AIME

20. Of the total 19.9 percent of payroll in OASDI costs that are forecast for 2075 (Board of Trustees 1999), 2.59 percent are for DI benefits, roughly 0.28 percent are for young survivors (including children), and roughly 1.6 percent are OASI benefits at ages sixty-five and above for people who converted from DI benefits when they reached the full-benefit age. The DI estimate comes directly from Board of Trustees (1999). The other two estimates rely on Table II.H2 in the 1999 trustees' report, which provides estimates of the number of beneficiaries of each type in future years and weights these estimates by the average benefit levels for each type of beneficiary in 1997 from the Annual Statistical Supplement to the *Social Security Bulletin.*

21. This is similar to the long-run growth rate of the tax base of 1.1 percent that is assumed by the actuaries. One reason my estimate is larger is that my sample contains many more one-earner couples than the population retiring in 2075 will likely contain.

22. The approach I take in this paper is appealing because it shows women receiving a higher rate of return from Social Security than men, as their longer life expectancy would imply. Two other plausible approaches are less satisfactory. One would be to credit each spouse with only his or her own tax contributions and Social Security benefit. This would result in much higher measured rates of return for women (infinite in the case of nonworking spouses) and low rates of return for men, because it would give them no credit for the spouse benefits produced by their earnings history. This would be unsatisfactory because the men in married couples are clearly benefiting from their spouses' receiving enhanced benefits. Another approach would be to credit men with the entire benefit produced by their earnings histories, including the spouse benefit. This approach is unsatisfactory because it would calculate the rates of return for many wives as zero even though they are getting a "very good deal" from Social Security.

for two reasons: First, the AIME of the higher earner is likely to be a good measure of a household's socioeconomic class and will not be confounded by the large variation in the earnings levels of secondary earners. Indeed, because most higher earners work full-time for at least thirty-five years, this measure is similar to the potential earnings measures used in the studies by Coronado, Fullerton, and Glass (2000) and Gustman and Steinmeier (2001). Second, for most couples, the Social Security benefit they receive depends only on the AIME of the highest earner, providing no marginal benefit for work by the lower-earning spouse.[23] Thus, the AIME is the income measure around which the explicit redistribution in the Social Security system is based.

The second measure I use is the total covered earnings of both members of the couple (accumulated to age sixty-five at the relevant discount rate). The appeal of this second measure is that it allows for comparison with the many studies that analyze the impact of government programs on the income distribution using actual rather than potential income data, and it also corresponds to the Social Security tax base. This second measure of income may not, however, be satisfactory for welfare analysis, because a nontrivial portion of the variation in this measure is due to the labor-leisure (or market production versus home production) choice of the secondary earner and not simply to the earnings potential of the household.

1.5   Redistribution in the Current System

1.5.1   Overall Redistribution

The theoretical progressivity of the Social Security system can be seen in figure 1.1, which abstracts from all of the nonincome sources of redistribution by graphing the relationship between AIME and net transfers from Social Security for a hypothetical set of single adults with different earnings levels but identical timing of earnings throughout their lifetimes and identical life expectancies.[24] For comparison with the results to come, the transfers are calculated discounting at a 1.29 percent rate, which matches the aggregate internal rate of return on Social Security for the microsimulation sample, and the mortality table used is the average of those for white males and white females. Initially, transfers rise with income, as the Social Security benefit formula replaces 90 percent of the first $505 dollars of monthly earnings, reaching a maximum net present value of roughly

---

23. The Social Security Administration reports that 63 percent of women beneficiaries currently receive no marginal benefit from their own earnings and that this percentage is expected to fall to 40 percent in 2060 (National Economic Council 1998).

24. In a steady-state Social Security system in which the rate of return on Social Security is equal to the rate of wage growth, the timing of earnings would not matter.

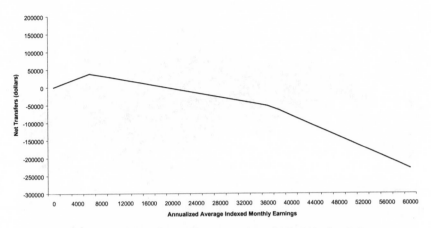

Fig. 1.1   Net transfers from Social Security for hypothetical single adults
Source: All figures are derived from author's calculations from a match of the 1990 and 1991 panels of the Survey of Income and Program Participation to Social Security administrative records.

$38,000 at an annualized AIME of $6,060.[25] Then they fall with income, first at a relatively gradual rate during the range over which the benefit formula replaces 32 percent of earnings, and then at a more rapid rate after the second bend point. Transfers are mostly negative in this figure because the single adults are not benefiting from spouse benefits. For an individual with an annualized AIME of $50,000, the net transfer is −$150,000.

Figure 1.2 shows the actual distribution of net transfers from Social Security with a discount rate of 1.29. In contrast to the striking theoretical relationship between income and net transfers from Social Security in the previous figure, figure 1.2 reveals that transfers can differ widely at a given level of household head AIME. Moreover, a substantial number of high-income individuals receive greater transfers than the typical low-income individual does. For example, 19 percent of individuals in the top AIME quintile receive transfers that are greater than the average transfer for people in the lowest AIME quintile, and 23 percent of top quintile individuals receive transfers that are greater than the average transfer received by people in the second lowest quintile.

Some of the variation in transfers at a given level of AIME can be attributed to the difference between the transfers received by men and women

---

25. The portion in which transfers rise with income can be thought of as similar to the phase-in region of the earned income tax credit in that it limits the amount of transfers to people with very small earnings who are likely to be unusual cases rather than full-time working poor.

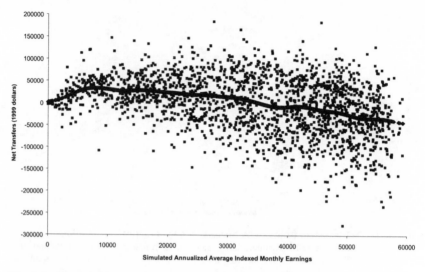

Fig. 1.2   Net transfers from Social Security by income, all individuals
Source: See figure 1.1.
Note: The points have been randomly jittered to preserve confidentiality.

in the same household—the wives receive larger transfers due to their longer life expectancies. This source of variation is highlighted in panels A and B of figure 1.3, which separates the male and female observations from figure 1.2 into separate plots. However, substantial variation remains in transfers at a given AIME even when one looks only at males. This variation is due to differences in life expectancies, marital status, the level of earnings of secondary earners, the share of earnings earned in years outside of the highest thirty-five years, and the timing of earnings over the lifetime.

Despite the wide spread of transfers at a given level of annualized AIME, it is important to emphasize that the kernel regression line in figure 1.2 showing mean transfers at a given level of income declines steadily with income (although the decline is not nearly as steep as the theoretical decline shown in figure 1.1). The regression line reaches a maximum of around $33,000 at an annualized AIME of $8,000 and falls to roughly −$25,000 at $50,000 of annualized AIME.

Figure 1.4 shows the distribution of internal rates of return from Social Security for the same sample. The average internal rate of return falls from around 4 percent down to around 1 percent as incomes rise. As with the transfer plots, there is wide variation in internal rates of return at a given level of AIME.

As discussed above, different definitions of income can lead to different interpretations of the strength of the relationship between income and the

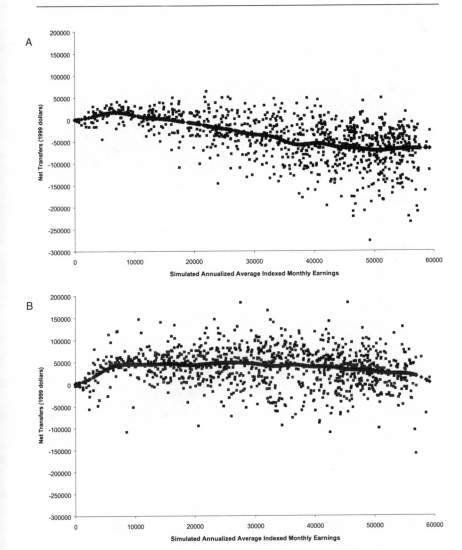

Fig. 1.3   **Net transfers from Social Security by income: *A*, males; *B*, females.**
Source: See figure 1.1.
Note: The points have been randomly jittered to preserve confidentiality.

transfers from Social Security. In figure 1.2, many of the individuals receiving very low transfers are people in married couples in which the secondary earner has substantial earnings. If the earnings of these secondary earners were included in the definition used for ranking household income, then these low-transfer families would be considered to have higher incomes, and the transfers would appear more progressive overall. Figure

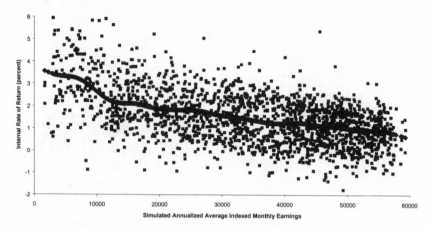

Fig. 1.4   Internal rates of return from Social Security by income
Source: See figure 1.1.
Note: The points have been randomly jittered to preserve confidentiality.

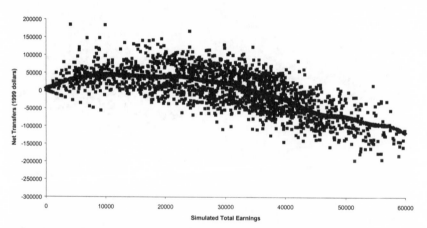

Fig. 1.5   Net transfers from Social Security by income, all individuals
Source: See figure 1.1.
Note: The points have been randomly jittered to preserve confidentiality.

1.5 shows transfers graphed against the total average annual earnings of both spouses. In addition to including the earnings of both spouses, it also includes all years of earnings, not just the highest thirty-five. The spread of transfers at a given level of earnings is now much tighter, largely because people with low returns due to a large amount of earnings that produce little or no marginal Social Security benefits are now classified as having higher earnings. To the extent that variations in earnings from secondary earners reflects a choice between home and market production rather than a difference in earning capacity, this total earnings measure of income may be a less satisfactory metric for ranking people than the measure based on the AIME of the primary earner.

The difference between the two measures of income can be seen in the first part of table 1.2, which presents internal rates of return, mean transfers, and lifetime net tax rates by income quintile under the two definitions of income. The first column presents the average annual earnings by quintile. The numbers for all beneficiaries and for the AIME quintiles are the AIME of the highest earner in the household, and therefore correspond to the results in figures 1.2 through 1.4. The last five rows use the total earnings measure, as in figure 1.5. Note that the average income under the more comprehensive measure can be lower than that in the less comprehensive measure because it is averaged over more years. The second column presents the average internal rate of return from Social Security by income quintile. These average rates of return are person weighted, not dollar weighted, and therefore the average internal rate of return for all beneficiaries (1.53 percent) exceeds the aggregate cohort rate of return (1.29 percent) mentioned above. Rates of return range from 2.70 to 0.85 for the AIME measure of income, and from 3.06 to the 0.35 for the total earnings measure. Thus low-income individuals clearly receive a higher rate of return from Social Security than higher-income individuals, and the difference between the rates of return of high-income and low-income individuals is greater when the individuals are ranked by total earnings than when they are ranked by the AIME of the primary earner.

The remaining six columns in the first part of table 1.2 show the net transfer from Social Security evaluated at age sixty-five and the lifetime net tax rate from Social Security. Results from each of these two measures are presented using discount rates of 1.29 percent (the cohort internal rate of return), 3 percent, and 5 percent. The lifetime net tax rate is calculated by dividing the net transfer from Social Security by the present value of lifetime covered earnings.[26]

At a discount rate of 1.29 percent, individuals in the lowest AIME quintile receive $26,375 more in Social Security benefits than they pay in taxes, and those in the 2nd quintile receive a net transfer of $17,932. In contrast, individuals in the highest AIME quintile pay $33,571 more in taxes than they receive in benefits. Those in the lowest quintile receive a net subsidy from Social Security equal to 6 percent of lifetime earnings, and those in the 2nd quintile receive a net subsidy of 1.7 percent, while those in the highest quintile face a net tax from Social Security equal to 2 percent of lifetime earnings.

It is worth noting that the composition of the lowest AIME quintile is

26. Because the denominator in this calculation is *covered* earnings, the lifetime net tax rates rise monotonically by income group. A measure of lifetime net tax rates that included earnings above the maximum level on which Social Security taxes are assessed would start to decline at income levels above the taxable maximum.

Table 1.2   Redistribution from Social Security in the Simulated 1925–29 Cohort

	Average Annual Earnings	Average Internal Rate of Return (%)	1.29% Discount Rate		3% Discount Rate		5% Discount Rate	
			Average Net Transfer ($)	Lifetime Net Tax Rate (%)	Average Net Transfer ($)	Lifetime Net Tax Rate (%)	Average Net Transfer ($)	Lifetime Net Tax Rate (%)
All beneficiaries	33,961[a] (349)	1.53 (0.03)	0	0	−119,897 (2,206)	6.6	−330,831 (4,273)	10.9
By Income Quintiles								
Lowest AIME quintile	10,434[a] (276)	2.70 (0.08)	26,375 (1,709)	−6.0	−22,103 (2,298)	3.3	−104,700 (4,793)	9.2
Second AIME quintile	25,338[a] (178)	1.71 (0.06)	17,932 (2,569)	−1.7	−87,150 (3,707)	5.6	−268,302 (6,798)	10.3
Third AIME quintile	36,735[a] (151)	1.32 (0.05)	−2,045 (3,346)	0.2	−137,748 (4,594)	6.7	−377,008 (7,822)	10.9
Fourth AIME quintile	45,379[a] (112)	1.16 (0.05)	−10,184 (3,400)	0.7	−160,330 (4,369)	7.0	−426,581 (7,162)	11.1
Highest AIME quintile	52,935[a] (125)	0.85 (0.04)	−33,571 (3,251)	2.0	−196,230 (4,082)	7.9	−486,393 (6,771)	11.5
Lowest total earnings quintile	11,791[a] (380)	3.06 (9.08)	38,516 (1,920)	−9.9	−4,887 (1,706)	0.8	−72,874 (2,902)	7.6
Second total earnings quintile	27,746[a] (408)	1.89 (0.04)	34,906 (2,182)	−3.8	−63,129 (2,102)	4.5	−224,223 (2,480)	9.7
Third total earnings quintile	38,880[a] (455)	1.46 (0.03)	14,836 (2,208)	−1.2	−114,118 (2,169)	6.0	−337,143 (2,381)	10.6
Fourth total earnings quintile	45,528[a] (431)	1.03 (0.03)	−14,535 (2,285)	1.0	−163,556 (2,055)	7.2	−432,772 (2,199)	11.2
Highest total earnings quintile	46,230[a] (407)	0.35 (0.03)	−75,256 (2,644)	3.9	−257,261 (3,250)	8.9	−594,333 (5,291)	12.1

By Demographic Characteristics

Men	36,002[a] (514)	0.78 (0.03)	−43,108 (1,692)	3.2	−169,944 (3,240)	8.4	−400,750 (6,564)	11.8
Women	32,207[a] (468)	2.18 (0.03)	37,047 (1,293)	−3.4	−76,887 (2,298)	4.7	−270,743 (4,892)	9.9
White	35,117[a] (355)	1.52 (0.03)	205 (1,456)	0.0	−122,827 (2,303)	6.6	−339,317 (4,433)	10.9
Black	19,798[a] (1,032)	1.64 (0.12)	−2,514 (4,241)	0.3	−84,001 (7,143)	6.7	−226,852 (13,644)	10.9
Hispanic[c]	19,328[a] (1,198)	2.46 (0.19)	14,249 (4,860)	−1.9	−57,480 (8,486)	5.3	−178,509 (17,052)	10.0
Less than high school	27,640[a] (515)	1.63 (0.05)	810 (2,162)	−0.1	−104,447 (3,551)	6.6	−290,876 (6,967)	10.9
High school	36,541[a] (494)	1.46 (0.04)	−693 (2,119)	0.1	−128,304 (3,291)	6.7	−353,529 (6,260)	10.9
More than high school	42,386[a] (809)	1.46 (0.06)	−10 (3,371)	0.0	−134,285 (5,129)	6.5	−365,204 (9,669)	10.8

Sources: This and following tables are derived from author's calculations from a match of the 1990 and 1991 panels of the Surveys of Income and Program Participation to Social Security administrative records.

Notes: Standard errors in parentheses. Dollar amounts are in 1999 dollars. Net transfers and lifetime net rate are accumulated to age 65.

[a] Average annual earnings measured as the annualized AIME. For married couples it is the AIME of the higher earner in the couple.

[b] Average annual earnings measured by the total earnings of the worker accumulated at the cohort rate of return. For married couples it is the sum of the earnings of the two spouses.

[c] Can be any race.

quite different from that of the other quintiles. Of the primary earners in the first quintile, 56 percent had fewer than thirty-five years of work in covered employment, compared with 22 percent in the 2nd quintile, 13 percent in the 3rd quintile, and less than 2 percent in the 4th and 5th quintiles. Of people in the 1st quintile, 20 percent are immigrants, compared with 5 percent in the other four quintiles. As Gustman and Steinmeier (1998) have shown, immigrants receive a very good deal from Social Security because they are credited with zeros in their earnings records for the years before they came to the United States, thereby appearing to have low lifetime earnings and benefiting from Social Security's progressive benefit formula. Many of the nonimmigrants in this 1st quintile are likely to have worked in noncovered sectors of the economy, and therefore their years with zero earnings are not true zeros.[27] Thus, an argument could be made for ignoring the results for the lowest-income quintile and focusing on the remaining four quintiles.

At higher discount rates, all income quintiles have negative transfers from Social Security on average, and the spread between the average transfers at different income levels grows. For example, at a discount rate of 1.29, there is a $51,000 difference in net transfers between the 2nd and 5th AIME quintiles; at a discount rate of 3 percent, this difference reaches $109,000; and at a discount rate of 5 percent it reaches $218,000. With the higher discount rates, lifetime net tax rates are positive at all income levels, but the variation in lifetime tax rates by income levels falls since with higher discount rates the progressive benefits (which occur later than the taxes) are reduced in importance relative to the proportional Social Security tax.

The second part of table 1.2 presents the analogous results broken down by sex, race, and level of education. As would be expected due to their lower mortality rates, women receive substantially larger transfers and rates of return than men. Discounted at the cohort rate of return of 1.29 percent, the average transfer for women is $37,047, while the average for men is −$43,108. Women receive a rate of return on the Social Security contributions of their household of 2.18 percent, compared with 0.78 percent for men.

Surprisingly, differences in transfers across race and education groups are generally not statistically significant, and differences in rates of return for these categories are only of borderline significance. For example, blacks receive an internal rate of return of 1.64 percent, compared to 1.52 percent for whites. The first column shows that AIMEs do differ substantially by race and education, but the progressive benefit formula is completely offset by the higher mortality in the lower-income groups. This can be seen

---

27. I attempted to exclude government workers (who in the past were not covered by Social Security) from my sample by dropping observations for individuals who could be identified in the SIPP work history topical module as having worked in the public sector or who were receiving income from a government pension. However, this procedure presumably did not identify all workers with public-sector experience.

Table 1.3   **The Impact of Differential Mortality on the Redistribution from Social Security**

	Using Mortality Tables that Vary by Age, Sex, Race, and Education		Using Mortality Tables that Vary by Only Age and Sex[a]	
	Internal Rate of Return (%)	Net Transfer at 1.29% Discount Rate	Internal Rate of Return (%)	Net Transfer at 1.29% Discount Rate
White	1.52	205	1.59	3,174
	(0.03)	(1,456)	(0.03)	(1,390)
Black	1.62	−2,514	2.19	18,259
	(0.12)	(4,241)	(0.11)	(3,453)
Hispanic[b]	2.46	14,249	2.70	22,664
	(0.19)	(4,860)	(0.18)	(4,461)
Less than high school	1.63	810	1.88	12,103
	(0.05)	(2,162)	(0.05)	(1,939)
High school	1.46	−693	1.52	1,905
	(0.04)	(2,119)	(0.04)	(2,008)
More than high school	1.46	−10	1.35	−8,355
	(0.06)	(3,371)	(0.07)	(3,483)

Source: See table 1.2.
Note: Standard errors in parentheses.
[a]Applies mortality tables for all white males and females to entire population.
[b]Can be any race.

clearly in table 1.3, which reproduces selected internal rate of return and net transfer results from table 1.2 and then adds results using mortality tables that vary only by sex (and not by race or education).[28] Whereas rates of return in different race and education groups are indistinguishable once differential mortality is accounted for, with uniform mortality rates low-income groups, such as blacks and people with less than high school education, have higher internal rates of return and transfers than the groups with higher average earnings.

In both sets of columns, Hispanics have returns and transfers significantly above those for whites and blacks. In this cohort, a large share of the Hispanics are immigrants, and as mentioned above, the progressive benefit formula strongly advantages immigrants with short periods of covered employment. In fact, the transfers for Hispanic immigrants are likely to be understated in these results. While precise lifetables for U.S. Hispanics are difficult to construct, the available evidence suggests that U.S. Hispanics (particularly Hispanic immigrants) have lower mortality rates than those for non-Hispanic whites, and my results do not take into account these lower mortality rates.[29]

28. Specifically, all men are assigned the white male mortality table and all women are assigned the white female mortality table.
29. For evidence on Hispanic mortality, see Sorlie et al. (1993) and Hummer et al. (1999).

1.5.2   Factors Offsetting Income-Related Redistribution

Table 1.4 contains results analyzing the extent to which spouse and survivor benefits and differential mortality reduce the amount of income-related redistribution accomplished by Social Security. The first column of the table contains the present value of Social Security taxes for each income quintile.[30] The second column contains the present value of Social Security benefits under two counterfactual assumptions. First, it calculates Social Security benefits with individuals receiving only their retired worker benefit and not spouse or survivor benefit. Second, it assumes that mortality rates vary only by sex and age and not by race and education. Thus, this column describes what the distribution of Social Security benefits would be if differential mortality and spouse and survivor benefits did not exist.

The next two columns remove each of these two counterfactual assumptions one at a time. Column (3) shows benefit levels with spouse and survivor benefits added in, but retaining the counterfactual assumption that mortality rates vary only by sex and age. Thus, the difference between column (3) and column (2) shows the impact of spouse and survivor benefits. Because spouse benefits are 50 percent of the benefit of the retired worker to whom the spouse is married, and survivor benefits are 100 percent of the benefit of the deceased retired worker, the size of these benefits is higher for those in the higher AIME quintiles. On average, individuals in the lowest AIME quintile gain $27,776 from the introduction of spouse and survivor benefits, individuals in the middle quintile gain $46,889, and individuals in the highest AIME quintile gain $52,158. Thus one could argue that the Social Security system implicitly values the time out of the labor force of women married to high-earning men more than that of women married to lower earners.

Viewed as a percentage increase, however, spouse and survivor benefits simply lead to an equal percentage increase in benefits across most of the quintiles, with a somewhat higher percentage increase in the benefits of the lowest-earning group. The bottom panel of the table shows benefit levels for each earnings quintile scaled so that the benefits for each group in column (2) equal 100. Introducing spouse and survivor benefits increases benefit levels by about 30 percent in the four highest quintiles and by about 40 percent in the lowest quintile. Thus, in evaluating the distributional implications of spouse and survivors benefits, one needs to have in mind a specific alternative for the extra revenue if it were not used for

30. These are the same values for Social Security taxes that underlie the basic results in tables 1.1 and 1.2. Mortality assumptions affect Social Security tax payments because my model incorporates the impact of mortality before age sixty-five. However, because the impact of different mortality assumptions on the present value of Social Security taxes paid by different income quintiles is extremely small, I ignore this effect in this table.

Table 1.4   The Impact of Spouse Benefits and Differential Mortality on Income-Related Redistribution from Social Security

	Present Value of Social Security Taxes	Present Value of Social Security Benefits		
		Using Mortality Tables Differing Only By Sex and Age, Assuming No Spouse or Survivor's Benefits	Using Mortality Tables Differing Only by Sex and Age	Using Mortality Tables Varying by Sex, Age, Race, and Education
All beneficiaries	184,413	140,283	184,413	184,413
Lowest AIME quintile	68,240	68,601	96,377	94,615
Second AIME quintile	158,675	137,918	178,014	176,606
Third AIME quintile	209,206	160,311	207,200	207,161
Fourth AIME quintile	231,752	166,345	220,663	221,568
Highest AIME quintile	258,485	170,333	222,491	224,915
		Scaled Benefit Levels		
Lowest AIME quintile		100	140.5	137.9
Second AIME quintile		100	129.1	128.1
Third AIME quintile		100	129.2	129.2
Fourth AIME quintile		100	132.7	133.2
Highest AIME quintile		100	130.6	132.0

Source: See table 1.2

Note: All present values are as of age 65.

these benefits. If the alternative were a proportional increase in all benefits or a reduction in the payroll tax, spouse benefits would have little impact on the amount of redistribution that occurs through Social Security. If the alternative is to raise the benefits or reduce the taxes of each beneficiary by an equal dollar amount, then spouse and survivor benefits cause substantial redistribution toward high-income households.

Differential mortality has a smaller impact on benefits levels, causing average lifetime benefits to fall in the lowest AIME quintile by about $3,330, or about 2 percent. In contrast, benefits rise in the highest AIME quintile by $2,424, or about 1 percent. These effects are somewhat smaller than the effects on education and race groups shown in table 1.3 because the income groups contain a mixture of the various race and education groups. Recent research by Deaton and Paxson (2001) suggests that income has a direct impact on mortality independent of race and education. Incorporating this direct effect of income would increase the effect of differential mortality on the benefit levels of the different income quintiles.

1.5.3   How Much Income-Related Redistribution is There?

The scatter plots and means make it clear that there is both a substantial amount of income-related redistribution occurring through Social Security and a substantial amount of redistribution that is not income related. However, the results presented so far do not provide a clear measure of the redistribution's total magnitude. While no summary measure of redistribution is perfect, a sense of the total magnitude is useful for understanding how important the income redistribution from Social Security is relative to other U.S. income-transfer programs and for considering how large an income-based transfer system would be needed to supplement an individual account-type Social Security system in order to preserve the current level of income-based redistribution.

The first row of table 1.5 shows that the present value of total Social Security benefits per birth year in my simulations is $460 billion.[31] Adding up the total transfers received by individuals receiving more than the cohort rate of return (which is also equal to the negative transfers of those receiving less than the cohort rate of return) results in total transfers of $60 billion, roughly 13 percent of total benefits. To measure the portion of these transfers that are income related, I replace each individual's transfer with the predicted transfer for a person of that income estimated by the kernel regression lines through the scatter plots in figures 1.2 and 1.5.[32] Adding up the income-related transfers calculated in this way produces an

---

31. This is an average over the five birth years, in 1999 dollars, discounting at the cohort rate of return of 1.29 percent.

32. An equivalent way to describe this measure of income-related transfers is that it is the total of all the transfers from individuals at income levels above the point where the average transfer becomes negative to people at income levels below that point.

Table 1.5   Measuring Aggregate Income-Related Redistribution from Social Security

	1.29% Discount Rate		3% Discount Rate		5% Discount Rate	
	$ billions	Share of Total Benefits (%)	$ billions	Share of Total Benefits (%)	$ billions	Share of Total Benefits (%)
Total present discounted value of benefits per birth year	460	100	396	100	342	100
Total transfers	60	13	99	25	192	56
Total income-related transfers using AIME measure of income	23	5	65	17	143	42
Total income-related transfers using total income measure of income	42	9	90	23	185	54

Source: See table 1.2.

estimate of $23 billion in income-related transfers under the AIME measure of income and $42 billion under the total-income measure of redistribution, suggesting that between 38 and 70 percent of Social Security transfers and between 5 and 9 percent of Social Security benefits go for income-related transfers. OASI benefit payments in 2001 are projected to be $373 billion dollars. Therefore, 5 to 9 percent would be between $19 and $34 billion of annual income-related transfers.

This measure of income-related transfers is quite sensitive to the discount rate used. At a discount rate of 3 percent, income-related transfers are between 17 and 23 percent of benefits, while at a discount rate of 5 percent they are between 42 and 54 percent.[33] This result is closely related to the point made earlier about the important interactions between intercohort and intracohort redistribution. When the interest rate used to discount Social Security benefits and taxes is lower than the cohort rate of return (as was the case for some early generations of beneficiaries), dollar measures of intracohort redistribution look regressive, because a large share of the windfalls go to upper-income beneficiaries with high benefit levels. In contrast, when the discount rate is above the cohort rate of return, dollar measures of the progressivity of the system show the high-

33. For discount rates above 1.29 percent, aggregate transfers are negative rather than zero. For these calculations, transfers for each individual are measured relative to the average dollar transfer for the cohort.

income individuals who pay higher amounts of taxes losing the most from
the low return on these tax payments.

In interpreting these results it is important to remember that the income
transfers from Social Security differ in a number of important ways from
transfers in other programs. First, because Social Security transfers vary
so much at each income level, crediting Social Security for accomplishing
the mean transfer at each income level exaggerates its effectiveness relative
to other income-transfer programs that give everyone at a given income
level the intended transfer.[34] That said, there are also advantages of transfers through Social Security. Lifetime income is almost surely a better measure of a person's true ability than income in a single year, and it is possible
that redistribution that occurs after retirement results in less distortion of
labor supply than redistribution that occurs during working years. Moreover, some of the redistribution that occurs for non–income-related reasons, like rewarding people with long life expectancies, could be desirable
if the goal is to ensure a constant replacement rate throughout retirement.

1.6   Discussion

Three other papers have recently provided evidence on the amount of
redistribution occurring through Social Security.[35] Although the papers
use different microsimulation models and often present different measures
of redistribution, the results, when comparable, are quite similar to the
ones in this paper and together suggest a consistent picture of Social Security's distributional effects. Caldwell et al. (1999) use a microsimulation
model based on projections of marriage and earnings patterns for postwar
generations. The net tax rates that they calculate for the 1990 birth cohort
(the cohort whose mortality patterns my results are calibrated to) range
from 6.2 percent in the first income decile to 8.9 percent in the 6th income
decile (and then fall in the upper deciles because their measure of income
is not capped at the Social Security taxable maximum).[36] These net tax
rates are somewhat lower than mine because Caldwell et al. assume a 14.6
percent OASI payroll tax in the long run, while I assume a 15.4 percent
tax rate. Gustman and Steinmeier (2001) use a microsimulation model
based on the Health and Retirement Survey. They emphasize that Social
Security looks less progressive after one groups individuals into house-

34. That is, the added variance from the Social Security transfers reduces utility relative
to a transfer that provided everyone at the income level with the mean transfer for that
income level.
35. The main work on all three of these projects occurred contemporaneously with my
work, and the various authors were not aware of each other's projects until the papers were
first presented.
36. These results come from discounting at a 5 percent rate of return.

holds and adjusts for variation in secondary earner levels than it does when one looks simply at retired worker benefits. Using a family measure of lifetime income that averages only those years with significant earnings, they find that the redistribution from Social Security increases benefits in the 2nd decile by 7 percent and reduces them by 7 percent in the 9th decile. Coronado, Fullerton, and Glass (2000) project future earnings and marriage patterns for a PSID-based sample. Ranking households by potential earnings and taking into account the fact that wages above the taxable maximum are not taxed, they conclude that, at a sufficiently high discount rate, Social Security is slightly regressive.

There are two important implications of my findings for Social Security reform. First, they suggest the magnitude of redistribution that an individual account–based plan would need to achieve in order to maintain the current level of redistribution from rich to poor. If distributionally neutral individual accounts completely replaced Social Security, the equivalent of $20 to $30 billion per year of redistribution from people with high lifetime earnings to people with low lifetime earnings would be required to maintain current levels of redistribution. In a distributionally neutral mixed plan in which individual accounts were responsible for only around one-third of the retirement income from Social Security, the equivalent of $7 to $10 billion per year in transfers would be required. However, because most individual account plans would mandate at least partial annuitization, such plans would not be distributionally neutral and would produce the same redistribution from short-lived to long-lived groups that occurs in the current system. This means that several billion additional dollars of transfers would be needed in an individual account plan in order for it to match the redistribution of the current system. Such transfers could be implemented in many ways. For example, contributions to individual accounts could be made in a redistributive way; payouts from the accounts of high earners could be taxed to subsidize payouts from the accounts of low earners; or general revenues could be used to provide supplemental payments to lower earners.

The second implication of these results for Social Security reform is that if no explicit steps are taken in an individual account–based plan to redistribute to groups with low life expectancies, then these groups could end up doing substantially worse than they do under the current system. In particular, blacks and high school dropouts currently receive rates of return from Social Security that are roughly the same as the population average, because the progressive benefit formula offsets the impact of their relatively high mortality rates. If an individual account–based plan required annuitization at a single price for everyone in the population, then the same effect of mortality on benefit payments would occur as in the current system, but there would not be the progressive benefit formula to offset it. Providing explicit redistribution as part of the individual accounts would be one way to ensure that these groups are not made worse off by Social Security reform. Other ways of offsetting the mortality effects include providing for bequests and coming up with sufficient additional resources in funding the account so that retirement income levels are preserved (see Feldstein and Liebman, chapter 7 in this volume).

In addition, these findings raise the question of how the Social Security benefit formula might be modified to align its distributional impact more closely with the theoretical impact shown in figure 1.1. There are two aspects to this modification: changing the average level of redistribution at different income levels and reducing the spread of transfers at a given income level. It would be relatively straightforward to increase transfers at low income levels and reduce them at higher income levels. The 90 percent factor in the PIA formula could be increased and the 32 and 15 percent factors reduced. Alternatively, if the goal was to concentrate the benefit increase on low earners, but not the atypical low earners in the 1st quintile, the range over which the 90 percent benefit factor applies could be extended, or a fourth range between 90 and 32 could be introduced.

Reducing the variation in transfers at a given level of income is more difficult and in some cases may not be desirable. Any retirement system that requires people to annuitize at a single rate will redistribute from those with short life expectancy to those with long life expectancy. One view of this sort of redistribution is that the correlation between income and life expectancy leads to perverse transfers from lower lifetime-income groups to higher lifetime-income groups. However, it is also possible to view people with longer life expectancies as having greater resource needs, in which case some redistribution to them could be desirable. Although it is unlikely that the political system would ever explicitly provide higher benefit levels for groups with lower life expectancy, adding bequest options similar to the ten-year certain options in private annuity plans would increase transfers to demographic groups with high mortality rates.[37] Reducing transfers between households with working and nonworking spouses could be accomplished by reducing spouse benefits (for example, by capping them at 50 percent of the PIA of the average earner) and raising worker benefits. Alternatively, secondary earners could receive a federal income tax credit for their payroll taxes at the end of the year. Because female earnings levels have increased in more recent cohorts, the importance of spouse benefits will decrease over time, and by some measures the progressivity of Social Security will increase.

---

37. If total benefits were held constant, providing bequests would of course require a reduction in retirement benefit levels.

1.7   Conclusion

Social Security provides income-related transfers that are between 5 and 9 percent of Social Security benefits paid, or $19 to $34 billion, at 2001 aggregate benefit levels (discounting at the 1.29 percent rate of return on Social Security earned by the microsimulation sample in this study). However, the range of transfers received at a given level of average lifetime income is quite wide. This wide variation is due to different mortality rates for people in different demographic groups, to variation in earnings levels by secondary earners, and to marital status differences, among other factors.

These results indicate that the income-based redistribution in the current Social Security system is fairly modest compared to the total benefits paid. However, it is worth emphasizing that income redistribution is only one of the benefits provided by Social Security, and some of the other benefits—such as the inflation-protected annuity and absence of market risk—may be particularly valuable to low-income families. Therefore, when we compare alternative systems to the current Social Security system, it will be important to determine not only whether they can raise the incomes and lower the poverty rates of low-income families, but also that they can provide a comparable amount of income security.[38]

References

Aaron, Henry. 1977. Demographic effects on the equity of Social Security benefits. In *The economics of public service,* ed. Martin Feldstein and Robert Inman, 151–73. London: MacMillan.

Board of Trustees of the Federal Old-Age, Survivors, and Disability Insurance Trust Fund. 1999. *The 1999 annual report of the Board of Trustees of the Federal Old-Age and Survivors Insurance and Disability Insurance Trust Funds.* Washington, D.C.: Social Security Administration.

———. 2001. *The 2001 annual report of the Board of Trustees of the Federal Old-Age and Survivors Insurance and Disability Insurance Trust Funds.* Washington, D.C.: Social Security Administration.

Boskin, Michael J., Laurence J. Kotlikoff, Douglas J. Puffert, and John B. Shoven. 1987. Social Security: A financial appraisal across and within generations. *National Tax Journal* 40 (3): 19–34.

Burkhauser, R., and J. Warlick. 1981. Disentangling the annuity from the redistributive aspects of Social Security in the United States. *Review of Income and Wealth* 27 (4): 401–21.

Burtless, Gary. 1994. Public spending on the poor: Historical trends and economic

---

38. Feldstein and Liebman (chapter 7 in this volume) show that a mixed plan adding 3 percent individual accounts on top of a pay-as-you-go system that continues to be funded with 12.4 percent of payroll can, in the long run, substantially reduce the percentage of Social Security recipients with benefits below the poverty line.

limits. In *Confronting poverty: Prescriptions for change,* ed. Sheldon Danziger, Gary Sandefur, and Daniel Weinberg, 51–84. New York: Russell Sage Foundation.

Caldwell, Steven, Melisssa Favreault, Alla Ganman, Jagadeesh Gokhale, Thomas Johnson, and Laurence J. Kotlikoff. 1999. Social Security's treatment of postwar Americans. In *Tax policy and the economy,* vol. 13, ed. James M. Poterba, 109–48. Cambridge: MIT Press.

Coronado, Julia, Don Fullerton, and Thomas Glass. 2000. The progressivity of Social Security. NBER Working Paper no. 7520. Cambridge, Mass.: National Bureau of Economic Research, February.

Deaton, Angus, and Cristina Paxson. 2001. Mortality, education, income and inequality among American cohorts. In *Themes in the economics of aging,* ed. David A. Wise, 129–70. Chicago: University of Chicago Press.

Duggan, James E., Robert Gillingham, and John S. Greenlees. 1993. Returns paid to early Social Security cohorts. *Contemporary Policy Issues* 11 (4): 1–13.

———. 1995. Progressive returns to Social Security? An Answer from Social Security records. U.S. Treasury Department. Working paper.

Elmendorf, Douglas, Jeffrey Liebman, and David Wilcox. 2001. Fiscal policy and Social Security reform in the 1990s. In *American economic policy in the 1990s,* ed. Jeffrey Frankel and Peter Orszag, forthcoming.

Garrett, Daniel M. 1995. The effects of differential mortality rates on the progressivity of Social Security. *Economic Inquiry* 33 (3): 457–75.

Gustman, Alan, and Thomas Steinmeier. 2000. Social Security benefits of immigrants and U.S. born. In *Issues in the economics of immigration,* ed. George Borjas, 309–50. Chicago: University of Chicago Press.

———. 2001. How effective is redistribution under the Social Security benefit formula? *Journal of Public Economics* 82 (1): 1–28.

Hummer, Robert A., Richard G. Rogers, Charles B. Nam, and Felicia B LeClere. 1999. Race/ethnicity, nativity, and U.S. adult mortality. *Social Science Quarterly* 80 (1): 136–53.

Hurd, Michael D., and John B. Shoven. 1985. The distributional impact of Social Security. In *Pensions, labor, and individual choice,* ed. by David A. Wise, 193–207. Chicago: University of Chicago Press.

Kitagawa, E. M., and P. M. Hauser. 1973. *Differential mortality in the United States: A study in socioeconomic epidemiology.* Cambridge: Harvard University Press.

McClellan, Mark, and Jonathan Skinner. 1997. The incidence of Medicare. NBER Working Paper no. 6013. Cambridge, Mass.: National Bureau of Economic Research, April.

National Economic Council, Interagency Working Group on Social Security. 1998.*Women and retirement security.* Washington, D.C.: National Economic Council.

Panis, Constantijn, and Lee Lillard. 1996. Socioeconomic differentials in the returns to Social Security. RAND Corporation Report no. DRU/1327/NIA. Santa Monica, Calif.: RAND.

Pappas, Gregory, Susan Queen, Wilbur Hadden, and Gail Fisher. 1993. The increasing disparity in mortality between socioeconomic groups in the United States: 1960 and 1986. *New England Journal of Medicine* 329 (2): 103–09.

Rogot, Eugene, Paul D. Sorlie, and Norman J. Johnson. 1992. Life expectancy by employment status, income, and education in the National Longitudinal Mortality Study. *Public Health Reports* 107 (4): 457–61.

Social Security Administration. 2000. *Fast facts and figures about Social Security.*

Office of Policy, Office of Research, Evaluation, and Statistics. Washington, D.C.: Social Security Administration.

Sorlie, Paul D., Erick Backlund, Norman Johnson, and Eugene Rogot. 1993. Mortality by Hispanic status in the United States. *Journal of the American Medical Association* 270 (20): 2464–68.

Steuerle, C. Eugene, and Jon M. Bakija. 1994. *Retooling Social Security for the twenty-first century.* Washington, D.C.: Urban Institute Press.

Comment   Gary Burtless

Jeffrey Liebman has written a very lucid, well-conceived, and sensibly executed chapter. Although it may not be apparent to most readers, the tabulations he performs are extremely difficult, not least because they are based on data in a complex file containing information from both the Survey of Income and Program Participation files (SIPP) and Social Security Earnings Records (SSER). These merged records contain confidential earnings data and are therefore rarely examined by academic researchers. Liebman's tabulations shed highly revealing light on some of the important income redistributive effects of the existing Social Security system.

My remarks will focus on one main question: How should we think about Liebman's analytical framework in comparison with other possible ways of viewing Social Security's redistributive effects?

The chapter's basic goal is to uncover the pattern of *within*-generation redistribution produced by the Social Security system. In particular, Liebman tries to highlight the pattern of redistributive Social Security impacts on lifetime or permanent income. Naturally, the findings of the paper reflect the framework in which they are derived. They provide estimates of redistribution within only one possible framework. Different frameworks would reveal a different set of redistributive impacts.

To take a trivial example, Liebman focuses on within-generation redistribution. He could extend the analysis, as many others have done, to examine the impacts of the system on *cross*-generational income distribution. Many critics of Social Security point out that the cross-generational redistribution sometimes benefits the better off at the expense of the less well off. High-income members of generations that received generous net transfers from Social Security, especially the generations that began collecting pensions before 1980, have obtained generous net transfers partly at the expense of low-income people in generations that will pay net taxes to Social Security. It is nonetheless the case that the system on average

Gary Burtless is a senior fellow in the economic studies program at the Brookings Institution.

provided transfers to earlier and poorer generations at the expense of later and richer generations. Moving to an advance funded, defined-contribution system and phasing out the pay-as-you-go system would eventually eliminate this kind of cross-generational redistribution and, with it, a type of redistribution that on average has favored the less well off. Liebman's analysis will miss this kind of redistribution.

Liebman could also extend the analysis, as the Office of the Actuary has attempted to do, to account for all of the insurance components financed by the OASDI tax. Disability Insurance (DI) and early Survivors Insurance benefits can begin long before age sixty, which is the earliest age at which the OASDI benefit stream enters Liebman's calculations. Some early benefits last long after age sixty, and these, too, are missed in Liebman's analysis. For example, the DI pension is converted to an Old-Age Insurance (OAI) pension when the disabled worker reaches the normal retirement age. The OAI pension is much higher than it would be in the absence of the DI program, however, because under the regular OAI benefit formula all of the years of postdisability low earnings would be counted when determining the pension. Simlarly, the survivor's pension that is based on a DI pension is usually higher than an ordinary survivor's pension. As the chapter notes in passing, the lifetime redistributive effects of DI and early survivors' pensions are much more helpful for people with low lifetime incomes than are ordinary OAI pensions, which naturally favor people with longer than average life expectancies. Thus, a lifetime analysis of all the components of OASDI would show redistributive effects that are much more favorable to people with low permanent income, who tend to become disabled and leave young survivors much more frequently than people with high permanent income (see Leimer 1999).

Finally, one can examine the redistributive impacts of Social Security from a one-year rather than a lifetime perspective. In response to my suggestion at the conference, Liebman has now added a table to the chapter with some one-year estimates. These estimates provide evidence on questions such as whether the people who pay OASDI taxes *this year* have higher net incomes than the people who collect this year's OASDI benefits, and how much the transfers shift this year's income distribution. All empirical studies known to me show that Social Security benefits are very important in reducing the inequality of this year's income, and Liebman's estimates confirm this as well (see Danziger and Weinberg 1994). They are probably more important, in fact, than the income tax in reducing the inequality of net income. If we permitted taxpayers to keep their OASDI taxes and withheld OASDI pensions from current beneficiaries, we would tilt the income distribution in favor of higher-income people and greatly expand the ranks of the poor. Even though the OASDI payroll tax is often criticized as regressive, it is progressive up to a family income of about $100,000 or $125,000 a year, primarily because wage and self-employment income (which is taxable under OASDI) represents a rising percentage of family income up through those income levels.

I recognize that one-year accounting perspectives are not very fashionable in economics. Most of us are confident that the longer-term (especially the lifetime) perspective is more illuminating when we think about income redistribution. The retired seventy-year-old often has less current income than the working thirty-five-year-old, but the *permanent* income of the seventy-year-old might easily be higher. In a lifetime perspective, it is bad redistributive policy for the lower-permanent-income thirty-five-year-old to be transferring resources to the higher-permanent-income seventy-year-old. (Liebman essentially measures permanent income using Average Indexed Monthly Earnings, or AIME.)

In one sense, this reasoning is beyond reproach, but in another it is highly misleading. One reason we have a Social Security system is the view that people will not take sensible precautions to insure themselves against known risks to themselves and their families—risks such as early death, disability, retirement, and extremely long life spans. When these risks become realities, many people are caught flat-footed and find themselves with too little savings to support themselves. Social Security requires workers to purchase insurance that partially protects them against these risks. The Social Security system imposes taxes on low-permanent-income thirty-five-year-olds to finance transfers to high-permanent-income seventy-year-olds. The transfers prevent high-permanent-income seventy-year-olds from becoming low-*actual*-income seventy-year-olds. To a large extent, this transfer mechanism succeeds in holding down poverty among aged and disabled Americans, including retired and disabled Americans who had middle-class incomes when they were at work. Liebman's analysis largely misses this redistributional effect of Social Security. It is a view of redistribution that rests on the plausible but incorrect theory that, in the absence of Social Security, workers would have successfully smoothed their consumption over their lifetimes. Many would have smoothed their consumption, but workers who would have failed to do so are protected by Social Security.

In interpreting the aggregate amount of redistribution that Liebman attributes to Social Security, it is important not to make the mistake of comparing this sum directly to the annual expenditures on other transfer programs. Consider the Earned Income Tax Credit (EITC), for example. From a lifetime perspective, many EITC recipients have incomes above the one-year threshold for EITC eligibility, and many of the people who pay additional income taxes to finance the EITC, including low-income childless workers, have incomes below the EITC eligibility threshold. Thus a sensible comparison would require taking the lifetime perspective on other transfer programs as well.

However, we will move away from the redistributive analyses that Jeff

Liebman did not perform to focus on the one he actually did. His interest is on the within-generation impacts of the system from a truncated lifetime perspective (truncated because it ignores benefits contributors obtain before age sixty). Contributors pay taxes while they are at work and collect benefits starting some time after age sixty. Liebman can easily calculate the return workers obtain on their taxes, given a convention for counting taxes and benefits. In Liebman's main analysis, if a worker's return exceeds her generation's average, she has obtained a net transfer. If her internal rate of return falls short of her generation's average, she has paid net taxes to the system.

Note that this is a different concept of net taxes and transfers than the one adopted by Jagadeesh Gokhale and Larry Kotlikoff in another paper at this conference. They use a benchmark ("fair market") discounting factor to assess contributions and benefits. If a worker's return falls short of this benchmark, she is classified as a net taxpayer. Since Gokhale and Kotlikoff use a benchmark return that is far higher than the average internal rate of return actually realized on Social Security contributions, they find a much higher percentage of contributors in each generation to be net taxpayers.

As noted, Liebman must establish a convention for counting a worker's taxes and contributions, that is, for assigning total contributions and benefits to individual workers. Liebman's convention is to assign to a worker all the worker's taxes when she is single and half her contributions when she is married. In addition, Liebman assigns to a person half the spouse's contributions when the person is married. An identical convention is used to assign benefits to individuals. All of individual i's benefits when person i is single, and half the combined husband-wife benefits when person i is married, are assigned to person i.

This is a straightforward and illuminating way to assign contributions and benefits, but it is not necessarily compatible with the philosophy behind the program. Social Security sometimes bases a person's benefits on the person's own earnings record and sometimes on the earnings record of another family member. The architects seem to have had in mind an insurance scheme in which contributors earned rights to benefits under designated circumstances (insurable events). When a sixty-one-year-old married contributor is taken to the undertaker, he bequeaths benefit entitlements to specified dependents (including his spouse). Franklin D. Roosevelt and Congress probably believed the stream of benefits flowing to the contributor's survivors was generated by the earlier stream of contributions made by the deceased worker. In the example I have just given, however, Liebman would assign one-half the worker's tax contributions and none of the benefits to the deceased worker and assign one-half the tax contributions and *all* of the benefits to the surviving spouse. This procedure will obviously produce large and apparently capricious redistribution between workers and their spouses, with high net transfers and internal rates of return for longer-lived spouses. The variance of returns would be enormous if Liebman had tabulated the actual benefit streams of people in his sample, since variations in mortality experience would lead to wide variation in lifetime benefits, but he instead tabulates individuals' expected benefit streams.

Unless I have overlooked something, however, a conceptual problem remains. The worker's contributions produce a set of benefit entitlements, some of which flow to the worker and some of which flow to the worker's surviving dependents. The expected benefits that go to a surviving dependent after the contributor has died do not appear as "returns" to the contributor, even though they are part of the entitlements that the contributor's taxes have purchased.

We could view contributions and benefits in a different way than does Liebman. All the benefits that flow from a Social Security earnings record, whether received by the contributor or his surviving dependents, could be assigned to that Social Security contributor. This alternative framework would certainly lift the measured internal rate of return on men's Social Security taxes and reduce the apparent return on women's taxes. I do not think this alternative procedure should be preferred to the one Liebman uses, but it is the framework implicitly used by many women's groups who criticize the antifemale bias of the Social Security system. They correctly point out that the current system does not give full credit to the OASDI contributions of working wives who are secondary family earners. On the margin, such earners receive little or no extra OASDI benefits for their contributions, because the family's main retirement and survivors' benefit will be determined by the earnings record of the higher-earning spouse. From this perspective, men's contributions are producing a higher rate of return than women's, exactly the opposite conclusion from the one reached in this chapter.

While I think that Liebman's procedure is sensible and informative, it should be clear that a different convention for assigning taxes and benefits would have produced sharply differing results. For many critics of Social Security (although not for me), the alternative convention seems more meaningful than the one adopted by Liebman.

Since Liebman emphasizes the perverse effect of spouse benefits on redistribution, I want to conclude with a brief discussion of those benefits. It seems to me that the architects of Social Security had in mind a society in which each family was mainly supported by one breadwinner and all men and women mated for life. They designed an old-age and survivors' program that attempted to offer "adequate" benefits at the least possible cost. Thus, they did not give large payments to the estates of contributors who died young, unless the deceased contributors left surviving dependents.

Social Security's architects obviously thought it cost 50 percent more to support a couple than a single person.[1] A worker's premium contributions for Social Security thus purchased a pension that was 50 percent larger if two people survived or, equivalently, a pension 33 percent smaller if just one person survived. Suppose instead that the architects had chosen to give individual pensions without dependent spouse supplements. To assure that surviving couples had large enough pensions to support themselves comfortably, the basic pension would have had to be higher than the one provided to single survivors under the current system. The higher basic pensions in turn would have required a higher contribution rate. From the point of view of holding down program cost, a system with no dependent spouse benefit supplements would have provided "wastefully" high benefits to surviving single people. Given the rise in women's labor force participation and expected lifetime earnings, the original design of spouse benefits now seems misconceived and leads to capricious and sometimes regressive redistribution. Liebman suggests a sensible strategy for limiting the cost of spouse supplements and improving the redistributive impact of the system: Put a flat cap on dependent spouse monthly benefits.

It seems to me, however, that the design of spousal and survivor benefits provides real insurance to workers that Liebman's analysis may miss. He takes the perspective of people who have already survived to age sixty and know whether they will enter old age as a single person or as part of a married couple. At that point, workers' marital statuses already largely determine whether they will be advantaged or disadvantaged under the OAI and survivors' program. Women, especially secondary earner married women, can expect to receive large benefits relative to their contributions; men and single women can expect to be far less favorably treated. People who enter old age as single people are doomed to obtain the modest rate of return that their marital status automatically produces under Social Security.

However, at age sixteen or twenty this outcome could not have been foreseen, or it would have been just one of several possible outcomes. At that early age, the person would reasonably think he or she could marry, that the (unknown) marriage partner could earn substantially more or less than oneself, that the marriage partner could remain alive until old age. All of the possible benefit entitlements that flow out of these events would have entered into the individual's assessment of the expected returns ob-

---

1. In this they disagreed with the analysts who developed the official U.S. poverty thresholds. The poverty thresholds imply that it costs just 26 percent more to support an aged couple than an aged single person. This simple difference between the implicit equivalence scales in Social Security (and other benefit programs) and the poverty thresholds explains much of the difference in poverty rates between the elderly in married-couple and single-person households. Liebman does not make a family-size correction in computing the permanent incomes (AIMEs) of individuals included in his analysis. Thus, couples and single people with the same AIME are treated as having an equivalent position in the income distribution.

tainable under Social Security. What looks like a bad deal at age sixty-two, when a person enters old age without a living marriage partner, might have seemed like a much more attractive proposition at age twenty-two, when a happy marriage with a long-lived partner was still a real possibility.

An important question, then, is whether it is enough to analyze the distributional consequences of Social Security for people who have already experienced most of the marital status changes they will experience over their lifetimes. Or should we instead take the perspective of workers at, say, age sixteen, before the full sequence of marriage spells and widowhood is known? My guess is that a large number of well-informed sixteen-year-olds would find Social Security insurance valuable, even though at age sixty they will sensibly conclude it provided them with a bad deal—because they have no surviving spouse.

Let me emphasize, however, that I find Liebman's analytical framework and tabulations illuminating and helpful. Their limitations are those of all such tabulations: They provide just one kind of assessment of the redistribution produced by the system. A different framework would provide a different—although not necessarily a better—assessment.

References

Danziger, Sheldon, and Daniel Weinberg. 1994. The historical record: Trends in family income, inequality, and poverty. In *Confronting poverty: Prescriptions for change,* ed. Sheldon Danziger, Gary Sandefur, and Daniel Weinberg, 38–44. Cambridge: Harvard University Press.

Leimer, Dean R. 1999. Lifetime redistribution under the Social Security program: A literature synopsis. *Social Security Bulletin* 62 (2): 43–51.

Discussion Summary

Laurence J. Kotlikoff questioned the large amount of dispersion in expected benefits for people with the same lifetime income. The author indicated that this dispersion is caused by a variety of factors including differential ex ante mortality, spousal benefits, and the timing of income.

Stephen Zeldes was concerned about the net present value calculations. Since the author used the average cohort rate of return instead of the significantly larger market-based rate of return to determine the net present value of benefits, Zeldes said there might be very different answers about the progressivity of the system if alternative rates of return were considered.

Because the marginal utility of income for the poor is so much higher than the marginal utility of income for the wealthy, *Jonathan Skinner* thought the paper's conclusions might be completely different if the utility value of redistribution were analyzed, rather than just the dollar amount of redistribution. The author agreed with this assessment and noted that it might be important to take into account the value of insurance provision as well as weigh the dollar amounts of redistribution differently at various levels of the income distribution.

Several participants believed that the heterogeneous mortality experiences seen in historical data would not have as strong an impact in the future. However, the author said that it was not at all clear that mortality rates will converge in the future and pointed to actuarial forecasts implying a relatively constant gap between the life expectancies of men and women and to evidence from the 1960s to the mid-1980s indicating that over that period the morality experience of blacks and whites failed to converge.

2

Guaranteed Income
SSI and the Well-Being
of the Elderly Poor

Kathleen McGarry

Social Security has done much to improve the well-being of the elderly, particularly the well-being of the poorest among the old. In 1960 approximately 35 percent of those aged sixty-five and over lived in poverty; today that figure is below 11 percent. Much of this decline has been attributed to increases in Social Security. Social Security has also improved the lives of our elderly citizens by other measures. In 1960, 40 percent of elderly widows lived with their children, but by 1990 less than 20 percent did so. This shift toward independent living has been viewed as a positive outcome of the increased income of the elderly. Labor force participation among older male workers has also fallen to roughly half of its 1960 rate, a phenomenon that has again been attributed by many researchers to the growth in Social Security.

Despite these gains, there remains a sizable fraction of the population for whom Social Security and other retirement resources do not provide an adequate standard of living. For these individuals, benefits are available from the Supplemental Social Security Income program (SSI), which provides a guaranteed income for all those aged sixty-five and over, as well as the blind and the disabled. Conditional on sufficiently low assets, there should be no elderly individual with monthly income below $484 (in 1997 dollars) or married couple with income below $726. In reality, however, many of the poor are not enrolled in SSI and subsist on incomes below these levels. In order to improve the well-being of the elderly, it is therefore

Kathleen McGarry is associate professor of economics at the University of California, Los Angeles, and a research associate of the National Bureau of Economic Research.

The author is grateful to Martin Feldstein, Wei-Yin Hu, Jeffrey B. Liebman, Bruce D. Meyer, and Robert Schoeni for helpful comments and to the National Bureau of Economic Research for financial support.

imperative that we first understand how SSI functions and what changes might be made to improve the financial situation of the eligible population. As the nation considers changes in Social Security, concurrent changes in SSI might be well-advised. Successful linkage of the two programs and implementation of any changes require a clear understanding of the current system and an investigation of the costs and consequences of such changes. Furthermore, analyses of the impact of Social Security reforms on the well-being of the poorest among the elderly strongly depend on the interaction of the two programs.

In this chapter I first describe the SSI program in its current form, focusing exclusively on the benefits and regulations applicable to the elderly. I use data from the Asset and Health Dynamics Study to examine the behavior of a population of elderly individuals with respect to the program guidelines and then hypothesize what modifications to the SSI program might be introduced and how these changes would alter poverty rates and program costs. I then discuss the relationship between Social Security and SSI and how the characteristics of the SSI program would alter the distributional impact of various Social Security reforms.

2.1   Description of the Supplemental Security Income

2.1.1   Program Overview[1]

The Social Security Act of 1935 established a mechanism whereby the federal government would assist states in providing cash assistance to the poor; for the poor elderly, this assistance came from state-run old age assistance (OAA) programs. In 1972 legislation was passed that replaced these state-run plans with the federal Supplemental Security Income Program, administered by the Social Security Administration (SSA).[2] In contrast to the state programs, which typically assessed individual need on a case by case basis, the federal SSI program provides a guaranteed income to all eligible individuals. In 1997 the income guarantees were $484 per month for a single individual living in his own home, and $726 for a couple. These amounts are reduced by one-third if the recipient lives in someone else's home and are adjusted yearly for inflation. For individuals with no other income, the income guarantee is the actual benefit they receive from SSI. For those with other sources of income, the SSI benefit is the difference between the income guarantee and their countable income. Countable income is distinct from current income in that the SSI program disregards some portion of a potential recipient's income. The disregards vary by in-

---

1. The information in this section is drawn primarily from the Social Security Administration (1997, 1999).

2. The SSI program also took the place of the state-run assistance programs of Aid to the Blind and Aid to the Permanently and Totally Disabled.

come source. The most important of these, as measured on a monthly basis, are the first $20 of unearned income (most likely Social Security benefits), the first $65 of earned income, and one-half of other earned income.[3] Because of the disregards, those eligible for SSI can have income somewhat above the guarantee, but no participant should have income below this legislated amount.

An asset test is also required for participation in SSI. To be eligible for benefits, individuals must have countable assets of less than $2,000, and couples must have less than $3,000. With respect to the determination of countable assets, the disregards are substantial. Most importantly, an owner-occupied home regardless of value and a car worth less than $4,500 are excluded.[4]

In addition to the federal program, states have the option of offering supplemental benefits. In 1997, twenty-six states offered supplements to elderly individuals (or couples) living independently, and a total of forty-four states offered at least some form of supplemental benefits, including payments aimed specifically at the blind, the disabled or those with particular medical needs. With these supplements, the benefits available to individuals can vary substantially across states. For example, the income guarantee for a couple living in California in 1997 was $1,122.20 ($396.20 above the federal level), while in New York the income guarantee for a couple was $828.50. If states choose to follow the same eligibility guidelines as the federal program with respect to such issues as the determination of countable income and assets, the SSA will administer the supplemental program on behalf of the state. If a state is willing to administer its own program, it is free to alter the eligibility requirements as it wishes, including imposing more (or less) stringent income and asset tests and providing supplemental benefits to only a subset of the population eligible for SSI (e.g., those with specific medical needs).[5]

Those eligible for SSI are also likely to be entitled to benefits from other programs. SSI recipients are eligible for food stamps in all states except California.[6] Also, SSI recipients in most states are categorically eligible for Medicaid and need file no other application to receive these benefits.[7]

---

3. If there is less than $20 unearned income, additional earned income can be disregarded. Other disregards are irregularly or infrequently received income of less than $20 per month, home energy assistance payments, tuition benefits, disaster relief, and the value of food stamps.

4. Other exclusions are life insurance with a face value of less than $1,500, burial plots, and household furnishings of less than $2,000.

5. In 1997, twenty-seven states administered their own supplemental programs, eleven states had programs administered by the Social Security Administration, five reported both levels of administration, and one supplemental program was administered at the county level (seven states had no optional supplemental program).

6. California incorporates the value of food stamps into its monthly benefit.

7. Forty states used SSI program guidelines to determine Medicaid eligibility. The remaining states used different criteria.

Medicaid itself represents a substantial financial transfer and therefore makes participation in the SSI program much more valuable.

Despite these potential benefits, the majority of SSI recipients remain poor. In 1997 the poverty lines for elderly singles and couples were $641.5 and $809.33 per month, somewhat above the federal SSI guarantees. Because of the existence of income disregards, particularly the larger disregard for earned income, some of those receiving SSI will have their incomes increased above the poverty line by the federal benefit. However, for the most part, the federal SSI program will have little effect on poverty rates. In contrast, the supplemental programs in some states are sufficiently generous that they do guarantee income above the poverty line. Income guarantees in 1997 were above the poverty level for singles in three states and for couples in twelve states. In addition, when the income disregards are taken into account, individuals in many other states may also have their total incomes raised beyond the poverty line. I examine this issue further in section 2.2.4.

2.1.2 Participation in Supplemental Security Income

One of the more surprising aspects of SSI is that many of those entitled to benefits are not enrolled in the program. Several earlier studies have demonstrated that only slightly more than one-half of those who appear to be eligible for SSI are actually receiving benefits (Menefee, Edwards, and Schieber 1981; McGarry 1996). These participation rates are lower than those found for the former Aid to Families with Dependent Children (AFDC) program (Fraker and Moffitt 1988) and roughly comparable with more recent evidence on participation in the food stamp program (Blank and Ruggles 1996).[8]

The literature has offered several hypotheses to explain this nonparticipation. (See Warlick 1979 for a detailed discussion of the various arguments.) It has been proposed that those who do not participate are not aware of the program or that the process of applying for benefits is too challenging either physically or intellectually. Alternatively, it has been suggested that the stigma attached to the receipt of welfare outweighs the value of the benefits (Moffitt 1983). Below I briefly investigate the correlates of nonparticipation for a sample of SSI-eligible individuals.[9] When considering the effectiveness of the SSI program in achieving its goal of a guaranteed minimum income, one must keep in mind these low participation rates. Similarly, analyses of the effect of changes in the SSI program on the distribution of income and program costs must account for changes in both eligibility and participation.

8. Fraker and Moffit (1988) estimated much lower food stamp participation rates than did Blank and Ruggles (1996), 38 percent versus approximately 60 percent.
9. Menefee, Edwards, and Schieber (1981), Warlick (1982), Coe (1985), and McGarry (1996) address this issue in detail.

2.2   Microdata Analysis

2.2.1   Asset and Health Dynamics Study Data

I use data from the Asset and Health Dynamics Study (AHEAD) to analyze the distributional aspects of the SSI program and its potential to affect the well-being of the elderly poor.[10] AHEAD provides a nationally representative sample of the population born in 1923 or earlier and their spouses. The respondents were first interviewed in 1993, when the age-eligible portion of the sample was approximately seventy years old or over. The entire sample consists of 8,222 individuals in 6,048 households.[11] The analyses presented here will use a single individual or married couple as the unit of analysis, and I will refer to each observation as a family unit.[12] AHEAD is ideal for this study because it contains a large sample of individuals, nearly all of whom meet the age requirements for SSI eligibility, as well as detailed information on income and assets that allows for accurate determination of eligibility based on the income and asset criteria.[13] This project also draws on a supplemental restricted use data file that contains geographic identifiers for the AHEAD respondents. Because SSI benefits can vary widely across states, this information is necessary if potential benefits are to be properly imputed. Below I note the difference in eligibility when state programs are ignored.

2.2.2   Eligibility

I determine eligibility for federal SSI benefits using the specific rules of the program as they existed in 1993, including both the income and asset tests (Social Security Administration 1993). The federal guarantees in that year were $422 and $633 for singles and couples.[14] I then calculate the amount of a state supplement to which the family unit (single individual

10. A detailed description of the survey is available in Soldo et al. (1997).
11. Included in these numbers are 189 spouses below age sixty-five who would not themselves be eligible for SSI, regardless of income. However, because federal law requires that a portion of the income of an age-ineligible spouse be deemed to the SSI applicant, it is important that these individuals be kept in the sample and their incomes known.
12. In some cases, other individuals are present in the household; these could be children, other relatives, or nonrelatives. The SSI program does not count the income of these other individuals when determining the benefit to which the eligible unit is entitled, but the income guarantees are reduced by one-third if the potentially eligible unit lives in the household of another. In my calculation of benefits I, too, impose this one-third reduction. In all other respects, I ignore these other individuals; I do not count their income when considering the poverty status of the individual or couple, nor do I use their presence to determine the appropriate poverty line.
13. Many earlier studies of participation in welfare programs did not have asset information and imputed asset eligibility based on income from assets.
14. A portion of the AHEAD sample was interviewed in 1994. Because the income measures refer to the preceeding month, I use 1994 SSI rules for all those interviewed after January 1994. The federal guarantees in 1994 were $446 and $669 (SSA 1994).

or married couple) would be entitled based on the state of residence and the guidelines of the SSI program particular to that state. The calculation of countable income is based on reports of monthly income in AHEAD, subtracting the appropriate disregards for earned and unearned income. In addition to the standard disregards, I exclude transfers received from family members or other individuals, because it is unlikely that these transfers are received with sufficient regularity to be reported to the government and included in countable income.

With respect to calculating asset eligibility, I am again able to follow the program guidelines nearly exactly. I exclude the value of the home, up to $1,500 in life insurance, and up to $4,500 in vehicle equity (the limit on the value of a car).[15]

Table 2.1 compares income and asset eligibility. The first part of the table reports the percentage of the sample that is eligible for either federal or state SSI, based on the application of the income and asset tests alone and jointly. It is apparent from these numbers that the income limits are much more likely to be binding than are the asset limits. Of the sample, 29.22 percent have countable assets below the SSI limits, while only 12.77 percent have income that is sufficiently low. Combining the two criteria, 8.75 percent of family units are eligible for benefits from federal and/or state SSI programs.

The characteristics of the 4 percent of the sample that are income eligible but not asset eligible merit discussion. Seventy-nine percent of these units have incomes below the poverty line (not shown), and in that sense seem to merit assistance, yet their wealth holdings prevent them from receiving any benefits. Thus, even if the income guarantees were raised to the poverty line and all eligible individuals participated in SSI, a fraction of the population would remain poor, at least until their assets were depleted. The wealth holdings of this group of income eligibles/asset ineligibles are relatively high: Mean wealth is $168,486 ($103,756 if housing wealth is excluded). Only 9 percent of this subsample have countable assets less than twice the limits set by SSI, while 23 percent have countable assets of over $100,000. Thus the asset test does serve to limit the participation of those who can finance some consumption with current wealth.

The state supplemental programs play a large role in increasing eligibility relative to the federal guidelines. The second part of table 2.1 highlights the effect by reporting the proportion of the sample eligible for SSI based

15. With respect to the exclusion of a car, I am unable to identify precisely its actual value. AHEAD obtains the value of all vehicles (cars, boats, motorcycles, etc.) in a single question. The respondent may therefore own more than one car, or may own other vehicles that would be included in countable assets, although this is unlikely for those with little in the way of other assets or income. The survey also does not ask about the value of household furnishings, so these are presumed to be less than the $2,000 limit allowed under SSI and not included as part of countable assets.

Table 2.1   Income and Asset Eligibility

	Asset Test		
Income Test	Ineligible	Eligible	Total
Eligibility using federal and state criteria			
Ineligible	66.75	20.47	87.23
	(3,709)	(1,416)	(5,125)
Eligible	4.02	8.75	12.77
	(238)	(685)	(923)
Total	70.78	29.22	100.00
	(3,947)	(2,101)	(6,048)
Using federal criteria only			
Ineligible	67.93	22.18	90.11
	(3,769)	(1,520)	(5,289)
Eligible	2.85	7.04	9.89
	(178)	(581)	(759)
Total	70.78	29.22	100.00
	(3,947)	(2,101)	(6,048)

Source: All tables are from author's calculations.

Notes: Percentages of all family units (weighted figures). Total numbers of family units in parentheses (unweighted).

on federal guarantees alone. Here, the fraction of income eligible falls from 12.8 when state supplements are included to 9.9 percent, and the fraction eligible after both the income and asset tests falls to 7 percent. The state supplemental programs thus serve to increase the eligible population by 24 percent.

2.2.3   Characteristics of Participants

When examining actual participation for the families in the sample, I find the same low participation rates observed in other studies. Participation status is unknown for 11 of the 685 eligible units. Of the remaining 674 units, 392 report that they are receiving benefits. When appropriately weighted,[16] these numbers imply a participation rate of 55.9 percent. Surprisingly, this rate is nearly identical to the 55 percent participation rate found in the 1973 and 1974 Survey of Low-Income Aged and Disabled (Menefee, Edwards, and Schieber 1981) and the 56 percent participation rate in the 1984 Survey of Income and Program Participation (SIPP; McGarry 1996).

Although the participation rate matches those of past studies, recent evidence suggests that estimates of participation in welfare programs from survey data may be downward biased due to underreporting of the receipt of benefits (see Bavier 1999). While it is obviously difficult to assess the

16. AHEAD oversampled individuals in heavily black and Hispanic neighborhoods, so weighting is necessary to achieve population representative statistics.

extent of misreporting, comparisons with administrative records indicate that it may be an important phenomenon. Giannarelli and Wheaton (2000) estimate that the Current Population Survey (CPS) captures approximately 75 percent of SSI receipts. Comparisons of reported benefits presented here with administrative records also indicate underreporting.[17] However, despite the likely biases, there are several reasons to believe that underreporting does not alter the conclusion that a large fraction of eligible individuals fails to enroll. First, SSI enrollment figures are far below those predicted by the SSA from its data (Kennedy 1982). Second, consistent with the results of survey data, outreach studies have found large numbers of eligible nonparticipants but have had little success in increasing enrollment (Comptroller General 1976). Finally, the similarity between the participation rate found here and that observed in SIPP is notable because SIPP is believed have unusually accurate reporting of income sources and, in particular, more complete reporting of SSI income than the CPS (Kalton, McMillen, and Kasprzyk 1986). However, to the extent that the receipt of SSI is underreported in AHEAD, the participation rate is an underestimate of the true probability of participation in the program, and costs and enrollment figures will also be biased downward.

Table 2.2 presents the means of several variables used in the subsequent analyses. I examine the characteristics of three distinct groups: those who are ineligible for SSI, those who are eligible and receiving benefits, and those who are eligible but not collecting these benefits.[18] The ineligible subsample is obviously better off in virtually every dimension than either of the other two groups, and their mean values are reported mainly for purposes of comparison. Mean income for this group, exclusive of SSI, is $1,915 per month, and their net worth is $195,142, or $118,952 when housing

17. The 1998 Green Book (U.S. House of Representatives 1998) cites an SSI participation rate of 56.3 for the elderly, nearly identical to that estimated here. However, the participation rates tabulated in the Green Book count the fraction of the elderly *poor* receiving SSI benefits, rather than the fraction of the *eligible* population. Because some elderly poor are likely to be ineligible for SSI due to asset holding, and some with incomes above the poverty line are likely to be eligible, given state supplements and income disregards, this measure is imprecise. However, if I calculate a similar statistic for the AHEAD sample (the fraction of those with income below the poverty line who report receiving SSI benefits) I find a participation rate of only 28 percent. The substantially lower level of reported benefits found with AHEAD relative to that using administrative records indicates that there may be a good deal of nonreporting of SSI benefits. The discussion of table 2.6 below indicates a similarly important degree of nonreporting with a comparison of payments. (In addition to underreporting of recipiency, there are several other factors affecting the comparisons between AHEAD and SSA data, all of which are likely to play a role. First, the AHEAD sample is representative of the noninstitutional population aged seventy and over, rather than all those aged sixty-five and over. Second, the definitions of poverty differ somewhat (see note 22); third, the AHEAD estimates are based on SSI *units* rather than individuals; and, finally, the AHEAD estimates use monthly rather than yearly measures of poverty status and recipiency.)

18. Among the ineligible population, 1.3 percent report income from SSI. Some of these individuals are likely misclassified due to reporting error, but others may actually be receiving benefits to which they are not entitled. The SSA (1982) has estimated that 4 percent of those receiving benefits are actually ineligible.

Table 2.2   **Means of Variables Used in the Analyses**

		Eligible	
	Ineligible	Participating	Not Participating
Income variables			
Monthly pre-SSI income ($)	1,915	288	429
	(41.0)	(11.1)	(19.6)
Calculated SSI benefit ($)	0.0	223	156
	(0.0)	(9.6)	(9.9)
Reported SSI income ($)	2.91	236	0.0
	(0.5)	(9.9)	(0.0)
Total income, including SSI ($)	1,918	517	429
	(41.0)	(9.5)	(19.6)
Has Social Security income (%)	0.95	0.72	0.83
	(0.003)	(0.023)	(0.022)
Has labor earnings (%)	0.11	0.010	0.044
	(0.004)	(0.005)	(0.012)
Asset variables			
Net worth ($)	195,142	11,696	28,155
	(5,620)	(1,285)	(2,896)
Net worth, excluding housing ($)	118,952	341	−606[a]
	(4,741)	(70)	(667)
Own home (0/1) (%)	0.74	0.32	0.50
	(0.006)	(0.02)	(0.03)
Value of home (positive, $)	102,877	35,315	57,709
	(2,457)	(3,016)	(4,226)
Demographic variables (for male in couples)			
Born in the United States (%)	0.92	0.75	0.79
	(0.004)	(0.02)	(0.02)
Age at immigration (if not native born)	24.3	43.3	36.6
	0.83	(2.30)	(3.26)
Age	77.44	78.88	78.67
	0.08	(0.35)	(0.44)
Schooling (years)	11.3	6.4	8.2
	(0.05)	(0.21)	(0.25)
Nonwhite (%)	0.07	0.38	0.28
	(0.004)	(0.03)	(0.03)
Poor health (head or spouse) (%)	0.14	0.36	0.22
	(0.005)	(0.05)	(0.02)
Married (0/1) (%)	0.41	0.16	(0.22)
	(0.007)	(0.02)	(0.03)
Widowed (female) (%)	0.39	0.57	0.51
	(0.007)	(0.03)	(0.03)
Living arrangements			
Lives alone or with spouse (%)	0.78	0.65	0.66
	(0.006)	(0.03)	(0.03)
Lives with children (%)	0.16	0.26	0.28
	(0.005)	(0.02)	(0.03)
Lives with others (%)	0.07	0.11	0.08
	(0.004)	(0.02)	(0.02)
N[b]	5363	392	282

[a] Negative mean wealth is due to one outlier (see text).

[b] Differs for some variables due to missing values. Participation status is missing for eleven eligible households, which are excluded from the table.

wealth is excluded. The average number of years of schooling (using the level of schooling of the male for couples) is 11.3, and 7 percent are nonwhite.

While none of those eligible for SSI benefits is well off, those who are actually receiving benefits are in substantially worse financial straits than those who are not. The participants have average monthly pre-SSI income of $288, compared to $429 for those not receiving benefits. This lower income corresponds to a higher expected benefit for the participants than for the eligible nonparticipants, $223 compared to $156. This calculated benefit agrees well with the SSI income reported by recipients: The mean value of SSI actually received is $236, and the correlation between the calculated and reported amounts is 0.74.[19] When reported SSI benefits are added to the income of the participants, their incomes actually *exceed* those of the eligible nonparticipants, with an average monthly income that is $88 greater. SSI thus makes a large difference in the economic well-being of these individuals.

With respect to asset levels, those who are receiving benefits have substantially lower net worth than eligible nonparticipants, $11,696 versus $28,155, and a lower probability of home ownership. For both groups, nonhousing wealth is nearly nonexistent. Mean wealth, excluding housing wealth, is $341 for participants, while for nonparticipants it is actually negative (the medians are both zero).[20] These means stand in sharp contrast to mean (nonhousing) wealth reported earlier for those who are income but not asset eligible; the mean for those household units is $103,756.

The Social Security program is typically viewed as providing nearly universal coverage, and in fact 95 percent of the ineligible sample are receiving Social Security benefits. However, many of the participants are not; only 72 percent of this subsample reported receiving Social Security in the previous month. One possible explanation for the lack of benefits is the immigrant status of this population. Whereas 92 percent of the ineligible sample were born in the United States, only 75 percent of the eligible participants and 79 percent of the eligible nonparticipants were born here. There is also a substantial difference across groups in the age at arrival for those who did immigrate, increasing from twenty-four years old among the ineligibles

19. The calculated amount is on average lower than the reported amount because individuals may receive higher than predicted state benefits due to special needs. For example, in California the guarantee for an individual needing "nonmedical out-of-home care" is $116 more per month than someone who does not. In Connecticut, individuals may receive additional benefits to pay for such items as meals-on-wheels programs ($73.50 per month for one meal a day). I account for these extra payments where the data permit me to do so (such as an extra payment to those not having kitchen facilities in California), but in most cases I am unable to assess these special needs and, using the state income guarantees for those living independently, err consistently on the side of lower benefits.

20. The negative mean value is the result of one observation with (nonhousing) debt of $100,000. If this observation is eliminated, the mean for this subsample is $694.

to forty-three years old among the eligible participants. This late arrival suggests that many of those eligible for SSI may not have a sufficient earnings history to qualify for Social Security benefits and may have low benefits if they do qualify.[21]

There is also a substantial difference across groups in marital status; 16 percent of the participants are married, compared to 22 percent of the nonparticipants. The majority of those who are not married are widowed women. Fifty-seven percent of the participants and 51 percent of the eligible nonparticipants are widows.

Participants are more likely to be nonwhite, have approximately two fewer years of schooling on average, and are much more likely to report being in poor health—36 versus 22 percent—than eligible nonparticipants. Perhaps surprisingly, living arrangements for the two groups of eligibles are similar, although participants are somewhat more likely to live with others. Both groups are substantially less likely to live independently and more likely to live with children than are those ineligible for benefits.

2.2.4 Supplemental Security Income and Poverty

As discussed previously, the levels of the federal guarantees relative to the appropriate poverty lines indicate that the effect of SSI on the poverty rate itself is likely to be small, even if the program has a large effect on the well-being of the elderly poor. One common measure of the degree of poverty is the "poverty gap," which is defined as the total dollar amount needed to raise all incomes to the poverty line. As shown in table 2.3, if SSI is excluded from income, the poverty rate for the entire sample is 17.2 percent,[22] and the poverty gap, weighted to represent the total for the relevant U.S. population, is $7.45 billion.[23]

The second row of the table considers the effects of the federal program alone. If all those who are eligible for federal benefits are assigned their expected amount, the fraction with income below the poverty line falls only slightly, but the poverty gap declines by 34 percent. Adding potential

21. Differences in immigration status by group are not due to a correlation between differences in levels of state supplemental benefits and the regional distribution of immigrants. The same pattern is evident if only federal eligibility is used.

22. The poverty rates presented here are somewhat higher than published poverty rates of the elderly for two reasons. First, for those elderly living with individuals other than a spouse, the income of these other individuals is not included in my measure of total income (nor is their presence included in the determination of the appropriate poverty line). I do so in order to measure well-being while abstracting from the decision to coreside. Obviously one of the ways poverty among the elderly can be reduced is through an increase in the number coresiding with children or others. It is not clear that the introduction of the dependent relationship improves the well-being of the elderly person. The second reason for the high poverty rate is that the sample is representative of those age seventy and over. Poverty increases sharply with age after sixty-five.

23. I remind the reader that the AHEAD sample is representative of the noninstitutional population age seventy and over and their spouses. In section 2.3.2, I discuss one method of inflating these figures to represent the values for the population age sixty-five and over.

Table 2.3   **Poverty with and without Supplemental Security Income (SSI)**

Income Measure	Poverty Rate (%)	Poverty Gap	
		$ billions	% Reduction
No SSI	17.2	7.45	—
All potential federal benefits paid	17.0	4.91	34.1
All potential benefits paid	15.9	4.43	40.5
Current recipiency patterns and benefits	16.2	5.30	28.9

Notes: The poverty gap is the total amount needed to increase all incomes to the poverty line. Figures are weighted to represent national yearly totals for the AHEAD sample.

state benefits for all eligible units (third row) decreases the poverty rate to 15.9 percent, and the poverty gap falls even further, for a total decline of 40 percent. Even with the relatively low level of take-up among eligibles, the reduction in the poverty gap is substantial. As shown in the final row, using current recipiency patterns (i.e., eligible nonparticipants receive zero benefits) and actual benefits, the poverty rate is just 1 percentage point lower than without SSI, but the poverty gap is nearly 30 percent smaller than the no-SSI value. These figures provide a clear indication of both the ability and potential of SSI to reach the poor elderly.[24]

Figure 2.1 illustrates graphically the change in the distribution of income for the poor. The sample used in the figure is the population with income below the poverty line in the absence of SSI. The horizontal axis measures the ratio of income to the poverty line in 10 percent intervals (0–10, 10–20, . . . 90–100), and the vertical axis measures the fraction of the sample in each interval. The dark bars depict the distribution if SSI is excluded from income, while the light bars show the expected distribution if all eligible units were to enroll in the program. The largest change comes in the very bottom of the distribution. In the absence of SSI, 11.5 percent of this poverty sample would have incomes equal to less than 10 percent of the poverty line. For single individuals this interval corresponds to monthly incomes of less than $58, indicating that they have virtually no income other than SSI; for couples the interval corresponds to income less than $73.[25] With 100 percent participation, the fraction with incomes this low decreases to just 1.3 percent.[26] There is also a sharp change in the fraction of the sample with incomes between 70 and 80 percent of the

24. It should be noted that if SSI benefits are underreported, then the effect of the current program on poverty is understated.

25. One would expect that if SSI were not available, other behaviors would change. Some individuals might save or work more prior to retirement, some might postpone retirement, and some might receive greater transfers from family and friends. Others, however, would have no alternative means of support.

26. All twelve family units who remain in this lowest decile are ineligible for SSI because of the asset test.

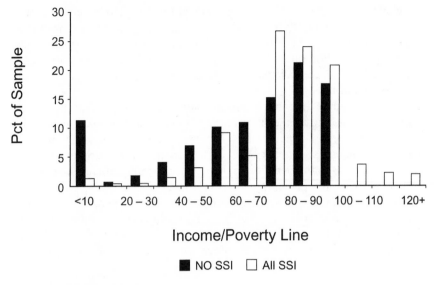

Income/Poverty Line

■ NO SSI   □ All SSI

Fig. 2.1   Distribution of income

poverty line. Federal SSI guarantees are equal to 73 percent of the poverty line for singles and 87 percent for couples. Because the majority of those eligible for benefits are single, the income of a substantial fraction of the population is increased to the 70–80 percent interval (although not to exactly 73 percent of the poverty line, because of the income disregards).

2.2.5   Correlates of Nonparticipation

Given the potential for improvement in their financial status, one might question the decision made by the eligible nonparticipants. Certainly the benefits to which the nonparticipating units are entitled are lower than those of the participants ($156 versus $223 on average), but they are still substantial, equal to 36 percent of average income. The choice is even more puzzling when one considers the relative stability of the income of the elderly and the likelihood that eligibility will remain unchanged for many years. Over a lifetime, the forgone benefits could represent a large sum.

To understand better the choice of nonparticipation, and to assess how participation rates would change in response to changes in benefits, I estimate a probit model for the probability of enrolling in SSI conditional on eligibility. The underlying theoretical model assumes that eligible units will enroll in SSI ($P_i = 1$) if the gain from the program (G_i) is greater than the associated costs (C_i). Thus,

$$P_i = \begin{cases} 1 & \text{if } G_i - C_i > 0, \\ 0 & \text{if otherwise.} \end{cases}$$

G_i depends in large part on the magnitude of the expected benefit (B_i), but may vary with characteristics of the individual such as health status. The variables used to measure G_i and C_i follow directly from the explanations for nonparticipation offered previously in the literature as summarized in section 2.1.2. The coefficient estimates for the reduced form specification are reported in table 2.4.

As was noted in the table of means, participation appears to be based largely on need, and this result is borne out in the regressions. The magnitude of the expected benefit, which is inversely related to pre-SSI income, has a positive and significant effect on the likelihood of participating. An increase of $100 in the benefit increases the probability of enrolling in the SSI program by 6.8 percentage points. Home ownership also has a large effect on participation, lowering the probability by 12.7 percentage points. As demonstrated above, net worth consists primarily of the value of a home. Its effect in the regression is to reduce significantly the probability of enrolling. Being married is associated with a significantly lower proba-

Table 2.4 **Probit Estimates of the Probability of Participating in SSI Conditional on Eligibility for Federal Benefits**

	Coefficient	Derivative
Potential benefit (×$100)	0.146	0.068
	(0.043)	
Net worth (×$10,000)	−0.068	−0.032
	(0.022)	
Own home (0/1)	−0.271	−0.127
	(0.156)	
Married (0/1)	−0.435	−0.203
	(0.156)	
Years of schooling (male in couple)	−0.047	−0.022
	(0.013)	
Nonwhite (male in couple)	0.054	0.025
	(0.106)	
Poor health (either spouse)	0.251	0.117
	(0.117)	
Receives Social Security (0/1)	−0.061	−0.028
	(0.190)	
Earnings (×$100)	−0.081	−0.038
	(0.219)	
Number of children	0.051	0.024
	(0.018)	
Urban resident (0/1)	−0.283	−0.132
	(0.112)	
N	674	
Mean of dependent variable	0.582	

Notes: Regression includes indicators for missing values of some variables and a constant term. Observations with missing values of the dependent variable are excluded.

bility of participation, a surprising result because, assuming that the expected benefit and net worth are constant, married couples have fewer resources per person and ought to be more in need of assistance.[27]

One of the explanations frequently offered for nonparticipation in welfare programs is that individuals do not know about the program (Daponte, Sanders, and Taylor 1999). The results here contradict this hypothesis. If there were informational barriers, one would expect those with more schooling to be more knowledgeable, as might those living in a urban area. Here both effects are associated with significant reductions in participation.[28] Furthermore, a primary method for informing people about SSI is through their receipt of Social Security. Those receiving Social Security are therefore more likely to have been informed about the program, but there is no effect on participation.

The effect of poor health is large and significant.[29] Those in poor health are 12 percentage points more likely to be enrolled. This large difference may come about through the interaction of Medicaid and SSI. As discussed previously, SSI participants are categorically eligible for Medicaid in most states, increasing the incentive for those with medical expenses to enroll in SSI. The link between Medicaid and SSI may also make enrollment more likely if those having received medical treatment for a prior illness were encouraged to enroll in SSI by the healthcare provider, ensuring that the provider was reimbursed by the accompanying Medicaid benefits.

The results in table 2.4 are consistent with those from earlier studies. While the decision to forgo SSI benefits remains a puzzle, there does seem to be strong evidence that enrollment is related to need, as measured both in terms of the magnitude of the expected benefit and other factors that proxy financial well-being. There appears to be little evidence of a correlation between proxies for informational barriers (schooling, Social Security receipt), the physical difficulty of enrolling (health, urban residence) or the intellectual difficulty (schooling). The observed relationships appear most consistent with a model wherein some cost—perhaps stigma, as hypothesized in Moffitt (1983)—discourages enrollment unless the marginal utility of the benefit is sufficiently large. The results also indicate that modifications to the SSI program that increase potential benefits or decrease the stigma associated with recipiency will increase the probability with which eligible households enroll and therefore increase the number of participants beyond that projected from a simple increase in eligibility.

---

27. SSI benefits and wealth are measured for the family unit. They are not scaled to be a per-person measure.

28. Schooling probably also proxies differences in lifetime income not captured by the income and asset variables.

29. Age was initially controlled for in the regression, but it had no effect on participation when income, assets, and health were included.

2.3 Possible Changes in Supplemental Security Income

A restructuring of the Social Security system may induce corresponding changes in the parameters of the SSI program. In this section I explore the potential effects of various changes in SSI guidelines on eligibility, costs, and poverty. I look first at the elimination of the asset test, then at the effects of increasing the income disregards and the income guarantees, and finally at a simplification of the determination of countable income. In all cases I consider only changes to the federal program and assume that states do not alter their benefit schedules or eligibility criteria in response. The results of these simulations are reported in tables 2.5–2.8.

It should be emphasized that any changes in the structure of Social Security or SSI are likely to induce changes in other economic behaviors, particularly savings, labor force participation, and the choice of living arrangements. Although these changes could well be significant, it is beyond the scope of this chapter to model these broader effects.

Because actual benefits and participation are not observed with these simulated changes, the comparisons presented here use the calculated benefits and probabilities of participation imputed from the estimated coefficients of the probit model. I estimate the total cost of each of the alternatives by weighting each eligible unit's expected benefit by its calculated probability of participating and summing these weighted amounts.[30] This cost is an underestimate of the true cost of the aged portion of the SSI program for several reasons. Most importantly, the sample in this paper excludes eligible individuals aged sixty-five to sixty-nine unless they are married to age-eligible persons, and also excludes those in nursing homes. (The size of the population aged sixty-five to sixty-nine is approximately 48 percent of the size of that aged seventy and over, and approximately 4 percent of the elderly are in nursing homes.) Second, as noted in footnote 19, my estimate of the expected benefit is biased downward because I cannot calculate the value of payments made for special needs. Finally, there are some in the sample whom I determine to be ineligible for benefits who are actually receiving payments from the SSI program. These amounts are not included in the calculations based on predicted benefits and participation. For similar reasons, the number of eligible and participating family units is not representative of all those who would be eligible in the U.S. population. Because of these limitations, I first report changes in eligibility, participation, and costs in percentage terms (table 2.5) and then adjust the baseline estimates for these biases and present estimated costs and participation levels for the population sixty-five and over (table 2.6).

---

30. This figure is calculated as $\Sigma_i (P_i \times \text{Benefit}_i)$ where P_i is the probability an eligible unit participates and Benefit_i is the benefit to which it is entitled.

Table 2.5 Impact of Alternative Eligibility Guidelines for SSI: Mean Benefits and Participation Rates

Plan	Initially Eligible			Newly Eligible			% Increase		
	Average Benefit	Probability of Participating	% Increase Costs	Average Benefit	Probability of Participating	% Increase Costs	Eligibility Units	Participating Units	Total Costs
Current program	195	56.7	—	—	—	—	—	—	—
No asset test	195	56.7	0.0	177	24.6	11.7	32.5	14.1	11.7
Unearned disregard equals $75	221	58.0	13.0	29	49.1	1.6	14.2	14.6	14.5
Guarantee raised to poverty line, with asset test	288	61.2	52.4	71	47.3	10.0	36.1	38.2	62.4
Guarantee raised to poverty line, no asset test	288	61.2	52.4	144	35.2	39.8	103.8	72.4	92.1
Social Security–based eligibility	201	57.8	−5.8	140	42.4	10.9	9.6	6.2	5.0

Notes: Benefits are determined by state and federal program parameters using reported values of income and assets. Participation probabilities are calculated using estimates in table 2.4 and observed characteristics. Increases in costs are calculated as the expected additional benefits paid to each group under each expansion relative to total payments under current rules.

Table 2.6   Impact of Alternative Eligibility Guidelines for SSI: Estimates of Total Cost
                   and Participation

	AHEAD Age 70+ (1)[a]		AHEAD Age 65+ (2)		SSA Age 65+ (3)	
Plan	Total Costs	No. of Units	Total Costs	No. of Units	Total Costs	No. of Units
Current program	2.78	1.04	4.28	1.60	6.07	2.07
No asset test	3.11	1.19	4.79	1.83	6.78	2.36
Unearned disregard equals $75	3.18	1.19	4.90	1.83	6.95	2.37
Guarantee raised to poverty line, with asset test	4.51	1.44	6.95	2.21	9.86	2.86
Guarantee raised to poverty line, no asset test	5.34	1.79	8.22	2.76	11.66	3.57
Social Security–based eligibility	2.92	1.10	4.49	1.70	6.37	2.20

Sources: Author's tabulations based on AHEAD and SSA data.

Notes: Costs are in billions of 1993 dollars, participation in millions of units. In column 1, estimates from reported SSI benefits in AHEAD correspond to the noninstitutional population born in 1923 or earlier (and their spouses). In column 2, estimates from column 1 are multiplied by 1.54 to include costs for those aged 65–69 and for those in nursing homes. In column 3, costs are based on published figures for total SSI benefits paid to the elderly in 1993. Number of SSI units is determined by dividing yearly costs by average benefits. SSA figures are multiplied by 1.43 to include benefits paid to those elderly originally classified as disabled or blind, and remaining so.

2.3.1   The Effects on Eligibility and Participation

The first row of table 2.5 reports benefits and participation under the current system. For the eligible population, the empirical model predicts a participation rate of 56.7 percent, nearly identical to the observed (weighted) rate of 55.9 percent.[31] The average calculated benefit for all 685 eligible units is $195 (the average of $223 and $156 in table 2.2).

Eliminating the Asset Test

In redesigning eligibility guidelines, one change that might be considered is an elimination of the asset test. It is often argued that such tests discourage savings, whereas an important goal of retirement policy is likely to be the encouragement of individual savings as a means of old age support. Furthermore, the asset test represents an additional administrative burden and, given the strict income limits and low participation rate, may not actually result in large changes in the participating population. By using the AHEAD data, one can simulate the effect of this change on program participation and costs. It is a relatively straightforward exercise to calculate the increase in eligibility—the number of families whose

---

31. The mean of the dependent variable in table 2.4 differs from 55.9 because it is not weighted by sampling probabilities.

countable income is below the guarantees but who have assets above the limit.[32] However, one also needs to determine what fraction of the newly eligible would choose to enroll in the program. I do so using the estimated effects from table 2.4 and the observable characteristics of each family unit.

With the elimination of the asset test, those eligible for SSI under the current program experience no change in eligibility or benefits and therefore no change in participation. The total number of eligible family units, however, increases by 32.5 percent. Because income and asset holding are positively correlated, the newly eligible have higher incomes and therefore lower expected benefits than those eligible initially, $177 compared to $195. Given the positive relationship between benefits are participation, and the negative relationship between net worth and enrollment, the newly eligible also have a substantially lower probability of enrolling in SSI than do those eligible under current rules. The probability of participating in SSI for the newly eligible is just 24.6 percent, compared to 56.7 for the initial sample. Based on the weighted sum of probabilities ($\Sigma_i P_i$), the expected increase in the participating population is 14.1 percent.

Using the expected benefits and the estimated probability of participation for each newly eligible unit to predict the additional cost associated with the expansion, I find that payments (exclusive of administrative expenses) increase by 11.7 percent.[33]

Increasing Unearned Income Disregard

The federal income guarantees are indexed for inflation and have increased every year since the program's inception. The asset limits have also grown over time. However, the income disregards have never been increased and remain at their initial levels—the first $65 of earned income and half of the remainder, and the first $20 of unearned income. One change in SSI that has been mentioned among policy makers is an increase in the disregard for unearned income from $20 to $75 per month.[34]

In the case of eliminating the asset test, the effects are felt only among the newly eligible. Here, however, there is both an increase in benefits

---

32. Here I consider eliminating the asset test for the federal program only. I assume that states maintain their current restrictions. The change in eligibility predicted here thus differs from that in table 2.1, where the asset test is eliminated at both levels.

33. These calculations (and those that follow) assume that the decision-making process does not change with the program expansions (i.e., that the estimated effects in table 2.4 remain valid). If the elimination of the asset test alters the desirability of enrollment, there will be changes in participation beyond those forecast here. For example, individuals may falsely believe that they are ineligible for SSI because they own a home. Eliminating the asset test might well reduce the prevalence of this misconception, changing the effect of home ownership on the participation decision. Similarly, some may view the asset test as an unpleasant requirement and refuse to apply for benefits if they need to provide such information. Again in this case, elimination of the asset test would increase enrollment beyond those who are newly eligible.

34. I thank Robert Schoeni for bringing this discussion to my attention.

among those previously eligible and an increase in the number eligible. Overall, the average benefit for the initially eligible subsample increases from $195 to $221: Those who were already participating initially see their average benefits increase from $223 to $249, and those who were eligible but not participating see an increase in their average benefits from $156 to $183 (breakdown by subgroup not shown). This increase in potential benefits will induce some of the eligible nonparticipants to enroll in SSI, and the average probability of participating for the entire eligible population increases slightly, from 56.7 to 58.0 percent. The increase in benefits and participation leads to an increase of 13 percent in costs for this group alone.

In addition to these changes, there is an increase of 14.2 percent in the number of eligible units. However, the expected benefit for the group of newly eligibles is small, averaging just $29 per month. Because of this low benefit, their average probability of participating is 49.1 percent, and the cost arising from the increase in eligibility is equal to just 1.6 percent of initial spending. Combining the additional costs for each group, the total increase in costs for this expansion is 14.5 percent over the initial amount.

Raising Guarantees to the Poverty Line

Several states offer supplements to SSI that effectively raise the incomes of the participating population to slightly above the poverty line. In considering plans to reduce or eliminate poverty among the elderly, one obvious solution is to raise the federal income guarantee to this level. This proposal has been discussed several times in the past (Zedlewski and Meyer 1989) and continues to be mentioned by policy makers. For those who live in states with guarantees above the poverty lines, the increase in federal benefits results in no change in their incomes: A greater fraction of their benefit will be paid for by the federal government, and a smaller fraction by the state, but there will be no increase in the total received. In contrast, those in less generous states could see a sizable increase in their monthly benefits, and some of those initially eligible but not enrolling at current levels may now find participation to be a more appealing option. At the same time, increasing the federal guarantees will also make more individuals eligible for the program and will increase participation along that avenue.

Increasing the federal guarantees to the poverty line—$577.50 per month for a single individual and $728.33 for a couple in 1993[35]—with no change in state programs results in a sharp increase in the average benefits for those who were initially eligible, from $195 to $288, and the probability of participating in SSI increases to 61 percent. The cost of this change is great, equal to 52 percent of initial expenditures.

35. $592.33 and $747.25 in 1994.

Increasing benefits also has a large effect on the number of eligible units, increasing the eligible population by 36 percent. However, as was the case when increasing the disregard, the expected benefit for the newly eligible is small, equal to $71, and their predicted participation rate is 47.3 percent. Given the relatively low benefits to which they are entitled, the expected additional outlay of SSI benefits for this group of newly eligible is just 10 percent of initial spending. The total increase in costs for this expansion is therefore equal to 62 percent of initial expenditures, with the vast majority of the increase accruing to those who were initially eligible.

This simulation assumed that the asset test remained in effect. The fifth row of table 2.5 reports the results of the same increase in income guarantees accompanied by an elimination of the asset test. This combination ensures that virtually all elderly will have the opportunity to increase their incomes above the poverty line.[36]

Those who were initially eligible for SSI are unaffected by the additional elimination of the asset test, and the increases in benefits and costs for this group are the same as in the previous example (fourth row). However, eliminating the asset test dramatically increases the eligible population, more than doubling its size. Following this change in eligibility, the participating population increases by 72 percent, 34 percentage points above the increase with no change in the asset test. Corresponding to the large increases in benefits and participation, there is a sharp increase in costs. In this expansion, expected payments increase by 92 percent.[37]

Using Social Security Income

The final alternative I investigate is basing eligibility and benefits on Social Security income alone, eliminating income disregards and conferring eligibility on those with Social Security income, rather than countable income, below the guarantee levels. This procedure would likely reduce administrative effort for both the SSA and the applicants, because Social Security benefits are readily observable by SSA and need not be reported or verified.[38] The drawback is that individuals with low Social Security benefits but with substantial other income could qualify for SSI, although with the asset test in place this group would be expected to be small.

36. It is possible that those who live with others and have the guarantees reduced accordingly could remain poor.
37. These figures reflect the percentage increases in the combined payments of the federal and state programs. Because the simulations assume that state programs are unchanged, in many cases the increase in the federal benefits will simply replace state spending. The percentage increase in federal costs is therefore larger than the overall increase. When guarantees are raised to the poverty line and the asset test remains in place, my calculations predict an increase in federal spending of 95 percent. If the asset test is eliminated, federal spending increases by 133 percent.
38. Administrative expenses for the SSI program are actually larger than for the OASDI program (SSA 2000). However, many of these costs are likely due to the disabled portion of the SSI program, not from the benefits going to the eligible elderly.

The cost of this change would obviously depend on the level of Social Security chosen as the cutoff for eligibility. In the AHEAD sample, the maximum Social Security benefits received by singles and couples eligible for *federal* SSI benefits under current rules are $441 and $644.[39] Because many family units are likely to have some income from sources other than Social Security, a reasonable choice of income limits might be the 90th percentiles—$418 for singles and $620 for couples.[40] Using these amounts as income guarantees, with no income disregards, results in a net increase in the eligible population of 9.6 percent, with a small number of those initially eligible for benefits becoming ineligible due to the elimination of income disregards and the slightly lower guarantee level.[41] Expected participation increases by the somewhat smaller amount of 6.2 percent. The total cost of this method is similar to the current program, with an increase in expenditures of 5 percent.

As noted earlier, these simulations are based on the assumption that the participation decision does not change when benefit formulas change. In this case in particular, the assumption may not be valid. One might imagine that if benefits were tied directly to low Social Security rather than to generally low income, the program might be viewed less as a welfare program and more as a supplement to Social Security itself, and participation rates could increase across the board.[42]

2.3.2 Costs of Changes

The increases in expected payments and the increases in the number of participating family units associated with each of these changes have thus far been expressed as percentage increases relative to the current program. Of particular relevance to policy makers and researchers is the cost of the SSI program for the entire elderly population. As noted above, the AHEAD sample does not provide such an estimate. By making some assumptions, however, it is possible to inflate the baseline amounts calculated from the AHEAD data to approximate the values for the population aged sixty-five and over. I make these adjustments in the first row of table 2.6 and then apply the estimated percentage increases for each hypothesized change (from table 2.5) to estimate the effects of the program expansions.

In the first row of table 2.6 I present the costs and the number of participating units for the current program using three different measures. In the

39. Because some states (notably California) have guarantees that are significantly higher than the federal levels, the maximum Social Security benefits among all eligibles (state and federal) are much higher at $897 and $1,180.

40. In this simulation, guarantees for 1994 are set by increasing the 1993 amounts to account for inflation.

41. Of the initially eligible, 91 percent remain eligible under the new rules.

42. The role of stigma, and indeed nonparticipation itself, could be eliminated in its entirety if the level of Social Security income were the only earnings test, the asset test were eliminated, and no application for SSI was required.

first set of columns I use the population weighted sums of observed bene- fits and participants for the AHEAD sample, $2.78 billion and 1.04 million participating units.[43] These figures are the totals relevant for the noninstitutional population aged seventy and over and their spouses. The numbers do not include the population aged sixty-five to sixty-nine, which is approximately 48 percent as large as that aged seventy and over, nor do they include the approximately 4 percent of elderly who live in nursing homes.[44] In column (2) I incorporate these omitted segments of the elderly population by simply multiplying the numbers in the first set of columns by 1.54 (1.48 × 1.04). This procedure yields a total cost of $4.28 billion in 1993 dollars and a total enrolled population of 1.6 million family units.[45] As an alternative estimate (column [3]), I use published figures from the SSA for SSI benefits to aged individuals in 1993 (SSA 1999). Using administrative data will correct for the possible underreporting of benefit receipt in AHEAD. The administrative values for 1993, $4.25 billion and $1.46 million, compare well with the inflated AHEAD numbers (not shown). However, these figures for aged recipients do not include those aged sixty-five and over who are receiving SSI but who initially enrolled in the program as a disabled or blind recipient. To approximate the totals for the entire population aged sixty-five and over, I multiply the $4.25 billion in benefits and the 1.46 million participating units by 1.43 to yield total estimated costs of $6.07 billion and a participating population of 2.07 million.[46] The difference in the size of the enrolled population between columns two and three suggests that, indeed, there might be a large amount of underreporting of SSI receipt in survey data.

The subsequent rows in the table provide cost and participant projections for each of the changes discussed in the previous section. As is evident from the percentage increases reported earlier, neither the elimination

43. Using reported benefits and recipiency corrects for any biases in my estimates based on calculated benefits and predicted probabilities.

44. If SSI benefits are underreported, then this figure is a downward biased estimate of the true cost of the program. Similarly, calculations of the increase in enrollment and costs are also likely to be incorrect.

45. Inflating the AHEAD numbers by 48 percent "overcorrects" for the omitted population, because spouses of age-eligible respondents who are sixty-five to sixty-nine are already included in the sample. The estimates for those sixty-five and over are further biased upward if one assumes that the younger elderly are better off than older cohorts due to differences in lifetime wealth and the predictions of the lifecycle hypothesis, and therefore less likely to be in need of SSI or to be receiving benefits.

46. Published statistics from the SSA report 616,799 disabled aged sixty-five and over and 21,588 blind receiving federally administered SSI benefits in 1993 (similar figures are not available for those receiving only state-administered benefits, approximately 7 percent of total recipients). These numbers total 43 percent of those categorized as aged recipients and receiving federally administered benefits. Also, although benefits are reported as the average amount per family unit, the number of recipients in published SSA tables refers to the number of *individuals*, not the number of units. In table 2.6 I calculate the number of SSI units by dividing total benefits (measured yearly) by average monthly benefits received (multiplied by twelve).

of the asset test nor the increase in the income disregard result in a substantial increase in costs or in the number enrolled. The 12–15 percent increases in costs shown in table 2.5 correspond to $500 to $700 million dollars when inflated to represent the population aged sixty-five and over, while the increases in the participating population are approximately 200,000 to 300,000 units (second and third rows of table 2.6).

The dramatic 92 percent cost increase associated with the poverty line guarantee and no asset test increases costs by approximately $4 to $5.5 billion and increases the number of enrolled families by 1 to 1.5 million. Even with this large expansion and the most expensive set of statistics, the total cost of the program remains below $12 billion.[47] This cost is best interpreted relative to other government programs: In 1993, total payments to the disabled segment of the SSI population were nearly $20 billion, payments to families in the AFDC were nearly $23 billion, and payments to food stamp beneficiaries were $22 billion.[48]

2.3.3 The Effects on Poverty

How much do these expansions actually benefit the elderly poor? Table 2.3 reported the potential for the current SSI program to reduce the poverty rate and the poverty gap. While the reduction in the poverty rate due to SSI was small, the reduction in the poverty gap was large, equal to a 30 percent decrease with current recipiency patterns. Table 2.7 shows the effects of the hypothesized changes to the SSI program on these measures. Using calculated benefits and predicted participation for the current program, the poverty rate is 16.4 percent and the poverty gap is $5.34 billion.[49]

Neither eliminating the asset test nor raising the disregard has a measurable effect on the poverty rate, and the reductions in the poverty gap associated with these changes are approximately 5 to 6 percent.

Of all the changes to SSI that have been discussed here, only the changes

47. The $4.25 billion in costs to aged recipients reported by the SSA represents federal costs of $3.10 billion and state costs of $1.15 billion. Assigning the same federal/state division to the inflated $6.07 billion in table 2.6 yields a division of expenditures of $4.43 for the federal government and $1.64 billion for the states. Applying the 95 and 133 percentage increases in federal spending (see note 37) to the $4.43 billion in federal expenditures under the current programs raises total federal costs to $8.6 billion and $10.3 billion under the two poverty line expansions.

48. It should be noted, however, that the increases in costs described here are limited to the direct cost of benefits from the SSI program. Because SSI recipients are likely to be categorically eligible for both food stamps and Medicaid, the true increase in costs may be much larger. Also, note that this simulation continues to assume less than full participation among the eligible population.

49. For comparison with the simulations, this calculation uses the calculated benefits (rather than reported) and predicted participation probabilities. The values reported in table 2.6 therefore differ slightly from those calculated on the basis of observed benefits and participation shown in the final row of table 2.3 ($5.3 billion). Note also that these numbers are not inflated to account for the age restrictions on the AHEAD sample. The reader can scale these numbers by 1.54 if such an estimate is desired.

Table 2.7   Impact of Alternative Eligibility Guidelines for SSI on the Poverty Gap

	Poverty Rate	Poverty Gap	
		$ billions	% Reduction
Current program	16.4	5.34	—
No asset test	16.4	5.09	4.7
Increase unearned disregard to $75	16.4	5.03	5.8
Guarantee raised to poverty line, asset test remains	12.4	4.02	24.7
Guarantee raised to poverty line, no asset test	11.0	3.37	36.9
Social Security–based eligibility guarantee equal 90% of maximum SS	16.3	5.45	−2.1

Note: All calculations use calculated benefits and predicted participation rates.

that raise benefits to the poverty line have a noticeable effect on the poverty rate, but the effects are large, even given the low participation rates. If federal guarantees are raised to the poverty line, the poverty rate (fourth row) falls from 16.4 to 12.4 percent. With a concurrent elimination of the asset test, poverty falls by an additional 1.4 percentage points, for a total decline of 33 percent. There is also large decline in the poverty gap in these two cases. When the asset test is left in place, the poverty gap falls by 25 percent, and with the additional elimination of the asset test it falls by 37 percent.

As shown in the final row, there is no change in the poverty rate with eligibility based on Social Security, but the poverty gap actually increases. This increase occurs because some SSI benefits in this regime accrue to those with incomes above the poverty line and therefore have no effect on the poverty gap, while some individuals with incomes below the poverty line lose their benefits. It is important to note that these declines are measured relative to the current program, which in and of itself provides a 30 percent reduction relative to situation without SSI. (As shown in table 2.3, the poverty rate with no SSI is 17.2 percent, and the poverty gap is $7.45 billion.)

2.3.4   Characteristics of the Newly Eligible

The preceding tables report the changes in participation, costs, and poverty associated with various changes in the parameters of the SSI program. Each of these changes will benefit a somewhat different subset of individuals. Table 2.8 presents the means of the regression variables for the newly eligible units under each of these scenarios. For comparison, the means of those initially eligible are reported in the first column.

By definition, those who become eligible when the asset test is elimi-

Table 2.8   **Means of Regression Variables for Newly Eligible under Alternative Changes in the SSI Program**

	Initially Eligible	Scenarios				
		(1)	(2)	(3)	(4)	(5)
Potential benefit	195	177	21	71	144	140
Net worth	19,028	185,278	16,346	24,043	100,010	31,342
Own home (0/1)	0.40	0.82	0.42	0.55	0.68	0.61
Married (0/1)	0.19	0.43	0.13	0.11	0.22	0.26
Years of schooling (male in couple)	7.17	10.43	7.23	8.03	9.43	9.42
Nonwhite (male in couple)	0.33	0.14	0.25	0.27	0.16	0.23
Poor health (either spouse)	0.30	0.17	0.29	0.28	0.20	0.17
Receives Social Security (0/1)	0.80	0.90	0.99	0.99	0.96	0.90
Number with earnings	0.02	0.04	0.09	0.07	0.05	0.15
Earnings (if positive)	179	62	30	188	222	597
Number of children)	3.3	2.6	2.8	3.0	2.6	3.0
Urban resident (0/1)	0.70	0.61	0.66	0.67	0.66	0.67
N	685	178	96	246	607	125

Notes: Scenario (1) corresponds to the elimination of the asset test. Scenario (2) corresponds to raising the disregard for unearned income to $75. Scenario (3) corresponds to raising guarantees to the poverty line with an asset test. Scenario (4) corresponds to raising guarantees to the poverty line with no asset test. Scenario (5) corresponds to using only SS income to determine eligibility.

nated have substantially higher levels of assets than those who are initially eligible. In this case, the mean value of wealth (including housing wealth) for the newly eligible is $185,278, nearly ten times that of the initial sample. This high wealth level is responsible for the low predicted probability of participating in SSI (24.6 percent) seen in table 2.5. The newly eligible are also twice as likely to own a home and to be married, and have over three more years of schooling on average.

In contrast, when the unearned income disregard is raised (scenario 2), those who become eligible must still meet the asset test, and mean assets are not changed noticeably. In fact, the population of newly eligibles is quite similar to those initially eligible. The largest differences are in the probability of receiving Social Security and of reporting positive earnings. Because nearly all those without Social Security are likely to be eligible for SSI benefits with the initial (lower) disregard, and because increases in the unearned income disregard act to increase the amount of Social Security that is excluded from countable income, virtually all of the newly eligible, 99 percent, are receiving Social Security.

Raising the benefit guarantees to the poverty line will again have little effect on asset levels, but will allow those with greater incomes to qualify for benefits. Thus, as shown in the column for scenario 3, while the newly eligible population is again nearly certain to have Social Security benefits and has a much higher level of earnings, assets are only slightly above those for the initially eligible subsample.

Eliminating the asset test along with the increase in the benefit guarantees again results in a newly eligible population with substantial net worth. The mean value of assets for this group is $100,010. The newly eligible have more schooling, are substantially more likely to own a home, and are less likely to be nonwhite or in poor health. They are also more likely to have Social Security income and income from earnings.

Finally, if Social Security income alone is used in determining eligibility, many of those with substantial labor earnings will be entitled to benefits. Because individuals can have unlimited labor earnings and still qualify for benefits, there is also a very large difference in the fraction with earnings, 2 versus 15 percent, and in mean earnings (over positive values), which increase from $179 to $597 per month.

2.4 Relationship Between Supplemental Security Income and Social Security

As plans to reform Social Security are discussed and their effects on the well-being of the population analyzed, it is important to keep in mind the potential interactions with SSI. One feature of the SSI program with important consequences for the role of Social Security in affecting the welfare of the elderly poor is the implicit tax on benefits. Because the benefit from SSI is equal to the difference between the income guarantee and countable income, any increase in unearned income (above the $20 disregard) reduces the SSI benefit dollar-for-dollar. Thus, for SSI participants, an additional dollar of Social Security income serves only to reduce the SSI benefit by one dollar, with no change in the total income of the recipient. Social Security payroll taxes paid by those eventually collecting SSI are therefore in some sense "wasted" because they realize no real benefits from the Social Security program itself.

One implication of this 100 percent tax is that those who expect to receive SSI should begin collecting Social Security at the earliest age of eligibility. There is no advantage to postponing retirement from age sixty-two to age sixty-five (or greater), since the higher benefit associated with later retirement does not result in an increase in income. With such a postponement, the individual simply loses the stream of benefits from age sixty-two to age sixty-five with no offsetting increase in income after age sixty-five. Because of this effect, changes in the normal retirement age for Social Security that leave unchanged the age for early retirement will have no effect on the decision by future SSI recipients of when to collect benefits. Furthermore, changes in Social Security benefit levels with no changes in the structure of SSI will have no effect on the incomes of the majority of SSI recipients.

A popular proposal for reforming Social Security is a move to a system of individual retirement accounts. (See Feldstein and Samwick 1998 for a discussion of such a plan, and Feldstein and Liebman, this volume, for estimates of its distributional effects.) Such a system would replace Social Security payroll taxes, at least in part, with contributions invested in private-sector financial instruments to be used to finance a worker's retirement. There are several avenues along which SSI would affect the operation and the redistributional aspects of such a system, depending on the requirements to annuitize account balances, the type of annuities available, and the provisions for leaving bequests.

First, as in the current system, those who expect to have balances low enough to qualify for SSI, regardless of the annuity type chosen, have little incentive to save because their total income will be determined exclusively by the SSI guarantees. Since savings rates are likely to be mandatory, this effect will show up as a work disincentive, similar to that in the current program. Along the same lines, if investments in individual retirement accounts are self-directed, those who expect to be eligible for SSI have an incentive to take inordinate risks with their portfolios because they will be unlikely to realize any benefit from savings with moderate returns and will be unaffected by losses.

There is also the question of the treatment of account balances. If individuals were permitted to retain the balance in an account after age sixty-five, in lieu of immediate mandatory annuitization, some provision for these balances would be necessary in the SSI asset test. One would not wish to disqualify from SSI all those with more than $2,000 in such an account, since such sums are small relative to the stream of Social Security benefits permitted under the current system. The accounting of these balances would be especially important for the disabled, who may qualify for benefits from SSI long before age sixty-five, but might be disqualified if balances in retirement accounts were included in countable assets.

A system of mandatory annuitization would raise different concerns, with implications for the choice of annuity types and death benefits. Brown (chapter 10 in this volume) shows that under a single life annuity with no bequests there is a sizable redistribution of wealth from those with short life expectancies (the poor) to those with long life expectancies (the rich). The magnitude of this redistribution is lessened if annuities have survivorship benefits. For those who will be eligible for SSI, the 100 percent tax on SSI benefits associated with an increase in annuity income means that differences between joint and single life annuities will be unimportant in most cases. If both the couple and the surviving spouse will be eligible for SSI, then changes in the magnitude of the annuity payment, arising from changes in the survivorship option, will alter the fractions of income coming from SSI and Social Security annuities, but will have no effect on total income. Regardless of the annuity policy, total income will be equal to the SSI guarantee.

A similar result follows for the choice of period-certain annuities. Period-certain annuities guarantee payment for a certain number of years even if the annuitant dies before the end of that time. If the annuitant does die before all guaranteed payments are paid, the remaining benefits are paid to his heirs. To finance this potential payout, payments during life from these period-certain annuities are reduced relative to what they would be with a straight life annuity. Brown shows that these period-certain annuities reduce the redistribution of resources from short-lived to long-lived individuals because they effectively increase the number of years of benefits for those with high mortality rates. Including SSI in such a calculation reinforces this effect. If the annuitant is eligible for SSI, the reduction in annuity payments needed to finance the period certain option will not reduce his income. Additionally, should he die before the end of the period, he will leave wealth to heirs at no cost to himself.

In addition to the choice of single or joint life, and straight life or period-certain annuities, individuals may be able to choose an annuity with a bequest option. This type of annuity would have the same effect on the redistribution of resources as a period-certain annuity. If given the option, an annuitant eligible for SSI who cares at least somewhat about his heirs will accept a reduction in the current flow of payments in order to guarantee a bequest, because he will not experience a corresponding reduction in actual income, with SSI payments making up the difference.

As this discussion illustrates, the distributional effects of alternative Social Security reforms can depend heavily on the interactions with SSI, and the details of any reform proposals need to consider the potential spill-over effects.

2.5   Discussion and Conclusions

The proposed privatization of Social Security raises a host of concerns over the best way to implement such a change. Chief among these concerns is how to provide for those elderly who reach old age with insufficient resources. When considering the needs of the elderly poor and possible methods to alleviate their poverty, it is instructive to examine the features of the existing SSI program and its success in improving the well-being of its target population. This chapter has addressed these issues.

In its current state, the SSI program has done much to improve the lot of the poorest elderly. While not eliminating poverty among the elderly, it has succeeded in raising the incomes of many of the poorest by a substantial amount. Under the current system, the poverty gap for the elderly (the amount of money needed to increase the incomes of all poor individuals to the poverty line) is 30 percent lower than it would be in the absence of SSI. Furthermore, for those enrolled in the program, SSI provides, on average, 42 percent of total monthly income. However, the potential for SSI to assist the elderly poor is even greater. Only 56 percent of those who appear to be eligible for benefits are actually enrolled in the program. If the participation rate of the current program were increased to 100 percent, the poverty gap could be reduced by an additional 11 percentage points.

This chapter explores the effects of several possible changes to the current SSI program. In simulating the changes in participation and costs, I control for the probability that eligible individuals may not enroll in the program. These simulations indicate that guaranteeing all elderly an income equal to the poverty line is potentially costly, increasing the current benefit outlays to the elderly by 62 percent with an asset test in effect, and by over 90 percent with the concurrent elimination of the asset test. Based on 1993 figures, this change results in an additional expenditure of approximately 5.5 billion dollars for the entire age-eligible population. However, because SSI payments to the elderly are dwarfed by those to the disabled, these changes are equal to increases of just 22 percent relative to the total payments in the SSI program. Other changes examined here have smaller cost increases, and correspondingly smaller improvements in the well-being of the elderly poor. Furthermore, because participation rates typically hover around 60 percent, the greatest costs and the greatest improvements in financial well-being will come from programs that also encourage higher rates of participation.

References

Bavier, Richard. 1999. An early look at the effects of welfare reform. Office of Management and Budget. Manuscript, March.

Blank, Rebecca, and Patricia Ruggles. 1996. When do women use Aid to Families with Dependent Children and food stamps? *Journal of Human Resources* 31 (1): 57–89.

Coe, Richard. 1985. Nonparticipation in the SSI program by the eligible elderly. *Southern Economic Journal* 51 (3): 891–97.

Comptroller General of the United States. 1976. Efforts made to locate and enroll potential recipients of the Supplemental Security Income Program for the aged, blind, and disabled. U.S. Department of Health, Education, and Welfare Publication no. HRD-76-105. Washington, D.C.: GPO.

Daponte, Beth Osborn, Seth Sanders, and Lowell Taylor. 1999. Why do low income households not use foodstamps? *Journal of Human Resources* 34 (3): 612–28.

Feldstein, Martin, and Andrew Samwick. 1998. The transition path in privatizing Social Security. In *Privatizing Social Security*, ed. Martin Feldstein, 215–260. Chicago: University of Chicago Press.

Fraker, Thomas, and Robert Moffitt. 1988. The effect of food stamps on labor supply: A bivariate selection model. *Journal of Public Economics* 35 (2): 25–56.

Giannarelli, Linda, and Laura Wheaton. 2000. Under-reporting of means-tested transfer programs in the March CPS. The Urban Institute. Manuscript, February.

Kalton, Graham, David B. McMillen, and Daniel Kasprzyk. 1986. Nonsampling error issues in the survey of income and program participation. SIPP Working Paper no. 8602. Washington, D.C.: U.S. Bureau of the Census.

Kennedy, Lenna. 1982. SSI: Trends and changes, 1974–1980. *Social Security Bulletin* 45 (7): 3–12.

McGarry, Kathleen. 1996. Participation of the elderly in SSI. *Journal of Human Resources* 31 (2): 331–58.

Menefee, John, Bea Edwards, and Sylvester J. Schieber. 1981. Analysis of nonparticipation in the SSI program. *Social Security Bulletin* 44 (6): 3–21.

Moffitt, Robert. 1983. An econometric model of welfare stigma. *American Economic Review* 73 (5): 1023–35.

Social Security Administration (SSA). 1982. Low income eligibility and participation in SSI. *Social Security Bulletin* 45 (5): 28–35.

———. 1993. *The Supplemental Security Income program for the aged, blind, and disabled: Selected characteristics of state supplementation programs as of January 1993.* Baltimore, Md.: Office of Supplemental Security Income, Social Security Administration.

———. 1994. *The Supplemental Security Income program for the aged, blind, and disabled: Selected characteristics of state supplementation programs as of January 1994.* Baltimore, Md.: Office of Supplemental Security Income, Social Security Administration.

———. 1997. *The Supplemental Security Income program for the aged, blind, and disabled: Selected characteristics of state supplementation programs as of January 1997.* Baltimore, Md.: Office of Supplemental Security Income, Social Security Administration.

———. 1999. *Social Security Bulletin Annual Statistical Supplement 1998.* Washington, D.C.: Social Security Administration.

———. 2000. SSA's accountability report for fiscal year 1997: Audited financial statements and notes. Available at [http:// www.ssa.gov/finance/97finstm.pdf].

Soldo, Beth J., Michael D. Hurd, Willard L. Rodgers, and Robert B. Wallace. 1997. Asset and Health Dynamics among the Oldest Old: An overview of the AHEAD study. *Journal of Gerontology* 52B:1–20.

U.S. House of Representatives. 1998. *Overview of entitlement programs: Background material and data on programs within the jurisdiction of the Committee on Ways and Means.* Washington, D.C.: GPO.

Warlick, Jennifer L. 1979. *An empirical analysis of participation in the supplemental security income program among aged eligible persons.* Ph.D diss. University of Wisconsin, Madison.

———. 1982. Participation of the aged in SSI. *Journal of Human Resources* 17 (2): 236–60.

Zedlewski, Sheila R., and Jack A. Meyer. 1989. *Toward ending poverty among the elderly and disabled through SSI reform.* Washington, D.C.: Urban Institute Press.

Comment   Bruce D. Meyer

This chapter provides an excellent background on the Supplemental Security Income (SSI) program. It also provides a nice description of who re-

Bruce D. Meyer is professor of economics at Northwestern University and a research associate of the National Bureau of Economic Research.

ceives SSI and how the benefits affect their income and poverty rates. The simulations of possible program expansions are well chosen and extremely useful. I will first summarize some of the key facts and findings in the chapter, then offer some caveats and discuss how the underreporting of SSI affects the results in the chapter. I will then offer some possible extensions to the analyses in the chapter.

There are a few main facts that are important to know about SSI. First, spending on the SSI aged is small, about $4.4 billion in 1997. Second, the typical maximum benefit is not especially high. The maximum monthly federal benefit, called the guarantee amount, was $484 for a single individual and $726 for a couple in 1997. There are state supplements to these benefits in many states. Third, average monthly benefits are much lower than the maximum benefit, due to deductions for other income and earnings. The average federal monthly payment was $235, while the average state monthly payment was $114.

The chapter features several key findings. First, there is substantial SSI nonparticipation. Only 56 percent of eligibles participate, though I believe this number is a sharp underestimate, for reasons I give below. The characteristics of eligible nonparticipants are mostly sensible. They tend to be eligible for lower benefits and to be healthier. They also are more educated and more likely to receive social security. This last result does not accord with the idea that those who are more likely to be informed are more likely to participate. Second, SSI substantially reduces poverty. SSI reduces the poverty rate among the elderly from 17.2 percent to 16.2 percent in the sample in the paper. More importantly, it creates a 29 percent reduction in the poverty gap (the amount of money needed to raise everyone to the poverty line), a much better measure of the effect on the poor. Third, SSI expansions would reduce poverty further at a fairly low cost. Raising the maximum benefit, the guarantee, to the poverty line along with eliminating asset limits for benefit receipt is the most extensive expansion considered. In 1993 this change would have raised the guarantee for a single individual from $422 per month to $577, and for a couple from $633 to $728. This reform would reduce the poverty rate another 5.4 percentage points and the poverty gap by just under 37 percent, at a cost of $5.6 billion.

Many of my earlier comments are reflected in McGarry's revisions to this chapter. However, there remain several key issues that have not been completely addressed. First, when extrapolating the results from the Asset and Health Dynamics (AHEAD) study sample to the aged SSI population in general, it would be useful to know how well the sample represents the aged SSI eligible population. The degree of confidence we have in the estimates would be greater if there were more discussion of this issue in the chapter. There are several reasons to be concerned that the sample is not very representative: There are indications of problems with the sample weights, and the sample frame seems to exclude most of the younger aged, those sixty-five to seventy, and persons in nursing homes.

Second, the underreporting of SSI receipt has serious consequences for the chapter's analyses yet is discussed only briefly. At least 20 percent of social insurance or welfare program recipients typically fail to report receipt in household surveys. This is not analogous to Planck's constant or Avogadro's number, but it is a reasonable rule of thumb. It appears that SSI reporting in the AHEAD data is no exception.

What, then, is the evidence of underreporting of program receipt in household data? Typically, one compares the weighted counts of recipients in a household survey to the totals from administrative sources. Bavier (1999) finds that about 19 percent of Aid to Families with Dependent Children (AFDC) recipients do not report receipt in the Survey of Income and Program Participation (SIPP), and over 20 percent do not report in the Current Population Survey (CPS). Hutchens (1981) reports that at least 38 percent of unemployment insurance (UI) recipients fail to report receipt in the CPS. Underreporting of UI receipt of almost this magnitude could also be inferred by the difference between take-up rates calculated using the survey and administrative data in the papers cited in Meyer (1995). Finally, it appears that this pattern holds for SSI, as Giannarelli and Wheaton (2000) find approximately 25 percent underreporting of SSI dollars in the CPS.

We turn now to the question of whether there is underreporting of SSI in AHEAD. McGarry finds a takeup rate of 56 percent in AHEAD. The 1998 *Green Book* reports the ratio of SSI recipients sixty-five and older (from administrative data) to the number of poor sixty-five and older (derived from survey data) to have been 0.56 in 1993 (U.S. House of Representatives 1998, 307). This number surely dramatically understates the participation rate, as many poor individuals and couples will not meet the SSI asset and income tests. To determine what fraction of the poor are in fact SSI eligible, table 2.5 of the chapter provides estimates. The chapter's estimate of the number of additional people eligible for SSI if the asset test were eliminated and the guarantee were raised to the poverty line is almost exactly what we need to calculate what fraction of the aged poor are in fact currently SSI eligible. Table 2.5 indicates that the number of eligibles would rise by 104 percent if the guarantees were raised to the poverty line and the asset test eliminated. Thus, taking this calculation from the chapter at face value implies that only about half of the poor are eligible for SSI and that the 56 percent take-up rate is really over 100 percent (which is possible given some noncompliance, i.e., ineligible recipients)! Now, a take-up rate of over 100 percent is clearly an overestimate, because some SSI recipients in very generous states are nonpoor, and because applying the 104 percent number from table 2.5 ignores that there are small income disregards in the SSI formula. Nevertheless, the upward biases in this alternative takeup calculation are probably not very large. The true takeup rate is probably far above the 56 percent figure reported in the chapter.

McGarry reports a similar underreporting calculation in note 17 of the chapter. Rather than adjust the number of poor to obtain just the eligibles, she calculates the ratio of the number of reported recipients to the number of poor in the AHEAD data. She finds a ratio of 0.28, which is exactly half the 0.56 reported in the *Green Book*. Again, this number suggests that SSI receipt is sharply underreported in the AHEAD data.

What are the implications of the true participation rate's being much higher than the 56 percent reported in the chapter? First, this information means that the problem of nonparticipation is much less severe, and that outreach efforts are less important to boost takeup rates. Second, the calculated effects of the current SSI program on the poverty rate and poverty gap are much larger than indicated in this chapter because many poor recipients are not reporting receipt. Third, the effects on poverty of expansions of the SSI program would also be bigger. Fourth, one should substantially revise the interpretation of the probit participation model results. The probit coefficients reflect the likelihood of reporting participation conditional on participating as much as they reflect the probability of participating conditional on eligibility.

Finally, there is a separate problem with the estimates of total budgetary costs of possible reforms that I now discuss. I would like to emphasize that I have confidence in only the third set of cost columns in table 2.6, labeled "SSA Age 65+." The other columns mistakenly extrapolate from cost figures that do not include the blind and disabled aged SSI recipients, even though they are included in the AHEAD data. As reported in the chapter notes, the total number of blind and disabled recipients is approximately 43 percent as large as that of the aged, so this is no small omission.

I close with a few comments regarding possible extensions of the chapter. It would be interesting to modify the simulations to include the Medicaid and food stamp costs and benefits that will generally accompany SSI eligibility. If additional people are made SSI eligible, they will generally become eligible for these other programs. Another interesting reform to consider would be federally provided benefits that reflect state living costs. The possibility of such benefits that would differ across states is discussed for welfare payments in National Research Council (1995).

It would also be interesting to know in more detail who receives SSI and how changes in Social Security would affect who receives it. In order to answer these questions, it would be useful to study why people are eligible for SSI. Are they nonimmigrants who are physically impaired, but not disabled enough to qualify for Disability Insurance (DI)? What fraction are disabled individuals are without a sufficient work history to qualify for DI? How would changes in DI eligibility rules affect the size of this population? What fraction are immigrants who have been in the country only a few years? What fraction are immigrants who have been in the country a long time, but have only a short work history? I ask these questions because the 1998 *Green Book* indicates that one-third of aged SSI recipients are blind or disabled and that 32.1 percent were aliens in 1995.

Other questions raised by this chapter include how Social Security reform proposals that change the number of quarters for eligibility affect SSI enrollment, costs, and poverty. Finally, what are the savings and work disincentives of the SSI program?

References

Bavier, Richard. 1999. An early look at the effects of welfare reform. Office of Management and Budget. Manuscript, March.

Giannarelli, Linda, and Laura Wheaton. 2000. Under-reporting of means-tested transfer programs in the March CPS. The Urban Institute. Manuscript, February.

Hutchens, Robert. 1981. Distributional equity in the unemployment insurance system. *Industrial and Labor Relations Review* 34 (3): 377–85.

Meyer, Bruce D. 1995. Lessons from the U.S. unemployment insurance experiments. *Journal of Economic Literature* 33 (March): 91–131.

National Research Council. 1995. *Measuring poverty: A new approach,* ed. Constance F. Citro and Robert T. Michael. Washington, D.C.: National Academy Press.

U.S. House of Representatives, Committee on Ways and Means. 1998. *Green book: Background material and data on programs within the jurisdiction of the Committee on Ways and Means.* Washington, D.C.: GPO.

Discussion Summary

Martin Feldstein highlighted the very limited current spending on impoverished elderly and the relatively small cost of moving this group up to the poverty line. *Christina Paxson* commented about the incentive changes created by increasing the size of SSI benefits. If benefits are sufficiently generous, people may decide to spend down their assets in order to qualify for benefits. Paxson also questioned the political feasibility of changing SSI for the elderly and leaving SSI for the young disabled untouched. This is particularly important because 85 percent of SSI expenditures are for the young disabled. The author confirmed that changing benefits for everyone eligible for SSI would be quite expensive, but indicated that changes to SSI for the elderly could be tied to changes in the Social Security system without disturbing the rest of the SSI program.

Charles Blahous felt that the paper provided evidence supporting the inclusion of stronger minimum benefit guarantees as part of Social Security instead of SSI. It seems that benefits are more likely to reach the intended recipients through OASDI and that using OASDI will remove the incentive to retire early because the minimum benefit guarantees could be actuarially adjusted. Certainly, the stigma issues associated with applications for SSI benefits would be eliminated. The author replied that the decision to replace SSI with minimum benefits in the Social Security system is up to policy makers. Clearly, the participation rate would be much higher if the minimum benefits were part of Social Security.

Leora Friedberg suggested that individuals could easily adjust the income received from their children in an effort to qualify for benefits. The author stated that transfers from family members are excluded from the calculations determining eligibility in the paper because it is not clear whether they are reported to the administrators of SSI.

Many participants asked for a more elaborate explanation of the low take-up rate for SSI benefits. The author indicated that the outreach efforts really try to enroll people, although there has not been a significant increase for enrollment rates. If the low take-up rate is caused by the stigma effect, then the benefits are not reaching the target population and there is a real problem. If people are actually getting help from family members and friends, then a low take-up rate may not be as great a concern.

Jeffrey B. Liebman thought that across-state comparisons might provide interesting results. In particular, do states that supplement SSI benefits have lower poverty rates? These data could be used to predict the effects of increasing benefits for the national program. The author believed that it would be very difficult to examine state-by-state differences because the samples are so small.

John B. Shoven wondered about the consequences of abolishing the asset test on the take-up rate. He noted that some eligible individuals may not participate in SSI because asset information must be submitted to the government. In the simulations, the author assumed that when the eligibility rules of the SSI program changed, the decision-making process for eligible individuals remained unchanged. However, this assumption may not be correct if people decide not to enroll because they must report their assets to the government or if people are unaware of the exact requirements and mistakenly believe that owning a home precludes eligibility. To the extent that removing the asset test eliminates the first problem and reduces the second, there would be an increase in the participation rate.

3

The Impact of Social Security and Other Factors on the Distribution of Wealth

Jagadeesh Gokhale and Laurence J. Kotlikoff

3.1 Introduction

As documented in Feldstein (1976) and Auerbach et al. (1995), the postwar period has witnessed a dramatic increase in the annuitization of the resources of America's elderly. Indeed, between 1960 and 1990, the annuitized share of resources of older men doubled, and that of older women quadrupled. Social Security is the main force behind this process, but Medicare and Medicaid as well as private pensions play an important role in replacing household wealth accumulation with survival-dependent old-age resource streams. Gokhale, Kotlikoff, and Sabelhaus (1996) suggest that the increased annuitization may explain the significant postwar rise in the propensity of the elderly to consume their remaining lifetime resources. Gokhale et al. (2001) consider a related point, namely, that increased annuitization will reduce bequests. This is particularly the case for lower-income households, who face Social Security taxation on all of their earnings and for whom Social Security replaces a higher share of preretirement income. Thanks to Social Security, these households have less to save, and less reason to save, than upper-income households. Thus, they arrive at old age with relatively little net worth available to bequeath. In differentially disenfranchising the children of the poor from the receipt of

Jagadeesh Gokhale is a senior economic advisor with the Federal Reserve Bank of Cleveland. Laurence J. Kotlikoff is professor of economics at Boston University and a research associate of the National Bureau of Economic Research.

The opinions expressed here are those of the authors and not necessarily those of Boston University, the Federal Reserve Bank of Cleveland, or the National Bureau of Economic Research. Laurence J. Kotlikoff thanks the National Bureau of Economic Research, the National Institute of Aging, and Boston University for research support.

inheritances, Social Security may be materially altering the distribution of wealth.

This chapter builds on Gokhale et al. (2001) in trying to understand how Social Security and other factors affect wealth inequality. Specifically, this chapter uses lifetime earnings data from the Panel Study of Income Dynamics (PSID) to calibrate Gokhale et al.'s (2001) bequest simulation model. The model features random death based on age-sex mortality probabilities, random fertility, assortative mating, heterogeneous human capital endowments, heterogeneous rates of return, the inheritability of human capital, progressive income taxation, and the partial annuitization through Social Security of households' retirement savings. Agents have no bequest motive. They live for a maximum of eighty-eight years, the first twenty-two as children, the second twenty-two as young married adults who have children, the third twenty-two as middle-aged adults raising children, and the last twenty-two as elderly individuals who die at random. Surviving spouses inherit all their partners' wealth but bequeath their own wealth in equal portions to their children.

Gokhale et al. (2001) use synthetic data generated by CORSIM—a micro simulation model—in conjunction with cross-section earnings data from the Survey of Consumer Finances (SCF) to calibrate the distribution of lifetime labor earnings. Surprisingly, their simulated distribution of wealth held by those reaching retirement closely matches that observed in the SCF. This is particularly true at the upper tail of the wealth distribution. In addition to matching the wealth distribution, Gokhale et al. decompose the influence of various factors, including Social Security, on wealth inequality. They show that, in the absence of Social Security, inheritances would reduce slightly the degree of wealth inequality. In Social Security's presence, however, they find that inheritances significantly exacerbate wealth inequality.

While intriguing, Gokhale et al.'s results should be viewed with caution, given the synthetic generation of lifetime earnings upon which they rely. This chapter attempts to alleviate that shortcoming by considering actual lifetime earnings as reported in the long PSID panel. The availability of actual lifetime earnings also permits a more accurate calibration of the degree of assortative mating and inheritability of skills. These advantages must be set against a key disadvantage: The PSID does not adequately capture the skewness in the upper tail of the distribution of lifetime earnings. Since the upper tail of the distribution of lifetime earnings plays such a key role in determining the upper tail of the distribution of wealth, this paper focuses on the shape of the distribution of wealth in the bottom half of the wealth distribution.

Because we are using the PSID to generate the distribution of lifetime earnings, and because the PSID data suggest a rather minor degree of assortative mating, our simulated distribution of wealth holdings among households reaching retirement is much less skewed than that reported in Gokhale et al. (2001). It is also less skewed than the 1995 SCF and 1984 PSID wealth distributions of married households aged sixty to sixty-nine.

Although we are less successful than Gokhale et al. (2001) in matching the upper tail of the wealth distribution, we continue to confirm Feldstein's (1976) finding that Social Security plays an important role in making wealth holdings less equal. The Gini coefficient for our simulated distribution of wealth is 16 percent higher in the presence of Social Security than in its absence, and Social Security raises the share of wealth held by the wealthiest 10 percent of retiring households by almost one quarter.

The paper proceeds in section 3.2 with a brief literature review. Section 3.3 draws heavily on Gokhale et al. (2001) in describing the model and proceeds to discuss the model's calibration. Section 3.4 presents results, and section 3.5 draws conclusions.

3.2   Related Literature

Harbury and Hitchens (1979) and Menchik (1979) are well-cited studies that connect the wealth of sons to the estates of their fathers. While suggestive, their data do not necessarily imply that inherited wealth is a source of inequality.[1] Nevertheless, they reinforced Meade's (1976) view that inheritances exacerbate wealth inequality—a conclusion supported by the theoretical model of Wilhelm (1997). Stiglitz (1969) and Atkinson and Stiglitz (1980) offered an alternative perspective: They showed that, under certain assumptions, a stable, egalitarian distribution of wealth would emerge if inheritances were distributed evenly among all of one's children.

The models by Becker and Tomes (1979) and Tomes (1981) go beyond these studies in examining the joint role that inheritances of financial wealth and earning power (human capital) play in determining whether intergenerational transfers are equalizing. Laitner (1979a, b) constructs a utility-maximizing framework in which parents care about both their own and their children's consumption, bequests must be nonnegative, and there is no inheritability of human capital. He shows that an equilibrium wealth distribution exists and that inheritances are equalizing if there is no assortative mating—an issue first examined by Blinder (1973). The studies of Meade (1964), Stiglitz (1969), Pryor (1973), Atkinson and Harrison (1978), and Atkinson (1980) also stress the role of imperfect correlation of spouses' inheritances in equalizing the distribution of inheritances.[2]

---

1. Their data record the total value of the father's estate, rather than the amount actually inherited by the son. Their findings may be explained, in large part, by the sons' inheritances of their fathers' human capital.

2. Theoretical work on taxation provides additional grounds for believing that inheritances are equalizing. Becker and Tomes (1979) and Atkinson and Stiglitz (1980) show that inheritance taxation can increase income inequality. However, if there are incomplete markets,

Early simulation studies of wealth inequality include Atkinson (1971), Flemming (1976), Oulton (1976), and Wolfson (1977). Their central finding is that, absent bequests, the life-cycle model is unable to explain the upper tail of the wealth distribution. Wolfson (1979) and Davies (1982) add bequests, specifically desired bequests, and generate much more realistic skewness in the distribution of wealth.

Flemming (1979) is the closest antecedent to our work. He, too, considers earnings heterogeneity and the inheritability of skills, but not marriage, assortative mating, or heterogeneity in the number and spacing of children. Flemming finds that wealth is much more unequally divided than earnings and that both unintended and intended bequests can markedly increase wealth inequality. Although many of our findings agree with Flemming's, we find that, in the absence of Social Security, unintended bequests serve to slightly reduce intragenerational wealth inequality.

3.2.1 Empirical Support for Excluding Altruism

Although Laitner and Juster (1996) provide some limited support for altruism, most recent studies do not. To be precise, Boskin and Kotlikoff (1985), Altonji, Hayashi and Kotlikoff (1992, 1997), Abel and Kotlikoff (1994), Hayashi, Altonji, and Kotlikoff (1996), Gokhale, Kotlikoff, and Sabelhaus (1996), Wilhelm (1996), and Hurd (1992) show that (a) the distribution of consumption across cohorts is very strongly dependent on the cross-cohort distribution of resources, (b) the distribution of consumption within extended families is very strongly dependent on the distribution of resources within extended families, (c) that taking a dollar from a child and handing it to parents who are actively transferring income to that child leads the parent to hand back only thirteen cents to the child, (d) that the very major postwar increase in the annuitization of the resources of the elderly has not been even partially offset by an increase in their holdings of life insurance, (e) that the vast majority of bequests are distributed equally among children independent of their economic needs, and (f) the presence of children does not influence postretirement dissaving. Individually and as a group, these studies constitute very strong evidence against intergenerational altruism, suggesting that most bequests may be unintended or motivated by nonaltruistic considerations—the modeling assumption made here.[3]

---

such as the market for educational loans considered by Loury (1981), redistributive taxation of bequests can reduce intragenerational inequality.

3. Of course, the Bill Gateses and Warren Buffets of the world are not making unintended bequests. Unlike most people, they may be able to afford their altruism because of their high levels of income. Stated differently, many households may be altruistic, but their degrees of altruism are so small that, given their resources, they choose not to allocate resources toward intentional, altruistically motivated bequests.

It is frequently observed that retired consumers save rather than dissave. Prima facie this might indicate a bequest motive in some form (Hurd 1990). However, Gokhale, Kotlikoff, and Sabelhaus (1996) and Miles (1997) point out that when wealth is calculated to include the capitalized value of Social Security receipts, it falls throughout retirement. Hurd also concludes from a careful analysis of panel and cross-section data that the evidence on wealth changes is consistent with the life-cycle hypothesis and the view that bequests are accidental.

Meade (1966) and Flemming (1976) provide a final reason to doubt the prevalence of altruistically motivated bequests. They pointed out that anything less than very strong altruism would not suffice to generate ubiquitous and significant bequests because the lifetime incomes of children significantly exceed those of their parents.

3.3   The Model and Its Calibration

This section describes the model's demographic structure, skill allocation, determination of inheritance, and consumption and saving behavior.

3.3.1   Demographics

Agents can live for eighty-eight periods, the first twenty-two of which they spend as children whose consumption is financed by their parents. All events, including earnings, consumption, marriages, births, deaths, and wealth transfers, occur at the end of each period. Agents marry on their twenty-second birthday. They give birth to children at ages twenty-two through forty-three, depending on their draw from a "birth matrix" described below. They also enter the work force on their twenty-second birthday and work through age sixty-six. They face positive probabilities of dying between ages sixty-seven and eighty-eight. The probability of an agent's dying on her eighty-eighth birthday, given that she has lived to that date, is 100 percent. The probabilities of dying at ages sixty-seven through eighty-seven are taken from U.S. mortality statistics.

The number, sexes, and timing of children born to each couple are determined randomly. This distribution is aligned to ensure that 2,000 males and 2,000 females are born each year. There is no population growth, so total annual births remain fixed through time.

3.3.2   Consumption and Saving Behavior

Agents' expected utilities are time-separable isoelastic functions of their own current and future consumption as well as that of their children through age twenty-two. Consider, as an example, the expected utility (EU) of a couple, aged twenty-three, who will have two children, one when the couple are aged twenty-five and the other when they are twenty-eight:

(1)
$$EU = \sum_{a=22}^{a=87} \beta^{a-22} (p_{ha} c_{ha}^{1-1/\sigma} + p_{wa} c_{wa}^{1-1/\sigma})$$
$$+ \delta \sum_{a=25}^{a=46} \beta^{a-22} c_{k1a}^{1-1/\sigma} + \delta \sum_{a=28}^{a=49} \beta^{a-22} c_{k2a}^{1-1/\sigma}.$$

In equation (1), the first summation considers the utility of each spouse from his or her own consumption at each possible age to which each could live. The second two summations consider the utility that the couple derive from the consumption of their two children. The terms c_{ha}, c_{wa}, c_{k1a}, and c_{k2a} refer, respectively, to the consumption of the husband, wife, first child, and second child when the couple is age a. The term β is the time-preference factor, σ is the intertemporal elasticity of substitution, and δ is the child consumption weighting factor.

As σ approaches zero, households become more and more reluctant to consume smaller amounts in the future than they consume in the present. Since the inverse of σ is the household's coefficient of relative risk aversion, a value of close to zero translates into a coefficient of risk aversion close to infinity. In our simulations, we assume that σ is very close to zero. Hall (1988) reports that there is "no strong evidence that the elasticity of intertemporal substitution is positive. Earlier findings of substantial positive elasticities are reversed when appropriate estimation methods are used."

Although Hall's findings are based on a highly stylized model, assuming that σ is very close to zero enormously simplifies the consumption decisions of our model's households. First, this assumption in conjunction with the assumption of a time preference rate equal to the interest rate means that households seek to maintain the same level of consumption over time for each spouse. Households also seek to maintain a constant level of consumption for their children, while they are children. Given the value of δ, this child consumption level equals 40 percent of the parental consumption level.

Most important, however, our assumption that σ is very close to zero means that households only consider their safe resources in deciding how much to consume at each point in time. Thus, households who expect to receive an inheritance, but are uncertain of receiving one (because all of their parents may live to age eighty-eight), will ignore this potential source of future income in making their current consumption and saving decisions.

At each point in time, married households will calculate the number of years of remaining life, multiply this amount by two (to take into account the presence of both spouses) and then add to the resulting value 0.4 times the number of years of consumption of their children. This total number of effective adult consumption years is then divided into the household's safe resources to determine consumption per effective adult. The household's safe resources consist of its wealth (which may reflect the receipt of past inheritances) plus the present value of its remaining lifetime labor earnings, which, by necessity, is assumed to be certain. Given the level of consumption per effective adult, it is straightforward to calculate total household consumption and subtract it from total household income to determine household saving.

We want to emphasize that inheritances affect consumption behavior, but only once they are received. There is no consumption out of potential future inheritances. Instead, households consider the worst-case scenario at each point in time and formulate their consumption and saving plans accordingly. Were we to assume a positive value of σ, households would take a gamble and consume more in the present in anticipation of a possible future inheritance. However, their decision as to how much to consume would be extraordinarily complex. The reason is that at certain ages they would have to take into account not simply their own resources, including their own wealth, but also those of their parents and grandparents, assuming their grandparents are still alive. Take, for example, a twenty-five-year-old couple with two sets of living parents and four sets of living grandparents. In deciding how much to consume, the household has to consider its own current wealth level as well as the wealth levels of all six parental and grandparental households. Formally, the dynamic program that the household must solve to determine how much to consume involves up to seven state variables, namely all seven of these wealth levels.[4] Unfortunately, solving dynamic programs with seven state variables appears to be beyond the capacity of current computers.[5]

3.3.3 Assortative Mating

Agents are assigned their marriage partners at age twenty-two on a partly systematic basis in which the probability of a match is higher the closer are the respective skill ranks of the two partners. Our assortative mating works as follows. We first construct for each year of the simulation a vector **A** containing 2,000 random numbers drawn from a uniform distribution with support (0, 1). Vector **A** is sorted in ascending order. Second, a vector **B** is constructed containing 2,000 random numbers from the same distribution but is left unsorted. Third, vector $\mathbf{C} = \alpha\mathbf{A} + (1 - \alpha)\mathbf{B}$ is constructed to yield a new vector of numbers between zero and one. Fourth, we associate with the first element of the **C** vector the integer 1, with the second element the integer 2, and so on up to the last element of **C**, to which we associate the integer 2,000. Fifth, we sort **C** such that **C** ends up in ascending

---

4. We say "up to" because during years in which the household is aged sixty-six and over, it has neither living parents nor living grandparents, and during years in which the household is aged forty-four through sixty-five, it has no living grandparents.

5. The fact that even supercomputers would have difficulty solving this problem in a reasonable amount of time raises the question of how mere mortals can actually deal with this complexity.

order and denote the associated integers as vector **R**. This vector is used to assign the husband's skill rank, j, for each female skill rank, where the female skills are aligned in ascending order), $i = 1 \ldots 2,000$.

For example, suppose that, for a given year, after the **C** vector has been generated and sorted in ascending order, the first three integers associated with the first three elements of the **C** vector are 3, 51, and 1,290. Then the most skilled twenty-two-year-old female in that year will be married to the 3rd most skilled twenty-two-year-old male, the 2nd most skilled twenty-two-year-old female will be married to the 51st most skilled twenty-two-year-old male, and the 3rd most skilled twenty-two-year-old female will be married to the 1,290th most skilled twenty-two-year-old male. The parameter α is chosen to reproduce the rank correlation coefficient between husbands' and wives' lifetime earnings, which we estimate in the PSID.

3.3.4   Inheritance of Skills

The procedure just described for correlating husbands' and wives' lifetime earnings is also used to determine the correlation between fathers' and sons' lifetime earnings as well as the correlation between mothers' and daughters' lifetime earnings. In each case, the relevant parameter is calibrated to reproduce the rank correlation coefficient observed between sons' (daughters') and fathers' (mothers') lifetime earnings. We use the assumption that if sons (daughters) inherit skills, they do so from their fathers (mothers), which, while both politically and genetically incorrect, maintains tractability of the distribution of earnings through time of males and females.

3.3.5   Fertility

An initial population (at time $t = 0$) of 4,000 thousand individuals (2,000 males and 2,000 females) was created for each age between zero and eighty-seven. This was done as follows: First, a matrix of "birth ages" was derived from a fertility simulation of CORSIM—a dynamic microsimulation model of the U.S. economy described in Caldwell et al. (1999). The simulation considered 40,434 females born between 1945 and 2000 and recorded their ages of giving birth if those ages fell between ages twenty-two and forty-three. For each female in our CORSIM sample, we stored this information in our CORSIM birth matrix, which accommodates a maximum of ten birth ages, five for male and five for female births. Thus, the matrix has 40,434 rows and ten columns. Table 3.1 shows the distribution of females in the CORSIM matrix by number and sex of births.

Because computer memory limitations allowed us to process only 4,000 individuals in each year of birth, we needed to pare down our birth matrix in such a way as to end up with a modified birth matrix that contains exactly 2,000 male births and 2,000 female births. We started by selecting

Table 3.1   **Distribution of Females by Number and Sex of Births at Ages 22 through 43**

	Female Births					
	0	1	2	3	4	5
Male Births			CORSIM Data			
0	20.68	**12.94**	**6.96**	**1.49**	**0.33**	**0.10**
1	**13.64**	**14.77**	**5.32**	**1.38**	**0.35**	0.13
2	**7.83**	**5.06**	**2.16**	**0.70**	0.24	0.12
3	**1.87**	**1.38**	**0.64**	0.23	0.12	0.05
4	**0.41**	**0.33**	0.17	0.12	0.08	0.00
5	**0.12**	0.13	0.11	0.05	0.00	0.00
		Birth Matrix Used in Simulation				
0	0.00	**13.00**	**9.00**	**2.20**	**0.55**	**0.15**
1	**16.05**	**22.40**	**6.45**	**1.60**	**0.50**	0.00
2	**12.20**	**7.15**	**2.50**	**0.80**	0.00	0.00
3	**2.85**	**0.95**	**0.75**	0.00	0.00	0.00
4	**0.40**	**0.40**	0.00	0.00	0.00	0.00
5	**0.10**	0.00	0.00	0.00	0.00	0.00

Source: Authors' calculations based on CORSIM birth matrix.

Notes: CORSIM data represent females with at least one but fewer than five births numbered 40434. Selections from the birth matrix are restricted to females with one through five births, male and female (shown in boldface type).

2,000 rows from the birth matrix. We performed selection at random and without replacement, except that rows containing more than five births were excluded. The total number of births in the selected 2,000-row matrix exceeded 4,000. Hence, we randomly eliminated male and female births in the rows of this matrix for rows containing more than one birth until we were left with precisely 2,000 male and 2,000 female births. This guaranteed that the 2,000 rows of the final birth matrix would generate exactly 2,000 female and 2,000 male births. Table 3.1 shows the distribution of females by the number and sex of their births in the birth matrix used in the simulation.

3.3.6 Populating the Model at Time Zero

We populated our model by first creating 2,000 male and 2,000 female old adults for each age between sixty-seven and eighty-eight. These males and females were then married to each other sequentially. Some of these oldsters were treated as dead when we initiated the simulation, but we needed to include their ghosts at this stage of our process of populating the model in order to establish complete family trees. Marriage was allowed only between people of the same age to be consistent with our assumption that marriage occurs at age twenty-two (i.e., that initial oldster males married initial oldster females when they were twenty-two and their brides were twenty-two). Family relationships were established by exchanging identification numbers.

In our next step, we drew from the 2,000 rows of the birth matrix at random (but without replacement) the middle-aged and young-adult children of the initial oldsters, ranging in age from twenty-four through sixty-six. In this process, we do not permit oldsters to bear children in their twilight years; rather, we are retrospectively considering the births of the initial oldsters when they were in their childbearing years.

Given that females give birth between the ages of twenty-two and forty-three, oldsters aged eighty-eight at the initiation of our simulation ($t = 0$) have children who are aged forty-five through sixty-six; oldsters aged eighty-seven at $t = 0$ have children aged forty-four through age sixty-five; and so on, until we reach oldsters aged sixty-seven at $t = 0$ who would have children aged between twenty-four and forty-five. Thus, at this stage of our populating procedure, exactly 4,000 (the full complement of) forth-five-year-olds and less then 4,000 thousand individuals at other ages between twenty-four and sixty-six have been created. The reason is that everyone (including oldster ghosts) who could have given birth to forty-five-year-olds has been considered, but not everyone who gave birth to those between ages twenty-four and forty-four and those between ages forty-six and sixty-six has been considered.

Because at this stage there are fewer than 4,000 middle-aged males and females at ages forty-six to sixty-six, additional middle-aged males and females are created for a total of 4,000 for each of these age groups. Next, all middle-aged males and females (those aged forty-five through sixty-six) were married at random, making sure that siblings were not married to each other. Next, the children of middle-aged adults were created, again taking draws without replacement from the birth matrix for females of a given age and then doing the same for females of another age until all females aged forty-five through sixty-six had been considered. The children produced by this process range in age from two through forty-four.[6] Given that we have already created the children of the $t = 0$ oldsters, the addition of these children leave us with exactly 2,000 males and 2,000 females aged twenty-three through forty-four—the young adults. The procedure just described was also used to marry the young adults.

The next step in the creation of the initial population was creating the children of the $t = 0$ young adults that were born at $t = -1$ or earlier. Each young-adult female was assigned a row of the birth matrix at random

---

6. Sixty-six-year-olds have children aged between twenty-three and forty-four; sixty-five-year-olds have children aged between twenty-two and forty-three; and so on through forty-five-year-olds, who have children aged between two and twenty-three.

without replacement, and children were created for all birth ages less than the age at $t = 0$ of the female in question. For example, a forty-four-year-old female's children were created for birth ages between twenty-two and forty-three, but a twenty-three-year-old's children are created only if her birth row assignment contains a birth age of twenty-two. That is, children that will be born at $t = 0$ or later were not created as yet. At the end of this process, exactly 2,000 males and 2,000 females had been created for each age between one and eighty-eight. The final step in creating the initial population was to kill off oldsters (i.e., make the ghosts disappear) according to their cumulative mortality probabilities.[7]

3.3.7 Populating the Model Through Time

In populating the model through time we do the following. First, for $t = 0$, we allocate at random and without replacement a row from the birth matrix to all twenty-two-year-old females. Second, we marry twenty-two-year-old males and females at random, or according to the assortative mating procedure described above. Third, we have females aged twenty-two to forty-three give birth as determined by their assigned birth matrix row, creating 2,000 newborn (zero-year-old) males and 2,000 newborn (zero-year-old) females. Fourth, we kill off oldsters at random according to the conditional probability of dying at their respective ages. The wealth of these oldsters is transferred to the surviving spouse or children. Finally, we age everyone by one year.

3.3.8 Using the Panel Study of Income Dynamics to Calculate Lifetime Earnings

The PSID began in 1968 with a representative sample of 5,000 U.S. households. The PSID has re-interviewed (or attempted to re-interview) the individuals from those households every year since that time, regardless of their demographic status, living arrangements, etc. Children of original PSID respondents have been followed after they have left their parents' households.

Forming longitudinal labor income profiles involves the following steps: First, labor income, family number, and sex variables for "head" and "wife" are extracted from the family file for year x and merged with the individual file by year-x family number, retaining only those observations that appeared in year x.[8] Step 1 is repeated separately for each year from

---

7. The mortality probabilities are based on U.S. mortality tables. Conditional mortality probabilities below age sixty-seven are set to zero, and the conditional mortality probability at age eighty-eight is set to unity. The probability of dying at age $= a$, d_a, is calculated as $d_a = (1 - \sigma_a) \Pi_{s=67}^{a-1} \sigma_s$, where σ_s is the conditional probability of surviving at age s.

8. The PSID's file structure comprises one cross-year individual file and several single-year family files. The cross-year individual file contains records for all individuals that ever ap-

1968 to 1993 to create twenty-six separate data files. Each data file is sorted by "family interview number" and "person number" respectively, and all are merged together to form a single "cross-year individual" file containing individual longitudinal labor income profiles.

The PSID reports annual labor income in nominal dollars. To place the income earned in different years on a comparable basis, we divide each year's values by the ratio of that year's Social Security Administration's average wage index to the average wage index in 1997. Using this wage index to rescale nominal labor income adjusts not only for inflation but also for labor productivity growth. We have selected 1997 as base year because that year's federal income tax rates and brackets are used to implement progressive income taxation in our simulation. Our motivation for controlling for productivity growth in forming lifetime earnings is simple: Our model does not account for productivity growth. Our next step is to sort the cross-year individual file by sex.[9]

Not all individuals appear in the PSID in each year between 1968 and 1993. Moreover, some individuals appear as "head" or "wife" for just a few years. To ensure a minimum number of data points from which to form lifetime earnings, we retained in our sample only those individuals who appear for at least ten years as "head" or "wife" between the ages of twenty-three and sixty-six.

Since the PSID spans only twenty-six years, it cannot provide us with earnings profiles for the full complement of forty-four years (from age twenty-three to age sixty-six) of earnings—the lifetime earnings profile as required by our simulation. Hence, we adopt a procedure for extrapolating each individual's labor income both backward and forward as required. First, we calculate average labor incomes for all males who appeared in the sample (as "head" or "wife") at each age between twenty-three and sixty-six.[10] This provides us with a benchmark age-earnings profile for males—M23–M66. This procedure is repeated for females to generate a corresponding benchmark profile for females—F23–F66.

Next, for each individual we calculate two average labor incomes for each person. A1 is the average labor income over the first five years of the

---

peared in the survey—whether these individuals were members of the original sample of households or households that formed after 1968. This individual file contains a "person number" variable indicating the response status for each individual, which can be associated with the family number to create a unique person identifier. Unfortunately, the cross-year individual file does not contain labor income for "head" and "wife" for all of the years. Hence it was necessary to select these variables from the single-year family files and merge them together to form individual longitudinal labor income profiles.

9. We classify appropriately female "heads" and male "wives."

10. Thus, those who appeared in the sample at their age twenty-three are included in the calculation of the average labor income for age twenty-three; those who appeared in the sample at age twenty-four are included in the calculation of the average labor income at age twenty-four, and so on through age sixty-six.

person's presence in the sample, and A2 is the average labor income over the last five years that the person is present in the sample (as "head" or "wife"). For example, if a female appeared in the sample at each age between thirty-five and fifty-four, A1 would be her average labor income at ages thirty-five through thirty-nine, and A2 would be average labor income at ages fifty through fifty-four. A1 is used to extrapolate her labor income backward—from age thirty-four through age twenty-three. Her imputed income at age thirty-four equals A1 times the ratio of F34 to the average of F35–F39; her imputed income at age thirty-three equals A1 times the ratio of F33 to the average of F35–F39, and so on. A similar procedure is adopted when extrapolating individuals' labor incomes forward—beyond their oldest age as a PSID "head" or "wife" (fifty-four for the male in the current example) through age sixty-six.

The sample of individuals for whom we could compute/impute lifetime earnings profiles in this manner included 4,706 males and 5,278 females. However, our simulation includes only 2,000 individuals of each sex. To arrive at 2,000 male and female lifetime earnings profiles, we proceed in the following manner. First, we replicate each of the 4,706 male and 5,278 female observations in proportion to their sample population weights. Second, we group to the nearest integer the "blown-up" males and females into 0.05 percentiles of the present value of lifetime earnings. Third, we pick the observation with the highest value of lifetime earnings in each of the 0.05 percentiles. This gives us 2,000 males and 2,000 females whose level and pattern of lifetime earnings are used in the simulation.

3.3.9   Calibrating the Degree of Assortative Mating and the Inheritability of Skills

Armed with the original (not blown up by population weights) lifetime earnings of the sample of 4,706 males and 5,278 females, we formed for each year of the PSID sample the rank correlation coefficients between (a) the lifetime earnings of husbands and their wives observed in that year and (b) the lifetime earnings of fathers (mothers) and sons (daughters) observed in that year. The average (across all the years) values of the husband-wife and same-sex parent-child rank correlation coefficients are 0.10 and 0.44, respectively. These coefficients are used to calibrate the parameters mentioned above.

Before proceeding, we should point out that the 0.10 husband-wife rank correlation coefficient is quite small relative to our priors. It is also much smaller than the 0.70 guesstimate used by Gokhale et al. (2001). Although this estimate suggests that assortative mating on the basis of lifetime earnings may not be an important factor, one should bear in mind that the PSID underrepresents upper-income earners for whom assortative mating may be much more important.

3.3.10   Bequests and Inheritances

When a spouse dies, the surviving spouse retains all the couple's marital wealth. That is, all bequests of married agents go to their spouses. When a widow or widower dies, or when both spouses die at the same time, the wealth of the decedent(s) is evenly divided among the children.

3.3.11   Initial Wealth Endowments and Length of the Simulations

We start each of our simulations by giving all adults at $t = 0$ an endowment of wealth of one unit. We then run the model for enough years into the future until the distribution of wealth of sixty-seven-year-olds, as well as the total amount of wealth in the economy, stabilizes. Since the asymptotic wealth distribution as well as the total level of wealth is independent of the initial level and distribution of wealth, the fact that we start with this particular initial endowment of wealth does not alter our results. In practice, both the wealth distribution of sixty-seven-year-olds and the total level of wealth converge well before 150 years in each of our simulations. Nonetheless, to guarantee consistency across simulations, we run each simulation for 150 years.

3.3.12   Including Interest Rate Heterogeneity

Different households face different rates of return on their portfolios because they systematically choose to hold different portfolios. To incorporate rate-of-return heterogeneity, we use data on the portfolio holdings of households from the 1995 SCF. Our first step entails classifying those household assets reported in the survey into several categories. Next, we assign a rate of return to each asset category and compute the portfolio-weighted rate of return that each household faces, given its portfolio of assets.[11] Finally, we compute the weighted frequency of households for

11. The asset categories are liquid assets, government bonds, private bonds and bond mutual fund shares, stocks and stock mutual funds, real estate, and other nonfinancial assets. Liability categories include mortgage and other debt. In forming a weighted average rate of return on each household's portfolio, we used the absolute value of liabilities. For liquid assets, we assumed the geometric average annual real rate of return (0.68 percent) on U.S. Treasury bills during the period 1926–97. For government bonds, we use the geometric average annual real rate of return on long- and intermediate-term government bonds between 1926 and 1997 (2.09 percent). For private bonds and bond mutual funds, we use the geometric average rate of return on long-term corporate bonds between 1926 and 1997 (2.52 percent). For stocks and stock mutual funds, we use the weighted average of real rates of return on large and small company stocks (8.00 percent). The weights for the two stock market returns were obtained from analysts at the Wilshire 5000 company. The source for the aforementioned average rates of return is the 1998 Yearbook published by Ibbotson Associates. The average rates of interest on mortgages and other real estate debt were constructed using data from Case and Shiller (1990), who report annualized excess returns (excess over the three-month T-bill return) on home purchases for each quarter between 1971 and 1986 in four large U.S. metropolitan areas. We computed the total returns

rates of return ranging from 0 to 10 percent or more in steps of 0.5 percent. This frequency distribution is used to randomly allocate the average rate of return within each step to households in the simulation. Households are assumed to earn their assigned rate of return in each year of their lives.

3.3.13   Additional Issues of Calibration

The mortality probabilities used in the analysis are those released by the U.S. Social Security Administration for 1995. The interest rate used in the simulations is 4 percent. To obtain a realistic shape of the age-consumption profile, we assume that the time preference factors generate a 1.5 percent growth in the planned path of consumption per equivalent adult through age sixty-five.[12] From age sixty-six through eighty-eight, planned consumption per equivalent adult remains constant. As mentioned, our fertility matrix is derived from simulating CORSIM. Its fertility module includes separate logistic functions for thirty different subgroups of women estimated using data from the National Longitudinal Survey.

The subgroups are distinguished by age, the presence of children, marital status, race, and work status. The regressors in the logits are age, duration of current marriage, earnings, family income, homeowner status, marital status, schooling status, work status, and duration since the birth of the women's two youngest children. In producing the larger birth matrix from which we selected 2,000 rows, we ran the CORSIM model from its start year of 1960 through 2000. In so doing, we used the entire panoply of CORSIM modules to assign CORSIM agents the various socioeconomic characteristics, such as work status, entering as regressors in the fertility logits.

3.4   Findings

Tables 3.2 and 3.3 describe the distributions of wealth resulting from eleven different simulations. Our base-case simulation incorporates mortality prior to age eighty-eight, assortative mating, heterogeneity in skills, inheritance of skills, life-cycle consumption growth, heterogeneity in rates of return, progressive income taxation, and a social security system with

---

by adding the annualized real T-bill return for each quarter, then calculated the geometric mean over the period of the study and averaged the rates of return over the four metropolitan areas. This procedure yields a real rate of return of 0.45 percent. Finally, the rate of return for mortgage and real estate debt was calculated as the geometric average nominal mortgage rate between 1973 and 1997 divided by the geometric average rate of inflation over the same period. This yielded 3.91 percent. The average real rate on other debt was assumed to be 13.54 percent of the rate applicable for 1995, obtained from the Statistical Abstract for the United States, 1998, table 820.

12. Actual consumption per equivalent adult prior to age sixty-six will differ from planned consumption if the household receives one or more inheritances.

Table 3.2   **Inequality and Bequest Flows: Base Case and Alternative Simulations**

Case	Simulation	Wealth Gini	Consumption Gini	Bequest/ Earnings	Cross-Generational Bequest/Earnings
1	Base case	0.336	0.283	4.5	1.5
2	No skill differences	0.097	0.045	4.3	1.4
3	No marital sorting	0.324	0.270	4.6	1.5
4	No inheritance of skills	0.327	0.277	4.6	1.5
5	No consumption growth	0.427	0.286	1.8	0.6
6	No interest rate heterogeneity	0.332	0.279	4.5	1.4
7	No progressive income taxes	0.436	0.317	3.2	1.0
8	No inheritances	0.325	0.287	0.0	0.0
9	No Social Security	0.278	0.271	10.6	3.4
10	No ceiling on SS taxable income	0.242	0.272	3.9	1.2
11	No inheritances and no Social Security	0.285	0.278	0.0	0.0

Source: Authors' calculations.

a ceiling on taxable income. The other ten simulations are variants on the base case that leave out one, or, in the case of simulation eleven, two of these elements.

The first row in table 3.2 shows results for our base-case simulation, including a wealth Gini of 0.336 and a consumption Gini of 0.283 among age-sixty-six households. The consumption Gini is smaller because consumption is financed in part by Social Security benefits, and these benefits are more evenly distributed than is net wealth. The first row also indicates that the steady-state flow of total bequests in our model is 4.5 percent of aggregate labor earnings, and the cross-generational flow is 1.5 percent of aggregate labor earnings. This cross-generational flow of bequests appears to be about half as large as in the actual U.S. economy. We say this because our own unpublished calculations using the 1962 and 1995 SCFs suggest that cross-generational bequests in the actual economy are roughly 3 percent of total labor compensation.[13]

Figure 3.1 graphs the first row of table 3.3—the wealth distribution of

13. In forming these calculations, we first benchmarked 1962 and 1995 SCF net worth and life insurance holdings to Federal Reserve Flow of Funds and American Council of Life Insurance respective reported aggregates. Next, we calculated the flow of bequests by age and sex by assuming that (a) single people with children leave their entire estates to their children, (b) married decedents leave 15 percent of their estates to their children, and (c) all decedents have the same age- and sex-specific mortality rates as those that prevailed in 1962 and 1994. Our estimated ratios of cross-generational bequests to total labor compensation are 0.030 for 1962 and 0.033 for 1994.

Table 3.3   Simulated Wealth Distributions

Case	Simulation	% of Wealth Held by Top								
		99	95	90	75	50	25	10	5	1
1	Base case	100.0	99.2	97.4	89.8	71.8	47.6	27.6	18.4	7.0
2	No skill differences	99.4	96.7	92.9	80.3	56.9	30.5	13.5	7.2	1.6
3	No marital sorting	100.0	99.1	97.2	89.3	71.0	46.7	26.8	17.8	6.6
4	No inheritance of skills	100.0	99.2	97.4	89.5	71.2	46.8	26.9	17.8	6.6
5	No consumption growth	100.0	99.5	98.2	92.2	76.9	54.9	35.4	25.1	10.3
6	No interest rate heterogeneity	100.0	99.3	97.5	89.7	71.6	47.1	27.1	17.9	6.5
7	No progressive income taxes	100.0	99.5	98.4	92.8	78.1	55.5	34.4	23.8	9.4
8	No inheritances	100.0	99.4	97.7	89.8	71.2	46.3	26.2	17.2	6.3
9	No Social Security	100.0	99.2	97.4	89.1	69.0	42.1	21.2	12.6	3.8
10	No ceiling on SS taxable income	100.0	99.1	97.0	87.8	66.8	39.4	18.9	10.7	2.9
11	No inheritances and no Social Security	100.0	99.4	97.7	89.6	69.5	42.4	21.3	12.7	3.9

Source: Authors' calculations.

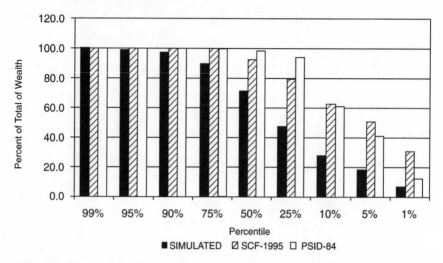

Fig. 3.1 Comparison of wealth distributions: simulated, SCF 1995, and PSID 1984

age-sixty-six couples generated by our base-case simulation. It also compares this distribution with wealth distributions of married couples whose heads are aged sixty to sixty-nine in (a) the 1995 SCF and (b) the 1984 PSID. As the figure makes clear, the concentration of wealth at the very top of the wealth distribution is much more substantial in the SCF. The SCF wealth Gini is 0.73—more than twice as large as our simulated Gini.

Why is our model generating too little skewness in the distribution of wealth compared to the SCF? The answer, we believe, is that (a) the PSID distribution of lifetime earnings is much less skewed than that of the actual economy, and (b) the skewness of lifetime earnings makes a significant difference in the skewness in our simulated distribution of wealth. To see the importance of our assumed degree of earnings inequality to our simulated wealth inequality, consider the results in the second rows of tables 3.2 and 3.3, which omit labor earnings heterogeneity. Without skill differences, the wealth Gini falls from 0.336 to 0.097. The fact that wealth inequality exists in the absence of skill inequality is due to differences across households in the number of timing of their children as well as in the rates of return earned on their saving.

The PSID earnings data from which we construct our male and female distributions of lifetime earnings is certainly much less skewed than the corresponding male and female cross-section distributions of earnings in the SCF. This would explain why the simulated wealth distribution in our base case is less concentrated than in the SCF.

However, it is harder to explain why the PSID's wealth concentration in the top tail is much greater than that simulated by the model. This may

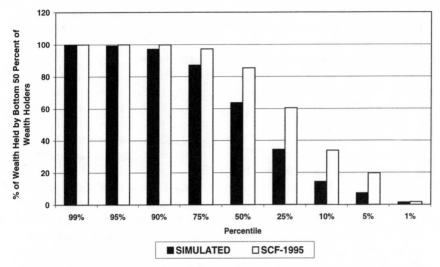

Fig. 3.2   Simulated and SCF-1995 distributions of wealth among bottom 50 percent of wealth holders

reflect a higher degree of underreporting of earnings among the rich than of underreporting of their assets. One way to test this possibility is to compare the distribution of wealth among the poorest (measured in terms of wealth) of our age-sixty-six simulated couples with the corresponding distribution of wealth among the poorest half of the SCF sixty- to sixty-nine-year-old couples. Figure 3.2 makes this comparison. While our model fits the distribution of the truncated data quite well at the very top of the tail, the fit in the rest of the top tail is not very good.

3.4.1   Determinants of Wealth Inequality

The remaining simulations in tables 3.2 and 3.3 examine other determinants of wealth inequality. Consider first the case 3 simulation, which eliminates assortative mating. Given the limited assortative mating we find in the data and incorporate in the base case, it is not surprising that eliminating assortative mating altogether makes very little difference to simulated wealth inequality. A second "nonfactor" with respect to the distribution of wealth is the inheritance of skills from parents. The source of agents' skills does not appear to have much impact on the cross-section distribution of wealth. This is clear from the case 4 simulation, which eliminates the inheritability of skills, leaving the Gini at essentially its base-case value.

The case 5 simulation eliminates consumption growth, which means that it alters the model's time-preference factors so that agents wish to have the same living standard per equivalent adult as they age. This smoothing of consumption generates more liquidity-constrained households that arrive at age sixty-six with zero wealth, which result, in turn, implies more wealth inequality. The wealth Gini in this case is 0.427—27 percent higher than in the base case.

The case 6 simulation turns off interest rate heterogeneity, which makes little difference to the distribution of wealth. The explanation here is that, other things being equal, households earning higher rates of return can afford to and do consume more at each point in time. Since accumulated assets reflect accumulated differences between past levels of earnings and consumption, this factor lowers the age-sixty-six wealth holdings of couples earning high rates of return. On the other hand, the smaller differences between past earnings and consumption are accumulated at a higher rate of return. This factor raises the age-sixty-six wealth holdings of high rate of return couples. According to the results, these two factors roughly cancel leaving wealth inequality essentially the same as in the case of no interest rate heterogeneity. In contrast to interest rate heterogeneity, progressive income taxation does play an important role in influencing wealth. In the case 7 simulation, this form of taxation is eliminated, raising the Gini coefficient from 0.336 to 0.436. Additionally, the share of wealth held by the top 1 percent of the wealth distribution rises from 7 percent to 9.4 percent.

3.4.2 The Role of Inheritances and Social Security in Wealth Inequality

How important are bequests and their associated inheritances to wealth inequality? The case 8 simulation addresses this question. It sets the probability of dying prior to age eighty-eight at zero. Compared to the base case, this experiment reduces wealth inequality only slightly. So, in the presence of Social Security, inheritances make the distribution of wealth more unequal. Is the same true if Social Security is absent? The answer, found by comparing cases 9 and 11, is no. With inheritances, but without Social Security, wealth inequality is somewhat smaller—the same finding reported in Gokhale et al. (2001).

How much does Social Security itself raise wealth inequality? Comparing the case 9 and 11 simulations reveals that the answer is a fair amount. Adding Social Security to the model's other features raises the wealth Gini by over 20 percent. It also almost doubles the share of wealth held by the top 1 percent of wealth holders. Figure 3.3 shows the impact of removing Social Security on the wealth levels of age-sixty-six couples at different percentiles of the wealth distributions. For those in the 75th percentile, eliminating Social Security would raise their age-sixty-six wealth by a factor of 2.55. In contrast, for those in the top 1 percentile, eliminating Social Security would raise their wealth by a factor of only 1.55.[14]

14. This difference would be greater still were we to assume that those who earn much higher than average earnings also earn much higher than average rates of return.

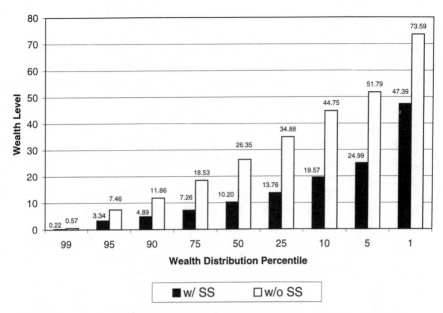

Fig. 3.3 **Average wealth holding within selected percentiles of the age-66 wealth distribution, with and without Social Security**

Why does Social Security increase wealth inequality? A small part of the reason, as previously mentioned, is that Social Security transforms inheritances into a disequalizing force. According to table 3.2, it also reduces the intergenerational flow of inheritances by over 50 percent. However, the main reason that Social Security is disequalizing is simply, as confirmed by the case 10 simulation, the ceiling that Social Security applies to its tax collection. This ceiling treats the lifetime rich more favorably than the lifetime poor. It also differentially annuitizes the lower classes. In the absence of the ceiling, the wealth Gini would be 0.242, compared to 0.336 in the base case, and the share of wealth held by the top 1 percent would be 2.9 percent, compared with 7 percent in the base case.

One can also assess the importance of Social Security to wealth inequality by considering how the wealth Gini varies with Social Security's load factor. As mentioned, our base case assumes that, for every dollar workers pay in Social Security payroll taxes, they receive thirty cents in retirement benefits, when both the taxes and benefits are measured in present value. A modest reduction in this load, such that workers receive back, in present value, thirty-five cents on each dollar contributed, would raise the wealth Gini from 0.336 to 0.363—that is, by about 10 percent. It would also, incidentally, lower the flows of both total and cross-generational bequests by 13 percent.

3.5 Conclusion

Given our use of the PSID, which undersamples very high-earning Americans, to calibrate the distribution of lifetime earnings, it is not surprising that our model fails to reproduce the extreme skewness of the top tail of U.S. wealth distribution. On the other hand, our analysis confirms the proposition first advanced by Feldstein (1976) and reemphasized by Gokhale et al. (2001) that Social Security exacerbates wealth inequality by leaving the lifetime poor with proportionately less to save, less reason to save, and a larger share of their old-age resources in a nonbequeathable form than the lifetime rich. In so doing, Social Security denies the children of the poor the opportunity to receive inheritances. Consequently, inheritances become a cause of wealth inequality rather than wealth equality. All told, Social Security appears to be raising wealth inequality, as measured by the Gini coefficient, by roughly one-fifth, substantially increasing the share of total wealth held by the richest members of society, and greatly reducing the flow of bequests to the next generation.

References

Abel, Andrew, and Laurence J. Kotlikoff. 1994. Intergenerational altruism and the effectiveness of fiscal policy: New tests based on cohort data. In *Savings and bequests,* ed. Toshiaki Tachibanaki, 167–96. Ann Arbor, Michigan: University of Michigan Press.

Altonji, Joseph, Fumio Hayashi, and Laurence J. Kotlikoff. 1992. Is the extended family altruistically linked? Direct tests using micro data. *American Economic Review* 82 (5): 1177–98.

———. 1997. Parental altruism and inter vivos transfers: Theory and evidence. *Journal of Political Economy* 105 (6): 1121–66.

Atkinson, Anthony B. 1971. The distribution of wealth and the individual life cycle. *Oxford Economic Papers* 23:239–54.

———. 1980. Inheritance and the redistribution of wealth. In *Public policy and the tax system,* ed. G. M. Heal and G. A. Hughes. London: Allen and Urwin.

Atkinson, Anthony B., and A. J. Harrison. 1978. *Distribution of personal wealth in Britain.* Cambridge: Cambridge University Press.

Atkinson, Anthony B., and Stiglitz, Joseph. 1980. *Lectures in public economics.* Singapore: McGraw-Hill.

Auerbach, Alan J., Jagadeesh Gokhale, Laurence J. Kotlikoff, John Sabelhaus, and David Weil. 1995. The annuitization of Americans' resources: A cohort analysis. NBER Working Paper no. 5089. Cambridge, Mass.: National Bureau of Economic Research, April.

Becker, Gary S., and Nigel Tomes. 1979. An equilibrium theory of the distribution of income and intergenerational mobility. *Journal of Political Economy* 87 (6): 1153–89.

Blinder, Alan S. 1973. A model of inherited wealth. *Quarterly Journal of Economics* 87 (4): 608–26.

Boskin, Michael J., and Laurence J. Kotlikoff. 1985. Public debt and U.S. saving: A new test of the neutrality hypothesis. *Carnegie-Rochester Conference Series on Public Policy* 23 (autumn): 55–86.
Caldwell, Steven, Melissa Favreault, Alla Gantman, Jagadeesh Gokhale, Thomas Johnson, and Laurence J. Kotlikoff. 1999. Social Security's treatment of postwar Americans. In *Tax policy and the economy,* vol. 13, ed. James M. Poterba, 109–48. Cambridge, Mass.: MIT Press.
Case, Karl E., and Robert J. Shiller. 1990. Forecasting prices and excess returns in the housing market. *AREUEA Journal* 18 (3): 253–73.
Davies, James B. 1982. The relative impact of inheritance and other factors on economic inequality. *Quarterly Journal of Economics* 97 (3): 471–98.
Feldstein, Martin. 1976. Social Security and the distribution of wealth. *Journal of the American Statistical Association* 71 (356): 800–07.
Flemming, John S. 1976. On the assessment of the inequality of wealth. In *Selected evidence submitted to the Royal Commission: Report no. 1, initial report of the standing reference,* 34–70. London: HMSO and Royal Commission on the Distribution of Income and Wealth.
———. 1979. The effects of earnings inequality, imperfect capital markets, and dynastic altruism on the distribution of wealth in life cycle models. *Economica* 46:363–80.
Gokhale, Jagadeesh, Laurence J. Kotlikoff, and John Sabelhaus. 1996. Understanding the postwar decline in United States saving: A cohort analysis. *Brookings Papers on Economic Activity* 1:315–90.
Gokhale, Jagadeesh, Laurence J. Kotlikoff, James Sefton, and Martin Weale. 2001. Simulating the transmission of wealth inequality via bequests. *Journal of Public Economics* 79:93–128.
Hall, Robert E. 1988. Intertemporal substitution in consumption. *Journal of Political Economy* 96 (2): 339–57.
Harbury, C. D., and D. M. W. N. Hitchens. 1979. *Inheritance and wealth inequality in Britain.* London: George Allen & Unwin.
Hayashi, Fumio, Joseph Altonji, and Laurence Kotlikoff. 1996. Risk-sharing between and within families. *Econometrica* 64 (2): 261–94.
Hurd, Michael D. 1990. Research on the elderly: Economic status, retirement and consumption & saving. *Journal of Economic Literature* 28:565–637.
———. 1992. Measuring the bequest motive: The effect of children on saving by the elderly in the United States. In *Savings and bequests,* ed. T. Tachibanaki, 111–36. Ann Arbor: University of Michigan Press.
Laitner, John. 1979a. Household bequests, perfect expectations, and the national distribution of wealth. *Econometrica* 47 (5): 1175–93.
———. 1979b. Household bequest behaviour and the national distribution of wealth. *Review of Economic Studies* 46 (3): 467–83.
Laitner, John, and F. Thomas Juster. 1996. New evidence on altruism: A study of TIAA-CREF retirees. *American Economic Review* 86 (4): 893–908.
Loury, Glenn. 1981. Intergenerational transfers and the distribution of earnings. *Econometrica* 49 (4): 843–67.
Meade, James E. 1964. *Efficiency, equality, and the ownership of property.* London: George Allen & Unwin.
———. 1966. Life-cycle savings, inheritance and economic growth. *Review of Economic Studies* 33:61–78.
———. 1976. *The just economy.* London: George Allen & Unwin.
Menchick, P. 1979. Intergeneration transmission of inequality: An empirical study of wealth mobility. *Economica* 46:349–62.
Miles, David. 1997. Demographics and saving: Can we reconcile the evidence? IFS Working Paper no. 97/6. London: Institute for Fiscal Studies.

Oulton, N. 1976. Inheritance and the distribution of wealth. *Oxford Economic Papers* 28:86–101.

Pryor, F. 1973. Simulation of the impact of social and economic institutions on the size distribution of income and wealth. *American Economic Review* 63:50–72.

Stiglitz, Joseph E. 1969. Distribution of income and wealth among individuals. *Econometrica* 37 (3): 382–97.

Tomes, Nigel. 1981. The family, inheritance, and the intergenerational transmission of inequality. *Journal of Political Economy* 89 (5): 928–58.

Wilhelm, Mark O. 1996. Bequest behavior and the effect of heirs' earnings: Testing the altruistic model of bequests. *American Economic Review* 86 (4): 874–92.

———. 1997. Inheritance, steady-state consumption inequality, and the lifetime earnings process. *Manchester School of Economic and Social Studies* 65 (4): 466–76.

Wolfson, M. 1977. *The causes of inequality in the distribution of wealth: A simulation analysis.* Ph.D. diss. Cambridge University, Cambridge, England.

———. 1979. The bequest process and causes of inequality in the distribution of wealth. In *Modelling the intergenerational transmission of wealth,* ed. J. D. Smith. New York: National Bureau of Economic Research.

Comment   R. Glenn Hubbard

I enjoyed this chapter very much, and I believe the research program in which Jagadeesh Gokhale and Larry Kotlikoff are engaged will make significant contributions to our understanding of the link between social insurance design and the distribution of wealth. The chapter's purported focus is Social Security, but this is true only in a narrow sense. The present chapter is better seen as part of a broader research program by the authors to explain the distribution of wealth and determinants of wealth inequality (see especially Gokhale et al., forthcoming).

My comments are organized as follows. First, I pose some open questions to frame the analysis in the chapter. Second, I briefly review the chapter's principal findings. Third, I focus on promising extensions of the chapter in research and policy analysis.

Open Questions

In the background of the chapter lie two important questions. Why might Social Security affect the distribution of wealth, and what non–Social Security factors explain the actual distribution of wealth?

At least four factors offer a link between Social Security and the distribution of wealth. First, intergenerational transfers in a pay-as-you-go system may reduce aggregate saving and capital accumulation, and crowd

R. Glenn Hubbard is chairman of the president's Council of Economic Advisers, on leave from posts as the Russell L. Carson Professor of Economics and Finance at Columbia University and a research associate of the National Bureau of Economic Research.

out the private wealth accumulation of many households. Second, Social Security may affect private intergenerational transfers and bequests. Third, even a fully funded and actuarially fair Social Security system would reduce saving on account of imperfections in private annuity markets; households wishing to annuitize more of their household wealth may reduce private saving accordingly. Fourth, even a funded, actuarially fair system can affect the saving of many households in the presence of borrowing constraints (that is, when households cannot borrow against future benefits).

These channels raise the open questions of why households save and why some households save very little. Early analysis of Social Security and saving focused on effects of the program on different generations in a life-cycle setting (Feldstein 1974; Auerbach and Kotlikoff 1987). Within a generation, insurance-market and capital-market imperfections can connect Social Security (and social insurance more broadly) to the distribution of wealth (Abel 1985; Hubbard and Judd 1987; Hubbard, Skinner, and Zeldes 1995). Even relatively complicated versions of life-cycle models, however, have difficulty in explaining the saving of the wealthy.

Toward that end, life-cycle models' predictions often fail to match the highly skewed distribution of wealth in U.S. microeconomic data. Why the rich save so much over their lifetimes remains an open question, in spite of recent analyses of heterogeneity in rates of time preference, market imperfections and precautionary saving, fiscal incentives, and household variation in access to different rates of return.

As I argue below, understanding links between Social Security and household wealth accumulation and sources of heterogeneity in household saving rates are important for interpreting the chapter's results and policy implications.

Findings of the Chapter

Under fairly reasonable assumptions, the model used by Gokhale and Kotlikoff can replicate many (though not all) features of the real-world distribution of U.S. household wealth. As sources of wealth inequality, the chapter focuses on uncertain lifetimes, skill differences within and across generations, annuitization of Social Security "wealth," and skewness in the distribution of households' lifetime earnings. In particular, the authors argue that annuitization of Social Security wealth—an element of the current Social Security system, but not necessarily an element of proposals to introduce individual Social Security accounts—can worsen household wealth inequality.

The chapter uses the CORSIM microsimulation model of the U.S. economy (see Caldwell et al. 1999) with parameters based on calibrations using data from the Panel Study of Income Dynamics (PSID). The basic model has a life-cycle structure. Households have a stochastic lifetime of up to eighty-eight periods. There are an equal number of males and females (fertility assumptions yield an equal match), with no population growth across cohorts. Marriage occurs at age twenty-two (the authors investigate both random and assortative mating).[1] In the base case, there are no differences in skill endowments; alternative cases consider contemporaneous skill differences (with and without assortative mating) and inherited skill differences.

Households' preferences are described by time-separable isoelastic functions of their own and future consumption, as well as that of their children through age twenty-two. While the basic structure used by the authors is standard among researchers employing life-cycle simulation models to study household consumption decisions, that structure begs deeper questions about saving decisions of very low- and very high-income households that may prove crucial for analysis of wealth inequality.

In their simulations, the authors assume a very low intertemporal elasticity of substitution in consumption, so that households effectively put great weight on their "safe" resources in deciding how much to consume at each point in time. The rate of interest is assumed to equal four percent per annum; time preference factors yield 1.5 percent annual growth in per capita consumption through age sixty-five. Mortality probabilities are taken from 1995 calculations by the Social Security Administration. Basic earnings and fertility matrices are taken from CORSIM. In general, the chapter might benefit from a bit more description of the calibration exercise and from sensitivity analysis; more discussion comparing the "earnings module" with other efforts using the PSID would also have been useful.[2]

The chapter's principal results are contained in tables 3.1 and 3.2, which report, respectively, for various simulations, Gini coefficients, and shares of total household wealth by wealth group. For the latter, the chapter also reports tabulations from the Federal Reserve's 1995 Survey of Consumer Finances.

Several features of the findings presented in tables 3.1 and 3.2 are partic-

---

1. Life doesn't have quite the feeling of Thornton Wilder's *Our Town* in the CORSIM model. Gokhale et al. (forthcoming), for example, describe marriage and death as follows: "22-year-old males and females were married to each other (at random, or according to their skill ranks, depending on the case being considered)," and "Oldsters were killed off at random according to the conditional probability of dying at their respective ages, and the existing wealth of those who just died was transferred to the surviving spouse (first) or children (equally)."

Previous simulation studies generally assumed that inheritances are unexpected and taxed away and redistributed (see, e.g., Hubbard and Judd, 1987; Hubbard, Skinner, and Zeldes, 1995; and Huggett 1996); this lack of emphasis on intentional bequests is consistent with the empirical work of Hurd (1992) and Gokhale, Kotlikoff, and Sabelhaus (1996). Previous work on intentional bequests and inheritability of skills (Flemming 1979) did not incorporate marriage.

2. Exploring differences between the present paper and the CORSIM approach in Gokhale et al. (forthcoming) might shed light on implications of key CORSIM assumptions. In the present paper based on the PSID, for example, assortative mating on the basis of lifetime earnings appears much less important than assumed by Gokhale et al. (forthcoming).

ularly noteworthy. While the predicted bequest flow in table 3.1 is significant, lifetime uncertainty per se (in the presence of Social Security) has a relatively modest effect on the wealth Gini; removing Social Security as well strengthens this effect.[3] More significant effects are traceable to skill differences. Removing desired consumption growth implies that households want to maintain an equivalent living standard as they age; as a consequence of this consumption smoothing, more liquidity-constrained households approach retirement with no wealth, increasing wealth inequality. Interest rate heterogeneity does not appear to be an important determinant of the wealth Gini (I return below to whether heterogeneity in rates of return is correctly measured). While the results of table 3.2 come closer to matching the SCF wealth shares than predictions of life-cycle models with no intra-cohort wealth and income variation, the model still fails to capture wealth accumulation at the top.

The villain of the inequality play is Social Security. In part, this reflects Social Security's effect on the distribution of inheritances. That is, annuitization of Social Security benefits increases inequality because high-income households have substantial annuitized wealth. In the model, the differential effect of Social Security annuitization traces principally to the fact that the payroll tax ceiling benefits high-lifetime-income households (see case 10 in table 3.1).

Even within the structure of the model, these effects of Social Security on household variation in wealth accumulation may be overstated. The authors' assumption of a "pure tax" rate (i.e., tax rate net of that fund benefits to the household) of 67 percent substantially exceeds estimates produced, for example, by the Congressional Budget Office (Mariger 1999). More important, a portion of any pure tax represents the servicing of debt incurred to provide unfunded benefits to previous generation. Hence one would not associate the removal of this tax with Social Security tax (as long as promised benefits will be paid from Social Security payroll tax revenues).

Ultimately, the value of the authors' approach to analyzing the contribution of Social Security to the distribution of household wealth derives at least in part from the model's effectiveness in explaining the distribution of wealth. While removing Social Security reduces the share of wealth held by the top one percent of households from 7 percent to 3.8 percent, the actual share in the 1995 data cited by the authors exceeds 30 percent.[4] This discrepancy is surely a topic for future research.

While the chapter's findings are thoughtful and suggestive, they seem to

---

3. In Gokhale et al. (forthcoming), the interaction of lifetime uncertainty and skill differences can be "leveling," in the sense that larger inheritances are predicted to be received by offspring with skill levels lower than those of their parents.

4. In Gokhale et al. (forthcoming), the authors attempt to address this problem by increasing the skewness of the distribution of lifetime earnings relative to that predicted by the PSID.

call for two extensions of the Gokhale-Kotlikoff research program—one on the "rich" and one on the "poor." First, how can one model more precisely sources of skewness in earnings and rates of return? In the Survey of Consumer Finances and the PSID, "entrepreneurs" (owners of active businesses) figure prominently in the upper tail of the distribution of wealth (see, for example, Gentry and Hubbard 1997, 1999; Quadrini 1997). For such households, capital-market imperfections could link saving and investment for such households, so that entrepreneurial "selection" and "investment" decisions can explain high preretirement saving rates for these households and slow dissaving in retirement (Gentry and Hubbard 1999, 2000).[5] Such considerations may be particularly important if wealth is required to exploit (business-related) skill differences, and they suggest the desirability of integrating determinants of household business saving in life-cycle simulation models.

Second, for low-lifetime-income households, how should one think about annuitization and welfare, as opposed to annuitization and saving? With imperfections in annuity markets, Social Security's mandatory annuitization may make these households better off, while reducing their saving (Hubbard and Judd 1987). In addition, more research is needed to shed light on the saving decisions of low-lifetime-income households—in particular, the extent to which they would save for retirement in the absence of Social Security's tax and mandatory annuitization elements.

While I believe these extensions are significant, I want to end where I began, complimenting Jagadeesh Gokhale and Larry Kotlikoff for their careful modeling and analysis of economic links between the structure of Social Security and the distribution of household wealth. Their chapter should be on the "recommended reading" list for serious students of Social Security reform.

References

Abel, Andrew B. 1985. Precautionary saving and accidental bequests. *American Economic Review* 75 (December): 777–97.
Auerbach, Alan J., and Laurence J. Kotlikoff. 1987. *Dynamic fiscal policy.* Cambridge: Cambridge University Press.
Caldwell, Steven, Melissa Favreault, Alla Gantman, Jagadeesh Gokhale, Thomas Johnson, and Laurence J. Kotlikoff. 1999. Social Security's treatment of postwar Americans. In *Tax policy and the economy,* vol. 13, ed. James M. Poterba. Cambridge: MIT Press.
Feldstein, Martin. 1974. Social Security, induced retirement, and aggregate capital accumulation. *Journal of Political Economy* 82 (September-October): 75–95.
Flemming, John S. 1979. The effects of earnings inequality, imperfect capital mar-

---

5. Recent research (Quadrini 1999; Quadrini and Rios-Rull 1997) indicates that such descriptions of entrepreneurial saving and investment are critical for explaining the share of wealth held by wealthy households in general equilibrium.

kets, and dynastic altruism on the distribution of wealth in life cycle models. *Economica* 46:363–84.

Gentry, William M., and R. Glenn Hubbard. 1997. Distributional implications of introducing a broad-based consumption tax. In *Tax policy and the economy,* vol. 11, ed. James M. Poterba, Cambridge: MIT Press.

———. 1999. Entrepreneurship and household saving. Columbia University, Graduate School of Business. Mimeograph.

———. 2000. Tax policy and entrepreneurial entry. *American Economic Review* 90 (May):

Gokhale, Jagadeesh, Laurence J. Kotlikoff, and John Sabelhaus. 1996. Understanding the postwar decline in United States saving: A cohort analysis. *Brookings Papers on Economic Activity.*

Gokhale, Jagadeesh, Laurence J. Kotlikoff, James Sefton, and Martin Weale. Forthcoming. Simulating the transmission of wealth inequality via bequests. *Journal of Public Economics.*

Hubbard, R. Glenn, and Kenneth Judd. 1987. Social security and individual welfare: Precautionary saving, borrowing constraints, and the payroll tax. *American Economic Review* 77 (September): 630–46.

Hubbard, R. Glenn, Jonathan Skinner, and Stephen P. Zeldes. 1995. Precautionary saving and social insurance. *Journal of Political Economy* 105 (April): 360–99.

Huggett, Mark. 1996. Wealth distribution in life cycle economies. *Journal of Monetary Economics* 38:469–94.

Hurd, Michael D. 1992. Measuring the bequest motive: The effect of children on saving by the elderly in the United States. In *Savings and bequests,* ed. T. Tuchibanaki, Ann Arbor: University of Michigan Press.

Mariger, Randall. 1999. Social security reform: A selective survey of the issues. Washington, D.C.: Congressional Budged Office, August.

Quadrini, Vincenzo. 1999. Entrepreneurship, saving, and social mobility. *Review of Income and Wealth* 45 (March): 1–19.

Quadrini, Vincenzo, and Victor Rios-Rull. 1997. Understanding the U.S. distribution of wealth. *Federal Reserve Bank of Minneapolis Quarterly Review* 21 (Spring): 22–36.

Discussion Summary

Jeffrey B. Liebman was interested in the effects of an investment-based system on bequests. In such a system with preretirement bequests, individuals from poor families will inherit more as a consequence of income related mortality. In addition, to the extent that individual accounts cause people with higher incomes to reduce other asset holdings resulting in little net new financial wealth, while lower-income individuals lack financial assets to substitute out of, individual accounts might make the wealth distribution more equal.

Martin Feldstein mentioned past work in which it was difficult to reconcile the existing financial wealth distribution with standard life-cycle saving models and the income distribution. However, if Social Security wealth was included with ordinary financial wealth, then the total wealth distribution was much more consistent with life-cycle saving models. If wealth is to be a measure of future consumption potential, then the present value of Social Security wealth should be included. However, liquid wealth provides options that an annuity (which may not have begun making payments) does not provide. For people who have not retired, wealth provides the option to take time when searching for a new employer and the ability to start a business or help one's children start a business. The present value of an annuity does not offer any of these opportunities. Therefore, it may be legitimate to focus on liquid wealth, especially when looking at younger people.

Stephen C. Goss did not find it particularly surprising that abolishing the current Social Security system has a dramatic effect on wealth when it is assumed that Social Security contributions do not create any wealth. He questioned whether it is appropriate to ignore Social Security wealth completely. In response, the authors said that when people express concern about wealth inequality, they are usually not talking about Social Security wealth. If social policy is to address this important issue, then it is important to examine wealth inequality in the absence of Social Security wealth.

Angus Deaton felt that while the PSID is not perfect, the SCF data set should not be considered the gold standard. Because the wealth distribution is very skewed, over-sampling the top end may help estimate the mean, but the upper percentiles will still be subject to a large amount of estimation error. For most models the wealth levels at the top of the distribution are not important and this is the data missing from the PSID. Furthermore, it is not necessary to build exotic behavior into simulations to generate large amounts of wealth inequality. The standard life-cycle model with earnings uncertainty implies that wealth inequality at the date of retirement is a very large number. Kotlikoff expressed doubt that a standard life-cycle model with earnings uncertainty could generate a Gini coefficient of 0.7.

R. Glenn Hubbard said that if the goal of the paper is to compare the poor to the middle class, then the approach taken in these simulations is fine; however, if the goal is to examine inequality for the entire wealth distribution, then it is important for the simulations to accurately reflect the behavior of the very wealthy—a group for whom the data are not very accurate.

Eytan Sheshinski emphasized the link between large unintended bequests and a lack of annuitization. He said it is a puzzle that middle and upper class people convert such a small percentage of their wealth into annuities.

Social Security and Inequality over the Life Cycle

Angus Deaton, Pierre-Olivier Gourinchas, and Christina Paxson

4.1 Introduction

This chapter explores the consequences of Social Security reform for the inequality of consumption across individuals. The basic idea is that inequality is at least in part the consequence of individual risk in earnings or asset returns. In each period, each person gets a different draw, of earnings or of asset returns, so that whenever differences cumulate over time, the members of any group will draw further apart from one another, and inequality will grow. Inequality at a moment of time is the fossilized record of the history of personal differences in risky outcomes. Any institution that shares risk across individuals, the U.S. Social Security system being the case in point, will moderate the transmission of individual risk into inequality, and it is this process that we study in this chapter. Note that we are not concerned here with what has been one of the central issues in Social Security reform, the distribution *between* different generations over the transition. Instead, we are concerned with the equilibrium effects of

Angus Deaton is the Dwight D. Eisenhower Professor of International Affairs and professor of economics and international affairs at the Woodrow Wilson School of Public and International Affairs, Princeton University, and a research associate of the National Bureau of Economic Research. Pierre-Olivier Gourinchas is assistant professor of economics at Princeton University and a faculty research fellow of the National Bureau of Economic Research. Christina Paxson is professor of economics and public affairs at the Woodrow Wilson School of Public and International Affairs, Princeton University, and a research associate of the National Bureau of Economic Research.

Angus Deaton and Christina Paxson acknowledge support from the National Institute on Aging through a grant to the National Bureau of Economic Research, and from the John D. and Catherine T. MacArthur Foundation within their network on inequality and poverty in broader perspectives. All the authors are grateful to Martin Feldstein, Laurence J. Kotlikoff, Jeffrey B. Liebman, and James M. Poterba for helpful comments and discussions.

different Social Security arrangements on inequality among members of any given generation.

A concrete and readily analyzed example occurs when the economy is composed of autarkic permanent income consumers, each of whom has an uncertain flow of earnings. Each agent's consumption follows a martingale (i.e., consumption today equals expected consumption tomorrow), and is therefore the cumulated sum of martingale differences, so that if shocks to earnings are independent over agents, consumption inequality grows with time for any group with fixed membership. The same is true of asset and income inequality, although not necessarily of earnings inequality: see Deaton and Paxson (1994), who also document the actual growth of income, earnings, and consumption inequality over the life cycle in the United States and elsewhere. An insurance arrangement that taxes earnings and redistributes the proceeds equally, either in the present or the future, reduces the rate at which consumption inequality evolves. With complete insurance, marginal utilities of different agents move in lockstep, and consumption inequality remains constant. Social Security pools risks and thus limits the growth of life-cycle inequality. Reducing the share of income that is pooled through the Social Security system, as envisaged by some reform proposals (such as the establishment of individual accounts with different portfolios or different management costs) but not by others (such as setting up a provident fund with a common portfolio and common management costs) increases the rate at which consumption and income inequality evolve over life in a world of permanent-income consumers. Even if inequality is not inherited from one generation to the next, and each generation starts afresh, partial privatization of Social Security will increase average inequality. While much of the discussion about limiting portfolio choice in new Social Security arrangements has (rightly) focused on limiting risk, such restrictions will also have effects on inequality.

Provided the reform is structured so that the poor are made no worse off, it can be argued that the increase in inequality is of no concern (see, e.g., Feldstein 1998), so that our analysis would be of purely academic interest. Nevertheless, the fact remains that many people—perhaps mistaking inequality for poverty—find inequality objectionable, so that it is as well to be aware of the fact if it is the case that an increase in inequality is likely to be an outcome of Social Security reform. There are also instrumental reasons for being concerned about inequality; both theoretical and empirical studies implicate inequality in other socially undesirable outcomes, such as low investment in public goods, lower economic growth, and even poor health (Wilkinson 1996).

The paper is organized as follows. Section 4.2 works entirely within the framework of the permanent income hypothesis (PIH). We derive the formulas that govern the spread of consumption inequality, and show how inequality is modified by the introduction of a stylized Social Security scheme. The baseline analysis and preliminary results come from Deaton and Paxson (1994), which should be consulted for more details, refinements, and reservations, as well as for documentation that consumption inequality grows over the life cycle, not only in the United States, but at much the same rate in Britain and Taiwan. The PIH is convenient because it permits closed-form solutions that show explicitly how Social Security is related to inequality. However, it is not a very realistic model of actual consumption in the United States, and it embodies assumptions that are far from obviously appropriate for Social Security analysis—for example, that consumers have unlimited access to credit, and that intertemporal transfers leaving the present value of lifetime resources unchanged have no effect on consumption. In consequence, in section 4.3, we consider richer models of consumption and saving that incorporate both precautionary motives for saving and borrowing restrictions. These models help replicate what we see in the data, which is the tendency of consumers to switch endogenously from buffer-stock behavior early in life to life-cycle saving behavior in middle age. The presence of the precautionary motive and the borrowing constraints breaks the link between consumption and the present value of lifetime resources, which both complicates and enriches the analysis of Social Security. Legal restrictions prevent the use of Social Security as a collateral for loans, and for at least some people such restrictions are likely to be binding.

Solutions to models with precautionary motives and borrowing constraints are used to document how Social Security systems with differing degrees of risk sharing affect inequality. We first consider the case in which all consumers receive the same rate of return on their assets. Our results indicate that systems in which there is less sharing of earnings risk—such as systems of individual accounts—produce higher consumption inequality both before and after retirement. An important related issue is whether differences across consumers in rates of return will contribute to even greater inequality. Somewhat surprisingly, we find that allowing for fairly substantial differences in rates of return across consumers has only modest additional effects on inequality. The bulk of saving, in the form of both Social Security and non–Social Security assets, is done late enough in life so that differences in rates of return do not contribute much to consumption inequality.

4.2 Social Security and Inequality under the Permanent Income Hypothesis

Section 4.2.1 introduces the notation and basic algebra of the permanent income hypothesis, while section 4.2.2 reproduces from Deaton and Paxson (1994) the basic result on the spread of consumption and income inequality over the life cycle. Both subsections are preliminary to the main analysis. Section 4.2.3 introduces a simplified Social Security system in an infinite horizon model with PIH consumers and shows how a Social Security tax at rate τ reduces the rate of spread of consumption inequality by the factor $(1 - \tau)^2$. Section 4.2.4 discusses what happens when there is a maximum to the Social Security tax, and section 4.2.5 extends the model to deal with finite lives and retirement and shows that the basic result is unaffected.

4.2.1   Preliminaries: Notation and the Permanent Income Hypothesis

It is useful to begin with the algebra of the PIH; the notation is taken from Deaton (1992). Real earnings at time t are denoted y_t. Individual consumption is c_t and assets A_t; when it is necessary to do so we shall introduce an i suffix to denote individuals. There is a constant real rate of interest r. These magnitudes are linked by the accumulation identity

$$(1) \qquad A_t = (1 + r)(A_{t-1} + y_{t-1} - c_{t-1}) \ .$$

Under certainty equivalence, with rate of time preference equal to r, and an infinite horizon, consumption satisfies the PIH rule, and is equal to the return on the discounted present value of earnings and assets:

$$(2) \qquad c_t = \frac{r}{1 + r} A_t + \frac{r}{1 + r} \sum_{k=0}^{\infty} \frac{1}{(1 + r)^k} E_t(y_{t+k})$$

for expectation operator E_t, conditional on information available at time t. It is convenient to begin with the infinite horizon case; we deal with the finite horizon case in section 4.2.5.

That consumption follows a martingale is made evident by manipulation of equation (2):

$$(3) \qquad \Delta c_t = \eta_t \equiv \frac{r}{1 + r} \sum_{k=0}^{\infty} \frac{1}{(1 + r)^k} (E_t - E_{t-1}) y_{t+k} \ .$$

"Disposable" income y_t^d is defined as earnings plus income from capital:

$$(4) \qquad y_t^d = \frac{r}{1 + r} A_t + y_t \ .$$

Saving is the difference between disposable income and consumption,

$$(5) \qquad s_t = y_t^d - c_t \, ,$$

which enables us to rewrite the PIH rule in equation (2) in the equivalent form (see Campbell 1987):

$$(6) \qquad s_t = -\sum_{k=1}^{\infty} \frac{1}{(1 + r)^k} E_t \Delta y_{t+k}$$

Assets are linked to saving through the identity (implied by equations [1] and [5]):

$$\Delta A_t = (1 + r)s_{t-1} \tag{7}$$

Finally, it is convenient to specify a stochastic process for earnings, y_t. It is convenient to do this by assuming that

$$\alpha(L)(y_t - \mu) = \beta(L)\varepsilon_t \tag{8}$$

for lag operator L and polynomials $\alpha(L)$ and $\beta(L)$ and white noise ε_t. As written, and under the usual conditions on the roots, earnings is stationary (around μ) and invertible. In fact, we can allow a unit root in $\alpha(L)$ with essentially no modification. (In the more realistic models in section 4.3, we will work with a process with a unit root but specified in logarithms.)

Given equation (8), we can derive explicit forms for the innovation to consumption (Flavin 1981):

$$\Delta c_t = \eta_t = \frac{r}{1 + r} \cdot \frac{\beta\left(\dfrac{1}{1 + r}\right)}{\alpha\left(\dfrac{1}{1 + r}\right)} \varepsilon_t , \tag{9}$$

so that consumption is a random walk and the innovation variance of consumption is tied to the innovation variance of earnings by the autocorrelation properties of the latter.

4.2.2   Spreading Inequality

Begin with the simplest illustrative case, in which earnings are white noise, and add an i suffix for an individual

$$y_{it} = \mu_i + \varepsilon_{it} = \mu_i + w_t + z_{it} , \tag{10}$$

where μ_i is the individual-specific mean of earnings, w_t is a common (macro) component, and z_{it} is an idiosyncratic component. The macro component w_t is also independently and identically distributed (i.i.d.) over time. Given equation (10), equation (3) implies

$$c_{it} = c_{it-1} + \frac{r}{1 + r} (w_t + z_{it}) . \tag{11}$$

As a result, if the idiosyncratic components are orthogonal to lagged consumption in the cross-section (which need not be true in each year but is true on the average by the martingale property), the cross-sectional variance of consumption satisfies

(12)
$$\text{var}_t(c) = \text{var}_{t-1}(c) + \frac{\sigma_z^2 r^2}{(1 + r)^2}$$

$$= \text{var}_0(c) + \frac{t\sigma_z^2 r^2}{(1 + r)^2}$$

so that consumption inequality is increasing over time.

Note that although equation (12) is derived for the variance of consumption, the increase in consumption variance is general, not specific to a particular measure of inequality. According to equation (11), the household distribution of consumption at t is the distribution of consumption at $t - 1$ plus uncorrelated white noise. Given that the mean is not changing, the addition of noise implies that the distribution of consumption at t is second-order stochastically dominated by the distribution of consumption at $t - 1$, so that any transfer-respecting measure of inequality, such as the Gini coefficient, the Theil inequality measure, or the coefficient of variation (but not necessarily the variance in logarithms), will show an increase of inequality over time.

In the i.i.d. case, saving is given by (see equation [6])

(13)
$$s_{it} = \frac{\varepsilon_{it}}{1 + r},$$

while assets satisfy

(14)
$$A_{it} = A_{it-1} + \varepsilon_{it-1}.$$

Because disposable income is the sum of consumption and saving, the change in disposable income satisfies

(15)
$$\Delta y_{it}^d = \frac{r\varepsilon_{it}}{1 + r} + \frac{\varepsilon_{it}}{1 + r} - \frac{\varepsilon_{it-1}}{1 + r} = \varepsilon_{it} - \frac{\varepsilon_{it-1}}{1 + r},$$

which implies, after some manipulation, that

(16)
$$\text{var}_t(y^d) = \text{var}_{t-1}(y^d) + \frac{\sigma_z^2 r^2}{(1 + r)^2}$$

$$= \text{var}_0(y^d) + \frac{t\sigma_z^2 r^2}{(1 + r)^2}.$$

Because the consumption variance is spreading, and because saving is stationary by equation (13), disposable income variance must spread at the same rate as the consumption variance. Note that earnings variance is constant given the stationarity assumption in equation (10), so that

(17)
$$\text{var}_t y = \sigma_\mu^2 + \sigma_z^2 = \text{constant}.$$

From equation (14), the variance of assets satisfies

(18) $$\text{var}_t(A) = \text{var}_0(A) + t\sigma_z^2 .$$

The rate of spread of the variance of assets is the variance of the idiosyncratic component of the innovation of earnings. At a real interest rate of 5 percent, this is 400 times faster than the rate of spread of the variance of consumption and of disposable income. From any given starting point, asset inequality among a group of individuals grows much faster than does consumption or disposable income inequality.

In the United States, the data on consumption, earnings, and income are consistent with the predictions of the theory. Deaton and Paxson (1994) use repeated cross-sections from the Consumer Expenditure Survey (CEX) to trace birth cohorts through the successive surveys, and find that cross-sectional consumption inequality for any given birth cohort increases with the age of the cohort. For example, the Gini coefficient for family consumption (family income) increases (on average over all cohorts) from 0.28 (0.42) at age twenty-five to about 0.38 (0.62) at age fifty-five. We shall return to these findings in section 4.3.

4.2.3 Social Security and the Spread of Inequality

Suppose that the government enacts a simple Social Security system. A proportionate tax on earnings is levied at rate τ, and the revenues are divided equally and given to everyone. We think about the (partial) reversal of this process as a stylized version of reform proposals that pays some part of each individual's Social Security tax into personal saving accounts; the precise mechanisms will be presented in section 4.3.2. We recognize that the establishment of personal accounts has other effects, some of which are not captured under our simple assumptions. Our concern here, however, is with the reduction in the pooling or risk sharing that is implied by removing a part of Social Security tax proceeds from the common pool and placing it in individual accounts. Such accounts provide smoothing benefits for autarkic agents who would not or cannot save on their own account, but they reduce the risk-sharing elements of the current system unless they are supplemented by other specifically risk-sharing features such as transfers from successful to unsuccessful investors.

Because of the infinite horizon and certainty equivalence assumptions, dividing up the revenues and returning them immediately is the same as giving them back later. The model assumes no deadweight loss. Denote before-tax earnings as y_{it}^b and retain the notation y_{it} for after-tax income, $(1 - \tau)y_{it}^b$. In the i.i.d. case we have

(19) $$y_{it} = (1 - \tau)(\mu_i + \varepsilon_{it}) + \tau\bar{\mu} ,$$

where the last term is the average revenue of the tax, which is given back to everyone. Equation (19) can also be written as

$$(20) \qquad y_{it} = \mu_i - \tau(\mu_i - \overline{\mu}) + (1 - \tau)\varepsilon_{it} .$$

Compared with the original earnings process in equation (10), there is a shift toward the grand mean—the redistributional effect of the Social Security system—together with a scaling of the innovation by $1 - \tau$, which is the risk-sharing component of the Social Security system. The redistribution will change consumption levels for everyone not at the mean, but will not affect the innovation of consumption equation (11), saving equation (13), asset equation (14), or disposable income equation (15), *except* that the original innovation must be rescaled by $1 - \tau$. In consequence, the variances of consumption, disposable income, and assets all evolve as before, but at a rate that is $(1 - \tau)^2$ times the original rate. If the Social Security tax is 12.4 percent, inequality (measured by the variance) will spread at 76.7 percent of the rate that it would in the absence of the system. Imagine an economy in equilibrium, with no inheritance of inequality and no growth in lifetime resources, so that the cross-sectional profile of consumption by age is identical to the lifetime profile of consumption for each cohort, and all consumption inequality is within-cohort inequality. With a working life of forty years and consumption variance originally growing at 5 percent, the imposition of a Social Security tax at 12.4 percent will reduce the cross-sectional standard deviation of consumption by a factor of 5.

In equations (19) and (20), we have not explicitly distinguished the macro common component of the innovation w_t from the idiosyncratic component ε_{it}. If we substitute to make the decomposition explicit, equation (20) becomes

$$(21) \qquad y_{it} = \mu_i - \tau(\mu_i - \overline{\mu}) + (1 - \tau)z_{it} + w_t ,$$

which shows that the common component is not insured. The change in consumption warranted by equation (21) is

$$(22) \qquad \Delta c_{it} = \frac{r}{1 + r}\left[w_t + (1 - \tau)z_{it}\right],$$

but only the second term in the brackets contributes to the spread in consumption variance, and the results are as stated previously.

4.2.4 Social Security with a Maximum

The PIH is not well suited to modeling a Social Security system in which taxes are paid only up to the Social Security maximum. The nonlinearity complicates the forecasting equations for earnings and eliminates the analytical tractability that is the main attraction of the formulation. However, in the spirit of a system with a maximum, it is worth noting what happens when there are two classes of people, one whose earnings never rise above the Social Security maximum, and one whose earnings never drop below the Social Security maximum. Equation (20) still gives after-tax income for the poor group, and inequality among them spreads as in the previous section. For the rich group, after-tax income is

$$(23) \qquad y_{it} = (1 - \tau)(\mu_i + \varepsilon_{it}) + \tau(\mu_i + \varepsilon_{it} - m)$$

$$+ \frac{(\tau\overline{\mu}_1 + \tau m)}{2},$$

where m is the Social Security maximum, $\overline{\mu}_1$ is mean earnings of the poorer group, and we have assumed that there are equal numbers in the two groups. (The first term is what is left if tax was paid on everything, the second term is the rebate of tax above the maximum, and the last term is the shared benefit.) Equation (23) can be rewritten as

$$(24) \qquad y_{it} = \mu_i - \frac{\tau(m - \overline{\mu}_1)}{2} + \varepsilon_{it},$$

which makes the straightforward point that those above the maximum no longer participate in the risk sharing, only in the redistribution. As a result, the Social Security system with the two groups will limit the rate of spread of inequality among the poorer group, but not among the richer group, although it will bring the two groups closer together than they would have been in the absence of the system.

4.2.5   Finite Lives with Retirement

With finitely lived consumers we can have a more realistic Social Security system, in which the taxes are repaid in retirement rather than instantaneously. One point to note about retirement is that it induces a fall in earnings at the time of retirement, a fall that enters into the determination of saving (see equation [6]). When there is a unit root in earnings, earnings immediately prior to retirement have a unit root, and so does the drop in earnings at retirement. In consequence, saving, which must cover this drop in earnings, is no longer stationary but integrated of order one, so that assets, which are cumulated saving, are integrated of order two. The spread of inequality in assets is therefore an order of integration faster than the spread of inequality in consumption and disposable income. However, this seems more a matter of degree than an essential difference.

People work until age R and die at age T. The consumption innovation formula is only slightly different:

$$(25) \qquad \beta_t \Delta c_t = \eta_t = \frac{r}{1 + r} \sum_{k=0}^{R-t} \frac{1}{(1 + r)^k} (E_t - E_{t-1}) y_{t+k},$$

where the annuity factor β_t is given by

$$(26) \qquad \beta_t \equiv 1 - \frac{1}{(1 + r)^{(T-t+1)}} = (1 + r)\beta_{t-1} - r .$$

From equation (25), we can write

$$(27) \qquad c_t = c_0 + \sum_{s=0}^{t} \beta_s^{-1} \eta_t .$$

Hence, in the i.i.d. case previously considered,

$$(28) \qquad \mathrm{var}_t(c) = \mathrm{var}_0(c) + \frac{r^2}{(1 + r)^2} \sigma_z^2 \sum_{s=0}^{t} \beta_s^{-2} .$$

With the Social Security scheme, after-tax earnings while working is

$$(29) \qquad \begin{aligned} y_{it} &= (1 - \tau)(\mu_i + \varepsilon_{it}) \\ &= (1 - \tau)\mu_i + (1 - \tau)(w_t + z_{it}) . \end{aligned}$$

With a uniform distribution of ages, the benefits while retired in year $R + s$ are

$$(30) \qquad \frac{R\tau(\overline{\mu} + w_{R+s})}{T - R} .$$

With certainty equivalence, only the expected present value of this matters (which is a constant given the i.i.d. assumption) so that, once again, although the levels of consumption are altered, there is no change to the innovation of consumption, nor to the rate at which the various inequalities spread.

These results would clearly be different with either an autocorrelation structure of the macro component of earnings such that current innovations had information about what will happen in retirement, although this issue seems hardly worth worrying about; or precautionary motives or borrowing restrictions, such that transactions that leave net present value unaffected can have real effects on the level and profile of consumption. Without quadratic preferences, and without the ability to borrow, we cannot even guarantee the basic result that uncertainty in earnings causes consumption and income inequality to increase with age. In consequence, we have little choice but to specify a model and to simulate the effects of alternative Social Security policies, and this is the topic of section 4.3. Of course, it might reasonably be argued that the purpose of Social Security is not well captured within any of these models, and that present-value neutral "forced" saving has real effects, not because of precautionary motives or borrowing restrictions, but because people are myopic or otherwise unable to make sensible retirement plans on their own. We are sympathetic to the general argument, but have nothing to say about such a case; without a more explicit model of behavior, it is not possible to conclude anything about the effects of Social Security reform on inequality.

4.3 Social Security with Precautionary Saving or Borrowing Constraints

4.3.1 Describing the Social Security System

When consumers cannot borrow, or when they have precautionary motives for saving, the timing of income affects their behavior. In consequence, we need to be more precise about the specification of the Social Security system and its financing. We assume that there is a constant rate of Social Security tax on earnings during the working life, levied at rate τ, and that during retirement, the system pays a two-part benefit. The first part, G, is a guaranteed floor that is paid to everyone, irrespective of their earnings or contribution record. The second part, V_i, is individual-specific and depends on the present value of earnings (or contributions) over the working life. We write S_i for the annual payment to individual i after retirement, so that

$$(31) \qquad S_i = G + V_i = G + \tilde{\alpha} \sum_{j=1}^{R-1} y_{ij}^b (1 + r)^{R-j}$$

$$= G + \alpha \sum_{j=1}^{R-1} y_{ij} (1 + r)^{R-j} \,,$$

where $\alpha = \tilde{\alpha}/(1 - \tau)$. The size of the parameter α determines the extent of the link between earnings in work and Social Security payments in retirement. When we consider the effects of different Social Security systems on inequality, we shall consider variations in α and G while holding the tax rate τ constant. As we shall see below, this is equivalent to devoting a larger or smaller share of Social Security tax revenues to individual accounts. When α is high relative to G (personal saving accounts), the system is relatively autarkic, and there is relatively little sharing of risk. Conversely, when G is large and α small (the current system), risk sharing is more important, and we expect inequality to be lower.

The government finances the Social Security system in such a way as to balance the budget in present-value terms within each cohort. If we use the date of retirement as the base for discounting, the present value of government revenues from the Social Security taxes levied on the cohort about to retire is given by

$$(32) \qquad \tau \sum_{j=1}^{R-1} \sum_{i=1}^{N} y_{ij}^b (1 + r)^{R-j} = \tau \sum_{j=1}^{R-1} Y_j (1 + r)^{R-j} \,,$$

where N is the number of people and Y_t is aggregate before-tax earnings for the cohort in year t. This must equal the present value at R of Social Security payments, which is

$$(33) \qquad \sum_{i=1}^{N}\sum_{j=R}^{T}(1 + r)^{R-j}\left[G + \tilde{\alpha}\sum_{j=1}^{R-1} y_{ij}^{b}(1 + r)^{R-j}\right].$$

The budget constraint that revenues equal outlays, that equation (32) equals equation (33), gives a relationship between the three parameters of the Social Security system, τ, G, and $\tilde{\alpha}$, namely

$$(34) \qquad G + \tilde{\alpha}\bar{y}^* = \frac{\tau\bar{y}^*}{\sum_{j=R}^{T}(1 + r)^{R-j}},$$

where $\bar{y}^*$ is the average over all consumers of the present value of lifetime earnings,

$$(35) \qquad \bar{y}^* = \left(\frac{1}{N}\right)\sum_{j=1}^{R-1}Y_j(1 + r)^{R-j}.$$

Equation (34) tells us that we can choose any two of the three parameters, G, α (or $\tilde{\alpha}$), and τ, and what is implied for the third. It also makes clear that, after appropriate scaling, and holding the guarantee fixed, increases in α—the earnings-related or autarkic part of the system—are equivalent to increases in the rate of the Social Security tax, given that the government is maintaining within-cohort budget balance.

The link between earnings-related Social Security payments and individual accounts can be seen more clearly if we reparameterize the system. Suppose that V_i, the earnings-related component of the Social Security payment, is funded out of a fraction of Social Security taxes set aside for the purpose, or equivalently, that a fraction φ of the tax is used to build a personal account, the value of which is used to buy an annuity at retirement. Equating the present value of each annuity V_i to the present value of contributions gives the relationship between α and φ,

$$(36) \qquad \varphi = \left(\frac{\tilde{\alpha}}{\tau}\right)\sum_{j=R}^{T}(1 + r)^{R-j}.$$

Hence, any increase in the earnings-related component of Social Security through an increase in α (or $\tilde{\alpha}$) can be thought of as an increase in the fraction of Social Security taxes sequestered into personal accounts. Equation (34), which constrains the parameters of the Social Security system, can be rewritten in terms of φ as

$$(37) \qquad G = \frac{\bar{y}^*\tau(1 - \varphi)}{\sum_{j=R}^{T}(1 + r)^{j-R}}.$$

Note also that the individual Social Security payment in equation (31) can be rewritten as

$$(38) \quad S_i = \frac{\tau}{\sum_{j=R}^{T}(1+r)^{R-j}}\left[(1-\varphi)\bar{y}^* + \varphi\sum_{j=1}^{R-1}y_{ij}^b(1+r)^{R-j}\right],$$

so that each person's Social Security benefits are related to a weighted average of their own lifetime earnings and the average lifetime earnings of their entire cohort.

If the above scheme were implemented for permanent-income consumers who are allowed to borrow and lend at will, the component of Social Security taxes that goes into personal accounts would have no effect on individual consumption nor, therefore, on its distribution across individuals. Although the scheme forces people to save, it is fair in present value terms, and so has no effect on the present value of each individual's lifetime resources. Moreover, although taxes are paid now and benefits received later, such a transfer can be undone by appropriate borrowing and lending. If the Social Security tax rate is τ, and a fraction φ is invested in a personal account, it is as if the tax rate were reduced to $\tau(1-\varphi)$, and the rate of increase in the consumption and income variance will be higher. Of course, none of these results hold if consumers are not allowed to borrow, or if preferences are other than quadratic.

4.3.2 Modeling Consumption Behavior

Although we shall also present results from the permanent income hypothesis, our preferred model is one with precautionary motives based on that in Gourinchas and Parker (2002) and Ludvigson and Paxson (2001), with the addition of retirement and a simple Social Security system. The specification and parameters are chosen to provide a reasonable approximation to actual behavior so that, even though it is not possible to derive closed-form solutions for the results, we can use simulations to give us some idea of the effects of the reforms.

Consumers have intertemporally additive isoelastic utility functions and, as before, they work through years 1 to $R-1$, retiring in period R and dying in period T. The real interest rate is fixed, but the rate of time preference δ is (in general) different from r, so that consumers satisfy the familiar Euler equation

$$(39) \quad c_t^{-\rho} = \beta(1+r)E_t(c_{t+1}^{-\rho}),$$

where ρ is the inverse of the intertemporal elasticity of substitution and $\beta = (1+\delta)^{-1}$. After-tax earnings, where taxes include Social Security taxes, evolves according to the (also fairly standard) nonstationary process

$$(40) \quad \ln y_t = \ln y_{t-1} + \gamma + \varepsilon_t - \lambda\varepsilon_{t-1},$$

which derives from a specification in which log earnings are the sum of a random walk with drift γ and white noise transitory earnings. The quantity λ is the parameter of the moving average process for the change in earnings and is an increasing function of the ratio of the variances of the transitory and random walk components, respectively. Consumers are assumed to be unable to borrow, which requires a modification of equation (39) (see below). One reason for this assumption is to mimic the United States, where it is illegal to borrow against prospective Social Security income. A second reason is to rule out the possibility that people borrow very large sums early in life to finance a declining consumption path over the life cycle. This prohibition could be enforced in other ways, such as the "voluntary" borrowing constraints in Carroll (1997) that result from isoelastic utility coupled with a finite probability of zero earnings. We do not find Carroll's income process empirically plausible, and it seems simpler to rule out borrowing explicitly rather than to choose the form of the earnings process to do so. Our calculations for the permanent income case are made with and without borrowing constraints, which will give some idea of the effects of the borrowing constraints in the other models.

Our procedure is as follows. Given values for the real interest rate, the rate of time preference, the intertemporal elasticity of substitution, the moving average parameter in income growth, and two out of three parameters of the Social Security system, we calculate a set of policy functions for each year of a forty-year working life. After retirement, there is no further uncertainty, and consumption can be solved analytically for each of the twenty years remaining. We assume that the Social Security system presented in section 4.3.2 has been in place for a long time, that its parameters are fixed, and that people understand how it works, including the government's intertemporal budget constraint. In particular, they understand the implications of innovations to their earnings for the value of their annuities in retirement. We do not require consumers to take into account the effects of successive macroeconomic shocks on the size of the Social Security guarantee G. Instead, we assume that the government sets G to the value that satisfies the budget constraint in expectation for each cohort, and that deficits and surpluses from cumulated macro shocks are passed on to future generations. There are, however, no macro shocks in the simulations reported below.

In each period of the working life, the ratio of consumption to earnings can be written as function of three state variables. These are defined as follows. Define cash on hand $x_t = A_t + y_t$, which, by equation (1), evolves during the working life $t < R$ according to

$$(41) \qquad x_t = (1 + r)(x_{t-1} - c_{t-1}) + y_t .$$

During retirement, for $t \geq R$,

(42)
$$x_t = (1 + r)(x_{t-1} - c_{t-1}) + S .$$

If w_t is the ratio of cash on hand to earnings, and θ_t the ratio of consumption to earnings, then equation (34) becomes, for $t < R$,

(43)
$$w_t = \frac{(1 + r)(w_{t-1} - \theta_{t-1})}{g_t} + 1 ,$$

where g_t is the ratio of current to lagged income, y_t/y_{t-1}. To derive corresponding equations for the dynamics of Social Security, define S_t as the current present value of the annual Social Security payment to which the consumer would be entitled if he or she earned no more income between year t and retirement. Hence, for $t < R$,

(44)
$$S_t = G(1 + r)^{-(R-t)} + \alpha \sum_{j=1}^{t} y_j (1 + r)^{t-j} ,$$

while for $t \geq R$, S_t is constant and given by equation (31). Noting that earnings in year R is zero, equation (44) satisfies, for $t \leq R$,

(45)
$$S_t = (1 + r)S_{t-1} + \alpha Y_t$$

and is constant thereafter. If we define σ_t, the ratio of S_t to current earnings and thus the "Social Security replacement rate," the corresponding evolution equation is

(46)
$$\sigma_t = \frac{S_t}{y_t} = (1 + r)\frac{\sigma_{t-1}}{g_t} + \alpha .$$

With borrowing constraints, which imply that consumption cannot be greater than cash on hand, or that the consumption ratio be no larger than the cash on hand ratio, the Euler equation (39) is modified to

(47)
$$\theta_t^{-\rho} = \max \left[\beta(1 + r)E_t(g_{t+1}^{-\rho}\theta_{t+1}^{-\rho}), w_t^{-\rho} \right].$$

We write the consumption ratio θ_t as a function of the cash on hand ratio w_t, the Social Security replacement rate σ_t, and the current innovation to earnings ε_t (which is required because, with positive λ, high earnings growth in one period predicts low earnings growth in the next), and then use equation (47) to solve backward for the policy function in each period, starting from the closed-form solution for consumption in the first year of retirement.

Armed with the policy functions, we simulate lifetime stochastic earnings profiles for each of 1,000 people. The logarithm of initial earnings is drawn from a normal distribution with mean $\ln (20,000)$ and a standard deviation of 0.65, the latter chosen to give an initial Gini coefficient that roughly corresponds to what we see in the data from the CPS. The drift (expected rate of growth) of earnings is set at 2 percent a year. For any given value of the replacement parameter α and the Social Security tax rate τ, the corresponding value of the Social Security guarantee G is set from equation (34) using actual realized earnings, which, as we have already noted, is potentially problematic if macro shocks are important. The value of G also gives the initial value of σ_t at the beginning of life. The calculated policy functions are then used to simulate life-cycle consumption for each of the 1,000 people, and these trajectories are used to assess lifetime inequality as a function of the design of the Social Security system. Different simulations use the same 1,000 sets of earnings realizations, so that comparisons across Social Security regimes reflect the regime parameters and not the specific draws.

4.3.3   Social Security Design and Inequality: Results with Constant Interest Rates

The model is solved under the following assumptions. The interest rate r is set at 3 percent, and the rate of time preference at either 3 or 5 percent. The drift of the earnings process is set at 2 percent a year, the moving average parameter λ to 0.4, and the standard deviation of the innovation (in logs) to be 0.25. The coefficient of relative risk aversion is set to 3, so that the intertemporal elasticity of substitution is one-third. We also include a certainty equivalent case, with and without borrowing restrictions, in which the rate of interest is set equal to the rate of time preference at 3 percent. There are four cases carried through the analysis: (1) isoelastic preferences, no borrowing, $r = 0.03$, $\delta = 0.05$; (2) isoelastic preferences, no borrowing, $r = 0.03$, $\delta = 0.03$; (3) quadratic preferences, no borrowing, $r = 0.03$, $\delta = 0.03$; and (4), quadratic preferences, borrowing allowed, $r = 0.03$, $\delta = 0.03$. The Social Security tax rate is set at its current value of 12.4 percent of before-tax earnings and there are no other taxes or benefits. The Social Security systems we consider are indexed on the level of the Social Security guarantee G, which takes the values ($0, $5,000, $10,000, $15,000, $20,000); given the tax rate, these values translate into corresponding values for α or, perhaps more revealingly, into values for φ, the share of the tax devoted to personal accounts (1, 0.811, 0.623, 0.434, 0.245). These different sets of parameters have quite different implications for the dispersion in Social Security payments among retirees. For example, our simulation results indicate that with a guarantee of $0, the person at the 10th percentile (ranked by the present value of lifetime earnings) receives an annual Social Security payment of $6,405, in contrast to a payment of $52,639 for the person at the 90th percentile. When the guarantee is increased to $20,000, this spread declines to $21,569 for the 10th percentile, and to $32,896 for the 90th.

Figure 4.1 shows the averages over the 1,000 consumers of the simulated

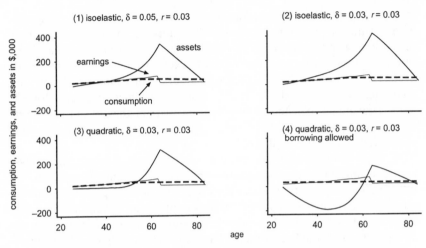

Fig. 4.1   Age profiles of consumption, earnings (inclusive of transfers), and assets for different specifications, _G_ = $5,000

trajectories of income (earnings prior to retirement and receipts from Social Security after retirement), consumption, and cash on hand (earnings plus assets excluding Social Security assets) for the four models all with _G_ set at $5,000. These graphs are shown to demonstrate that the various models do indeed generate standard life-cycle profiles. Earnings is the same in each of the three graphs. Consumption is flat over the life cycle in the certainty equivalent case when borrowing is allowed, but rises in the models with precautionary motives and borrowing constraints, and in the quadratic case with borrowing constraints. Indeed, the quadratic case with no borrowing (on the bottom left) and the isoelastic "impatient" case with no borrowing (top left) generate similar profiles. With more patient (lower δ) consumers in the top right panel, there is more accumulation during the working life, and assets prior to retirement are higher. The certainty equivalent consumers in the bottom right panel have expectations of earnings growth and so engage in substantial borrowing early in life but, even so, have some net assets prior to retirement.

Figure 4.2 shows the average consumption profiles for the four different models (in the four panels, as before) and for the five different Social Security schemes (in each panel). To a first approximation, and with the tax rate held fixed, the choice of system has no effect on the lifetime profile of consumption. Figure 4.2 also shows more clearly than figure 4.1 the lifetime shape of consumption in the four models: Precautionary motives or borrowing restrictions drive the increase in consumption over the working period; in the top left panel, where impatience is greater than the interest rate, consumption declines after retirement once all uncertainty is resolved. For the cases with precautionary motives or borrowing restrictions, average consumption during retirement is somewhat higher in the regimes with the higher minimum guarantee. This appears to be a consequence of the borrowing constraints. Those consumers who draw poor earnings throughout their lives, and who would like to borrow against their Social Security but cannot, have higher consumption in retirement when the guarantee becomes available. In effect, such consumers are being forced to save for higher consumption in retirement than they would choose if left to themselves. Such effects are absent in the pure certainty equivalent case where borrowing is allowed.

Figure 4.3 plots the Gini coefficients of consumption by age and shows how consumption inequality evolves in the various models and for the different Social Security systems. The Gini coefficients, together with inter-quartile ranges of the logarithm of consumption, are given in numerical form in table 4.1. In all of the models, consumption inequality is higher at all ages the lower the Social Security guarantee (the higher the fraction of taxes invested in personal accounts) and the more autarkic the system. A higher guarantee with its associated lower limit to lifetime earnings causes consumption inequality to be lower from the start of the life cycle, though the early effects are strongest in the pure certainty equivalent case, and manifest themselves only later in life in the models with borrowing constraints. With a higher guarantee, and less in individual accounts, the system has more sharing, so that individual earnings innovations have less effect on consumption because the good (or ill) fortune will be shared with others. Although this sharing is implemented only after retirement, because consumption is smoothed over the life cycle, the effect on inequality works at all ages to an extent determined by the assumptions about prefer-

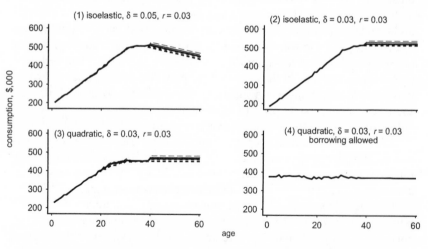

Fig. 4.2 Consumption profiles under different specifications and alternative Social Security rules

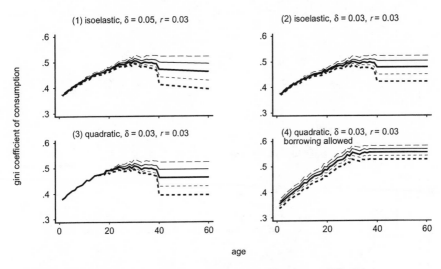

Fig. 4.3   Consumption inequality for different specifications and Social Security systems

ences, growth, and borrowing constraints. When borrowing constraints are imposed in an environment with earnings growth, consumption smoothing is inhibited, and the effects of risk sharing on inequality are more apparent in the later than in the earlier phases of the life cycle. These results are not sensitive to the choice of inequality measure. The interquartile ranges, although somewhat jumpier, display patterns that are similar to the Gini coefficients.

Figure 4.3 also shows a sharp drop in consumption inequality after retirement, particularly when the guarantee in the Social Security system is relatively large. Once again, this comes from the borrowing constraints and the inability of lifetime unlucky consumers to borrow against the Social Security system. These people have very low consumption immediately prior to retirement, which exaggerates inequality. The effect vanishes as Social Security becomes available and their consumption rises. In the cases where the guarantee is large, there is also some decline in inequality prior to retirement. Although no theoretical reason prohibits this, we have not so far developed a convincing explanation of why it should occur. Panel 1 of figure 4.3 also shows a small decline in consumption inequality during retirement. This is due to the combination of borrowing constraints and impatience ($r < \delta$). Unconstrained consumers choose declining consumption paths during retirement (at a constant and common rate of about 0.64 percent per year), while those who are constrained simply consume their constant Social Security income. The result is a compression of the distribution of consumption.

Table 4.1   Gini Coefficients for Consumption and Interquartile Ranges for Logarithm of Consumption, with Different Social Security Plans

Age	G = $0		G = $5,000		G = $10,000		G = $15,000		G = $20,000	
	Gini	IQR	Gini	IQR	Gini	IQR	Gini	IQR	Gini	IQR
	Isoelastic preferences, r = 0.03, δ = 0.05, borrowing constraints									
25	0.37	0.910	0.37	0.905	0.37	0.903	0.37	0.900	0.37	0.894
29	0.41	1.034	0.40	1.024	0.40	1.020	0.40	1.018	0.40	1.011
34	0.44	1.024	0.43	1.011	0.43	1.011	0.43	1.009	0.43	0.998
39	0.46	1.098	0.46	1.079	0.46	1.082	0.45	1.079	0.45	1.064
44	0.48	1.190	0.47	1.177	0.47	1.175	0.47	1.173	0.46	1.154
49	0.50	1.283	0.50	1.249	0.49	1.243	0.49	1.236	0.48	1.230
54	0.52	1.304	0.51	1.240	0.51	1.194	0.50	1.180	0.49	1.176
59	0.52	1.287	0.51	1.199	0.50	1.122	0.49	1.056	0.48	1.035
64	0.52	1.292	0.50	1.204	0.47	1.098	0.44	0.993	0.41	0.896
69	0.52	1.292	0.50	1.204	0.47	1.093	0.44	0.986	0.41	0.876
74	0.52	1.292	0.50	1.201	0.47	1.089	0.44	0.976	0.40	0.859
79	0.52	1.292	0.50	1.191	0.46	1.086	0.43	0.956	0.40	0.835
84	0.52	1.288	0.49	1.189	0.46	1.066	0.43	0.934	0.39	0.812
	Isoelastic preferences, r = 0.03, δ = 0.03, borrowing constraints									
25	0.37	0.899	0.37	0.888	0.37	0.880	0.36	0.876	0.36	0.872
29	0.40	1.033	0.40	1.016	0.40	1.010	0.40	1.007	0.39	1.000
34	0.43	1.011	0.43	0.992	0.43	0.984	0.42	0.982	0.42	0.970
39	0.46	1.092	0.45	1.068	0.45	1.054	0.44	1.049	0.44	1.039
44	0.47	1.164	0.46	1.136	0.46	1.123	0.46	1.118	0.45	1.104
49	0.50	1.238	0.49	1.205	0.48	1.181	0.48	1.173	0.47	1.168
54	0.52	1.283	0.51	1.216	0.50	1.161	0.49	1.127	0.48	1.113
59	0.52	1.275	0.51	1.191	0.49	1.115	0.48	1.039	0.48	0.985
64	0.52	1.284	0.50	1.207	0.47	1.130	0.45	1.033	0.42	0.931
69	0.52	1.284	0.50	1.207	0.47	1.130	0.45	1.033	0.42	0.931
74	0.52	1.284	0.50	1.207	0.47	1.130	0.45	1.033	0.42	0.931
79	0.52	1.284	0.50	1.207	0.47	1.130	0.45	1.033	0.42	0.931
84	0.52	1.284	0.50	1.207	0.47	1.130	0.45	1.033	0.42	0.931

Quadratic preferences, r = 0.03, δ = 0.03, borrowing constraints

Age	IQR	Gini	IQR	Gini	IQR	Gini	IQR	Gini	IQR	Gini
25	0.918	0.38	0.918	0.38	0.918	0.38	0.918	0.38	0.918	0.38
29	1.050	0.41	1.050	0.41	1.050	0.41	1.050	0.41	1.050	0.41
34	1.067	0.44	1.067	0.44	1.067	0.44	1.067	0.44	1.067	0.44
39	1.167	0.47	1.167	0.47	1.167	0.47	1.166	0.47	1.165	0.47
44	1.231	0.49	1.229	0.48	1.227	0.48	1.224	0.48	1.218	0.48
49	1.327	0.51	1.296	0.50	1.291	0.49	1.283	0.49	1.276	0.49
54	1.315	0.53	1.233	0.51	1.177	0.50	1.157	0.50	1.152	0.49
59	1.287	0.53	1.184	0.50	1.093	0.49	1.045	0.48	1.009	0.48
64	1.298	0.52	1.183	0.46	1.050	0.43	0.929	0.39	0.815	0.39
69	1.298	0.52	1.183	0.46	1.050	0.43	0.929	0.39	0.815	0.39
74	1.298	0.52	1.183	0.46	1.050	0.43	0.929	0.39	0.815	0.39
79	1.298	0.52	1.183	0.46	1.050	0.43	0.929	0.39	0.815	0.39
84	1.298	0.52	1.183	0.46	1.050	0.43	0.929	0.39	0.815	0.39

PIH: Quadratic preferences, r = 0.03, δ = 0.03, no borrowing constraints

Age	IQR	Gini	IQR	Gini	IQR	Gini	IQR	Gini	IQR	Gini
25	0.899	0.37	0.872	0.36	0.845	0.36	0.818	0.35	0.792	0.34
29	1.029	0.41	0.996	0.39	0.965	0.39	0.934	0.38	0.903	0.37
34	1.061	0.45	1.025	0.43	0.990	0.43	0.955	0.42	0.922	0.41
39	1.193	0.48	1.149	0.46	1.107	0.46	1.066	0.45	1.026	0.44
44	1.333	0.51	1.280	0.48	1.229	0.48	1.180	0.47	1.133	0.46
49	1.455	0.54	1.389	0.52	1.328	0.52	1.270	0.51	1.215	0.50
54	1.515	0.57	1.442	0.55	1.377	0.55	1.316	0.54	1.258	0.53
59	1.526	0.57	1.457	0.55	1.388	0.55	1.323	0.54	1.262	0.53
64	1.560	0.57	1.493	0.55	1.422	0.55	1.356	0.54	1.294	0.53
69	1.560	0.57	1.493	0.55	1.422	0.55	1.356	0.54	1.294	0.53
74	1.560	0.57	1.493	0.55	1.422	0.55	1.356	0.54	1.294	0.53
79	1.560	0.57	1.493	0.55	1.422	0.55	1.356	0.54	1.294	0.53
84	1.560	0.57	1.493	0.55	1.422	0.55	1.356	0.54	1.294	0.53

Source: Authors' calculations.

Notes: "Gini" refers to the Gini coefficient for consumption. IQR is the interquartile range of the logarithm of consumption. PIH is the permanent income hypothesis.

Overall, the results in figure 4.3 and table 4.1 show that as we move from one extreme to the other, from putting everything into individual accounts and giving no guarantee (a Social Security system than confines itself to compulsory saving) to a guaranteed floor of $20,000 with only one-fourth of Social Security taxes going to personal accounts, the Gini coefficient of consumption increases by between 5 and 6 percentage points on average over the life cycle, less among the young, and more among the old. This is a large increase, exceeding the increase in consumption inequality in the United States during the inequality boom from the early to the mid-1980s. For example, the Gini coefficient of total consumption for urban households from the U.S. Consumer Expenditure Survey rose from 0.37 in 1981 to 0.41 in 1986.

Table 4.2 shows "poverty rates" by age for the different models and Social Security systems. An individual is defined as being in poverty if annual consumption is less than $10,000. This poverty threshold was arbitrarily chosen, but it delivers total poverty rates that are not very different from those in the United States. For example, with G equal to $5,000, the total poverty rate is 12.5 percent for the first model. We are more concerned with how poverty varies with age than with its level. The age profiles of poverty are similar for the first three models, in which there are borrowing constraints. Poverty rates decline up to retirement age: Constrained consumers are more likely to be poor when they are young, and earnings are low. Poverty in retirement depends on the value of the Social Security guarantee. When the guarantee is greater than or equal to the poverty threshold, poverty in retirement must equal zero. For smaller values of the guarantee, the poverty rate in retirement is generally less than during working years. However, in one case—that of isoelastic preferences and $r < \delta$—the poverty rate grows during retirement. In this case, impatient consumers reduce consumption over time, and increasingly fall below the threshold.

The fourth model, with quadratic preferences and no borrowing constraints, yields very different results. Poverty rates increase with age up to retirement. Average consumption is constant over the life cycle, and the increasing dispersion in consumption with age implies that consumers will increasingly fall below the threshold. Increases in the poverty rate cease at retirement. However, Social Security guarantees in excess of the poverty threshold do not eliminate poverty, since (in this model) individuals are free to borrow against the guarantee during working years. Higher Social Security guarantees do, in fact, reduce poverty, but they do so at all ages, by making lifetime wealth more equal across individuals.

Figure 4.4 compares our simulated patterns of inequality over the life cycle with those calculated from the data in the CEX and reported in Deaton and Paxson (1994). By construction, the life-cycle profile of simulated earnings inequality is similar to the actual profile. Simulated consumption

Table 4.2   **Poverty Rates (fraction of age group with consumption less than $10,000) with Different Social Security Plans**

Age	$0	$5,000	$10,000	$15,000	$20,000
			G		
Isoelastic preferences, r = 0.03, δ = 0.05					
25	0.239	0.238	0.238	0.237	0.238
29	0.210	0.209	0.207	0.207	0.207
34	0.177	0.176	0.175	0.175	0.175
39	0.158	0.153	0.153	0.153	0.153
44	0.146	0.140	0.143	0.142	0.139
49	0.133	0.127	0.127	0.128	0.128
54	0.120	0.115	0.116	0.117	0.117
59	0.119	0.104	0.103	0.106	0.105
64	0.119	0.061	0.000	0.000	0.000
69	0.123	0.069	0.000	0.000	0.000
74	0.134	0.073	0.000	0.000	0.000
79	0.141	0.076	0.000	0.000	0.000
84	0.144	0.081	0.000	0.000	0.000
Isoelastic preferences, r = 0.03, δ = 0.03					
25	0.264	0.262	0.258	0.258	0.258
29	0.228	0.227	0.225	0.225	0.225
34	0.186	0.185	0.179	0.178	0.178
39	0.155	0.154	0.153	0.150	0.150
44	0.141	0.135	0.134	0.134	0.134
49	0.129	0.115	0.115	0.115	0.114
54	0.118	0.106	0.099	0.098	0.098
59	0.112	0.095	0.091	0.093	0.094
64	0.113	0.067	0.000	0.000	0.000
69	0.113	0.067	0.000	0.000	0.000
74	0.113	0.067	0.000	0.000	0.000
79	0.113	0.067	0.000	0.000	0.000
84	0.113	0.067	0.000	0.000	0.000
Quadratic preferences, r = 0.03, δ = 0.03					
25	0.195	0.195	0.195	0.195	0.195
29	0.186	0.186	0.186	0.186	0.186
34	0.163	0.163	0.163	0.163	0.163
39	0.152	0.152	0.152	0.152	0.152
44	0.149	0.149	0.149	0.149	0.149
49	0.144	0.141	0.138	0.139	0.139
54	0.138	0.129	0.125	0.125	0.126
59	0.147	0.126	0.118	0.123	0.124
64	0.135	0.073	0.000	0.000	0.000
69	0.135	0.073	0.000	0.000	0.000
74	0.135	0.073	0.000	0.000	0.000
79	0.135	0.073	0.000	0.000	0.000
84	0.135	0.073	0.000	0.000	0.000

(*continued*)

Table 4.2   (continued)

			G		
Age	$0	$5,000	$10,000	$15,000	$20,000
Quadratic preferences, r = 0.03, δ = 0.03, no borrowing constraints					
25	0.055	0.047	0.036	0.030	0.014
29	0.082	0.068	0.054	0.043	0.030
34	0.116	0.100	0.085	0.068	0.051
39	0.153	0.143	0.125	0.114	0.097
44	0.202	0.187	0.175	0.149	0.134
49	0.247	0.224	0.203	0.183	0.163
54	0.260	0.242	0.221	0.194	0.170
59	0.277	0.259	0.234	0.209	0.192
64	0.280	0.264	0.239	0.212	0.197
69	0.280	0.264	0.239	0.212	0.197
74	0.280	0.264	0.239	0.212	0.197
79	0.280	0.264	0.239	0.212	0.197
84	0.280	0.264	0.239	0.212	0.197

Source: Authors' calculations.

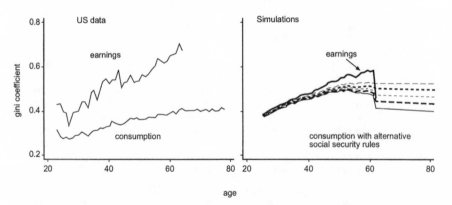

Fig. 4.4   Actual and simulated inequality of earnings and consumption

inequality (from the "impatient" isoelastic case) is too high relative to the actuals; perhaps the borrowing restrictions are preventing consumption from being sufficiently smoothed. Nevertheless, the upward drift of consumption inequality is very much the same in the data as in the simulations, which also show the effects on inequality of the different Social Security designs.

In figures 4.5 and 4.6 we turn to the life-cycle pattern of inequality in assets, in figure 4.5 for assets excluding Social Security wealth, and in figure 4.6 including Social Security wealth. The permanent income model is excluded from these comparisons because average wealth is negative for much of the life cycle. Total wealth at any given age is defined as the sum

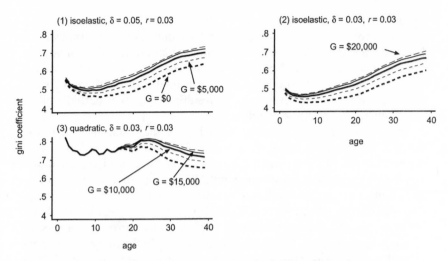

Fig. 4.5   Gini coefficients for assets, excluding Social Security assets

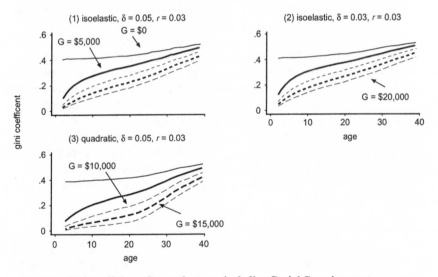

Fig. 4.6   Gini coefficients for total assets, including Social Security assets

of non–Social Security assets A_t and the present discounted value at t of receiving G from retirement R to death T, plus the accumulated balance in the personal saving account, if any. Making the Social Security system more autarkic by holding the Social Security tax constant and devoting more of the revenue to personal accounts and less to a universal guarantee has the opposite effect on inequality of non–Social Security wealth than it does on the inequality of consumption. This is because of the substitutability between saving for retirement inside and outside the Social Security system. If we examine the profiles of asset accumulation by age (not shown here), average non–Social Security accumulations are larger the smaller is the fraction of the Social Security tax invested in individual accounts. There is a similar substitutability in asset inequality; when there is a large Social Security floor for everyone, the resulting equality is partially offset by inequality in private accumulation.

The different patterns of asset inequality for the quadratic case in the bottom left panel, as opposed to the isoelastic cases in the top panels, are associated with the fact that a substantial fraction of the quadratic consumers are credit constrained up until around age forty, so that inequality is high at early ages because so many consumers have exactly nothing. The offsetting of private wealth against Social Security wealth only shows up once the majority of consumers are accumulating private assets, at which point they are no longer credit constrained. In the cases with isoelastic preferences, the borrowing constraints are binding for only a small fraction of young consumers; the variability of earnings and the convexity of marginal utility is enough to overcome impatience and the expected growth of earnings.

When we come to figure 4.6, which shows the inequality of all assets, we see the "standard" pattern restored; the more autarkic the system and the larger the fraction of Social Security taxes devoted to private accounts, the larger is the inequality of assets. Note that the Gini coefficients for *all* assets are much lower than those for private assets; even with personal accounts, the addition of Social Security to private wealth makes the distribution of wealth much more equal. As with consumption, asset inequality rises with age, but does so most rapidly in the cases where insurance is greatest, so that the differences in asset inequalities across the various schemes diminish with age. Even so, the most autarkic systems are the most unequal at all ages.

4.3.4   Social Security Design and Inequality: Results with Variable Interest Rates

The results on asset inequality, and to a lesser extent those on consumption inequality, are likely to be seriously affected by our assumption that everyone earns the same rate of return on their assets. Under some of the early proposals for reform—for example, those from the largest group in the Gramlich report—one of the great virtues of personal accounts was seen as the freedom given to individual consumers to choose their own portfolios. More recent proposals have tended to favor severe restrictions on portfolio choice, perhaps restricting consumers to a limited menu of approved funds, which themselves must adhere to strict portfolio rules. Clearly, allowing different people to obtain different returns adds a new source of inequality, in both assets and in consumption. If, for example, the funds for the minimum guarantee G were invested in a common fund at rate r, as above, but the personal accounts obtained different rates of return for different individuals, either because of their individual portfolio choices or because of differential management fees, then a move to personal accounts can be expected to increase inequality by more than in the calculations presented thus far. Alternatively, if the limited menu of funds offered different risk-return tradeoffs, and if high earners chose higher returns because they are less risk averse, the availability of the menu would likely translate into higher consumption inequality.

It is not obvious how to construct a model with differential asset returns that is both realistic and computationally tractable. We have so far considered only one simple case. Personal accounts are invested in one of eleven mutual funds, and consumers must choose among them at the outset of the working life. The eleven mutual funds have rates of return from 2.5 to 3.5 percent per year. One can think of the funds as having identical (Standard & Poor's 500) portfolios, but management fees range from zero to 1 percentage point; the equilibrium is maintained by differential advertising and reporting services. We allocate our 1,000 consumers randomly to the eleven mutual funds, with equal probability of receiving any one interest rate; this is a conservative procedure, and inequality would presumably be higher if those with higher earnings were more financially sophisticated and systematically chose the no-load funds. We assume that consumers are forced to convert their retirement accounts into annuities at retirement (using the interest rate to which they have been assigned), and also that the Social Security system gives each consumer a guaranteed amount of $5,000 per year after retirement in addition to the annuity.

The results indicate that there is virtually no increase in consumption inequality before retirement, and very little after retirement, associated with assigning different consumers to different fixed interest rates. The top panel of figure 4.7 shows the Gini coefficient for consumption for the cases described above, with dispersion in interest rates, and the case in which all consumers receive the same interest rate of 3.0 percent. This result may not be not surprising, considering that most saving (whether private or through the Social Security system) is done late in life, when income is high, so that those that receive lower interest rates do not have wealth at retirement that is much lower than those with higher interest rates. Consider, for example, a group of 1,000 consumers whose incomes follow the process described above, each of whom pays 12.4 percent in taxes, 81 percent of which is allocated to private Social Security accounts (thereby generating enough government revenue to fund a $5,000 guaranteed payment to each during retirement). If each member of the group receives an interest rate of 2.5 percent, the average private Social Security account balance upon retirement will equal $278,597. This number will be 22.4 percent higher, or $341,014, with an interest rate of 3.5 percent. The percentage difference in total retirement wealth, including the equalizing guarantee of $5,000 per year, is even smaller, and the difference in average consumption

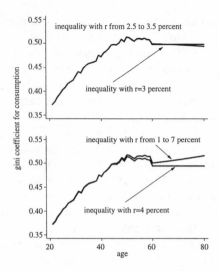

Fig. 4.7   The effects on consumption inequality of a distribution of interest rates

in the first year of retirement for the two interest rates is less than $5,000. This difference is for a spread of one full percentage point; in the exercise conducted above, most consumers have interest rates between the extremes, so there is even less of an effect on overall inequality.

Even with a much wider spread of returns, there is only a modest effect on inequality. The bottom panel of figure 4.7 shows the case in which consumers are distributed over (fixed) rates of return from 1 percent to 7 percent, compared with the case in which all get 4 percent. This can be thought of as the case in which consumers make a choice between equities and bonds at the beginning of their working careers and may never change thereafter. Because the spread is wider, there is more inequality than before, but the effects are modest compared with the other issues examined in this chapter.

It is important to note that assigning consumers to different but fixed rates of interest will not necessarily have the same affects as allowing the interest rate to vary randomly over time for individual consumers. In future work, we plan to examine how interest rate risk, as opposed to interest rate dispersion, affects inequality.

References

Campbell, John Y. 1987. Does saving anticipate declining labor income? An alternative test of the permanent income hypothesis. *Econometrica* 55:1249–73.

Carroll, Christopher. 1997. Buffer-stock saving and the life-cycle permanent income hypothesis. *Quarterly Journal of Economics* 112:1–55.

Deaton, Angus. 1992. *Understanding consumption.* Oxford, England: Clarendon Press.

Deaton, Angus, and Christina Paxson. 1994. Intertemporal choice and inequality. *Journal of Political Economy* 102:437–67.

Feldstein, Martin S. 1998. Is income inequality really a problem? In *Income inequality issues and policy options: A symposium sponsored by the Federal Reserve Bank of Kansas City,* 357–67. N.p.: Federal Reserve Bank of Kansas City.

Flavin, Marjorie. 1981. The adjustment of consumption to changing expectations about future income. *Journal of Political Economy* 89:974–1009.

Gourinchas, Pierre-Olivier, and Jonathan A. Parker. 2002. Consumption over the life-cycle. *Econometrica* (forthcoming).

Ludvigson, Sydney, and Christina H. Paxson. 2001. Approximation bias in linearized Euler equations. *Review of Economics and Statistics* 83:242–56.

Wilkinson, Richard. 1996. *Unhealthy societies: The afflictions of inequality.* London: Routledge.

Comment   James M. Poterba

This is an innovative and important chapter that provides new evidence on how Social Security programs affect the distribution of lifetime resources. The chapter presents an elegant analytical treatment of the issues surrounding lifetime inequality and retirement transfer programs. It considers how a somewhat stylized version of the current U.S. Social Security system would affect the degree of inequality in lifetime consumption, and it also explores how a shift toward an individual accounts Social Security system might affect inequality. The chapter provides a very useful starting point for analyzing more complex Social Security arrangements, and many of my comments will focus on potential directions for such extensions. One very attractive feature of the analysis is the presentation of both Gini coefficients for consumption inequality as well as summary statistics for the fraction of the population at different ages that has consumption below a "poverty line" level.

The chapter begins with an elegant treatment of how a simple Social Security system would affect the inequality of consumption, saving, and assets in a stylized economy. The analysis begins with a very general insight. A Social Security system that taxes each worker's earnings at a fixed

James M. Poterba is the Mitsui Professor of Economics at the Massachusetts Institute of Technology, and both a research associate of and director of the public economics research program at the National Bureau of Economic Research.

rate, and then pays each worker a benefit that is tied to the average earnings level in the population, reduces the variance of consumption and of net-of-tax incomes. If infinitely lived consumers populate the economy, and these consumers save in accordance with the life-cycle hypothesis, then it is possible to derive analytical results for the steady-state variance of consumption with and without the simplified Social Security system.

While the insights from such a model are quite general, the numerical results may fail to describe the impact of actual Social Security programs for two reasons. First, actual Social Security systems do not tax all workers at the same rate, and transfer back a fixed share of economy-wide income. Taxable earnings are often subject to limits, and benefit formulae often incorporate progressive elements that transfer larger amounts, per dollar of taxes paid, to low- than to high-earning individuals. Such programmatic details would be straightforward to incorporate in a somewhat more detailed model of lifetime income and consumption inequality.

The second difficulty with the stylized model in the first part of the chapter is that a substantial body of empirical evidence suggests that many households do not behave in accordance with the simple life-cycle hypothesis. This concern motivates the second part of the chapter, which uses a richer model of consumer behavior, incorporating precautionary motives for saving, to estimate how current and modified Social Security programs could affect consumption inequality. The chapter is careful to consider several different specifications of preferences and to illustrate the sensitivity of key findings to various assumptions. The results are presented both in terms of standard inequality measures, such as the Gini coefficient, and by calculating the fraction of households who experience consumption levels below a prespecified threshold.

The chapter yields several findings of broad interest and importance. First, Social Security systems that levy taxes on realized earnings, but provide benefits that depend in part on aggregate earnings, typically reduce the inequality of lifetime consumption. The current defined benefit (DB) system in the United States has some elements of such a system. Programs of this type reduce inequality in consumption both before and after retirement, and they can have a particularly large impact on the inequality of postretirement consumption when there is a large "guarantee level" that provides a consumption floor for Social Security recipients. With such a guarantee, many households will choose not to save at all for retirement, instead relying on the guarantee level to provide their retirement consumption.

Second, shifting from a DB Social Security system with a guaranteed benefit floor to a system of individual accounts will increase consumption inequality both before and after retirement. The postretirement increase in inequality arises largely from the greater link between preretirement earnings and postretirement resources in individual accounts rather than redistributive defined-benefit systems. The preretirement increase in consumption inequality results in part from the saving adjustments that individuals make in response to the shifting Social Security system. Even if the share of earnings devoted to individual accounts was the same as the share collected by the taxes that finance a DB pension plan, there could be endogenous changes in the saving behavior of individuals and in the resulting pattern of preretirement consumption. This is an important insight, and one that must be considered in future studies of Social Security and inequality.

Third, the numerical results suggest that allowing for differences in the rates of return earned by different individuals within an individual accounts system has a relatively modest impact on the inequality of lifetime consumption. This result seems surprising at first, since one would imagine that greater return variability would result in greater variability of postretirement consumption. While variable rates of return work in this direction, they have a modest effect because most retirement saving is done in the few years before retirement, so the period of time over which differences in returns compound is relatively short. The modest incremental increase in consumption inequality is also, to some extent, a reflection of the very substantial degree of inequality in lifetime income, which translates into heterogeneity in postretirement consumption.

The chapter represents an important start on the very substantial task of modeling how public policies such as Social Security may affect consumption inequality. There are many productive directions in which the current analysis could be extended, however, to provide more information on what might actually happen in a personal accounts retirement system. The remainder of this comment outlines several such directions.

One natural extension is to allow for possible correlation between the rate of return that investors earn on their individual accounts and the level of their lifetime income. There is some evidence from 401(k)-type plans, reported in Poterba and Wise (1998), that higher-income households tend to hold a higher fraction of their 401(k) balances in stocks rather than bonds. Since stocks have historically provided investors with a higher return than bonds, this raises the prospect that those with higher incomes may earn better returns on their individual accounts, on average. Such a correlation would magnify the degree of inequality in retirement resources. It might be particularly important if individuals choose focal values in their asset allocation, such as 0, 50, or 100 percent stock.

A second potentially useful extension would recognize the potential feedback from the Social Security system to the structure of pretax earnings. The current analysis treats the pretax income distribution as given. Yet Social Security systems that tax individuals on their earnings, and return to them a fraction of the economy-wide average earnings at some future date, have incentive effects similar to those of more standard individual income taxes. If redistributive DB Social Security systems are recognized as having different incentive effects than individual accounts systems in which individuals can invest a fraction of their earnings, then it is possible that labor supply would be different under the two systems. If higher tax rates generally discourage labor supply, then one would expect a more compressed distribution of pretax incomes in the DB case than in the individual accounts case. More generally, the possibility that different Social Security systems have different levels of deadweight loss raises a host of additional issues for analysis, because policies that change the distribution of resources and affect consumption inequality would also affect the aggregate pool of resources.

A third potential extension would be to recognize that Social Security benefits are typically paid to two members of a household, because both husbands and wives are eligible to receive benefits. Recent work by Gustman and Steinmeier (1999) suggests that a very substantial part of the redistribution that the current Social Security program carries out on an individual basis is undone when one considers redistribution across households. The households with higher lifetime incomes often have secondary earners who receive net benefits with larger present discounted values (in relative terms) than the secondary earners in lower-income couples. Some of this effect operates through differential mortality of secondary earners in different types of households, and some operates through differences in lifetime earning histories. The central message of this work is that considering couples rather than individuals is a key step for analyzing Social Security policies. The framework developed in this paper could be extended to consider marriage and to create households with two earnings streams.

A fourth, and particularly ambitious, extension of the current work would involve using actual earnings histories rather than simulated earnings histories to evaluate Social Security redistribution. There is undoubtedly more information in the history of actual earnings processes than in the stylized set of earnings histories generated by the stochastic models in the present chapter. Actual earnings histories are increasingly available for research purposes—for example, in conjunction with the Health and Retirement Survey. It would be intriguing to learn whether the patterns of consumption inequality that emerge in the current analysis are broadly confirmed if the analysis is based on actual earnings experience.

The authors of the present chapter have tackled one of the central issues in the analysis of Social Security reform. There is little doubt that substantive discussions of Social Security reform in the political arena will turn not only on distributional issues across generations, which have received much attention in the academic literature, but also on how reform will affect the distribution of resources within cohorts. This chapter provides a very valuable set of insights for addressing within-cohort redistribution, and it is sure to stimulate further work.

References

Gustman, Alan L., and Thomas L. Steinmeier. 1999. How effective is redistribution under the Social Security benefit formula? Dartmouth College, mimeograph.

Poterba, James, and David Wise. 1998. Individual financial decisions in retirement saving plans and the provision of resources for retirement. In *Privatizing Social Security*, ed. Martin Feldstein, 363–93. Chicago: University of Chicago Press.

Discussion Summary

Martin Feldstein asked about the relative importance of the timing of contributions, because those who contributed early would get the advantage of more years of compound interest. The authors explained that with high wage growth, most income occurs at the end of the life cycle. Consequently, almost all contributions are made at the end of the life cycle, and the impact of compound interest is negligible. The more significant factor is inequality in earnings, not timing of contributions.

John B. Shoven felt that it was important to examine inequality of opportunities, but not necessarily inequality of outcomes. If people are informed and given a broader menu, then the extra choice allows people to maximize their utility better: It should not be argued that increased choice is terrible because it increases inequality. The authors responded with two points. First, most of the inequality comes from earnings inequality, which is not really chosen in this model. Second, society seems to be concerned about choices that are made voluntarily, but are very bad decisions ex post. For instance, Teachers Insurance and Annuity Association (TIAA-CREF) has increased the choices, but has limited those choices in some ways because it is worried about people's voluntarily choosing to become very poor.

Laurence J. Kotlikoff indicated that the traditional life-cycle picture, high nonasset income followed by lower nonasset income during retirement, does not seem to correspond with data in the United States. If Social Security, Medicare, and Medicaid are part of net nonasset income, cohorts going through the life cycle now have net nonasset income that rises through retirement. The number of people in old age who are borrowing constrained seems to be important. Hence, an accurate profile of net nonasset income is vital to examining this issue. In addition, if Social Security is actuarially unfair, then the ceiling on taxable earnings implies that the lower-income classes are affected more severely by this unfairness. Very wealthy people have avoided most of the actuarial penalties of Social Security, and their consumption will be proportionately higher when compared to everyone else. In this situation, Social Security might actually increase consumption inequality. The authors acknowledged the second observation, but said it would be difficult to build an earnings ceiling into their model for various technical reasons.

Alan Gustman mentioned that when redistribution is examined by family, about half of the redistribution in the current system disappears. The amount of redistribution within the family depends on the number of years worked by the spouse. While he could understand the difficulties preventing the inclusion of these factors in the model, Gustman believed that a large amount of risk sharing and redistribution occurs between family members.

5

Long-Run Effects of Social Security Reform Proposals on Lifetime Progressivity

Julia Lynn Coronado, Don Fullerton,
and Thomas Glass

5.1 Introduction

Most observers agree that the U.S. Social Security system must be reformed. Although the original "pay-as-you-go" (PAYGO) system was converted to a partially funded system in 1983, promised future benefits still exceed expected future taxes—especially by the time the baby boom population bulge is finished retiring. When converted into 1995 dollars, the "intermediate" projected deficit for the year 2075 is $480 billion, or just less than 4 percent of projected gross domestic product (GDP; U.S. Social Security Administration 1998).

In addition to serving as a mandatory retirement saving program, Social Security is a program of social insurance with many redistributive elements. The program redistributes income not only from current working generations to the retired, but also between families of a given generation in different circumstances. The benefits formula is highly progressive in that it provides a greater replacement rate for workers with lower lifetime earnings. Benefits well in excess of taxes paid are also provided to spouses who do not work, to survivors of deceased workers, and to women in general (because they tend to live longer than men). Any reform will alter

Julia Lynn Coronado is an economist at the Federal Reserve Board of Governors. Don Fullerton is the Addison Baker Duncan Centennial Professor of Economics at the University of Texas, and a research associate of the National Bureau of Economic Research. Thomas Glass is a consultant with Glass & Company in Austin, Texas.

The model used in this chapter reflects helpful comments from Henry Aaron, Charles Blahous, Angus Deaton, Martin Feldstein, Stephen C. Goss, Jeffrey B. Liebman, Gib Metcalf, James M. Poterba, and Jonathan Skinner. The authors are grateful for support from the National Bureau of Economic Research (NBER). Any opinions expressed are those of the authors and not those of the Federal Reserve Board or NBER.

redistribution under the program, and many proposals give careful consideration to this issue. In general, the current system is considered to be progressive, and most proposals seek to maintain or enhance that degree of progressivity.

In this chapter, we estimate the implied changes to the progressivity of the current system from four specific reform proposals. We focus on the retirement portion of the program and the redistribution between the rich and poor of a given generation, giving special attention to how we classify economic well-being. We take a steady-state approach in that we assume people work and retire under a given system. Thus, we do not address intergenerational redistribution or the issue of transition costs from the present system to any given new system. To define who is rich or poor, we use an estimate of *lifetime potential* income—the present value of the total value of one's time. We also pool the resources of husbands and wives. A spouse of a high earner who chooses to stay at home is therefore not misclassified as "poor" under our methodology. We use a large data set of almost 2,000 individuals and classify them into five lifetime income groups. We calculate the present value of the Social Security taxes paid and benefits received for each individual. The difference is divided by lifetime potential income to provide a lifetime "net tax rate." If this net tax rate rises across the five income groups, the system (or reform) is deemed progressive.

We evaluate how four specific reform proposals would alter redistribution from rich to poor. The proposals were chosen to represent the broad spectrum of possible approaches to reforming Social Security. One set of reforms would either privatize the system or switch to a system based entirely on mandatory individual accounts with benefits that depend on contributions (e.g., Feldstein and Samwick 1998). Transition costs aside, such a plan does not redistribute, but provides benefits equal to the present value of one's own contributions. In our model, the net tax rate under such a system is zero, and the redistributive consequences of this type of reform are the same as the "repeal" of Social Security. Second, we evaluate the proposal of the National Commission on Retirement Policy (NCRP; 1999). This plan redirects 2 percentage points of the payroll tax into defined contribution individual accounts, and it dramatically cuts other benefits to balance the Social Security budget at that reduced tax rate. Third, we look at the plan of Aaron and Reischauer (1998), which suggests smaller specific changes without fundamentally altering the nature of Social Security. In order to close the long-run imbalances, this plan relies heavily on higher returns generated by investing the trust fund in private financial markets. Fourth, we calculate effects of the Moynihan (1999) plan that depletes the current Social Security trust fund through lower tax rates now and then switches to true PAYGO financing.

The model used in this chapter was developed elsewhere to evaluate the progressivity of the current Social Security system (Coronado, Fullerton, and Glass 2000). In that analysis, we found that the current system redistributes little, if anything, from rich to poor. In the current chapter, we find that each of the proposed reforms is a somewhat regressive change to the current system.

The next two subsections describe our model and review the existing literature on the redistributive effects of Social Security. Section 5.2 provides more detail on the model, and section 5.3 provides more detail on the four reforms. Section 5.4 discusses our basic results, and section 5.5 discusses the sensitivity of those results to alternative assumptions. Section 5.6 concludes.

5.1.1 Overview of the Model

We assume that all working years and retirement years come under a single Social Security system. Thus, we assess long-run redistributive effects of the current system and of several reforms. Within this steady-state context, we take account of the ways in which Social Security redistributes across groups defined by income, gender, and marital status. That is, while we report only the redistributions between lifetime income quintiles, we account for heterogeneity within each such quintile. Thus we capture the fact that different income groups have different proportions of individuals who are single or married, male or female, and employed continuously or sporadically, and who have different mortality rates.

We use twenty-two years of wage rates from the Panel Study of Income Dynamics (PSID) to estimate wage rate profiles for different kinds of individuals (household heads, full-time secondary workers, and part-time secondary workers). The estimated coefficients are used to project each individual's wage rates before and after the sample period, so that each individual has a complete wage profile from age twenty-two to sixty-six (extended through age sixty-nine for plans with retirement at age seventy). The wage rate for each year is multiplied by a total time endowment to calculate potential earnings, and the present value of this endowment is used to categorize individuals into quintiles from rich to poor. Lifetime resources for husbands and wives are pooled so that they are always classified in the same quintile.

Next, for each quintile, actual earnings are used to estimate earnings profiles. We estimate Tobit earnings regressions and again use the coefficients to project out-of-sample earnings for each individual, so that each member of our sample has a complete lifetime earnings history. We then derive income-differentiated mortality rates, and we use those mortality probabilities with constructed earnings histories to calculate each individual's expected lifetime Social Security taxes and benefits. Finally, we add over the individuals in each quintile to determine the net impact of Social Security on each group under the current system and proposed reforms.

Using actual earnings data is one of the important innovations of our model. As noted below, previous studies use stylized groups, or smoothly estimated profiles for each group. In contrast, the use of actual earnings data allows us to incorporate differential effects of human capital investment, illnesses, child rearing, and other events that affect earnings and may lead individuals to enter and exit the labor force. We also give special attention to differential mortality rates by gender, race, and lifetime income.

Distributional effects of the current system also represent the effects of a major reform, namely, the repeal of Social Security or complete privatization. In addition, we calculate effects of three specific reforms, and we compare the progressivity of those reforms to a proportional cut in all benefits (with a comparable overall net tax rate). For each plan, we plot the net tax rate as a function of income. We compare the slopes of these curves because of our interest in long-run redistributions between rich and poor, but we ignore the levels of these curves because our model does not capture redistributions between current generations and long-run future generations.

5.1.2 Overview of Existing Literature

The Social Security system takes taxes from both a high-wage person and a low-wage person during working years, and it provides benefits to both individuals when retired. We wish to measure how much of this money is transferred between individuals, rather than merely transferred from the working years to the retirement years of the same person.

Initial tax incidence studies like Pechman and Okner (1974) used groupings based on annual income. This type of study would find that the Social Security system is progressive, but it aggregates unlike individuals. The low-annual-income group may include both the working poor and those who have retired from a high-earning career. Some later studies like that of Auerbach and Kotlikoff (1987) include lifetime profiles and lifetime decision making in order to determine how Social Security redistributes between young and old. However, this study does not distinguish between different lifetime income groups of the *same* cohort.[1]

Although much work has focused on intergenerational effects of the Social Security system, Aaron (1977) initiates a growing literature on intragenerational redistribution. Some researchers use arbitrary levels of income for different groups. For example, of the studies by Hurd and Shoven (1985) and Boskin et al. (1987), each uses three groups (e.g., median income, half the median, and five times the median).[2] The approach of using

---

1. Nelissen (1998) finds substantial differences between annual incidence and lifetime incidence for social security in the Netherlands.

2. Panis and Lillard (1996) set the low group at full-time minimum wage earnings, the middle group at social security's average earnings, and the high group at the social security

arbitrarily set income levels has tremendous computational appeal. However, the calculation of Social Security benefits depends not only on the level of lifetime earnings. Recent years often receive more weight, and some years with zero earnings can be dropped from the calculation. Thus, the benefits received by each group depend on the shape of the earnings profile and the variance from one year to the next. For these reasons, we estimate a nonlinear profile separately for each group. We retain actual earnings data from the sample period and use actual and constructed years of data with zero earnings. Each group has different proportions of individuals with different numbers of zero-earnings years that can be dropped from the benefit calculations (as in Williams 1998).

Some studies have used actual Social Security records to examine issues of redistribution (Burkhauser and Warlick 1981); Hurd and Shoven 1985; and Liebman, chap. 1, this volume). Duggan, Gillingham, and Greenlees (1993) use records for more than 32,000 workers from the Continuous Work History Sample of Social Security records. While using Social Security records would better identify Social Security earnings histories, two important elements are missing from the available extracts. First, the observed amount of earnings is generally capped at the annual Social Security wage cap, yet only data with wage rates above the cap can fully capture the regressivity of Social Security taxes that exempt higher wages.[3] Second, and equally important, records for individuals are not linked with records of spouses.

Fullerton and Rogers (1993) also estimate profiles separately for twelve different lifetime income groups and use them to calculate the incidence of various taxes, but they do not look at Social Security benefits. More recently, Altig et al. (1997) employ the same twelve lifetime income groups in their model of tax incidence, and Kotlikoff, Smetters, and Walliser (1998) use that model to look at Social Security. These computational general equilibrium models can calculate the effects of Social Security reforms on factor returns in each period, but each of the twelve groups is assumed to contain homogeneous individuals. Since everyone in a group must work the average amount for that group, these general equilibrium models cannot incorporate heterogeneity, such as the existence of a fraction in each group that has zero earnings.

For these reasons, we do not attempt to build a general equilibrium model. The point of this chapter is to make use of actual data on diverse individuals within each lifetime income group. We can thus use the fact that each group has a different proportion of individuals with zero-

---

tax wage cap. Similar procedures are followed by Myers and Schobel (1983), Steuerle and Bakija (1994), and Garrett (1995).

3. The true earnings can be estimated, however. For example, Fox (1982) uses information on the time of year that an individual reaches the wage cap to infer the full annual earnings.

earnings years, of individuals who qualify for spousal benefits, and of individuals who receive fewer benefits because they die earlier. In this way, we can look at distributional impacts of specific elements of the Social Security system.[4]

The literature on distributional impacts of specific elements of the Social Security system is sparse. Flowers and Horwitz (1993) examine the spousal benefit, whereby low-earner spouses can draw the greater of their own computed benefit or one-half of the higher-earning spouse's benefit. They demonstrate that the spousal benefit calculation is progressive when compared to an own-benefit calculation. This result is driven by their finding that higher-income families consist of spouses with more-equal earnings and that lower-income couples have more disparate earnings. Our data imply the opposite: more-equal earnings among couples with low wages. Also, Panis and Lillard (1996) use a low-medium-high income structure to examine three basic reforms: the increase of the retirement age, the increase of payroll taxes, and the decrease of benefits. The effects of these reforms on progressivity are not clear.

Starting with Aaron (1977), some have introduced differential mortality into the analysis. Rofman (1993) uses a data set that matches demographic information from the Current Population Survey with Social Security information on earnings, benefits, and mortality. However, Duleep (1986) reports that mortality information is severely underreported in the Social Security records, especially for working-age individuals and minorities. Garrett (1995) uses mortality estimates from a literature search, while Panis and Lillard (1996) extract mortality information from the PSID. Since high-income people live longer, several studies show that accounting for income-differentiated mortality seriously dampens the progressivity of Social Security (e.g., Steuerle and Bakija 1994; Duggan, Gillingham, and Greenlees 1995; and Panis and Lillard 1996).

Finally, Caldwell et al. (1999) use a large microsimulation model to construct lifetime earnings for many heterogeneous individuals. This model starts with the 1960 Census Public-Use Microdata Sample and uses estimated transition probabilities to "grow" the sample in one-year intervals. For each person, they simulate the next year's income and work status. Thus, as in our study, they capture differences in race, gender, the number of zero-earnings years, differential mortality, and wage rates above the cap. They focus primarily on intergenerational redistributions, finding that, although early generations received a good rate of return, postwar generations receive smaller and even negative rates of return.

4. By concentrating on dollar flows, however, we miss the effect of this social insurance program on the utility of risk-averse individuals (see Geanakopolos, Mitchell, and Zeldes 1998). The benefits of risk reduction may be larger for low- or high-income individuals. Lee, McClellan, and Skinner (1999) calculate such effects for Medicare.

5.2 Lifetime Earnings Profiles and Net Benefits from Social Security

In this section we describe the data and methodology used to obtain lifetime earnings profiles, to estimate mortality probabilities that differ by lifetime income, and to calculate net taxes from Social Security. A more detailed description is provided in the appendix. We use the PSID for the years 1968 to 1989, which gives us twenty-two years of actual earnings data for a sample of the population.[5] We select a sample consisting of 1,086 heads and 700 wives that is 66 percent of the representative cross-section. The use of a reduced sample suggests the possibility of bias in our econometric estimates and our conclusions about the progressivity of Social Security. However, we do not believe our results are biased, for reasons discussed in the appendix.

The PSID provides only twenty-two years of actual data. In order to obtain complete profiles of earnings from age twenty-two through age sixty-six for each of our sample members, we want to be able to generate out-of-sample earning observations.[6] We do this by estimating earnings regressions and using the estimated coefficients to generate the needed observations. However, as Fullerton and Rogers (1993) demonstrated using data from the PSID, earnings profiles can have significantly different shapes for different lifetime income groups. We therefore estimate separate earnings regressions for different lifetime income classes.

Our model is somewhat stylized in that we ignore inheritances and transfers. Our measure of annual income is based on wages, which are zero for a retired person. Lifetime income is the present value of that annual income. Note that capital income from life-cycle saving is *not* part of lifetime income. If the present value of consumption must equal the present value of labor income, then capital income merely reflects rearrangements in the timing of consumption.

5.2.1 Lifetime Income

We want to estimate a separate earnings regression for each lifetime income class, and we want a measure of lifetime income that accurately reflects economic well-being. To begin, we calculate an annual wage rate for each member of our sample by dividing annual earnings by hours

---

5. While data are currently available through 1992, our model was constructed several years ago when data were available only through 1989.

6. We assume that people work until the future normal retirement age of sixty-seven, claim social security benefits at that point, and do not work after retirement. While the majority of people retiring in the past decade have claimed early retirement, they receive a reduction in benefits that is supposed to be actuarially fair. However, early retirees have less education and are more likely to be retiring from blue-collar jobs, indicating that they have lower lifetime incomes (U.S. Congressional Budget Office 1999).

worked. To construct a wage rate for every year of each sample member's working life, we first use all positive wage observations to estimate log wage profiles.[7] We estimate separate log wage regressions for heads, full-time working wives, and part-time working wives. The results of these regressions can be found in the second main section of the appendix. We regress the log of the wage rate on an individual fixed effect and other variables like age, age squared, and age cubed. Because we have a fixed effect for each individual, we cannot use variables that do not vary over time (like race or gender). However, we do include age *interacted* with education, race, and gender. Using the resulting fixed effects and coefficients, we then fill in missing observations during the sample period and observations outside the sample period. The appendix details how we assign a wage rate to women who have no earnings histories. Nonworking wives do engage in household production, and assigning them a zero wage may incorrectly place them in a low lifetime income group for the distributional analysis. Thus, for each individual, we have a wage rate for every year of entire economic life from age twenty-two to sixty-six.

We then use this wage rate and multiply it in each year by 4,000 hours to represent the year's labor endowment. This product represents the potential earnings of the individual and therefore serves as a measure of his or her material well-being.[8] Using this endowment allows us to abstract from the actual labor-leisure choice, since someone who chooses to work less and consume more leisure might be just as well off as someone who decides to work more and consume less leisure. Using potential income also avoids the distortion introduced by the fact that home production does not show up in the data under hours worked. The wage rate is a measure of earning power that reflects experience, talent, and education.[9]

Once we have a complete wage profile for each of our heads and wives for ages twenty-two to sixty-six, we calculate individual gross lifetime income as

$$(1) \qquad LI = \sum_{t=1}^{45} \frac{w_t \times 4,000}{(1 + r)^{t-1}} ,$$

where t indexes the forty-five years in the individual's economic lifetime relevant for Social Security, ages twenty-two to sixty-six, and where the individual could work a maximum of eighty hours per week for fifty weeks

7. This estimation of a whole life's wage profile takes advantage of the fact that some individuals are in the sample during the early part of their working lives and others are in the sample for the latter part.
8. For sensitivity analysis, we show net tax rates with two other measures of income: the present value of actual earnings, and the present value of potential earnings, where leisure is valued at the average wage rate for the sample instead of the individual's wage rate.
9. On the other hand, our model may overstate the value of time at home to the extent that it represents sick days or unemployment.

per year. Through most of our analysis, we use a value of 2 percent for r, the real discount rate. Later, we see the effect of changing the discount rate.

As couples generally pool their resources, it would be inappropriate to place husbands and wives individually into separate lifetime income groups. The low-wage wife of a high-wage husband is not "poor." We therefore combine the lifetime income of the husband and wife, and divide by two to obtain individual lifetime income for each of them. We can now deal with each member of our sample as an individual and categorize them into five lifetime income groups. The 1st quintile has the lowest income, the 5th quintile the highest income.

5.2.2   Earnings Profiles

Once we have classified people into lifetime income groups based on what we feel to be an appropriate measure of economic well-being, we estimate regressions for actual earnings. For each quintile, using our data from the PSID, the third main section of the appendix describes how we estimate separate earnings regressions for heads, habitually working wives, and occasional working wives, for a total of fifteen regressions. We use both positive and zero earnings observations in a Tobit framework.

Because the Tobit framework is nonlinear, we do not include fixed effects, as their inclusion would imply inconsistent parameter estimates. The exclusion of fixed effects also means we can use variables in these earnings regressions that do not vary over time, such as education, race, and gender. For each regression for the heads, we begin with independent variables for age, age squared, age cubed, education, education squared, the product of age and education, a dummy for whether the head is female, age interacted with the female dummy, and a dummy for whether the head is white. We then eliminate the variables that were insignificant. We follow a similar procedure for habitually working wives and occasionally working wives.

We next use the estimated coefficients from our earnings regressions to simulate earnings observations for the out-of-sample years for all individuals in our sample.[10] We do not use these coefficients to fill in zero earnings observations during the sample period, because we are interested in actual earnings, and years spent out of the labor force are relevant for calculating the costs and benefits of Social Security. In fact, we also simulate a representative number of zero earnings years for the out-of-sample portions of each earnings profile.

5.2.3   Income-Differentiated Mortality

It is a stylized fact that people with higher lifetime incomes tend to live longer, a fact that can dampen the progressivity of the benefit structure of

---

10. These imputations are independent of each other and are not serially correlated.

the Social Security system. We derive a set of mortality probabilities that vary by race, gender, and our measure of potential lifetime income, so that we can examine the impact of differential mortality on redistribution. Standard mortality tables extend only to age eighty-five and are differentiated only by sex and race. As the fourth part of the appendix describes, we extend these data in three ways. First, we extend the tables to age ninety-nine. Second, since individuals with low incomes have higher mortality rates than the population as a whole, we modify the standard tables by using available information on mortality differentiated by annual income. Third, we then use that information to construct mortality tables that are differentiated among our lifetime income quintiles. In later sections, we use these tables to compute expected present values of Social Security taxes and benefits.

Standard mortality tables are provided in *Vital Statistics of the United States* (U.S. Department of Health and Human Services 1993).[11] For 100,000 individuals alive at age zero, the table shows the number surviving at each age from one through eighty-five. Based on standard mortality tables, a hypothetical twenty-two-year-old white male has probabilities of survival to age twenty-three of 99.83 percent, survival to age sixty-five of 75.82 percent, and survival to age eighty-five of 22.34 percent. We multiply the tax that would be due or the benefit that would be received at each age by the probability of attaining that age, and then calculate the present value of these expected cash flows.

The National Center for Health Statistics obtains death certificates from all U.S. states and constructs four "current life tables" (for white males, white females, nonwhite males, and nonwhite females). Since 31 percent of the population is still alive at age eighty-five, the fourth section of the appendix describes how we extend the tables through age ninety-nine. These expanded mortality tables allow us to weight tax payments and benefits by the probability of being alive in each year from age twenty-two to ninety-nine.

Many studies have noted that mortality rates for the poor are higher than average. *A Mortality Study of 1.3 Million Persons* (Rogot et al. 1992) provides a rich source of data on this phenomenon. They show the observed number of deaths for each annual income class of each race, gender, and ten-year age group. For each such cell, we divide observed deaths (O) by the expected deaths (E) that would occur if all income classes of that group had the same mortality rate. We then apply that O/E ratio to each cell in the extended mortality tables. Among white males aged twenty-five

11. An alternative source of data for our analysis of a hypothetical future cohort would be projected mortality tables from the Social Security Administration (SSA), which incorporate projected increases in life expectancies. Using the SSA's probabilities would decrease the net tax rate for everyone, as people live longer and draw benefits longer, but it would have no effect on our adjustments for mortality probabilities that differ by lifetime potential income and so would not substantively alter our conclusions on redistribution.

to thirty-four, for example, those in the poorest annual income group die at a rate that is 168 percent of the average, while those in the richest annual income group die at rate that is only 61 percent of the average. For non-white females of the same age, the poor die at a rate that is 186 percent of the average, while the rich die at a rate equal to 44 percent of the average.

Although we have the annual household income of each individual in our sample for each year, we do not use only the corresponding annual income group's *O/E* ratio for that person in that year to weight mortality probability. Using annual income would imply that an individual with a steeply hump-shaped earnings profile would have a probability of dying that falls dramatically during high annual income years and then rises again during low annual income years. We do not believe that the same individual's probability of death changes that rapidly with annual income, jumping over other individuals in the same age cohort whose annual incomes are not so volatile. Instead, the probability of dying is more likely affected by the individual's *lifetime* income. To address this issue, our procedure described in the fourth section of the appendix is based on the relative ranking of each individual's lifetime income. Basically, a person in a particular percentile of the lifetime income distribution is assigned the *O/E* ratio of a person in the same percentile of the annual income distribution.[12]

5.2.4 Social Security Taxes Paid

We next compute the value of Social Security taxes for each person in each year, following the provisions of the Social Security Administration. This tax is commonly called the FICA (Federal Insurance Contributions Act) tax. It is collected on earned income and consists of three portions: Old Age and Survivors Insurance (OASI), Disability Insurance (DI), and Hospitalization Insurance (HI, also known as Medicare). The proceeds from these taxes are deposited into three separate trust funds, and benefits are paid from the appropriate fund. The program has become almost universal—95 percent of all employment in the United States is covered.[13]

The tax is deducted from employees' pay at a rate of 7.65 percent of wages, but employers match those deductions for a total tax of 15.3 percent. Self-employed individuals pay the entire 15.3 percent tax annually with their income tax returns. Both the employee and employer shares of the tax are collected on wages up to an annual maximum amount of taxable earnings—the Social Security wage cap ($76,200 for the year 2000).

12. Thus, even if two retirees have the same low annual income, the one with higher lifetime income is assumed to have a lower mortality probability.

13. Coverage may be excluded for the following: federal civilian workers hired before 1984 who have not elected to be covered; railroad workers who are covered under a similar but separate program; certain employees of state and local government who are covered by their state's retirement programs; household workers and farm workers with certain low annual incomes; persons with income from self employment of less than $400 annually; and persons who work in the underground, cash, or barter economy, who may illegally escape the tax.

This cap is adjusted automatically each year with the average earnings level of individuals covered by the system, thereby accounting for both real wage growth and inflation.

Since an objective of our research is to measure each worker's net Social Security tax burden, the question arises: How much of the total FICA tax does the worker bear? Using only the statutory incidence (the worker's half) would yield much lower burdens than using the combined employer and employee portions. Hamermesh and Rees (1993, 212) review empirical work on payroll tax incidence and conclude that the worker bears most of the employer's share of the tax through reduced wages. We therefore base our estimates on the combined employer and employee tax.[14]

Our focus is the retirement portion of the Social Security system, not the DI or HI portions. Of the total 15.3 percent tax rate, 2.9 percent is for Medicare (HI), leaving 12.4 percent for Old Age, Survivors and Disability Insurance (OASDI). This is the rate cited and modified by certain reform proposals, even though 1.8 percent goes to DI. The remaining 10.6 percent is for OASI, and this is the tax in our model.[15] The OASI portion of the tax is paid directly to the OASI Trust Fund, which is used to pay all retirement benefits. We ignore the DI and HI portions of the tax, as well as benefits paid from the DI and HI Trust Funds. In essence, we assume that no one becomes disabled prior to retirement. If sample members have few earnings observations because they became disabled, they are treated as any other workers with many years out of the labor force.

Our sample from the PSID includes observed and constructed earnings for each individual from age twenty-two until retirement. To obtain steady-state taxes and benefits under current law, however, we look at a hypothetical future cohort with a birth year of 1990. We therefore take N_{oij}, the "observed" nominal earnings of individual i in year j, and we convert it to the corresponding future individual's nominal earnings, N_{fij}, using the ratio of projected average earnings in the future year (AE_{fj}) to observed average earnings in the PSID sample year (AE_{oj}):

$$(2) \qquad N_{fij} = N_{oij} \frac{AE_{fj}}{AE_{oj}}.$$

14. Panis and Lillard (1996) point out that because the employer's portion of the payroll tax is deductible against the employer's income tax, the net cost to the employer is lower than the full amount of the payroll tax paid. Like Panis and Lillard, however, and for comparability with other studies, we treat the entire payroll tax as the employee's cost of social security coverage. In effect, we look at the social security system only, without any income tax. The combined incidence is not equal to the sum of the parts, but we cannot say whether the income tax affects the incidence of social security, or social security affects the incidence of the income tax.

15. These allocation percentages are for the year 2000 and beyond. Congress "temporarily" increased the portion going to DI for the years 1994 to 1996, followed by a reduction for 1997–1999. The 1997 allocation is OASI = 10.7 percent, DI = 1.7 percent, and HI = 2.9 percent.

Since 1951, the Social Security Administration has computed average earnings, the average annual earnings of all workers covered under the Social Security Act. We project this average earnings into the future using assumptions about future real wage growth and inflation.[16]

In our study, we calculate the present value at age twenty-two of mortality-adjusted Social Security taxes and benefits through age ninety-nine. Again, we assume that each person works and retires under a given system. The probability P_{ij} of individual i being alive at age j is conditional on being alive at age twenty-two, and it is computed from the constructed tables (for each age-race-sex-income cell) as the number in cell i alive at age j divided by the number in cell i alive at age twenty-two. We then calculate $E(\text{SST}_{ij})$, the expected Social Security tax of person i in year j, as

$$(3) \qquad E(\text{SST}_{ij}) = \left[T \times \min\left(N_{ij}, \text{CAP}_j\right)\right] \times P_{ij},$$

where T is the combined OASI tax rate (which is constant with unchanged law), CAP_j is the maximum nominal earnings subject to the OASI tax (which increases with inflation), and P_{ij} is the probability that person i is alive at age j. These amounts are used to compute the present value of Social Security taxes paid.

5.2.5   Social Security Benefits

Under the provisions of the Social Security Act, benefits are calculated from a progressive formula based on the individual's average indexed monthly earnings (AIME). Our calculations follow the Social Security Administration's computation of AIME upon the individual's retirement. In particular, earnings prior to age sixty are indexed to average wages in the year the individual attains age sixty. Only earnings at or below the taxable cap in each year are considered. The method of indexing is to multiply the nominal earnings in year j by the ratio of average earnings in the year age sixty was attained to average earnings in year j. Earnings after age sixty are not indexed. A person who works from age twenty-two through age sixty-six (retiring on his or her sixty-seventh birthday) would have a total of forty-five years of earnings. Under the act, only the highest thirty-five years are considered, so the ten lowest years will be dropped. The AIME is the simple average of the indexed earnings in those thirty-five highest-earnings years.[17]

Next, the primary insurance amount (PIA) is calculated as 90 percent

---

16. We use actual inflation and growth to scale observed PSID years up to 1995. Since amounts in future years are indexed, the subsequent inflation and growth rates are set to zero.

17. The language of the act specifies dropping the *five* lowest years of earnings through age sixty-one. Then, if the worker has years of earnings after age sixty-one that are higher than some earlier years' earnings, the higher earnings from after age sixty-one will replace those lower earnings. The net effect for a worker retiring at age sixty-seven is to drop the ten lowest years.

of AIME up to the first bend point, plus 32 percent of AIME in excess of the first bend point but less than the second bend point, plus 15 percent of AIME in excess of that second bend point. The fact that only capped earnings are used to calculate AIME provides a de facto maximum benefit. In 1995, the bend points were \$426 and \$2,567. If AIME were \$3,200, for example, the PIA would be calculated as follows:

$$(4) \qquad PIA = 0.90 \times (426) + 0.32 \times (2,567 - 426)$$
$$+ 0.15 \times (3,200 - 2,567) = \$1,163.47 .$$

Like the cap on earnings, the bend points are adjusted annually by the proportional increase in average earnings. We calculate this PIA for each worker in the sample.

A retiree is entitled to a benefit equal to the PIA upon "normal" retirement at age sixty-seven. A worker may still choose to retire as early as age sixty-two, with reduced benefits.[18] In contrast, if a worker elects to delay receipt of benefits to an age as late as seventy, the eventual benefits are permanently increased by 5 percent per year of delay. Our calculations below ignore these provisions for early or late retirement, as we assume workers (and their spouses) always choose the normal retirement age,[19] which for our hypothetical cohort under the current system is sixty-seven.

In addition to retirement benefits for covered workers, the OASI Trust Fund provides certain benefits to the spouse and other dependents of retired or deceased workers. The spouse of a retired worker can receive the greater of the benefit based on the spouse's own earnings, or one-half of the PIA of the retired worker (designated as the "spousal benefit"). The spouse of a deceased worker can receive the higher of the benefit based on the spouse's own earnings, or 100 percent of the benefit to which that worker was entitled. The benefit based on the deceased worker's benefit is called the "survivor benefit." We ignore nonspousal survivor benefits; in aggregate they are relatively minor.[20]

Our calculations of these amounts are detailed in the fifth main section of the appendix. We use each individual's observed and constructed earnings to compute AIME, PIA, the spousal benefit (SpBen), and the survivor

18. This early retirement penalty is a permanent reduction in the PIA of 5/9 percent for each early month (6.67 percent for each early year). For example, workers retiring at age sixty-four when the normal retirement age is sixty-seven would receive a benefit for the rest of their lives that is reduced by 20 percent.

19. This assumption does not affect progressivity unless the chosen date of retirement differs by income. If low-income individuals tend to die earlier, then they might optimally retire earlier, so the availability of this option might be progressive.

20. In 1996, a total of \$302.9 billion in benefits was paid from the OASI trust fund. Of that total, \$288.1 billion was paid to retired workers or their spouses, and only \$14.8 billion (4.9 percent) was paid for the other survivor and miscellaneous benefits (U.S. Social Security Administration 1997, table 4A.5).

benefit for the surviving spouse (SurvBen) in exact accordance with provisions of the act.

5.2.6   Present-Value Net Tax Rates

After we calculate the mortality-adjusted tax and benefit in each year for each individual in each of our lifetime income quintiles, we compute the present value, at age twenty-two, of the benefits to be received minus the taxes paid. We then add over the individuals in each lifetime income quintile. We divide by the present value at age twenty-two of the lifetime endowment (discounted at the same rate) to arrive at an effective net tax rate for each group. A system that takes exactly the same fraction of income for all groups is "proportional," whereas a system that takes a higher fraction of the income of the rich (poor) is deemed progressive (regressive).

The discount rate should reflect a real rate of return that would be available to participants in the system and that would provide for the same certainty as does the Social Security system. The trustees of the Social Security system currently used a rate of 2.8 percent for their long-term estimate of real returns in their 1998 report.[21] Ibbotson Associates (1998) reports on historic rates of return for various portfolio investments. For the period 1935 to 1997, the average inflation rate was 4.0 percent, and the nominal return on intermediate-term U.S. Treasury obligations was 5.4 percent, so the real rate of return was 1.4 percent.

For one choice of discount rate we use 2 percent, which lies between the forecast rate earned by the OASI Trust Fund on its investments (2.8 percent) and the historical average of real returns on government bonds reported by Ibbotson (1.4 percent).[22] To test the sensitivity of results, we also use a discount rate of 4 percent. As shown below, the choice of rate affects not only the absolute size of the present value gains or loss for each group but also the pattern of progressivity.

5.3   Proposed Reforms and their Treatment in our Model

Our evaluation of Social Security reform is limited in many respects. First, because we focus on distributional effects, we ignore behavioral effects such as changes in labor supply or saving. Second, since we cannot

21. In arriving at that rate, they forecast inflation at a long-term rate of 3.5 percent, and a nominal interest rate of 6.3 percent on the special-issue U.S. Treasury obligations that are purchased by the OASI trust fund. Whether to use a before-tax or after-tax discount rate depends on one's assumption about what alternative retirement investments are available.

22. Other studies of social security redistribution have used rates on either side of 2 percent. Myers and Schobel (1983) use 2 percent, Hurd and Shoven (1985) use 3 percent, Boskin et al. (1987) use 3 percent, Duggan, Gillingham, and Greenlees (1993) use 1.2 percent, Steuerle and Bakija (1994) use 2 percent, and Gramlich (1996) uses 2.3 percent. In contrast, Caldwell et al. (1999) use 3, 5, or 7 percent.

evaluate all of the many suggested reform proposals, we focus on only four of the major ones. Third, since most of these proposals are still evolving, we evaluate only versions that were available in written form in early 1999. Fourth, since each such proposal is too complicated to capture fully in our model, we really just evaluate "stylized" versions of these reforms. In particular, since we consider only long-run provisions, we ignore any phase-in of a change in the normal retirement age.[23] Since we assume everybody retires at that normal retirement age, we also ignore the effects of proposed changes in the early retirement age. Additionally, since we have only one "discount rate" in our model, with no consideration of risk, we cannot capture the welfare effects of any plan to switch some of the Social Security trust fund from government bonds to investments in corporate stocks and bonds.

Because we miss some of these ways in which each reform might raise net revenue, especially during the transition, we cannot comment on the extent to which each reform might close the existing Social Security deficit. Each plan extends the solvency of the program to seventy-five years. Some extend solvency indefinitely, while others have large annual cash flow deficits at the end of seventy-five years. Thus each of the plans evaluated is different in present value, and the long-run features that we consider raise different amounts of net revenue for each plan. As a consequence, some of the plans appear in our model to have higher overall net tax rates than others. We emphasize, however, that our goal is to compare the progressivity of these plans and not their overall net tax rates.

As described above, we do capture the major long-run provisions of Social Security that determine taxes and benefits for individuals in different circumstances. We now describe proposed changes to these provisions, as summarized in table 5.1. Column (1) of this table represents the current system. It does not list all features of the current system, only the main ones that would be reformed by one of the plans.

5.3.1 The Feldstein-Samwick Plan

A number of proposals would completely privatize Social Security. The proposal outlined by Feldstein and Samwick (1998) is typical of these plans. It specifies a transition from the current system to one in which the benefits are equivalent to those guaranteed under the current system, but in which these benefits in the long run are funded entirely by mandatory contributions to individual accounts made over a lifetime. The balances in

---

23. Legislation already enacted will increase the retirement age by two months each year beginning in the year 2000, so that by 2005 the normal retirement age will be sixty-six. Another two month per year increase will begin in 2017, resulting in a normal retirement age of sixty-seven after the year 2021. All of the reform proposals we consider would eliminate the pause from 2005 to 2017 and reach the new higher normal retirement age sooner.

Table 5.1 Summary of Long-Run Provisions of Social Security and Proposed Reforms

	Current System (1)	NCRP (2)	Aaron & Reischauer (3)	Moynihan (4)
Captured by our model				
OASDI tax rate (%)	12.4	10.4 (2% into ISA)	—	11.4, 10.4, 11.4, 12.4, 12.7, 13.4 (PAYGO)
Wage cap in 2003 (% taxed)	$82,800 (85)	—	—	$97,500 (87)
PIA factors (%)	90, 32, 15	90.00, 21.36, 10.01	—	—
Minimum benefit	Yes	Increases to AIPL	—	—
NRA	67	70	—	70
AIME (included years/drop years)	35/10	43/5	38/7	38/10
Spousal benefit	1/2	1/3	1/3	—
Survivor's benefit	max(hus,wife)	—	3/4 (hus+wife)	—
COLA	Indexes by CPI	Reduces CPI by 0.5 percentage points	(fix CPI)	Reduces CPI by 1.0 percentage point
Not captured by our model				
Earliest eligibility age (EEA)	62	65	64	—
State and local government workers	Most	All new	All new	All new
Earnings test	Cut benefits by 1/3	Eliminate at age 70	—	Eliminate at age 62
Tax on Social Security benefits	Above threshold	—	Like private pension	Like private pension
Investment in the trust fund	Government bonds	—	Part into corporate stocks and bonds	—

Notes: A dash means no change from current system. Other abbreviations and subtleties are described in the text.

the individual accounts would be invested in private debt and equity markets.

We do not explicitly model the Feldstein-Samwick plan, or any other plan based on individual accounts, as such plans involve little or no redistribution (except to the extent that some privatization plans include minimum benefits and survivor benefits).[24] In our modeling framework, such plans are equivalent to the repeal of the system. Our model is better suited to capturing the effects of reforms that do not alter the basic tax and benefit nature of the current system. Thus, in our model, the effects of the Feldstein-Samwick plan are the opposite of the effects of the current Social Security system.

5.3.2   The National Commission on Retirement Policy (NCRP) Plan

The 1999 NCRP proposal is also associated with the names of Senators Breaux and Gregg and Representatives Kolbe and Stenholm. One version is a defined benefit (DB) plan based on the current OASDI tax rate, but we evaluate only the other version, which sets aside 2 percentage points of each person's tax into a mandatory individual saving account (ISA). Since each retired individual receives back his or her own ISA, plus earnings, such a mandatory savings plan does not redistribute between members of a generation in the long run. It has a net present value tax of zero for each individual and therefore does not enter our calculations. The remaining "tax and benefit" portion of this plan is scaled back from current law. As shown in the first row of table 5.1, the OASDI tax rate is cut from 12.4 percent to 10.4 percent.[25] The next row shows that this plan does not change the wage cap.

With taxes cut substantially, closing the Social Security deficit means that benefits must be cut dramatically. The NCRP plan cuts benefits in several ways. The largest cut is in the calculation of benefits called the PIA in equation (4). In that calculation, "PIA factors" are applied to AIME between the bend points. As shown in the third row of table 5.1, the long-run NCRP plan would still provide 90 percent of AIME up to the first bend point, but the 32 percent rate between the two bend points is cut to 21.36 percent, and the 15 percent rate above the second bend point is cut to 10.01 percent. Thus, benefits are cut disproportionately for high-income individuals. This change is progressive, even in a lifetime context, as we confirm below.

In fact, this plan adds benefits to low-income individuals, another pro-

---

24. Also, individual accounts that require annuitization at a single rate will retain some redistribution due to differential mortality (see Brown, chap. 10 in this volume).

25. These reforms state changes in terms of the current 12.4 percent OASDI rate, as shown in the table. However, 1.8 percentage points of that tax go to disability insurance (DI), and we model only OASI. With the 2 points diverted into ISA accounts, the 10.6 percent OASI rate becomes 8.6 percent.

gressive change. Current law has a small "minimum benefit" that depends on the number of quarters of earnings but that can reach as high as $6,235 per year (at 1995 levels, but indexed). As indicated in the next row of table 5.1, the NCRP plan would raise this minimum benefit to the indexed "aged individual poverty level" (AIPL), which was $7,761 in 1995 (a 24 percent increase).

The next biggest cut in benefits occurs through the NCRP's increase in the ultimate normal retirement age (NRA) from sixty-seven to seventy.[26] This change is regressive for three reasons. First, it means that individuals will work and pay taxes for more years, and those taxes are generally regressive because they apply only to earnings below the wage cap. Second, it means that individuals will retire later and receive benefits for fewer years. Because the benefit schedule is progressive, that cut in benefits is regressive. Third, because of income-differentiated mortality, the higher retirement age means that low-income individuals have a disproportionate increase in their chance of dying before they receive retirement benefits.

The NCRP plan also changes the number of years' earnings used in the AIME calculation. Current rules use thirty-five years, which means that ten years of low earnings can be dropped from the calculation. This includes the five years that can be dropped before the AIME calculation at age sixty-two and the additional five years of earnings after age sixty-two that can be used to replace lower earnings from before sixty-two. The NCRP plan says it would "include earnings for all years," and we interpret this to mean all years up to the AIME calculation. Since the NCRP plan raises the early retirement age (and AIME calculation) from sixty-two to sixty-five, the individual can still use five subsequent years of earnings (until retirement at age seventy) to replace lower earnings from before sixty-five. In other words, effectively, five years still can be dropped.[27]

Under current law, any married retiree can receive the higher of his or her own benefit or half of what the spouse receives. This latter option is called the spousal benefit. The next row of table 5.1 shows that the NCRP plan would allow only one-third of the spouse's benefits. This cut would most affect any person whose income is low relative to his or her spouse, but remember that we do not count that person as "poor" (because we

---

26. Like other reforms considered here, the NCRP plan would also later increase the NRA above age seventy to account for subsequent increases in longevity (to maintain a constant number of expected years of life after retirement). We cannot model this provision as an increase in the retirement age, unless we were also to raise survival probabilities (which would roughly *maintain* the expected number of years of benefits).

27. In Coronado, Fullerton, and Glass (1999), we use the same model to analyze the redistributive impact of specific reform components. We found any reduction in the number of drop years allowed to be a regressive reform. Including the low-earning years reduces AIME somewhat more for low-income workers because they have more zero-earning years. In addition, that decline in AIME reduces benefits at the 90 percent PIA factor for individuals below the first bend point, and it reduces benefits at a low PIA factor for those with income above the bend points.

assume each person gets half of the couple's total income). Perhaps surprisingly, this change is slightly progressive. As it turns out, middle- and high-income couples have more disparate incomes and make greater use of the spousal benefit.

While the current system is fully indexed for inflation, it uses the Consumer Price Index (CPI). This index has been criticized for overstating inflation and therefore scaling up benefits by more than necessary amounts to maintain living standards for retired beneficiaries. The NCRP plan, like other reform plans, would require a downward revision in the CPI, which would raise some net revenue. If the issue were described only in terms of accurate indexation for inflation, then we would not be able to capture this provision. If the Bureau of Labor Statistics does not change the CPI, however, the reform says that benefits will be indexed explicitly to the CPI minus 0.5 percentage points. We model that change as a real cut in benefits. Specifically, real benefits fall at 0.5 percent per year, starting at the age of retirement. Because the benefit schedule is progressive, any cut in benefits would normally be regressive. However, benefits are cut more for those who live longer and continue to experience real benefit cuts each year. Since high-income individuals live longer, this particular form of benefit cut has uncertain effects. As it turns out, the net effect of this provision is somewhat regressive in our model.

Thus, some aspects of the NCRP plan are progressive, and some are regressive. Our calculations below will show the net effects of all these changes together. Table 5.1 also lists a few provisions that are not captured by our model. The NCRP plan would also raise the age for early retirement from sixty-two to sixty-five (to match the three-year increase in the NRA from sixty-seven to seventy). It would extend OASDI coverage to all state and local government employees hired after 1999. Under current law, if a Social Security beneficiary works after normal retirement age, retirement benefits are reduced by $1 for every $3 earned above a certain threshold. This feature is not captured in our model, because we assume no earnings after retirement. The NCRP plan would also eliminate this retirement earnings test for individuals after NRA (seventy).

5.3.3   The Aaron and Reischauer (A&R) Plan

Any reform plan must face fundamental choices about the very nature of Social Security. The current system is partially funded, so a reform could raise revenue and create a fully funded program, or it could return to the original pay-as-you-go (PAYGO) idea. The current system is explicitly a transfer program that redistributes from workers to retirees, to those with low income, to nonearning spouses, and to women (because they live longer). Any reform could choose either to remove these transfer elements or to enhance them.

Rather than make wholesale changes to Social Security, the plan devised by Aaron and Reischauer (1998) would "fix" the current system. It would "close the projected long-term deficit and make Social Security better reflect current social and economic conditions, while preserving Social Security's fundamental character" (96). As a consequence, this plan tinkers with a number of provisions in ways that individually raise a bit of revenue while closing a significant portion of the projected shortfall by investing the trust fund in private debt and equity markets.

The A&R plan is summarized in column (3) of table 5.1. As it turns out, many of these changes appear at the bottom of the column, under features "not captured by our model." The A&R plan would raise the earliest eligibility age (EEA) from sixty-two to sixty-four (to match the currently provided two-year increase in the NRA from sixty-five to sixty-seven). Like other plans, it would cover all new state and local employees. Whereas current law collects income tax on Social Security benefits only above some threshold, the A&R plan would tax Social Security benefits just as if it were a private pension.[28] As mentioned above, the A&R plan would also raise some money by transferring part of the Social Security Trust Fund from government bonds to higher-yielding corporate stocks and bonds. We use only one discount rate, ignoring different risk premia, so we do not capture this provision either. We might note, however, that many of these ignored provisions have no obvious implications for redistribution.

The top of column (3) shows the provisions of the A&R plan that *are* captured in our model. First, this plan would change the number of years of earnings used in the AIME calculation from thirty-five to thirty-eight. Including more low-earning years means that AIME is reduced, and thus benefits are lower. The calculation still drops four years before the AIME calculation, and it still uses three more years (from sixty-four to sixty-seven) to substitute for earlier low-earning years. Thus it drops the seven lowest-earning years to age sixty-seven. Like the NCRP plan, the A&R plan would raise a bit of money by cutting the spousal benefit from one-half to one-third of the benefits of the higher-earning spouse. As mentioned above, the reduction in the number of dropped years is regressive and the reduction in the spousal benefit somewhat progressive—at least by our measurements, according to which each spouse's well-being is based on half of the couple's lifetime income.

Next, the A&R plan makes a change to the "survivor's benefit," which currently allows a widow or widower to receive his or her own benefit or the deceased spouse's benefit (whichever is larger). In the table, this rule is represented by "max (hus, wife)." Instead, the A&R plan would provide three-

---

28. That means it would exempt the amount that was already subjected to income tax (such as the employee's payroll tax share, which comes out of taxable income), but it would tax the rest of social security benefits—since those dollars have not yet been subject to income tax.

quarters of the *combined* benefits of both spouses ("3/4[hus+wife]"). The logic for this change is based on the cost of living for one person compared to the cost for two together. Compared to current law, however, it provides more benefits to some individuals and less to others. If two spouses had the same earnings, for example, then either person's survival benefit would become three-quarters of the total, which is 50 percent *more* than under current law (according to which either person would get half of the total). If a lower-earning spouse had own benefits of less than one-third of those of the higher-earning spouse, then either person's new survivor's benefit would be less than under current law.[29] In our calculations, this particular provision is found to be progressive. As mentioned above, low-income couples tend to have more similar incomes, since both must work at low-paying jobs. Equal incomes gain from this reform provision. Middle- and high-income couples tend to have more disparate incomes, since they can afford for one person to stay at home, and thus gain less or actually lose from this proposal.

Finally, the A&R plan would undertake unspecified corrections in the CPI. The reasoning is the same as that described above, namely, that the current CPI has been criticized for growing too quickly. This plan would leave those corrections to the economics experts, however, and not subtract any number of points from the CPI. With the system fully indexed to an accurate measure of inflation, we assume that real benefits are maintained.

Again, some of these provisions are progressive and some regressive. Most are small, however, and so the overall progressivity of the A&R plan is not expected to differ much from that of current law. As we show below, the A&R plan is slightly more progressive than the current Social Security system.

5.3.4   The Moynihan Plan

In terms of fundamental choices about the nature of Social Security, Senator Moynihan's 1999 reform proposal would head in a different direction. Whereas the 1983 changes raised revenue to generate a partially funded Social Security trust fund, this plan would return to PAYGO. The current trust fund would be drawn down by a temporary *reduction* in the current 12.4 percent OASDI tax rate to 11.4 percent (for the years 1999–2000) and to 10.4 percent (for 2001–2024). Then, when the trust fund is depleted, and that tax on a smaller number of workers is not enough to cover the benefits for a larger number of retirees, the rate would have to rise again to 11.4 percent (for 2025–29), 12.4 percent (for 2030–44), 12.7 percent (for 2045–54), 13.0 percent (2055–59), and 13.4 percent thereafter. These numbers are summarized in the top of column (4) of table 5.1.

---

29. The break-even point is the point at which one's benefit is one-third of the higher-earning spouse's benefit, because $(3/4)(1 + 1/3) = \max(1/3, 1)$.

Since our model considers only the long-run provisions of these reforms, the Moynihan plan must be represented by the 13.4 percent tax rate. We show results with the 13.4 percent rate in our tables below. In the long run, with this rate, overall net tax rates on all individuals are substantially higher than for the other reforms (and higher than for current law). The reason is that this plan disperses the trust fund to those of us in current generations—by lowering *our* overall net tax rates. For this reason, results below also show the effects of the Moynihan plan with the low 10.4 percent rate.

The wage cap was $76,200 in year 2000, and it is projected to reach $82,800 in 2003. As indicated in the second row of the table under the current system, this wage cap will cover about 85 percent of wages. This percentage has been falling, because high wage rates have been growing faster than average wages. The Moynihan plan would raise the wage cap to $97,500 in 2003, which would cover about 87 percent of wages, and it would still be indexed thereafter. We calculate the real increase in the long-run wage cap for our model. This change is progressive, because it collects additional payroll tax from those above the current wage cap. On the other hand, we should note, the increase in the OASDI tax rate to 13.4 percent is regressive, given any wage cap, because it collects only from those below the cap. Again, our model can calculate the net effect on progressivity.

The Moynihan plan also speeds up the currently scheduled increase in the NRA to sixty-seven, and it continues that increase to the age of seventy (for those retiring in 2073 and later). This change is regressive, for three reasons mentioned above: First, individuals pay the regressive payroll tax for more years; second, they receive the progressive benefit schedule for fewer years; third, low-income workers also die sooner, so the fall in their survival probability from age sixty-seven to seventy is greater than for high-income workers.

Because it increases the normal retirement age by three years (from sixty-seven to seventy), the Moynihan plan also increases the number of years of earnings in the AIME calculation by three (from thirty-five to thirty-eight). The lowest ten years of earnings are still ignored. This change is regressive, for reasons mentioned in note 27.

Like the NCRP, the Moynihan plan requires a reduction in the index used to maintain real benefits after retirement. If those corrections are not made within the CPI, then benefits will be indexed by the CPI minus 1 percentage point. We model this change as a 1 percent cut in real benefits each year after retirement.

The bottom of column (4) of the table indicates the provisions of the Moynihan plan that are not captured by our model. Like other reforms, it extends coverage to all new state and local workers. Like the NCRP plan, it eliminates the current earnings test for those beyond the retirement age who work. While the NCRP plan would eliminate this test at age seventy, the Moynihan plan would eliminate it at age sixty-two. Finally, like the

A&R plan, the Moynihan plan would change the income tax to cover all Social Security benefits as if they were private pensions.

5.4 Results

Our initial simulations use the enacted provisions of the Social Security Act, applied to a future cohort born in 1990. Results are presented in table 5.2.The last row shows the overall average *un*discounted taxes paid minus benefits received, in thousands of dollars per person. The reason for showing undiscounted net taxes is to shed some light on the overall solvency of the Social Security system. Our model cannot project actual inflows and outflows, since we do not use demographic forecasts, but a conceptual point can be made about solvency in a world with unchanging demographics: With a constant number of entering twenty-two-year-olds in each of the sex-race-income cells in our model, the undiscounted sum of taxes paid per individual ($103,200) equals the sum of taxes paid by all ages alive at one time. Similarly, the undiscounted sum of benefits ($164,900) is the sum of benefits paid out to all ages alive at one time. On this basis, the current Social Security system loses the difference ($61,700 per twenty-two-year-old) each year.[30]

Column (1) of table 5.2 shows the present value net tax as a fraction of lifetime potential income for each quintile under the current system. This net tax rate rises from 0.62 percent for the lowest-income quintile to 1.01 percent for the highest-income quintile. Thus, current law is progressive, but not uniformly so. The highest net tax rate applies to the middle-income quintile (1.07 percent). The benefit structure is progressive, even on a lifetime basis, but that progressivity is largely offset by the regressive tax system (which exempts earnings above the wage cap) and by various features of the system that tend to favor high-income groups (like the fact that high-income individuals tend to live longer and therefore receive benefits longer).

A large number of recent articles on Social Security reform have dealt with privatization of the system or other large-scale overhauls of the program (e.g., Kotlikoff, Smetters, and Walliser 1998). If complete privatization were to provide actuarially fair returns, with no redistributions between individuals, then the effects of complete privatization in our model are exactly the reverse of those of the current Social Security system. Thus, the results in this first column for the current system can be viewed as the distributional impact of an extreme reform—the repeal of Social Security.

---

30. If we multiply this $61,700 figure by the number of twenty-two-year-olds alive in 1994 (about 3.7 million), we get a total loss of about $228 billion per year. This figure lies between the "low" and the "high" deficit projected by the U.S. Social Security Administration (1998). As mentioned above, their "intermediate" projected deficit for the year 2075 is $480 billion in 1995 dollars, but that includes DI and pertains to a larger population.

Table 5.2   Long-Run Distributional Impacts of Social Security Reform

Lifetime Income Quintile	Net Social Security Tax Rates (%)						
	Current System (1)	Feldstein & Samwick (2)	NCRP (3)	Aaron & Reischauer (4)	Moynihan (with 10.4% payroll tax) (5)	Moynihan (with 13.4% payroll tax) (6)	Equal % Benefit Cut
1	0.62	0.00	1.83	0.68	2.38	4.05	1.56
2	0.74	0.00	1.91	0.95	2.30	3.84	1.59
3	1.07	0.00	2.15	1.25	2.58	4.18	1.89
4	0.96	0.00	1.96	1.15	2.34	3.79	1.70
5	1.01	0.00	1.77	1.15	2.24	3.52	1.60
Changes in Net Social Security Tax Rates from Current System							
1		−0.62	1.21	0.06	1.76	3.43	0.94
2		−0.74	1.17	0.21	1.56	3.10	0.85
3		−1.07	1.08	0.18	1.51	3.11	0.82
4		−0.96	1.00	0.19	1.38	2.83	0.74
5		−1.01	0.76	0.14	1.23	2.51	0.59
Total undiscounted taxes minus benefits, in $ thousands per person	−61.7	0.0	−5.6	−55.4	−8.0	23.1	−30.8

Source: Authors' calculations.

Note: See text for abbreviations.

Because the current system is progressive, its repeal would be a regressive change.

Feldstein and Samwick (1998) do not suggest the repeal of the current system, but instead outline a plan to make it solvent and actuarially fair. Most importantly, their plan deals with the costs of a transition that honors the current promise of benefits to existing generations. That transition does not emerge in our long-run model. If the Feldstein-Samwick plan is actuarially fair in the long run, then it does not take net taxes from anyone. Column (2) of table 5.2 shows these zero net tax rates in the top panel and the change from current law in the bottom panel. To the extent that our calculations accurately reflect the long-run progressivity of the current system, the change to zero tax rates would be a regressive change, but not uniformly regressive.

The results in table 5.2 are illustrated in figure 5.1, where the net tax rate for the current system is the lowest of these six lines, rising from 0.62 percent for the first income group to 1.07 percent for the middle group and 1.01 percent for the high-income group. The Feldstein-Samwick plan would be represented by the horizontal axis, with zero tax rates for all groups.

The NCRP plan has both progressive and regressive elements. It would lower the regressive payroll tax by 2 percentage points and make the benefit schedule more progressive, but it would also cut benefits by raising the retirement age, by including more years of earnings in the benefit calculation, and by reducing the CPI by 0.5 percentage points. Since benefits are generally progressive, these benefit cuts are regressive. The net effects of all these changes are shown for the NCRP plan in column (3) of table 5.2. The net tax rate on the lowest-income group would rise to 1.83 percent, but the rate on the highest-income group would rise to only 1.77 percent. Again, the middle group pays the highest tax rate (2.15 percent). The bottom panel of table 5.2 shows that the increase in tax rate is highest for the group whose income is lowest. Thus, the reform is a regressive change to the current system. On the other hand, figure 5.1 shows that the NCRP system overall is fairly flat, with a net tax rate of around 2 percent of lifetime income for all groups.

The bottom of the NCRP column in table 5.2 shows the annual shortfall. By raising the net tax rate for everyone, the NCRP plan is able to reduce the annual shortfall as measured in our model from $61,700 per person to only $5,600 per person (and provisions that we do not capture may raise the rest of the needed revenue to balance the Social Security budget). Yet (one might ask) if "balance" means that all Social Security benefit payments are covered by payroll taxes, then why is the net tax rate still positive (at about 2 percent of lifetime income)? A zero balance in our model is represented by total taxes equal to benefits without discounting, to represent all cohorts alive at one time. In contrast, the net tax rate in

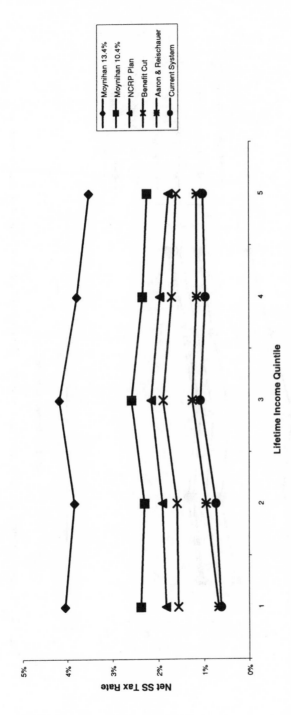

Fig. 5.1 Net social security tax rates under current system and proposed reforms (using 2 percent discount rate)

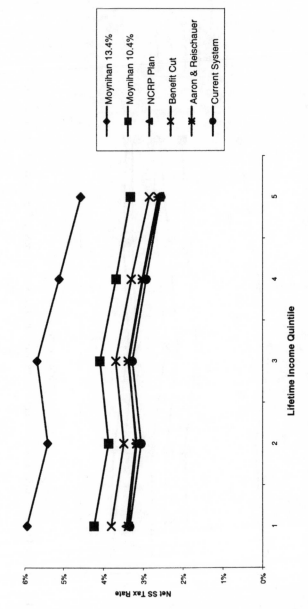

Fig. 5.2 Net social security tax rates under current system and proposed reforms (using 4 percent discount rate)

our model is the discounted present value of one's taxes minus one's own benefits during life. Since taxes come before benefits, discounting means that the present value of taxes outweigh the present value of benefits, for a positive net tax rate.[31]

Aaron and Reischauer (1998) make less dramatic modifications to Social Security. As indicated earlier, they would raise some revenue in ways not captured in our model, and they would reduce benefits by raising the number of years of earnings included in the benefit calculation (from thirty-five to thirty-eight). This provision is regressive in our model. The A&R plan would also cut the spousal benefit from one-half to one-third, and it would change the survivor's benefit to three-fourths of the combined benefits of husband and wife. These changes are both somewhat progressive. Column (4) of table 5.2 shows that the net effect is slightly progressive. The lowest-income group's net tax rate rises only slightly, from 0.62 percent to 0.68 percent, but the highest-income group's net tax rate rises from 1.01 percent to 1.15 percent. In figure 5.1, the A&R plan begins near the current system and raises net tax rates only slightly with income.

The Moynihan plan receives two columns in table 5.2 (and two curves in figure 5.1). Column 5 shows the long-run effects of the Moynihan plan with a 10.4 percent payroll tax (which actually only applies to years 2001–2024). Even with this reduced tax, however, net tax rates all rise to at least 2.3 percent because this plan incorporates major benefit cuts. It raises the retirement age to seventy, includes more low-earning years in the benefit calculations, and reduces indexing by 1 percentage point. Effectively, each person's real benefits are cut by 1 percent per year. Because benefits are progressive, these benefit cuts are regressive. On the other hand, the cut in regressive payroll taxes is progressive. Our table and figure show the net effects, where this version of the Moynihan plan has a very flat net tax rate (2.38 percent on the lowest-income group and 2.24 percent on the highest-income group).[32] By removing the small amount of progressivity of current law, the change is regressive. Tax rates rise by 1.76 percent for the poor group and by 1.23 percent for the rich.

31. However, the net tax rates in this table bear no direct relationship to the annual shortfall shown in the last row. According to the logic in the text, an unfunded PAYGO system would have zero annual deficit but positive net tax rates. In contrast, a fully privatized system would have zero taxes *and* zero benefits, for a zero annual balance and zero net tax rates. A fully funded tax and benefit scheme could have a zero net tax rate overall but positive annual taxes minus benefits. A related problem not captured in these numbers is that a reform plan may be designed to balance the social security budget in a present value sense, and not necessarily in each year of the long run we calculate. The difference is the transition. A plan may employ higher positive net tax rates in the long run just to help pay for the currently promised but unfunded benefits to the current generations.

32. This column is a bit misleading because it uses a short-run tax rate (10.4 percent in 2001–24) with a long-run retirement age (which takes effect in the year 2065). Similarly, the column with the 13.4 percent tax rate probably overstates the effects of this plan. The truth may lie in between.

The other version of the Moynihan plan employs the eventual 13.4 percent tax rate (after year 2060) and is reflected in column (6) of the table. Net tax rates rise even more, ranging from 4.05 percent for the lowest-lifetime-income group to 3.52 percent for the highest-lifetime-income group. Again the change is regressive, to the point that the entire system is now regressive. As shown in the figure, these net tax rates all lie well above those of any other plan. The reason is related to the switch back to PAYGO. This plan depletes the current partial funding of Social Security. Without a trust fund that earns a rate of return, eventual tax rates must be much higher to balance the Social Security budget year by year.

Current law may not be a relevant comparison, however, if it is not sustainable. Even if policy makers omit these reforms and do nothing, the budget shortfall may necessitate eventual cuts in benefits or increases in taxes. Therefore, as an alternative basis of comparison, we also show the effects of a proportionate cut in benefits (in column [7] of table 5.2). Somewhat arbitrarily, we set this benefit cut to eliminate half of the current shortfall in our model. This amount of benefit cut aids comparability, because it places the net tax rates near the middle of the reform plans (see figure 5.1). The result is 18.9 percent less benefits for all individuals.

Because the Social Security benefit formula is progressive, we expect this cut in benefits to be regressive. In fact, the wish to avoid the regressivity of this eventual "forced" cut in benefits would seem to be a reason that policy makers wish to plan ahead by designing their own reforms now. As it turns out, however, this do-nothing approach is no more regressive than the other planned approaches. In table 5.2, the net tax rate rises from 1.56 percent on the poor group to 1.89 percent on the middle group, and then falls back to 1.60 percent on the rich group. In figure 5.1, the line that represents this proportional benefit cut has the same shape as the lines for the reform plans: mostly flat, with some tendency to rise in the middle of the lifetime income distribution.

5.5 Sensitivity Analysis

We now vary some of the crucial assumptions of the model and observe how much these assumptions affect our results. Instead of showing many additional numbers in tables, however, we show only figures. Comparison to figure 5.1, then, reveals important differences.

First, we consider an increase in the discount rate from 2 percent to 4 percent. As discussed in section 5.2.6, this discount rate is supposed to reflect the alternative rate of return available to savers. Most studies of Social Security use a rate like our 2 percent, but Caldwell et al. (1999) and others argue that the rate should be higher. If so, results might more closely resemble the results with a 4 percent discount rate in figure 5.2.

As is immediately evident from a comparison of figures 5.1 and 5.2, an increase in the discount rate makes *all* of these Social Security systems more regressive. Recall that all plans have offsetting effects: Payroll taxes in all plans are regressive (because of the wage cap) and benefits in all plans are progressive (because of the formula). Yet taxes are paid before retirement, and benefits are received after. Therefore, a higher discount rate reduces the weight on these later progressive benefits, and it thereby increases the relative weight on the earlier regressive taxes. Figure 5.2 shows that net tax rates now slope down for the current system and all reform plans. One plan is not really more regressive than another. The order of the plans is about the same as before, with the lowest net tax rates for current law, followed by A&R, the benefit cut, and the Moynihan plan. The Moynihan plan with a 13.4 percent payroll tax rate still has net tax rates significantly above the other plans. One other noteworthy point is that *all* systems have higher net tax rates than in figure 5.1. The increase in the discount rate reduces the present value of taxes, but it reduces the present value of benefits by more.

Second, we consider a redefinition of lifetime income. Up to this point, we have argued that lifetime potential income should include the value of leisure and time spent at home. We wish to classify individuals from those who are well off to those who are not, and that time at home provides part of the well-being of those individuals. Consider, for example, one individual who works forty hours per week at $10 per hour and another individual who works twenty hours per week at $20 per hour. Previous studies that classify individuals by actual earnings would put both of these individuals into the same income group. Instead, we argue that the second individual is "richer" because he or she has the same take-home pay as well as the extra twenty hours per week at home to care for children, cook dinner, clean house, do the gardening, or just relax.

These are the reasons that we assign each individual 4,000 hours per year valued at that individual's wage rate. As a consequence, however, this "potential" income may be about twice the value of actual earnings (of a person who works about 2,000 hours per year). When we use this larger measure of potential earnings in the denominator of our net Social Security tax rate calculation, the resulting net tax rates are lower than in other previous studies.

To make our results more comparable to those from previous studies. figure 5.3 provides net tax rates based on actual earnings. Specifically, the present value of Social Security taxes minus benefits is divided by the present value of actual earnings for each group. We do not reclassify individuals into quintiles based on actual earnings. (For comparability with the basic results in figure 5.1, we return to the 2 percent discount rate of figure 5.1.)

When the measure of income in the denominator is cut approximately in half, the net tax as a fraction of income is about twice the size it was

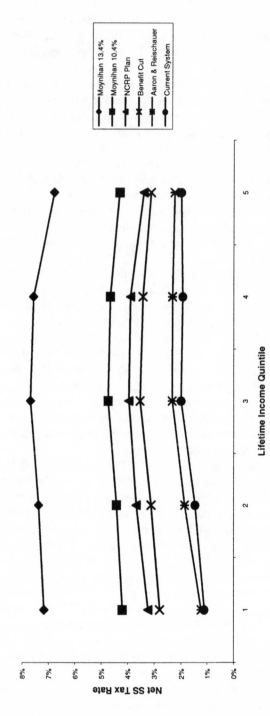

Fig. 5.3 Net social security tax rates under current system and proposed reforms (as a percentage of actual earnings, using 2 percent discount rate)

before. Otherwise, figure 5.3 looks much like figure 5.1. The current Social Security system has the lowest overall net tax rates and is slightly progressive. The A&R plan features net tax rates that are not much higher and slightly more progressive. The proportional benefit cut has the next higher net tax rates, and it is fairly proportional (rather than progressive). The NCRP plan is then followed by the Moynihan plans, where all are approximately proportional. The high-rate Moynihan plan looks a bit more regressive than the others (just as in figure 5.1).

Finally, we consider a different redefinition of lifetime income. Even if all agree that an individual's well-being includes the value of time at home, we could still debate the price at which to value that leisure. Up to this point, leisure has been valued at the individual's wage rate. To the extent that an individual can choose what amount to work, an hour at home must be worth at least that individual's wage rate, or else that person would instead have worked that hour.

A problem with this valuation, however, is that a given hour of leisure activity is worth more to a high-wage person than to a low-wage person. Implicitly, the assumption is that the high-wage person receives more well-being or more enjoyment from each hour of leisure. As an alternative, we consider a measurement based on a common set of prices to evaluate all goods that different individuals receive. This alternative measurement takes the view that a person is classified as well off if he or she receives more goods: more food, more furniture, or more leisure. To determine whether one person's bundle is worth more than another person's bundle, the researcher would use a given price per unit of each good (such as food, furniture, or leisure). Actual income or actual total expenditure *does* value purchased goods at the same prices for all individuals, and it can be augmented to value leisure at the same price for all individuals. To value all units of leisure at the same price, we use the average of all individuals' wage rates. The results are shown in figure 5.4.

With all individuals' time at home valued at the same wage rate, figure 5.4 shows that all Social Security plans look more progressive. To explain this result, note that the revaluation of leisure *reduces* potential income for the high-income group (which raises their net tax rate as a fraction of income) and *raises* potential income for anyone with less than the average wage rate (which lowers their net tax rate as a fraction of income). The important point is simply that the characterization of any tax system as regressive or progressive depends substantially on the definition of "income"—a term for which we have no unambiguous definition.

Otherwise, again, the differences between the plans are similar to those in other figures above. The current system has the lowest overall net tax rates. The A&R plan's tax rates are slightly higher and slightly more progressive. The "benefit cut" is next, followed by the NCRP plan and the

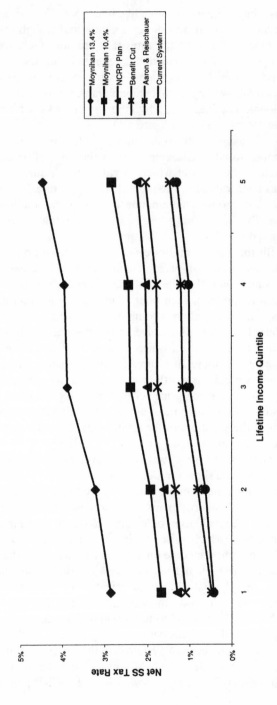

Fig. 5.4 Net social security tax rates under current system and proposed reforms (valuing leisure at average wage rate, using 2 percent discount rate)

Moynihan plan. All look progressive in figure 5.4, but one is not noticeably more or less progressive than any other.

5.6   Conclusion

This chapter uses a lifetime framework to address questions about the progressivity of Social Security and proposed reforms. We use a large sample of diverse individuals to calculate lifetime income, to classify individuals into income quintiles, and then to calculate the present value net tax in each group. We note, however, that this type of calculation does not answer all questions. In addition to redistributing between income groups, Social Security also redistributes between groups based on age, gender, or family size, redistribution not shown in our results. Also not addressed here are questions about effects of Social Security reform on labor supply, savings, and the government budget.

Recent Social Security reform proposals have many large apparent differences. Some would raise revenue to fund all future promises, and others would deplete the current partial trust fund and return to PAYGO financing. Some would remove implicit transfers between groups, and others would enhance them. Some cut the payroll tax, and others increase it. The retirement age may be raised or not, and the benefit formula may be changed or not.

In a lifetime context, we find that these provisions tend to offset each other's effects on progressivity. Each plan has both regressive and progressive elements, so the net effect is not necessarily a great deal different from the current system. Despite these many differences between the reform plans, we find that they have similar effects on overall progressivity. In our basic calculations, the slightly progressive current system would be slightly more progressive in the A&R plan, and it would become slightly regressive in each of the other plans. The pattern of progressivity is affected by alternative assumptions, but it is affected in similar ways for the current system and proposed reforms. None of these reforms greatly alters the current degree of progressivity on a lifetime basis.

Appendix 5A
Data and Methodology

This appendix is divided into five parts, describing respectively the selection of the sample from the PSID, the estimation of log wage regressions and calculation of potential lifetime earnings, the estimation of earnings profiles, the derivation of income-differentiated mortality, and the calculation of Social Security benefits.

Data and Sample Selection

We use the PSID for the years 1968 to 1989, which gives us twenty-two years of data for a sample of the population. We select our sample based on three criteria. First, our sample members are not taken from the low-income subsample of the PSID. While the data contain weights so that the low-income sample can be merged with the representative sample, we felt that the representative sample provided sufficient data for our purposes. Second, we require that sample members remain in the sample for the entire period. Survey respondents may have died, or may have simply decided that the survey was no longer worth their time, and we judged that including individuals such as these was not worth the possible distortion in the data and additional computational work required to track these individuals. Third, we only include individuals whose relationship to head status did not change during the sample period.

Because of these criteria, we cut off a group of individuals who were less than thirty in 1968. We disproportionately eliminate women from the sample, because the PSID always classifies the man of a couple as the head of household. A single man who marries during the period remains head of household and is included in our sample, but a single woman who marries does not maintain the same relationship to head status for the whole period and would be excluded.

Our final sample consists of 1,086 heads and 700 wives. It captures 66 percent of the original, non–low-income PSID sample, including 92 percent of heads and 66 percent of wives. Because we did not extract data for those who dropped out of the sample or changed their relationship to head status, we cannot formally test whether their exclusion biases the parameters in our wage and earnings regressions. As reflected in table 5A.1, however, the observable characteristics of our sample are remarkably similar to the original sample. We therefore believe it is unlikely that our econometric estimates are significantly biased, or that our sample selection skews the conclusions we draw about the progressivity of the Social Security system and various reform proposals.

Log Wage Regressions and the Calculation of Potential Lifetime Income

As our analysis is intended to reflect a steady state, we abstract from real economic growth that occurred during our sample period. We want to isolate life-cycle movements in wages so that our wage profiles will not be specific to one generation during a particular time frame. Adjusting for economic growth and inflation yields lifetime wage profiles that can be used to analyze the distributional impact of Social Security in a more general, structural sense. We therefore adjust the nominal wage rate using

Table 5A.1   **Sample Selection**

	Original PSID Sample	Sample Used in Analysis
Number of people	2,780	1,786
Under age 30 (%)	36	25
Education of head (%)		
High school diploma	33	32
College degree	12	12
Education of wife (%)		
High school diploma	46	50
College degree	8	7
Race of head (%)		
White	92	94
Black	7	5

the Social Security Administration's Average Wage Index, which reflects growth in average nominal wages over the sample period. Using this index to deflate wages removes the effects of both inflation and real growth in wages.

We want to estimate a separate wage regression for working wives and household heads, but we question the idea of pooling the positive observations of the wives who work consistently throughout the sample with those who work only occasionally. We found that a woman would have to work at least 750 hours a year throughout her working life, an amount slightly less than half time in order for own Social Security benefits to be greater than the spousal benefits she could receive based on her husband's earnings (assuming she earns the same wage as her husband). Thus, we divide the working wives into two groups based on whether or not they averaged at least 750 hours of work per year throughout the sample. We ran our log wage regressions separately for the two groups, and then ran another one pooling the two groups, in order to perform an F-test. The results suggest that these two groups should indeed be analyzed separately. We therefore estimate three log wage regressions: for household heads, habitually working wives, and occasionally working wives.

We regress the log of the wage rate on an individual fixed effect and other variables like age, age squared, and age cubed. Because we have a fixed effect for each individual, we cannot use variables that do not vary over time (like race or gender). However, we do include age interacted with education, race, and gender. For the heads of household, we use all positive observations of wages, which gives us 19,130 observations on our 1,086 heads. The results of this regression are shown in table 5A.2. Using the resulting fixed effects and coefficients, we then fill in missing observations during the sample period and observations outside the sample period so that each individual has a wage rate for every year of his entire economic life from age twenty-two to sixty-six.

Table 5A.2   Log Wage Regression for Heads of Household

Independent Variable	Coefficient	T-Statistic
Age	0.1343	6.26
Age^2	−0.003313	−8.53
Age^3	0.000026	9.55
Age × education	0.003669	4.87
Age^2 × education	−0.0000326	−4.52
Age × female	−0.0239	−1.89
Age^2 × female	0.000306	2.11
Age × white	0.0167	1.32
Age^2 × white	−0.000240	−1.67
Individuals		1,086
N		19,130
Adjusted R^2		0.57

For each of the two groups of working women, we take all positive observations and regress the log of the wage rate on an individual fixed effect and variables for age and the interaction between age and education. The PSID does not have a race variable for the wives in the sample. For the wives who averaged more than 750 hours of work annually, we have 5,413 observations on 311 women. for those who work occasionally, but less than 750 hours, we have 2,292 observations on 296 wives. The results of the log wage regressions for the two groups of working wives can be found in table 5A.3. For these two groups, we again use the estimated fixed effects and coefficients to fill in missing observations within the sample and to simulate observations outside the sample, so that each woman has a complete wage profile. To each of the ninety-three women who did not work at all we assign the median fixed effect from the occasional workers and then use the coefficients from this group's regression to fill in an entire profile of potential hourly wages. Using the wage profile for each individual, we calculate the present value of potential lifetime income. We use this income to delineate quintiles.

The Estimation of Earnings Profiles

For each of our five lifetimes income quintiles, we estimate three new regressions for actual earnings of heads, habitually working wives, and part-time working wives. Our dependent variable is actual annual earnings. As above, we deflate earnings by the Social Security Administration's Average Wage Index to adjust for both inflation and real economic growth. Since earnings represent a continuous variable truncated at zero, we use a tobit framework for estimation. Here we assume that earnings are the product of optimal hours of work and a wage rate that is exogenous to the individual. Optimal hours of work can be positive or negative, so optimal earnings can be described as a latent variable, y^*:

Table 5A.3   **Log Wage Regressions for Wives**

Independent Variable	Habitual Workers	T-Statistic	Occasional Workers	T-Statistic
Age	0.0493	1.25	0.0104	0.102
Age²	−0.000647	−0.949	0.000985	0.522
Age³	0.0000018	0.399	−0.0000111	−1.03
Age × education	−0.000252	−0.106	−0.00538	−0.965
Age² × education	0.0000085	0.344	0.0000262	0.419
Individuals		311		296
N		5,413		2,292
Adjusted R²		0.55		0.36

$$y_i^* = \mathbf{X}_i \beta + \varepsilon_i \, ,$$

where $\mathbf{X}$ is a vector of personal characteristics that determine the individual's wage and desired hours of work. We assume that observations of zero hours worked imply that desired hours of work are less than or equal to zero. Actual earnings, y, are observed only if y^* is greater than zero. If y^* is less than or equal to zero, then actual earnings are zero:

$$y_i = y_i^* \quad \text{if} \quad y_i^* > 0$$

$$y_i = 0 \quad \text{if} \quad y_i^* \le 0 \, .$$

In the first stage described above, in which we divide people into lifetime income quintiles, our dependent variable was log wages. Thus we use generalized least squares estimation with individual fixed effects. In this second stage, the tobit model is nonlinear. We judged that the additional programming effort to include fixed effects in our tobit estimation was not worth while, given that such estimation also implies inconsistent parameter estimates (Heckman and MaCurdy 1980). By excluding fixed effects in this stage, we are able to include race, gender, and education variables in the earnings regressions without interacting them with age. For each regression for the heads of household, we begin with independent variables for age, age squared, age cubed, education, education squared, the product of age and education, a dummy variable for whether the head is female, age interacted with the female dummy, and a dummy for whether the head is white. We then eliminate variables that are insignificant. The results of the regressions for heads can be found in table 5A.4. For wives who averaged more than 750 hours of work a year, we begin with age, age squared, age cubed, education, education squared and the product of age and education. We again eliminate the insignificant regressors. Results for these regressions can be found in table 5A.5. We follow a similar procedure for

Table 5A.4   Tobit Earnings Regressions for Heads

Independent Variable	(Poorest) First Quintile	Second Quintile	Third Quintile	Fourth Quintile	(Richest) Fifth Quintile
Constant	-8,132.46	-30,327.00	-2,488.82	-85,422.40	-11,116.00
	(1.76)	(6.13)	(10.20)	(12.75)	(5.83)
Age	1,059.26	1,961.75	2,389.17	4,521.45	6,722.26
	(5.50)	(9.92)	(7.82)	(22.55)	(12.54)
Age^2	-13.64	-23.02	-35.43	-50.39	-90.61
	(6.64)	(10.61)	(14.62)	(22.44)	(20.95)
Age × education			54.67		107.59
			(4.72)		(4.85)
Education	636.43	2,069.38	-3,554.69	2,811.77	-1,912.73
	(6.03)	(4.93)	(2.96)	(3.77)	(1.79)
Education^2	-5.45	-60.97	84.76	-93.01	
	(5.35)	(3.25)	(2.47)	(3.18)	
Female	-15,432.50	-36,378.60	-8,338.69	-7,919.65	-28,415.50
	(5.46)	(5.73)	(5.80)	(5.05)	(12.22)
Age × female	148.24	548.23			
	(2.73)	(4.53)			
White	1,785.82		2,505.66	5,242.61	13,890.80
	(2.63)		(1.91)	(3.59)	(5.19)
Sigma	15,012.6	16,429.6	17,149.2	18,262.5	34,386.6
	(81.64)	(85.09)	(84.32)	(89.81)	(92.16)
% positive observations	90	93	95	96	95

Notes: T-statistics are in parentheses. Sigma is the standard error of the regression.

Table 5A.5   Tobit Earnings Regressions for Habitually Working Wives

Independent Variable	(Poorest) First Quintile	Second Quintile	Third Quintile	Fourth Quintile	(Richest) Fifth Quintile
Constant	−14,128.30	−4,324.50	17,493.00	22,901.90	29,809.20
	(2.53)	(0.59)	(1.18)	(1.11)	(0.54)
Age	1,100.17	947.28	−2,154.25	−4,597.56	−11,867.60
	(7.62)	(4.56)	(1.98)	(3.09)	(5.75)
Age^2	−12.60	−15.03	75.45	142.90	333.48
	(9.51)	(7.52)	(2.91)	(3.97)	(6.79)
Age^3			−0.68		−2.85
			(3.44)		(7.56)
Age × education	10.33	46.05		−1.30	
	(1.38)	(3.74)		(4.64)	
Education	−1,371.47	−1,788.95	190.00	3,522.40	15,155.10
	(2.27)	(3.06)	(1.52)	(3.39)	(2.14)
$Education^2$	64.97			−88.25	−510.36
	(3.18)			(2.13)	(2.10)
Sigma	6,392.47	8,777.50	10,216.40	11,548.40	15,471.30
	(52.55)	(46.22)	(48.26)	(39.36)	(37.76)
% positive observations	84	83	84	85	84

Notes: *T*-statistics are in parentheses. Sigma is the standard error of the regression.

wives who average less than 750 hours of work per year, and these results can be found in table 5A.6.

To simulate out-of-sample observations, we multiply the independent variables of each individual by the appropriate coefficients from his or her group's earnings regression. In addition, we include a random component, which we obtain by using the estimated standard error of each group's regression (shown in tables 5A.4–5A.6) to generate a normally distributed random variable. This random component is intended to represent unforeseen circumstances that affect earnings. It also means that individuals with the same observed characteristics will not have exactly the same earnings profile. Simulated earning observations are thus calculated as

$$\hat{y}_i = \mathbf{X}_i \hat{\beta} + \hat{\varepsilon}_i \, ,$$

where $\hat{\beta}$ is the vector of estimated coefficients from our earnings regressions, and $\hat{\varepsilon}_i$ is the random component obtained by using the standard error of the regression to generate a random variable. Using this procedure, both positive and zero observations are generated. We found that the number of zeros generated for each group is consistent with the number of zero observations observed for that group during the sample years.

Derivation of Extended, Income-Differentiated Mortality

To extend the mortality tables from age eighty-five through ninety-nine, we make three assumptions. First, we assume that the probability of remaining alive beyond age eighty-five decreases annually by a constant amount (Faber and Wade 1983). Second, we set to zero the probability of remaining alive after age ninety-nine. This age seems a reasonable cut-off point, since less than 0.7 percent of all Social Security beneficiaries are older than ninety-five (U.S. Social Security Administration 1997). Third, given these two conditions, we find the constant annual change in the probability each year for each sex-race group such that the resulting set of probabilities yields the same life expectancy at age eighty-five as in the *Vital Statistics* (U.S. Department of Health and Human Services 1993).

Table 7 in Rogot et al. (1992) shows information on actual deaths in the sample for each annual income group, within each race-sex-age group. For example, consider white males, ages twenty-five to thirty-four. For each range of income (e.g., $10,000 to $14,999 in 1980 dollars), their table shows the number of individuals in their sample ($N = 14,563$), the number of observed deaths during the sample period ($O = 115$), and the number of deaths that would be expected if all income groups had the same mortality rate ($E = 92.2$). They then divide to calculate the Observed/Expected ratio ($O/E = 1.25$). Actual deaths in that low-income group are 25 percent higher than what would be expected using tables not differentiated by income.

We know the annual income of every individual in our PSID sample, so

Table 5A.6   Tobit Earnings Regressions for Part-time Working Wives

Independent Variable	(Poorest) First Quintile	Second Quintile	Third Quintile	Fourth Quintile	(Richest) Fifth Quintile
Constant	2,738.87	2,049.33	−27,560.40	−29,957.00	108,105.00
	(1.06)	(0.13)	(2.83)	(5.88)	(4.26)
Age	−68.30	−2,970.23	1,505.06	739.21	−10,479.20
	(1.58)	(3.14)	(5.60)	(5.03)	(5.72)
Age^2		86.98	−16.69	−9.12	267.93
		(4.06)	(5.73)	(5.49)	(6.28)
Age^3		−0.69			−2.156
		(4.30)			(6.69)
Age × education		−50.12			
		(3.59)			
Education	−409.04	4,947.28	−2,579.50	1,870.71	1,219.79
	(2.96)	(4.24)	(1.78)	(2.59)	(7.05)
Education^2		−119.18	138.56	−58.73	−12.19
		(2.86)	(2.25)	(2.01)	(7.53)
Sigma	9,067.14	6,708.64	9,759.96	7,926.30	12,086.00
	(17.96)	(25.78)	(24.70)	(35.60)	(30.62)
% positive observations	31	28	26	39	34

Notes: *T*-statistics are in parentheses. Sigma is the standard error of the regression.

we need to exclude the "unknown income" category from the table in Rogot et al. (1992). If we simply ignored this category, the overall O/E ratio would not be 1.0 for all income groups together. For this reason, we recalculate the expected deaths based on the subset of their individuals for which income is known, and recalculate O/E ratios for each group. The average of these new O/E ratios is 1.0, as desired. We then apply the appropriate ratio to each cell. Results for twenty-five to thirty-four-year-olds are shown in the top half of table 5A.7.

Finally, since annual income is volatile, we do not want to apply these annual-income-differentiated O/E ratios to the annual income of each person each year. Instead, we base differential mortality on lifetime income, in three steps. First, after we compute the present value of lifetime income for each of the 1,786 individuals in our PSID sample, we assign each a ranking compared to all individuals in our sample. For example, an individual whose lifetime income ranks 432 our of the 1,786 individuals is ranked in the 24th percentile. Second, for each of the annual income groups in table 5A.7, we likewise determine percentile rankings based on income (shown in the third column). Third, for each individual in our sample, we match the percentile of his or her lifetime income to the percentile for the same age-race-sex category in table 5A.7. For example, a white female aged twenty-seven who has lifetime income at the 24th percentile would be matched to the $10,000–14,999 annual income group (which lies between the 18th percentile and the 36th percentile). That individual would then be assigned that group's O/E ratio for white females (1.17). Finally, this ratio is used to scale the probability of death for that individual's age, sex, and race in the *Vital Statistics* (which are not differentiated by income).

A remaining problem, however, is related to causality: Our procedure essentially uses the individual's income as a determinant of death, even though the annual income levels in table 5A.7 may be determined in part by illness immediately preceding death. This problem is somewhat mitigated by the fact that the CPS data used by Rogot et al. (1992) is based on total combined family income, rather than just the decedent's income.

Calculation of Social Security Benefits

Every variable in this appendix is specific to each individual, but we drop the index i for expositional simplicity. For an unmarried individual, the Social Security benefit at age j is

$$\text{BEN}_j = \text{PIA}_j \times \text{CPI}_{62,j},$$

where PIA is the primary insurance amount and $\text{CPI}_{62,j}$ is the cumulative inflation index from age sixty-two to the age at which the benefit is computed. Then the mortality-adjusted benefit is

Table 5A.7   **Ratio of Observed Deaths to Expected Deaths (O/E) for Each Race-Sex Group**

Annual Family Income	Number (N)	Percentile	O/E White Male	O/E White Female	O/E Other Male	O/E Other Female
		Ages 25–34				
< $5,000	11,670	6.31	1.68	1.51	1.54	1.86
$5,000–9,999	22,085	18.25	1.20	0.97	0.81	1.01
$10,000–14,999	33,331	36.27	1.28	1.17	1.36	1.01
$15,000–19,999	32,231	53.70	1.12	0.76	0.71	0.84
$20,000–24,999	30,729	70.31	0.80	0.97	0.92	0.36
$25,000–49,999	48,375	96.47	0.73	0.94	0.72	0.44
> $49,999	6,529		0.61	1.15	0.72	0.44
N	184,950		81,461	85,047	7,752	10,690
		Ages 65–74				
< $5,000	13,386	6.65	1.39	1.23	1.15	1.06
$5,000–9,999	20,418	49.83	1.19	1.06	0.99	1.00
$10,000–14,999	13,774	70.13	0.98	0.88	0.95	0.85
$15,000–19,999	7,082	80.57	0.75	0.93	0.79	0.91
$20,000–24,999	4,868	87.75	0.79	0.74	0.92	0.85
$25,000–49,999	6,669	97.62	0.73	0.80	0.79	0.87
> $49,999	1,614		0.59	0.79	0.79	0.87
N	67,841		27,245	34,727	2,452	3,417

Source: Rogot et al. (1992, table 7).
Note: The "expected" number of deaths is based on the overall death rate within the age-sex-race category, not differentiated by income, while "observed" deaths are the actual number of deaths in each income group.

$$E_{22}(\text{BEN}_j) = \text{BEN}_j \times P_j ,$$

where $E_{22}(\text{BEN}_j)$ is the expected value at age twenty-two of the benefit to be received at age j, and P_j is the conditional probability of survival to age j, given survival to age twenty-two. For married individuals, the basic benefit is computed in the same manner. We compute the spousal benefit for the wife (or analogously, the husband) as

$$\text{SpBEN}_j = 0.5 \times \text{SBEN}_{js} ,$$

where SpBEN_j is the spousal benefit at wife's age j, SBEN_{js} is the husband's PIA adjusted for inflation to age js, and js is the husband's age when the wife is age j. Similarly, we calculate the survivor benefit as

$$\text{SurvBEN}_j = \text{SBEN}_{js} ,$$

where SurvBEN_j is the wife's survivor benefit after the death of the husband. If the other spouse is alive, we assume that a married individual receives the greater of his or her own benefit (BEN) or the spousal benefit (SpBEN). If the other spouse is deceased, the individual receives the greater of his or her own benefit (BEN) or the survivor benefit (SurvBEN). Using PH_j and PW_j for the husband's and wife's survival probabilities, the husband's mortality-adjusted benefit is

$$E_{22}(HBEN_j) = PH_j[PW_j \, Max(BEN_j, SpBEN_j)$$
$$+ (1 - PW_j) \, Max(BEN_j, SurvBEN_j)],$$

where $E_{22}(HBEN_j)$ is the expected value at age twenty-two of the husband's benefit. This expected value includes only the dollars going directly to husband. A symmetrical calculation is made to determine the wife's mortality-adjusted benefit:

$$E_{22}(WBEN_j) = PW_j[PH_j \, Max(BEN_j, SpBEN_j)$$
$$+ (1 - PH_j) \, Max(BEN_j, SurvBEN_j)].$$

We then compute the present value of expected taxes and benefits at age twenty-two for each individual, using alternative values for the constant real discount rate r:

$$PVTAX = \sum_j \frac{E_{22}(SST_j)}{(1 + r)^{j-22}},$$

$$PVBEN = \sum_j \frac{E_{22}(BEN_j)}{(1 + r)^{j-22}}.$$

References

Aaron, Henry J. 1977. Demographic effects on the equity of Social Security benefits. In *The economics of public services,* ed. M. Feldstein and R. P. Inman, 151–73. London: Macmillan.
Aaron, Henry J., and Robert D. Reischauer. 1998. *Countdown to reform.* New York: Century Foundation Press.
Altig, David, Alan J. Auerbach, Laurence J. Kotlikoff, Kent A. Smetters, and Jan Walliser. 1997. Simulating U.S. tax reform. Washington, D.C.: Congressional Budget Office.
Auerbach, Alan J., and Laurence J. Kotlikoff. 1987. *Dynamic fiscal policy.* New York: Cambridge University Press.
Boskin, Michael J., Laurence J. Kotlikoff, Douglas J. Puffert, and John B. Shoven. 1987. Social Security: A financial appraisal across and within generations. *National Tax Journal* 40 (March): 19–34.
Burkhauser, Richard V., and Jennifer Warlick. 1981. Disentangling the annuity from the redistributive aspects of Social Security. *Review of Income and Wealth* 27 (December): 401–21.
Caldwell, Steven, Melissa Favreault, Alla Gantman, Jagdeesh Gokhale, Thomas Johnson, and Laurence J. Kotlikoff. 1999. Social Security's treatment of postwar

Americans. *Tax policy and the economy,* vol. 13, ed. James M. Poterba, 109–48. Cambridge, Mass: MIT Press.

Coronado, Julia Lynn, Don Fullerton, and Thomas Glass. 1999. Distributional impacts of proposed changes to the Social Security system. *Tax policy and the economy,* vol. 13, ed. James M. Poterba, 149–86. Cambridge, Mass.: MIT Press.

———. 2000. The progressivity of Social Security. NBER Working Paper no. 7520. Cambridge, Mass.: National Bureau of Economic Research, February.

Duggan, James E., Robert Gillingham, and John S. Greenlees. 1993. Returns paid to early Social Security cohorts. *Contemporary Policy Issues* 11 (October): 1–13.

———. 1995. Progressive returns to Social Security? An answer from Social Security records. Research paper no. 9501. Washington, D.C.: U.S. Treasury Department, Office of Economic Policy.

Duleep, Harriett Orcutt. 1986. Measuring the effect of income on adult mortality using the longitudinal administrative record data. *Journal of Human Resources* 21 (spring).

Faber, Joseph F., and Alice H. Wade. 1983. *Life tables for the United States: 1900–2050.* Actuarial Study no. 89. Washington, D.C.: Social Security Administration, Office of the Actuary.

Feldstein, Martin, and Andrew Samwick. 1998. The transition path in privatizing Social Security. In *Privatizing Social Security,* ed. Martin Feldstein, 215–63. Chicago: University of Chicago Press.

Flowers, Marilyn, and John B. Horowitz. 1993. Distributional implications of the Social Security spouse benefit. *Southern Economic Journal* 60 (October): 490–94.

Fox, Alan. 1982. Earnings replacement rates and total income: Findings from the retirement history study. *Social Security Bulletin* 45 (October): 3–23.

Fullerton, Don, and Diane Lim Rogers. 1993. *Who bears the lifetime tax burden?* Washington, D.C.: Brookings Institution.

Garrett, Daniel M. 1995. The effects of differential mortality rates on the progressivity of Social Security. *Economic Inquiry* 7 (July): 457–75.

Geanokopolos, John, Olivia S. Mitchell, and Stephen P. Zeldes. 1998. Social Security money's worth. NBER Working Paper no. 6722. Cambridge, Mass.: National Bureau of Economic Research, September.

Gramlich, Edward M. 1996. Different approaches for dealing with Social Security. *Journal of Economic Perspectives* 10 (summer): 55–66.

Hamermesh, Daniel S., and Albert Rees. 1993. *The economics of work and pay.* New York: Harper Collins College Publishers.

Heckman, James J., and Thomas E. MaCurdy. 1980. A life cycle model of female labor supply. *Review of Economics Studies* 47 (January): 47–74.

Hurd, Michael D., and John B. Shoven. 1985. The distributional impact of Social Security. In *Pensions, labor, and individual choice,* ed. David A. Wise. Chicago: University of Chicago Press.

Ibbotson Associates. 1998. *Stocks, bonds, bells, and inflation 1998 yearbook.* Chicago: Ibbotson Associates.

Kotlikoff, Laurence J., Kent A. Smetters, and Jan Walliser. 1998. Social Security: Privatization and progressivity. *American Economic Review* 88 (May): 137–41.

Lee, Julie, Mark McClellan, and Jonathan Skinner. 1999. Who benefits from Medicare? In *Tax Policy and the Economy* 13, ed. James M. Poterba, chap. 3. Cambridge, Mass.: MIT Press.

Moynihan, Daniel Patrick. 1999. Social Security Solvency Act of 1998: Brief description of provisions. Washington, D.C.: U.S. Senate. Unpublished paper.

Myers, Robert J., and Bruce D. Schobel. 1983. A money's-worth analysis of Social Security retirement benefits. *Society of Actuaries Transactions* 35 (October): 533–61.

National Commission on Retirement Policy (NCRP). 1999. The twenty-first century retirement security plan. Washington, D.C.: Center for Strategic and International Studies.

Nelissen, Jan H. M. 1998. Annual versus lifetime income redistribution by Social Security. *Journal of Public Economics* 68 (May): 223–49.

Panis, Constantijn W. A., and Lee A. Lillard. 1996. Socioeconomic differentials in the returns to Social Security. RAND Labor and Population Program Working Paper Series no. 96–05. Santa Monica, Calif.: RAND Distribution Services.

Pechman, Joseph A., and Benjamin A. Okner. 1974. *Who bears the tax burden?* Washington, D.C.: Brookings Institution.

Rofman, Rafel Paulino. 1993. *Social Security and income distribution: Mortality and equity in pension plans.* Ph.D. diss. University of California, Berkeley.

Rogot, Eugene, Paul D. Sorlie, Norman J. Johnson, and Catherine Schmitt. 1992. *A mortality study of 1.3 million persons by demographic, social, and economic factors: 1979–1985 follow-up.* NIH Publication no. 92–3297. Bethesda, Md.: National Institutes of Health.

Steuerle, C. Eugene, and Jon M. Bakija. 1994. *Retooling Social Security for the twenty-first century: Right and wrong approaches to reform.* Washington, D.C.: Urban Institute Press.

U.S. Congressional Budget Office. 1999. *Raising the earliest age for Social Security benefits.* Washington, D.C.: U.S. Congressional Budget Office.

U.S. Department of Health and Human Services. 1993. *Vital statistics of the United States: 1989.* Hyattsville, Md.: Public Health Service, Centers for Disease Control and Prevention, National Center for Health Statistics.

U.S. Social Security Administration. 1997. *Annual statistical supplement, 1997.* Washington, D.C.: GPO.

———. 1998. *The 1998 annual report of the board of trustees of the Federal Old Age and Survivors Insurance and Disability Insurance Trust Funds.* Washington, D.C.: GPO.

Williams, Roberton C. III. 1998. Equity in Social Security benefit determination: The effect of ignoring some working years. Department of economics, Stanford University. Unpublished paper.

Comment   Stephen C. Goss

This chapter presents an analysis of the progressivity of the Social Security Old Age, and Survivors Insurance (OASI) program across groups separated by the level of lifetime potential earnings. The authors calculate the net Social Security tax (the difference between the present values of taxes paid and benefits receive) under present law and under four proposals designed to restore long-range solvency for OASDI. The net tax is expressed in relative terms, as a percentage of the lifetime potential earnings for each group, and is referred to as a net tax rate. Progressivity is defined as the state in which the net tax rate rises as lifetime potential income rises.

This chapter makes a real contribution to the analysis of progressivity

Stephen C. Goss is chief actuary of the U.S. Social Security Administration.

in Social Security, providing a potentially useful measure for assessing the degree of progressivity across proposed formulations of Social Security. This kind of assessment should help policy makers achieve a balanced understanding of the implications of different reform proposals.

This discussion reviews briefly the measures of money's worth that have evolved and how these measures have provided a basis for assessing progressivity in the Social Security program. Finally, I make a number of suggestions for improving the calculations using this approach and for the specific calculations presented in this chapter.

Measures of Money's Worth

The net tax (the negative of the "net subsidy" referred to by Steuerle and Bakija 1994) is one of a family of "money's worth" measures. Another, the "money's worth ratio," is the ratio of the present value of expected benefits to expected taxes. Like the net tax, the money's worth ratio requires selection of a discount rate. In each case, the benefits under the plan in question are being effectively compared to the benefits that could have been achieved by investing the same taxes in a defined-contribution account that realized a rate of return equal to the assumed discount rate.

A third measure is the internal rate of return, i.e., the constant real rate of return on taxes for each generation that would just allow the taxes to pay for benefits under the plan. If the internal rate of return is less than the assumed discount rate for the other measures, then the net tax is positive and the money's worth ratio is less than 1.0. Comprehensive estimates using each of these three measures for a range of proposals were presented in appendix 2 of volume 1 of the report of the 1994–96 Advisory Council on Social Security.

All of these measures are sensitive to accurate and consistent measurement of both taxes and benefits. Because these measures compare the differences between two large values (taxes and benefits) that tend to be fairly similar in size, even small inconsistencies can be magnified into large errors.

Measurement of Progressivity

Progressivity may be assessed in a number of ways. A plan with a decreasing internal rate of return (or a decreasing money's worth ratio) as the earnings level increases has traditionally been referred to as progressive. This kind of progressivity is observed for the current U.S. Social Security program even though the payroll tax, taken alone, is regressive. (Earnings above $72,600 are not taxed for 1999.) The regressivity of the tax is irrelevant in this case because earnings above the taxable maximum amount are not considered in computing benefits.

Steuerle and Bakija (1994) used the net subsidy to illustrate that for the first several decades during which the OASDI program was maturing, the net subsidies were greater for high earners than low earners, even though internal rates of return and money's worth ratios were lower for high earners. This implied a kind of regressivity of the program even though standard analysis of internal rates of return indicated otherwise. Use of the net subsidy concept in analyzing progressivity assumes that amounts of taxes and benefits that are equal in discounted present value can be ignored. Thus, the difference between discounted benefits and taxes is taken to represent the net gain or loss (subsidy or tax).

The authors of this paper have transformed the net tax (net subsidy) to a relative form, the net tax rate, which is far more useful for assessing progressivity than is the net tax itself. The authors choose to divide the net tax by *total potential* lifetime earnings and categorize workers with the same measure.

This choice has the effect of portraying a program with a maximum taxable amount as less progressive at higher earnings levels than does the internal rate of return. If, for example, we had a program that provided a money's worth ratio of 0.8 for all participants, this would mean a net tax of 20 percent of the present value of each worker's taxes. With a 10 percent payroll tax rate, this would then mean a net tax rate of 2 percent of taxable earnings for all workers, indicating a program that is neither progressive nor regressive. However, with the authors' definition of the net tax rate, a worker with a lifetime earnings level that is double the taxable limit would have a net tax rate of only 1 percent, which suggests a regressive program.

In addition, the use of potential rather than actual earnings to categorize workers dampens the extent to which the current benefit formula appears to be progressive. Under this approach, a worker who works only twenty years and thus benefits from the weighted benefit formula is categorized as if he or she had worked at the same wage rate for all years from entry into the workforce until retirement. This has the effect of diluting the tendency for lower benefit-to-tax ratios in the class of high-lifetime-income workers. The authors provide an illustration of the effect of using actual rather than taxable earnings in the denominator of the net tax rate in figure 5.3. It is unclear whether workers were reclassified on the basis of lifetime actual rather than potential earnings. If not, it would be useful to add a figure with this reclassification.

For the sake of comparison (sensitivity analysis), it would also be useful to add a graph showing net tax rates where the net tax is divided by actual taxable earnings. This would isolate the tendency to show regressivity at higher earnings levels from the inclusion of nontaxable earnings. It would include only the tendency toward regressivity that is due to different mortality assumed by earnings class. A further graph assuming no difference in mortality by income level would also isolate this effect.

Unlike the internal rate of return and the money's worth ratio, the authors' choice of the net tax rate (as percent of total earnings) translates the regressivity of the tax alone into the program itself. Doing this is consistent with a view that any net tax that is needed to support the program should be assessed proportionally on *total* earnings, unlimited by the program taxable maximum. Consistent with this view, however, would be an intent to distribute any net subsidy (if the net tax is in aggregate negative) proportionally by total rather than taxable earnings. As with measures of money's worth, assessment of progressivity is extremely sensitive to proper and consistent measurement of the values of benefits and taxes.

Progressivity for the Whole Program

The Social Security program is a complex and highly integrated package of benefits, so it is very difficult to separate out particular benefits and the associated taxes. As discussed below, money's worth analysis and progressivity analysis are best performed for the program as a whole. This chapter, like most analyses of Social Security, focuses only on retirement benefits. Because workers with lower earnings have not only higher mortality but also higher disability incidence, focusing only on retirement benefits understates the overall progressivity of the Social Security program. If analysis cannot readily be extended to include expected disability benefits, then the effect of this omission should be described.

Measurement of Benefits and Taxes

In developing a measure like the net tax rate, accurate and consistent measurement of taxes and benefits is critical. While the intention of the authors is primarily to analyze progressivity, the absolute levels of their estimated net tax rates provide a meaningful measure of money's worth, whether intentional or not. The absolute level of the net tax rates is very sensitive to any bias in estimates of benefits or taxes. For example, if benefits are understated by 10 percent, then estimates of the net tax rate will be overstated by much more than 10 percent.

Progressivity analysis would also be affected if, for example, disability benefits are excluded (as they are in this chapter and in most such analyses). While workers with lower earnings tend to die younger, a regressive influence, they also tend to become disabled more, a progressive influence. (Note that the average primary insurance amount (PIA) for new male disabled worker awards in 1997 was 15 percent below the average PIA for new male retired worker awards. This means the average earnings level for disabled workers is more than 15 percent below that for retired workers.) If expected disability benefits cannot be included in the analysis, the effect of their exclusion on program progressivity should be noted.

Matching OASI Benefits and Taxes

The authors acknowledge that in comparing OASI taxes (ultimately 10.6 percent of taxable earnings) to OASI benefits simulated only for retirees plus their aged spouses and aged surviving spouses, their analysis excludes about 5 percent of OASI benefits that are paid from the OASI trust fund to (young) survivors. This exclusion could be partially remedied if the analysis was restricted to workers who survive with certainty to the normal retirement age (NRA). The current approach of modeling death between ages twenty-two and NRA (sixty-seven) includes the taxes paid by workers who die prematurely, but excludes much or all of the benefits associated with such deaths. This tends to understate net tax rates but may have little effect on progressivity.

However, the current analysis also excludes an additional, larger category of benefits, retirement benefits payable to "disability conversions." The Disability Insurance taxes (ultimately 1.8 percent of taxable earnings) pay only for disability benefits until a disabled worker reaches the NRA. At that point, the disabled worker is converted to retired worker status and receives benefits from the OASI trust fund. The cost of these benefits after disability conversion represents a form of extended disability insurance, in large part, that is financed from OASI taxes. Thus, if the analysis is restricted to retirement benefits commencing at NRA, and the expected value of disability conversion benefits is excluded, then the portion of the OASI tax that finances this insurance should also be excluded. The total cost of disability conversion benefits is about 10 percent of OASI retirement-benefit cost, so the "premium" for this insurance is significant portion of this amount.

In fact, due to the complex integration of benefits, the only way to assure a comprehensive match between taxes and benefits for Social Security, and to assure comprehensive analysis of progressivity for the program, is to include *all* OASDI benefits and taxes. This requires modeling of young survivor benefits, disability benefits, and disability conversion benefits, in addition to retirement and aged survivor benefits. If this is done, then the comparison to the total OASDI payroll tax rate is straightforward. This is the approach used for the estimates in appendix 2 of volume 1 of the report of the 1994–96 Advisory Council on Social Security. Where this cannot be done because of data limitations, the effects of the limitation should be discussed.

Mortality

The authors use mortality tables from the *Vital Statistics of the United States 1989* (U.S. Department of Health and Human Services 1993). These tables are based on "period" mortality data for experience around the year

1990. However, the authors simulate "a hypothetical future cohort with a birth year of 1990" for their analysis. The authors cite the probabilities of a twenty-two-year-old white male's surviving to ages sixty-five and eighty-five as 75.8 percent and 22.3 percent, respectively. However, projected mortality specifically for the 1990 birth cohort used in trustees' report projections (see the U.S. Social Security Administration's Actuarial Study no. 107 [1992]) indicate probabilities of 83.2 percent and 35.9 percent for all males. Moreover, where the authors cite that 31 percent of the population is still alive at age eighty-five, while Actuarial Study no. 107 indicates that this percentage is expected to be 45 percent for the cohort born in 1990. Differences of this magnitude would have very substantial effects on net tax rates and may influence progressivity.

The authors should consider using projected mortality for the 1990 birth cohort. If the *Vital Statistics* life tables are used, then the description of the hypothetical workers should be modified to indicate the use of 1990 period mortality with ultimate program benefit and tax provisions for the simulation.

Mortality by Income

The authors make a very sensible choice in assigning relative mortality at each age based on lifetime average earnings, rather than earnings at that age. However, because the underlying data provided by Rogot et al. (1992) are based on current income rather than lifetime income, there is some element of inconsistency. The authors do point out that the fact that the Rogot data are family income from the Current Population Surveys (CPS) means that the relative level at each age may not be very far off from the relative lifetime level of earnings.

Appendix table 5A.7 provides relative mortality factors by income only for the age group twenty-five to thirty-four. It would be useful to add these factors for other age groups used in the analysis, most importantly for ages sixty-five and older.

Assumed Retirement at Age Sixty-Seven

The authors assume that all workers would work until reaching their NRA (sixty-seven) if they do not die earlier. In fact, a large proportion of insured workers currently begin receiving benefits well before reaching the NRA. This tendency is expected to continue in the future.

The marginal increase in PIA (the unreduced benefit) for work after benefit eligibility at age sixty-two is small relative to the additional taxes paid because of the weighting in the benefit formula and the inclusion of only the highest thirty-five years in the Average Indexed Monthly Earnings (AIME). Thus, assuming that all workers work until age sixty-seven significantly understates money's worth and overstates the net tax. To the extent that workers with lower earnings retire earlier, assuming retirement at age sixty-seven for all workers results in a systematic underestimate of the actual progressivity that exists in the program.

For the National Commission on Retirement Policy (NCRP; 1999) and Moynihan (1999) plans, increases in the NRA above sixty-seven are said to be regressive largely because the methodology assumes that the hypothetical worker will always delay retirement to the NRA. If workers continue to retire more nearly at the earliest eligibility age (sixty-two) in the future, then increase in the NRA will be more nearly equivalent to an across-the-board benefit reduction for workers of all earnings levels. This would have a far smaller effect on progressivity. The chapter should point out that most of the effect of increasing NRA on progressivity results from the assumption that retirement age will rise directly.

Early Retirement Reduction Factors

Note 6 in the chapter suggests that for low-paid workers who tend to have higher mortality rates, the actuarial reduction factors are "likely to be too great." In fact, the tendency is the opposite. Higher mortality implies a larger actuarial reduction for earlier retirement, so that universal reduction factors are relatively more favorable for groups with higher mortality, like men. It should be further noted, however, that disabled persons have substantially higher-than-average mortality, so that workers becoming initially entitled to retirement benefits at ages sixty-two and over have an expected mortality that is lower than the average for the population as a whole.

Treatment of Stock Returns and Inclusion of Individual Accounts

Three of the four proposals considered depend significantly on investment in stock for the payment of future benefits. The Aaron and Reischauer (A&R) plan (1998) increases advance funding in the trust funds substantially and invests a part of the Social Security trust funds in stock and other private securities. The assumption of a higher return for stock (7 percent real) than for government bonds (3 percent real) allows a given tax rate to provide more benefits. Thus, the assumed higher rate of return for stock is automatically incorporated in the relationship between benefits and taxes under the A&R plan.

For the hypothetical, fully privatized, fully defined-contribution proposal (associated with Feldstein and Samwick 1998), and the individual account portion of the NCRP plan, the authors assume that the present values of taxes (contributions) and benefits (distributions) are equal. This implicitly assumes that the real yield on individual account investments is equal to only 2 percent. However, assuming a 7 percent real yield for stock and a 3 percent real yield for government bonds with a universal real discount rate of 2 percent, the expected present value of investments in defined-contribution individual accounts would be greater than the amount of the initial investment. While the theory of risk-adjusted returns argues against portraying this expected gain, it should not be ignored for the defined-contribution plans if it is reflected in the A&R plan (and the defined benefit portions of the other plans).

For the sake of consistency, the authors should include the expected gains from stock and bond investment in the defined-contribution individual accounts. The alternative would be to leave the treatment of individual investments alone (at an implicit 2 percent real rate of return) but to modify the benefits provided under the defined benefit program so that they are affordable with only a 2 percent return on trust fund investments.

Changes in the Consumer Price Index (CPI) or Cost of Living Adjustment (COLA)

Three of the plans include a provision that specifies or anticipates a change in the CPI or COLA. The authors have included the effect on benefits of this change for two of the plans, Moynihan and NCRP, because the reduction in COLA is more nearly specified, regardless of what action the Bureau of Labor Statistics takes. The effect of the change on benefits was not reflected in A&R because that plan anticipates more than it specifies a change. the treatment of CPI/COLA change should perhaps be made consistent (either by including for all or excluding for all) for two reasons. First, a portion of the change in CPI anticipated by these plans has already occurred with the implementation of geometric weighting in the CPI earlier this year. Second, while A&R do not specify the COLA change, the estimates that result in the estimated long-range solvency for the plan assume that the changes will occur with certainty.

Equal Benefit Cuts Under Current Law

Recognizing that the payroll tax rates provided under current law are not sufficient to provide long-range solvency, the authors develop an alternative "Equal % Benefit Cut" alternative. The 18.9 percent benefit cut is assumed to eliminate about one-half of the long-range shortfall. If benefit levels were gradually reduced to extend solvency of the current program on a roughly pay-as-you-go basis, a 30 percent cut would be required for the cohort born in 1990. For the sake of consistency with the other plans, which all are estimated to achieve long range solvency, this equal percent benefit cut should perhaps be set at 30 percent.

Other Clarifications

A number of small issues about the specification of the proposals to reform Social Security might be clarified before publication. For example, the provision in the NCRP plan to include all years of earnings in the numerator of the AIME would do so literally. This means that AIME would no longer be a true average, but a ratio with potentially more years of earnings in the numerator than the number of years in the denominator. Another example is the 75 percent of couple benefits for widow(er)s in the A&R proposal. This provision is intended to provide 75 percent of the sum the couple would be receiving if both were still alive. Thus, the lower-earning spouse would contribute to the couple benefit either his own worker benefit or one-third of the spouse's worker benefit, whichever is higher. Accordingly, 75 percent of the couple benefit could not be less than benefit provided under current law.

References

Aaron, Henry J., and Robert D. Reischauer. 1998. *Countdown to reform.* New York: Century Foundation Press.
Feldstein, Martin, and Andrew Samwick. 1998. The transition path in privatizing Social Security. In *Privatizing Social Security,* ed. Martin Feldstein, 215–63. Chicago: University of Chicago Press.
Moynihan, Daniel Patrick. 1999. Social Security Solvency Act of 1998: Brief description of provisions. Washington, D.C.: U.S. Senate. Unpublished paper.
National Commission on Retirement Policy (NCRP). 1999. The 21st century retirement security plan. Washington, D.C.: Center for Strategic and International Studies.
Rogot, Eugene, Paul D. Sorlie, Norman J. Johnson, and Catherine Schmitt. 1992. *A mortality study of 1.3 million persons by demographic, social, and economic factors: 1979–1985 follow-up.* NIH Publication no. 92-3297. Bethesda, Md.: National Institutes of Health.
Steuerle, C. Eugene, and Jon M. Bakija. 1994. *Retooling Social Security for the twenty-first century: Right and wrong approaches to reform.* Washington, D.C.: Urban Institute Press.
U.S. Department of Health and Human Services. 1993. *Vital statistics of the United States: 1989.* Hyattsville, Md.: Public Health Service, Centers for Disease Control and Prevention, National Center for Health Statistics.
U.S. Social Security Administration. 1992. *Life tables for the United States Social Security area 1900–2080.* Actuarial Study no. 107, Social Security Publication no. 11-11536. Washington, D.C.: Social Security Administration.

Discussion Summary

Because disability and life insurance programs have different consequences for income redistribution, *Martin Feldstein* suggested that the issues raised by modifying the retirement portion of the Social Security system should be kept separate from the disability insurance program. The decision to keep a pay-as-you-go disability system can be independent of the proposed changes in the old age insurance program.

Charles Blahous argued that the version of the NCRP plan modeled in this chapter differs in important ways from the actual NCRP plan, making the results in the paper difficult to interpret and possibly misleading. In addition, he questioned whether the chapter's methodology was appropriate for comparing plans of different sizes. In particular, comparing an across-the-board cut in benefits to less drastic cuts with other very progressive changes should imply that the NCRP plan is more progressive than the straight benefit cut option. However, the results in the chapter seem to suggest otherwise. In addition, Blahous noted that it is not a coincidence that the plans assessed with the highest net Social Security tax rates have the highest percentage of costs met through payroll taxes, because general revenue requirements above Social Security payroll taxes are not considered. Finally, there is some inconsistent treatment between plans when calculating net tax rates. For example, the portion of the NCRP plan with the improved rate of return—the individual account portion—is ignored while the remaining segment with the lower rate of return is considered. This introduces significant problems when comparing plans. The authors described various changes outlined by the NCRP plan. Their explanation for the regressive appearance of the NCRP plan compared to straight benefit cuts is the large reduction in the number of drop years as well as the increase in the retirement age. According to the authors, the reduction of drop years is the most regressive reform component that they have analyzed.

Gary Burtless did not think that redistribution to the long-lived at the expense of the short-lived should be considered as a shortcoming of the redistributive impact of different plans. This redistribution is inherent when mandatory annuitization is imposed for everyone using the same annuity table, but this is not fundamental to Social Security. This type of redistribution could be avoided by eliminating annuitization completely or by using annuity tables that varied with life expectancy.

A number of participants were concerned about the chapter's approach to modeling plans that adjust Social Security's cost-of-living provisions. Plans that specified that benefits would be indexed at a rate below the growth rate of the CPI were penalized, but proposals that redefined the CPI in a way that would likely reduce its growth rate were not penalized. Since the two approaches would produce the same decrease in benefits, they should produce equivalent results.

6

Social Security's Treatment of Postwar Americans
How Bad Can It Get?

Jagadeesh Gokhale and Laurence J. Kotlikoff

6.1 Introduction

As currently legislated, the U.S. Social Security system represents a bad deal for postwar Americans. Of every dollar postwar Americans have earned or will earn over their lifetimes, over five cents will be lost to the Old-Age and Survivor Insurance System (OASI) in the form of payroll taxes paid in excess of benefits received. OASI's 5 percent lifetime net tax rate can also be described in terms of the internal rate of return it delivers to contributors. This rate—1.86 percent—is less than half the rate currently being paid on inflation-indexed long-term government bonds, which are much safer. Of course, Social Security is an insurance as well as a net tax system. However, if it is viewed as an insurance company, it is clear that the insurance OASI sells (or, rather, forces households to buy) is no bargain. The load charged averages sixty-six cents per dollar of premium.

The bad deal that Social Security offers postwar Americans is, of course, payback for the great deal it offered and still offers prewar Ameri-

Jagadeesh Gokhale is a senior economic advisor with the Federal Reserve Bank of Cleveland. Laurence J. Kotlikoff is professor of economics at Boston University and a research associate of the National Bureau of Economic Research.

The authors thank Carolyn Weaver for critically important comments on various stages of this research. They also thank David A. Wise and Martin Feldstein for their careful reviews and comments on the paper. Steven Caldwell and his colleagues provided data from their CORSIM microsimulation model that plays a critical role in this study. Laurence J. Kotlikoff thanks the National Bureau of Economic Research, Boston University, and the National Institute of Aging for research support. The authors thank Economic Security Planning, Inc., for permitting the use for this study of Social Security Benefit Calculator—a detailed OASDI tax and benefit calculator. All opinions expressed here are strictly those of the authors and are not necessarily those of the Federal Reserve Bank of Cleveland, Boston University, the National Bureau of Economic Research, or the National Institute of Aging.

cans.[1] These generations were enrolled during the beginning of Social Security and received very generous benefits compared with their tax contributions to the system. That postwar Americans are receiving less than a market rate of return on their contributions is not news. What is news is the precise degree to which postwar Americans are being hurt by the system. Understanding their treatment necessitates an actuarial approach because Social Security's benefit payout depends on the vagaries of longevity, fertility, marital arrangements, and lifetime earnings. Capturing the full range of these outcomes requires longitudinal data that follow individuals from their initial encounters with the OASI system through the end of their lives. Coronado, Fullerton, and Glass (1999, as well as their chapter 5 in this volume), Liebman, and Feldstein-Liebman (chapters 1 and 7, respectively, in this volume) use past longitudinal data for individuals or cohorts and then project future data for their observations. Our study takes a different approach, namely simulating complete lifetime histories for individuals. The data used here are from CORSIM, an extensive microsimulation model developed by Steven Caldwell and his colleagues at Cornell University (see Caldwell 1996; Caldwell and Morrison 1999).

Caldwell et al. (1999) married CORSIM's simulated data to a highly detailed Social Security benefit estimator developed by Economic Security Planning, Inc., as part of its financial planning software package, ESPlanner. The resulting study, which produced a range of findings, including those mentioned above, adopted one major counterfactual assumption—that Social Security would be able to deliver on its benefit promises without raising its rate of taxation. Unfortunately, this assumption is far from the reality. Instead, Social Security faces a staggering long-term funding problem. According to the system's own actuaries, meeting promised benefit payments on an ongoing basis requires raising the OASDI 10.8 tax rate immediately and permanently by two-fifths!

This paper uses the machinery developed in Caldwell et al. (1999) to study how bad Social Security's treatment of postwar Americans would be if Social Security maintains its pay-as-you-go (PAYGO) structure, but either raises payroll taxes or cuts benefits to bring the system's finances into present value balance. The alternatives include immediate tax increases, elimination of the ceiling on taxable payroll, immediate and sustained benefit cuts, an increase in the system's normal retirement ages beyond those currently legislated, a switch from wage to price indexing in calculating benefits, and a limit on the price indexation of benefits. The choice among these and other alternatives has important consequences in determining which postwar generations and which members of those generations pay for the system's long-term funding shortfall.

---

1. Saying that prewar Americans received a good deal from Social Security and that postwar Americans are, as a result, receiving a bad deal is a positive, not a normative statement. Some may view this outcome as generationally just, while others view it as exploitive.

The paper proceeds in section 6.2 with a brief literature review. Section 6.3 describes CORSIM and ESPlanner's Social Security Benefit Estimator.[2] Section 6.4 reviews the findings of Caldwell et al. (1999). Section 6.5 describes ten alternative tax increases and benefit reductions that would improve the system's present value finances and proceeds to show the distribution of the additional burden that these policies impose both across postwar cohorts and across different demographic groups within each postwar cohort. This section also reports the contribution that each policy option makes to shoring up the system's finances. Section 6.6 summarizes the main points of the chapter and concludes.

6.2 Some Relevant Literature

A number of past studies have examined Social Security's treatment of its participants by focusing on stylized cases—particular types of married couples and single individuals who differ by age of birth, sex, race, and lifetime earnings and who all live for the same number of years. These studies include Nichols and Schreitmueller (1978), Myers and Schobel (1993), Hurd and Shoven (1985), Boskin, Kotlikoff, Puffert, and Shoven (1987), Steuerle and Bakija (1994), and Diamond and Gruber (1997).

Steuerle and Bakija's 1994 study is fairly representative of the past literature and may be the best-known prior study. It considers three alternative lifetime wage patterns: low, average, and high, where "low" refers to 45 percent of the average value of Social Security–covered earnings, "average" refers to the average value of Social Security–covered earnings, and "high" refers to the value of the maximum taxable level of Social Security–covered earnings. For each cohort reaching age sixty-five between the years 1940 and 2050, Steuerle and Bakija calculate the lifetime net benefits from Social Security for singles and married couples for alternative sets of these three lifetime wage patterns. For example, they consider married couples in which both spouses have low earnings, one spouse has low earnings and the other average earnings, and one spouse has average earnings and the other high earnings. Steuerle and Bakija use their assumed earnings trajectories to compute retirement, dependent, and survivor benefits. In the case of survivor benefits, the authors consider all possible truncations of the earnings trajectories resulting from all possible alternative dates of early death, although not from any other sources. Each of the various state-contingent benefits is actuarially discounted to form a lifetime net benefit.

Steuerle and Bakija's 1994 findings generally accord with those of previous studies: They show that today's and tomorrow's workers will fare much worse under Social Security than current and past retirees; that men are being disadvantaged relative to women; and that single individuals and

2. This section draws heavily on Caldwell et al.'s (1999) description of CORSIM and ESPLanner's benefit calculator.

two-earner couples face higher net taxes than do single-earner couples. The authors also claim that "for most of Social Security's history, the system has been regressive within generations. That is, within a given cohort of retirees, net transfers have been inversely related to need: people with the highest lifetime incomes have tended to receive the largest absolute transfers above and beyond what they contributed."[3]

Like our paper, the 1999 study by Coronado, Fullerton, and Glass represents a different approach—namely, considering the dispersion of all potential outcomes. However, unlike in our paper, Coronado, Fullerton, and Glass examine actual data (from the Panel Study of Income Dynamics), rather than synthetic data. Their paper represents a real step forward in determining exactly how postwar Americans are being treated. Although their focus is on postretirement benefits and they do not include as much detail in their calculation of OASI benefits, their findings are broadly consistent with those presented here and in Caldwell et al. (1999).

6.3   CORSIM and ESPlanner's Social Security Benefit Calculator

As mentioned, we use two tools in our analysis—CORSIM, a dynamic microsimulation model, and ESPlanner's Social Security benefit calculator—to calculate OASI lifetime net taxes (taxes paid less benefits received) for baby boomers and their children.

6.3.1   CORSIM

CORSIM begins in 1960 with the representative sample of Americans surveyed in the 1960 U.S. Census Public-Use Microdata Sample. This data set is a one-in-one-thousand sample, which means that one of every thousand Americans alive in 1960 is included. The census survey provides much, but not all, of the information needed as baseline data. The remaining information is imputed to the 1960 sample from a variety of sources. CORSIM "grows" the 1960 sample demographically and economically in one-year intervals through the year 2100. Demographic growth refers to

---

3. Steuerle and Bakija's study pays careful attention to detail and provides an impressive and extensive array of calculations. However, it raises five concerns. First, in considering only uninterrupted earnings histories, the study omits a potentially very important source of intra- and intergenerational heterogeneity in lifetime Social Security net benefits. Second, in assuming fixed lifetime marital status, the study ignores the role of divorce and remarriage in altering Social Security net benefits. Third, in assuming that receipt of Social Security retirement benefits starts at workers' ages of normal retirement, the study ignores benefit reductions for age, delayed retirement credits, benefit recomputation, and the earnings test—all of which can materially affect Social Security's lifetime net benefits. Fourth, the study uses an extremely low real interest rate, just 2 percent, in discounting future net benefits. Fifth, in failing to consider workers who earn above the taxable maximum, the study fails to capture an important regressive element of the system—the fact that for very high-income single individuals and couples, Social Security's net lifetime taxation is a smaller fraction of lifetime earnings than it is for Steuerle and Bakija's "high" earners.

birth, death, and immigration, entry into the marriage market, family formation, family dissolution, and the attainment of schooling. Economic growth refers to working or not working, choosing annual weeks worked, and determining weekly labor earnings.[4]

As detailed in Caldwell et al. (1996), these and other CORSIM processes are determined by over 1,000 distinct equations, hundreds of rule-based algorithms, and over 5,000 parameters. Data used to estimate and test the separate equation-based modules were drawn from large national Microdata files, including High School and Beyond (HSB), the National Longitudinal Survey (NLS), the National Longitudinal Survey of Youth (NLS-Y), the Panel Study of Income Dynamics (PSID), the National Longitudinal Mortality Study (NLMS), the Survey of Consumer Finances (SCF), and the U.S. Census Public Use Microdata Sample (PUMS). Data used to construct the rule-based modules and to compute alignment factors are drawn from another six files plus miscellaneous sources.

CORSIM's alignment procedures ensure that the model's modules, which are, in part, deterministic and, in part, stochastic, are benchmarked, on a year-by-year basis, to historical and projected future aggregates. These aggregates are typically group specific, such as the average earnings of white females ages nineteen to twenty-five who are married with children in the home and working part time. Benchmarking is performed by calculating group-specific alignment factors, which are applied within each group to the values of the sample member's predicted continuous variable (such as earnings) and probabilities (such as the chance of divorcing). These adjustment factors are then used in a second pass of the model through the population.[5]

Our CORSIM data were produced by running CORSIM from 1960 through 2100. From this master sample, we selected (a) all never-married males and females born between 1945 and 2000 who lived to at least age fifteen, (b) all males born between 1945 and 2000 who married women born between 1945 and 2010 and lived to at least age fifteen, and (c) all females born between 1945 and 2000 who married males born between 1945 and 2000, all of whom lived to at least age fifteen. Selecting the sample in this manner omits (a) males born between 1945 and 2000 who married females born either before 1945 or after 2010 and (b) females born between 1945 and 2000 who married males born either before 1945 or after 2000. Thus, at the early end of the sample we lose some males who married

---

4. CORSIM's other economic processes include consumption expenditures; saving; federal, state, and local income and property taxation; individual asset holdings; inheritance; and disability.

5. For example, if the model generates fewer (more) than the expected number of births in a given period, the fertility probabilities for women of childbearing age in the period are scaled upward (downward). One can scale continuous variables in a simple linear fashion or by using more complex nonlinear methods.

older women and some women who married older men. At the late end of the sample we lose some males who married very much younger women and some females who married younger men.

Whatever bias this selection process introduces should be absent for cohorts born in the central years of our sample. For these cohorts, we are presumably omitting very few, if any, observations. Take, for example, those born in 1965. The males born in 1965 who are left out of the sample are those who either married women twenty or more years older than themselves or married women forty-five or more years younger than themselves. Those females born in 1965 who are omitted from the sample either married males twenty or more years older than themselves or married males thirty-five or more years younger than themselves.

Sample Size

Table 6.1 decomposes the number of observations by birth cohort, lifetime earnings quintile, sex, race, and education. The total number of sample observations in 68,688 individuals. The observations are almost equally divided among men and women. They are also fairly evenly distributed across our eleven cohorts defined over five years of birth (six years for the youngest cohort). For convenience, we refer in the text to each of the cohorts by their oldest members' year of birth. Thus cohort 45 refers to those born between 1945 and 1949, cohort 50 refers to those born between 1950 and 1954, and so on up through cohort 90, which refers to six, rather than five, separate birth cohorts, specifically, those born in the years 1995 through 2000.

Sixteen percent of the observations are nonwhite, and 41 percent have one or more years of college education. These percentages increase for successive cohorts. Eleven percent of cohort 45 is nonwhite, compared with 21 percent of cohort 95. Thirty-one percent of cohort 45 observations have at least one year of college education, compared with 46 percent of observations in cohort 95.

The table sorts observations into three lifetime earnings quintiles: the lowest 20 percent of lifetime earners, the middle 20 percent of lifetime earners, and the top 20 percent of lifetime earners. "Lifetime earnings" is defined as the present value of an individual's annual earnings from age eighteen through the end of his or her life discounted at a 5 percent real interest rate. The lifetime earnings quintiles are defined with respect to the overall distribution of lifetime earnings. *This quintile definition holds even when we consider results for specific demographic groups.* Thus, when we refer to the non–college educated in the highest quintile of the lifetime earnings distribution, we do not mean the 20 percent highest earners among those without a college education, but rather those of the non–college educated who end up among the top 20 percent of *all* lifetime earners. As one would expect (and as table 6.1 shows), 29 percent of all female

Table 6.1   Number of Observations by Present Value of Earnings Quintiles

Birth Cohort	All				White				Nonwhite			
	Lowest	Middle	Highest	All	Lowest	Middle	Highest	All	Lowest	Middle	Highest	All
1945–49	1,000	1,000	1,001	5,001	912	875	923	4,448	88	125	78	553
1950–54	1,209	1,209	1,209	6,045	1,090	1,031	1,076	5,279	119	178	133	766
1955–59	1,415	1,415	1,416	7,076	1,254	1,217	1,286	6,208	161	198	130	868
1960–64	1,273	1,273	1,274	6,366	1,110	1,103	1,124	5,507	163	170	150	859
1965–69	1,171	1,171	1,173	5,857	1,015	958	1,028	4,980	156	213	145	877
1970–74	1,121	1,121	1,121	5,605	957	912	960	4,676	164	209	161	929
1975–79	1,109	1,109	1,109	5,545	928	924	930	4,582	181	185	179	963
1980–84	1,265	1,265	1,269	6,329	1,044	1,035	1,068	5,232	221	230	201	1,097
1985–89	1,319	1,319	1,322	6,598	1,091	1,076	1,123	5,434	228	243	199	1,164
1990–94	1,366	1,366	1,368	6,832	1,089	1,068	1,145	5,489	277	298	223	1,343
1995–2000	1,486	1,486	1,490	7,434	1,168	1,152	1,231	5,848	318	334	259	1,586

Birth Cohort	Men				College				Non-College			
	Lowest	Middle	Highest	All	Lowest	Middle	Highest	All	Lowest	Middle	Highest	All
1945–49	210	513	791	2,462	238	249	456	1,530	762	751	545	3,471
1950–54	272	569	891	2,925	353	367	546	2,036	856	842	663	4,009
1955–59	362	660	986	3,418	425	475	630	2,459	990	940	786	4,617
1960–64	324	620	841	3,013	389	448	614	2,386	884	825	660	3,980
1965–69	322	563	808	2,859	377	456	552	2,292	794	715	621	3,565
1970–74	323	546	779	2,735	399	478	607	2,450	722	643	514	3,155

(continued)

Table 6.1 (continued)

Birth Cohort	Men				College				Non-College			
	Lowest	Middle	Highest	All	Lowest	Middle	Highest	All	Lowest	Middle	Highest	All
1975–79	297	522	730	2,661	424	494	599	2,477	685	615	510	3,068
1980–84	334	663	885	3,139	504	584	721	2,912	761	681	548	3,417
1985–89	371	604	891	3,130	501	598	757	3,014	818	721	565	3,584
1990–94	398	651	928	3,294	532	591	750	3,108	834	775	618	3,724
1995–2000	428	779	1,023	3,699	558	656	854	3,420	928	830	636	4,014

Birth Cohort	Women				Men, White, College				Women, Nonwhite, Non-College			
	Lowest	Middle	Highest	All	Lowest	Middle	Highest	All	Lowest	Middle	Highest	All
1945–49	790	487	210	2,539	45	103	351	744	50	41	9	194
1950–54	937	640	318	3,120	72	153	391	977	63	70	33	279
1955–59	1,053	755	430	3,658	85	207	410	1,104	76	80	30	310
1960–64	949	653	433	3,353	88	170	375	1,011	71	64	35	300
1965–69	849	608	365	2,998	81	166	344	945	59	59	30	267
1970–74	798	575	342	2,870	99	180	372	1,011	72	63	26	269
1975–79	812	587	379	2,884	93	172	339	981	66	52	37	277
1980–84	931	602	384	3,190	92	233	427	1,219	77	65	35	318
1985–89	948	715	431	3,468	109	229	454	1,250	90	70	41	351
1990–94	968	715	440	3,538	119	193	449	1,248	118	94	52	411
1995–2000	1,058	707	467	3,735	110	276	517	1,424	154	78	57	487

Source: Author's calculations.

observations fall in the lowest lifetime earnings quintile, compared to only 12 percent in the highest quintile. Similar remarks apply to the distribution of observations for the nonwhite and non–college educated groups.

Longevity

Since Social Security pays its benefits in the form of annuities, how long one lives is a critical factor in determining how much one benefits from the system. Table 6.2 reports average ages of death by cohort and demographic group. As one would expect, later-born cohorts live longer, females outlive males, whites outlive nonwhites, and those with a college education outlive those without. The average age of death for the first five cohorts is 79.5, compared with 81.1 for the last five. Across the entire sample, females outlive males by 6.3 years, but this gap in longevity narrows somewhat between the earliest and latest cohorts. The longevity gaps between whites and nonwhites of about two years, and between the college educated and non–college educated of about 1.5 years, are fairly stable over time.

There is also a clear correlation between lifetime earnings and average length of life. Part of this correlation runs from earnings to lifespan; in other words, the mortality probabilities used in the CORSIM model are smaller the higher is the level of earnings. However, part runs from lifespan to earnings: Those with shorter lifetimes have fewer years during which to work and may, for that reason, have lower lifetime earnings. Across all cohorts, the difference in longevity between those in the bottom and those in the top quintiles is 1.2 years. However, if one looks within male and female subpopulations, these differences are much larger. Compare, for example, highest- and lowest-quintile life expectancies for men who are in cohort 85. The difference is 7.1 years. For females in the same cohort, the gap is 2.8 years between the top and bottom quintiles.[6]

Longevity differences between the college-educated and non–college educated are worth noting. As mentioned, there is a significant college–non-college difference in average longevity. Given the level of education, however, there is very little difference in life expectancies across lifetime income quintiles. Indeed, college graduates in the lowest quintile of the lifetime earnings distribution have a higher life expectancy than do non-college graduates in the top quintile. Thus, education appears to trump income in explaining longevity.

6. Note that the male and female cohort 85 gap in life expectancies between lowest and highest quintiles are smaller than the corresponding gap for male and female observations combined. The reason is that in forming the overall life expectancies, low quintile males and high quintile females receive relatively little weight because there are relatively few of them. This weighting pattern makes the average life expectancy of all those in the lowest quintile closer to that of females in that quintile and makes the average life expectancy of all those in the highest quintile closer to that of males in that quintile. Since, other things being equal, males have lower life expectancies than do females, this weighting pattern reduces the size of the top-bottom quintile gap relative to the gaps of either sex calculated separately.

Table 6.2 Average Age of Death by Present Value of Earnings Quintiles

Birth Cohort	All				White				Nonwhite			
	Lowest	Middle	Highest	All	Lowest	Middle	Highest	All	Lowest	Middle	Highest	All
1945-49	79.1	78.8	79.6	79.1	79.6	79.2	79.5	79.3	74.7	75.6	81.2	76.7
1950-54	79.6	77.9	79.4	78.9	80.1	78.2	79.4	79.1	74.8	76.4	79.9	77.4
1955-59	79.5	79.2	80.0	79.5	80.0	79.4	80.2	79.8	75.5	77.8	78.9	77.6
1960-64	79.9	79.3	81.3	79.9	80.4	79.8	81.4	80.2	77.0	76.3	81.1	78.2
1965-69	79.0	80.1	81.7	80.2	79.6	80.0	81.5	80.4	75.1	80.7	82.7	79.2
1970-74	80.0	81.3	81.2	80.7	80.5	81.6	81.0	81.0	77.1	80.2	82.8	79.2
1975-79	80.2	80.8	82.0	81.0	80.7	80.7	82.0	81.3	77.7	80.9	81.6	79.7
1980-84	81.1	81.0	82.1	81.1	82.1	81.0	82.2	81.4	76.7	80.6	81.8	79.6
1985-89	80.9	81.6	82.7	81.5	81.6	81.8	82.7	81.9	77.5	80.4	82.9	79.9
1990-94	80.7	80.9	82.4	81.2	81.5	81.1	82.8	81.5	77.7	80.1	80.8	79.8
1995-2000	80.0	80.2	81.0	80.6	80.7	80.7	81.4	81.0	77.7	78.4	79.2	78.9

Birth Cohort	Men				College				Non-College			
	Lowest	Middle	Highest	All	Lowest	Middle	Highest	All	Lowest	Middle	Highest	All
1945-49	70.2	74.3	78.3	75.8	80.4	81.0	79.5	80.4	78.8	78.0	79.7	78.5
1950-54	69.2	74.5	77.9	75.3	80.2	78.7	79.4	79.5	79.3	77.5	79.5	78.6
1955-59	71.6	75.4	78.4	76.0	81.4	79.4	81.2	80.3	78.7	79.1	79.1	79.1
1960-64	71.9	76.0	79.8	76.6	80.7	80.7	82.0	80.8	79.6	78.6	80.6	79.4

Year	Women				Men, White, College				Women, Nonwhite, Non-College			
1965–69	70.7	75.6	80.1	76.9	79.7	80.7	82.1	80.9	78.7	79.8	81.3	79.8
1970–74	71.9	78.8	79.8	77.3	80.6	82.3	81.0	81.4	79.6	80.5	81.5	80.2
1975–79	72.4	77.3	79.7	77.6	81.6	81.9	83.0	82.1	79.4	79.8	80.8	80.1
1980–84	73.8	77.8	80.5	77.8	82.6	81.9	82.5	82.0	80.2	80.2	81.6	80.4
1985–89	73.8	78.5	80.9	78.3	82.0	82.7	82.9	82.4	80.2	80.6	82.4	80.8
1990–94	74.2	77.2	81.0	78.2	80.9	81.3	82.7	81.6	80.6	80.6	82.1	80.8
1995–2000	74.6	77.3	79.7	78.0	80.9	80.3	81.5	81.3	79.5	80.1	80.3	80.0
1945–49	81.5	83.5	84.5	82.2	74.4	75.0	78.3	77.7	80.2	79.8	84.0	79.8
1950–54	82.6	80.9	83.8	82.3	73.1	75.2	77.7	76.3	83.4	77.7	84.0	80.7
1955–59	82.2	82.5	83.8	82.8	72.2	76.2	79.7	77.3	80.0	80.5	82.7	81.2
1960–64	82.7	82.6	84.2	82.9	72.6	78.7	80.6	77.7	79.9	77.6	83.7	79.9
1965–69	82.2	84.4	85.1	83.4	69.6	75.1	80.2	77.5	80.7	85.1	84.6	83.0
1970–74	83.2	83.7	84.5	83.9	74.9	79.4	79.3	78.3	82.1	82.5	85.0	81.7
1975–79	83.1	83.8	86.2	84.1	75.3	76.5	81.4	79.2	79.8	83.4	84.3	82.8
1980–84	83.8	84.4	85.9	84.4	78.9	77.8	81.2	78.9	78.1	82.2	84.0	82.0
1985–89	83.7	84.1	86.5	84.4	76.6	79.8	81.2	79.8	78.4	82.4	86.3	81.6
1990–94	83.4	84.3	85.4	83.9	75.5	77.4	82.2	79.4	82.2	83.5	87.1	82.5
1995–2000	82.2	83.4	83.8	83.2	75.5	77.7	80.6	79.4	80.5	80.8	80.8	81.2

Source: Author's calculations.

Lifetime Earnings

Table 6.3 shows the huge gulf that separates high and low earners with respect to the present value of lifetime earnings. For cohort 45, average lifetime earnings in the top quintile are thirty-three times those in the bottom quintile. For cohort 95, the corresponding factor is thirty-nine. The table also shows that postwar males have much higher average lifetime earnings than do postwar females. In cohort 85, for example, females average $398,300 in lifetime earnings, compared with $731,800 for males. This over-$300,000 differential is much larger than the white-nonwhite and college-non–college educated differentials in cohort 85. Indeed, in this cohort, the white-nonwhite differential is less than $100,000 and the college-non–college differential is less than $200,000. In combination, these differentials can be very sizeable, although their interactions are not necessarily positive. Take white, college-educated males in cohort 85 and non-white, non–college educated females in the same cohort. The lifetime earnings difference, which is in excess of $500,000, is nonetheless smaller than the sum of the separate male-female, white-nonwhite, and college educated-non–college educated differentials.

Although lifetime earnings are higher in general for men than for women, for whites than for nonwhites, and for the college-educated than for the non–college educated, these differences do not necessarily extend to within-quintile comparisons. For example, the lowest quintile males have lower lifetime earnings than the lowest quintile females.

Another prominent feature of table 6.3 is the growth over time in lifetime earnings measured in 1998 dollars. This reflects historic as well as projected growth in real wages. As a comparison of results for different members of cohorts 1945–49 and 1995–2000 makes clear, lifetime earnings of successive generations are growing much more rapidly for women than for men, and somewhat more rapidly for whites than for nonwhites and for the college-educated than for the non–college educated.

6.3.2   ESPLanner's Social Security Benefit Calculator (SSBC)

ESPLanner's OASI benefit calculator calculates retirement, spousal, widow(er), mother, father, children, and divorcee benefits as well as OASI taxes. It does so by taking into account Social Security's earnings test, family benefit maximums, actuarial reductions and increases, benefit recomputations, eligibility rules, the ceiling on taxable earnings, and legislated changes in normal retirement ages. Although the benefit calculator considers the OASI system in great detail, it leaves out the disability insurance (DI) portion of Social Security as well as the Supplemental Security Income (SSI) program. It also ignores the taxation of Social Security benefits under federal and state income taxes. Both of these omissions lead to an understatement of Social Security's redistribution from the lifetime rich to the lifetime poor.

Table 6.3

Table 6.3 Average Present Value Earnings by Present Value of Earnings Quintiles

Birth Cohort	All				White				Nonwhite			
	Lowest	Middle	Highest	All	Lowest	Middle	Highest	All	Lowest	Middle	Highest	All
1945–49	33.4	254.8	1,107.7	394.6	33.0	254.9	1,112.8	399.3	38.0	254.4	1,046.8	356.4
1950–54	33.4	248.8	1,117.7	394.1	33.7	248.9	1,129.2	398.1	31.1	247.9	1,024.0	366.6
1955–59	36.2	251.9	1,307.1	435.4	36.5	252.3	1,319.3	445.0	34.4	249.5	1,186.1	366.4
1960–64	35.4	241.8	1,465.3	464.4	35.7	241.3	1,452.7	466.5	33.3	244.5	1,560.2	451.1
1965–69	34.5	253.4	1,435.8	466.8	34.6	253.6	1,451.8	478.0	33.6	252.2	1,322.1	402.9
1970–74	35.6	255.4	1,509.0	481.5	35.2	255.7	1,504.9	487.0	38.4	253.8	1,533.4	453.7
1975–79	37.8	263.9	1,516.6	489.3	38.1	264.4	1,546.9	499.4	36.5	261.6	1,359.3	440.9
1980–84	36.3	274.5	1,671.7	529.4	35.8	274.9	1,725.7	546.3	38.7	272.3	1,384.6	448.9
1985–89	41.8	284.3	1,773.3	556.5	41.7	284.5	1,802.2	571.3	41.9	283.2	1,610.2	487.5
1990–94	43.6	292.2	1,717.1	552.4	42.7	293.3	1,736.5	568.3	47.1	288.5	1,617.7	487.5
1995–2000	48.3	325.0	1,872.6	605.7	49.0	325.7	1,899.3	628.3	45.9	322.4	1,745.8	522.3

Birth Cohort	Men				College				Non-College			
	Lowest	Middle	Highest	All	Lowest	Middle	Highest	All	Lowest	Middle	Highest	All
1945–49	21.6	258.8	1,105.0	549.2	31.9	258.0	1,185.2	514.1	33.9	253.8	1,042.8	341.9
1950–54	27.5	251.1	1,129.8	533.8	32.1	251.0	1,208.7	490.3	34.0	247.8	1,042.7	345.2
1955–59	32.8	256.8	1,325.3	570.7	35.5	251.8	1,414.8	533.2	36.5	252.0	1,220.8	383.3
1960–64	33.2	243.2	1,519.2	611.1	34.2	239.8	1,629.6	588.5	35.9	242.8	1,312.5	390.0
1965–69	31.4	255.6	1,459.0	605.7	33.3	253.1	1,556.2	557.4	35.1	253.5	1,328.8	408.5
1970–74	34.5	257.6	1,466.8	607.9	35.2	256.2	1,613.6	581.1	35.9	254.7	1385.4	404.2

(*continued*)

Table 6.3   (continued)

Birth Cohort	Men				College				Non-College			
	Lowest	Middle	Highest	All	Lowest	Middle	Highest	All	Lowest	Middle	Highest	All
1975–79	38.1	265.3	1,551.4	630.7	36.6	266.6	1,587.0	572.2	38.6	261.7	1,433.9	422.3
1980–84	33.9	279.2	1,636.0	668.9	36.4	276.1	1,787.8	634.4	36.2	273.1	1,519.0	440.0
1985–89	41.2	285.7	1,815.2	731.8	42.6	285.8	1,818.8	659.3	41.3	283.0	1,712.4	470.1
1990–94	39.3	295.2	1,718.8	705.4	41.1	295.1	1,862.6	662.0	45.2	290.1	1,540.6	461.0
1995–2000	46.4	329.0	1,881.9	768.1	47.1	330.4	2,027.5	739.5	49.0	320.7	1,664.7	491.7

Birth Cohort	Women				Men, White, College				Women, Nonwhite, Non-College			
	Lowest	Middle	Highest	All	Lowest	Middle	Highest	All	Lowest	Middle	Highest	All
1945–49	36.6	250.6	1,117.7	244.6	15.8	264.4	1,202.4	733.1	37.5	248.0	1,089.3	242.6
1950–54	35.1	246.7	1,083.7	263.1	23.6	257.8	1,247.9	677.2	24.3	250.1	942.1	278.9
1955–59	37.4	247.7	1,265.4	308.9	27.3	258.2	1,485.6	729.3	24.3	247.8	1,111.8	286.0
1960–64	36.2	240.4	1,360.7	332.6	29.8	240.9	1,665.4	794.8	31.0	250.8	1,081.0	298.8
1965–69	35.7	251.2	1,384.5	334.3	27.0	257.3	1,639.4	787.6	29.0	256.2	1,151.1	309.9
1970–74	36.1	253.2	1,605.1	361.1	29.1	257.6	1,561.2	753.1	31.3	251.4	1,425.6	311.7
1975–79	37.8	262.7	1,449.6	358.7	31.6	267.1	1,700.7	786.5	34.0	268.6	1,403.3	366.6
1980–84	37.1	269.2	1,753.9	392.2	28.4	280.4	1,763.4	824.2	31.2	263.4	1,048.2	330.4
1985–89	42.0	283.1	1,686.6	398.3	37.7	288.1	1,931.5	909.8	38.0	275.4	1,560.6	379.9
1990–94	45.3	289.6	1,713.6	410.0	31.1	302.1	1,868.5	890.6	46.7	289.8	1,390.9	373.8
1995–2000	49.1	320.6	1,852.4	444.8	42.1	335.6	2,091.9	1,002.1	42.3	314.5	1,741.6	403.5

Source: Author's calculations.

Calculation of OASI benefits is extremely complex. The *Social Security Handbook* describing the rules governing these benefits runs over 500 pages. Even so, on many key points, the *Handbook* is incomplete and misleading. This assessment is shared by the Social Security senior actuaries who were consulted in developing SSBC. Their assistance, which proved invaluable, came in the form of both extensive discussions and the transmittal of numerous documents detailing various aspects of Social Security's benefit formulae. The Social Security actuaries also introduced us to their ANYPIA program, which calculates primary insurance amounts (PIAs). Unfortunately, ANYPIA considers only one person at a time and does not permit the calculation of multiple, interdependent benefits of household members. Consequently, ANYPIA did not provide an alternative to developing SSBC, although we have used it, where possible, to check SSBC's accuracy. We refer readers to Caldwell et al. (1998) for a detailed discussion of SSBC's calculation of each type of benefit.

6.4   OASDI's Treatment of Postwar Americans Assuming No Tax Hikes or Benefit Cuts

Tables 6.4 through 6.6 summarize a number of the findings in Caldwell et al. (1999) about Social Security's treatment of current generations assuming no future change in Social Security tax and benefit provisions. Table 6.4 reports cohort-specific OASI lifetime net tax rates for the lowest, middle, and highest lifetime earnings quintiles and for different demographic groups. These tax rates are calculated by dividing (a) the sum of lifetime net taxes of all individuals in a given cell by (b) the sum of those individuals' lifetime earnings. These lifetime variables are present values (discounted at a real rate of 5 percent), measured in 1998 dollars and calculated as of the year the individual is age eighteen. The taxes and benefits used in forming the lifetime net tax rate are all OASI taxes paid by cell members *plus* those paid by their employers and all OASI benefits received by cell members. Thus, spousal and widow(er) benefits are credited to the recipients—the dependent spouse or widow(er)—and not to the spouse who paid the taxes that procured those benefits. For example, a spousal benefit paid to a husband is counted as his benefit notwithstanding the fact that the benefit is based on his wife's earnings record.

Table 6.5 reports cohort-specific OASI internal rates of return, again broken down by lifetime earnings quintiles. The cell-specific internal rates of return were determined by finding the discount rate that equated the present value of the aggregate tax payments of cell observations to the present value of the aggregate benefit receipts of cell observations.

Table 6.6 shows cell-specific OASI equivalent wealth tax rates. These tax rates are calculated by (a) present valuing to age sixty-five (accumulating to age sixty-five or, as appropriate, discounting to age sixty-five) all

Table 6.4   Lifetime Net Tax Rates by Present Value of Earnings Quintiles

Birth Cohort	All				Men				White				Nonwhite				College				Non-College			
	Lowest	Middle	Highest	All	Lowest	Middle	Highest	All	Lowest	Middle	Highest	All	Lowest	Middle	Highest	All	Lowest	Middle	Highest	All	Lowest	Middle	Highest	All
1945–49	-4.2	6.1	5.0	5.3	2.2	6.8	5.2	5.8	-4.3	6.1	4.9	5.3	-3.8	6.4	5.2	5.7	-6.0	5.5	4.8	5.0	-3.7	6.3	5.1	5.6
1950–54	-7.9	5.1	4.9	4.8	1.8	5.9	5.0	5.4	-8.0	5.0	4.9	4.7	-7.0	5.5	5.3	5.3	-9.4	4.7	4.5	4.5	-7.3	5.2	5.3	5.0
1955–59	-5.0	5.5	5.0	5.1	2.1	6.5	5.2	5.6	-5.1	5.4	5.0	5.0	-4.2	6.0	5.5	5.6	-6.7	5.4	4.6	4.8	-4.4	5.6	5.5	5.3
1960–64	-4.6	5.9	4.9	5.2	2.7	6.7	5.0	5.6	-4.6	5.7	5.0	5.2	-4.1	6.6	4.4	5.1	-6.0	5.5	4.4	4.8	-4.0	6.1	5.5	5.6
1965–69	-3.9	6.0	5.3	5.5					-4.0	5.9	5.3	5.5	-3.2	6.0	5.6	5.8								
1970–74	-3.4	5.7	5.3	5.4					-3.8	5.7	5.3	5.4	-1.7	6.1	5.0	5.4								
1975–79	-3.7	5.8	5.4	5.5					-3.2	5.7	5.3	5.4	-5.9	6.2	6.0	5.9								
1980–84	-4.8	5.6	5.3	5.4					-5.2	5.5	5.2	5.3	-3.2	5.8	6.2	6.0								
1985–89	-4.0	5.5	5.0	5.1					-4.3	5.3	5.0	5.1	-2.9	6.0	5.3	5.5								
1990–94	-3.5	5.4	5.3	5.3					-4.5	5.3	5.3	5.3	.0	5.8	5.3	5.5								
1995–2000	-2.9	5.5	5.4	5.4					-3.3	5.3	5.3	5.2	-1.4	6.2	5.9	5.9								

1965–69	3.7	6.8	5.4	5.9	-6.3	5.9	4.9	5.2	-2.8	6.0	5.8	5.8
1970–74	3.7	6.4	5.6	5.9	-4.3	5.4	5.0	5.2	-3.0	6.0	5.7	5.7
1975–79	4.0	6.5	5.5	5.9	-5.1	5.6	5.1	5.3	-2.8	5.9	5.7	5.7
1980–84	4.1	6.3	5.6	5.9	-6.1	5.4	5.0	5.2	-3.9	5.7	5.7	5.7
1985–89	2.2	6.1	5.1	5.5	-4.6	5.1	4.9	5.0	-3.7	5.7	5.2	5.3
1990–94	1.9	6.1	5.5	5.7	-5.3	5.3	5.0	5.1	-2.5	5.5	5.8	5.6
1995–2000	1.3	5.9	5.5	5.7	-4.9	5.4	5.0	5.0	-1.8	5.5	6.0	5.8
			Women			Men, White, College				Women, Nonwhite, Non-College		
1945–49	-5.2	5.4	4.0	4.3	1.5	6.5	5.0	5.4	-4.8	6.1	3.9	5.1
1950–54	-10.1	4.3	4.6	3.7	.5	5.7	4.5	4.9	-22.2	5.1	4.8	4.5
1955–59	-7.2	4.7	4.7	4.2	1.3	6.4	4.6	5.0	-14.1	5.6	5.5	5.0
1960–64	-6.8	5.0	4.8	4.6	4.1	6.2	4.6	5.1	-6.7	6.3	6.1	5.9
1965–69	-6.4	5.1	5.1	4.9	2.3	7.1	4.9	5.4	-13.6	5.6	6.5	5.8
1970–74	-6.2	5.1	4.7	4.6	3.3	6.2	5.4	5.6	-8.7	5.6	5.2	5.2
1975–79	-6.5	5.1	5.0	4.7	2.8	6.5	5.0	5.4	-12.0	5.7	5.7	5.2
1980–84	-7.7	4.8	4.7	4.5	2.0	6.2	5.2	5.6	-11.1	5.3	7.3	6.0
1985–89	-6.4	4.9	4.7	4.6	.7	5.6	4.9	5.2	-8.1	5.4	5.6	5.4
1990–94	-5.4	4.8	5.0	4.7	.6	6.0	5.1	5.4	-1.2	5.2	5.3	5.3
1995–2000	-4.6	5.0	5.2	4.9	-.2	5.6	5.0	5.1	-3.1	5.7	5.9	5.6

Source: Author's calculations.

Table 6.5   Internal Rates of Return by Present Value of Earnings Quintiles

Birth Cohort	All				White				Nonwhite			
	Lowest	Middle	Highest	All	Lowest	Middle	Highest	All	Lowest	Middle	Highest	All
1945–49	5.7	2.4	.8	1.9	5.7	2.5	.8	2.0	5.7	2.1	1.0	1.9
1950–54	6.7	2.6	.8	2.1	6.7	2.7	.8	2.1	6.7	2.2	1.0	1.9
1955–59	6.2	2.6	.7	1.9	6.2	2.6	.7	1.9	6.1	2.3	.7	1.9
1960–64	6.0	2.6	.6	1.8	6.0	2.6	.6	1.8	6.0	2.0	.7	1.7
1965–69	5.9	2.6	.7	1.8	5.9	2.6	.7	1.8	5.8	2.6	.9	1.9
1970–74	5.8	2.8	.6	1.8	5.9	2.8	.6	1.8	5.4	2.6	.9	1.9
1975–79	5.8	2.7	.8	1.9	5.7	2.7	.8	1.9	6.2	2.5	.8	1.9
1980–84	6.0	2.8	.7	1.9	6.1	2.8	.7	1.9	5.7	2.6	.7	1.8
1985–89	5.9	2.9	.9	2.0	6.0	3.0	.8	2.0	5.7	2.6	1.0	2.0
1990–94	5.8	2.9	.9	2.0	6.0	2.9	.9	2.0	5.0	2.6	.8	1.9
1995–2000	5.7	2.8	.6	1.9	5.8	2.9	.7	1.9	5.4	2.3	.3	1.7

Birth Cohort	Men				College				Non-College			
	Lowest	Middle	Highest	All	Lowest	Middle	Highest	All	Lowest	Middle	Highest	All
1945–49	4.3	1.6	.5	1.0	6.0	2.8	.8	1.9	5.7	2.3	.9	2.0
1950–54	4.3	1.8	.5	1.1	6.9	2.9	.9	2.0	6.6	2.5	.8	2.1
1955–59	4.3	1.7	.4	1.0	6.4	2.7	.8	1.8	6.0	2.5	.5	1.9
1960–64	4.0	1.7	.3	.9	6.2	2.9	.8	1.8	5.9	2.4	.5	1.8

						Men, White, College			Women, Nonwhite, Non-College		
1965–69	3.7	1.7	.9	6.3	2.7	.8	1.8	5.6	2.5	.6	1.8
1970–74	3.7	2.1	1.0	5.9	3.0	.6	1.8	5.7	2.6	.7	1.9
1975–79	3.6	2.0	1.1	6.0	2.9	.9	1.9	5.6	2.6	.6	1.9
1980–84	3.6	2.2	1.1	6.2	2.9	.8	1.8	5.9	2.7	.7	2.0
1985–89	4.3	2.3	1.3	6.0	3.1	.9	2.0	5.8	2.7	.8	2.1
1990–94	4.4	2.2	1.3	6.1	3.0	.9	1.9	5.6	2.8	.9	2.1
1995–2000	4.6	2.4	1.3	6.1	2.9	.7	1.9	5.4	2.8	.5	1.9
	Women										
1945–49	5.9	3.0	1.7	4.5	1.7	.5	.9	5.9	2.5	1.7	2.6
1950–54	7.0	3.2	1.6	4.8	1.9	.5	1.0	9.1	2.5	1.4	2.6
1955–59	6.5	3.1	1.3	4.5	1.8	.5	.9	8.2	2.5	1.0	2.5
1960–64	6.4	3.2	1.2	3.3	2.1	.4	.8	6.5	2.1	.9	2.0
1965–69	6.3	3.2	1.3	4.2	1.6	.4	.8	8.2	2.9	1.0	2.4
1970–74	6.3	3.2	1.2	3.9	2.2	.2	.8	6.8	2.8	1.1	2.5
1975–79	6.3	3.2	1.4	4.0	2.0	.6	.8	7.2	2.8	1.0	2.5
1980–84	6.5	3.3	1.3	4.4	2.1	.5	1.1	7.3	2.9	1.0	2.4
1985–89	6.3	3.3	1.4	4.8	2.6	.6	1.0	6.5	2.8	1.1	2.4
1990–94	6.1	3.3	1.3	4.8	2.3	.7	1.2	5.3	3.0	1.6	2.5
1995–2000	6.0	3.2	.9	5.1	2.5	.6	1.3	5.7	2.7	.4	2.2

Source: Author's calculations.

Table 6.6   Wealth Tax Rates by Present Value of Earnings Quintiles

Birth Cohort	All				White				Nonwhite			
	Lowest	Middle	Highest	All	Lowest	Middle	Highest	All	Lowest	Middle	Highest	All
1945–49	−35.3	61.5	75.6	66.3	−35.1	60.9	75.7	66.2	−37.4	65.8	74.7	67.1
1950–54	−89.9	56.3	75.0	63.3	−90.6	55.5	75.0	63.0	−82.5	61.3	74.6	65.3
1955–59	−54.8	57.8	76.9	66.0	−55.9	57.1	76.9	65.9	−45.6	61.7	76.9	66.3
1960–64	−46.5	58.4	77.7	67.7	−47.2	57.2	77.7	67.6	−41.1	65.6	77.6	68.7
1965–69	−38.1	58.1	77.8	68.1	−39.1	58.0	77.9	68.2	−31.2	58.7	76.6	67.2
1970–74	−33.7	55.6	78.2	67.5	−36.9	54.9	78.4	67.5	−16.7	58.7	76.6	67.5
1975–79	−35.9	56.7	77.4	67.0	−31.8	56.1	77.4	67.0	−57.6	59.8	77.1	67.0
1980–84	−46.8	55.0	77.6	67.1	−50.8	54.5	77.6	67.1	−30.1	57.5	77.3	67.4
1985–89	−40.0	53.6	76.7	65.7	−42.4	52.5	76.9	65.6	−28.5	58.4	75.7	66.1
1990–94	−34.7	53.6	75.9	65.4	−44.7	52.6	75.8	65.2	−.5	57.3	76.8	66.6
1995–2000	−28.9	53.8	77.5	65.8	−32.6	51.8	77.0	65.2	−14.3	60.6	79.5	68.3

Birth Cohort	Men				College				Non-College			
	Lowest	Middle	Highest	All	Lowest	Middle	Highest	All	Lowest	Middle	Highest	All
1945–49	20.6	69.4	77.4	74.5	−51.2	56.0	76.2	67.5	−30.7	63.3	75.0	65.6
1950–54	20.0	65.3	76.7	72.4	−109.5	53.7	74.7	64.6	−82.5	57.4	75.2	62.5
1955–59	22.3	66.4	78.6	73.7	−74.8	56.8	75.9	66.9	−46.8	58.3	77.7	65.3
1960–64	26.5	66.4	79.2	74.6	−60.3	54.4	77.1	68.2	−40.6	60.5	78.2	67.4

Top panel:

Period									Women, Nonwhite, Non-College			
1965–69	36.4	66.7	79.3	74.8	−64.3	57.7	77.3	68.6	−26.8	58.4	78.2	67.7
1970–74	36.1	62.1	79.5	74.1	−42.2	52.6	78.6	68.5	−29.1	57.9	77.7	66.6
1975–79	39.6	64.3	79.4	73.8	−50.6	55.2	76.5	67.4	−27.5	57.9	78.4	66.6
1980–84	39.7	61.7	78.9	73.5	−59.5	53.1	77.4	68.1	−38.3	56.6	77.8	66.1
1985–89	21.4	59.7	78.3	72.2	−45.4	50.5	76.5	66.6	−36.5	56.2	77.1	64.7
1990–94	19.1	60.6	76.8	71.1	−51.4	52.9	76.0	66.6	−24.8	54.2	75.8	64.3
1995–2000	13.2	58.1	78.0	70.6	−49.5	53.4	77.0	66.4	−17.3	54.1	78.1	65.2

Bottom panel:

Period	Women				Men, White, College				Women, Nonwhite, Non-College			
1945–49	−43.1	53.2	67.8	49.8	13.8	67.9	77.9	75.2	−45.2	60.0	66.2	56.4
1950–54	−115.7	48.0	70.0	46.7	5.7	64.2	76.5	72.8	−250.8	56.7	70.4	54.7
1955–59	−78.7	49.7	72.8	53.3	14.0	65.1	77.6	74.1	−160.2	57.7	74.5	58.1
1960–64	−69.8	50.6	74.5	57.3	39.6	61.8	78.6	75.2	−68.5	64.6	75.8	64.2
1965–69	−62.5	50.0	74.3	57.4	23.6	68.1	79.1	75.7	−127.4	53.2	75.7	60.0
1970–74	−61.3	49.4	75.2	57.0	31.3	60.2	80.1	75.4	−84.0	54.5	75.3	59.4
1975–79	−63.8	49.9	73.1	56.4	29.9	64.9	78.1	73.7	−121.8	54.9	75.2	58.7
1980–84	−75.8	47.3	74.4	56.4	19.1	62.2	78.6	74.3	−107.6	53.0	75.3	60.1
1985–89	−63.6	48.4	73.2	55.7	7.3	55.8	78.2	72.6	−80.4	54.4	74.8	60.2
1990–94	−54.0	47.2	74.0	56.8	5.9	59.8	76.5	71.6	−11.4	50.8	70.3	59.6
1995–2000	−44.7	48.9	76.3	58.1	−2.3	55.1	77.1	70.0	−29.6	55.6	79.4	63.0

Source: Author's calculations.

lifetime OASI taxes paid by all cell members, (b) doing the same for all lifetime OASI benefits received by all cell members, and (c) forming the number one minus the ratio of the collective within-cell lifetime benefits to the collective within-cell lifetime taxes. Again, a 5 percent rate of discount is used in finding present values. If the lifetime benefits of cell members equal their lifetime taxes, the implicit OASI wealth tax rate equals zero. If lifetime benefits of cell members are zero, the implicit wealth tax rate is 100 percent.

The reason we refer to this tax rate as an implicit wealth tax is that the accumulated-to-age-sixty-five lifetime tax payments of cell members would be the extra net wealth they would have at age sixty-five if (a) there were no OASI program, (b) all OASI payroll tax contributions were saved and invested by cell members as a group, and (c) these savings earned a real rate of return of 5 percent.[7] If the OASI wealth tax rate is 0.66, this means that Social Security has, in effect, taxed away two-thirds of that net wealth when the surviving cell members reach age sixty-five. Another way to think about OASI is that it represents an insurance policy. From this perspective, the contributions are insurance premiums and the implicit wealth tax is the load charged by the OASI insurance company. A wealth tax rate of 0.66 translates into a load of 66 cents per dollar of premium.

Since we are pooling together the outcomes of all cell observations in forming the cell entries in tables 6.4 through 6.6 as well as subsequent tables, we are making actuarial calculations. Individuals who die young and receive benefits for only a few years are pooled with those who die old and receive benefits for many years. Individuals who parent multiple children and, if they die when the children are young, endow their children with child survivor benefits and their spouses with mother/father benefits, are pooled with those who have no children and, therefore, generate no such benefits. Individuals who are married for ten or more years and, because they have the right constellation of earnings and death dates vis-à-vis their spouses, provide their spouses with spousal and survivor benefits, are pooled with both individuals who never married and with individuals who marry but are divorced before ten years and, consequently, disqualify their former spouses for such benefits.[8,9]

---

7. We take a 5 percent real rate of return as a reasonable approximation of available market rates of return, comprising of a risk-free rate of 3.5 percent and a risk premium of 1.5 percent.

8. Since surviving spouses are eligible for survivor benefits provided they have been married for nine or more months, we refer here only to the case of marriages of less than ten years that end in divorce in which a spouse dies after the couple has divorced.

9. Note that we allocate benefits to recipients rather than to the individuals whose earnings records generated the benefits. Hence, load factors are likely to be understated for those demographic groups who receive sizable benefits based on the earnings of individuals belonging to some other demographic group. Women, for example, have lower earnings and live longer than men on average and, therefore, receive spousal and survivor benefits based on

6.4.1 Lifetime Net Tax Rates Under the Existing System

Table 6.4 documents several key features of the current OASI system. First, with the exception of cohort 50, lifetime net tax rates exceed 5 percent for almost all postwar cohorts. Second, there is no clear cohort time trend. Younger cohorts are not, under current law, generally facing higher lifetime net tax rates than older cohorts. Third, lifetime net tax rates are negative for members of all cohorts who fall within the lowest 20 percent of their cohort's lifetime earnings distribution. Fourth, the lifetime net tax rates of the middle class (the middle or 3rd quintile of the lifetime earnings distribution) exceed those of the highest quintile of the lifetime earnings distribution.

Thus, the current OASI system represents an overall bad deal for postwar Americans when viewed from an actuarial perspective. One might expect the deal to be worsening over time, given that the OASI tax rate has risen over time. However, life expectancy has increased, and work expectancy has decreased. Hence, younger postwar cohort members are receiving benefits for more years and paying taxes for fewer years than are older postwar cohort members.

The OASI program significantly hurts Americans as a group, but it also significantly helps poor postwar Americans. Take, for example, members of cohort 80 in the lowest lifetime earnings quintile. OASI is, in effect, handing them 4.8 cents on balance for every dollar they earn. Although the system is highly progressive at the bottom of the lifetime earnings distribution, it is somewhat regressive at the top. The regressive nature of the system arises from the ceiling on covered earnings that limits the payroll tax contributions of high earners as well as the benefits high earners receive. Although high earners are facing somewhat lower rates of lifetime net OASI contributions than the middle class, they are still paying, in absolute terms, much more than the middle class. To see this, multiply, for example, table 6.4's 5.3 percent lifetime net tax rate for the highest quintile in cohort 80 by $1,671,700—cohort 80's average lifetime earnings. The resulting $88,600 is over five times the corresponding absolute net tax of $15,372 paid, on average, by members of cohort 80's middle quintile.

Table 6.4 breaks down the lifetime net tax rates by demographic group. Men pay about 1 percent more of their lifetime earnings to OASI in net taxes than do women. The higher male net tax rates obtain even within the same lifetime earnings quintiles. Indeed, the poorest one-fifth of males in each cohort all face positive lifetime net tax rates, whereas the poorest one-fifth of women in each cohort all face negative lifetime net tax rates.

---

their husbands' earnings histories. The opposite would be true for men. Hence, in drawing conclusions about the size of load factors, it may be appropriate to focus on average wealth tax rates across all groups.

These results reflect males' shorter life expectancies and less frequent receipt of OASI dependent and survivor benefits. Nonwhites, because of their shorter life expectancies, face slightly higher (about a third of a percentage point) lifetime OASI net tax rates than do whites. This is true within as well as across lifetime earnings quintiles. College-educated workers face somewhat lower lifetime OASI net tax rates (about three-fifths of a percentage point) than non–college educated workers. This difference is particularly pronounced among college-educated and non–college educated observations in the first quintile.

6.4.2   Internal Rates of Return Paid by the Existing System

Table 6.5 indicates that postwar cohorts, as a group, are receiving a roughly 2 percent rate of return on their OASI contributions. Relative to the nearly 4 percent safe rate of return currently available on inflation-indexed long-term government treasury bonds, 2 percent is quite low, particularly given the fact that future OASI tax payments and benefit receipts are highly uncertain. Indeed, the nonidiosyncratic component of these tax payments and benefit receipts is closely linked to overall labor productivity growth. Because labor productivity growth is highly correlated with the economy's performance, which, in turn, is highly correlated with the performance of the stock market, the stock market's real rate of return may be a reasonable rate to compare with the 2 percent being paid Social Security. The average real return on the stock market since 1926 is 7.7 percent—a very far cry from 2 percent!

While postwar Americans are, as a group, receiving a quite low rate of return from the system, the poorest among them are earning a very respectable return—roughly 6 percent. The counterpart of this much better deal for the poor is a much worse deal for those in the top quintile. Their rate of return is below 1 percent. In addition to this large difference between rates of return for high and low earners, there is a large difference in rates of return between men and women. The differences between male and female internal rates of return are smaller at higher quintiles. In the case of cohort 70, for example, the difference is 2.6 percentage points in the lowest quintile versus 0.8 percentage points for the highest quintile. This may reflect the fact that a larger fraction of women in the lower lifetime earnings quintiles have longer spells of nonparticipation in the labor market. Hence, women in these quintiles may collect benefits based on their spouses' earnings records with greater frequency than do men—making their benefits larger relative to their earnings. In contrast, women in higher lifetime earnings quintiles mostly collect benefits based on their own earnings records. Their internal rates are, nevertheless, larger than those of men because women collect survivor benefits based on the spouses' higher earnings records and because they possess greater longevity.

The differences between male and female internal rates of return are smaller for later cohorts. For cohort 95, for example, the difference in the lowest quintile is only 1.4 percentage points. In the highest quintile, it is only 0.5 percentage points. The decline in the difference for later cohorts may reflect the increase over time in women's labor force participation— leading to fewer women's collecting benefits based on the spouse's earnings records. Interestingly, and unlike the lifetime net tax measure, the rate-of-return criterion suggests that nonwhites fare just as well as whites and that the non–college educated fare just as well as the college-educated.

6.4.3 Implicit Wealth Taxes Levied by the Current System

Table 6.6 shows the point made above, that roughly two-thirds of every dollar paid by postwar Americans to the OASI system represents a pure tax. Since two-thirds of the 10.6 percent OASI nominal tax rate equals 7.1 percent, the average effective OASI tax rate is 7.1 percent. For high earners, the implicit tax rate is close to eight cents on each dollar earned up to the covered earnings ceiling. For low earners, the system not only pays back in full each dollar paid in, but also provides about forty-five cents on the dollar as a subsidy. Not all poor individuals receive a subsidy, however. None of the poorest fifth of males in the eleven cohorts can expect to get back more than they pay in. Instead, they can expect that for each dollar paid in taxes, they will receive back only seventy-three cents in benefits; that is, they will lose twenty-seven cents per dollar contributed to OASI. Poor women, on the other hand, can anticipate receiving benefits equal to 1.67 cents per dollar paid in (a subsidy of sixty-seven cents). OASI's implicit wealth tax rates are also higher for nonwhites than whites and for the college-educated than the non–college educated.

6.5 Alternative Policies to Shore Up Social Security's Finances

This section examines ten potential policy reforms, all of which have been popularly discussed, that would help shore up Social Security's long-term finances. To set the stage for their analysis, we first point out that the system's present value budget imbalance is very much larger than is generally understood or being publicly acknowledged by the system's trustees.

6.5.1 Social Security's Financial Dilemma

How large is the total present value imbalance of the OASI system? If we discount all future taxes and benefits at a 3 percent real rate, we arrive at a present value imbalance of $8.1 trillion.[10] This figure represents the

10. While we follow the actuaries in using a 3 percent real discount rate in assessing the present value budget impact of alternative policies, a 3 percent discount rate seems far too low for the individual money's worth calculations we make in forming lifetime net tax rates and implicit OASDI wealth taxes. Why? Because future OASI taxes and benefits are highly uncertain and, from an individual perspective, should be discounted for their risk. One could

difference between (a) the present value of all future benefit payments and (b) the sum of the present value of future payroll tax revenue plus the current OASI trust fund.[11]

The immediate and permanent tax hike required to generate $8.1 trillion more in present value and, thus, eliminate the OASI budget imbalance is 4 percentage points or 38 percent of the post-2000 OASI tax rate of 10.6 percent.[12] This requisite 38 percent tax hike is over twice the required rate increase reported in the *1999 Trustee's Report of the Social Security Administration.* The discrepancy between the tax hike that is needed and the one the trustees say is needed is easily explained. Unlike our calculation, the *Trustees' Report* uses a truncated projection horizon—seventy-five years—which ignores the enormous deficits forecast in years seventy-six and thereafter.

One might think that looking out seventy-five years is far enough, but with each passing year, another "out-year" is added to the current seventy-five-year projection horizon. If these out-years involve large deficits, the current seventy-five-year present value imbalance will worsen. This is precisely what has been happening since 1983, when the Greenspan Commission "saved" Social Security. Indeed, about one-third of the current seventy-five-year long-term imbalance in Social Security's finances reflects the fact that since 1983, sixteen years of very large deficits have been added to the seventy-five-year projection horizon. Another third of the seventy-five-year imbalance that has arisen since 1983 reflects mistakes the actuaries made in their forecasting techniques. The final third reflects overly optimistic assumptions the actuaries made about the growth of taxable payroll, take-up rates of disability benefits, and demographics.

The size of the tax hike (38 percent) needed to produce present value balance, not just over the next 75 years but over the entire long run, is even more remarkable given that it was calculated using the relatively optimistic "intermediate" demographic and economic assumptions. Two assumptions in the intermediate set seem particularly sanguine. One is that improvements in longevity will slow down over the next several decades compared with the rate of such improvements observed over the past twenty years. Indeed, if one believes the intermediate longevity forecast, it will

argue that the actuaries should also risk adjust their discount rate in assessing the system's long-term finances.

11. In forming the present values, we use SSA's most recent projections of payroll tax revenue and OASI benefits. We take average annual growth rates of OASI taxes and benefits during the final twenty years of the seventy-five-year projections and grow the year-75 taxes and benefits through the year 2300. Discounting the difference between taxes and benefits at a real discount rate of 3 percent per year, adding the current value of the OASI trust fund, and making an adjustment for the post-2300 imbalance yields the total present value imbalance reported in the text.

12. In a telephone conservation, Social Security's deputy chief actuary, Stephen C. Goss, indicated that he also finds a 38 percent present value imbalance, although his calculations include the DI system. According to Goss, the tax hike required to balance the OASDI system in present value would be 4.7 percentage points.

take the United States until the middle of the next century to achieve the current Japanese life expectancy. The other assumption is real wage growth. Here the actuaries assume a growth rate that is over twice that observed, on average, over the past quarter century.

Under more pessimistic but arguably more realistic assumptions, an immediate and permanent payroll tax hike of more than 6 percentage points and close to 50 percent is needed to ensure that the present value of all future OASDI taxes plus the combined OASDI trust funds equal the present value of all future OASDI benefits. If such a tax hike is not enacted in the short term, even larger tax hikes will be required in the long term. Alternatively, Social Security benefits will have to be dramatically reduced.

6.5.2   Alternative OASI Reforms

All of the reforms we examine are based on the assumption that Social Security continues to finance its benefits on a PAYGO basis. The first two of the ten policies considered here were also examined in Caldwell et al. (1999). These are an immediate and permanent 38 percent increase in the OASI payroll tax rate and an immediate and permanent 25 percent cut in all OASDI benefits. The benefit cut policy generates roughly the same amount of saving in present value as the tax hike and suffices to eliminate Social Security's long-term fiscal imbalance when measured in present value. Our third policy is entitled "Accelerated Increase in the NRA." This policy raises the normal retirement age (NRA) by six months per year after the year 2000 until the normal retirement age is raised to seventy by the year 2010.[13] The fourth policy uses the consumer price index (CPI) rather than the OASI nominal wage index, to index average monthly covered earnings in forming recipients' Average Indexed Monthly Earnings (AIME). Unlike the OASI nominal wage index, which reflects both inflation and improvements in labor productivity, the CPI reflects only inflation. Hence, in placing past earnings on an equal footing with current earnings, CPI indexing provides a credit against inflation during the interim years, but none for productivity growth. Because productivity growth is generally positive, this method reduces progressively the contribution of earnings that accrued earlier during a worker's lifetime and results in a lower AIME. A lower AIME, in turn, yields a lower PIA—the retirement benefit that the worker would receive if he or she begins to collect at the applicable NRA. Note that this policy does not alter the scheduled growth in the bend points used in calculating workers' PIAs from their AIMEs.[14]

---

13. Those achieving age sixty-five during the year 2001 are assigned an NRA of sixty-five years and six months; those achieving age sixty-five during the year 2002 are assigned NRA = sixty-six, and so on, until the NRA reaches seventy.

14. The PIA equals 90 percent of the first X dollars of AIME plus 32 percent of the AIME exceeding X dollars but less than Y dollars plus 15 percent of the AIME in excess of Y dollars. The nominal values X and Y (the bend points) are announced each year by the Social

Our fifth policy maintains the current formula for calculating initial benefits, but once these benefits commence, they increase over time, not by
the CPI, but by the CPI minus 1 percent. The sixth policy is called "Stabilize Real Per Capita Benefits." This policy calculates retirees' primary insurance amounts as prescribed by current law, but then reduces these
amounts by post–year-2000 growth in labor productivity. This growth reduction factor means that real OASI benefit levels do not keep pace with
economy-wide increases in labor productivity and real wages. The seventh
policy maintains the current benefit formula in all respects except one: It
grows the bend points used in the calculating PIAs according to inflation
rather than the growth in the OASI wage index. Consequently, as real
wages grow, successive generations of retirees will find themselves experiencing real "bracket creep," meaning that the benefits of an ever larger
percentage of retirees will be computed using the less progressive parts of
the benefit formula.

The eighth policy eliminates the ceiling on taxable earnings but does not
alter the method of determining benefits, so earnings that are above what
would otherwise be the ceiling will be included by OASI in the calculation
of benefits. The ninth policy is equivalent to the previous one except for
this last feature: It collects taxes without any earnings ceiling but calculates benefits based on the existing earnings ceiling provisions that apply
to the future as well as the present. The tenth and final policy increases
the years used in computing covered workers' AIME from thirty-five to
forty years.

6.5.3 Impact of the Alternative Policies on OASI's Unfunded Liability to Postwar Americans

As mentioned, policies 1 and 2 (the 38 percent immediate and permanent hike in the OASDI tax rate and the 25 percent immediate and permanent benefit cut) both suffice, under the Social Security actuaries' intermediate assumptions, to bring the system's finances into present value
balance when its future net cash flows are discounted at a 3 percent real
rate of return. Both policies generate approximately $8 trillion more in net
taxes when measured in present value. These additional net taxes would
be paid not only by postwar Americans but also by other Americans either
alive now or expected to be born in the future.

Table 6.7 shows how these two policies as well as our other eight would
affect the net taxes (taxes minus benefits) that postwar Americans will pay,
measured in present value. The first row of this table indicates that, under

---

Security Administration and are scheduled to increase at the rate of growth of average wages
lagged by two years. For example, the bend points for 1999 are obtained by multiplying the
corresponding 1979 bend point amounts by the ratio between the national average wage
index for 1997 ($27,426.00) and that for 1977 ($9,779.44). These results are then rounded to
the nearest dollar.

Table 6.7   **Change in Social Security's Net Liability to Postwar Generations**

Policy	Present Value Imbalance	Change from Current Rules
Current rules	1,172.9	
1 38% tax hike beginning in year 2000	−2,874.0	−4,046.9
2 25% benefit cut beginning in year 2000	−2,004.3	−3,177.2
3 Accelerated increase in NRA	−1,089.7	−2,262.5
4 CPI indexing of covered earnings	145.9	−1,026.9
5 Indexing benefits by CPI minus 1%	−231.0	−1,403.9
6 Stabilize real per capita benefits	−3,312.7	−4,485.6
7 Freeze bend points in real terms	−194.9	−1,367.7
8 Eliminate taxable earnings ceiling	−1,048.5	−2,221.4
9 Eliminate taxable ceiling without benefit change	−2,276.7	−3,449.6
10 Increase computation years from 35 to 40	737.9	−435.0

Source: Author's calculations.

current policy, postwar Americans' future benefits exceed their future taxes by about $1.2 trillion; thus, the present value of postwar Americans' future net taxes is negative. This is hardly surprising, given that the baby boom generation is nearing retirement.

Although OASI's $1.2 trillion unfunded net OASI liability to postwar Americans is large, it represents less than 15 percent of the total $8.1 trillion present value budget gap identified above. Thus, the overwhelming majority of OASI's present value imbalance consists not of obligations to postwar Americans but of obligations to the Americans born before 1945—most of whom are now retired.

As table 6.7 indicates, all ten of the policies reduce the system's liability to postwar Americans. Indeed, eight of the ten policies wipe out the liability entirely; of these, six transform postwar Americans' net tax payments into a major implicit asset of the system by making their future benefits far smaller in present value than their future taxes. Take policy 1, the 38 percent tax hike. This policy reduces the unfunded net OASI liability to postwar Americans by over $4 trillion! To put it more directly, this policy forces postwar Americans to resolve, on their own, almost 50 percent of the system's current long-term fiscal imbalance. The same can be said of policies 2, 6, and 9.

6.5.4   Lifetime Net Tax Rates Under Alternative Policies

Tables 6.8 through 6.10 show the impact on lifetime net tax rates of our ten different methods of dealing with OASI's long-term funding shortfall. These tables present results for all members of cohorts 45, 70, and 95, cross-classified by lowest, middle, and highest quintiles of lifetime earnings. They also consider three different real discount rates—our bench-

Table 6.8   **The Impact of Potential OASI Reforms on Lifetime Net Tax Rates, All Observations ($r = 5\%$)**

	Quintile of Average Benefits			
	Lowest	Middle	Highest	All
Birth cohort 1945–49				
1 Current rules	−4.2	6.1	5.0	5.3
2 38% tax hike beginning in year 2000	−3.9	6.4	5.3	5.7
3 25% benefit cut beginning in year 2000	−0.2	7.1	5.4	6.0
4 Accelerated increase in NRA	−1.7	6.9	5.4	5.9
5 CPI indexing of covered earnings	−3.0	6.4	5.1	5.6
6 Indexing benefits by CPI minus 1%	−2.5	6.5	5.1	5.6
7 Stabilize real per capita benefits	−2.3	6.6	5.2	5.7
8 Freeze bend points in real terms	−3.8	6.3	5.0	5.4
9 Eliminate earnings ceiling	−4.4	6.1	5.3	5.5
10 Eliminate earnings ceiling without benefit change	−4.2	6.1	5.4	5.6
11 Increase computation years from 35 to 40	−3.5	6.3	5.0	5.4
Birth cohort 1970–74				
1 Current rules	−3.4	5.7	5.3	5.4
2 38% tax hike beginning in year 2000	−1.1	8.4	7.1	7.6
3 25% benefit cut beginning in year 2000	0.0	6.9	5.7	6.1
4 Accelerated increase in NRA	−1.6	6.5	5.6	5.9
5 CPI indexing of covered earnings	−2.2	6.1	5.4	5.6
6 Indexing benefits by CPI minus 1%	−1.9	6.2	5.4	5.7
7 Stabilize real per capita benefits	1.9	7.5	5.9	6.5
8 Freeze bend points in real terms	−2.2	6.3	5.5	5.8
9 Eliminate earnings ceiling	−4.1	5.7	7.7	6.9
10 Eliminate earnings ceiling without benefit change	−3.4	5.7	8.2	7.3
11 Increase computation years from 35 to 40	−2.6	5.9	5.3	5.5
Birth cohort 1995–2000				
1 Current rules	−2.9	5.5	5.4	5.4
2 38% tax hike beginning in year 2000	0.9	9.3	8.0	8.4
3 25% benefit cut beginning in year 2000	0.4	6.7	5.8	6.1
4 Accelerated increase in NRA	−1.3	6.2	5.6	5.8
5 CPI indexing of covered earnings	−1.7	5.9	5.5	5.6
6 Indexing benefits by CPI minus 1%	−1.5	5.9	5.5	5.6
7 Stabilize real per capita benefits	6.8	9.0	6.6	7.5
8 Freeze bend points in real terms	−0.9	6.4	5.7	5.9
9 Eliminate earnings ceiling	−3.3	5.5	8.2	7.1
10 Eliminate earnings ceiling without benefit change	−2.9	5.5	8.7	7.5
11 Increase computation years from 35 to 40	−2.2	5.7	5.4	5.5

Source: Author's calculations.

Table 6.9   **The Impact of Potential OASI Reforms on Lifetime Net Tax Rates,
All Observations ($r = 7\%$)**

	Quintile of Average Benefits			
	Lowest	Middle	Highest	All
Birth cohort 1945–49				
1 Current rules	4.7	8.4	5.9	6.9
2 38% tax hike beginning in year 2000	5.0	8.6	6.1	7.1
3 25% benefit cut beginning in year 2000	6.5	8.9	6.0	7.2
4 Accelerated increase in NRA	5.9	8.8	6.0	7.2
5 CPI indexing of covered earnings	5.2	8.6	5.9	7.0
6 Indexing benefits by CPI minus 1%	5.4	8.6	5.9	7.0
7 Stabilize real per capita benefits	5.6	8.7	5.9	7.0
8 Freeze bend points in real terms	4.9	8.5	5.9	6.9
9 Eliminate earnings ceiling	4.6	8.4	6.1	7.0
10 Eliminate earnings ceiling without benefit change	4.7	8.4	6.1	7.0
11 Increase computation years from 35 to 40	5.0	8.5	5.9	6.9
Birth cohort 1970–74				
1 Current rules	3.4	8.1	6.2	6.9
2 38% tax hike beginning in year 2000	5.6	10.5	7.9	8.8
3 25% benefit cut beginning in year 2000	5.1	8.7	6.4	7.2
4 Accelerated increase in NRA	4.3	8.5	6.3	7.1
5 CPI indexing of covered earnings	4.0	8.3	6.2	7.0
6 Indexing benefits by CPI minus 1%	4.1	8.3	6.3	7.0
7 Stabilize real per capita benefits	6.1	9.0	6.5	7.4
8 Freeze bend points in real terms	4.0	8.4	6.3	7.0
9 Eliminate earnings ceiling	3.1	8.1	8.6	8.4
10 Eliminate earnings ceiling without benefit change	3.4	8.1	8.8	8.5
11 Increase computation years from 35 to 40	3.8	8.2	6.2	6.9
Birth cohort 1995–2000				
1 Current rules	3.7	7.8	6.3	6.9
2 38% tax hike beginning in year 2000	7.5	11.7	9.0	10.0
3 25% benefit cut beginning in year 2000	5.3	8.4	6.5	7.2
4 Accelerated increase in NRA	4.5	8.2	6.4	7.1
5 CPI indexing of covered earnings	4.3	8.0	6.4	7.0
6 Indexing benefits by CPI minus 1%	4.3	8.0	6.4	7.0
7 Stabilize real per capita benefits	8.5	9.6	6.9	7.9
8 Freeze bend points in real terms	4.7	8.3	6.5	7.2
9 Eliminate earnings ceiling	3.5	7.8	9.2	8.7
10 Eliminate earnings ceiling without benefit change	3.7	7.9	9.5	8.8
11 Increase computation years from 35 to 40	4.1	7.9	6.3	6.9

Source: Author's calculations.

Table 6.10   **The Impact of Potential OASI Reforms on Lifetime Net Tax Rates,
All Observations ($r = 3\%$)**

	Quintile of Average Benefits			
	Lowest	Middle	Highest	All
Birth cohort 1945–49				
1 Current rules	−23.0	1.9	3.3	2.5
2 38% tax hike beginning in year 2000	−22.5	2.4	3.8	3.0
3 25% benefit cut beginning in year 2000	−14.3	3.9	4.1	3.9
4 Accelerated increase in NRA	−17.8	3.5	4.1	3.6
5 CPI indexing of covered earnings	−20.3	2.5	3.5	2.9
6 Indexing benefits by CPI minus 1%	−18.8	2.7	3.7	3.1
7 Stabilize real per capita benefits	−18.9	2.8	3.7	3.1
8 Freeze bend points in real terms	−21.9	2.1	3.5	2.7
9 Eliminate earnings ceiling	−23.4	1.9	3.7	2.7
10 Eliminate earnings ceiling without benefit change	−23.0	1.9	4.0	2.9
11 Increase computation years from 35 to 40	−21.4	2.2	3.4	2.7
Birth cohort 1970–74				
1 Current rules	−17.9	0.9	3.7	2.7
2 38% tax hike beginning in year 2000	−15.5	3.9	5.6	5.0
3 25% benefit cut beginning in year 2000	−10.8	3.3	4.4	4.0
4 Accelerated increase in NRA	−14.4	2.5	4.2	3.5
5 CPI indexing of covered earnings	−15.3	1.7	3.9	3.1
6 Indexing benefits by CPI minus 1%	−14.4	2.0	4.0	3.3
7 Stabilize real per capita benefits	−7.0	4.7	4.8	4.7
8 Freeze bend points in real terms	−15.4	2.0	4.1	3.3
9 Eliminate earnings ceiling	−19.4	0.8	5.9	4.0
10 Eliminate earnings ceiling without benefit change	−17.9	0.9	6.8	4.7
11 Increase computation years from 35 to 40	−16.3	1.3	3.7	2.8
Birth cohort 1995–2000				
1 Current rules	−17.4	0.8	3.7	2.5
2 38% tax hike beginning in year 2000	−13.5	4.6	6.3	5.5
3 25% benefit cut beginning in year 2000	−10.5	3.2	4.5	3.9
4 Accelerated increase in NRA	−14.0	2.1	4.2	3.4
5 CPI indexing of covered earnings	−14.8	1.5	3.9	3.0
6 Indexing benefits by CPI minus 1%	−14.1	1.7	4.0	3.1
7 Stabilize real per capita benefits	3.1	7.9	6.0	6.6
8 Freeze bend points in real terms	−13.1	2.5	4.4	3.6
9 Eliminate earnings ceiling	−18.3	0.7	6.2	4.1
10 Eliminate earnings ceiling without benefit change	−17.4	0.8	7.2	4.7
11 Increase computation years from 35 to 40	−15.9	1.1	3.8	2.7

Source: Author's calculations.

mark rate of 5 percent, a high rate of 7 percent, and a low rate of 3 percent. The group of 32 tables which supplement this paper, which are posted at [http://www.NBER.org/data-appendix/gokhale01] results broken down by demographic subgroup.

Observe first the 5 percent discount rate results for policies 1 and 2 in table 6.8. Implementing either policy would raise the lifetime net tax rates of all postwar generations. However, the two policies have quite different intergenerational incidence. The tax hike hits later generations much harder than it does earlier ones. The benefit cut affects all generations roughly the same. Consider cohorts 45 and 96. The tax hike policy raises cohort 45's lifetime net tax rate from 5.3 percent to just 5.7 percent, but it raises cohort 95's lifetime net tax rate from 5.4 to 8.4 percent. In contrast, the benefit cut policy leaves cohort 45's and 95's lifetime net tax rates at 6.0 percent and 6.1 percent, respectively. Clearly, earlier generations fare better under the tax hike because they have limited remaining labor earnings that are subject to the higher payroll tax rate. In the case of the benefit cut, all generations are similarly hurt because none has yet begun to receive Social Security retirement benefits, which is the lion's share of OASI benefits.

Both of these policies are tougher on the lifetime low earners than on the lifetime high earners in terms of their impact on lifetime net tax rates. For those in the lowest quintile in cohort 95, a 38 percent tax hike means losing close to four cents more per dollar earned to the system.[15] For their contemporaries in the highest quintile, the policy means losing only 2.6 percent more per dollar earned. Under the benefit cut policy, these differences are much more striking. The poorest one-fifth of cohort 95 lose 3.3 percent of their lifetime incomes, whereas the richest fifth lose only 0.4 percent. Finally, it is worth noting that for the bottom quintile in cohort 95 both the tax hike and benefit cut policies transform OASI from a net subsidy into a net tax.

How do policies 3 through 10 compare with policies 1 and 2? In terms of their impact on lifetime net tax rates, the answer is that they fall between policies 1 and 2. Several points are, however, worth stressing. First, policy 3 (the accelerated increase in NRA) hurts older cohorts more than younger cohorts. For example, the overall increase in the lifetime net tax rate for cohort 45 is 0.6, whereas it is only 0.4 for cohort 95. This occurs because current rules already incorporate an increase in the NRA.[16] The accelera-

---

15. This percentage point increase precisely equals that required for eliminating the OASI imbalance.

16. Under current rules, the NRA is scheduled to increase from sixty-five for those who will achieve age sixty-five in 2002 or earlier to sixty-six for those who will achieve age sixty-five between the years 2007 and 2019. Thereafter, the NRA will increase from sixty-six for those achieving age sixty-five before the year 2020 to sixty-seven for those achieving age sixty-five in 2025.

tion of the increase in NRA hits those about to retire in the near future particularly hard. For example, those reaching age sixty-five in the year 2010 would have a normal retirement age of sixty-six under current rules, but seventy under policy 3. In contrast, the NRA of those reaching age sixty-five after 2022 will increase from sixty-seven under current rules to seventy under policy 3.

Second, policies 6, 7, 8, and 9 ("Stabilize Real Per Capita Benefits," "Eliminate Earnings Ceiling," and "Eliminate Earnings Ceiling without Benefit Change") hurt younger cohorts much more than older ones. Policy 6 eliminates the real growth in benefits under the current system associated with economy-wide productivity growth. Hence, later retiring generations, whose benefits would otherwise be higher than the benefits of those retiring earlier, lose the most from this policy. As mentioned earlier, policy 7 imposes bracket creep: Slower growth in nominal bend point values exposes a greater fraction of each person's AIME to the relatively progressive regions of the PIA formula. Under policy 8, the incremental lifetime earnings subject to payroll taxes are much larger for younger than for older generations because a greater fraction of the former generations' working lifetimes lies the future. However, because of the progressive benefit formula, younger generations' benefits do not keep pace with the increase in their lifetime payroll taxes. The effect is even more pronounced when benefits are held constant under policy 9.

Third, policy 6 (and, to a lesser extent, policy 7) is extremely tough on poor members of young cohorts. For the bottom quintile of cohort 95, policy 6 transforms OASI's 2.9 percent of lifetime earnings net subsidy into a 6.8 percent net tax and leaves this quintile with a higher net tax rate than the top quintile! Note that this policy has a much bigger impact than does policy 4 ("CPI Indexing of Covered Earnings") on the lifetime net tax rates of poor members of young cohorts. The same can be said of middle- and upper-income young cohort members. The reason is that policy 6 directly eliminates all growth in benefits due to overall real wage growth, whereas policy 4 works by reducing the AIME. For those at the upper range of the distribution of lifetime earnings, a 1 percent reduction in the AIME translates into only a 0.15 percent reduction in benefits under policy 4. Policy 7 ("Freeze Bend Points in Real Terms") is particularly damaging to the lifetime poor because it pushes them into lower marginal benefit brackets.

Fourth, policy 9—raising the earnings ceiling without concomitant benefit increases (without permitting the higher covered earnings to be included in the calculation of AIME)—is particularly grievous on young cohort members in the highest lifetime earnings quintile. As can be verified in the bottom panel of table 6.8, policy 9 raises the lifetime net tax rate of cohort 95's top 20 percent of lifetime earners by 3.3 percentage points. In contrast, the poorest members of this cohort experience no change in their lifetime net tax rates.[17]

Fifth, policy 10 ("Increase Computation Years from 35 to 40) leaves unchanged the lifetime net tax rates of the top earning quintiles, whereas it raises those of the lowest and middle quintiles. The lowest quintile in each cohort is especially hard hit. The reason is that members of this quintile have many years in their earnings histories during which they do not work. Including those years in calculating AIME lowers their AIMEs and, thus, their benefit levels.

6.5.5   The Sensitivity of the Results to the Choice of Discount Rates

Tables 6.9 and 6.10 repeat the analysis of table 6.8 but assume discount rates of 3 and 7 percent, respectively. Comparing the same policy across the three tables indicates that the level of lifetime net tax rates is highly sensitive to the choice of discount rates. For example, under current law and assuming a 3 percent discount rate, the lifetime net tax rate of the lowest lifetime earnings quintile in cohort 70 is −17.9 percent. Assuming a 5 percent discount rate, it is −3.4 percent, and assuming a 7 percent discount rate, it is 3.4 percent. Hence, a 400 basis point swing in the choice of the discount rate transforms the OASI system from a huge net subsidy to the poor to a small net tax. The same experiment—moving from a 3 percent to a 7 percent discount rate—raises the current-rules lifetime net tax rate of the middle quintile from 0.8 percent to 7.8 percent, a very dramatic increase.

In contrast, for the highest quintile in cohort 70, the absolute increase in the lifetime net tax rate (in moving from a 3 to a 7 percent discount rate) is only 2.5 percentage points. One reason for this difference is that the lifetime poor have shorter workspans. This makes the denominators of the lifetime net tax rates of the poor less sensitive to the discount rate than the numerators, which makes the net tax rate itself more sensitive. A second reason is that the lifetime poor are paying relatively little in OASI taxes compared to the benefits they receive. This means that changes in the discount rate change the present value of benefits by substantially more than they do the present value of taxes. This point becomes abundantly clear when one considers the case in which taxes equal benefits on an annual basis. In this case, the lifetime net tax rate is zero regardless of the discount rate.

Given the substantial sensitivity of the calculated lifetime OASI net tax

---

17. In the case of policy 8, the lowest quintiles in all cohorts experience declines in their lifetime net tax rate. The explanation is that many of the observations in these quintiles receive benefits based on their spouses' earnings record and these benefits go up when all of their spouses' earnings are included in the calculation of dependent and survivor benefits, not simply their spouses' earnings up to the covered earnings ceiling.

rates to the assumed discount rate, it is worth pondering which discount rate is most appropriate to use in this context. The answer depends on one's view of the risk of OASI taxes and transfers. If one views these flows as no more risky than, say, the repayment of government debt, the appropriate discount rate would be the real return offered by inflation-indexed treasury bonds. If, on the other hand, these flows are not only risky but subject to fluctuations in line with the stock market, then the expected return on the stock market would be the appropriate benchmark. In the former case, a real discount rate of between 3 and 4 percent would be justified. In the latter case, a rate around 7 percent should be chosen.

As Baxter and King (2001) pointed out, the method of wage-indexing Social Security benefits and the positive correlation between real wage growth and the stock market, suggests that both Social Security taxes and benefits move with the stock market. On the other hand, there are ample examples of changes in Social Security benefit rules that have not coincided with stock market fluctuations. How these political risks would affect the appropriate rate at which to discount Social Security benefits is a subject we are currently researching.

6.5.6   Lifetime Net Tax Rates of Demographic Groups Under Alternative Policies

The male and female results, based on the benchmark 5 percent discount rate, are displayed in website tables 1 and 2. These tables show the same general patterns across policy alternatives as table 6.8. Males and females would generally rank the policy alternatives in the same way, provided they were in the same earnings quintile within the same cohort. As an example, take cohort 95. For middle-income males in this group, the tax hike policy produces the highest net tax rate—9.8 percent. For the bottom quintile males, policy 6 ("Stabilize Real Per Capital Benefits") is the worst, leaving this group facing a 7.9 percent lifetime net tax rate—a full 1.3 percentage points higher than the corresponding rate facing those in the top quintile of this cohort. Moreover, for the top quintile of males, eliminating the earnings ceiling with no benefit change is the worst alternative, producing an 8.7 percent lifetime net tax rate. Middle quintile and bottom quintile females are both harmed the most by policy 6, but in the case of middle quintile females, the tax hike policy is almost as bad; and, like the top quintile males, the top quintile females find policy 9 the worst overall.

Whites and nonwhites within the same cohort and quintile would also rank the policy changes the same. This is also the case for the college-educated and non–college educated. As web site tables 3 through 6 confirm, the really adverse policies for cohort 45 members, regardless of their race or education, are policy 2 and policy 1. For those in the middle quintile of cohort 95, policies 1 and 6 are the worst policies, independent of race and education. If, on the other hand, one does not control for quintile, it is clear that certain policies that are worse for the high earners are better for nonwhites than whites, and for the non–college educated than for the college-educated, because the former groups are overrepresented in the lower quintiles. Policy 9 is an example. For cohort 95, this policy would lower the nonwhite/white and non–college educated/college-educated lifetime net tax rate differentials from 0.7 to 0.1 and from 0.8 to −0.5 percent, respectively.

Web site tables 7 and 8 show the impact of the proposed reforms on college-educated, white males, on the one hand, and non–college educated, nonwhite females on the other. Again, how individual members of these groups fare is primarily a matter of their cohort, their quintile, and the policy selected. However, if one fails to consider quintile position, policies 8 and 9 are particularly detrimental to white, college-educated males relative to nonwhite, non–college educated females.

6.5.7   Internal Rates of Return Under Alternative Policies

Table 6.11 considers how the ten policies alter internal rates of return. With the exception of the benefit cut and accelerated increase in NRA policies, the reforms produce rather small changes in overall internal rates of return for cohort 45. For cohort 95, however, the story is quite different. Six of the ten policies reduce the overall internal rate of return by 0.5 or more percentage points. Policy 6, which stabilizes real benefits, produces a negative 2.3 percent rate of return. This is to be expected, given that the policy cuts initial benefits based on a compound productivity growth factor.

Higher earners in all three cohorts experience the sharpest reductions in internal rates of return. In cohort 95, four of the ten policies reduce the internal rates of return of those in the top quintile by 0.9 percentage points or more. Policy 6 lowers the internal rate of return of those in the top quintile in cohort 95 from 0.6 percent to −3.8 percent! Of the ten policies, eight leave top quintile earners in cohort 95 with negative to very close to zero rates of return.

While all ten policies substantially lower rates of return earned by the lifetime high earners, only policy 6 dramatically reduces the rate of return earned by the lifetime poor, and only in the case of cohort 95. Take, as an example, the tax hike policy. For the bottom quintile in cohort 95, the internal rate of return declines from 5.7 percent to 4.8 percent. Although this may seem small, its also consistent with table 6.7's finding that the policy raises this group's lifetime net tax rate by 3.8 percentage points— not a small amount. The point that must be kept in mind, then, is the standard one about the power of compound interest; in this context, it means that small differences in internal rates of return can translate into very large differences in lifetime net tax rates.

As expected, policy 9 (eliminating the earnings ceiling without changing

Table 6.11   **The Impact of Potential OASI Reforms on Internal Rates of Return, All Observations**

	Lowest	Middle	Highest	All
Birth Cohort 1945–49				
0 Current rules	5.7	2.4	0.8	1.9
1 38% tax hike beginning in year 2000	5.7	2.3	0.5	1.7
2 25% benefit cut beginning in year 2000	5.0	1.6	−0.1	1.1
3 Accelerated increase in NRA	5.3	1.8	0	1.3
4 CPI indexing of covered earnings	5.5	2.2	0.6	1.7
5 Indexing benefits by CPI minus 1%	5.5	2.1	0.4	1.6
6 Stabilize real per capita benefits	5.4	2.1	0.4	1.6
7 Freeze bend points in real terms	5.7	2.3	0.7	1.8
8 Eliminate earnings ceiling	5.8	2.4	0.6	1.9
9 Eliminate earnings ceiling without benefit change	5.7	2.4	0.4	1.8
10 Increase computation years from 35 to 40	5.6	2.3	0.7	1.8
Birth Cohort 1970–74				
0 Current rules	5.8	2.8	0.6	1.8
1 38% tax hike beginning in year 2000	5.2	2.0	−0.2	1.1
2 25% benefit cut beginning in year 2000	5.0	1.9	−0.2	1.0
3 Accelerated increase in NRA	5.4	2.3	0.1	1.3
4 CPI indexing of covered earnings	5.5	2.5	0.4	1.6
5 Indexing benefits by CPI minus 1%	5.5	2.4	0.2	1.5
6 Stabilize real per capita benefits	4.5	1.4	−0.9	0.4
7 Freeze bend points in real terms	5.5	2.4	0.2	1.5
8 Eliminate earnings ceiling	5.9	2.8	0.2	1.5
9 Eliminate earnings ceiling without benefit change	5.8	2.8	−0.7	1.1
10 Increase computation years from 35 to 40	5.6	2.7	0.6	1.7
Birth cohort 1995–2000				
0 Current rules	5.7	2.8	0.6	1.9
1 38% tax hike beginning in year 2000	4.8	1.9	−0.4	0.9
2 25% benefit cut beginning in year 2000	4.9	2.0	−0.3	1.0
3 Accelerated increase in NRA	5.3	2.3	0.1	1.4
4 CPI indexing of covered earnings	5.4	2.6	0.4	1.7
5 Indexing benefits by CPI minus 1%	5.4	2.5	0.2	1.5
6 Stabilize real per capita benefits	2.0	−1.3	−3.8	−2.3
7 Freeze bend points in real terms	5.2	2.2	−0.1	1.2
8 Eliminate earnings ceiling	5.8	2.8	0.1	1.5
9 Eliminate earnings ceiling without benefit change	5.7	2.8	−0.8	1.1
10 Increase computation years from 35 to 40	5.5	2.7	0.5	1.8

Source: Author's calculations.

benefits) significantly reduces the internal rates of return for those in the highest quintile, especially for later-born cohorts. The patterns shown in table 6.11 are reproduced to varying degrees in web site tables 9 through 16, which break down the policy effects on internal rates of return by demographic subgroup. Policy 3 (the accelerated increase in NRA) affects older men more than older women, but the same is not true for younger men versus younger women. For example, the internal rate of return (not controlling for quintile) falls by 0.9 percentage points for men but only by 0.5 percentage points for women in cohort 45. In contrast, the corresponding changes are 0.6 percentage points for men and 0.5 percentage points for women in cohort 95. This result may arise because the longevity difference between men and women is greater for cohort 45 than for cohort 95. As a result, postponing the NRA affects men more than women in the older cohort, but this effect is not as pronounced for younger men versus women. Web site tables 9 through 16 reveal no other significant differences across demographic groups with respect to the manner in which internal rates of return respond to particular policy changes.

6.5.8 Implicit Wealth Tax Rates Under Alternative Policies

Table 6.12 shows how OASI implicit wealth taxes, calculated at a 5 percent discount rate, would be altered by the ten policies. Each policy would raise implicit tax rates for all postwar cohorts, but for the oldest cohorts the effects would be small. In the case of cohort 45, the current rules implicit tax rate is 66.3 percent. Policy 2 (the explicit benefit cut) produces the largest increase in this tax rate, but the increase is only to 74.8 percent. For cohort 95, the implicit tax rate under current law is 65.8 percent. Policy 6 generates the greatest increase in this tax rate, to 91.5 percent; policy 2 generates the second greatest increase, to 75.2 percent.

The increases in implicit wealth tax rates are more dramatic for the bottom quintile of cohort 95. This quintile faces a negative current rules tax rate equal to −28.9 percent, meaning the government is returning in benefits 1.289 cents per dollar paid in taxes. Policies 1, 2, and 6 reverse the sign of this group's implicit tax rate. Indeed, policy 6 raises the tax rate all the way to 67.1 percent. For the top quintile in cohort 95, six of the policies generate implicit wealth tax rates in excess of 80 percent; policy 6 imposes an implicit tax rate of 94.4 percent. Web site tables 17 through 24 provide demographic breakdowns of these results. As in the case of lifetime net tax rates and internal rates of return, the basic patterns of policy impacts experienced by the overall samples in each cohort carry over to the demographic subgroups.

Tables 6.13 and 6.14 consider how the implicit wealth tax rates would differ when calculated based on either a 3 percent or a 7 percent real discount rate. The answer is that they would differ enormously. Under current rules, the lowest quintile of cohort 70 faces a negative 175 percent

Table 6.12   **The Impact of Potential OASI Reforms on Implicit Wealth Tax Rates, All Observations ($r = 5\%$)**

	Quintile of Average Benefits			
	Lowest	Middle	Highest	All
Birth cohort 1945–49				
1 Current rules	−35.3	61.5	75.6	66.3
2 38% tax hike beginning in year 2000	−31.6	62.7	76.7	67.6
3 25% benefit cut beginning in year 2000	−1.5	71.4	81.7	74.8
4 Accelerated increase in NRA	−14.1	69.4	81.6	73.6
5 CPI indexing of covered earnings	−24.8	64.6	77.1	68.8
6 Indexing benefits by CPI minus 1%	−20.9	65.3	77.9	69.6
7 Stabilize real per capita benefits	−19.4	66.1	78.5	70.3
8 Freeze bend points in real terms	−31.3	62.8	76.7	67.5
9 Eliminate earnings ceiling	−37.1	61.3	75.3	66.3
10 Eliminate earnings ceiling without benefit change	−35.3	61.5	77.1	67.3
11 Increase computation years from 35 to 40	−29.0	63.0	76.3	67.5
Birth cohort 1970–74				
1 Current rules	−33.7	55.6	78.2	67.5
2 38% tax hike beginning in year 2000	−8.8	64.8	82.8	74.3
3 25% benefit cut beginning in year 2000	−0.1	67.0	83.7	75.8
4 Accelerated increase in NRA	−16.0	63.1	82.2	73.1
5 CPI indexing of covered earnings	−21.6	59.4	79.6	70.2
6 Indexing benefits by CPI minus 1%	−18.9	60.1	80.4	70.9
7 Stabilize real per capita benefits	18.3	73.3	86.8	80.4
8 Freeze bend points in real terms	−21.9	60.9	81.2	71.6
9 Eliminate earnings ceiling	−39.8	55.1	79.7	70.1
10 Eliminate earnings ceiling without benefit change	−33.6	55.7	84.7	73.6
11 Increase computation years from 35 to 40	−25.9	57.3	78.6	68.7
Birth cohort 1995–2000				
1 Current rules	−28.9	53.8	77.5	65.8
2 38% tax hike beginning in year 2000	6.5	66.5	83.7	75.2
3 25% benefit cut beginning in year 2000	3.6	65.7	83.1	74.5
4 Accelerated increase in NRA	−12.5	60.8	81.1	71.1
5 CPI indexing of covered earnings	−16.6	57.7	78.9	68.6
6 Indexing benefits by CPI minus 1%	−15.2	58.1	79.7	69.2
7 Stabilize real per capita benefits	67.1	88.8	94.4	91.5
8 Freeze bend points in real terms	−8.8	62.6	82.4	72.9
9 Eliminate earnings ceiling	−32.7	53.6	79.9	69.5
10 Eliminate earnings ceiling without benefit change	−28.8	53.9	84.8	72.8
11 Increase computation years from 35 to 40	−21.5	55.6	77.9	67.0

Source: Author's calculations.

Table 6.13   **The Impact of Potential OASI Reforms on Implicit Wealth Tax Rates, All Observations ($r = 7\%$)**

	Quintile of Average Benefits			
	Lowest	Middle	Highest	All
Birth cohort 1945–49				
1 Current rules	38.7	82.2	88.2	83.8
2 38% tax hike beginning in year 2000	40.1	82.6	88.5	84.2
3 25% benefit cut beginning in year 2000	53.8	86.8	91.2	87.9
4 Accelerated increase in NRA	49.2	86.0	91.1	87.4
5 CPI indexing of covered earnings	43.4	83.7	88.9	85.0
6 Indexing benefits by CPI minus 1%	44.5	83.8	89.2	85.2
7 Stabilize real per capita benefits	45.9	84.4	89.6	85.7
8 Freeze bend points in real terms	40.5	82.8	88.7	84.4
9 Eliminate earnings ceiling	38.0	82.2	87.8	83.6
10 Eliminate earnings ceiling without benefit change	38.7	82.2	88.7	84.1
11 Increase computation years from 35 to 40	41.7	82.9	88.5	84.4
Birth cohort 1970–74				
1 Current rules	33.5	78.6	89.4	84.2
2 38% tax hike beginning in year 2000	45.2	82.7	91.5	87.3
3 25% benefit cut beginning in year 2000	50.2	84.1	92.1	88.2
4 Accelerated increase in NRA	42.6	82.3	91.4	87.0
5 CPI indexing of covered earnings	39.3	80.4	90.1	85.5
6 Indexing benefits by CPI minus 1%	40.0	80.6	90.4	85.7
7 Stabilize real per capita benefits	59.4	87.2	93.6	90.5
8 Freeze bend points in real terms	39.3	81.2	90.9	86.2
9 Eliminate earnings ceiling	30.7	78.3	89.8	85.2
10 Eliminate earnings ceiling without benefit change	33.5	78.7	92.3	86.9
11 Increase computation years from 35 to 40	37.7	79.4	89.7	84.8
Birth cohort 1995–2000				
1 Current rules	36.4	77.1	89.0	83.2
2 38% tax hike beginning in year 2000	53.9	83.4	92.0	87.8
3 25% benefit cut beginning in year 2000	52.4	83.1	91.8	87.5
4 Accelerated increase in NRA	44.7	80.6	90.8	85.8
5 CPI indexing of covered earnings	42.3	79.1	89.7	84.6
6 Indexing benefits by CPI minus 1%	42.5	79.1	90.0	84.7
7 Stabilize real per capita benefits	83.8	94.5	97.3	95.9
8 Freeze bend points in real terms	46.3	81.5	91.4	86.7
9 Eliminate earnings ceiling	34.5	77.0	89.9	84.8
10 Eliminate earnings ceiling without benefit change	36.4	77.2	92.4	86.4
11 Increase computation years from 35 to 40	40.2	78.1	89.2	83.8

Source: Author's calculations.

Table 6.14   **The Impact of Potential OASI Reforms on Implicit Wealth Tax Rates, All Observations ($r = 3\%$)**

	Quintile of Average Benefits			
	Lowest	Middle	Highest	All
Birth cohort 1945–49				
1 Current rules	−196.1	19.2	50.9	30.9
2 38% tax hike beginning in year 2000	−185.0	22.9	54.2	34.9
3 25% benefit cut beginning in year 2000	−121.8	39.9	63.3	48.4
4 Accelerated increase in NRA	−152.3	35.3	62.8	45.6
5 CPI indexing of covered earnings	−173.0	25.7	53.8	36.1
6 Indexing benefits by CPI minus 1%	−160.6	28.0	56.1	38.4
7 Stabilize real per capita benefits	−161.2	28.8	56.7	39.1
8 Freeze bend points in real terms	−187.3	21.9	53.1	33.4
9 Eliminate earnings ceiling	−200.2	18.9	51.9	32.0
10 Eliminate earnings ceiling without benefit change	−196.1	19.3	55.5	34.1
11 Increase computation years from 35 to 40	−182.6	22.3	52.3	33.5
Birth cohort 1970–74				
1 Current rules	−175.0	8.9	55.6	33.7
2 38% tax hike beginning in year 2000	−122.1	29.1	65.7	48.6
3 25% benefit cut beginning in year 2000	−105.9	32.1	66.8	50.5
4 Accelerated increase in NRA	−140.8	23.8	63.5	44.7
5 CPI indexing of covered earnings	−149.4	16.5	58.4	39.1
6 Indexing benefits by CPI minus 1%	−140.5	19.1	60.6	41.2
7 Stabilize real per capita benefits	−68.2	45.1	73.1	59.8
8 Freeze bend points in real terms	−150.8	19.6	61.7	42.0
9 Eliminate earnings ceiling	−189.6	7.9	60.1	40.3
10 Eliminate earnings ceiling without benefit change	−175.0	9.0	70.0	47.3
11 Increase computation years from 35 to 40	−159.4	12.3	56.5	36.0
Birth cohort 1995–2000				
1 Current rules	−170.9	7.5	54.7	31.4
2 38% tax hike beginning in year 2000	−96.4	32.9	67.2	50.2
3 25% benefit cut beginning in year 2000	−102.8	31.1	66.1	48.8
4 Accelerated increase in NRA	−137.6	21.1	62.1	41.9
5 CPI indexing of covered earnings	−145.2	15.1	57.5	36.9
6 Indexing benefits by CPI minus 1%	−138.8	17.0	59.6	38.7
7 Stabilize real per capita benefits	30.5	77.4	88.7	83.0
8 Freeze bend points in real terms	−128.8	24.9	64.6	45.6
9 Eliminate earnings ceiling	−179.5	6.8	60.5	39.7
10 Eliminate earnings ceiling without benefit change	−170.7	7.8	70.1	46.3
11 Increase computation years from 35 to 40	−155.9	11.1	55.6	33.7

Source: Author's calculations.

implicit tax rate when the discount rate is 3 percent, and a 33.5 percent implicit tax rate when the discount rate is 7 percent. For middle quintile members of cohort 70, seventy-seven cents of every dollar contributed to OASI is a tax if one accepts a 7 percent discount rate; only nine cents of every dollar is a tax if one does the calculation with a 3 percent discount rate.

6.5.9   Benefit Reductions of Retirees by Quintiles of Average Social Security Benefits

Our final set of tables, table 6.15 and web site tables 25 through 32, shows how the various policies alter the average OASI benefits received by a subset of observations in cohorts 45, 70, and 90—namely, those who receive benefits for at least one year after reaching age sixty-two. In these tables, rather than classify observations within the three cohorts on the basis of lifetime earnings quintiles, we sort the observations based on quintiles of average OASI benefits received after reaching age sixty-two. Before sorting the observations, we calculate for each observation the average amount of benefits received (in 1998 dollars) over only the years in which the observation is age sixty-two or older and actually receives benefits. Since roughly 40 percent of retired American households appear to be living almost exclusively from Social Security benefits, the lowest quintile of Social Security benefit recipients represents individuals for whom Social Security income is critically important.

Under current rules, average benefits are generally higher in constant 1998 dollars for later retiring cohorts—reflecting the projected growth in benefits due to real wage growth. This statement is not true for those in the lowest quintile of average benefits, presumably because this cohort (and others close to it) will bear the brunt of the increase in the NRA already scheduled to occur during the first two decades of the next century.

Among the ten policies considered here, policies 1 and 9 do not affect OASI benefits at all. Policy 2 generates precisely what it is supposed to: a 25 percent benefit cut across all cohorts and quintiles. Policy 3 (the accelerated increase in NRA) reduces benefits by less than policy 2 across all cohorts and quintiles. It hurts earlier born generations by more because, given the increase in NRA already scheduled under current rules, policy 3 exposes these cohorts to a larger increase in NRA compared to later born generations. Although in dollar terms policy 3 hurts those in the highest quintiles the most, it reduces the benefits of the benefit-poor by more in percentage terms. For cohort 95, for example, it reduces the average benefit by $921 at the lowest quintile, a 19 percent reduction, and by $3,338 at the highest quintile of average benefits, a 12 percent reduction.

Policy 4 (CPI indexing of Covered Earnings) exhibits a similar pattern across quintiles to that of policy 2. In percentage terms, it harms the benefit-poor by more than the benefit-rich. In this case, however, the reason is that a marginal reduction in the AIME of better-off individuals does

Table 6.15   **The Impact of Potential OASI Reforms on Average Benefits, All Observations**

	Quintile of Average Benefits			
	Lowest	Middle	Highest	All
Birth cohort 1945–49				
1 Current rules	3,814	8,612	17,203	9,614
2 38% tax hike beginning in year 2000	3,814	8,612	17,203	9,614
3 25% benefit cut beginning in year 2000	2,863	6,518	12,968	7,267
4 Accelerated increase in NRA	2,871	6,881	13,695	7,620
5 CPI indexing of covered earnings	3,450	7,883	16,243	8,931
6 Indexing benefits by CPI minus 1%	3,438	7,680	15,401	8,589
7 Stabilize real per capita benefits	3,374	7,644	15,241	8,532
8 Freeze bend points in real terms	3,695	8,364	16,494	9,271
9 Eliminate earnings ceiling	3,814	8,651	18,735	9,949
10 Eliminate earnings ceiling without benefit change	3,814	8,612	17,203	9,614
11 Increase computation years from 35 to 40	3,599	8,279	16,742	9,274
Birth cohort 1970–74				
1 Current rules	3,757	9,313	20,305	10,757
2 38% tax hike beginning in year 2000	3,757	9,313	20,305	10,757
3 25% benefit cut beginning in year 2000	2,830	7,054	15,264	8,108
4 Accelerated increase in NRA	3,048	7,781	17,203	9,008
5 CPI indexing of covered earnings	3,284	8,505	19,112	9,928
6 Indexing benefits by CPI minus 1%	3,363	8,239	18,013	9,537
7 Stabilize real per capita benefits	2,287	5,760	12,415	6,601
8 Freeze bend points in real terms	3,410	8,354	17,602	9,445
9 Eliminate earnings ceiling	3,757	9,410	27,425	12,254
10 Eliminate earnings ceiling without benefit change	3,757	9,313	20,305	10,757
11 Increase computation years from 35 to 40	3,511	8,949	19,973	10,421
Birth cohort 1995–2000				
1 Current rules	4,919	12,212	26,868	14,143
2 38% tax hike beginning in year 2000	4,919	12,212	26,868	14,143
3 25% benefit cut beginning in year 2000	3,688	9,258	20,188	10,643
4 Accelerated increase in NRA	3,998	10,336	23,530	12,040
5 CPI indexing of covered earnings	4,317	11,172	25,204	13,049
6 Indexing benefits by CPI minus 1%	4,401	10,847	24,034	12,610
7 Stabilize real per capita benefits	1,216	3,143	6,903	3,606
8 Freeze bend points in real terms	4,078	10,108	21,246	11,275
9 Eliminate earnings ceiling	4,921	12,355	35,777	16,028
10 Eliminate earnings ceiling without benefit change	4,919	12,212	26,868	14,143
11 Increase computation years from 35 to 40	4,602	11,742	26,378	13,696

Source: Author's calculations.

not translate into a proportional reduction in their benefits because they face lower marginal PIA rates. Policy 5 (Indexing benefits by CPI minus 1 percent) yields the most uniform percentage reduction in average benefits across all cohorts and quintiles—about 11 percent. At 75 percent, policy 6 (Stabilizing Real Per Capita Benefits) generates very large benefit reduction for cohort 95. The reduction is a sizable 40 percent for cohort 70 and is only 11 percent for the oldest cohort. The percentage reductions for the respective cohorts are uniform across quintiles.

As expected, policy 7 generates a larger percentage benefit reduction for the youngest cohort—about 20 percent overall. As mentioned earlier, this occurs because the bracket-creep effect is most severe for later born generations. Policy 8 leads to an *increase* in future benefits for the middle and highest quintiles of all cohorts, but this effect is strongest in percentage terms for members of the highest quintile of cohort 70. Their average annual benefit (conditional on receiving a benefit) increases by more than $7,000—an increase of 35 percent over that under current rules. Finally, policy 10 (Increasing Computation Years from 35 to 40) leads to fairly modest reductions in average benefits across all cohorts and quintiles. Tables 36 through 43 (located on the web site) report reductions in average benefits by demographic group; the benefits reductions in these tables are similar to those in table 35.

6.6 Summary and Conclusion

This paper uses CORSIM, a dynamic microsimulation model developed by Steven Caldwell and his colleagues, and Economic Security Planner's detailed Social Security benefit calculator to study how potential reform of Social Security's OASI program would affect postwar Americans. We consider ten alternative reforms, including a major and immediate increase in the OASI tax rate, a major and immediate cut in benefits, an accelerated increase in the age of normal retirement, two alternative methods of moving from wage-indexed to price-index benefits, and the elimination of the ceiling on taxable payroll. We present results for different postwar cohorts and different lifetime earnings groups within those cohorts and decompose these results by sex, race, and education. We also demonstrate the sensitivity of certain of our results to the choice of real discount rate.

Our measures of the impacts of reform are four: how the reforms alter OASI lifetime net tax rates, internal rates of return, implicit wealth tax rates, and average benefit levels received by retirees. Regardless of which measure we examine, the message of our paper is clear: Reforms to the OASI system of the type needed to bring the system's finances into present value balance are likely to greatly worsen OASI's treatment of postwar Americans. Although sex, race, and education play a role in determining current and prospective OASI treatment of postwar Americans, the primary determinant of this treatment is an individual's cohort and position in the distribution of lifetime earnings.

The youngest postwar generations have the most to worry about in this regard because tax increases will affect them over their entire working careers and benefit cuts will be fully phased in when they retire. Under current law, today's newborns are slated to surrender five cents of every dollar earned to the OASI system in taxes paid net of benefits received. That lifetime net tax rate could rise as high as 8 percent under some of the reforms being contemplated by Social Security's actuaries. For the poorest members of today's newborn generation, a number of the reforms would transform the system from a net subsidy to a net tax. For the highest-earning members of today's newborn generations, some of the reforms translate into large negative internal rates of return on contributions and implicit wealth taxes of close to 100 percent.

To conclude, this paper assumes the OASI system will continue to run on a PAYGO basis and considers alternative reforms to achieve financial solvency. Each is highly unpleasant. However, some reforms are more even-handed than are others with respect to their distribution of additional fiscal burdens both across and within generations. Microsimulation analysis of the kind presented here can help policy makers better sugar-coat what will inevitably be a bitter pill.

References

Baxter, Marianne, and Robert King. 2001. "The role of international investment in a privatized Social Security system. In *Risk aspects of investment-based Social Security reform,* ed. M. Feldstein and J. Campbell, 371–428. Chicago: University of Chicago Press.

Boskin, Michael J., Laurence J. Kotlikoff, Douglas J. Puffert, and John B. Shoven. 1987. Social security: A financial appraisal across and within generations. *National Tax Journal* 40 (1): 19–34.

Caldwell, Steven B. 1996. CORSIM 3.0 technical and user documentation. Cornell University, Department of Sociology. Unpublished Manuscript.

Caldwell, Steven B., Melissa Favreault, Alla Gantman, Jagadeesh Gokhale, Thomas Johnson, and Laurence J. Kotlikoff. 1999. Social Security's treatment of postwar Americans. In *Tax policy and the economy,* vol. 13, ed., James M. Poterba, 109–48. Cambridge, Mass.: MIT Press.

Caldwell, Steven B., and Richard J. Morrison. 1999. Validation of longitudinal dynamic microsimulation models: Experience with CORSIM and DYNACAN. In *Microsimulation and the new millennium: Challenges and innovations.* New York: Cambridge University Press.

Coronado, Julia Lynn, Don Fullerton, and Thomas Glass. 1999. Distributional impacts of proposed changes to the Social Security system. In *Tax policy and the economy,* vol. 13, ed. James M. Poterba, 149–86. Cambridge, Mass.: MIT Press.

Diamond, Peter, and Jonathan Gruber. 1997. Social Security and retirement in the U.S. NBER Working Paper no. 6097. Cambridge, Mass.: National Bureau of Economic Research, July.

Hurd, Michael D., and John B. Shoven. 1985. The distributional impact of Social Security. In *Pensions, labor, and individual choice,* 193–222. ed. David Wise, Chicago: University of Chicago Press.

Myers, Robert J., and Bruce D. Schobel. 1993. An updated money's-worth analysis of Social Security's retirement benefits. *Transactions of the Society of Actuaries* 44:247–75.

Nichols, Orlo R., and Richard G. Schreitmueller. 1978. Some comparisons of the value of a worker's Social Security taxes and benefits. Actuarial Note no. 95. Baltimore, Md.: U.S. Social Security Administration, Office of the Actuary.

Steuerle, C. Eugene, and Jon M. Bakija. 1994. *Retooling Social Security for the 21st century.* Washington, D.C.: Urban Institute Press.

Comment   David A. Wise

Jagadeesh Gokhale and Laurence Kotlikoff have written a very informative paper. I like it. The results of their analysis are very sobering, and perhaps even suggest, as the authors put it, "how bad Social Security's treatment of postwar Americans would be under alternative tax increases and benefit cuts." The most striking conclusion is that balancing the Social Security budget would require a 4 percentage point, or 38 percent, increase in the OASI current 10.6 percent tax rate. The very high tax rates and low internal rates of return posited for most participants, while perhaps not new ideas, are also depressing. Finally, the differential effect of potential reforms on different lifetime income groups should inform future discussion of reform proposals.

The analysis is based on "synthetic" data, which at first aroused my suspicions, but the benchmark evidence that the authors present has left me more comfortable with these data. The results are likely to be very sensitive to some key assumptions, however, and I would like to emphasize a few of these. Perhaps the most important is the assumed discount rate. In addition, to compare the results with those of the Social Security Trust Fund actuaries, a few additional simulations would be informative, and I will mention those as well.

Data and Benchmarks

The analysis is based on key inputs from Caldwell et al. (1999), the CORSIM synthetic data, and the Social Security Benefit Calculator

David A. Wise is the John F. Stambaugh Professor of Political Economy at the John F. Kennedy School of Government, Harvard University, and the director for Health and Retirement Programs at the National Bureau of Economic Research.

(SSBC). The authors produced their data by running the CORSIM model from the year 1960 to 2100 and selecting a master sample of particular groups born between 1945 and 2000. This sample is separated into three lifetime earnings quintiles—lowest, middle, and highest (discounting at 5 percent from age eighteen to the end of life). The CORSIM data begin with a sample from the 1960 U.S. Census. The census data are supplemented with data from many other sources, including the data from the High School and Beyond Survey, National Longitudinal Survey, the Panel Study of Income Dynamics, the Survey of Consumer Finances, and others. CORSIM "grows" the sample demographically and economically to 2100, based on a large number of equations and rule-based algorithms. The process seems very complicated. My inclination is to be very suspicious of such data files, but I was for the most part reassured by the benchmarking described by the authors.

For example, the longevity of the synthetic data groups seems to correspond rather well to "actual" data. The average longevity is 79.5 for the five oldest cohorts and 81.1 for the five youngest. The most recent Decennial Life Tables, by comparison, show "cross-sectional" life expectancy of 75.4 years. In Gokhale and Kotlikoff's calculations, the life expectancy of women is 6.3 years longer than that of men. The life tables show a difference of 6.7 years. According to Gokhale and Kotlikoff, however, whites live only about two years longer than nonwhites, which is much less than the life tables' difference of 4.9 years. The paper does correctly present a substantial correlation between earnings and life expectancy. For example, men in the highest quintile in the 1985 cohort live 7.1 years longer than men in the lowest quintile. The paper's account of differences by education is also persuasive. With respect to income, those in the highest quintile earn over their lifetimes thirty-three to thirty-nine times as much as those in the lowest quintile. This compares rather well with the lowest versus the highest decile of lifetime earnings reported in Venti and Wise (2001), based on the Social Security earnings histories of HRS respondents. We found that the top decile earned about forty-six times as much as the bottom decile, with no correction for the top coding at the Social Security covered earnings limit.

The SSBC ignores the disability insurance part of Social Security and leaves out federal and state taxes of SS benefits. This calculator is extremely detailed and seems to have been subjected to much checking.

Summary of Results

Because Gokhale and Kotlikoff's results are presented in such a quantity of lengthy tables, I have tried to summarize the key results here. The first results reported in the paper (tables 6.4–6.6) are reproduced from Caldwell et al. and are summarized in the next two figures, which show lifetime tax rates, internal rates of return, and wealth taxes by quintile for

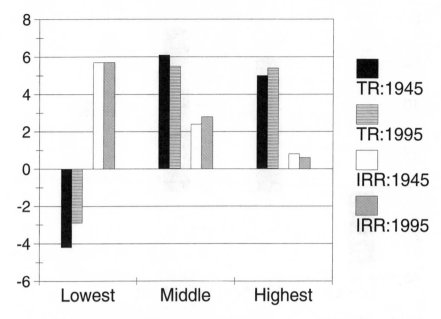

Fig. 6C.1   Tax Rates and Internal Rates of Return

the 1945 and 1995 cohorts. The lifetime tax rate is given by (PVT − PVB)/ PVE, where PVT is the present value of lifetime taxes, PVB is the present value of benefits, and PVE is the present value of lifetime earnings. The wealth tax is given by 1 − PVB/PVT. Both the wealth tax and the tax rate are calculated based on a real discount rate of 5 percent (to which I will return below). The internal rate of return is determined by choosing the discount rate such that PVB = PVT. These results show low tax rates and rather high internal rates of return for the lowest quintile and high tax rates and low internal rates of return for the middle and especially the highest quintiles.

The analysis new to this paper examines the distributional effects of potential Social Security reforms. For example, many reforms would have a disproportionate effect on the lowest income quintile. This is shown with respect to the tax rate for the 1945 cohort in the next figure. The figure shows changes from the tax rates under the current rules. (The labels are shorter versions of the labels on the authors' tables beginning with table 6.8.) The following figure shows the effect on tax rates for the 1995 cohort.

Time Horizon and Life Expectancy

These results, like those based on any projections, are subject to many assumptions and conventions. I would like to mention three in particular which are likely to have an important effect on the conclusions. First, the

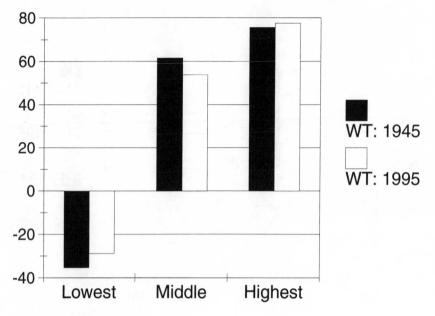

Fig. 6C.2   Wealth Taxes

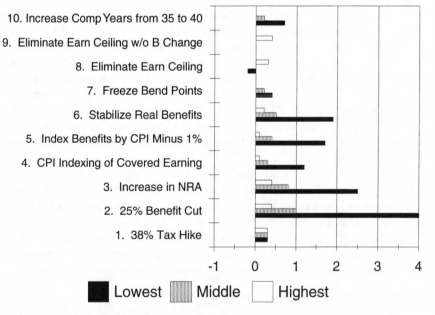

Fig. 6C.3   Tax Rate Change by Quintile: C1945

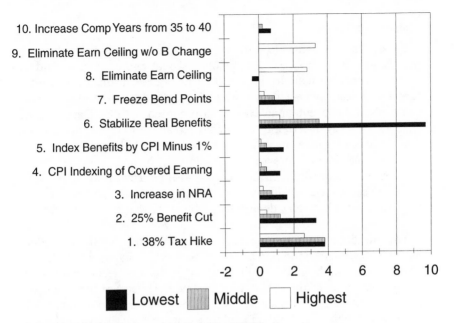

Fig. 6C.4   Tax Rate Change by Quintile: C1995

authors conclude that to balance the Social Security budget would require an immediate 4 percentage point, or 38 percent, increase in the OASI current 10.6 percent tax rate. This is more than twice the rate projected by the Social Security Trust Fund actuaries. The authors' explanation is that the Social Security actuaries use a seventy-five-year projection horizon, while their results are based on projections through the year 2100. I believe it would strengthen the results reported in the paper if the authors also reported results that correspond to the seventy-five-year horizon used by the actuaries, confirming that these data yield the trustees' results when their convention is used.

Second, longevity assumptions built into the CORSIM data seem to correspond closely to (and perhaps reflect) the Social Security intermediate demographic assumptions. Many prominent demographers believe, however, that actual future realized life spans will be much greater than the longevity assumptions used here, and the authors emphasize this fact. Indeed, one demographer has told me that he would not be surprised if the average girl baby born today lived 100 years. Whatever the truth, death rates are likely to see declines much greater than those assumed in these data, which yield the results reported here. More rapid, and I would say more realistic, declines would suggest a much larger Social Security liability under the current program provisions and much larger benefits, than the results the authors report.

Discount Rate

Finally, the discount rate assumptions can have a very large effect on the results. The authors use a 5 percent discount rate to make individual money's worth calculations, arguing that this rate is justified because future Social Security benefits are risky. They are indeed risky. Many events could result in benefits much less than promised benefits. Demographic changes are a key uncertainty, as emphasized above. "Errors," like the one that led to double indexing in the 1970s, are another. The political process could change the plan provisions substantially. Nonetheless, the "right" rate could be higher or lower than authors assume. Thus, it would be informative to see some calculations showing how much the discount rate matters. Here let me simply demonstrate that I believe it would matter a great deal.

The authors assume a 5 percent real discount rate for the individual money's worth calculations. The Social Security actuaries use 3 percent (the rate that Gokhale and Kotlikoff use to assess the effect of reforms on the present value of the Social Security budget). Because the calculated tax rates and wealth taxes are very sensitive to the assumed discount rate, perhaps Gokhale and Kotlikoff could present some sensitivity analysis to demonstrate the degree to which this rate matters. The potential sensitivity to the discount rate can perhaps be demonstrated by observing the relationship between the internal rate of return, a data-determined calculation, and the wealth tax and the tax rate, which are based on an assumed 5 percent discount rate. Recall that the relationship between the discount rate and the ratio of the present value of benefits to the present value of taxes looks like the line marked by squares in the figure below. The internal rate of return is determined by finding the discount rate such that PVB = PVT, so that the ratio is one. Thus, when the discount rate is equal to the internal rate of return, both the wealth tax [1 − PVB/PVT] and the tax rate [(PVT − PVB)/PVE] are equal to zero. For example, if the internal rate of return is 5 percent and the discount rate is 5 percent, both will be zero. Then, for discount rates below 5 percent, PVB > PVT, and both the wealth tax and the tax rate will be negative. For discount rates greater than 5 percent, PVB < PVT, and both the wealth tax and the tax rate will be positive.

For example, consider the internal rate of return and the wealth tax for all nonwhite persons in the lowest quintile in the 1990 cohort. The internal rate of return is 5.0 percent, and because the assumed discount rate is also 5.0 percent, both the wealth tax (I presume except for rounding error) and the tax rate are zero. However, for the 1985 cohort in the same quintile, the internal rate of return is 5.7 percent, the discount rate is less than the internal rate of return, and the wealth tax and tax rate are negative. For persons in the middle quintile in the 1985 cohort, the internal rate of return is only 2.6 percent, so the assumed discount rate is much larger than the internal rate of return, and the wealth tax and tax rate are very large.

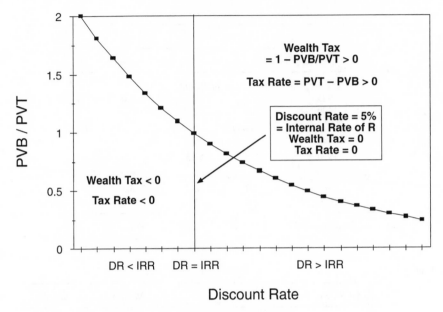

Fig. 6C.5   Discount Rate, Tax Rate, and Wealth Tax

The point of the example is to emphasize the sensitivity of the calculated wealth taxes and tax rates to the assumed discount rate. Both would be much lower if the assumed discount rate were lower and much higher if the assumed discount rate were higher.

As another example, consider the internal rate of return and the wealth tax of all women. The internal rate of return for the middle quintile in the 1945 cohort is 3.0, and the wealth tax is large—53.2 percent. If the assumed discount rate were 3 percent instead of 5 percent, the wealth tax for this group would be zero. The wealth tax for all other cohorts in the middle quintile would be negative. The wealth taxes for the lowest quintile would be more negative than they are. The wealth taxes of the highest quintile would still be positive, but much lower than the Gokhale and Kotlikoff estimates. On the other hand, if the discount rate were 7 percent, all of the wealth taxes would be greater than zero, even for the lowest quintile—except for the 1950 cohort, for which the wealth tax would be zero.

As emphasized above, there is no "correct" discount rate, and I have no reason to believe the one chosen by Gokhale and Kotlikoff is either too high or too low, but I believe some sensitivity analysis would demonstrate the substantial relationship between the assumed discount rate and the implied wealth taxes and tax rates.

In short, the results of this paper are striking and sobering. They ought to be used to help inform the current financial status of the Social Security

Table 6C.1

		Quintile	
Cohort	Lowest	Middle	Highest
Internal Rate of Return			
1985	5.7	2.6	1.0
1990	5.0	2.6	0.8
Wealth Tax			
1985	−28.5	58.4	75.7
1990	−0.5	57.3	76.8
Tax Rate			
1985	−2.9	6.0	5.3
1990	0.0	5.8	5.3

Note: All nonwhite data.

Table 6C.2

	Internal Rate of Return, by Quintile			Wealth Tax, by Quintile		
	Lowest	Middle	Highest	Lowest	Middle	Highest
1945	5.9	3.0	1.7	−43.1	53.2	67.8
1950	7.0	3.2	1.6	−115.7	48.0	70.0
1955	6.5	3.1	1.3	−78.7	49.7	72.8
1960	6.4	3.2	1.2	−69.8	50.6	74.5
1965	6.3	3.2	1.3	−62.5	50.0	74.3
1970	6.3	3.2	1.2	−61.3	49.4	75.2
1975	6.3	3.2	1.4	−63.8	49.9	73.1
1980	6.5	3.3	1.3	−75.8	47.3	74.4
1985	6.3	3.3	1.4	−63.6	48.4	73.2
1990	6.1	3.3	1.3	−54.0	47.2	74.0
1995	6.0	3.2	0.9	−44.7	48.9	76.3

system, the gains or losses that current participants are receiving from the system, and the distributional effects of potential reforms of the current system.

References

Caldwell, Steven B., Melissa Favreault, Alla Gantman, Jagadeesh Gokhale, Thomas Johnson, and Laurence J. Kotlikoff. 1999. Social Security's treatment of postwar Americans. In *Tax policy and the economy,* vol. 13, ed. James M. Poterba, 109–48. Cambridge: MIT Press.
Venti, Steven F., and David A. Wise. 2001. Choice, change, and wealth dispersion at retirement. In *Issues in aging in the United States and Japan,* ed. Seiritsu Ogura, Toshiaki Tachibanaki, and David A. Wise. Chicago: University of Chicago Press. Forthcoming.

Discussion Summary

Gary Burtless described two reasons for the low rates of return for postwar generations. First, there was a large gift to the early generations of contributors that later generations are paying for with their payroll taxes. Second, the investment portfolio for the Social Security Trust Fund is extremely conservative and earns a much lower expected rate of return than the benchmark rate of return used to calculate the discount rate used in this paper. Even if we ignore the gift given to past generations, Social Security would still appear to be a bad deal for current contributors under the calculations in this paper. Burtless added that applying a discount factor of 5 percent would show that almost all insurance would have astoundingly high load factors. The authors defended their 5 percent discount rate, noting that the average internal rate of return for postwar Americans is 1.9 percent, while inflation-indexed government bonds have a return of more than 4 percent. Even if Social Security benefits are considered to be riskless assets (which they are not), it is clear that people are not receiving a good deal.

Burtless also believed that the calculation of tax burdens that people pay under the system is based on the assumption that all of the taxes that support these payments are indeed paid for by the worker. To the extent that labor does respond to taxation, employers will bear some of the tax burden, and, therefore, all of the tax contributions should not be added to the ledger as in this paper.

Charles Blahous emphasized the difference between the tax burden from Social Security taxes and the total tax burden. Around the year 2015 the federal government will have to use general revenue to pay the Social Security Trust Fund, and by 2030 the burden on general revenue will be approximately 5 percent of payroll. Clearly, the total tax burden will be much higher for workers entering the labor force in 2015. Consequently, the internal rate of return for the Social Security system depends on both the Social Security taxes and the general revenue requirements.

Martin Feldstein pointed out that the magnitude of the tax burden on future generations would be even higher if deadweight losses were considered.

7

The Distributional Effects
of an Investment-Based
Social Security System

Martin Feldstein and Jeffrey B. Liebman

In this paper we study the distributional impact of a change from the existing pay-as-you-go (PAYGO) U.S. Social Security system to one that combines both PAYGO and investment-based elements.[1] Such a transition can avert the large tax increases that would otherwise be necessary to maintain the level of benefits promised under current law as life expectancy increases. According to the Social Security actuaries (Board of Trustees 1999), retaining the existing PAYGO system would eventually require raising the current 12.4 percent Social Security payroll tax rate to about 19 percent to maintain the current benefit rules or cutting benefits by more than one-third in order to avoid a tax increase. In contrast, previous research showed that adding an investment-based component with savings equal to 2 percent of covered earnings to the existing 12.4 percent

Martin Feldstein is the George F. Baker Professor of Economics, Harvard University, and the president of the National Bureau of Economic Research. Jeffrey B. Liebman is an associate professor of public policy at the John F. Kennedy School of Government, Harvard University, and a faculty research fellow of the National Bureau of Economic Research.

The authors are grateful to Jeffrey Brown, Glenn Ellison, Kathleen Feldstein, Stephen C. Goss, James M. Poterba, David Pattison, Elena Ranguelova, and other conference participants for discussions about this research, and to Joyce Manchester, Olivia Mitchell, and Kent Smetters for comments on an earlier draft. The authors thank Joshua Pollet, Peter Spiegler, Elisabeth Welty, and Ying Qian for excellent research assistance. Martin Feldstein acknowledges financial support from the Ford Foundation. Jeffrey B. Liebman acknowledges support from the Russell Sage Foundation and the National Institute on Aging. This research was conducted while Liebman was also a Bureau of the Census research associate at the Boston Research Data Center. Research results and conclusions expressed are those of the authors and do not necessarily indicate concurrence by the Bureau of the Census. This paper has been screened by a Census Bureau employee to insure that no confidential data are revealed.

1. For a discussion of the distributional impact of the existing Social Security system see Liebman (chap. 1 in this volume), Coronado, Fullerton, and Glass (2000), Gustman and Steinmeier (2000) and the classic papers by Hurd and Shoven (1985) and Boskin et al. (1987).

PAYGO system would be sufficient to maintain the benefits promised under current rules without any increase in tax rates (Feldstein and Samwick 1997, 1998a, b).

Most proposed investment-based systems would increase the link between a worker's earnings and the worker's retirement benefits, potentially reducing the amount of redistribution that occurs through the Social Security system. Critics of investment-based plans have been concerned that such plans, even if desirable for a typical employee, might reduce the retirement income of low-paid workers or surviving spouses relative to what they would get from Social Security, and might therefore increase the extent of poverty among the aged. Our analysis shows that this need not be the case, even in plans that make no special effort to maintain or increase redistribution, provided that sufficient funding is contributed to the investment-based component (and current funding levels are continued for the PAYGO component).

To analyze the actual distributional effect of a shift to a mixed system of Social Security funding, we use a rich data set of government administrative records on the lifetime earnings of a cohort of workers and spouses who retired in the early 1990s combined with a government survey of the same individuals. More specifically, we use the 1990 and 1991 panels of the Survey of Income and Program Participation (SIPP) matched to Social Security Administration (SSA) data on earnings and benefits. We simulate the impact of alternative potential reforms using the cohort of individuals from the SIPP-SSA match who were born between 1925 and 1929 (and were therefore between the ages of sixty-one and sixty-five in 1990) and present results in a way that can be taken to represent the impact of the reforms on the entire cross-sectional population of aged Social Security beneficiaries at a point in time. We use these data to study who the likely future gainers and losers would be after a transition to such a system as well as to analyze some of the options for increasing the progressivity in such a system that have been proposed in the recent public debate on Social Security reform.

We focus our analysis on the benefits for retirees and their surviving spouses, excluding disability benefits and benefits for children and non-aged parents. Financing this portion of the overall Old Age, Survivors and Disability Insurance (OASDI) program with pure PAYGO financing would require raising the relevant portion of the Social Security payroll tax from 9.4 percent, where it stands today, to 15.4 percent by 2075.[2] The

---

2. Of the total 19.9 percent of payroll in OASDI costs that are forecast for 2075, 2.59 percent are for disability insurance (DI) benefits, roughly 0.28 percent are for young survivors (including children), and roughly 1.6 percent are OASI benefits at ages sixty-five and above for people who converted from DI benefits when they reached the normal retirement age. The DI estimate comes directly from the Board of Trustees (1999) report. The other two estimates rely on table II.H2 in that report, which provides projections of the number of

mixed system that we analyze leaves the portion of the payroll tax allocated for retirement benefits at 9.4 percent and supplements this with a 3 percent contribution to personal retirement accounts that invest in a stock-bond portfolio. While the 3 percent account contributions require extra resources in the next few decades compared with a completely PAYGO system,[3] in the long run they replace the 6 percentage point increase in payroll tax rates that would otherwise be necessary.[4] We assume that the future PAYGO benefits are reduced by the same proportion as the tax revenue (i.e., by 39 percent, since 6 percent is 39 percent of 15.4 percent) and analyze how the sum of the remaining PAYGO benefits and the personal retirement account (PRA) annuities received by each individual compares to the social security benefits that would be paid with the full 15.4 percent tax.

We assume that a worker's personal retirement account is annuitized at the person's retirement date, using a single unisex mortality series for every worker. Each spouse in a married couple is required to obtain a joint and survivor's annuity that pays the widow(er) two-thirds of the benefit the couple received when both spouses were alive. We further assume that accounts are split equally upon divorce and that workers who die before age sixty-five bequeath their accounts to their surviving spouse, if they have one, and to any other designee if they do not. The annuities in our simulations are variable annuities that allow beneficiaries to continue to receive the same rate of return in retirement as workers receive in that year.

Our principal finding is that in the long run virtually all of the demographic groups that we examine would receive higher average benefits under a mixed system with an investment-based component than they would receive under current Social Security rules with a substantially higher tax cost. There would also be a smaller share of individuals with benefits below the poverty line than under a pure PAYGO system that maintained current law benefit rules. Taking into account the lower cost of funding the mixed system in the long run—a 3 percent saving contribution rather than a 6 percent rise in the tax rate—also implies higher internal rates of return on the taxes-plus-savings in the fully phased-in mixed system than on the taxes paid in the pure PAYGO system. Transition generations would also

---

beneficiaries of each type in future years and weight these projections by the average benefit levels for each type of beneficiary in 1997 from the *Annual Statistical Supplement* (U.S. Social Security Administration 1999a).

3. The additional resources could come from a temporary increase in the payroll tax or from transfers from general revenue. Feldstein and Samwick (2000) present a third mechanism: borrowing by the trust fund with subsequent repayment made possible by the returns to the increased capital accumulation.

4. Thus total contributions in the mixed plan are 15.4 percent: a payroll tax of 12.4 (9.4 percent for retirement and 3.0 percent for DI and young survivors) plus the 3.0 percent for PRAs. In the long run, this is substantially less than the 19 percent payroll tax that would be necessary in total to continue the PAYGO system. In both plans there is also revenue from the taxation of benefits. In the mixed plan, we allocate all of this revenue to finance DI benefits and benefits for young survivors.

experience higher retirement benefit levels than under current Social Security rules, and again this would apply to virtually all demographic groups. However, these generations might also face higher contribution rates.[5]

Our individual data permit us to go beyond comparing group means to analyze the full distribution of the benefits that individuals would receive under the two different systems. These comparisons show that the overwhelming majority of individuals would have higher benefits with the investment-based system than with the pure PAYGO system. The relatively small number of individuals who would receive less from the investment-based system is further reduced when the effects of the Supplementary Security Income (SSI) program are taken into account.

These basic conclusions remain true even if the future rate of return in the investment-based component of the mixed system is substantially less than past experience implies. We repeat our analysis for various demographic groups and individuals on a "low rate of return" assumption, which assumes that the rate of return in the investment-based portion is so low that the odds are 9 to 1 that it would be exceeded in practice. Even in this worst 10th percentile case, there are few individuals who would be significantly worse off under the mixed system than they would be under the pure PAYGO system.

Note that, by comparing the benefits under the mixed plan to the full Social Security benefits promised under current law, we are setting a high standard for the mixed plan. Many proposed Social Security reform plans would reduce benefits compared with current law. If we were to compare the mixed plan to such a plan, the results would be much more impressive.

We also explore two options for increasing redistribution to individuals with low incomes or retirees with low benefits. We find that, without any increase in the total cost of the PRA deposits, such a system can provide beneficiaries who have low lifetime incomes with the same average percentage increase in benefits as higher-income beneficiaries, while still allowing most high-income individuals to have higher benefits in the investment-based system than in the PAYGO system. Moreover, such funding of the PRAs substantially diminishes the chance that lower-income families will have lower benefits than under current law in the case that financial market performance does not achieve its historic average.

The paper begins in section 7.1 with a review of the basic economics of converting from a PAYGO system to a system that is wholly or partially investment-based. Section 7.2 then discusses the data and technical assumptions used in our calculations. The analysis of results begins with the simplification of the extreme case of a pure investment-based system. Section 7.3 examines the effects of such a system on the mean benefits of

5. See note 3.

different demographic groups, the fraction of each group that would gain or lose from such a shift, and the effect on the number of people who would potentially be in poverty. Section 7.4 then goes beyond these averages and proportions to look at each individual and assess the distribution of gains and losses within each demographic group. With this simplified, extreme case as background, section 7.5 then examines a more realistic mixed system in which the current 12.4 percent OASDI payroll tax rate continues and is supplemented by a 3 percent saving rate in PRAs instead of the 6 percent tax rate increase that would be needed to fund current law benefits. Section 7.6 then considers the effect of substituting a low probability, poor return performance that has only about one chance in ten of occurring. Finally, section 7.7 modifies the assumption that the PRA deposits are a fixed percentage of each individual's covered earnings to consider PRA deposits that are either the same dollar amount for all participants or a combination of a fixed dollar amount and a portion of earnings. Section 7.8 concludes.

7.1 Investment-Based Social Security Reform: The Economics of Prefunding

The SSA Office of the Actuary projects that rising life expectancies and continued low rates of fertility will reduce the ratio of workers to beneficiaries from 3.4 today to 2.0 in the year 2035 and 1.8 in 2075. This aging of the population implies that, in order to maintain the level of benefits promised under current law under a (largely) PAYGO system, OASDI taxes would have to rise from the current level of 12.7 percent of payroll (including both the 12.4 percent payroll tax and revenue from the taxation of benefits) to 19.9 percent of payroll in the year 2075, an increase of 57 percent.[6] As we noted above, financing the current law rules for retiree benefits alone would require increasing the tax rate by 6 percent of covered earnings, from 9.4 percent of earnings to 15.4 percent of earnings.

This large future tax increase (or the equivalent benefit cut) can be averted by prefunding future Social Security benefits. Prefunding involves setting aside resources today that would otherwise be consumed and allowing them to accumulate until they are needed to finance retirement benefits in the future. The basic intuition is that one dollar in benefits thirty-five years from now can be funded by setting aside a much smaller amount today.

---

6. Some academic demographers suggest that the needed tax increase could be even higher (Lee and Tuljapurkar 1998). It is important to note that the tax increase is not a temporary phenomenon associated with the retirement of the baby boom generation; rather, it is a permanent change associated with long-run demographic trends.

From the standpoint of the entire economy, additional savings today earns a real rate of return equal to the pretax marginal product of capital, which is likely to be around 7.5 percent.[7] Thus, $100 of retirement benefits (in today's prices) thirty-five years from now could, in principle, be financed by setting aside only $7.96 today: In other words, the present value of $100 in thirty-five years discounting by a real return of 7.5 percent ($7.96 = $100/[1.075]^{35}).

Four points about this rate of return are worth emphasizing. First, the rate of return earned through prefunding can be obtained for the economy as a whole only by increasing national saving. Simply shifting funds into private assets that would otherwise be used for reducing national debt (as do some plans for investing the trust fund in equities as well as some carve-out individual account plans) would merely move returns from the private to the public sector without increasing total national resources.[8]

Second, all of the economic logic behind prefunding applies whether the prefunding occurs through collective investing on behalf of the Social Security trust fund or through individual retirement savings accounts. Although there are serious arguments both for and against collective investing,[9] we believe that it is highly unlikely that the political system would adopt the magnitude of prefunding discussed in this paper unless the prefunding occurs through private savings accounts.

Third, prefunding comes at a cost. It requires the current generation to give up consumption in order to make future generations (with higher standards of living) better off. The logic behind prefunding is that the high rates of return on additional savings imply that current generations must give up only a little consumption to prevent future generations from giving up a large amount of consumption. Equivalently, if individuals today accept a slightly higher tax rate than would otherwise be necessary, it will be possible to avoid a much larger tax increase in the future. Whether this tradeoff is worth making depends on one's view of the intergenerational social welfare function (see Feldstein 1996 and the explicit calculations presented in Feldstein and Samwick 1997, 1998b) and the increased excess burden that would be caused by higher future tax rates.[10]

---

7. Poterba (1998) estimates that the pretax marginal product of corporate capital is 8.5 percent. Since some capital may be invested in housing or abroad, the marginal product for all capital could be somewhat lower than this. In addition, the increase in the capital stock could cause the marginal product of capital to fall. Feldstein and Samwick (1997) show that with Cobb-Douglas production technology, the reduction in the marginal product would be about 20 percent in the long run.

8. Elmendorf and Liebman (2000) examine the impact of Social Security reform on national saving.

9. See, for example, Diamond (2000) and the comments on it by Feldstein (2000).

10. The low rates of observed saving by the current generation is not evidence that current workers would oppose this transfer to future generations. Private savers cannot (outside of tax-favored retirement accounts) earn the pre–income tax rate of return on their saving; thus, their saving is distorted by the income tax. In addition, the need for a government-provided

Fourth, part of the national return to incremental saving accrues to governments through taxes. Even when those savings are invested in stocks and bonds in "tax exempt" PRAs, a portion of the total return is collected by the federal, state, and local governments in the form of corporate profits taxes and business property taxes. While in principle these incremental tax revenues could be rebated to the investment-based Social Security accounts (just as the federal government transfers the income taxes collected on Social Security benefits to the Trust Fund), we recognize that such transfers may be politically unlikely, especially with respect to the taxes collected by state and local governments. Thus, in the calculations that follow, we underestimate the total return to the economy by assuming that the investment-based PRAs earn the return on a balanced stock-bond portfolio, a return that, therefore, is after all taxes paid at the corporate level.

More specifically, we assume a portfolio with 60 percent stock (the Standard & Poor's 500 portfolio) and 40 percent corporate bonds, a balance that reflects the ratio in which corporations finance their capital accumulation. The real logarithmic return on such a portfolio in the half century from 1946 to 1995 was 5.9 percent. We subtract 40 basis points for administrative costs to obtain the 5.5 percent real return that we use in most of our calculations. We discuss in section 7.3 why this understates the actual mean return since 1946, and in section 7.6 we explicitly recognize the uncertainty of this return and analyze a low-probability "poor portfolio performance" case.

To assess the extent to which prefunding can reduce the required PAYGO tax rate, it is necessary to consider the implicit rate of return on the PAYGO system. In the long run, the PAYGO system has an implicit rate of return equal to the rate of growth of the Social Security tax base (Samuelson 1958). According to Board of Trustees (1999), that tax base will expand in real terms by about 1.1 percent per year over the next seventy-five years as labor force growth averages 0.2 percent per year and real taxable wage growth averages 0.9 percent per year.

The comparison of the 1.1 percent growth rate for the payroll tax base and the 5.5 percent rate of return on investment-based accounts shows the profound effect that prefunding can have on the cost of financing future Social Security benefits. Consider an individual who works from age twenty-five to age sixty-five and then retires with a life expectancy of nearly twenty more years. To illustrate this case, we approximate the costs of financing each $100 of benefits under the two systems by assuming that all of the contributing or saving is performed at the midpoint of the working years (age forty-five) and all of the benefits are paid at age eighty. With this thirty-five-year time span, each $100 in retirement benefits requires

---

Social Security retirement system is largely predicated on the inability of individuals to make far-sighted saving decisions.

contributions to the PAYGO system of $\$100/(1.011)^{35} = \$68.18$ or savings in the investment-based system of $\$100/(1.055)^{35} = \$15.35$. Thus, each dollar of tax required in a PAYGO system with a 1.1 percent implicit rate of return can be replaced by $15.35/68.18 = 0.225$ dollars in an investment-based system with a 5.5 percent rate of return.

These calculations imply that the 15.4 percent long-run OASI tax could, in principle, be replaced with a 3.5 percent PRA saving rate (i.e., 0.225×15.4 percent $= 3.5$ percent). Alternatively, a pure prefunded system could use a saving rate that is higher than this 3.5 percent in order to achieve a higher expected benefit, to provide a cushion against the possibility of a lower-than-expected rate of return, and to ensure that even those individuals who receive a higher-than-average return from the current Social Security system come out with higher benefits under the reformed system. Therefore, in this paper we assume a 9 percent PRA saving rate—a rate that is only slightly more than half (58 percent) of the required long-run PAYGO tax rate.

The relative cost of investment-based and PAYGO benefits (i.e., 0.225) can also be used in evaluating the mixed system by calculating the cost of avoiding the 6.0 percent increase in the tax rate—from 9.4 percent to 15.4 percent—that would be necessary to finance retirement benefits under the current PAYGO Social Security system. This calculation implies that a 1.35 percent PRA saving rate can replace a 6.0 percent increase in the payroll tax rate. The analysis of the mixed system in this paper assumes instead a 3.0 percent PRA saving rate. This is only half of the increase that would be required in the long run with the pure PAYGO but provides both a higher level of expected benefits and a cushion against the risk of a lower rate of return.

It is important to emphasize that the analysis in this paper deals with only the long-run situation in which the demographic change has increased the cost of the PAYGO system and the alternative plans are fully phased in. In practice, of course, it would be necessary to go through a transition period in which the population is aging and the new funding system is gradually put into place. Thinking about the pure funded case shows the nature of the transition problem and how it can be solved in practice. Nearly all of the 12.4 percent OASDI payroll tax is currently needed to pay benefits to current retirees, survivors, and disabled beneficiaries. Over time, this will grow to 19.9 percent if no investment-based component is introduced. The 0.225 percent relative cost factor implies that the 19.9 percent could be financed in the long run by saving 4.47 percent of covered earnings. However, adding that 4.47 percent to the 12.4 percent at the start of the transition would no doubt be a politically unacceptable burden. It is unnecessary, however, to resort immediately to the long-run funding rate. A gradual transition is possible in which the saving rate begins at less than its long-run value and increases gradually as the rising level of investment-based benefits makes it possible to reduce the PAYGO tax rate. Feldstein and Samwick (1997) show how the current 12.4 percent can be gradually replaced with a much lower prefunded investment-based system by increasing the initial combination to 14.4 percent and then gradually bringing that total down to less than the initial 12.4 percent.

The distributional impact during the transition period will depend on the exact timing of the PAYGO benefit declines relative to the distribution of the PRA annuities. Throughout the transition, a smaller fraction of benefits will come from the individual accounts and a larger fraction from the traditional defined benefit Social Security system than will be the case at the end of the transition. If the cuts in traditional Social Security benefits are phased in at the same rate at which the individual accounts accumulate, then retirees in the transition generations will also have higher expected retirement benefits than under current law. However, some transition individuals may also pay higher total contribution rates than under current law. We do not consider any of these transition issues in the current paper.

7.2   The Microsimulation Model[11]

As we noted above, our microsimulation model is based on a match of the 1990 and 1991 panels of the SIPP to SSA earnings and benefit records for the same individuals. We select SIPP sample members who were born from 1925 through 1929 and construct lifetime earnings and marital histories from age twenty-one through age sixty-four using the administrative records and the SIPP topical module on marriage. We then simulate the sample members' Social Security benefit levels under today's Social Security rules (rather than under the ones they actually experienced) and simulate their PRA accumulations under the alternative policy rules outlined in the previous section.

The strength of our simulation model is that it reflects the full range of experience of the different individual members of an actual cohort, including periods of unemployment, childrearing, low earnings, divorce, and so forth. Because we have forty years of actual covered earnings for each sample member as well complete marital histories, we can be confident that our results portray the full range of distributional outcomes that would have occurred for this cohort if it had experienced these alternative Social Security systems.[12] Compared with other microsimulation models used to study the distributional implications of Social Security reform, we rely little on projected or imputed data. Because we are particularly

---

11. Readers who are not interested in the technical description of our method can go directly to the next section.
12. We ignore behavioral responses to these alternative Social Security rules.

concerned about the lower tail of the benefit distribution, our ability to observe extreme cases and to reflect the complicated cross-correlations between marital status, earnings, retirement, and mortality is important.

Our data have two drawbacks, however. The first is that the future cohorts affected by Social Security reform will differ along important dimensions from the cohort that we study. In particular, women in future cohorts of retirees will reach retirement having had much more extensive labor market experience, and marriage rates will be lower, particularly in some lower-income populations. Second, we have to make some imputations to account for spouses who were absent at the time of the 1990–91 SIPP (due to death or divorce) and because our administrative earnings data were truncated at the Social Security taxable maximum. The full details of our matching and imputation methods are described in the data appendix.

Once we have constructed complete earnings and marital histories, we calculate benefit streams for ages 60 through 100. We assume that sample members claim benefits at their actual retirement age (obtained from Social Security benefit records). For the individual account plans, we similarly assume that sample members annuitize their accounts at the same age at which they chose to start receiving Social Security benefits or at age sixty-five, whichever is earlier.[13] We then calculate Social Security benefits at each age from 60 to 100.[14] For married and divorced sample members, we calculate separate benefit streams corresponding to the benefits the sample member would receive if his or her spouse were still alive and if the spouse were dead (assuming that the sample member were still alive).

Using these benefit streams, we construct a simulated cross section of Social Security beneficiaries by treating each benefit year as an observation and weighting each observation by the probability that the sample member is alive in that year. For married and divorced individuals, the weights on each of the two benefit streams account additionally for the probability that the spouse is alive. We use mortality tables classified by age, race, sex, and education, thereby incorporating socioeconomic differences in mortality. Brown, Liebman, and Pollet (in the appendix to this volume) constructed these mortality tables by fitting a Gompertz-Makeham function to data from the 1979–85 National Longitudinal Mortality Study (NLMS) using nonlinear least squares. The period life tables estimated from the NLMS were used to create mortality ratios (at each single year of age) for each race-education-sex group relative to the overall mortality rate for the relevant sex. These ratios were then applied to SSA life tables for males and females born in 1990 to produce the mortality

13. This assumption is made to facilitate comparisons between the different systems. In practice, it would probably make more sense to have a standard annuitization age in order to avoid adverse selection problems.
14. Benefits vary by age because they can depend on whether the sample member's spouse has begun receiving benefits yet.

Table 7.1   **Characteristics of Sample**

	1925–29 Cohorts at Time of 1990 and 1991 SIPP (%)	Simulated Cross Section of Beneficiaries (%)
Male	46.1	41.0
Female	53.9	59.0
Married (including separated)	73.7	52.8
Widowed	13.6	38.0
Divorced	8.6	5.8
Never married	4.1	3.4
White (and other)	92.4	93.2
Black	7.6	6.8
Hispanic (can be either race)	4.3	4.0
Less than high school	30.8	28.8
High school	53.5	55.5
More than high school	15.9	15.6
Age 60–61	n.a.	2.4
Age 62–64	n.a.	10.7
Age 65–75	n.a.	40.0
Age 75–85	n.a.	29.2
Age 85+	n.a.	17.6
Unweighted sample size	2,720	Up to 41 benefit years × 2,720
Weighted sample size	3.424 million (per birth year)	71.156 million

Source: All tables are derived from authors' calculations from match of the 1990 and 1991 panels of the Survey of Income and Program Participation to Social Security administrative records.
Note: n.a. = not applicable.

tables used in this paper. Potential benefit years with zero benefits are not included in the sample. For example, only widows who take benefits at age sixty have observations at age sixty.[15]

Table 7.1 displays two sets of means for our sample. The first column displays the means for our 2,720 sample members, weighted for sampling and to correct for sample attrition due to imperfect matching to administrative data. At the time of the SIPP surveys, 54 percent of the members of our five-year cohort were female, 74 percent were married, and 92 percent were white. Column (2) presents weighted means for our simulated

15. We adopted this cross-sectional methodology after seeing a similar approach used by David Pattison at the Social Security Administration. However, our approach differs from that used in studies such as Social Security Administration (1999b) because we do not discount the benefit levels back to age sixty-five, as SSA does. We believe that our approach better represents the cross-sectional distribution of all beneficiaries and does not underweight older beneficiaries, particularly older widows.

cross section of beneficiaries. Thus, each of the 2,720 sample members contributes up to forty-one observations from age 60 to 100 weighted by the probability that he or she survives to that time. As would be expected, due to the lower mortality rates of women, a higher fraction of this simulated cross section of beneficiaries is female (59 percent). The fraction that is married declines as spouses die. Thus, in the simulated cross section of beneficiaries, 53 percent are married, as compared to 74 percent at the time of the SIPP, and 38 percent are widow(er)s, as compared to 14 percent at the time of the survey. Similarly, the fraction that is black is lower in the simulated cross section because of higher mortality rates for blacks than for whites.

7.3   A Pure Prefunding System

Although our primary interest is in the distributional effect of a mixed system that combines the existing PAYGO finance with an investment-based component, we begin our analysis in the current section by considering the analytically pure case of completely replacing the traditional PAYGO financing with a prefunding system of individual accounts. Because there are different possible combinations of PAYGO and investment-based systems, the pure prefunding system provides a useful limiting case. It also exaggerates the distributional effects and makes them easier to study.

We follow the procedure described above to compare the benefits that the retirees in our sample would receive in a pure prefunded system (after it is fully phased in) with the benefits that they would receive under the existing PAYGO Social Security rules (which we will refer to as the individual's benchmark Social Security benefits.) Our focus in this section is only on the beneficiaries and the amounts of benefits that they would receive. In section 7.4 we combine this information with the different amounts that these individuals would pay during their working years either as taxes for the Social Security program or as savings deposited into the PRAs. This allows us to calculate the internal rates of return and net present value for different subgroups as a way of assessing the net distributional consequences of the shift from tax-financed Social Security benefits to the funded PRA system.

Although a complete shift to a pure investment-based system has occurred in several countries, other nations have combined PAYGO defined-benefit systems with defined-contribution investment-based prefunding. A system that combines some prefunding with a portion of the traditional PAYGO finance would have a muted effect on distribution compared to the pure prefunding system examined in the current section. We examine one such mixed system in section 7.5, in which we assume that the current PAYGO tax rate continues to exist and that benefits are scaled down to the amount that could be financed by such a tax rate with the older population that will prevail in the year 2075, the date that we use for comparing the two systems.[16]

Currently, OASDI benefits are 10.8 percent of payroll (the fact that this is lower than the 12.4 percent OASDI payroll tax explains the existence of the Social Security surplus). However, some of these benefit payments are for disability benefits and other benefit categories, such as children and young widows, that we do not model. Using numbers from Board of Trustees (1999), we calculate that the cost of the portion of the OASDI program that we simulate in this paper will rise from 9.4 percent of payroll today to 15.4 percent of payroll in the year 2075. The most direct comparison of the fully phased-in version of the prefunded system with the existing PAYGO system would assume that the retirees pay the same 15.4 percent of their wages each year during their working lives under both systems, with those funds going to pay concurrent benefits under the PAYGO system and being invested in the PRAs in the prefunded system. However, since one of the advantages of the prefunded system is that it would allow a lower rate of contribution in the long run than the tax rate of the PAYGO system, our analysis assumes that individuals contribute only 9 percent of their covered earnings to their PRAs during their working lives. This represents a 42 percent reduction in the cost of providing for their retirement income relative to the 15.4 percent required in the PAYGO system. As we noted above, we examine the implications of this reduction for the internal rate of return and for the net present value in different subgroups in section 7.5.

Our analysis assumes that individuals invest in a way that produces a 5.5 percent real rate of return on their PRA contributions after allowing for administrative costs of 0.4 percent.[17] As we noted above, 5.9 percent has been the mean for the period 1946 to 1995 of the logarithmic real return on a portfolio consisting of 60 percent stocks (the Standard & Poor's 500 index) and 40 percent corporate bonds. Four comments about this rate of return are warranted.

First, 5.9 percent is the return to investors on the portfolio of stocks and bonds and therefore understates the overall return to the nation of the incremental savings generated in the PRA accounts. To the extent that

16. Although we do not explicitly model the transition to the pure prefunded system, the mixed system that we study in section 7.5 indicates the nature of the distributional effects that might be observed along such a path.

17. Administrative costs of 0.4 percent are about twice the rate charged by efficient equity index funds such as the Vanguard fund. Bond funds generally have lower charges than equity funds. Teachers Insurance and Annuity Association College Retirement Equity Fund (TIAA-CREF) now offers a variable annuity with an administrative cost of 0.37 percent. These existing funds must incur expenses in collecting funds that would be avoided in a system in which funds are deposited annually in individual accounts by the government. For a discussion of these issues, see the NBER volume on the administrative costs of Social Security reform edited by Shoven (2000) and the paper by Goldberg and Graetz (2000).

those savings are invested in corporate capital, they generate taxes to the federal, state, and local governments, including both corporate profits taxes and property taxes. This extra tax revenue permits reductions in other taxes or increases in government spending. We make no attempt to calculate how this extra benefit would be distributed in the population.

Second, the 5.9 percent mean return is the mean of the logarithmic annual returns. The corresponding mean return of the ordinary level rates of return is about one full percentage point higher, or 6.9 percent.[18]

Third, ending the postwar sample period in 1995 excludes the 125 percent rise in share prices between 1995 and 1999 as well as the significant—if smaller—rise in bond prices since that time. Extending the period through 1999 would raise the rate of return from 6.9 percent for 1946–95 to about 7.5 percent for 1946–99. Understating the actual average past rate of return in these two ways provides a margin of safety for the year-to-year fluctuations of the rate of return in the future and for the possibility that the stock market is particularly vulnerable to a downward correction at the present time.

Fourth, we provide explicit calculations in section 7.6 of the distributional effect of a prefunded system with a substantially lower rate of return, substituting 3.5 percent for 5.5 percent. The statistical analysis reported in Feldstein and Ranguelova (1998) shows that historic experience implies that an annuity with a cumulative rate of return higher than 3.5 percent would be experienced in 90 percent of the realizations from the process that generated the observed rates of return between 1946 and 1995.[19]

Table 7.2 compares the mean benefits that would be paid to various retiree groups under existing PAYGO Social Security rules with the PRA annuities that they would receive from the investment-based accounts with the net 5.5 percent real rate of return. For each population group we also note the percentage of beneficiaries whose PRA annuities would be greater than or equal to the benefits that those individuals would receive from the Social Security program.[20] In addition, we show the percentage of individuals whose benefits are lower than the poverty line under the current law Social Security rules and in the PRA system.

---

18. The log-normal approximation for the rate of return implies that $E(1 + R) = \exp [E(r) + 0.5 \text{ var } (r)]$, where R is the level rate of return, r is the logarithmic rate of return, $E(x)$ is the expected value of x, and var (x) is the variance of x. Since $E(r) = 0.059$ and var $(r) = (0.125)^2 = 0.016$, the mean of the level return is given by $E(1 + R) = \exp (0.067) = 1.069$, i.e., a 6.9 percent real level rate of return.

19. Some additional variance could arise because individuals would be allowed to choose among various mutual fund managers. However, this additional variance would be quite small. Chevalier and Ellison (1999) estimate that the standard deviations of excess returns (relative to the market) of large growth and income mutual funds is around 3.5 percent. Since our estimates use a market standard deviation of 12.5 percent, accounting for the extra 3.5 percent spread would increase our overall standard deviation by less than 5 percent.

20. If benefit levels under both plans are below the SSI guarantee, we treat the two plans as providing equal retirement benefits.

Table 7.2   Comparison of Benefit Levels from 9% Personal Retirement Accounts versus Social Security

	Average Benefit Levels			% with Retirement Benefits Below Poverty Line	
	Current-Law Social Security	PRAs Funded with 9% of Payroll (5.5% rate of return)	% of Beneficiaries with PRA Benefits ≥ SS Benefits	Current-Law Social Security	PRA
All beneficiaries	9,291	21,414	97.9	18.9	9.2
		Married Couples			
Men	8,425	17,152	97.8	13.7	9.2
Women	8,185	17,582	97.2	13.5	9.1
Whites	8,413	17,657	97.6	12.9	8.5
Blacks	6,229	10,850	96.1	29.5	22.6
Hispanics	5,896	9,123	86.4	38.7	31.4
Less than high school	7,613	15,476	97.5	16.5	12.0
High school	8,227	17,652	98.1	13.4	8.9
College and above	9,440	19,074	96.3	10.5	6.2
Lowest Lifetime Income Quintile	3,899	5,189	92.8	71.4	49.9
2nd Quintile	6,610	11,270	94.4	13.8	7.3
3rd Quintile	8,504	16,871	97.6	3.9	2.7
4th Quintile	9,462	21,339	99.8	2.2	1.6
Highest Quintile	10,478	24,240	100.0	1.9	1.3

(continued)

Table 7.2   (continued)

	Average Benefit Levels			% with Retirement Benefits Below Poverty Line	
	Current-Law Social Security	PRAs Funded with 9% of Payroll (5.5% rate of return)	% of Beneficiaries with PRA Benefits ≧ SS Benefits	Current-Law Social Security	PRA
Widowed, Divorced, and Never Married					
Men	11,120	26,264	98.7	22.4	8.7
Women	10,112	25,837	98.1	25.6	9.4
Early widow/divorce	8,249	22,044	99.0	45.8	14.6
Whites	10,673	26,933	98.2	21.8	8.0
Blacks	7,562	16,484	98.9	53.3	20.5
Hispanics	7,961	18,316	95.2	46.8	27.3
Less than high school	9,135	22,684	98.4	34.5	12.8
High school	10,932	28,329	98.8	18.9	6.2
College and above	12,475	28,316	95.7	13.3	7.9
Lowest Lifetime Income Quintile	5,414	9,651	96.0	94.1	41.7
2nd Quintile	9,310	21,196	98.3	18.7	1.0
3rd Quintile	11,564	29,521	97.8	1.8	1.5
4th Quintile	12,947	35,819	99.9	0.0	0.0
Highest Quintile	14,722	41,210	100.0	0.0	0.0

All of these calculations assume that the beneficiaries begin receiving benefits at their actual age of claiming benefits or at age sixty-five, whichever is earlier.[21] The dollar amounts that we report are per retiree. This convention implies that a married couple receives twice the benefits that we report. Under the Social Security system, the per-retiree benefit for a married couple is calculated by adding the retiree benefit of the primary earner plus the spouse benefit or the second earner's benefit, whichever is higher, and then dividing the sum by two. In the investment-based options, the PRA annuities of both members of a married couple are combined and the sum is divided by two. Recall that the simulation assumes that retirees experience their actual earnings histories, restated in 1999 dollars, and will receive benefits under the current (1999) law benefit rules. When an individual reaches the age at which he claims benefits, his PRA balance is fully annuitized. Those individuals who die prematurely bequeath their PRA balances to their spouse, if they have one, or to someone else if they have no spouse. All amounts are in 1999 dollars and wage levels.

The top line of the table shows (in column [1]) that the average annual current-law Social Security benefit in our sample of retirees, funded with a 15.4 percent payroll tax, would be $9,291.[22] By contrast, PRA annuities for the same group of individuals with the same earnings histories, funded with 9 percent of covered earnings, produce a mean annuity of $21,414 (column [2]). The mean annuity is thus more than twice as high under the PRA system as under current Social Security rules, even though the 9 percent funding rate is only slightly more than half of the 15.4 percent payroll tax rate required in the long run for the PAYGO Social Security system with the current benefit rules.[23] Column (3) reports that 98 percent of all beneficiaries would have PRA annuities that were greater than or equal to the benefits they would receive from Social Security under current law.

---

21. We simulate benefit levels under the current normal retirement age of sixty-five, even though we are considering a fully phased-in system that would exist after the retirement age has been raised to sixty-seven (or higher). We do this because we do not want to bias the results of our analysis in favor of personal retirement accounts by assuming no behavioral responses to the benefit cuts implicit in raising the retirement age. In doing so, we tilt our results in favor of the traditional Social Security system, in assuming that the benefits we simulate could be afforded with 15.4 percent of payroll. In fact, if the NRA of sixty-five were maintained, PAYGO Social Security benefits would cost more than 15.4 percent of payroll.

22. In comparison, the SSA reports average benefits actually received by new beneficiaries (retired workers, husbands/wives, and widows) of $8,000 in 1997. Accounting for wage growth between 1997 and 1999 would eliminate about one-third of the gap between the two averages. In addition, our simulation model assumes that workers faced a taxable maximum that was equivalent to current levels throughout their careers, raising their covered earnings relative to those of actual retirees.

23. The two mean annuities could be made equal by cutting the PRA saving rate from 9.0 percent to only 4.0 percent—which is only about one-fourth of the 15.4 percent payroll tax needed to fund the current law Social Security benefits with the future demographics and projected earnings. While it would be interesting to examine the distributional effects of the shift to a pure prefunded systems with different saving rates, we do not pursue this here.

Finally, columns (4) and (5) report the effect of the reform on the percentage of retirees whose total income would be below the poverty level on the basis of their Social Security or PRA benefits taken alone. We say "benefits taken alone" to emphasize that this makes no allowance for Supplemental Security Income payments or other sources of retirement income (private pensions, federal and state government pensions, private savings, earnings, etc.) Columns (4) and (5) show that the Social Security benefits taken alone would leave 18.9 percent of beneficiaries below the poverty line, although this would fall to 9.2 percent with the PRA system. Thus, PRA prefunding, using a saving rate that is less than 60 percent of the tax rate that would be required for PAYGO Social Security, cuts the potential poverty rate by more than half.

The rest of the table provides similar information for several different population subgroups. In every group, the mean PRA annuity substantially exceeds the mean benefits that would be paid under current law Social Security rules, the number of beneficiaries who would receive more from the PRA annuity substantially exceeds the number who would receive more from Social Security, and the potential poverty rate under Social Security rules is substantially higher than it would be in the PRA system. After commenting on some of these comparisons, we will look at a graphic representation of the outcomes for individual beneficiaries that indicates the extent to which some individuals would receive less from the PRA system than they would receive under existing Social Security rules.

Although all of the subgroups do substantially better with the PRA system than with the traditional Social Security, there are differences in the extent to which this is true. Some of these differences might have been expected, but we found others surprising.

Married individuals gain relatively less on average than other groups. The mean PRA annuity of $17,152 for married men is 2.04 times the Social Security benefits of $8,425 per person for the same individuals. The ratio is similar (2.15) but not identical for married women.[24] By comparison, the ratio of PRA benefits to current law Social Security benefits is 2.36 for nonmarried (widowed, divorced, or never married) men and 2.56 for nonmarried women.[25] This reflects two things. First, many married couples gain from the existing Social Security rule that gives benefits of 150 percent of the benefit of the primary earner whenever that amount is greater than what the couple would have received on the basis of their

24. The amounts for married women are not the same as the amounts for married men because only individuals born between 1925 and 1929 are included in the calculations. Thus, both members of married couples are not always in the sample.

25. Note that although the per-person benefits are higher for the single retirees of all sorts, the benefits for the married couples with the male in the age range are twice $17,152, or $34,304—substantially higher than the household benefits in the other groups.

individual earnings, even if the secondary earner had little or no earnings. Second, under the PRA system that we simulate, women who become widows after both spouses claim benefits receive a retirement benefit that is two-thirds of what the couple was receiving. In contrast, Social Security provides widows with benefits that range between one-half and two-thirds of the couple's benefit, depending on the relative earnings of the two spouses. Moreover, if the widow's husband dies before claiming benefits in the PRA program, the widow inherits the account balance and eventually annuitizes it (as well as her own account if she has not previously claimed benefits either) at a single life rate.

This explains why widows and widowers have not only greater proportional gains but also substantially more per capita benefits than married individuals. Divorced individuals also do well under the PRA plan relative to Social Security, especially if their former spouse is still alive or if their marriage lasted for fewer than ten years. Social Security provides spouse benefits to divorced spouses that are only one-half of the benefit received by the former spouse while the former spouse is still alive (this prevents the system from creating an incentive for divorce). Moreover, the system provides no benefits to divorced spouses from marriages that lasted fewer than ten years. In contrast, our PRA plan splits the accounts of the two spouses at the time of divorce regardless of the length of the marriage, and therefore often results in higher benefits.

The poverty figures in columns (4) and (5) show that married couples that depend exclusively on the Social Security or PRA benefits are less likely to be below the poverty level than the unmarried retirees (widows, widowers, divorcees, and those who were never married). However, the shift from Social Security to the PRA benefit reduces the below-poverty portion by much more among these high-poverty unmarried groups than among the married. For example, although the proportion of married women who would be in poverty on the basis of Social Security benefits alone falls from 13 percent to 9 percent, the proportion of nonmarried women who would be in poverty falls from 26 percent to 9 percent.

Women who become widowed or divorced at an early age are particularly vulnerable under current Social Security rules. A woman who is widowed at age fifty and does not remarry will receive benefits based on her own earnings record (which may have large gaps during child-raising years or may only begin at age fifty) or on the limited earnings record of her husband, often leaving her with relatively low benefits when she turns sixty-five. The PRA system provides her with substantially more benefits when she retires because the amount in her husband's account passes to her if he dies before age sixty-five and accumulates value through the investment return.

The situation is similar for women who become divorced at an early age and do not remarry. The combination of account splitting at the time of divorce and the long period over which to earn investment returns generally results in higher benefits than they receive under Social Security.

This advantage of the PRA system is shown in the row marked "Early widows and divorcees," which refers to women who were widowed or divorced before the age of fifty and not remarried before retirement. We combine the young widows and young divorcees for this calculation because the sample of each taken separately would be too small. Their mean benefit under current Social Security rules would be only $8,249, while their PRA annuities would be $22,044, a ratio of 2.67 and therefore substantially higher than the ratio for married men and women. Ninety-nine percent of the PRA annuities of these young widows and divorcees would exceed the Social Security benefits that they would receive under current rules. The percentage of "young widow and divorcees" whose benefits at retirement age are below the poverty line declines from 46 percent under current rules to 15 percent in the PRA system.

Table 7.2 also presents separate results for whites, blacks and Hispanics. All three groups gain substantially from the switch, even those who are divorced, widowed, or never married. The mean gain is larger for whites than for blacks, but the reduction of the proportion of retirees who are potentially in poverty is greatest among blacks, a decline from 53 percent to 21 percent among unmarried blacks. Thus, the shift to the PRA system is potentially much more important for blacks than it is for whites in combating poverty in old age.

Another way of assessing how the shift would affect different socioeconomic groups is to compare the potential effect on households with different primary earner education levels. All three of the education groups enjoy a more than doubling of mean benefits among both the married and the single, but the relative gain is lower among those with a college education (2.02 when married and 2.27 with unmarried) than among those with a high school education (2.15 and 2.59) or those with less than a high school education (2.03 and 2.48). The reduction in poverty is greatest among the unmarried with less than a high school education; the proportion that potentially receives less than the poverty level falls from 35 percent to 13 percent among those with less than a high school education.

The greater relative gain among those with less than a college education is surprising at first, because it is natural to think that the less educated group would have lower incomes and therefore, given the nature of the Social Security rules, would have higher benefits relative to previous earnings (and thus to PRA benefits) than those with more education and earnings. The contrary observed result may reflect the greater likelihood that married college attendees are more likely to be in a couple in which the wife receives benefits as a spouse rather than as a retired worker, a situation that raises the value of Social Security benefits relative to lifetime earnings. The college educated group also has lower age-specific mortality rates, increasing the expected number of years of benefits.

Table 7.2 also presents results by lifetime income, defined as the Average Indexed Monthly Earnings (AIME) of the higher earner in the household. The overall pattern suggests that the reductions in potential poverty are the greatest in the lower-income quintiles, while upper-income households have the largest proportional gains from switching to a PRA system. This classification must be regarded with great caution, however, since many of those who are classified as being in the lowest quintile on the basis of their covered earnings may have worked for state governments or for the federal government for much of their lives and may not have actually had low incomes. The distributional results are therefore more meaningful for the other four quintiles. Education and race may also be better factors with which to assess how the reform would affect those with lower lifetime earnings. Finally, it is important to emphasize that all income groups benefit substantially from the shift, and that the reductions in potential poverty are largest for those most at risk.

7.3.1   Comparing Individual Benefits

We now go beyond the comparison of the mean benefits and other summary statistics for each of the demographic groups shown in table 7.1 to examine how each of the individuals in our sample would do under the two systems. Figure 7.1 compares the simulated annual annuity benefits from the PRA accounts (the vertical axis) to the simulated annual social security benefits under current law (the horizontal account) for all beneficiaries. As in table 7.2, the PRA benefits are based on contribution of 9 percent of earnings, approximately 58 percent of the 15.4 percent payroll tax that would be required to finance the PAYGO OASI Social Security benefits for those who retire in 2075. Each point in the figure represents an individual in the sample weighted to represent the population sampling weight and the survival probabilities, as described in section 7.2 of this paper. To conform to Bureau of the Census restrictions on disclosing information on individuals, each point has been slightly modified from the actual location by adding random noise, a process known as "random jittering" in the statistical literature. This procedure does not change the overall appearance of the figure in a perceptible way. Note that the scale of the two axes is different; the annual Social Security benefits (horizontal scale) range from zero to $20,000 per beneficiary, and the PRA annuities for the same individuals range from zero to $60,000.

The ray from the origin represents equal values of simulated Social Security benefits and simulated PRA annuities. Any point above the line corresponds to an individual who would receive more from the PRA system based on a 9 percent contribution rate than from the Social Security system despite the substantially higher 15.4 percent tax rate. The figure

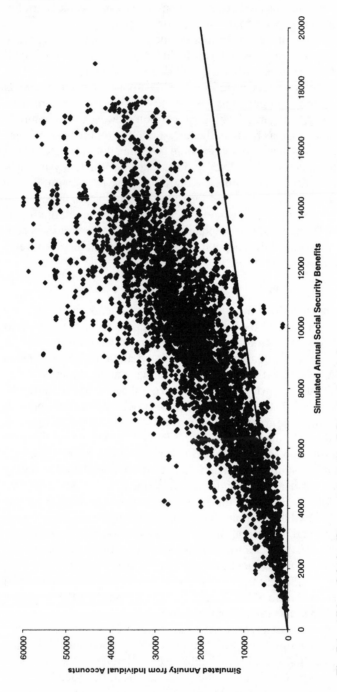

Fig. 7.1   All beneficiaries (9 percent accounts, 5.5 percent return)
Source: All figures are derived from authors' calculations from match of the 1990 and 1991 panels of the Survey of Income and Program Participation to Social Security administrative records
Note: The points have been randomly jittered to preserve confidentiality.

illustrates the statistic in table 7.2 that nearly all individuals would receive more from the PRA system than from the Social Security system.

The figure goes beyond that summary statistic by showing the Social Security benefit level and the PRA annuity of each individual in our sample who would gain or lose in the shift to a prefunded system and the magnitude of the net gain or loss. It is clear that most of those who appear to lose from the shift are individuals with relatively low Social Security benefits. It is significant, therefore, to consider the role that Supplemental Security Income (SSI) would play in supplementing both the regular Social Security benefits and the PRA annuities. SSI is a federal government program that currently provides means-tested supplemental benefits so that the combination of regular Social Security benefits, other income (from assets, pensions, and work), and the SSI benefit together provide a specified minimum income. Since our figures are benchmarked to 1999 income levels, the relevant SSI amounts are $6,000 per year for a single individual and $9,012 per year for a couple. This implies that incomes below $4,506 per person in married couples and $6,000 for unmarried individuals should not be observed under either the Social Security system or the PRA system.[26]

To show the implication of this in a clear way, figure 7.2 repeats the points in figure 7.1 for married individuals and adds vertical and horizontal lines corresponding to the federal SSI guarantee level (i.e., $4,506); to make the points clearer, we limit the range to individuals with Social Security benefits up to $12,000 per person. No point inside this SSI box would be observed in practice. Note that some individuals with Social Security benefits at or below the SSI level will have PRA benefits above that level, and some with Social Security benefits above the SSI level will receive only the SSI level of benefits under the PRA program. The diagonal line from the origin still shows the equal value combinations of Social Security benefits and PRA annuity payments, but any point inside the SSI box will be raised to the SSI level.

Any point below the diagonal line but inside the SSI box will not correspond to lower benefits under the actual PRA system because of the SSI supplement. The key point to note is that in the presence of the SSI guarantee there are very few points in which the PRA system provides lower income than the Social Security system.[27]

26. Some individuals who appear to be eligible for SSI payments do not take up their SSI benefits. McGarry (chap. 2 in this volume) discusses this issue.

27. If a beneficiary had sufficient other income to be ineligible for SSI, then it would be possible for a person with a point in the bottom right portion of the SSI box to have lower income in a PRA system than under Social Security. However, no one would end up with total income below the federal SSI standard. The cost of the SSI program would also be reduced since the PRA benefits would raise the incomes of many of those who now qualify for SSI benefits.

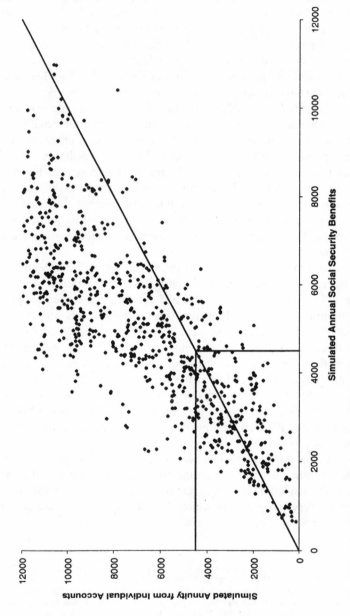

Fig. 7.2 Married poor (9 percent accounts, 5.5 percent return)
Source: See figure 7.1.
Note: The points have been randomly jittered to preserve confidentiality.

Figure 7.3 shows the combinations of Social Security benefits and PRA annuity levels for women who are not married at retirement age (i.e., are widowed, divorced, or never married). There are very few points in which the PRA benefit would be less than the Social Security benefit. When the benefit levels in the two systems are adjusted for SSI—that is, each individual's retirement income has been adjusted up to the SSI level if it would otherwise be below this level—the small number of potential losers is substantially reduced. Only those points that are outside the "SSI box" and below the diagonal line would receive lower benefits.

The results are even more striking for young widows and divorcees (figure 7.4), in which case virtually all of the individuals in the sample would be better off under the PRA system than under existing Social Security rules.

Figure 7.5 presents the same analysis for black individuals. Almost all members of this group would receive higher retirement benefits under the PRA plan with a 9 percent contribution rate than under the Social Security plan with the 15.4 percent tax rate—often very much higher benefits. Although some members of this group with low Social Security benefits would have even lower PRA annuities, this would rarely occur in practice because of the SSI program.

Figure 7.6 shows a similar analysis for individuals in households in which the primary earner had less than a high school education. Again, virtually every member in this group would have a higher retirement income in the PRA system, and SSI would eliminate many of those shortfalls that remain.

7.4 Taking Taxes into Account: Internal Rates of Return and Net Present Values

The analysis of section 7.3 focused on the benefits that individuals would receive under the two systems. Although we noted that the 9 percent long-run rate of contribution to the PRA system would be substantially less than the corresponding 15.4 percent long-run tax required to fund the PAYGO system, our analysis did not take this into account explicitly. We now remedy that omission by comparing the internal rates of return and the net present values of different population subgroups under the current Social Security rules with the rates of return and net present values that those groups would have in the PRA system.[28]

The rate-of-return calculations for the PRA system are sensitive to the PRA annuity assumptions and to the bequest rules. All PRA balances are fully annuitized when the individual reaches retirement. Although an actuarially fair PRA system would give each individual the same rate of

---

28. It is important to emphasize that these rates of return are after the transition to the new system is complete. During part of the transition to the PRA system, contribution rates might be higher under the PRA system than under the PAYGO system.

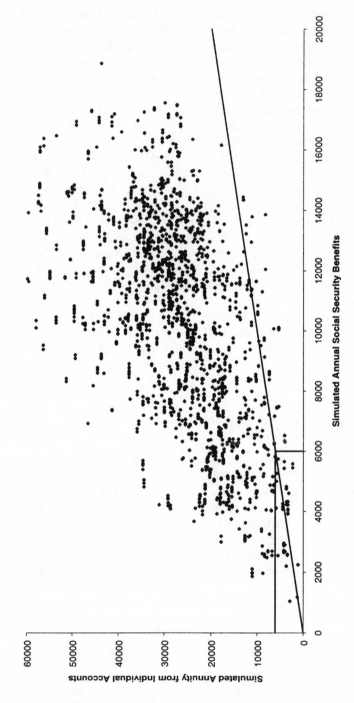

Fig. 7.3 Widowed, divorced, and never married women (9 percent accounts, 5.5 percent return)
Source: See figure 7.1.
Note: The points have been randomly jittered to preserve confidentiality.

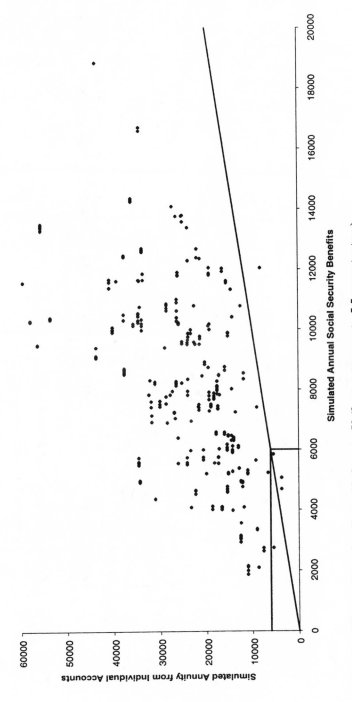

Fig. 7.4 Women widowed or divorced before age 50 (9 percent accounts, 5.5 percent return)
Source: See figure 7.1.
Note: The points have been randomly jittered to preserve confidentiality.

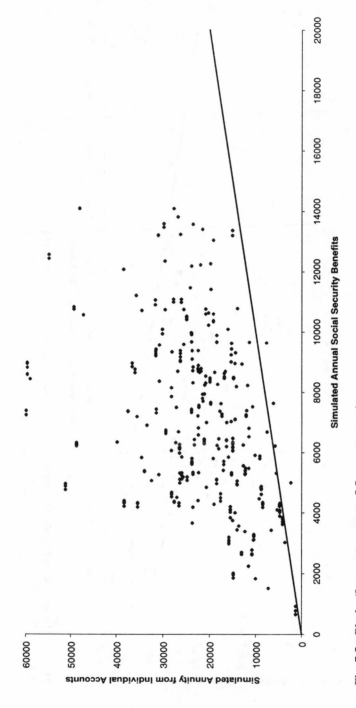

Fig. 7.5 Blacks (9 percent accounts, 5.5 percent return)
Source: See figure 7.1.
Note: The points have been randomly jittered to preserve confidentiality.

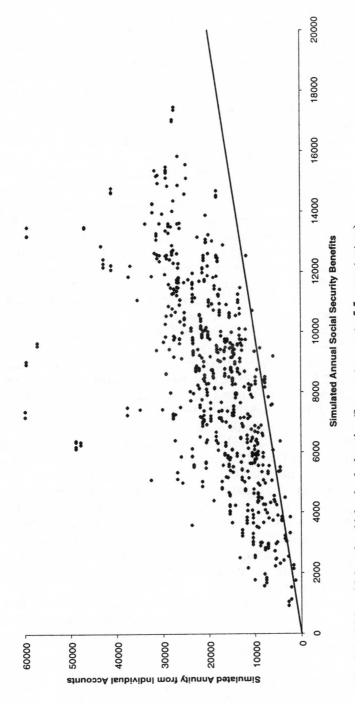

Fig. 7.6 Males with less than high school education (9 percent accounts, 5.5 percent return)
Source: See figure 7.1.
Note: The points have been randomly jittered to preserve confidentiality.

return, we noted above that we assume that the PRA annuities would be calculated using a single uniform unisex mortality table. The PRA system therefore gives a higher rate of return to those groups that have higher life expectancies, a difference that is particularly important in favoring women relative to men. With respect to bequests, we assume that a married individual who dies before age sixty-seven bequeaths his PRA balance to the spouse, if he or she has one, and to someone else if there is no spouse.

The internal rate of return is calculated for each individual as follows. For individuals who are never married, we calculate the internal rate of return on the stream that begins with the taxes paid by the individual and the individual's employer at a combined 15.4 percent rate and switches to the benefits that the individual receives in each year, with each year weighted by the probability that the individual is alive at that age, using the age-sex-race-education mortality probabilities described above. For married couples, one-half of the combined payroll taxes paid by the couple in each year that they are married is assumed to be paid by each individual (in years in which the spouses were not married, the entire payroll tax is attributed to the spouse who paid the tax). When the individuals receive benefits as a couple, half of the total benefit in each year is assumed to be received by each. When one of the couple dies, the remaining benefits are attributed only to the surviving spouse. The same procedure is followed for divorce: the divorced individual is assumed to pay half of the couple's combined payroll tax while married and to receive the relevant benefits after divorce.[29] In each situation, the internal rate of return for each individual in the couple is then based on these calculated tax payments and benefit receipts. From the SIPP marriage topical module we observe annual marital status for each individual including up to three marriages and divorces. Rates of return are reduced to account for the payroll taxes paid by cohort members who died before the time of the SIPP survey. Implicitly, we assume that all deceased members of the cohort had earnings when they were alive that were equal to the average earnings of a person in the same sex-age-race-education subgroup. Rates of return are increased to account for the bequests by cohort members who died while single and before claiming benefits. The full amount of the bequest is treated as a benefit accruing to the sex-age-race-education subgroup of the decedent, and he or she is assumed to have had a PRA equal to the subgroup average for people of his or her age.

Our estimates of the internal rate of return in each subgroup are performed for the aggregate taxes and benefits in the relevant subgroup. Thus, individuals with higher earnings and benefit levels receive more weight in the internal rate-of-return calculations.

---

29. Recall that, at the time of a divorce, the PRA balances of the two individuals are combined and divided equally between them.

For the sample as a whole, the switch from the PAYGO system to the PRA system raises the rate of return from about 1.4 percent in the unfunded Social Security system[30] to 5.5 percent in the PRA system. Although the difference between the two rates of return is substantially greater for some population groups than it is for others, reflecting the redistribution implied by the Social Security rules and the differences in PRA returns due to the use of a single unisex mortality table for calculating the PRA annuity payments, it is also true that all of the subgroups that we consider experience substantial rate-of-return increases.

Table 7.3 presents results for each of the subgroups for which an internal rate of return can be calculated. This is straightforward for the classifications that can be identified of age twenty-one: sex, race, and education. We do not present results for marital status since it is not generally known at age twenty-one and varies over an individual's lifetime.

It is tempting to say that the groups with the biggest increase in rate of return benefit most from the shift, and in some sense this is true. However, such a comparison does not take into account the relative magnitudes of the tax and of the saving deposits under the two systems. A given rise in the internal rate of return is worth more in absolute amount when the magnitude of the tax and saving deposit is larger. We therefore also present estimates of the net present value of the time paths of payments and receipts for the Social Security and PRA systems.

The first column of table 7.3 shows the internal rates of return of the current PAYGO Social Security system for different population subgroups. We use our age-sex-race-education life tables to calculate the probability that each such person is alive to pay the tax in each year of his or her working life and to receive the Social Security benefit at each age. Because we are modeling the fully phased-in systems, we assume that the individuals (and their employers) pay 15.4 percent of their covered earnings in each year (from age twenty-one to their retirement age). The corresponding PRA calculations in column (2) assume that the individuals and/or their employers contribute 9 percent of their covered earnings and receive a 5.5 percent net rate of return on their contributions subject to the same mortality tables.

Women receive a higher return under Social Security than men because of their greater longevity and lower earnings; column (1) shows a return of 0.62 percent for men and 1.95 percent for women. The difference between women and men increases slightly if we shift to the PRA system, in which case we see an increase of 4.04 percent for men (to 4.66 percent) and an

---

30. This is the rate of return on Social Security contributions for the cohort that we study. Different cohorts would have different rates of return, but after the baby boom demographic transition, all groups would receive approximately the rate of growth of real money wages.

Table 7.3   Comparison of Internal Rates of Return and Net Present Values from 9% Personal Retirement Accounts versus Social Security

| | Internal Rate of Return | | Net Present Value at Age 21 (per capita) | | | | | |
| | Current-Law Social Security (1) | PRAs Funded with 9% of Payroll (5.5% rate of return) (2) | 1% Discount Rate | | 3% Discount Rate | | 5% Discount Rate | |
			SS (3)	9% PRA (4)	SS (5)	9% PRA (6)	SS (7)	9% PRA (8)
All beneficiaries	1.35	5.54	11,510	186,992	−26,475	48,414	−31,911	5,176
Men	0.62	4.66	−11,323	132,172	−36,166	28,484	−36,895	−2,975
Women	1.95	6.24	32,554	237,515	−17,543	66,782	−27,318	12,688
Whites	1.36	5.55	12,070	194,859	−27,328	50,487	−32,987	5,458
Blacks	1.27	5.38	5,461	101,982	−17,257	26,013	−20,285	2,126
Hispanics	1.81	5.71	16,572	113,596	−11,835	29,881	−16,783	3,901
Less than high school	1.32	5.49	8,439	150,566	−22,658	39,020	−27,142	3,899
High school	1.39	5.62	13,470	206,310	−27,660	54,046	−33,768	6,408
College and above	1.30	5.34	11,114	196,585	−30,536	48,521	−35,614	3,493

increase of 4.29 percent for women (to 6.24 percent), primarily reflecting the use of the unisex life table.

The results by race are quite interesting. Whites and blacks receive essentially the same rate of return under Social Security, with blacks receiving slightly less (1.27 percent) than whites (1.36 percent). Blacks do not receive a higher rate of return from Social Security, despite their lower incomes, because of differences in mortality rates: blacks are more likely to die before they receive any benefits and, should they reach age sixty-five, to die earlier than whites who reached that age. More specifically, if we look only at those who live to age sixty-five, the internal rate of return for blacks is slightly higher than for whites, demonstrating how important mortality before age sixty-five is in racial differences in returns.[31]

Under the PRA, the gains for the two groups are very similar, with whites receiving slightly higher rates of return than blacks because both groups are assumed to purchase annuities at the same rates, even though whites have a greater life expectancy.

Columns (3) through (8) contrast the net present value of the benefits and taxes for each of these groups, using three alternative real discount rates. We regard the 3 percent real rate (used in columns [5] and [6]) as approximately the value that could be obtained *after tax* by an investor who could invest in the PRA portfolio of stocks and bonds. As a sensitivity test, we repeat this analysis for real discount rates of both 1 percent and 5 percent. All other things being equal, a group that has had higher incomes throughout its life will pay more payroll tax in the Social Security program and make larger contributions in the PRA system; it will therefore have a larger positive net present value (NPV) if its internal rate of return exceeds the discount rate and a larger negative NPV if its internal rate of return is less than the discount rate.

The first row shows that for the average participant the lifetime NPV of the PAYGO Social Security system is negative (−$26,475) when discounting at 3 percent (column [5]). In contrast, with the PRA system the lifetime NPV for the average participant (shown in column [6]) is a positive $48,414. With a 1 percent discount rate, both systems have positive present values (columns [3] and [4]) but the difference between the two widens: $186,992 in the PRA and $11,510 with Social Security. A 5 percent discount rate makes the Social Security NPVs more negative and reduces the NPV of the PRA system to a smaller positive amount. The higher the discount rate, the smaller the overall NPV difference between the two systems.

As would be expected, the higher rates of return that women receive in

31. As we explained above, these rates of return are based on the total taxes and benefits for the population subgroup; i.e., these are the weighted average of the individual rates of return with weights equal to the amount of taxes paid and benefits received. A simple unweighted average shows a higher return for blacks than for whites. See Liebman (chap. 1 in this volume) for more detail.

both the current Social Security system and the PRA system translate into more favorable NPVs for women than for men. Results for the other demographic groups are similarly straightforward.

7.5   A Mixed System: PAYGO Plus Investment-Based

Although the pure investment-based system that we examined in sections 7.3 and 7.4 provides a useful benchmark, it is not a realistic prospect for the United States. The countries that adopted pure investment-based systems are ones in which the traditional PAYGO systems were generally regarded by the public as bankrupt, corrupt, and in need of fundamental reform. That is not the situation in the United States. The Social Security program is highly regarded, and the public is seeking a way of maintaining the system ("saving Social Security") without the large tax increase that would be required if the pure PAYGO system continued.

As we noted above, several countries now operate social security retirement systems that include both traditional defined benefits financed on a PAYGO basis and an investment-based defined contribution benefit.[32] Proposals for such a hybrid system have been made in the United States by academic researchers, advisory groups, and politicians. The proposal that we examine in this section would maintain a PAYGO system with a tax of 12.4 percent of payroll. An estimated 3 percent of the 12.4 percent (along with the revenue that is collected from the taxation of benefits) would be needed to continue the disability benefits provided in current law as well as benefits for young survivors. Because retirement benefits will require 15.4 percent of payroll in the year 2075, the 9.4 percent of the payroll tax that remains after providing for disability insurance (DI) would be sufficient to finance 61 percent of current law benefits. This plan would supplement these reduced PAYGO benefits (implemented as an across-the-board reduction in all retirement benefits) with a PRA system with contributions equal to 3 percent of covered earnings—half of the 6 percent of earnings increase that would be required in the 15.4 percent pure PAYGO financing.[33]

Table 7.4 shows the effects of this mixed system for the same population subgroups discussed above. The resulting benefits for the mixed system are of course a hybrid of the pure Social Security benefits shown in column (1) and the benefits that would result from a pure PRA system (shown in column [2] of table 7.2). More specifically, the benefits shown in column (2) of table 7.4 are approximately equal to 61 percent of the pure Social

32. See Feldstein (1998) for discussions of such mixed systems in Australia and the United Kingdom, and Feldstein and Siebert (2001) for discussions of reform in Europe.

33. Both systems receive additional revenue from the taxation of benefits. In the mixed system, these revenues are used to continue to provide full (i.e., not reduced to 61 percent) DI benefits.

Table 7.4   Comparison of Benefit Levels from Mixed Plan and Social Security

	Average Benefit Levels		% of Beneficiaries with Mixed Plan Benefits ≧ SS Benefits	% with Retirement Benefits Below Poverty Line	
	Current-Law Social Security	Mixed Plan (5.5% rate of return)		Current-Law Social Security	Mixed Plan
All beneficiaries	9,291	12,898	96.2	18.9	13.1
		Married Couples			
Men	8,425	10,941	96.3	13.7	12.2
Women	8,185	10,935	95.0	13.5	11.2
Whites	8,413	11,102	95.7	12.9	11.1
Blacks	6,229	7,478	95.8	29.5	25.8
Hispanics	5,896	6,696	78.7	38.7	33.0
Less than high school	7,613	9,879	95.9	16.5	14.6
High school	8,227	10,984	95.9	13.4	11.3
College and above	9,440	12,211	95.0	10.5	9.0
Lowest Lifetime Income Quintile	3,899	4,147	89.1	71.4	63.7
2nd Quintile	6,610	7,855	88.9	13.8	9.9
3rd Quintile	8,504	10,896	95.7	3.9	3.1
4th Quintile	9,462	12,979	99.5	2.2	2.0
Highest Quintile	10,478	14,576	100.0	1.9	1.8

(continued)

Table 7.4 (continued)

| | Average Benefit Levels | | % of Beneficiaries with Mixed Plan Benefits ≧ SS Benefits | % with Retirement Benefits Below Poverty Line | |
	Current-Law Social Security	Mixed Plan (5.5% rate of return)		Current-Law Social Security	Mixed Plan
	Widowed, Divorced, and Never Married				
Men	11,120	15,649	97.4	22.4	12.9
Women	10,112	14,882	96.5	25.6	15.4
Early widow/divorce	8,249	12,462	98.1	45.8	25.1
Whites	10,673	15,595	96.7	21.8	12.6
Blacks	7,562	10,183	97.9	53.3	34.8
Hispanics	7,961	11,041	91.7	46.8	40.0
Less than high school	9,135	13,225	97.2	34.5	21.7
High school	10,932	16,221	97.6	18.9	9.4
College and above	12,475	17,173	92.6	13.3	10.3
Lowest Lifetime Income Quintile	5,414	6,574	94.1	94.1	66.9
2nd Quintile	9,310	12,838	95.7	18.7	3.0
3rd Quintile	11,564	17,010	96.1	1.8	0.8
4th Quintile	12,947	19,967	99.8	0	0
Highest Quintile	14,722	22,864	100.0	0	0

Security benefits shown in column (1) of table 7.2 (the ratio of the 9.4 percent current PAYGO OASI tax to the 15.4 percent that would be required in the pure Social Security system) plus three-ninths of the 9 percent pure PRA benefits shown in column (2) of table 7.2.

The relative gains among the different marital groups are qualitatively similar to the pure case of table 7.2, but more muted. On average, beneficiaries see their per capita annual benefits increase by $3,607 or 39 percent, despite the substantial reduction in the cost of financing the combined package. The gain among married couples is around $2,600 per person, a 30 percent rise over the traditional Social Security benefit. The relative gain is greater among the other marital status groups: unmarried women, for example, gain 47 percent. Potential poverty reduction is also greatest among these groups; for women who are widowed, divorced, or never married, the potential poverty rates are reduced from almost 26 percent with the current Social Security law to 15 percent with the mixed system. Women gain more than men, a reflection of the unisex life tables and the greater annuities received by widows. More specifically, the gains average 30 percent for married men and 41 percent for unmarried men. In contrast, married and unmarried women gain 34 percent and 47 percent. Those women who were widowed or divorced by the age of fifty have an even greater relative gain, rising by 51 percent. The potential poverty rate for this group is cut from over 45 percent to 25 percent.

Although whites gain more than blacks, the potential poverty reduction among blacks is more substantial than among whites. Hispanics gain relatively least because a substantial share of the Hispanics in our sample are immigrants for whom the current Social Security rules provide a very high return on contributions.[34] When the change is assessed in terms of the impact on potential poverty, it is the unmarried blacks who benefit most, with potential poverty falling from 53 percent to 35 percent. Hispanics benefit less because they have less time in the country as PRA participants during which to benefit from the PRA accumulation.

When beneficiaries are classified by the education of the highest earner in the household, the smallest proportional gain tends to go to those with more than a high school education. This group with the highest education level does well under the traditional Social Security rules, because the wives in this group are most likely to receive benefits as spouses. The group with less than a high school education also has the greatest gain when measured by the reduction in poverty.

When we examine income in table 7.4, we see that all groups gain, although the higher quintiles receive the largest percentage increases in ben-

34. On the impact of Social Security rules on immigrants, see Gustman and Steinmeier (2000) and Liebman (chap. 1 in this volume).

efits. The first two quintiles, however, have the largest reductions in potential poverty.

7.5.1   Comparing Individual Benefits

More than 95 percent of the retirees would receive more from the mixed system than from the pure Social Security system. The proportion of gainers differs among the various groups but exceeds 90 percent in all groups except for married Hispanics, whose gain is limited by the large fraction of immigrants in this group.

The scatter plots showing the way that individuals are affected are similar to the pure PRA results shown in section 7.3, but reveal a reduced difference between the social security benefit and the mixed system benefit for each individual. Any point that is above the equal-benefit line in the pure PRA scatter diagrams (implying that the PRA benefit exceeds the Social Security benefit) will continue to be above the line in the mixed system, but with the distance reduced. We therefore present only four scatter diagrams for comparison with the earlier results.

Figure 7.7 shows the results for all beneficiaries. The key results to notice are that most people are above the equal benefit line, that the points are more tightly clustered near the line than they were before, and that the people who are below the line tend to be below it by a very small amount.

Figure 7.8 refers to women who are divorced or widowed before age fifty and do not remarry and can be compared to figure 7.4 in section 7.3. Virtually all of the points are above the equal benefit line, with only a handful of individuals who are both below the line and outside the SSI box.

Figure 7.9, for blacks, shows that almost all the points are above the line and that the few below it tend to reflect levels of income at which the individuals would be eligible for SSI. In short, nearly all of these individuals would be better off with the mixed system than with traditional Social Security.

Finally, figure 7.10 shows that the results for the low education group (i.e., males with less than a high school education) are similar. The losses are small and mostly in the income range for which SSI would be available. The gains for the gainers are substantially larger than the losses for the losers.

7.5.2   Internal Rates of Return and NPVs in the Mixed System

Table 7.5 presents the internal rate of return and net present value calculations for the mixed system and compares those calculations with the corresponding estimates for the pure Social Security system. The mixed plan produces an overall internal rate of return of 3.07 percent, reflecting the 1.4 percent on the PAYGO portion and the 5.5 percent on the PRA portion. The differences among the subgroups follow the same pattern as for the pure PRA option but in a muted way. The gain in NPV (calculated as of age twenty-one) averages $27,666 for all beneficiaries using a 3 percent discount rate.

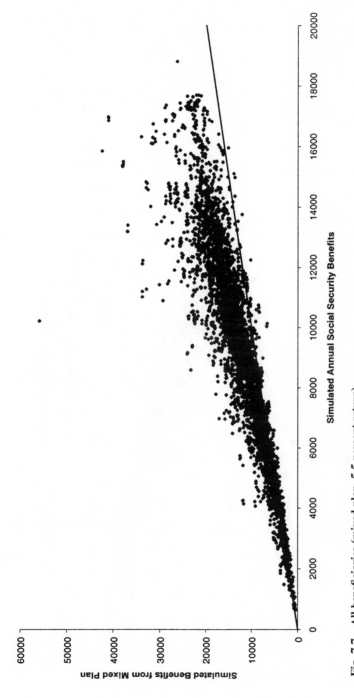

Fig. 7.7   All beneficiaries (mixed plan, 5.5 percent return)
Source: See figure 7.1.
Note: The points have been randomly jittered to preserve confidentiality.

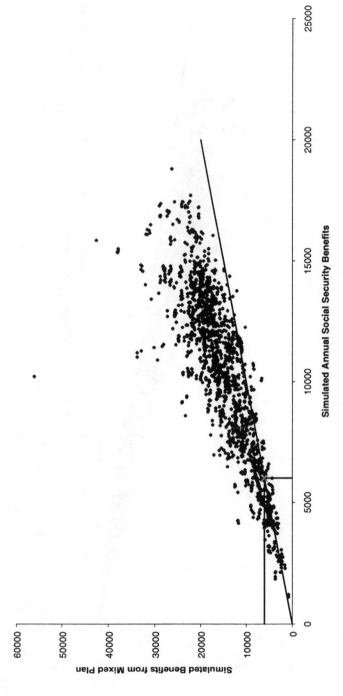

Fig. 7.8 Widowed, divorced, and never married women (mixed plan, 5.5 percent return)

Source: See figure 7.1.

Note: The points have been randomly jittered to preserve confidentiality.

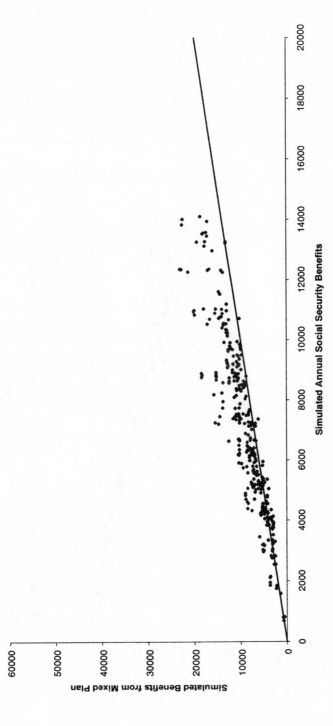

Fig. 7.9   Blacks (mixed plan, 5.5 percent return)
Source: See figure 7.1.
Note: The points have been randomly jittered to preserve confidentiality.

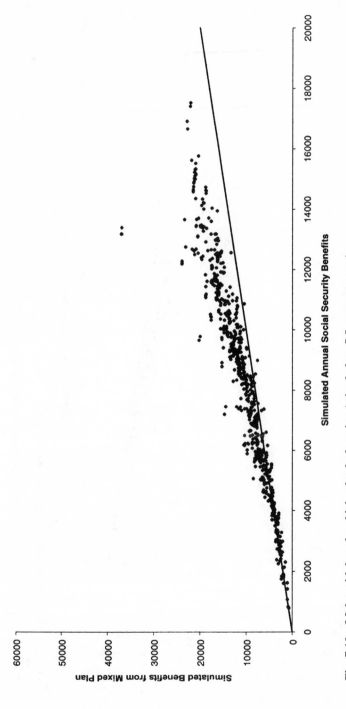

Fig. 7.10   Males with less than high school education (mixed plan, 5.5 percent return)
Source: See figure 7.1.
Note: The points have been randomly jittered to preserve confidentiality.

Table 7.5   Comparison of Internal Rates of Return and Net Present Values from Mixed Plan versus Social Security

	Internal Rate of Return		Net Present Value at Age 21 (per capita)					
			1% Discount Rate		3% Discount Rate		5% Discount Rate	
	Current-Law Social Security (1)	Mixed Plan (5.5% rate of return) (2)	SS (3)	Mixed Plan (4)	SS (5)	Mixed Plan (6)	SS (7)	Mixed Plan (8)
All beneficiaries	1.35	3.07	11,510	71,991	−26,475	1,191	−31,911	−17,154
Men	0.62	2.27	−11,323	39,809	−36,166	−11,301	−36,895	−22,853
Women	1.95	3.71	32,554	101,651	−17,543	12,705	−27,318	−11,902
Whites	1.36	3.07	12,070	74,695	−27,328	1,214	−32,987	−17,801
Blacks	1.27	3.09	5,461	42,779	−17,257	941	−20,285	−10,162
Hispanics	1.81	3.38	16,572	50,282	−11,835	3,814	−16,783	−8,408
Less than high school	1.32	3.05	8,439	58,577	−22,658	748	−27,142	−14,459
High school	1.39	3.12	13,470	79,425	−27,660	2,223	−33,768	−17,951
College and above	1.30	2.91	11,114	74,356	−30,536	−1,592	−35,614	−20,169

7.6   The Risk of Low Investment Returns

Our analysis until now has assumed that the PRA accounts earn a real return of 5.5 percent. We now examine the effects on different population subgroups and individuals of the risk that the return earned in PRA accounts will be very much lower than it would have been in the past.

As we noted in section 7.3, the mean logarithmic real return on a balanced portfolio of 60 percent stock (the Standard & Poor's 500) and 40 percent corporate bonds for the fifty-year period 1946 through 1995 was 5.9 percent. We subtract 0.4 percent for administrative costs to arrive at the 5.5 percent that we used in these analyses. As we explained above, using the mean logarithmic return understates the mean of the actual level returns by about one percentage point, allowing a margin of safety for fluctuations in the investment return. A further reduction of nearly one percentage point results from not extending the sample to 1999.

Our examination in this section draws on the Feldstein and Ranguelova (1998) and Feldstein, Ranguelova, and Samwick (2001) analyses of the investment risks in an investment-based or mixed system. Those analyses showed that the benefits generated by a pure PRA system with a 6.0 percent PRA saving rate or by a mixed system with a 2.3 percent PRA saving rate (and continuation of the current PAYGO tax rate) have a very high probability of exceeding the traditional Social Security benefits. Those analyses presented calculations for a representative agent with average earnings and not for an actual sample of individuals of the type that we study here.

We now use the disaggregated sample data to examine whether there are some demographic groups that would be more adversely affected by investment risk than others. We do not perform the same kind of full analysis of the complete distribution of returns that Feldstein and Ranguelova performed for the representative agent. Instead, we focus on a particular low probability "pessimistic" scenario and evaluate the effects on different population groups if this outcome occurs. More specifically, we assume that, instead of a 5.5 percent real rate of return, the PRA account earns only 3.5 percent. Simulations based on the mean-variance experience from 1946 through 1995 imply that this would be at the 10th percentile of the probability distribution of the annuity payments that would be earned by an individual who had contributed in every year from age twenty-one through age sixty-six. Thus, there is essentially a 90 percent probability based on past experience with the variability of returns that the representative individual's PRA annuity would be greater than the PRA benefit based on a 3.5 percent return.[35]

---

35. More explicitly, we calculated the 3.5 percent as the average level return at the 10th percentile of the 10,000 simulations of the portfolio return performed in Feldstein and Ranguelova (1998). This 3.5 percent return can be compared to the 4.1 real return implicit in

We begin this analysis with the pure investment-based case. In our judgment, this involves more risk of benefit reductions than most individuals would want. This risk could be reduced or eliminated by the type of PAYGO supplementary benefit (conditional on the PRA portfolio return) that is examined in Feldstein and Ranguelova (1998) and Feldstein, Ranguelova, and Samwick (2001). An alternative possibility is that a cohort that learns at age forty-five or fifty that it has received an unusually low rate of return might decide to increase the PRA savings above the 9 percent, reducing the risk of shortfalls in retirement, while still paying substantially less than the 15.4 percent payroll tax that would be required in the pure PAYGO system.

Alternatively, this risk might be reduced or eliminated by private options that provide guarantees of minimum benefits in exchange for some reduction in average or maximum returns. We do not explore any of these ideas here. Nor do we discuss the role that a means-tested program like SSI might play. Instead, we discuss the pure investment-based system briefly and then turn to the more realistic mixed system. The reduced dependence on the investment-based component in the mixed system substantially lowers the risk to individuals. Other ways of reducing the shortfall below the Social Security benchmark and the fraction of individuals whose benefits are below the poverty level are discussed in the next section.

Table 7.6 shows that, with a 3.5 real rate of return, the mean PRA benefit for all retirees would be $10,938, about 18 percent higher than the mean PAYGO Social Security benefits. Thus, in more than 90 percent of the possible rate-of-return outcomes, the pure PRA system would produce a mean benefit for all retirees that exceeds the corresponding mean of the traditional Social Security benefits.

Comparing the remaining rows of columns (1) and (2) shows that, even in this "10th percentile low return scenario," the mean PRA benefit exceeds the mean traditional Social Security benefit in most demographic subgroups that we study (the exceptions being married blacks and Hispanics and the bottom two income quintiles). Thus, among married couples the mean benefit in this low-return case would be roughly $8,900 per person ($17,800 per couple) or 7 percent more than the mean Social Security benefit. For unmarried women, the relative gain is substantially greater: a 30 percent increase, from $10,112 to $13,122. Although there are differences among the groups, the key point is that even in this very poor performance case the mean PRA benefit is higher than the mean Social Security benefit for almost every subgroup, even though the 15.4 percent tax rate is replaced by a 9 percent saving rate. Table 7.7 shows internal rates of return and net present values corresponding to this lower return sample.

---

the current price for Treasury Inflation Protected Securities and to the 3.0 percent interest rate assumed by the Social Security Board of Trustees as the future real return on Treasury bonds in the Social Security Trust Fund.

Table 7.6   Comparison of Benefit Levels from 9% Personal Retirement Accounts with Lower Returns versus Social Security

	Average Benefit Levels			% with Retirement Benefits Below Poverty Line	
	Current-Law Social Security	PRAs Funded with 9% of Payroll (3.5% rate of return)	% of Beneficiaries with PRA Benefits ≧ SS Benefits	Current-Law Social Security	PRA
All beneficiaries	9,291	10,938	72.1	18.9	21.5
		Married Couples			
Men	8,425	8,796	64.4	13.7	20.0
Women	8,185	9,007	69.6	13.5	20.2
Whites	8,413	9,047	67.5	12.9	19.0
Blacks	6,229	5,639	51.6	29.5	43.3
Hispanics	5,896	4,836	47.4	38.7	53.0
Less than high school	7,613	7,913	63.6	16.5	23.7
High school	8,227	8,993	68.5	13.4	20.8
College and above	9,440	9,935	66.8	10.5	13.7
Lowest Lifetime Income Quintile	3,899	2,593	61.6	71.4	92.5

2nd Quintile	6,610	5,812	32.5	13.8	32.9
3rd Quintile	8,504	8,649	51.1	3.9	6.4
4th Quintile	9,462	10,946	81.9	2.2	2.2
Highest Quintile	10,478	12,430	90.0	1.9	1.9
Widowed, Divorced, and Never Married					
Men	11,120	13,491	72.3	22.4	21.3
Women	10,112	13,122	80.1	25.6	23.8
Early widow/divorce	8,249	10,602	77.4	45.8	36.4
Whites	10,673	13,715	78.4	21.8	20.2
Blacks	7,562	8,453	74.1	53.3	27.6
Hispanics	7,961	9,368	72.2	46.8	53.5
Less than high school	9,135	11,478	78.7	34.5	31.5
High school	10,932	14,400	79.4	18.9	17.5
College and above	12,475	14,784	71.2	13.3	15.8
Lowest Lifetime Income Quintile	5,414	4,827	75.9	94.1	84.5
2nd Quintile	9,310	10,845	63.5	18.7	19.4
3rd Quintile	11,564	15,063	78.5	1.8	2.9
4th Quintile	12,947	18,323	90.9	0.0	0.0
Highest Quintile	14,722	20,903	91.8	0.0	0.0

Table 7.7 Comparison of Internal Rates of Return and Net Present Values from Personal Retirement Accounts with Lower Return versus Social Security

| | Internal Rate of Return | | Net Present Value at Age 21 (per capita) | | | | | |
| | Current-Law Social Security (1) | PRAs Funded with 9% of Payroll (3.5% rate of return) (2) | 1% Discount Rate | | 3% Discount Rate | | 5% Discount Rate | |
			SS (3)	9% PRA (4)	SS (5)	9% PRA (6)	SS (7)	9% PRA (8)
All beneficiaries	1.35	3.53	11,510	69,640	−26,475	6,981	−31,911	−10,192
Men	0.62	2.66	−11,323	40,574	−36,166	−4,081	−36,895	−15,068
Women	1.95	4.22	32,554	96,427	−17,543	17,176	−27,318	−5,698
Whites	1.36	3.53	12,070	72,577	−27,328	7,337	−32,987	−10,538
Blacks	1.27	3.41	5,461	37,903	−17,257	3,139	−20,285	−6,452
Hispanics	1.81	3.67	16,572	43,381	−11,835	5,150	−16,783	−5,240
Less than high school	1.32	3.47	8,439	55,291	−22,658	5,061	−27,142	−8,817
High school	1.39	3.61	13,470	77,621	−27,660	8,645	−33,768	−10,429
College and above	1.30	3.35	11,114	72,065	−30,536	5,133	−35,614	−12,350

Although the mean PRA benefits compare favorably with the mean Social Security benefits, a significant fraction of individuals would receive less in PRA benefits than they would have received from Social Security. Among all the individuals in our sample, only 72 percent would receive PRA benefits as large as their benchmark Social Security benefits; see column (3) of table 7.6. The gap between PRA benefits and Social Security benefits in theses cases, however, is not large. Among those with lower benefits under the PRA plan, 51 percent have benefits that are within 15 percent of their benchmark Social Security benefits. To put this reduction into perspective, it is helpful to bear in mind that the 9 percent saving rate is equivalent to less than two-thirds of the tax that would otherwise have to be paid for the Social Security benefits and that the adverse effect shown in table 7.6 occurs only in the worst 10 percent of possible outcomes.

Table 7.8 presents the results for the "10th percentile low return scenario" in the mixed system with PRA saving of 3 percent and a PAYGO OASI tax rate unchanged at 9.4 percent. Despite this very poor investment performance, the overall average combined benefit still exceeds the current law Social Security benchmark. Married men experience an average loss of 3 percent, although most unmarried subgroups have higher means in the mixed PRA system even with this lowest 10th percentile return.

The last two columns of table 7.8 show that the impact of the shift on potential poverty is usually negligible in this case of the lowest 10th percentile return. Stated differently, if the investment experience is better than the lowest 10 percent of cases that can be expected on the basis of the postwar record, there will be a reduction in the potential poverty among retirees.

The estimates in column (3) show that only 54 percent of beneficiaries would receive benefits from the mixed system that were greater than or equal to the current law PAYGO in this worst 10th percentile case.[36] The differences, however, are usually fairly small. Of the individuals with lower benefits under the mixed plan, 87 percent have benefits that are less than 15 percent below those in the current law Social Security system.

This is shown in figure 7.11 by the fact that almost all of the points lie very close to the equal benefit line, with the more substantial departures above the line rather than below. The differences are not large and could again be offset by a conditional government payment that fills the shortfall, by a midcareer adjustment in the cohort PRA saving rate, by private market guarantee arrangements, or by modifying the PRA contributions in the way discussed in the next section. Table 7.9 shows internal rates of

36. Recall that when both plans produce benefit levels below the SSI guarantee, the plans are considered to provide equal benefits. Under the mixed plan with low returns, SSI costs would be higher than under the PAYGO approach. However, the additional costs would be less than 2 percent of total retirement benefits.

Table 7.8   Comparison of Benefit Levels from Mixed Plan with Lower Returns and Social Security

| | Average Benefit Levels | | % of Beneficiaries with Mixed Plan Benefits ≧ SS Benefits | % with Retirement Benefits Below Poverty Line | |
	Current-Law Social Security	Mixed Plan (3.5% rate of return)		Current-Law Social Security	Mixed Plan
All beneficiaries	9,291	9,406	53.7	18.9	20.8
		Married Couples			
Men	8,425	8,156	39.0	13.7	17.5
Women	8,185	8,077	50.1	13.5	17.9
Whites	8,413	8,232	44.5	12.9	16.7
Blacks	6,229	5,741	35.4	29.5	38.9
Hispanics	5,896	5,267	37.1	38.7	48.5
Less than high school	7,613	7,358	40.5	16.5	21.2
High school	8,227	8,098	49.0	13.4	17.9
College and above	9,440	9,165	36.9	10.5	12.4
Lowest Lifetime Income Quintile	3,899	3,282	59.6	71.4	87.9

2nd Quintile	6,610	6,035	16.9	13.8	23.7
3rd Quintile	8,504	8,155	27.4	3.9	4.9
4th Quintile	9,462	9,515	52.1	2.2	2.2
Highest Quintile	10,478	10,639	59.4	1.9	1.9

Widowed, Divorced, and Never Married

Men	11,120	11,392	54.7	22.4	22.5
Women	10,112	10,643	68.1	25.6	25.0
Early widow/divorce	8,249	8,648	69.8	45.8	41.8
Whites	10,673	11,189	64.7	21.8	21.5
Blacks	7,562	7,506	62.9	53.3	51.6
Hispanics	7,961	8,058	62.5	46.8	53.0
Less than high school	9,135	9,490	66.0	34.5	33.3
High school	10,932	11,578	66.6	18.9	18.6
College and above	12,475	12,663	53.0	13.3	14.8
Lowest Lifetime Income Quintile	5,414	4,966	68.0	94.1	92.5
2nd Quintile	9,310	9,387	48.7	18.7	18.6
3rd Quintile	11,564	12,191	67.6	1.8	1.6
4th Quintile	12,947	14,135	75.6	0.0	0.0
Highest Quintile	14,722	16,095	70.6	0.0	0.0

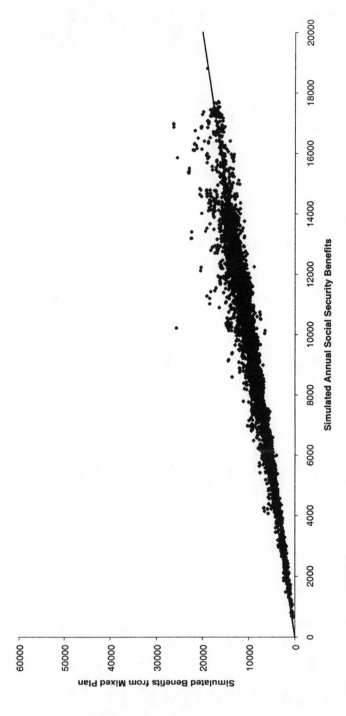

Fig. 7.11 All beneficiaries (mixed plan, 3.5 percent return)
Source: See figure 7.1.
Note: The points have been randomly jittered to preserve confidentiality.

Table 7.9 Comparison of Internal Rates of Return and Net Present Values from Mixed Plan with Lower Return versus Social Security

| | Internal Rate of Return | | Net Present Value at Age 21 (per capita) | | | | | | |
| | Current-Law Social Security (1) | Mixed Plan (3.5% rate of return) (2) | 1% Discount Rate | | 3% Discount Rate | | 5% Discount Rate | |
			SS (3)	Mixed Plan (4)	SS (5)	Mixed Plan (6)	SS (7)	Mixed Plan (8)
All beneficiaries	1.35	2.12	11,510	32,797	−26,475	−12,658	−31,911	−22,297
Men	0.62	1.35	−11,323	9,241	−36,166	−22,174	−36,895	−26,893
Women	1.95	2.74	32,554	54,507	−17,543	−3,889	−27,318	−18,060
Whites	1.36	2.12	12,070	33,862	−27,328	−13,205	−32,987	−23,152
Blacks	1.27	2.22	5,461	21,288	−17,257	−6,750	−20,285	−13,055
Hispanics	1.81	2.49	16,572	26,794	−11,835	−4,470	−16,783	−11,476
Less than high school	1.32	2.11	8,439	26,694	−22,658	−10,635	−27,142	−18,729
High school	1.39	2.16	13,470	36,466	−27,660	−12,943	−33,768	−23,579
College and above	1.30	2.00	11,114	32,830	−30,536	−16,065	−35,614	−25,455

return and net present values corresponding to this lower return example for the mixed plan.

7.7 Redistributive Funding of Personal Retirement Accounts

In previous sections, we have shown that most of the time a PRA system funded with contributions that are proportional to earnings can provide essentially all demographic and income groups with a combination of higher benefit levels and lower levels of taxation than would be available under a purely PAYGO system. Moreover, the reductions in potential poverty are largest for the groups that are most at risk of poverty. Nonetheless, higher income groups tend to receive benefit increases from a PRA system relative to the Social Security system that are larger than those of lower income groups.[37] Furthermore, low–lifetime income workers remain at greatest risk of falling into poverty if financial markets perform worse in the future than they have historically. Although some analysts are concerned that an investment-based system would increase the inequality of benefits, it is important to emphasize that the plans that we study in this paper produce an increase in the income of virtually all retirees and will likely reduce rates of poverty among the elderly.[38]

Redistributive funding of personal retirement accounts can increase the relative gains for low-income households and reduce the risk that lower-than-expected returns will leave them in poverty.[39] A wide range of different funding formulas to achieve this have been suggested. In this section, we consider two simple funding formulas that have been discussed in the policy debate. We present options in the context of our mixed plan. Therefore, we continue to assume PAYGO benefits equal to 61 percent of current law benefits but replace the PRA saving equal to 3 percent of covered earnings with alternative contributions that have the same aggregate cost. More specifically, 1 percent of covered earnings for each employee[40] has the same total cost as $300 per worker (in 1999 dollars, indexed to average

37. The presence in our sample of government workers with low covered earnings exaggerates the percentages of low-income workers relative to what we will expect to see in future cohorts. However, it has little impact on our estimates of the relative gains and losses by workers at a given income level.
38. See Feldstein (2000) for a discussion of different distributive goals.
39. An alternative approach to protecting lower-income beneficiaries is to reduce the traditional Social Security benefits by relatively less for this group.
40. More accurately, 1 percent of the covered earnings of workers who meet the current Social Security requirement of annual earnings of $3,000 a year. Many individual account plans require a minimum level of earnings to qualify for an annual contribution, a requirement designed to reduce administrative costs associated with very small accounts. In the redistributive options that we are discussing, a minimum earnings threshold is likely to be necessary to prevent people from gaming the system by working for only a few hours during the year but still earning a full contribution.

Table 7.10   **Comparison of Average Benefit Levels under Different Redistributive Funding Options for Personal Retirement Accounts in the Mixed Plan**

	Current-Law Social Security	3% of Payroll Accounts (5.5% return)	1.5% of Payroll + $450 per Worker (5.5% return)	$900 per Worker (5.5% return)
	Married Couples			
Lowest Lifetime Income Quintile	3,899	4,147	4,856	5,564
2nd Quintile	6,610	7,855	8,447	9,040
3rd Quintile	8,504	10,896	10,809	10,722
4th Quintile	9,462	12,979	12,330	11,680
Highest Quintile	10,478	14,576	13,433	12,290
Whites	8,413	11,102	10,783	10,464
Blacks	6,229	7,478	8,128	8,778
Hispanics	5,896	6,696	7,219	7,741
	Widowed, Divorced, and Never Married			
Lowest Lifetime Income Quintile	5,414	6,574	8,422	10,270
2nd Quintile	9,310	12,838	14,129	15,420
3rd Quintile	11,564	17,010	17,195	17,380
4th Quintile	12,947	19,967	19,115	18,263
Highest Quintile	14,722	22,864	20,981	19,099
Whites	10,673	15,595	15,819	16,044
Black	7,562	10,183	11,770	13,357
Hispanics	7,961	11,041	12,028	13,014

wages thereafter). In the first option, the individual accounts contributions are a flat amount of $900 per worker, while in the second the annual contributions into the PRA accounts are 1.5 percent of the worker's covered earnings plus $450.

Table 7.10 shows mean benefits by income quintile for Social Security and the three different formulas for funding the PRAs under a 5.5 percent investment return. Notice that under the accounts funded with 3 percent of covered earnings, the increase in benefits relative to Social Security rises from 19 percent in the 2nd quintile to 39 percent in the 5th quintile among married couples, and from 38 percent in the 2nd quintile to 55 percent in the 5th quintile among the unmarried. In contrast, the middle plan, which mixes flat contributions and earnings-related contributions, replicates the progressivity of Social Security with roughly equal percentage increases for each quintile: 28 percent for the 2nd quintile, 30 percent for the 4th quintile, and 28 percent for the 5th quintile among married couples; and

Table 7.11   **Percent with Retirement Benefits below the Poverty Line under Different Redistributive Funding Options for Personal Retirement Accounts in the Mixed Plan with a 10th Percentile Return**

		Mixed Plan		
	Current-Law Social Security	3% of Payroll Accounts (3.5% return)	1.5% of Payroll + $450 per Worker (3.5% return)	$900 per Worker (3.5% return)
Married Couples				
Lowest Lifetime Income Quintile	71.4	87.9	78.6	71.9
2nd Quintile	13.8	23.7	21.0	20.0
3rd Quintile	3.9	4.9	5.3	6.5
4th Quintile	2.2	2.2	2.2	2.5
Highest Quintile	1.9	1.9	1.9	2.0
Whites	12.9	16.7	15.3	14.7
Blacks	29.5	38.9	31.9	29.1
Hispanics	38.7	48.5	38.8	36.6
Widowed, Divorced, and Never Married				
Lowest Lifetime Income Quintile	94.1	92.5	85.2	68.0
2nd Quintile	18.7	18.6	12.4	9.3
3rd Quintile	1.8	1.6	0.8	1.5
4th Quintile	0.0	0.0	0.0	0.0
Highest Quintile	0.0	0.0	0.0	0.0
Whites	21.8	21.5	18.4	14.7
Black	53.3	51.6	45.6	36.8
Hispanics	46.8	53.0	47.8	36.3

from 52 percent in the 2nd quintile to 48 percent in the 4th quintile, and 43 percent in the 5th quintile, among the unmarried. The plan with flat contributions is substantially more redistributive than Social Security, increasing benefits by 37 percent in the 2nd quintile, 23 percent in the 4th quintile, and only 17 percent in the 5th quintile among married couples. A similar pattern occurs among the unmarried. The relative increases for blacks and Hispanics are quite a bit higher in the redistributive plans as well.

Table 7.11 focuses on the poverty impact of the three plans in the case in which the market performs poorly—a 3.5 percent return. It is clear that the more redistributive plans reduce the risk to the lowest income beneficiaries. For example, under the proportional-to-earnings approach, 19 percent of widowed, divorced, or never-married individuals in the 2nd quintile have benefits below the poverty line if the market performs poorly. In contrast, only 12 percent have benefits below poverty in the 1.5 percent plus $450 plan, and only 9 percent in the $900 per covered worker plan.

7.8 Conclusion

Investment-based Social Security reform provides a way to prevent the benefit cuts and payroll tax increases that would otherwise be necessary, adjustments that would likely have deleterious impacts on those who depend most heavily on Social Security. Nonetheless, critics of investment-based Social Security reforms have argued that by increasing the link between earnings and benefits, this approach threatens the progressivity of the system and could lead to additional poverty among the elderly. This paper shows that this need not be the case. We find that essentially all demographic and income groups can benefit from an investment-based system with a lower saving rate than the projected long-run PAYGO tax, and that the potential reductions in poverty are the largest for those most at risk of poverty. A mixed system that combines the investment-based accounts and PAYGO benefits can achieve such results, even if financial markets perform extremely poorly. Finally, we show how alternative contributions to PRAs can enable an investment-based system to equal or exceed the redistribution in the current U.S. Social Security system.

Appendix

Our data set is created by matching the 1990 and 1991 panels of the SIPP to SSA records on earnings from 1951 through 1993 (the Summary Earnings Record, or SER) and benefit records from 1995 (the Master Beneficiary Record, or MBR) for the same individuals.

From the public-use sample of the SIPP, we selected all individuals from the first wave of each SIPP panel who were aged sixty or above in 1990 (individuals who were sixty years or above at the start of the 1990 panel, sixty-one years or above at the start of the 1991 panel). We also used variables on marital history from the wave-two topical module of the SIPP. We included data on spouses of people in the age range, even if they themselves were not in the age range. Our ultimate unit of observation is the individual, so a married couple with two individuals in the appropriate age range would be counted as two observations. However, for programming purposes, married couples were stacked into one observation. We then matched these observations to the SER and disgarded observations that did not match to earnings.

Next we created our cohort—individuals who were born from 1925 through 1929. We chose 1929 as a cutoff because it ensures that we can observe earnings through age sixty-four for everyone in the sample (our earnings data extend through 1993). We wanted as narrow an age group as possible so that we would not have age groups that had already lost significant numbers of Social Security beneficiaries due to death. However, given our modest sample sizes, we decided to use five birth-years of data. We dropped individuals whose year of birth in the SER was more than five years from their year of birth in the SIPP.

For the never-married and married individuals, the SIPP-SER match produced the earnings data necessary for our simulation.[41] For previously married individuals, however, the former spouse is not in our data set, so we do not have the spouse's SER earnings record. For many of these individuals (those receiving spouse benefits, widow(er) benefits, or dually entitled worker benefits), we were able to obtain the former spouse's Primary Insurance Amount (PIA, and therefore their AIME) by further matching to the MBR. For the rest (those receiving retired worker benefits only), we imputed a spouse PIA using the correlation between respondent and spouse PIA for similar individuals from the New Beneficiary Survey—an older sample that obtained earnings and benefit records for former spouses of sample members. We dropped disabled individuals (and any couple with a disabled member) and unstacked married couples so that each individual in the couple counts as an observation if both spouses were members of the 1925 to 1929 birth cohort.

Once we had a former spouse's PIA for the previously married individuals, we calculated an AIME by inverting the Social Security benefit formula. We then calculated (separately for men and women) the average share of earnings earned in each year for people in our sample with earnings histories and generated an earnings record for the missing spouses by spreading their AIME according to the average share of earnings earned in each year, subject, of course, to the constraint that a former spouse of a widow or widower could not have earnings in years after his or her death.

The earnings data report earnings only up to the taxable maximum for the year. In the past, the taxable maximum was much lower relative to average earnings than it is today. In order to be able to simulate the current Social Security rules, we imputed a level of earnings above the taxable maximum for sample members with earnings at the taxable maximum. We did this by estimating a two-limit Tobit regressed on a constant (i.e., with no other independent variables) separately for men and women for each year between 1951 and 1990. The level of earnings is fit very well by a normal distribution until a percentile that is above the current taxable maximum. The regressions produced an estimate for mean earnings and a regression error. Using these parameter estimates, we randomly drew from a normal distribution with the appropriate mean and variance until each topcoded observation was replaced with a draw above the topcode.

Based on the sample member's earnings history and the earnings history

---

41. In some cases, we were required to impute earnings at the beginning or end of the career if the 1951–93 period did not include all years from age twenty-one to age sixty-four.

of the spouse, we calculated Social Security benefits. Our calculations incorporate nearly all of the retirement benefit provisions, including covered worker requirements, the minimum benefit, spouse benefits, survivor benefits, and reductions for claiming benefits before the normal retirement age. We do not simulate the delayed retirement credit (instead assuming that everyone in our sample claims benefits by age sixty-five), nor do we have adequate information with which to implement government pension offset provisions.

References

Board of Trustees. 1999. *The 1999 Annual report of the Social Security trustees.* Washington, D.C.: Social Security Administration.

Boskin, Michael J., Laurence J. Kotlikoff, Douglas J. Puffert, and John B. Shoven. 1987. Social Security: A financial appraisal across and within generations. *National Tax Journal* 40 (3): 19–34.

Chevalier, Judith, and Glenn Ellison. 1999. Career concerns of mutual fund managers. *Quarterly Journal of Economics* (May): 389–432.

Coronado, Julia, Don Fullerton, and Thomas Glass. 2000. The progressivity of Social Security. NBER Working Paper no. 7520. Cambridge, Mass.: National Bureau of Economic Research, February.

Diamond, Peter. 2000. Administrative costs and equilibrium changes with individual accounts. In *Administrative aspects of investment-based Social Security reform,* ed. John Shoven, 137–62. Chicago: University of Chicago Press.

Elmendorf, Douglas W., and Jeffrey B. Liebman. 2000. Social Security reform and national savings in an era of budget surpluses. *Brookings Papers on Economic Activity,* no. 2:1–71.

Feldstein, Martin. 1996. The missing piece in policy analysis: Social Security reform. *American Economic Review* 86 (2): 1–14.

———. 1997. Don't waste the budget surplus. *Wall Street Journal.* 4 November.

———. 2000. Comment on "Administrative costs and equilibrium charges in individual accounts." In *Administrative aspects of investment-based social security reform,* ed. John Shoven, 162–69. Chicago: University of Chicago Press.

———. Ed. 1998. *Privatizing Social Security.* Chicago: University of Chicago Press.

Feldstein, Martin, and Elena Ranguelova. 1998. Individual risk and intergenerational risk sharing in an investment-based social security system. NBER Working Paper no. 6839. Cambridge, Mass.: National Bureau of Economic Research, December.

Feldstein, Martin, Elena Ranguelova, and Andrew Samwick. 2001. The transition to investment-based social security when portfolio returns and capital profitability are uncertain. In *Risk aspects of investment-based social security reform,* ed. J. Campbell and Martin Feldstein, 41–81.

Feldstein, Martin, and Andrew Samwick. 1997. The economics of prefunding Social Security and Medicare benefits. *NBER Macroeconomics Annual 1997.* Cambridge, Mass.: MIT Press.

———. 1998a. Potential effects of two percent personal retirement accounts. *Tax Notes* 79 (5): 615–20.

———. 1998b. The transition path in privatizing Social Security. In *Privatizing Social Security,* ed. Feldstein, 215–60. Chicago: Chicago University Press.

———. 2000. Allocating payroll tax revenue to personal retirement accounts. *Tax Notes* 87 (12): 1645–52.

Feldstein, Martin, and Horst Siebert, eds. 2001. *Social security pension reform in Europe.* Chicago: University of Chicago Press (forthcoming).

Goldberg, Fred, and Michael Graetz. 2000. Reforming social security: A practical and workable system of personal retirement accounts. In *Administrative aspects of investment-based social security reform,* ed. John B. Shoven, 9–37. Chicago: University of Chicago Press.

Gustman, Alan, and Thomas Steinmeier. 2000. Social Security benefits of immigrants and U.S. born. In *Issues in the economics of immigration,* ed. George Borjas, 309–50. Chicago: University of Chicago Press.

Hurd, Michael D., and John B. Shoven. 1985. The distributional impact of Social Security. In *Pensions, labor, and individual choice,* ed. David A. Wise, 193–207. Chicago: University of Chicago Press.

Lee, Ronald, and Shripad Tuljapurkar. 1998. Uncertain demographic futures and Social Security finances. *American Economic Review* 88 (2): 237–41.

Poterba, James. 1998. The rate of return to corporate capital and factor shares. *Carnegie-Rochester Conference Series on Public Policy* 48 (June): 211–46.

Samuelson, Paul. 1958. An exact consumption-load model of interest with or without the social contrivance of money. *Journal of Political Economy* 66: 467–82.

Shoven, John B., ed. 2000. *Administrative aspects of investment-based social security reform.* Chicago: University of Chicago Press.

Social Security Administration. 1999a. *Annual statistical supplement to the Social Security bulletin.* Washington, D.C.: Social Security Administration.

———. 1999b. Information on the distributional effects of various Social Security solvency options by gender and income. Washington, D.C.: Social Security Administration. Available at [http://www.ssa.gov/policy/pubs/memDistImp.pdf].

Comment   John B. Shoven

This paper addresses a matter of first-order importance—the distributional consequences of privatization and partial privatization plans for Social Security. The authors use a rich data source—the Survey of Income and Program Participation (SIPP) data—and supplement it with Social Security earnings and benefit records. This allows them to observe a diverse group of individuals in terms of earnings histories, health events, marriage and divorce, and retirement behavior. The main finding of the paper is that all groups (women, men, whites, blacks, Hispanics, and those with different levels of education and lifetime incomes) and the vast majority of individuals would be better off in retirement with either full privatization or partial privatization. This is true if the investment portfolio modeled—60 percent stocks and 40 percent corporate bonds—has a geo-

John B. Shoven is the Charles R. Schwab Professor of Economics at Stanford University and a research associate of the National Bureau of Economic Research.

metric average real rate of return of 5.5 percent net of expenses. The authors convincingly argue that this is a conservative assumption for the mean future outcome based on the actually realized returns between the years 1946 and 1995. To give the readers a sense of the sensitivity of their results to risk in financial markets, the authors repeat their analysis using a real return of 3.5 percent net of expenses. They argue that Monte Carlo simulations based on the distribution of annual returns observed between 1946 and 1995 indicate that a 3.5 percent return over a career would represent about a 10th percentile outcome.

I do have a few qualms about the analysis, most of them concerning the issue of the riskiness of private financial market returns. The paper evaluates the new systems after the transition from the existing Social Security program. Effectively, the authors are evaluating how people would fare under the new systems between 2075 and 2115 or so. No one can be sure that financial market returns earned between 1946 and 1995 will be representative of what might happen late in the twenty-first century (and beyond). Retirement behavior, spells of unemployment, and patterns of marriage and divorce might also be quite different for people born more than 100 years after their particular SIPP data individuals. My intuition is that we should increase the standard deviation of the return distribution to reflect the fact that the period under consideration is so far in future.

Moreover, the low-return simulation (3.5 percent net of expenses) roughly equals the current real return on safe inflation-indexed U.S. government bonds. However, a poor return from a risky strategy must be lower than the return on a safe strategy in order for the observed financial market returns to make sense. Otherwise, the risky portfolio absolutely dominates the safe one, and prices (and returns) should adjust. This issue is related to the equity premium puzzle literature and cannot be sorted out in this discussion or this paper. It is my sense, however, that a 3.5 percent real rate of return is too high to use for an evaluation of the downside risk of accumulating a 60–40 portfolio late in this century. Even if it does represent a 10th percentile outcome of the future return distribution (of which I am skeptical), policy makers might want to carefully consider worse outcomes than that—for instance, what is the 1st percentile outcome, and how much importance should be placed on the truly unlikely bad outcomes?

The partial privatization plan examined involves holding the existing payroll tax fixed, reducing defined benefit promises to live within that budget constraint, and supplementing the defined benefit promises with the annuitized proceeds of 3 percent individual accounts. The new mandatory 3 percent accounts are only half as burdensome as the 6 percent increase in the payroll tax that would be necessary to maintain the current system's benefit structure with pay-as-you-go financing. Feldstein and Liebman model the partial privatization plan as cutting current defined benefit

promises across the board by 39 percent. They then show that the 3 percent accounts with a 5.5 percent real return more than make up the defined
benefit promise reductions for almost everyone.

Although the vast majority of individuals receive higher benefits with
partial privatization if the real return is 5.5 percent, it is somewhat disturbing that a disproportionate number of those people who are worse off
are poor. For most of these cases, the authors appeal to Supplemental
Security Income (SSI) to argue that the benefits of these poor individuals
would be supplemented in such a way that they are no worse off. However,
a shortcoming of this argument is that these SSI payments must come
from somewhere. The authors do not count the increase in SSI payments
as a cost of switching to the new system. In the event that the accounts
earn only 3.5 percent, only 43 percent of the population are in a better
position than they would be under current law benefits. For blacks and
Hispanics, fewer than 10 percent of the households would do better than
under current law. Similarly, less than 10 percent of those in the two lowest
income quintiles enjoy benefits as high as those in the current law. The
fraction of elderly households in poverty is slightly greater with the mixed
plan and the low return outcome than with current benefits. These results,
taken together with my concern that the 3.5 percent scenario is too optimistic for the poor outcome simulation, cause me to question the attrac-
tiveness of the mixed plan modeled in this paper.

Many proposed partial privatization plans, such as the Committee for
Economic Development (CED) plan and the Individual Accounts plan of
the Social Security Advisory Board, reduce the benefits of those with low
lifetime income by a lower percentage than those with higher lifetime incomes. This is accomplished by revising the PrimaryInsurance Amount
(PIA) formula. Currently, the formula has three brackets for converting
Average Indexed Monthly Earnings (AIME) into PIA—a 90 percent
bracket, a 32 percent bracket, and a 15 percent bracket. The CED plan ad-
vocates going to a 90/22.4/10.5 percent set of brackets. That is, they would
not reduce the formula at all for those with very low AIMEs. The Individual Accounts plan does much the same. The plan modeled in this Feldstein-
Liebman paper involves across-the-board 39 percent reductions in the
defined benefits. This reduction plan could be revised in such a way as to
protect the lifetime poor more. The extreme plan in this regard is the Personal Security Accounts plan of the Social Security Advisory Board,
which involves a flat defined benefit amount for all full career participants.

Another drawback of this analysis is that the authors do not consider
behavioral responses by the individuals in the program. Their results suggest that middle- and high-income individuals would gain a great deal
from switching to a partially privatized system. However, many of these
individuals already own stocks and bonds. If they are forced to save in the
new Social Security savings accounts, they may simply adjust their own

saving and asset allocation decisions. The forced saving component of the new program may only affect those who currently are not saving much.

One could also question whether assigning everyone a 60 percent stocks and 40 percent bonds portfolio is desirable. I would favor giving people more choice than this. Risk-averse households should choose a higher percentage of bonds (or perhaps inflation-indexed bonds) whereas less risk-averse people should choose more stocks. Of course, the more choice the system offers, the greater the need for financial education.

Although I have been emphasizing the aspects of the paper that bother me, I should repeat that I think that this is an important paper concerning a crucial issue. It has already been added to the reading list of my Ph.D. course in public finance. My proposal for further work in this area would be to apply this methodology to the actual reform proposals in existence and to do more research on the uncertainty of financial returns in the distant future.

Discussion Summary

Laurence J. Kotlikoff liked many of the provisions of the investment-based system analyzed by the authors but wished the authors had explicitly specified a transition path. Kotlikoff believed that it is important to discuss the transition because this is essentially a zero sum game from a present value perspective. Without changing the degree of excess burden, it is not possible to improve one person's situation without making somebody else worse off. In this paper, nobody seems to be losing. He added that if the elderly are not taxed to fund the transition, then the long run is truly a long way away. The authors said that it was not feasible to consider all aspects of Social Security reform in one paper and that in other papers Feldstein and Samwick had spelled out some alternative transition paths. The authors agreed that there is a tradeoff between the well-being of different generations and that it is not possible to make everyone better off. However, with a discount rate that reflects the *after-tax* rate of return, the present value of the transition is positive. The future generations who are made better off in a plan like this will be richer than current generations. Thus, there is a trade-off, and that is why the discount rate and the implicit social welfare function become important.

Martin Feldstein emphasized that the focus of the paper is on the long-run distributional impacts. What happens to women who become widowed or divorced at an early age? What happens to the number of elderly living poverty? He explained that the investment-based plan really does do well by these disadvantaged groups and better in terms of poverty reduction. This paper uses the earnings histories of real people who get divorced and have long spells of unemployment and consequently avoids the standard criticisms faced by models with representative agents or only a few different hypothetical individuals. Therefore, these results are particularly reassuring.

Stephen Zeldes thought it was important to clarify the nature of the paper. While the paper explains that the transition is not evaluated, this explanation gets lost in the conclusions. Zeldes also felt that the combination of prefunding and individual retirements accounts is not necessary. Although he understands the view that it is not politically feasible to maintain the current system with prefunding, this argument should be spelled out more clearly. It might be fruitful to consider an alternative comparison between individual retirement accounts and a prefunded defined benefit system. The authors agreed that it might be possible to prefund within the current system, although prefunding of the magnitude envisioned in this paper implies that the government would own more than 30 percent and possibly more than 50 percent of the stock market. The authors questioned whether this was wise or politically feasible.

Peter Orszag outlined another political concern. Is it realistic to assume that individual accounts can be restricted to index funds? Administrative costs of only 40 basis points might be reasonable for index funds but are probably too low for other funds. The authors mentioned that the College Retirement Equity Fund offers low-cost variable annuities with a fee of 37 basis points, which covers managing the portfolio as well as managing the annuity. *James M. Poterba* indicated that for index funds 40 basis points is quite generous, because the Vanguard Index 500 is 19 basis points.

Peter Orszag also pointed out that if the individual account plan moves some of the very poor into Supplemental Security Income (SSI), then it is important to count these additional costs, especially because SSI eligibility triggers Medicaid eligibility. *Jeffrey B. Liebman* responded that most of the time the mixed plan resulted in savings for SSI and that only under very bad market outcomes would SSI spending increase.

Distributional Effects in a General Equilibrium Analysis of Social Security

Laurence J. Kotlikoff, Kent Smetters, and Jan Walliser

8.1 Introduction

This paper reviews and extends our recent general equilibrium analyses of the distributional effects of Social Security. The model is based on the Auerbach and Kotlikoff (1987) model, which computes the perfect foresight transition path of a life-cycle economy consisting of multiple overlapping generations. However, unlike the original Auerbach-Kotlikoff model, the new version of the model includes intragenerational heterogeneity and a much more detailed specification of U.S. fiscal institutions.[1] The latest version of the model, which is still in a very preliminary state, incorporates a more realistic pattern of births and length of life.

We reach six conclusions. First, Social Security's privatization can substantially raise long-run living standards. However, achieving these gains will take a considerable amount of time and will entail some welfare losses to transition generations. Second, Social Security's privatization helps the long-run poor even absent any explicit redistribution mechanism. This reflects both the opportunity cost of the current pay-as-you-go system as well as the impact of privatization on capital deepening. Third, privatizations that feature voluntary rather than compulsory exit from the old system

Laurence J. Kotlikoff is professor of economics at Boston University and a research associate of the National Bureau of Economic Research. Kent Smetters is assistant professor of insurance and risk management at the Wharton School, University of Pennsylvania, and a faculty research fellow of the National Bureau of Economic Research. Jan Walliser is in the Fiscal Affairs Department of the International Monetary Fund.

The authors thank the National Bureau of Economic Research, the Smith Richardson Foundation, the National Institute of Aging, and Boston University for research support.

1. Prior applications of the AKSW Model include Kotlikoff (1996), Kotlikoff, Smetters, and Walliser (1997, 1998a, b, and 1999a, b), and Altig et al. (1997).

have particularly low transition costs and particularly favorable macroeconomic and distributional consequences despite the adverse selection they entail. Fourth, privatizations, like those advocated by the World Bank (1994), that provide a flat (minimum) benefit, can actually make the long-run poor worse off relative to privatizations without a flat benefit because they pay-as-you-go finance the flat benefit with a significant payroll tax. Fifth, combining privatization with a progressive match to contributions benefits the lifetime poor relative to privatization without a match. Sixth, when America's aging is considered, the long-run gains to Social Security's privatization are greater because the status-quo alternative entails a substantial long-run increase in the rate of payroll taxation.

The paper proceeds in section 8.2 with a review of some of the recent simulation literature on Social Security. Section 8.3 describes our base model, which does not include our newest enhancements to the demographic structure. Section 8.4 uses the model to explore privatization. The results presented here draw on Kotlikoff, Smetters, and Walliser (1997, 1998a, b, and 1999a, b). Section 8.5 presents some very preliminary results using the demographic variant of the model. Section 8.6 concludes.

8.2   Literature Review

Feldstein's (1974) seminal article on Social Security's impact on national saving has, over the years, stimulated a plethora of related studies. The majority of these have been theoretical and empirical, but a growing number involve simulating Social Security's dynamic general equilibrium effects within macroeconomic models that have microeconomic foundations. Early contributions here include Kotlikoff (1979), Auerbach and Kotlikoff (1983), and Seidman (1986). These papers confirmed Feldstein's theoretical prediction and empirical finding that unfunded Social Security systems significantly reduce nations' long-run capital intensivities and living standards. Kotlikoff and Auerbach-Kotlikoff examined how introducing "pay-as-you-go" (PAYGO) Social Security would worsen an economy's economic position, notwithstanding induced changes in retirement behavior. Seidman's in contrast, appears to be the first to study the economic gains from eliminating unfunded Social Security.

More recent contributions include Auerbach and Kotlikoff (1987), Auerbach et al. (1989), Hubbard and Judd (1987), Hansson and Stuart (1989), Arrau and Schmidt-Hebbel (1993), Kotlikoff (1996), Hubbard, Skinner, and Zeldes (1994a, b, and 1995), Kotlikoff, Smetters, and Walliser (1997, 1998a, b, and 1999a, b), Huang, İmrohoroğlu, and Sargent (1997), and İmrohoroğlu, İmrohoroğlu, and Joines (1995, 1999), Knudsen et al. (1999), Fougere and Merette (1998, 1999), Schneider (1997), Raffelhuschen (1993), Cooley and Soares (1999a, b), Huggett and Ventura (1999), De Nardi, İmrohoroğlu, and Sargent (1999), Galasso (1999), and others. These studies have included a range of additional important factors, including demographics, land, earnings uncertainty, liquidity constraints, and majority voting on the system's continued existence. They have also examined the different ways a transition to a privatized Social Security system could be financed.

8.3 Description of Our Model

This section describes our base model as well as its calibration and solution methods. It draws heavily on similar descriptions in Altig et al. (2001), Kotlikoff, Smetters, and Walliser (1999a, b), and the review presented in Kotlikoff (2000). Section 8.5 describes how the model presented in this section is currently being modified to more accurately capture demographics. We report some very preliminary simulation results in that section.

8.3.1 Demographic Structure

The model contains a fixed number of overlapping cohorts. Each period in the model corresponds to a year. Adults live for fifty-five years (from age twenty-one through seventy-five). Like that of Fullerton and Rogers (1993), our model incorporates intragenerational heterogeneity in the form of twelve lifetime-earnings groups. Each group has its own initial skill level and its own longitudinal age-skill profile. The twelve groups also have distinct bequest preferences. Our model has both advantages and disadvantages relative to Fullerton and Rogers's (1993) model. Some of the advantages are the inclusion of a Social Security system, a detailed description of non–Social Security taxes, the existence of government debt and endogenous bequests, and the ability to compute the economy's perfect-foresight transition path. The principal disadvantage is the lack of a highly detailed production sector that includes multiple sectors and intermediate production. However, the omission of this production sector detail may matter little for our purposes, because the Social Security policies we examine do not differentially affect particular industries or types of capital goods.

8.3.2 Preferences and Budget Constraints[2]

Each j-type agent who begins her economic life at date t chooses perfect-foresight consumption paths (c), leisure paths (l), and intergenerational transfers (b) to maximize a time-separable utility function of the form.

$$(1) \quad U_t^j = \frac{1}{1 - \frac{1}{\gamma}} \left\{ \sum_{s=21}^{75} \beta^{s-21} \left(c_{s,t+s-21}^{j\,1-1/\rho} + \alpha l_{s,t+s-21}^{j\,1-1/\rho} \right)^{\left[\left(1-\frac{1}{\gamma}\right) / \left(1-\frac{1}{\rho}\right) \right]} + \beta^{54} \mu^j b_{75,t+54}^{j\,1-1/\gamma} \right\}.$$

In equation (1), α is the utility weight on leisure, γ is the intertemporal elasticity of substitution in the leisure-consumption composite, and ρ is

---

2. This description of the model draws heavily on Kotlikoff, Smetters, and Walliser (1999).

the intratemporal elasticity of substitution between consumption and leisure. The parameter μ^j is a j-type specific utility weight placed on bequests left to each child when the agent dies. The term $\beta = 1/(1 + \delta)$, where δ is the rate of time preference, is assumed to be the same for all agents.

Letting $a_{s,t}^j$ be capital holdings for type j agents, of age s, at time t, maximization of equation (1) is subject to a sequence of budget constraints given by

$$(2) \qquad a_{s+1,t+1}^j = (1 + r_t)(a_{s,t}^j + g_{s,t}^j) + w_{s,t}^j(E_{s,t}^j - l_{s,t}^j) - c_{s,t}^j$$

$$- \sum_{k \in \tilde{T}} T^k(B_{s,t}^{j,k}) - Nb_{s,t}^j$$

$$l_{s,t}^j \leq E_{s,t}^j$$

where r_t is the pretax return to savings, $g_{s,t}^j$ are gifts received from parents, $E_{s,t}^j$ is the time endowment, $b_{s,t}^j$ denotes bequests made to each of the $N = (1 + n)^{20}$ children, and the functions $T^k(\cdot)$ with tax base arguments $B_{s,t}^{j,k}$ determine net tax payments from income sources $k \in \tilde{T} = \{C, K, W, Y, P\}$. $T^C(\cdot)$, $T^K(\cdot)$, $T^W(\cdot)$, $T^Y(\cdot)$, and $T^P(\cdot)$ are consumption taxes, capital income taxes, wage taxes, income taxes, and Social Security payroll taxes, respectively. Social Security benefits are represented in equation (2) as negative taxes with the base switching at the point of retirement from the contemporaneous payroll base to average indexed yearly earnings in the preretirement years. All taxes are collected at the household level, and the tax system includes both a personal income tax and a business profits tax. The bases for the wage and payroll taxes are smaller than total labor income due to the base reductions discussed below.

An individual's earning ability is an exogenous function of her age, her type, and the level of labor-augmenting technical progress, which grows at a constant rate λ. We concentrate all skill differences by age and type in an efficiency parameter ε_s^j. Thus, the wage rate for an agent of type j and age s is $w_{s,t}^j = \varepsilon_s^j w_t$, where w_t is the growth-adjusted real wage at time t. ε_s^j increases with age to reflect not only the accumulation of human capital, but also technical progress. To permit balanced growth for our specifications of preferences given the restriction on leisure shown in equation (2), we assume that technical progress also causes the time endowment of each successive generation to grow at rate λ.[3] More precisely, if $E_{s,t}^j$ is the endowment of type j at age s and time t, then $E_{s,t}^j = (1 + \lambda)E_{s,t-1}^j$, for all s, t, and j. Notice that the endowment $E_{s,t}^j$ depends only on an agent's year of birth. Because E grows at rate λ from one cohort to the next, there will be no underlying trend in w_t. The growth-adjusted earnings ability profiles take the form

---

3. See Auerbach et al. (1989) for a more complete discussion of this strategy for dealing with balanced growth.

$$(3) \qquad\qquad \varepsilon_s^j = e^{a_0^j + a_1^j s^2 + a_3^j s^3}.$$

Values of the a coefficients for j-type groups 1 through 12—in ascending order of lifetime income—are based on regressions fitted to the University of Michigan's Panel Study of Income Dynamics and are taken from Altig et al. (2001). Groups 1 and 12 comprise the bottom and top 2 percent of lifetime wage income earners, and groups 2 and 11 the remaining 8 percent of the top and bottom deciles. All other groups constitute 10 percent of the population. For example, group 3 is the second decile of lifetime-wage income, group four the third decile, and so on up to group 10. The estimated longitudinal age-earnings-ability profiles are scaled to include the effects of technical progress. Given our benchmark parameterization, peak hourly wages valued in 1996 dollars are $4.00, $14.70, and $79.50 for individuals in classes 1, 6, and 12, respectively. More generally, steady-state annual labor incomes derived from the model's assumptions and the endogenous labor supply choices range from $9,000 to $130,000. As discussed below, these calculations do not yet include labor compensation in the form of fringe benefits.

Bequests are received by children, with interest, at the beginning of the period after they are made by their parents. We restrict all parental transfers to bequests, so that $b_{s,t}^j = 0$, for $s \neq 75$, and $g_{s,t}^j = 0$, for $s \neq 56$. In the steady state, therefore, $g^j = b^j$, for all j (where we have dropped the age subscripts for convenience). The parameters μ^j are derived endogenously for the initial steady state such that the ratio of the bequest to economy-wide mean income corresponds to the ratio originally estimated by Menchik and David (1982) and updated by Fullerton and Rogers (1993). Bequests range from $4,800 to $450,000 for the lowest and highest lifetime earnings classes, respectively.

The benchmark values for δ, γ, ρ, and n are those in Auerbach and Kotlikoff (1987). The parameter α is chosen so that agents devote, on average, about 40 percent of their available time endowment (of sixteen hours per day) to labor during their prime working years (real-life ages of roughly twenty-one to fifty-five).

8.3.3   The Non–Social Security Government Budget Constraint

At time t, the government collects tax revenues and issues debt (D_{t+1}), which it uses to finance government purchases of goods and services (G_t) and interest payments on the existing stock of debt (D_t). Letting φ^j be the fraction of j-type agents in each generation, the non–Social Security part of the government's budget constraint evolves according to

$$(4) \quad D_{t+1} + (1 + n)^t \sum_{j=1}^{12} \varphi^j \sum_{s=21}^{75} (1 + n)^{-(s-21)} \sum_{k \in \{\overline{T}-P\}} T^k(B_{s,t}^{j,k}) = G_t + (1 + r_t)D_t.$$

The exclusion of Social Security taxes in equation (4) reflects the fact that Social Security currently uses self-financing earmarked taxes.

Government expenditures are assumed to be unproductive and generate no utility to households.[4] The values of G_t and D_t are held fixed per effective worker throughout the transition path. Any reduction in government outlays resulting from a change in the government's real interest payments is passed on to households in the form of a lower tax rate. The level of government debt, D_t, was chosen such that the associated real interest payments equal about 3.5 percent of national income in the initial steady state. The statutory tax schedules (described below) generate a level of revenue above debt service such that the benchmark steady-state ratio of government purchases, G_t, to national income equals 0.239. These values correspond very closely to the corresponding 1996 values for the combined local, state, and federal government in the United States.

8.3.4   Non–Social Security Taxes

The benchmark tax system in our initial steady state is designed to approximate the salient aspects of the 1996 U.S. (federal, state, and local) tax and transfer system. It features a hybrid tax system (incorporating wage-income, capital-income, and consumption tax elements) and payroll taxation for the Social Security and Medicare programs. To adjust for tax evasion, we reduce income taxes by 2.6 percentage points. This adjustment is consistent with the degree of tax evasion reported in Slemrod and Bakija (1996). In the various alternative tax structure experiments, we assume that evasion reduces the postreform tax base (income net of deductions and exemptions) by the same percentage as before the reform. Thus, the level of tax evasion falls when the tax base shrinks. We approximate the hybrid current U.S. tax system by specifying a progressive wage-income tax, a flat capital-income tax, a flat state income tax, and a flat consumption tax.

Wage Income Taxation

The wage-income tax structure has four elements: (a) a progressive marginal rate structure derived from a quadratic approximation to the 1996 federal statutory tax rates for individuals; (b) a standard deduction of $4,000 and exemptions of $5,660 (which assumes 1.2 children per agent, consistent with the model's population growth assumption); (c) itemized deductions—applied only when they exceed the amount of the standard deduction—that are a positive linear function of income estimated from data reported in the *Statistics of Income;*[5] and (d) earnings-ability profiles

---

4. Since G remains fixed in all of our experiments, incorporating G into the utility function is unimportant.

5. The data used in this estimation were taken from all taxable returns in tax year 1993. The function was obtained by regressing deductions exclusive of mortgage interest expense on the midpoints of reported income ranges. (The deduction of interest expense on home mortgages was included in our calculation of the capital-income tax rate, as we will subsequently describe.) The regression yielded a coefficient of 0.0755 with an R^2 equal to 0.99.

that are scaled to incorporate pension and nonpension components of labor compensation.[6]

The model's initial economy-wide average marginal tax rate on wage income is about 21 percent, roughly the figure obtained from NBER's TAXSIM model as reported in Auerbach (1996). The average wage-income tax rate equals 12.1 percent. For all individuals in the highest lifetime income class (group 12), the average effective marginal tax rate on labor income is 28.6 percent. The highest realized effective marginal tax rate is 34 percent. For lifetime income class six—whose members have peak labor earnings of about $35,000—the average tax rate and average marginal tax rate are 10.6 and 20.0 percent, respectively. For the poorest class (group one), the corresponding rates are zero and 5.5 percent.[7]

Capital Income Taxation

Following Auerbach (1996), we assume that income from residential and nonresidential capital are taxed at flat rates of 6 percent and 26 percent, respectively. Given the roughly equal amounts of these two forms of capital, the effective federal marginal tax rate on total capital income is 16 percent. However, this rate applies only to new capital. Existing capital faces a higher tax rate, which, given depreciation schedules, is estimated to be 20 percent. We model this gap by assuming that all capital income faces a 20 percent tax, but that 20 percent of new capital may be expensed, thereby generating a 16 percent effective rate on new capital.

State Income Taxation

In addition to the federal taxation, both capital and wage income are subject to a proportional state income tax of 3.7 percent. This value corresponds to the amount of revenue generated by state income taxes in 1996 divided by national income.

Consumption Taxation

Consumption taxes in the initial steady state reflect two elements of the existing tax structure. First we impose an 8.8 percent tax on consumption expenditures consistent with values reported in the National Income and Product Accounts on indirect business and excise revenues. However, because contributions to both defined benefit and defined contribution pension plans receive consumption tax treatment, we levy an additional 2.5

6. Benefits as a function of adjusted gross income were kindly provided by Jane Gravelle of the Congressional Research Service and Judy Xanthopoulos of the Joint Committee on Taxation, respectively. On the basis of this information, we regressed total benefits on AGI. The regression yielded a coefficient of 0.11295 with an R^2 equal to 0.99. In defining the wage-tax base, we therefore exempt roughly 11 percent of labor compensation from the base calculations.

7. The average marginal rate for people with the lowest income exceeds zero due to positive shadow tax rates in peak earnings years.

percent tax on household consumption goods expenditures to account for the indirect taxation of labor compensation in the form of pension benefits (Auerbach 1996). This 2.5 percent tax replaces the wage tax that otherwise would apply to labor compensation in the form of fringe benefits.

8.3.5 Social Security, Medicare, and Disability

The model has a social insurance system that incorporates Social Security Old Age and Survivors Insurance (OASI), Social Security Disability Insurance (DI), and public health insurance taking the form of Medicare (HI). OASI benefits are calculated according to the progressive statutory bend-point formula. U.S. Social Security benefits are based on a measure of average indexed monthly earnings (AIME) over a thirty-five-year work history. The AIME is converted into a primary insurance amount (PIA) in accordance with a progressive formula. In particular, the 1996 benefit formula has two bend points. The PIA is calculated as 90 percent of the first $437 of AIME, 32 percent of the next $2,198 of AIME, and 15 percent of AIME above $2,198. We approximate the benefit formula with a sixth-order polynomial, which is applied to the dollar-scaled AIME generated by the model. This polynomial approximation is very accurate with $R^2 = 0.99$. We achieve replacement values between 25 and 75 percent for the lifetime richest and lifetime poorest, respectively. Since approximately 50 percent of Social Security benefits are paid to survivors and spouses, we multiply benefits by a factor of two.

In ignoring spousal benefits and the fact that the rich live longer than the poor, we may be overstating the program's degree of progressivity. The papers by Liebman and by Coronado, Fullerton, and Glass (chapters 1 and 5 in this volume) investigate how these factors influence progressivity.

An earmarked tax applied to wage income up to a limit of $62,700—the earnings ceiling in 1996—is used to pay for OASI benefits. Define $\omega_{s,t}^j \equiv w_{s,t}^j(E_{s,t}^j - l_{s,t}^j)$ as the wage income earned by the j-type agent who is age s in year t. Also define $\overline{\omega}_{65,t}^j$ as the average indexed annual earnings for the j-type agent aged sixty-five at time t. Labor income earned before turning age sixty-five is adjusted upward by the growth rate of the economy in calculating $\overline{\omega}_{65,t}^j$. Payroll taxes at time t—with retirement benefits modeled as negative taxes—equal

$$
(5) \qquad T^P(B_{s,t}^{j,k}) = \begin{cases} \tau \cdot \omega_{s,t}^j & ; \ s \leq 64, \ \omega_{s,t}^j \leq \$62,700 \\ \tau \cdot \$62,000 & ; \ s \leq 64, \ \omega_{s,t}^j > \$62,700 \\ -2 \cdot R(\overline{\omega}_{s,t}^j) \cdot \overline{\omega}_{s,t}^j & ; \ s > 64 \end{cases}
$$

where $R(\cdot)$ is the statutory replacement rate function.

Budget balance for a self-financing PAYGO Social Security system with earmarked taxes at time t requires:

Macro Effects

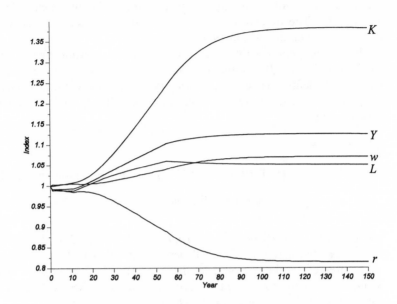

Remaining Lifetime Utility

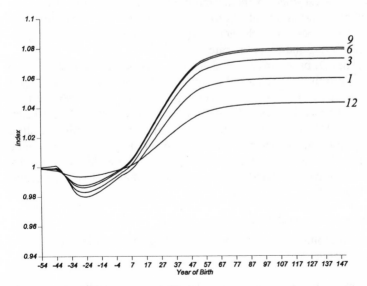

Fig. 8.1   Payroll tax finance of transition

(6) $$\sum_{j=1}^{12} \phi^j \sum_{s=21}^{75} (1 + n)^{-(s-21)} T^P(B_{s,t}^{j,P}) = 0$$

The value of τ is solved for endogenously as a function of benefit rules via equation (6). The value of τ is 9.9 percent in the initial steady state, which is close to its actual value in 1996.[8]

The net marginal tax rate is a component of the consumer's first-order conditions. Let $PVT(\omega_{s,t}^j)$ and $PVB(\omega_{s,t}^j)$ be the present value of payroll taxes and benefits, respectively, for the j-type agent age s at time t. The net marginal tax rate for those below the earnings ceiling in each case considered herein is

(7) $\theta(\omega_{s,t}^j) =$

$$\left\{ \begin{array}{l} \tau \cdot [1 - PVB'(\omega_{s,t}^j) / PVT'(\omega_{s,t}^j)]\,; \;\; \text{full perception linkage} \\ \tau\,; \;\; \text{no perception linkage} \end{array} \right\}$$

where $PVB'(\cdot) = \partial\, PVB(\cdot)/\partial\omega$ and $PVT'(\cdot) = \partial\, PVT(\cdot)/\partial w\omega$. The simulations presented herein assume full perception—that is, that agents correctly foresee how the payroll taxes they pay relate to their future benefits. Simulations for the no-perception case can be found in Kotlikoff, Smetters, and Walliser (1999a). Under full perception, the net marginal tax rates are typically relatively higher for both richer and younger agents. The higher rates for richer agents reflect the progressive manner in which Social Security benefits are calculated. The higher rates for younger agents reflect the compound interest effect of being required to save in a Social Security system whose internal rate of return is less than after-tax rate of return to capital (reported below). Rich agents whose labor income exceeds the payroll tax face a zero marginal tax rate.

The HI and DI programs are modeled very simply. The HI and DI levels of lump-sum transfers are picked to generate payroll tax rates of 2.9 percent and 1.9 percent, respectively, corresponding to their 1996 statutory rates. Like the OASI taxes, DI contributions apply only to wages below $62,700. The HI tax, in contrast, is not subject to an earnings ceiling. Lump-sum HI and DI benefits are provided on an equal basis to agents above and below age sixty-five, respectively. In the simulations using the new model, we have updated the payroll tax rates and payroll tax ceiling to their 1999 values.

8.3.6   Aggregation and Technology

Aggregate capital (K) and labor (L) are obtained from individual asset and labor supplies as

---

8. The employer-employee combined payroll tax equaled 10.52 percentage points. About 1 percentage point represents a net increase to the Social Security trust fund.

(8) $K_t = (1 + n)^t \sum_{j=1}^{12} \phi^j \sum_{s=21}^{75} (1 + n)^{-(s-21)} a_{s,t}^j - D_t$,

(where, recall, D_t is government debt at time t) and

(9) $L_t = (1 + n)^t (1 + \lambda)^{-t} \sum_{j=1}^{12} \phi^j \sum_{s=21}^{75} (1 + n)^{-(s-21)} \varepsilon_s^j (E_{s,t}^j - l_{s,t}^j)$.

Output (net of depreciation) is produced by identical competitive firms using a neoclassical, constant-returns-to-scale production technology. The aggregate production technology is the standard Cobb-Douglas form

(10) $Y_t = A K_t^\theta L_t^{1-\theta}$,

where Y_t is aggregate output (national income) and θ is capital's share in production. Denote the capital-labor ratio as κ. The time-t competitive posttax capital rate of return equals

(11) $r_t = \dfrac{\theta A \kappa_t^{\theta-1}(1 - \tau_t^K) + q_{t+1} - q_t}{q_t}$.

where $q_t = (1 - z_t \tau_t^K)$ is Tobin's q at time t and z is the level of capital investment expensing.

Given our parameter choices, the nondemographic version of the AKSW Model generates a pretax interest rate of 9.3 percent, a net national saving rate of 5.3 percent, and a capital/national-income ratio of 2.6. Consumption accounts for 73.4 percent of national income, net investment for 5.2 percent, and government purchases of goods and services for 21.4 percent. These figures are close to their respective 1996 NIPA values. The posttax interest rate equals 0.08 and is calculated following Auerbach (1996).

8.3.7 Solving the Model

The model uses a Gauss-Seidel algorithm to solve for the perfect foresight general equilibrium transition path of the economy. The calculation starts with a guess for certain key variables and then iterates on those variables until a convergence criterion is met. The solution involves several steps and inner loops that solve for household-level variables before moving to an outer loop that solves for the time paths of aggregate variables and factor prices.

Our optimization problem includes the constraint that leisure not exceed the endowment of time (equation [2]). For those households who would violate the constraint, the model calculates shadow wage rates at which they exactly consume their full-time endowment. The household's budget constraint is kinked due to the tax deductions applied against wage income. A household with wage income below the deduction level faces marginal and average tax rates equal to zero. A household with wage income above the deduction level faces positive marginal and average tax rates. Due to the discontinuity of the marginal tax rates, it may be optimal for some households to locate exactly at the kink. Our algorithm deals with this problem as follows. We identify households that choose to locate at the kink by evaluating their leisure choice and corresponding wage income above and below the kink. We then calculate a shadow marginal tax rate from the first-order conditions that puts those households exactly at the kink. This procedure generates optimal forward-looking leisure and consumption choices for all periods of life.

The payroll tax ceiling introduces additional complexity by creating a nonconvexity in the budget constraint. For those above the payroll tax ceiling, the marginal tax rate on labor falls to zero. We evaluate the utility on both sides of the nonconvex section and put households on the side that generates highest utility.

The sequence of calculations follows: An initial guess is made for the time paths of aggregate factor supplies as well as for the shadow wage rates; shadow tax rates; endogenous tax rates; the separate OASI, DI, and HI payroll tax rates; and the Social Security and Medicare wealth levels. The corresponding factor prices are calculated along with the forward-looking consumption, asset, and leisure choices for all income classes in each current and future cohort. Shadow wages and shadow taxes are calculated to ensure that the time endowment and the tax constraints discussed above are satisfied. Households' labor supplies and assets are then aggregated by both age and lifetime income class at each period in time. This aggregation generates a new guess for the time paths of the capital stock and labor supply. The tax rate, which is endogenous for the particular simulation, is updated to meet the relevant revenue requirement. OASI, HI, and DI payroll tax rates are also updated to preserve the PAYGO financing of these benefits.[9] The new supplies of capital and labor generated by the household sector of our model are weighted on an annual basis with the initial guess of these supplies to form a new guess of the time path of these variables. The algorithm then iterates until the capital stock and labor supply time paths converge.

8.4 Simulation Results

This section describes the results of six simulations. Additional simulations, which are presented in the next section, include some preliminary results of our model with enhanced demographics. The label "Year of Birth" in the tables and figures refers to the year of an agent's birth relative to the year the reform begins. Thus, for example, the index "−10" refers to a person born ten years before the reform. The index "1" refers to a person born the year the reform begins.

---

9. Note that the Social Security replacement rate and absolute level of Medicare benefits are exogenous.

8.4.1   The Choice of the Tax Used to Privatize Social Security

Simulations 1 through 3 study how different methods of financing the transition to a privatized Social Security system affect the macroeconomy, different cohorts, and different lifetime income classes within each cohort. In these simulations, participation in the new system is mandatory, and privatization entails (a) having workers contribute to private accounts, (b) paying retirees and workers in retirement those Social Security benefits that they had accrued as of the time of the reform, and (c) financing these accrued Social Security benefits during the transition with either a payroll tax, an income tax, or a consumption tax.

Since our model does not include liquidity constraints, privatizing Social Security contributions simply requires setting the model's Social Security payroll tax rate to zero. Since agents are able to borrow against any government-stipulated saving, there is no mechanical need to add a formal private pension system to the model to which workers are forced to contribute. Doing so would not change any agents' labor supply or consumption behavior. This said, it is worth noting that in the particular economies simulated here, only the poorest 10 percent of agents actually seek to borrow against their future Social Security benefits. Hence, prohibiting borrowing in our model would not materially alter our findings.

To provide existing retirees at the time of the reform their full accrued benefits, we wait ten years until after the reform is announced to start phasing out Social Security benefits. Since benefits in the economy's initial steady state are provided for the ten years between agents' ages forty-six and fifty-five, the ten-year delay in cutting benefits permits the ten initial generations of retirees to receive the same benefits they would have enjoyed absent the reform. Starting in the eleventh year of the reform, benefits are phased out by 2.2 percent (of the baseline benefits) per year for forty-five years. This phase-out pattern is designed to approximate the provision to initial workers of the full value in retirement of those benefits they had accrued as of the time of the reform.

In simulations 1 and 3, which use, respectively, a payroll tax and a consumption tax to finance benefits, the tax rates applied are proportional. Simulation 2 raises progressive income tax rates to finance transition benefits. This is accomplished by increasing the two components of the income tax, the progressive wage tax and the proportional capital income tax, so that the average wage tax and the average capital income tax change proportionally. The macroeconomic changes in factor supplies along the economy's transition path alter the income tax base used to finance government purchases. In order to maintain a constant level of government purchases per effective worker in each transition, we adjust income tax rates along the transition path even in those simulations in which income taxes are not used to pay the benefits accrued under Social Security.

Macroeconomic Effects

The top panels of figures 8.1 through 8.3 and the first three rows of tables 8.1 through 8.5 show the macroeconomic impact of the three alternative methods of financing the transition. In tables 8.1, 8.2, and 8.3, the capital stock, labor supply, and output are measured per twenty-one-year-old. In simulations 1 through 6, which are generated by our base model discussed above, the percentage changes are relative to the initial steady-state values of the variables in question.

The first thing to note is that all three simulations generate the same long-run outcome. This is to be expected, since in the long run Social Security is fully phased out and the tax used to pay for benefits during the transition equals zero. The long-run economic impact is considerable. Compared to the initial steady state, the economy's capital stock ends up 39.0 percent higher, its labor supply 5.5 percent higher, and its output 13.0 percent higher. The relative changes in factor supplies effect a 7.1 percent rise in the long-run real wage rate and an 18.6 percent decline in the interest rate.

Although all three policies do the same long-run macroeconomic good, they differ markedly with respect to their short-run macroeconomic impact and the speed with which they approach their common steady state. Consumption tax finance, by imposing a relatively heavy burden on the initial elderly (who have the highest consumption propensities due to their proximity to their terminal state), crowds in capital formation from the initiation of the reform onward. In contrast, wage taxation generates essentially no additional capital formation during the first decade of the policy. Indeed, even after twenty-five years, the capital stock is only 5.2 percent larger than its initial value. Income tax finance of the transition is even worse on this score. It actually reduces the capital stock for more than a quarter of a century after the reform begins. At the quarter-century mark, the capital stock is 4.6 lower than its starting value. The differences in these results are quite striking and serve as an important lesson to those advocating privatization. However, most proposals to privatize Social Security, which, incidentally, do not rely on consumption-tax finance, may still entail rapid attainment toward the new steady state if they phase out benefits under the old system at a faster rate. The trade-off, however, is that this might cause greater harm to initial retirees and workers.

Welfare and Distributional Effects

The bottom panels of figures 8.1–8.3 and the first three sections of table 8.6 show the winners and losers within and across generations of the three alternative ways of financing the transition. The first thing to note is that all agents alive in the long run, regardless of their lifetime income class, are better off as a result of Social Security's privatization. The welfare

Macro Effects

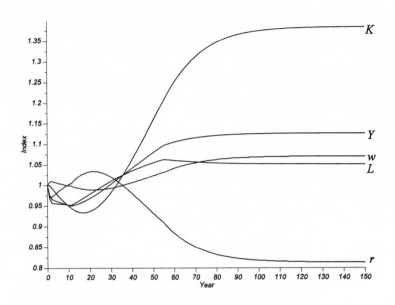

Remaining Lifetime Utility

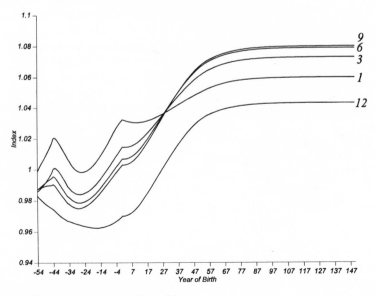

Fig. 8.2   Income tax finance of transition

Macro Effects

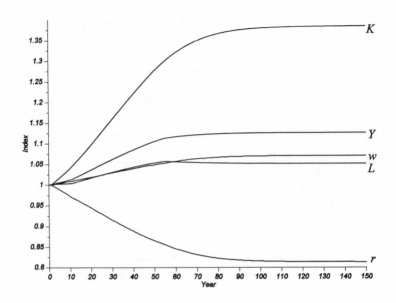

Remaining Lifetime Utility

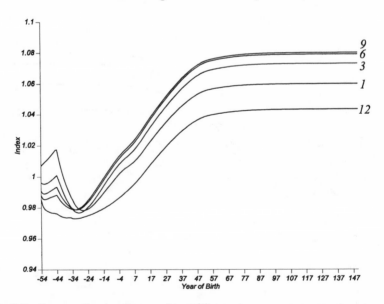

Fig. 8.3 Consumption tax finance of transition

Table 8.1   **Percentage Change in Capital Stock**

			Year of Transition			
Run	Experiment	Transition Tax	5	10	25	150
1	Privatization	W	0.0	0.1	5.2	39.0
2	Privatization	Y	−2.4	−5.0	−4.6	39.0
3	Privatization	C	1.8	4.1	12.8	39.0
4	Voluntary privatization	C	1.5	3.8	14.2	39.0
4+	Voluntary privatization	C	1.5	3.5	11.0	39.0
5	Privatization with flat benefit	Y	−2.8	−5.7	−8.7	12.4
6	Privatization with progressive match	Y	−3.4	−7.1	−9.7	35.4
7*	Current policy in demo model	W	5.9	19.3	52.7	26.0
8*	Privatization in demo model	W	6.9	21.9	61.8	112.1

Notes: C = consumption tax. W = payroll tax. Y = income tax. All runs are relative to initial steady state except for starred runs, which are relative to year one.

Table 8.2   **Percentage Change in Labor Supply**

			Year of Transition			
Run	Experiment	Transition Tax	5	10	25	150
1	Privatization	W	−1.1	−1.1	1.8	5.5
2	Privatization	Y	−4.5	−4.7	0.0	5.5
3	Privatization	C	0.3	0.4	2.4	5.5
4	Voluntary privatization	C	−0.2	0.0	2.4	5.5
4+	Voluntary privatization	C	0.8	0.8	0.9	5.5
5	Privatization with flat benefit	Y	−4.7	−4.9	−2.9	1.2
6	Privatization with progressive match	Y	−6.7	−7.3	−3.0	4.0
7*	Current policy in demo model	W	−3.8	−1.8	2.5	−4.4
8*	Privatization in demo model	W	−3.6	−1.6	5.4	5.0

Notes: C = consumption tax. W = payroll tax. Y = income tax. All runs are relative to initial steady state except for starred runs, which are relative to year one.

gains—measured as full remaining lifetime wealth equivalent variations—vary from 6.0 percent for the lowest lifetime earners, to over 8 percent for the middle- and upper-income lifetime earnings, to only 4.4 percent for the highest lifetime earners. Hence, Social Security's privatization improves the welfare across all income classes for those born in the long run and is, broadly speaking, progressive when measured with respect to its

Table 8.3   Percentage Change in Income

Run	Experiment	Tax that Finances Accrued Social Security Benefits	Year of Transition			
			5	10	25	150
1	Privatization	W	−0.8	−0.7	2.6	13.0
2	Privatization	Y	−4.0	−4.8	−1.5	13.0
3	Privatization	C	0.6	1.3	4.9	13.0
4	Voluntary privatization	C	0.2	1.0	5.2	13.0
4+	Voluntary privatization	C	1.0	1.5	3.3	13.0
5	Privatization with flat benefit	Y	−4.2	−5.1	−4.4	3.9
6	Privatization with prog match	Y	−5.9	−7.2	−4.7	11.1
7*	Current policy in demo model	W	−1.5	3.1	13.3	2.4
8*	Privatization in demo model	W	−1.1	3.8	17.3	25.2

Notes: C = consumption tax. W = payroll tax. Y = income tax. All runs are relative to initial steady state except for starred runs, which are relative to year one.

Table 8.4   Percentage Change in Wages

Run	Experiment	Tax that Finances Accrued Social Security Benefits	Year of Transition			
			5	10	25	150
1	Privatization	W	0.4	0.5	0.8	7.1
2	Privatization	Y	0.5	0.0	−1.0	7.1
3	Privatization	C	0.4	0.9	2.4	7.1
4	Voluntary privatization	C	0.4	0.9	2.8	7.1
4+	Voluntary privatization	C	0.2	0.7	2.4	7.1
5	Privatization with flat benefit	Y	0.5	−0.2	−1.5	2.7
6	Privatization with prog match	Y	0.9	0.1	−1.8	6.8
7*	Current policy in demo model	W	2.4	5.0	10.5	7.1
8*	Privatization in demo model	W	2.6	5.4	11.3	19.2

Notes: C = consumption tax. W = payroll tax. Y = income tax. All runs are relative to initial steady state except for starred runs, which are relative to year one.

long-run welfare effects. This may seem surprising, given that Social Security benefits are very progressive, and one might think that losing them should be very important to the lifetime poor. However, the opportunity cost of investing in Social Security is quite high even for a poor person because its internal rate of return is quite low relative to the private market return. Moreover, the system's taxes are regressive due to the ceiling on

Table 8.5 **Percentage Change in Interest Rates**

Run	Experiment	Tax that Finances Accrued Social Security Benefits	Year of Transition			
			5	10	25	150
1	Privatization	W	−1.0	−1.4	−2.5	−18.6
2	Privatization	Y	−1.5	0.0	3.2	−18.6
3	Privatization	C	−1.1	−2.7	−6.9	−18.6
4	Voluntary privatization	C	−1.2	−2.7	−7.8	−18.6
4+	Voluntary privatization	C	−0.5	−1.9	−6.8	−18.6
5	Privatization with flat benefit	Y	−1.4	0.6	4.7	−7.6
6	Privatization with prog match	Y	−2.6	−0.2	5.4	−17.9
7*	Current policy in demo model	W	−7.0	−13.6	−25.9	−18.8
8*	Privatization in demo model	W	−7.5	−14.8	−27.5	−41.1

Notes: C = consumption tax. W = payroll tax. Y = income tax. All runs are relative to initial steady state except for starred runs, which are relative to year one.

Table 8.6 **Percentage Change in Remaining Lifetime Utility for Selected Income Classes**

Class	Year of Birth						
	−54	−25	−10	1	10	25	150
Run 1							
1	0.0	−2.0	−1.3	−0.6	0.1	2.2	6.0
3	−0.1	−1.7	−1.1	−0.4	0.5	3.0	7.4
6	−0.1	−1.4	−0.8	−0.2	0.8	3.3	8.0
9	−0.1	−1.2	−0.7	−0.1	0.9	3.5	8.1
12	−0.1	−0.6	−0.4	−0.1	0.3	1.5	4.4
Run 2							
1	−0.1	−0.2	1.6	3.2	3.1	3.5	6.0
3	−1.4	−1.6	0.0	1.4	1.7	3.3	7.4
6	−1.3	−2.1	−0.7	0.7	1.1	3.2	8.0
9	−1.2	−2.4	−1.0	0.3	0.8	3.1	8.1
12	−1.7	−3.6	−3.6	−3.0	−2.5	−0.2	4.4
Run 3							
1	0.7	−2.1	−0.6	0.5	1.3	3.2	6.0
3	−0.4	−2.0	0.0	1.2	2.1	4.2	7.4
6	−0.9	−1.7	0.3	1.6	2.6	4.8	8.0
9	−1.2	−1.6	0.5	1.7	2.7	4.9	8.1
12	−1.5	−2.5	−1.8	−1.0	−0.1	1.7	4.4
Run 4							
1	0.5	−2.2	−1.0	0.9	1.6	4.2	6.0
3	−0.3	−2.7	−0.2	1.6	2.4	5.2	7.4

(*continued*)

Table 8.6   (continued)

| | | | | Year of Birth | | | |
Class	−54	−25	−10	1	10	25	150
6	−0.6	−2.8	0.3	2.0	2.9	5.8	8.0
9	−0.8	−2.8	0.5	2.2	3.1	5.9	8.1
12	−1.0	−2.9	−1.6	−0.6	0.1	2.5	4.4
Run 4+							
1	0.5	−0.8	−0.8	0.5	1.0	2.8	6.0
3	−0.2	−1.3	−0.5	1.2	1.8	3.8	7.4
6	−0.6	−1.4	0.1	1.7	2.2	4.3	8.0
9	−0.8	−1.4	0.3	1.8	2.4	4.4	8.1
12	−1.0	−2.3	−1.7	−0.9	−0.4	1.3	4.4
Run 5							
1	−0.1	1.8	3.1	4.3	4.1	4.2	5.7
3	−1.4	−0.5	0.6	1.7	1.7	2.3	4.8
6	−1.3	−1.6	−0.5	0.6	0.5	1.4	4.4
9	−1.2	−2.1	−1.0	0.0	−0.1	1.0	4.1
12	−1.7	−3.6	−3.9	−3.4	−3.5	−3.4	0.5
Run 6							
1	−0.2	0.9	3.2	5.3	5.0	5.3	8.0
3	−1.8	−1.3	0.7	2.6	2.7	4.2	8.4
6	−1.6	−2.4	−1.0	0.7	0.9	2.9	8.1
9	−1.6	−3.2	−1.8	−0.4	−0.1	2.2	7.7
12	−2.1	−4.9	−5.0	−4.3	−4.1	−1.7	3.5
Run 8*							
1	−0.01	−2.36	−2.29	−1.49	−0.88	2.11	7.68
3	0.01	−1.86	−1.76	−1.12	−0.46	2.53	8.26
6	0.02	−1.41	−1.22	−0.57	0.25	3.47	9.60
9	0.02	−1.17	−0.95	−0.33	0.54	3.79	9.94
12	0.03	−0.37	−0.18	0.06	0.45	1.89	5.99

Note: All runs are relative to initial steady state except starred run, which is relative to utility under the current policy transition.

taxable earnings. The poor benefit more than the very rich from the privatization of Social Security because the regressiveness of the payroll tax outweighs the progressivity of the benefit schedule.

While everyone alive in the long run wins due to the privatization of Social Security, their winnings come at the price of reduced welfare for initial and intermediate generations. However, the different financing mechanisms spread out the transitional losses quite differently. Consumption tax financing (simulation 3) is hard on initial older generations because it raises resource using a wealth levy. Increasing progressive tax rates (simulation 2), however, hits them even harder. The wage tax transition is the least painful for the oldest retirees alive at the time of the reform, as they pay no wage taxes. Despite the fact that funding Social Security is simply a redistribution mechanism between generations that does *not* improve *efficiency* (that is, unless people do not perceive their Social Security tax-benefit linkage properly), it can be shown that greater funding can increase *social welfare* provided that the social welfare function places enough weight on the utility of future generations (Feldstein 1995, 1998). This is an important point for policy makers to keep in mind, because they influence the distribution of resources across generations.

8.4.2   Making Privatization Voluntary

A mandatory privatization plan may face less chance of being enacted than one that provides workers the choice to simply opt out of Social Security. Indeed, most actual privatizations have given people the choice. This was true, for example, in Chile and Argentina, and in the case of other major reforms in Latin America; only new workers were forced into the new system. In the United Kingdom, even new workers are allowed to choose between the traditional public pension system and private accounts. Allowing for choice leads those agents whose present values of future Social Security taxes (PVT) exceed the present value of their future benefits (PVB) (including benefits already accrued) to opt out of the existing system.

Permitting voluntary exit from Social Security involves three elements: (a) eliminating both future payroll taxation as well as all future benefit claims for those who opt out, (b) collecting payroll taxes from and paying benefits to those who stay in, and (c) using general revenue to finance the gap between payroll taxes collected and benefits received. Agents who stay in Social Security face the same payroll tax rate and receive the same benefits that they would under current law. Agents endogenously decide whether or not it is better for them to opt out of Social Security, taking into account the entire future path of factor prices and tax rates. Since the opting-out decision of one agent affects the decision of other agents via changes in factor prices, the simulation iterates until a final competitive (Nash) equilibrium is arrived at.

Providing workers with the option to leave Social Security may sound more generous than forcing them to leave with only their accrued benefits, but the opposite is actually the case. Consider first those who opt out of Social Security. In so doing, they forfeit all the benefits they have accrued up to that point in their working careers. Hence, compared with compulsory privatization, which guarantees the full value of accrued benefits, voluntary privatization is less generous. Next, consider those who decide to stay in the old system. In so doing, they ensure that they will receive their past accrued benefits (also provided by a compulsory system), but the price for so doing is staying in a system which, at the margin, may represent a net tax: For those remaining in the old system, each dollar contributed in the future may deliver additional benefits that total less than a dollar in expected present value.

In the actual simulation, the loss of their accrued benefits leads most existing workers to remain in the old system. On the other hand, all agents younger than twenty-five years of (real-life) age opt out, as do all future agents. Since the System's benefits are provided on a progressive basis, one would expect the opting-out cutoff age for high earners to be larger than that for low earners. This indeed turns out to be the case. High earners in their mid-thirties choose to opt out, whereas the poorest agents opt out only through age twenty-seven.

Macroeconomic Effects

To be sure, only a fraction of initial workers voluntarily leave the Social Security System under opting-out, which means that they will eventually collect full benefits, whereas they would have collected only partial benefits under the forced phase-out considered earlier. However, those that do leave forfeit their right to collect any future Social Security benefits, whereas they would have collected at least some benefits under the forced privatization plan considered earlier. On net, the aggregate decrease in Social Security wealth is about the same over time between the two options. This is shown in simulation 4, which reports the results seen when agents are given the choice to remain in the current system or to opt out. The transition, which is depicted in figure 8.4, is financed via a consumption tax, similar to simulation 3, that forces participation. Notice that the intermediate impact on macroeconomic variables is about the same for both simulations. For the case of income tax financing (not shown), opting out outperforms forced participation.

Welfare and Distribution

Compared with forced participation, opting out does a slightly better job of protecting the welfare of the initial elderly. Whereas the welfare of oldest agents alive at the time of the reform in income class 6 is reduced by 0.9 percent in simulation 3, it is reduced by 0.6 percent in simulation 4. For members of income class 12, who hold even more wealth and therefore are even more exposed to the wealth levy associated with consumption tax financing, these values are 1.5 percent and 1.0 percent, respectively. Opting out leads to a smaller need to increase consumption taxes immediately, because some payroll tax revenue is still being collected from those who remain in Social Security. Opting out, however, leaves middle-aged agents alive at the time of the reform (e.g., those born in year of birth −25) because many of them choose to remain in Social Security (and, therefore, pay a high payroll tax) and must help pay for, via a consumption tax, the revenue that is lost when younger and higher-earning workers opt out of Social Security.

To address the welfare impact that opting out has on middle-aged workers alive at the time of the reform, simulation 4+ considers the same opting-out experiment but with a "plus": Workers who remain in Social Security must pay only half the current tax rate. The immediate payroll

Macro Effects

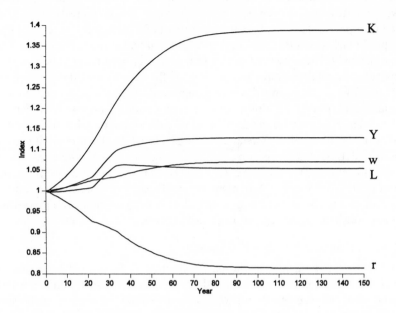

Remaining Lifetime Utility

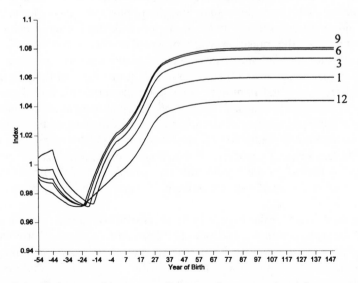

Fig. 8.4 Opting out with new payroll tax equal to present law value, consumption tax finance of transition

tax revenue lost from this policy change is offset, in large part, by the decrease in the number of workers choosing to opt out. Eventually all new workers, however, choose not to participate in Social Security, even at a reduced payroll tax rate, because the rate of return they can receive in the capital market is sufficiently higher than the internal rate of return to Social Security. The net effect of this policy change is to reduce the revenue collected from those alive at the time of the reform and therefore push more of the burden toward future generations. This is why simulation 4+ leads to a slower transition relative to simulations 3 and 4, as shown in the tables. However, on the distributional side, simulation 4+ more evenly distributes the burden associated with privatization, both over time and across lifetime income groups. While the utility of a middle-aged agent (born in year −25) of income class 1 decreases by 2.1 percent in simulation 3, it decreases by only 0.8 percent in simulation 4+. This change comes, in part, at the cost of future transitional workers, who gain from privatization in both cases, but less so in simulation 4+.

8.4.3   Privatization with a Flat Benefit

The World Bank has, in the past, encouraged developing countries to include a "first pillar" as part of their reforms. This first pillar is a flat benefit that is received by all workers independent of their contribution level. Although an attempt to protect the poor, the first pillar has two major drawbacks. First, the tax used for its finance adds a work disincentive. Second, the flat benefit is typically financed on a PAYGO basis and therefore vitiates most of the potential long-run gains from privatizing the old system. We investigate this policy by (a) providing a wage-indexed flat minimum annual benefit that equals $6,000, (b) paying a weighted average of the old OASI and the new flat minimum benefit during the transition, and (c) financing the transition with a progressive income tax.

As tables 8.1 and 8.2 and figure 8.5 indicate, the long-run increases in capital and labor under this policy are less than one-third of their values in the absence of a flat minimum benefit. Furthermore, the added work disincentives associated with financing the minimum benefit reduce labor supply by almost 3 percent after the first twenty-five years of the transition, compared to no reduction for simulation 2. Less labor supply translates into less saving by workers, less national saving, and less domestic investment. Indeed, in the twenty-fifth year of this policy, the economy's capital stock and output are, respectively, 8.7 percent and 4.4 percent below their initial values.

How does adding a flat benefit to an income tax–financed policy alter the well-being of the poor in the long run? The surprising answer, provided in the fifth section of table 8.6, is that makes them worse off relative to privatization without the flat benefit. In the long run, the welfare of the poorest earners is 5.7 percent higher than in the initial steady state,

Macro Effects

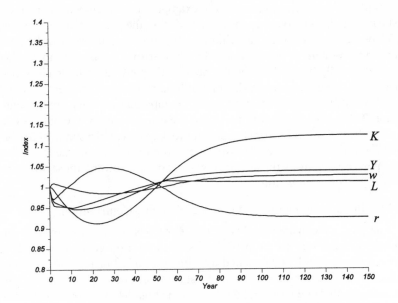

Remaining Lifetime Utility

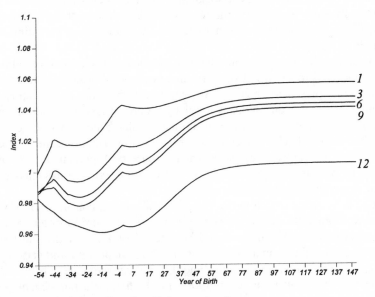

Fig. 8.5   Flat minimum benefit with income tax finance

whereas without a flat benefit (simulation 2), it is 6.0 percent higher. Although the flat benefit harms the long-run poor, it substantially improves the well-being of the initial poor. For example, those members of the lowest earnings class who are born ten years before the policy is enacted enjoy a 3.1 percent improvement in welfare in simulation 5 compared to a 1.6 percent improvement in simulation 2. In contrast to the long-run poor, who are only mildly harmed by the flat benefit, the long-run middle class and rich are substantially harmed. For the long-run highest earners, welfare rises by only 0.5 percent in simulation 5, compared to 4.4 percent in simulation 2. For those long-run members of earnings class 6, the flat benefit lowers the welfare gain from 8.0 percent to 4.4 percent. To summarize, the inclusion of the flat benefit redistributes from those alive in the long run, but particularly from those with higher earnings, toward those who are poor during the transition.

8.4.4   Privatization with a Progressive Matching Contribution

The plan we consider in this section envisions having the government match contributions to the privatized system on a progressive basis. The government's match is calculated as a function of labor income and falls steadily as a percentage of earnings, starting at about 5 percent for the poorest. In absolute terms, it increases from about $470 at annual earnings of $10,000 to around $840 for annual earnings of $21,000 and remains constant thereafter. On a lifetime basis, the match provides a transfer to the poor whose long-run value exceeds the flat minimum benefit by 30 percent. Workers fully incorporate in their labor supply and saving decisions the marginal subsidy associated with the progressive contribution match. In order to compare the results of this option to those of the flat benefit, an income tax is used to finance the transition, including the match.

As tables 8.1 through 8.5 and figure 8.6 indicate, this method of helping the poor leads to the worst short-run macroeconomic outcomes of all the simulations presented thus far. By year twenty-five, the capital stock is smaller by 9.7 percent, labor is lower by 3 percent, and national income is down by 4.7 percent. However, unlike the flat benefit, whose general equilibrium feedbacks worsen the plight of the long-run poor, the progressive matching contribution raises their welfare by 8 percent in the long run. The primary sacrificers here are those in the top earnings classes of their respective cohorts.

The progressive match performs quite well when a consumption tax is used to finance the transition (which is not shown here in order to save space; see Kotlikoff, Smetters, and Walliser 1999a). All of the short-run and long-run gains to macroeconomic variables are positive and very similar to those shown in simulation 3, and the long-run gains are substantially larger relative to using a consumption tax to finance a flat benefit. For

Macro Effects

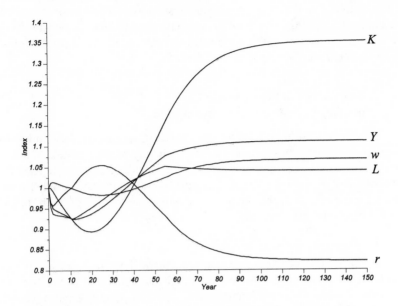

Remaining Lifetime Utility

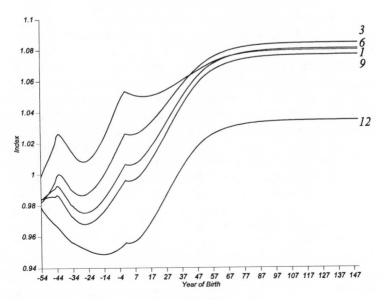

Fig. 8.6 Progressive match with income tax finance

example, the capital stock increases by 39 percent under the progressive match but by only 23 percent under the flat benefit. For national income, these values are 12.4 and 7.5 percent, respectively. These results confirm the importance of the choice of the tax base used to finance the transition. They also indicate that there are ways to help the long-run poor without hurting those who are poor in the short run.

8.5   Preliminary and Future Work: Including More Realistic Demographics

This section outlines how we are currently modifying the model described in the previous section. We have already made a large amount of progress toward this end, but we are not yet satisfied enough with the model's design and calibration to regard our simulations as final. Hence, we offer the results in this section as a "sneak peek"—but a high-quality one—into our work at hand.

8.5.1   The New Model

Our current work expands the treatment of demographics in four dimensions. First, it permits much more realistic patterns of births. Second, it permits a more realistic length of life. Third, it permits a more realistic age-distribution of inheritances. Fourth, it permits the economy to initiate its transition from arbitrary initial demographic conditions; in other words, the initial period's population age distribution is not necessarily stable.

Births and Children

In the new version of the model, children derive utility from consumption and leisure from birth through age twenty-one. These levels of child utility enter their parents' utility function in a linearly additive manner. The form of this utility function is identical to that of the adults'. It is a time separable CES function and runs through the child's twenty-first year of age. The child utility functions are multiplied by a child-utility preference parameter. They are also multiplied by the number, which could be a fraction, of children per parent. Because parents give birth to children (or, to be more precise, give birth to fractions of children) at different ages, each parent's utility function has a child utility function for each of the different ages at which a child is born. Children are assumed to have a wage of zero prior to reaching age twenty-one. Consequently, they choose to supply no labor. On the other hand, they do consume when young. Their consumption is determined by their parents and enters their parents' budget constraints.

The new model features a realistic distribution of births by the age of parents instead of assuming that all children arrive when the parents reach age twenty-one. Newborns of each cohort are allocated to adults over age twenty-one based on the actual age-distribution of new mothers observed in U.S. data. For example, if thirty-year-old females give birth to 5 percent of newborns each year in the United States, 5 percent of the model's newborns each year are assigned as children to that year's thirty-year-olds. There is nothing in the mathematics of our model that precludes adults' giving birth to fractions of children in a given year. This allows us to avoid having to separately track those agents in a given cohort who do and do not have children in a given year. Instead, we can focus on the average agent in a particular income class and generation.

Length of Life

Average longevity in the United States has increased by about two years since the original Auerbach and Kotlikoff (1987) model and will continue to do so in the future. Thus, the fifty-five-period model, in which people are independent economic actors for fifty-five years, was updated to allow for sixty periods, or whatever age the programmer chooses. We are in the process of indexing this age to the year index, so that longevity can increase over time. We may also make longevity differ by income class if we can find suitable empirical data to match. As it stands now, an agent is an independent actor for sixty years, which means that agents live for a total of eighty-one years (the first twenty-one years as dependents).

Inheritances

A parent's utility from bequests is also modified in the new version of the model. Specifically, this utility is multiplied by the number of children the parent has when he or she reaches the maximum age of life and passes on. However, all recipients of bequests are no longer the same age. Instead, we assume that decedents divide their bequests evenly among all their offspring and that their offspring receive these inheritances at whatever age they have achieved as of the time of the parent's death.

Calibration

In calibrating the new model's demographics, we use the Social Security Administration's projections of aggregate annual births to determine the size of each successive cohort. In addition, we use the current age distribution of the U.S. population to populate our model in the first year of the transition. We do not assume a stable initial distribution of the U.S. population.

We have not yet calibrated the model to our full satisfaction. This includes fully matching the model's initial wealth and initial Social Security benefit distributions to their empirical counterparts. Some of the short-run results presented below might reflect this fact, although the medium- to long-run results tend to be fairly robust to a reasonable range of choices for the model's initial conditions. Also, we currently assume that those in the top three lifetime income classes, representing the top 20 percent of the wage distribution, face only the inframarginal Social Security tax in each period of their lives; consequently, for this group, the marginal Social Security tax is always zero. All wage groups below the top three are assumed to face the Social Security tax rate at the margin. Although this assumption is likely to lead to very little bias, we plan to implement the procedure used in our base model in the near future that takes into account the kink in the budget constraint arising from the ceiling on payroll taxation. Finally, the aggregate variables produced by our model are measured per twenty-one-year-old. That is, they are normalized by the number of agents who are who are entering their first year of independent economic activity.

8.5.2   Preliminary Simulation Results

Simulating the Demographic Transition Under Current Policy

Simulation 7 considers how the Social Security system will fare over time if there is no change in the PAYGO nature of the program. Given the projected aging of the U.S. economy and the concomitant projected growth in Social Security benefits, Social Security payroll tax rates will have to rise if no other financing mechanism is put into place. Indeed, simulation 7, entitled "Current Policy in Demo Model," eventuates in a 5 percentage point rise in the payroll tax rate. This is the bad news about the demographic transition. The good, and somewhat surprising, news is that, notwithstanding Social Security's problem, the nation's aging is a positive thing for the economy overall if we look out to the medium term. Table 8.3 documents this point. It shows that output per twenty-one-year-old is 2.5 percent lower five years from now (year 1 in the simulation), but 12.9 percent higher twenty-five years from now. In the very long run, after the nation's population distribution has stabilized, output per twenty-one-year-old is only 3.3 percent higher than its current value.

The explanation for this unusual growth pattern is the medium-term capital deepening arising from the large numbers of baby boomers arriving at retirement with significant holdings of capital. Since the work force coming behind them is relatively small in size, there is a substantial rise in the capital-labor ratio. For example, in the twenty-fifth year of the transition, the capital-labor ratio is 47 percent higher than its initial value. This capital deepening translates into almost a 10 percent rise in the real wage in the medium term and an 8 percent rise in the real wage in the long term.

Privatization in the Demographic Model

Our final simulation, number 8, enacts the privatization policy of simulation 1. Social Security benefits are phased out after ten years, and transition costs are financed with a proportional labor tax on wages. As tables 8.1 through 8.5 indicate, compared to the status quo/current policy transition (simulation 7), privatization in the demographic model (simulation 8) produces an even more dramatic improvement in the economy's medium- as well as long-run positions. According to table 8.3 and the top panel in figure 8.7, privatization raises living standards twenty-five years out by 18.8 percent, and in the long run by 20 percent. Associated with this policy is a 56 percent increase in the capital-labor ratio by year 25 and a corresponding 11.1 percent rise in real wages. The combination of capital deepening and reduced payroll taxation generates a significant medium-term increase in labor supply. In year 25, labor supply is 7.0 percent above its initial (year 1) value, compared to only 2.7 percent above in the current-policy demographic simulation.

Table 8.6 and figure 8.7 display the welfare effects associated with privatization using wage-tax finance. Welfare changes are measured relative to the utility levels that the particular agents in each generations would have enjoyed under the status-quo (baseline) policy, which is considered in simulation 7. There are four things here worth emphasizing. First, as in the nondemographic version of our model (see simulation 1), all lifetime earnings groups alive in the long run experience substantial welfare gains from Social Security's privatization. Second, the lifetime poor alive in the long run experience a much higher welfare gain than do the lifetime rich. Third, these long-run gains are larger in the nondemographic model because the long-run payroll tax rate would otherwise be 5 percentage points higher. Fourth, the short-run welfare losses to initial younger workers are larger in the demographic model because of the need to pay the retirement benefits of the large baby boom cohorts.

8.6 Conclusion

The U.S. Social Security system is in trouble. Its projected future expenditures exceed its projected means of paying for those expenditures by more than one-third. Addressing Social Security's fiscal imbalance is inevitable. How it is done will affect current and future generations of Americans, not just through their payment of payroll taxes and their receipt of benefits, but also through the real wages and real rates of return they earn on their labor supply and savings. Hence, understanding these effects necessitates a general equilibrium analysis. This paper provides such an analysis. It shows that privatizing Social Security can generate significant long-run economic gains for the lifetime poor as well as the lifetime rich. However, achieving these gains comes at the expense of some welfare losses to transition generations. It also requires patience, since even the best-designed privatization of Social Security will take years to significantly

Macro Effects

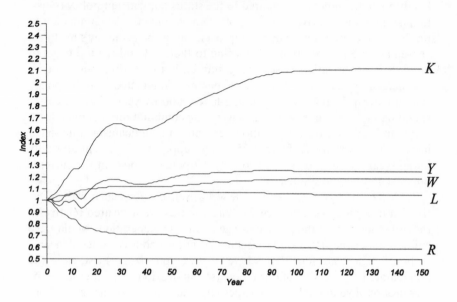

Remaining Lifetime Utility

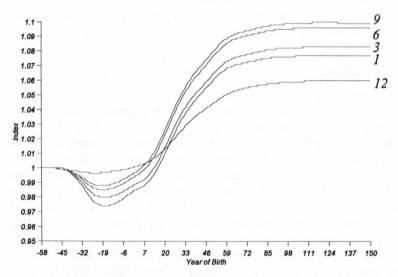

Fig. 8.7 Payroll tax finance of transition (demo)

affect the economy. Finally, it requires avoiding flat benefits and other measures that may seem progressive but that end up doing more harm than good to those who are poor in the long run.

References

Altig, David, Alan Auerbach, Larry Kotlikoff, Kent Smetters, and Jan Walliser. 2001. Simulating U.S. tax reform. *American Economic Review* 91 (3): 574–95.

Arrau, Patricio, and Klaus Schmidt-Hebbel. 1993. Macroeconomic and intergenerational welfare effects of a transition from pay-as-you-go to fully funded pensions. Paper of the Policy Research Department, Macroeconomics and Growth Division. Washington, D.C.: World Bank.

Auerbach, Alan J. 1996. Tax reform, capital accumulation, efficiency, and growth. In *Effects of Fundamental Tax Reform,* ed. Henry J. Aaron and William G. Gale, 29–82. Washington, D.C.: Brookings Institution.

Auerbach, Alan J., and Laurence J. Kotlikoff. 1983. National saving, economic welfare, and the structure of taxation. in *Behavioral simulation methods in tax policy analysis,* ed. Martin S. Feldstein, 459–93. Chicago: University of Chicago Press.

———. 1987. *Dynamic fiscal policy.* Cambridge, England: Cambridge University Press.

Auerbach, Alan, Robert Hageman, Laurence J. Kotlikoff, and Giuseppe Nicoletti. 1989. The economics of aging populations: The case of four OECD economies. *OECD Staff Papers.*

Cooley, Thomas F., and Jorge Soares. 1999a. A positive theory of Social Security based on reputation. *Journal of Political Economy* 107 (1): 135–60.

———. 1999b. Privatizing Social Security. *Review of Economic Dynamics* 2 (3): 731–55.

De Nardi, Mariacristina, Selahattin İmrohoroğlu, and Thomas J. Sargent. 1999. Projected U.S. demographics and social security. *Review of Economic Dynamics* 2 (3): 575–615.

Feldstein, Martin S. 1974. Social Security, induced retirement, and aggregate capital accumulation. *Journal of Political Economy* 82:905–26.

———. 1995. Would privatizing Social Security raise economic welfare? NBER Working Paper no. 5281. Cambridge, Mass.: National Bureau of Economic Research.

———. 1998. Introduction to *Privatizing Social Security,* ed. Martin S. Feldstein, 1–29. Chicago: University of Chicago Press.

Fougere, Maxime, and Marcel Merette. 1998. Economic dynamics of population aging in Canada: An analysis with a computable overlapping-generations model. Paper presented at the Canadian Public Economics Study Group, Ottawa, Canada. May.

———. 1999. Population aging, intergenerational equity and growth: Analysis with an endogenous growth, overlapping generations model. In *Using dynamic general equilibrium models for policy analysis.* ed. Glenn W. Harrison, Svend E. Hougaard Jensen, Lars Haagen Pedersen, and Thomas F. Rutherford, 13–52, 325–362. Amsterdam: North Holland.

Fullerton, Don, and Diane Lim Rogers. 1993. *Who bears the lifetime tax burden?* Washington, D.C.: Brookings Institution.

Galasso, Vincenzo. 1999. The U.S. Social Security system: What does political sustainability imply? *Review of Economic Dynamics* 2 (3): 698–730.

Hansson, Ingemar, and Charles Stuart. 1989. Social Security as trade among living generations. *American Economic Review* (December): 1182–95.

Huang, He, Selo İmrohoroğlu, and Thomas Sargent. 1997. Two computational experiments to fund social security. *Macroeconomic Dynamics* 1:7–44.

Hubbard, Glenn R., and Kenneth L. Judd. 1987. Social Security and individual welfare: Precautionary saving, borrowing constraints, and the payroll tax. *The American Economic Review* 77 (4): 630–46.

———. 1994a. The importance of precautionary motives in explaining individual and aggregate saving. *Carnegie-Rochester Conference Series on Public Policy* 40:59–125.

———. 1994b. Why do people save? *The American Economic Review* 84 (2): 174–79.

———. 1995. Precautionary saving and social insurance. *Journal of Political Economy* 103 (2): 360–99.

Huggett, Mark, and Gustavo Ventura. 1999. "On the Distributional Effects of Social Security Reform," *Review of Economic Dynamics,* 2(3), July, 498–531.

İmrohoroğlu, Ayse, Selahattin İmrohoroğlu, and Douglas H. Joines. 1995. A life cycle analysis of social security. *Economic Theory* 6:83–114b.

———. 1999. Social security in an overlapping generations economy with land. *Review of Economic Dynamics* 2 (3): 638–65.

Kotlikoff, Laurence J. 1979. Social security and equilibrium capital intensity. *Quarterly Journal of Economics* (May): 233–54.

———. 1996. Privatizing social security: How it works and why it matters. In *Tax policy and the economy,* Vol. 10, ed. James M. Poterba, 1–32. Cambridge, Mass.: MIT Press.

Kotlikoff, Laurence J. 2000. The A-K model: Its past, present, and future. In *Using dynamic general equilibrium models for policy analysis,* forthcoming, ed. Glenn W. Harrison, Svend E. Hougaard Jensen, Lars Haagen Pedersen, and Thomas F. Rutherford, 13–52. Amsterdam: North Holland.

Kotlikoff, Laurence J., Kent Smetters, and Jan Walliser. 1997. The economic impact of privatizing Social Security. In *Redesigning social security,* ed. Horst Siebert. 327–48. Tübingen, Germany: Mohr Siebeck.

———. 1998a. Opting out of social security and adverse selection. NBER Working Paper no. 6430. Cambridge, Mass.: National Bureau of Economic Research, February.

———. 1998b. Social security: Privatization and progressivity. *Papers and Proceedings of American Economic Review* 88 (2): 137–41.

———. 1999a. Privatizing social security in the U.S.: Comparing the options. *Review of Economic Dynamics* 2 (3): 532–74.

———. 1999b. Privatizing U.S. Social Security: A simulation study. In *Pension systems: From crisis to reform,* ed. Klaus Schmidt Hebbel. Washington, D.C.: World Bank. Forthcoming.

Knudsen, Martin B., Lars Haagen Pedersen, Toke Ward Petersen, Peter Stephensen, and Peter Trier. 1999. A dynamic CGE analysis of the Danish aging problem. In *Using dynamic computable general equilibrium models for policy analysis.* North Holland. Forthcoming.

Menchik, Paul L., and Martin David. 1982. The incidence of a lifetime consumption tax. *National Tax Journal* 35 (2): 189–203.

Raffelhuschen, Bernd. 1993. Funding social security through pareto-optimal conversion policies. In *Public pension economics,* ed. Bernhard Felderer, 105–31. Journal of Economics/Zeitschrift fur Nationalokonomie, Suppl. 7.

Schneider, Ondrei. 1997. Dynamic simulation of pension reform. Charles University, CERGE-EL, Prague. Mimeograph.

Seidman, Laurence S. 1986. A phase-down of social security: The transition in a life cycle growth model. *National Tax Journal,* 39:97–107.

Slemrod, Joel, and Jon M. Bakija. 1996. *Taxing ourselves: A citizen's guide to the great debate over tax reform.* Cambridge, Mass.: MIT Press.

World Bank. 1994. *Averting the old age crisis.* Washington, D.C.: World Bank.

Comment   James E. Duggan and David W. Wilcox

The paper by Kotlikoff, Smetters, and Walliser (KSW) represents a progress report on—and an extension of—a research program of very impressive proportions. Surely, this must be one of the most ambitious simulation research programs in economics, whether measured in terms of the importance of the topic, the length of time that the authors have remained with the project, or the range of features they have incorporated into their model.

We organize our comment into two main sections. First, we highlight three specific observations about various aspects of the paper. Then we move to a more general assessment of the adequacy of the basic approach used by KSW—and countless others—as a means of conducting distributional analysis of the Social Security system.

Specific Observations

It is ironic that the last time one of us (Wilcox) had the pleasure of serving as a discussant at an NBER conference, it was also of a Smetters paper, the objective of which was to highlight the financial risk associated with ownership of equities. In particular, the earlier Smetters paper argued that the burden of equity-related risk should be evaluated at the prices paid by private market participants. Given the important role that equities play in the current paper, and the striking results reported in the earlier paper, future effort might be directed toward examining whether additional insights could be gained by marrying these two branches of Smetters's research.

A second observation pertains to the use of the word "privatization" in this paper. The positive welfare effects that obtain in the new steady state do not stem from linking an individual's Social Security benefit to the

The views expressed in this note are those of the authors and may not reflect the official views of the Treasury Department. The authors thank John Hambor and Chris Soares for helpful discussions.

James E. Duggan is a senior economist in the Office of Economic Policy at the U.S. Treasury Department. David W. Wilcox is deputy director in the Division of Research and Statistics at the Federal Reserve Board.

investment outcome of an account in that person's name and under his or her individual control. Rather, the welfare benefits simply reflect the result demonstrated by Peter Diamond (1965), that when the economy is on the right side of the golden rule, steady-state utility is higher in a funded system than in an unfunded system. In short, the welfare gains estimated by KSW have nothing to do with "privatization" as most people understand that term, and all of the benefits outlined by KSW could equally be captured in a prefunded system that preserves the essential contours of the current system.[1]

Finally, we question the characterization of some of the results as demonstrating that "privatization" is "progressive" (see, for example, the discussion of table 8.6 in section 8.4). It is true that, in most or all of these simulations, the poor are better off by more than the top 2 percent of the population, but they are also better off by *less* than everyone else for whom results are shown. This does not answer to our definition of a progressive reform.

The More General Question

In the remainder of this comment, we focus on one element of KSW's model, namely the representation in the model of the mechanism that generates Social Security benefits. The goal will be to assess the adequacy of the approach taken by KSW, using some administrative data available to us at the Treasury Department. KSW have enforced some simplifications of reality, with the objective of keeping the model computationally and conceptually tractable. The important question is not whether the model is simpler than reality—it is—but, rather, whether the simplifications could materially affect the conclusions of some analyses KSW might undertake in the future, recognizing that (a) the authors intend to use the model to address questions in which general-equilibrium considerations may be particularly germane, and (b) they also intend to examine (as the title of their paper states) the distributional effects of various policy experiments.

One common approach in setting up a simulation model is to specify a small number of worker/beneficiaries, each with an exogenous earnings trajectory. This is the approach that historically has been taken, for example, by the Social Security actuaries, with their "steady low earners," "steady average earners," and "steady high earners."

KSW go one better than this by specifying the lifetime skill profiles of a small number of worker/beneficiaries as well as their preferences over consumption and leisure. Importantly, this allows labor supply to respond endogenously to changes in factor prices. Nonetheless, individuals with

---

1. See Geanakoplos, Mitchell, and Zeldes (1998) for a careful typology of Social Security systems and reforms.

the preferences assumed by KSW will always choose at least some work (assuming a positive wage rate) and will experience a smooth earnings trajectory over their lifetimes, much like the ones specified by the actuaries.

Weaknesses of the Typical Approach

At least in its simplest form, the approach taken by KSW and countless other authors suffers from some notable shortcomings, at least for some purposes: It cannot be used to analyze issues related to gender, because there is (in the simplest models) no distinction between males and females. Likewise, it cannot be used to analyze issues related to survivor benefits, because there is no concept of premature death. Nor can it be used to analyze issues related to spousal benefits, because there is no concept of marriage.

Even the ability to examine issues related to income may be more limited than it first appears. For example, labor force attachment is markedly more intermittent for lower-income workers than for higher-income workers, yet, in the typical approach, all earnings trajectories show each worker/beneficiary with positive earnings every year of working life. Depending on the question under investigation, this could be a material shortcoming.

Solutions to These Problems

All of the issues raised above could be addressed by increasing (possibly greatly) the number of earnings trajectories considered. For example,

- To address the issue of gender, one could double the number of trajectories and label half as "women" and the other half as "men."
- To address the issue of survivor benefits, one could impose an empirically realistic distribution of death dates for each gender. Some workers would die young, some at intermediate ages, and some in old age.
- To address the issue of spousal benefits, one could allow an empirically realistic amount of "marriage" to take place, with an appropriate matching of age and lifetime-income characteristics.

The proper means of addressing the issue of intermittent labor force attachment is less apparent, but a good start might involve building in the idea that, for many workers, employment is more a binary variable than continuous. The modifications that are advertised at the end of the paper are interesting and useful, but will not fundamentally address any of the issues raised here.

Evaluating the Seriousness of the Problem

Do the simplifications inherent in the baseline model involve important loss of accuracy in answering specific questions? The remainder of this comment provides some evidence on that question. The results that follow are based on two primary data files from the Social Security Administration (SSA): the 1 percent 1996 Continuous Work History Sample (CWHS) and the Master Beneficiary Record (MBR). The CWHS is a record of 1951–96 annual earnings for workers in covered employment, and the MBR is a record of benefits paid to those workers when they retire (or become disabled) and to nonworkers who become eligible on the basis of a worker's eligibility (spouses, children, etc.). We also utilize data on the earnings histories of auxiliary beneficiaries extracted from SSA's Master Earnings File.

We formed a subsample of just over 95,000 retired-worker (76 percent), spouse (11 percent), and widow (13 percent) beneficiaries born during the years 1924 to 1928. In the spirit of KSW, we classified observations according to the distribution of age-sixty-five benefits. For those beneficiaries who died before age sixty-five, or who started receiving benefits after age sixty-five, we imputed an age-sixty-five benefit by indexing the benefit closest to that age based on legislated changes in benefits. Our benefit classification scheme mimics the twelve KSW income categories: the first two percentiles, the next eight percentiles, deciles two to nine, the 91st–98th percentiles, and the top two percentiles. The second column of table 8C.1 shows the means and standard deviations of age-sixty-five benefits for retired workers by benefit class. (For purposes of this table we omitted spouses and widows.)

The third column shows, for the same subsample, the benefit amounts that would be paid based on the mean earnings trajectory for each benefit class. The greatest discrepancies between the second and third columns occur at the lower and top benefit classes.

It is interesting to note that the benefit classes are demographically very nonhomogeneous. For example, figure 8C.1 shows the distribution of males and females by benefit class based on actual benefits. Most women are in the lower end of the distribution and most men in the upper end. This suggests that Social Security reforms that affect different income classes differently will also affect men and women differently.

We constructed age-earnings profiles for the beneficiary sample described above for ages twenty-five to sixty-five using actual historical covered earnings data from the CWHS for primary workers and from the SSA's Master Earnings File for auxiliary beneficiaries. Figure 8C.2 shows these profiles for three beneficiary classes, the first two percentiles, the 5th decile, and the top two percentiles. The differences in magnitude and shape are remarkable, even if expected. Earnings for the top benefit class peak past age sixty, but ten to fifteen years earlier for the first and fifth classes. Of course, there is no reason that the underlying structure of KSW's model should not closely resemble these results.

The more pressing issue is that mean age-earnings profiles may obscure important underlying labor force patterns, and—interacting with a highly

Table 8C.1   **Age-65 Social Security Benefit Distribution (1999 dollars)**

Benefit Class	Mean Actual Benefit in $ (Standard Deviation)	Benefit Based on Mean Earnings Trajectory (in $)
1st and 2nd percentiles	1,234 (334)	2,227
3rd–10th percentiles	2,767 (591)	2,423
2rd decile	4,446 (335)	3,427
3th decile	5,330 (200)	4,038
4th decile	6,135 (290)	5,489
5th decile	7,276 (358)	6,426
6th decile	8,645 (423)	7,994
7th decile	10,038 (382)	9,460
8th decile	11,245 (294)	11,784
9th decile	12,417 (493)	12,752
91st–98th percentiles	14,465 (629)	14,167
Top 2 percentiles	16,766 (1,303)	14,846

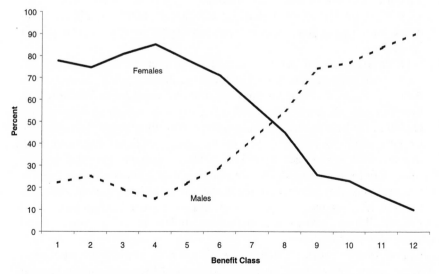

Fig. 8C.1   Male-female percentage distribution by age-65 benefits

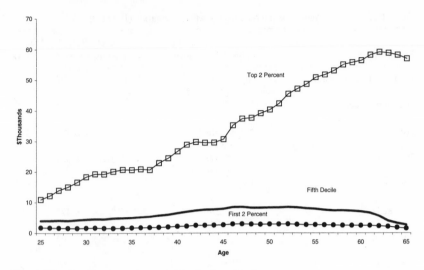

Fig. 8C.2   Real age-earnings profiles by benefit class

nonlinear benefit system—may generate misleading results. As we noted above, low-income individuals generally exhibit more intermittent labor force participation than higher-income individuals. This can be seen in figure 8C.3, which shows the differential incidence of years with zero earnings across the benefit classes, limiting the computation to the highest thirty-eight years of earnings. The percentage is very high for the lowest benefit classes but relatively small for the highest classes. Separate results for men and women (not shown) suggest that women have a higher incidence than men of years with no earnings, especially in the upper benefit classes.

Of course, the real issue of interest is whether the considerations we have raised suggest that some distributional analysis might be materially distorted. As a case study for this question, we have examined the distributional impact of increasing the number of years' worth of earnings included in the benefit formula from thirty-five to thirty-eight. (This change to the system has been a feature of many congressional and think-tank proposals for Social Security reform.) While this oft-proposed change in the benefit formula provides a convenient vehicle for illustrating our point, it is probably not the most consequential example. For example, the same types of effects would emerge in proposals to create individual accounts if the contribution into the account is zero unless annual earnings exceed some nonzero threshold.

The effect on worker benefits of such a change depends on whether it causes more low earnings to be added to the AIME and on the level of AIME. Workers with steady earnings in all years would be unaffected.

Workers with low or zero earnings for the thirty-sixth through thirty-eighth years, on the other hand, would be affected most. Due to the progressive structure of the benefit formula, changes in the AIME result in larger changes for beneficiaries with low earnings and conversely for high earners.

We evaluated the effects of such a proposal on over 14,000 retired workers born in 1928 by first computing age-sixty-five retirement benefits under current law and then recomputing those benefits with the computation period increased by three years. Our results for males and females are summarized in figure 8C.4. Benefit reductions are uniformly higher for females than for males and larger for low- than for high-beneficiary classes.

Conclusion

We believe that the results described above illustrate a generic shortcoming of simulation models based on a very limited representation of heterogeneity in the population. To be clear, we believe that KSW have taken a useful step in introducing heterogeneity into their model. An interesting question—the answer to which we do not know—is whether at the current stage they have achieved only an uncomfortable middle ground, having introduced enough heterogeneity to invite contemplation of specific realistic reforms, but not enough to be able to deliver accurate answers.

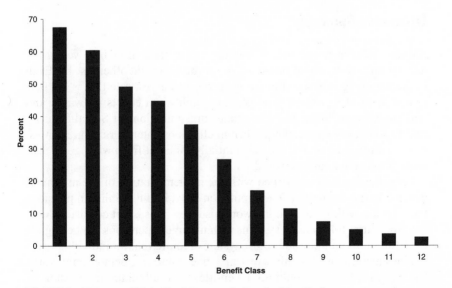

Fig. 8C.3   Percent of high 38 with zero earnings by benefit class

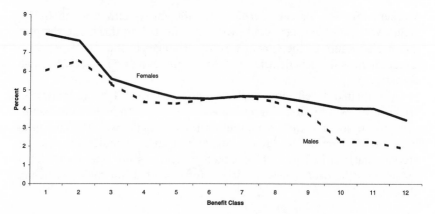

Fig. 8C.4   Percentage reduction in benefits from increasing the computation period by 3 years

Reference

Geanakoplos, John, Olivia Mitchell, and Stephen P. Zeldes. 1998. Would a privatized social security system really pay a higher rate of return? In *Framing the social security debate: Values, politics, and economics,* ed. R. Douglas Arnold, Michael J. Graetz, and Alicia H. Munnell, 137–56. Washington, D.C.: National Academy of Social Insurance.

Discussion Summary

Martin Feldstein noted that it was important that, after fifty years, the interest rate is only about one-tenth lower than it would otherwise be. Even in the very long run, the simulation shows an interest rate that is 8.5 percent instead of 9 percent. The general equilibrium effects on wages and real incomes are larger. However, long-run simulations of Social Security reform that ignore general equilibrium effects on interest rates are not assuming interest rates that are substantially different from what good general equilibrium analyses would imply.

Gary Burtless was concerned with the implementation of the minimum pension in the simulation. The simulation provides full minimum pensions for everyone without examining work histories. This is not consistent with the procedures followed by systems with minimum pensions. To be eligible for a full minimum pension, most systems require that an individual earn a minimum amount for thirty or thirty-five years. If a person only works twenty years, then he would not be entitled to a full minimum pension.

Andrew A. Samwick indicated that simplifications in general equilibrium models might lead to poor calibrations of the remaining parameters. For example, if the model is not designed to have precautionary saving, then the simulated consumers derived from the model's calibration will be more patient than the real consumers used to calibrate the model. Consequently, the evolution of the capital stock may be incorrect.

9

The Economics of Bequests in Pensions and Social Security

Martin Feldstein and Elena Ranguelova

One of the apparent advantages of Social Security and of private pensions is that they provide an annuitized form of retirement income that allows retirees to avoid "wasting" some of their lifetime accumulation in the form of unintended bequests.[1] In practice, however, individuals generally choose to forgo the potential gain from full annuitization in order to have the prospect of providing a bequest with some of their lifetime accumulation.

For example, given the choice between an ordinary life annuity (for the retiree or the retiree and spouse) and a "ten-year certain" annuity that provides that benefits continue for at least ten years even if the annuitant dies, most participants in defined contribution TIAA-CREF plans select the ten-year certain annuity.[2] More generally, the participants in virtually all defined contribution plans choose to bequeath the entire value of their accumulated accounts if they die before reaching retirement age instead of committing those funds to an annuity at an earlier preretirement age.[3]

Martin Feldstein is the George F. Baker Professor of Economics at Harvard University and president of the National Bureau of Economic Research. Elena Ranguelova was a PhD student at Harvard while this chapter was being completed; she now works for Lehman Brothers, Inc..

The authors are grateful to John Campbell, Jeffrey B. Liebman, James M. Poterba, and Andrew A. Samwick for useful discussions, and to Andrew A. Samwick for some of the analytic data used here.

1. See Brown, Mitchell, and Poterba (1999) for estimates of the utility gain that an egoistic retiree who does not place any utility value on making a bequest obtains by being able to annuitize retirement assets.

2. The Teachers Insurance and Annuity Association College Retirement Equity Fund (TIAA-CREF) is the largest private pension plan, with more than $250 billion in assets. Among male retirees, 74 percent now choose some period of certain benefits in addition to a life annuity.

3. This paper provides an estimate of the increased value of the annuity that would be possible if individuals used their accumulated funds to purchase annuities during their preretirement years.

Moreover, countries that have adopted investment-based Social Security programs to supplement or replace traditional pay-as-you-go (PAYGO) systems also generally provide for bequests both when individuals die before retirement and when they die during their retirement years.[4] For many people, an attraction of supplementing the existing PAYGO Social Security system in the United States with an investment-based system is that it would give middle- and lower-income individuals the opportunity to accumulate wealth and make significant bequests. Recent legislative proposals for investment-based supplements to the U.S. Social Security program provide for such bequests.[5] The ability to provide bequests in this way is also regarded as an advantage of using individual retirement accounts rather than a single government fund as a way of achieving an investment-based supplement to Social Security.

A mechanism for making significant bequests is attractive both to those who would receive the bequests and those who would make the bequests. The financial assets that heirs receive in this way would, if saved and spent gradually, allow them to maintain consumption in the face of substantial financial risks, including long-term unemployment, large uninsured health expenditures, or substantial property losses. In addition, financial assets give individuals the ability to quit an undesirable job and seek new work or to undertake entrepreneurial activities.[6] The ability to make such bequests to children or grandchildren is appealing to those who would make them because it provides an opportunity to express generosity at the end of life (Bernheim and Severinov 1998) and because it offers the "strategic" advantage of strengthening filial loyalty (Bernheim, Shleifer, and Summers 1985).

Although it might be argued that individuals who want to make bequests could save explicitly for this purpose, it is the lack of foresight and self-discipline to accumulate for their own old age that justifies mandatory Social Security pensions. This same inability to do long-term saving can also justify helping individuals to make the bequests that they would like to make but lack the ability to achieve.[7]

The provision of bequests is also a matter of practical program design in a system of investment-based personal retirement accounts. Although

4. See Feldstein (1998) and World Bank (1994) for descriptions of the investment-based systems in a number of countries.

5. These include the explicit proposals that have been put forth by Senators Moynihan and Kerry, by Senators Gramm and Domenici, and by Senators Gregg and Breaux. The provision of bequests was also a feature of the two individual account proposals contained in the report of the official Social Security Advisory Council.

6. Rosen, Holtz-Eakin, and Joulfaian (1993) show that moderate-sized bequests increase significantly the probability that individuals will begin entrepreneurial activities.

7. Bequests are, of course, an uncertain way of helping children and grandchildren. An explicit form of saving to make nonrandom gifts might in principle be a useful supplement to a pension system with bequests.

retirees could in principle be required to annuitize their accumulated assets at retirement with no provision for bequests, those individuals who die before retirement must be allowed to make bequests unless the government taxes away the entire value of their accumulated assets at death or requires that all preretirement saving be invested in the form of annuities as it accumulates. Foreign experience and the revealed preferences in private defined contribution plans in the United States imply that neither of those would be popular options.

Previous academic analyses of investment-based Social Security reforms have ignored the possibility of bequests, implicitly assuming that all saving would be invested in annuities both during working years and after retirement (see, for example, Feldstein and Samwick 1997, 1998a, b; Kotlikoff 1996, 1998). In contrast, the present paper examines a variety of possible options for bequests before retirement and during the retirement years. Although our calculations use the individual employee as the unit of analysis, the level of projected PAYGO benefits to which we compare the investment-based annuities corresponds to the Social Security actuaries' projections for the benefits of retirees, spouses, survivors, and the disabled.[8] The bequests that we study here are therefore supplementary to these additional benefits that are specified in current law.

We examine three types of issues about such bequests. First, we ask how expensive such bequests would be in terms of the saving rate necessary to support such bequests without reducing the associated annuities. Alternatively, we ask how much of an annuity reduction different bequest rules would require if the saving rate used to fund the investment-based pensions was not raised when bequests were introduced. Next, we examine the probability distribution of bequests by size and by timing under different bequest options. Finally, we consider the macroeconomic consequences of bequests on capital accumulation.

9.1 Personal Retirement Accounts and Preretirement Bequests

In an investment-based system, individuals accumulate a fraction of each year's wages in personal retirement accounts (PRAs) during working years and receive annuities during retirement. The deposits to these accounts may be financed by the individuals themselves, by their employers, or by the government. The deposits may be set at a level that permits the resulting annuities to fully replace the PAYGO system of benefits or at a level that only supplements a PAYGO system. The issues of who funds the accounts and of whether the accounts are intended to replace the existing PAYGO system or to supplement the existing system are not directly rele-

---

8. About one-third of the total cost of benefits is for the additional benefits for spouses, survivors, dependents, and the disabled.

vant to our analysis.[9] The structure of the calculations makes it clear that the size of the annuities and of the bequests is proportionate to the saving rate. Although we analyze a level of saving that could fully replace the existing PAYGO system in the long run, readers can consider the effect of smaller investment-based programs by a proportionate reduction in all of our dollar amounts.

In a system with no preretirement bequests, the individual is implicitly required to buy a retirement annuity with each year's PRA deposit. The rate of return on the preretirement saving of those who survive in any given year is therefore the sum of the ordinary market return on the assets in the account plus the increased value that results from receiving a share of the assets of those who died during the year.

More specifically, consider a cohort of individuals who enter the labor force at age twenty-one. Let N_s be the number of individuals of the cohort who are alive and working at age s, let w_s be the annual wage of the representative individual in that cohort in year s, let α be the fraction of wages contributed each year to the PRAs,[10] and let R_s be the investment return in that year. If bequests are not permitted, the funds that are owned by those who die at age s are automatically reinvested in the accounts of those who remain alive, as they would be in an actuarially fair annuity. During the preretirement period, those who live to the end of their sth year will have accumulated (as a cohort) an amount

$$(1) \qquad M_s = (1 + R_{s-1})M_{s-1} + \alpha w_s N_s \ ,$$

where M_s is the aggregate PRA balance for the cohort as a whole. A representative member of the cohort who survives to age s will therefore have accumulated

$$(2) \qquad A_s = (1 + R_{s-1})A_{s-1} + \alpha w_s + (1 + R_{s-1})\frac{(N_s - N_{s-1})A_{s-1}}{N_s} \ ,$$

where the term $([N_s - N_{s-1}]A_{s-1})/N_s$ indicates the amount transferred to each survivor's account in year $s - 1$ from those who died during that year.

Permitting bequests of the accumulated account balances during the preretirement years changes this accumulation by eliminating the increment in equation (2) that comes from the accounts of those who died dur-

---

9. Feldstein and Samwick (1997, 1998b) analyze plans based on employee-employer contributions that would eventually replace the existing tax-financed system completely. Feldstein and Samwick (1998a, 1999) describe a plan to use government deposits in individual accounts to supplement the benefits that could be financed with the existing level of Social Security payroll taxes. Feldstein, Ranguelova, and Samwick (1999) analyze both types of plan in a stochastic environment.

10. Saving in PRAs is based on wages up to the maximum earnings taxed under Social Security. This maximum was $68,400 in 1998.

ing the year. The value of the assets of an individual who survives to age t (and therefore the magnitude of that individual's bequest if he or she dies in that year) evolves according to

$$(3) \qquad A_s = (1 + R_{s-1})A_{s-1} + \alpha w_s \ .$$

To assess the magnitude of the potential bequests and the effect of bequests on the amount accumulated at age sixty-six, we use the cohort of individuals who are twenty-one years old in the year 1998 and the age-specific mortality rates for this cohort as projected by the Social Security actuaries in the *Statistical Supplement to the Social Security Bulletin*. We look at a representative individual in this cohort who has mean age-specific earnings in each year, again using the projections of the Social Security actuaries.

9.2 A Model of Uncertain Investment Returns

Our analysis assumes that the PRA balances are invested in a portfolio consisting of 60 percent stocks and 40 percent corporate bonds. The accumulation of assets in the PRAs and the annuities and bequests at each age reflect the uncertain returns on these assets.

To analyze this uncertainty, we assume that the PRA portfolio is continually rebalanced to maintain 60 percent equities and 40 percent debt.[11] We use the Standard & Poor's 500 index and a Salomon Brothers corporate bond index as proxies for the stock and bond investments. Both indexes are assumed to follow a geometric random walk with drift. This implies that the log returns for each type of asset are serially independent and identically distributed with given mean and variance. Thus, if p_{es} and p_{bs} are the log levels of the equity and bond indexes at time s, we assume

$$p_{es} = p_{e(s-1)} + \mu_e + u_{es}$$

and

$$p_{bs} = p_{b(s-1)} + \mu_b + u_{bs} \ ,$$

where μ_e and μ_b are the mean drift per period in the logarithmic value of equities and bonds, while $u_e \sim$ independently and identically distributed (i.i.d.) $N(0, \sigma_e^2)$ and $u_b \sim$ i.i.d. $N(0, \sigma_b^2)$. The covariance between the stock and bond returns is σ_{eb}.

With a continuously compounded 60-40 equity-debt portfolio, the log

---

11. This ratio is selected to correspond approximately to the debt-to-equity ratio of U.S. corporations so that the rate of return on capital at the corporate level can correspond to the return to these portfolio investments without considerations of the relative yields on debt and equity. The 60–40 ratio is also a common ratio used by corporate pensions.

level of the overall portfolio would satisfy the following random walk if there were no additions or payouts:

$$p_s = p_{s-1} + \mu + u_s$$

with $u \sim$ i.i.d. $N(0, \sigma^2)$. To derive the values of μ and σ^2 we use the lognormal property of the returns.

More specifically, if μ_i^* is the mean return on asset i in level form, the mean return on the 60-40 portfolio is the weighted average $\mu^* = 0.6 \mu_e^* + 0.4 \mu_b^*$. Because we assume the log returns to be normally distributed, $\mu_i^* = \mu_i + 0.5 \sigma_i^2$. This implies that

$$\mu + 0.5\sigma^2 = 0.6(\mu_e + 0.5\sigma_e^2) + 0.4(\mu_b + 0.5\sigma_b^2) ,$$

where

$$\sigma^2 = 0.36\sigma_e^2 + 0.16\sigma_b^2 + 0.48\sigma_{eb} .$$

From these two equations and the measured mean and variance of the log returns on stocks and bonds, we can derive the log return on the portfolio and the variance of that return.

The Center for Research in Security Prices (CRSP) data for the postwar period from 1946 through 1995 imply that for stocks and bonds the mean log real rates of return were 7.0 percent and 3.3 percent.[12] The corresponding standard deviations are 16.6 percent for stocks and 10.4 percent for bonds. The covariance of the stock and bond log returns is $\sigma_{eb} = 0.0081$. Taken together, these parameters imply an average log real rate of return on the 60-40 portfolio of 5.9 percent with a standard deviation of 12.5 percent.

In the analysis that follows, we reduce the mean log return from 5.9 percent to 5.5 percent to reflect potential administrative costs.[13]

Although the equation for p_s describes the way that the logarithmic value of the PRA account would evolve during the accumulation years if there were no external additions, the actual individual PRAs would be augmented annually by a fraction α of the individual's wage and, when there are no preretirement bequests, by the distributed share of the PRA balances of those members of the cohort who die during the year. These are shown in equations (2) and (3) above. Since those equations are stated in level rather than logarithmic form, the value of $1 + R_s = \exp(r_s)$ where r_s is the logarithmic rate of return in period s implied by $r_s = p_s - p_{s-1} = \mu + u_s$.

---

12. The bond rate of return is based on the Salomon Brothers' AAA bond returns, adjusted to a more typical corporate bond yield by adding 2 percentage points.

13. This estimate of the administrative cost may be compared with the cost of about 0.2 percent charged now in indexed equity funds by mutual fund companies like Vanguard and Fidelity. Bond funds generally have lower administrative charges.

We use equation (3) to simulate 10,000 evolutions of the PRA values for each year from age 21 through 100, taking into account the mortality probabilities and the stochastic distribution of returns. Our stochastic simulations recognize the uncertainty of the future mean return as well as the annual variations in returns around that future mean. For each of the 10,000 simulations, we begin by drawing a mean rate of return from a distribution with a mean of 0.055 and a standard deviation of 0.0177, the standard error or the mean estimate based on our fifty-year sample of observations. We then generate an eighty-year series of returns that have this mean and a standard deviation of 0.125.

We assume that individuals save 6 percent of their wages each year in PRA accounts and that the PAYGO tax declines from the initial 12.4 percent to zero. For comparison, the Social Security actuaries project that the current PAYGO tax rate of 12.4 percent will have to rise to more than 18 percent in a purely tax-financed PAYGO system in order to provide the benefits that are promised in the Social Security law. In contrast, we show in this paper that, with no bequests and a saving rate of 6 percent, the median annuity at age sixty-seven is 2.05 times the future Social Security benefits promised in current law (which we call the "benchmark benefits") and that there is a 90 percent probability that the PRA annuity at age sixty-seven will equal or exceed 76 percent of the benchmark benefit.[14] Since the benchmark PAYGO benefit replaces approximately 40 percent of the preretirement wage, the median annuity based on a 6 percent replacement rate would correspond to a replacement rate of 81 percent. The mean annuity exceeds the median and corresponds to 2.98 times the benchmark benefits.

9.3   The Distribution of Preretirement Bequests

We now study the annuity financed by a 6 percent saving rate to see the effects of mortality risk and investment uncertainty on the distribution of bequests. Table 9.1 shows the implied distribution of preretirement bequests of different sizes for individuals who die at different ages between twenty-five and sixty-seven. These bequests are all based on the potential experience of a representative individual who earns the mean wage[15] and who makes annual saving deposits of 6 percent of that wage to a PRA. The distribution of bequest values reflects the variation in rates of return on the assets in the PRAs. Column (1) shows the annual age-specific

---

14. For a more complete analysis of these risk issues, see Feldstein and Ranguelova (1998).
15. The mean wage is the mean of the wage distribution subject to the ceiling on the taxable earnings for Social Security ($68,400 in 1998) and adjusted for multiple excess wages. The multiple excess wages adjustment accounts for the fact that some individuals who receive wages from more than one employer may earn less than the taxable ceiling at each job but that their total earnings may exceed that ceiling.

Table 9.1   **Distribution of Preretirement Bequests, 6.0% Saving Rate**

| | | | Bequest Size | | | Probability that Bequest Exceeds Multiples of Mean Wage | | | |
	Mortality Rate (1)	Cumulative Probability of Bequest (2)	Mean ($000) (3)	Standard Deviation ($000) (4)	Mean Wage ($000) (5)	1× (6)	2× (7)	3× (8)	4× (9)
Age									
25	0.0010	0.004	5	1	29.0	0.000	0.000	0.000	0.000
30	0.0013	0.009	14	4	30.5	0.001	0.000	0.000	0.000
35	0.0016	0.016	29	10	32.1	0.311	0.007	0.000	0.000
40	0.0019	0.025	51	21	33.7	0.801	0.174	0.027	0.005
45	0.0023	0.035	83	42	35.4	0.953	0.528	0.216	0.086
50	0.0034	0.047	128	78	37.2	0.986	0.762	0.479	0.284
55	0.0054	0.067	193	138	39.1	0.995	0.880	0.675	0.490
60	0.0085	0.097	285	241	41.1	0.998	0.930	0.797	0.653
65	0.0142	0.143	417	420	43.2	0.998	0.958	0.868	0.758
67	0.0172	0.168	487	518	44.1	0.998	0.967	0.888	0.791

Source: These calculations are based on 10,000 two-stage simulations. First we generate the log mean return by drawing from a distribution with mean 0.055 and a standard deviation of 0.0177. We then generate an eighty-year series of annual returns that have this mean and a standard deviation of 0.125.

Notes: All dollar amounts are in 1998 prices. The representative individuals in this simulation have the mean age-specific covered earnings in each year. Six percent of these wages are deposited annually to the personal retirement accounts.

mortality rates, the probabilities that an individual of that age will die and leave a bequest. The cumulative probability of leaving a bequest (i.e., the probability of dying by that age conditional on being alive at age twenty-one) is shown in column (2).

The mean and standard deviation of those bequests, in thousands of 1998 dollars, is shown in columns (3) and (4). For comparison, the corresponding mean wage projected for that year is shown in column (5).[16] The simulation of 10,000 forecasts is used to calculate the probabilities that the bequest will exceed various multiples of the future mean wage; these probabilities are shown in columns (6) through (9).

The mean bequests grow rapidly with age, from just $5,000 for those who die at age twenty-five to $128,000 at age fifty, and more than $400,000 for those who die just before retirement. Even by age thirty-five, the mean bequest of an individual who has had average earnings all his life would be nearly as large as the average earnings in that year. By age fifty, the mean bequest is more than three times mean earnings. Recall that this is with a 6 percent saving rate. If the saving rate were limited to 2 percent of earnings, as it might be in a system that combines PAYGO and investment-based components, these means and standard deviations would be reduced by a factor of three.

The increasing relative variance of the bequest size (seen by comparing columns [4] and [3]) reflects the fact that the annual returns follow a random walk, causing the variance of the return to grow with time. The probability distributions described in columns (6) through (9) show that those who die in middle age are increasingly likely to leave bequests that are a significant multiple of the average wage at the time of their death. Thus, among fifty-year-olds who die, virtually all bequests exceed the average wage, 76 percent of bequests exceed twice the average, and 48 percent exceed three times the average wage.

In considering these values, it should be recalled that the cost of providing these preretirement bequests while maintaining the 6 percent PRA saving rate is to reduce the funds available to finance annuities among the vast majority of individuals who do not die before reaching retirement age. The payment of preretirement bequests reduces the mean accumulation of assets at age sixty-six by 14 percent, causing the annuities to decline by the same percentage. Table 9.2 shows the effect of providing preretirement bequests on the distribution of the variable annuity payments. We report the variable annuity payments as a fraction of the "benchmark benefits"— the benefits promised to each cohort under the Social Security law.[17] The first three columns show the cumulative probability distributions of

---

16. This is also the mean of the truncated distribution, with all wages at or above the ceiling truncated as if they are at the celing and adjusted for multiple excess wages.

17. See section 9.4 for a description of the variable annuities.

Table 9.2   Effects of Preretirement Bequests on the Distribution of the Variable Annuity Payments as a Fraction of Benchmark Social Security Benefits

	No Bequests (6% saving rate)			Preretirement Bequests (with associated saving rates)					
				Age 67		Age 77		Age 87	
Cumulative Probability	Age 67	Age 77	Age 87	6%	7%	6%	7%	6%	7%
0.01	0.38	0.21	0.12	0.34	0.40	0.18	0.21	0.10	0.12
0.02	0.45	0.26	0.16	0.40	0.47	0.23	0.26	0.15	0.17
0.05	0.59	0.38	0.26	0.52	0.61	0.34	0.39	0.22	0.26
0.10	0.76	0.55	0.39	0.67	0.78	0.48	0.56	0.34	0.40
0.20	1.04	0.81	0.63	0.91	1.07	0.71	0.83	0.55	0.65
0.30	1.34	1.12	0.92	1.17	1.36	0.98	1.14	0.81	0.94
0.40	1.66	1.47	1.30	1.44	1.68	1.28	1.50	1.13	1.32
0.50	2.05	1.90	1.78	1.78	2.08	1.65	1.92	1.54	1.80
0.60	2.49	2.46	2.42	2.16	2.52	2.14	2.49	2.10	2.45
0.70	3.16	3.24	3.36	2.73	3.19	2.81	3.27	2.90	3.39
0.80	4.17	4.60	4.90	3.59	4.19	3.96	4.62	4.24	4.94
0.90	6.12	7.29	8.60	5.26	6.13	6.29	7.34	7.42	8.66
0.95	8.50	10.99	13.31	7.29	8.50	9.44	11.02	11.45	13.35
0.98	12.14	17.02	22.53	10.43	12.17	14.60	17.04	19.37	22.60
0.99	15.24	22.21	31.41	13.06	15.24	19.00	22.17	26.88	31.36

Source: These calculations are based on 10,000 two-stage simulations. First we generate the log mean return by drawing from a distribution with mean 0.055 and a standard deviation of 0.0177. We then generate an eighty-year series of annual returns that have this mean and a standard deviation of 0.125.

Notes: Benchmark Social Security Benefits are the future benefits projected for the individuals who are 21 in 1998, based on current Social Security rules. The representative individuals in this simulation have the mean age-specific covered earnings in each year. Six percent of these wages are deposited annually to the personal retirement accounts.

annuity payments relative to benchmark benefits for retirees at ages sixty-seven, seventy-seven, and eighty-seven with no preretirement bequest and a 6 percent saving rate. The next six columns show the same cumulative distributions, but for the case in which individuals can bequeath their accounts if they die before age sixty-seven. For this case, we consider PRA saving rates of 6 percent and 7 percent.

The results indicate that permitting preretirement bequests does not significantly increase the risk to retirees and that the increased risk can be fully offset by raising the PRA saving rate from 6 percent to 7 percent. With that increase in the saving rate, the risk distribution of annuity payments with preretirement bequests is essentially the same as the distribution with no bequests and a 6 percent saving rate. The median benefit with the 7 percent saving rate and preretirement bequests is 2.08 times the benchmark benefit level (column [6]), virtually unchanged from the 2.05 times the benchmark value with the 6 percent saving rate and no bequests (column [2]). The corresponding values at the 10th percentile of the distribution are 0.78 times the benchmark and 0.76 times the benchmark. The similarity continues at the higher age levels shown in table 9.2.

The logic of the calculation is such that the same 17 percent proportional increase in the saving rate would be sufficient for any initial saving rate. For example, a PRA annuity that is intended to supplement rather than replace the tax-financed retirement Social Security benefits would produce essentially the same distribution of annuities with either a 2.00 percent saving rate and no bequests or a 2.33 percent saving rate and preretirement bequests.

9.4 Postretirement Bequests

The magnitude of potential bequests is increased substantially if retirees can bequeath some part of their postretirement income as well as their preretirement accumulation. We consider first how a variable annuity system would work and then examine a variety of alternative bequest options, assessing the cost in terms of reduced annuities or increased preretirement savings needed to produce those bequests. We begin with a life annuity for the retiree alone and then extend our analysis in section 9.5 to a double life annuity for the retiree and a spouse.

Our analysis assumes that the postretirement annuity is financed with the same stock-bond mix that the individuals had during the preretirement years. When there is no postretirement bequest, we assume that the individual receives variable annuity payments that adjust according to the changes in the value of the PRA account balance caused by changes in market rates of return. More specifically, in a standard variable annuity contract, the "baseline" annuity benefit that would be paid at age sixty-seven (on an annuity purchased at age sixty-six) reflects the PRA assets at the beginning of the individual's sixty-sixth year, the expected mortality rates at all future ages, and the assumption that the future return will be equal to the expected portfolio rate of return (5.5 percent in the current context). Each year the actual size of the variable annuity payment is increased or decreased from the initial value in proportion to the change in the market value of the PRA assets relative to the market value that would have prevailed if the expected 5.5 percent return had actually occurred.

More explicitly, let A_{66} be the value of the assets that the individual has accumulated at the beginning of the sixty-sixth year, let R be the expected real rate of return on the portfolio of assets used to finance the retirement annuity, and let $p_{s|66}$ be the probability of reaching age s conditional on being alive at age sixty-six. The actuarial present value (APV) at age sixty-six of a fixed real annuity of \$1 for life beginning at age sixty-six is then

$$\text{APV} = \sum_{s=67}^{s=100} p_{s|66}(1 + R)^{-(s-66)} \, ,$$

where we assume that all individuals alive at age 99 die at the end of the 100th year. Since the PRA account has assets equal to A_{66} when the annuity is established, the annual annuity that the individual would receive in the sixty-seventh year is $a_{67} = A_{66}/\text{APV}$ if the expected return of R is actually realized in the sixty-sixth year. In practice, of course, the actual rate of return varies from year to year. The annuity payments are adjusted in proportion to the annual changes in the asset value in such a way that the accumulated fund of the individuals with survival probabilities $p_{s|66}$ is exhausted over the thirty-four-year potential retirement period. If R_s is the actual rate of increase of the asset value during year s, the value of the annuity paid in that year is $a_{67} = (A_{66}/\text{APV})([1 + R_{66}]/[1 + R])$. Similarly, the annuity at age sixty-eight reflects the changes in the market value of the assets during the sixty-sixth and sixty-seventh years: $a_{68} = a_{67}([1 + R_{67}]/[1 + R]) = (A_{66}/\text{APV})([1 + R_{67}]/[1 + R])([1 + R_{66}]/[1 + R])$.

These annuity payments leave no room for postretirement bequests in the sense that, for the birth cohort as a whole, the annuity payments between ages 67 and 100 just exhaust the aggregate value of the assets that had been accumulated at age sixty-six. It is possible, however, to reduce each annuity payment by some factor k and provide for a bequest at the time of the retiree's death. The value of k will depend on the particular bequest rule. We now consider two of the many possible types of possible bequest rules: (a) rules that combine actuarial life annuities and N-year certain payouts, and (b) a residual balance bequest rule that provides a lifetime annuity but also a bequest equal to the original accumulated PRA balance at the time of retirement (A_{66}) supplemented by the increases in the nominal account value resulting from investment returns until the time of death and reduced by the sum of the actual annuities paid to the retiree. Our use of a variable annuity (i.e., one in which the annuitant takes the risks associated with investing in a stock-bond portfolio) precludes bequest rules that promise a fixed dollar payment at death.[18]

Table 9.3 compares the costs and benefits of the different postretirement bequest rules. All of the options are assumed to include full *preretirement* bequests. The basic PRA saving rate in these simulations is 6 percent of wages.

The first row corresponds to the case (studied in section 9.3) in which there is a preretirement bequest but no postretirement bequest. With the 6 percent saving rate, the mean value of the annuity at age sixty-seven in 10,000 simulations is equal to 2.57 times the benchmark Social Security benefit in current law; this is shown in column (2). The corresponding median annuity, shown in the fifth column of table 9.2, is 1.78 times the benchmark benefit. The annuity reduction factor (column [1]) is the constant proportionality factor, k, by which the specified postretirement bequest reduces all annuity benefits relative to the benefits that would be paid with the preretirement bequest but no postretirement bequest. By definition, $k = 1$ for the "No Bequest" option of the first row. The "Required PRA Saving Rate" shown in column (3) is the saving rate required to have the same mean annuities at each retirement age as the option with no postretirement bequest based on a 6 percent saving rate (i.e., $6.0/k$).

9.4.1 Ten-Year and Twenty-Year Certain Annuities

In private pension plans, a popular alternative to a pure life annuity is an option that provides for a minimum number of years of annuity payments even if the retiree dies during those years. Two common forms are the "ten-year certain life annuity" and the "twenty-year certain life annuity." If the retiree dies after this specified period, there is no bequest.

The proportional reduction in the regular life annuity that is required to permit a ten-year certain payment is calculated by equating the actuarial present value of the regular life annuity ($\Sigma_{s=67 \text{ to } 100} a_s p_{s|66}[1 + R]^{-(s-66)}$) to the sum of a fixed ten-year reduced annuity ($\Sigma_{s=67 \text{ to } 76} k a_s [1 + R]^{-(s-66)}$) and the actuarial present value of the similarly reduced life annuity beginning eleven years after retirement ($\Sigma_{s=77 \text{ to } 100} k a_s p_{s|66}[1 + R]^{-(s-66)}$), where $1 + R = E(e^{r(s)})$ is the expected value of the gross return. The value of k calculated in this way implies that the preretirement saving rate that would be required to maintain the initial annuity distribution is simply the basic saving rate divided by the value of k because that raises the PRA assets at the time of retirement by the factor $1/k$.

The results for ten-year and twenty-year certain annuities are shown in the second and third rows of table 9.3. A ten-year certain payment reduces the available annuity by only 6 percent (i.e., by the factor $k = 0.94$ in

---

18. In practice it would, of course, be possible to have a portion of the funds in a fixed annuity, so that a fixed dollar payment at death could be promised.

Table 9.3   **Effects of Alternative Postretirement Bequest Rules**

Postretirement Bequest	Annuity Reduction Factor (1)	Relative Mean Annuity (2)	Required PRA Saving Rate (3)	Distribution of Bequests with 6% Saving Rate		Distribution of Bequests with Adjusted Saving Rate	
				Mean (4)	Standard Deviation (5)	Mean (6)	Standard Deviation (7)
None	1.00	2.57	6.00	0.00	0.00	0.00	0.00
10-year certain	0.94	2.41	6.42	0.52	0.66	0.56	0.71
20-year certain	0.83	2.13	7.26	1.51	2.35	1.83	2.84
Residual balance	0.71	1.83	8.46	2.49	3.73	3.51	5.26

Notes: Column 2 depicts the mean PRA annuity at each age relative to the Social Security "benchmark" benefit. Column 3 depicts the PRA saving rate required to make the mean annuity at each age equal to the value with no postretirement bequests. The mean and standard deviations of bequests in columns (5) through (8) are stated as the present value of bequests discounted to age 67 and stated as multiples of the mean wage when the cohort was aged 66.

column [1]). The ability of a 6 percent reduction in the annuity payment to compensate for the fact that the annuity will be paid for at least ten years even if the retiree dies before age seventy-seven reflects the relatively low mortality probability during those years. With the basic 6 percent saving rate, the mean annuity at age sixty-seven is still 2.41 times the benchmark Social Security benefit. Achieving the same mean annuity with the ten-year certain payment as with no postretirement bequest requires increasing the 6 percent saving rate by a factor of $1/k = 1.064$ to a saving rate of 6.42 percent (shown in column (3)).

The postretirement bequests are separate from the preretirement bequests and, for the cohort as a whole, are in addition to them. For any individual, the mean expected bequest is p(death before age sixty-seven) $*$ (mean preretirement bequest) $+ (1 - p$[death before age sixty-seven]) $*$ (mean postretirement bequest.)

Columns (4) and (5) show the mean and standard deviation of the postretirement bequests that would be available with the basic 6 percent saving rate. These bequest values are the present values as of age sixty-seven (discounting at the expected return on the PRA balances) and are reported as a multiple of the projected mean wage in the year that the cohort reached age sixty-seven ($44,087 in 1998 dollars). The value of 0.52 in column (4) of the second row implies that the mean of the postretirement bequests in the 10,000 simulations has a present value as of age sixty-seven of $22,925. Associated with this mean present value of bequests is a standard deviation shown in column (5). In interpreting this standard deviation, it should be noted that the distribution is lognormal and therefore not symmetric.

With the adjusted saving rate that is needed to maintain the same distribution of annuity payments that would prevail with no postretirement bequests—a saving rate of 6.42 percent—the value of the bequests rises by the same proportional amount. The mean bequest shown in column (6) is 0.56 times the mean wage in the year that the cohort reaches age sixty-seven.

A twenty-year certain rule means that the annuity payments continue after death until at least the time when the retiree would have been eighty-seven years old even if he dies before then. The extra ten years of guaranteed payments at a time when the mortality rate is increasing rapidly require a further reduction in benefits of 11 percent of the standard benefit, from 94 percent of the standard annuity with the ten-year certain rule to 83 percent with the twenty-year certain rule. However, even with this reduction, the 6 percent PRA saving rate implies a mean annuity at age sixty-seven that is still 2.13 times the benchmark Social Security benefit. To offset this decrease and achieve the same annuity distribution that would occur with no postretirement bequest requires increasing the 6 percent saving rate to 7.26 percent.

Columns (4) and (5) show the mean and standard deviation of the present value of postretirement bequests that would be available with the basic 6 percent saving rate, reported as a multiple of the mean wage in the year that the cohort reached age sixty-seven. The mean present value bequest as of age sixty-seven with the 6 percent saving rate is $66,571; this rises to $80,679 if the saving rate is adjusted to 7.26 percent.

9.4.2 Residual Balance Annuities

An alternative type of bequest rule would give heirs the actuarial value of the remaining lifetime annuity payments at the time of the retiree's death. This is equivalent to the original account value at the time of retirement (A_{66}) reduced by the sum of the annuities actually paid and supplemented by the increases (or decreases) in the nominal account values resulting from the investment returns. More explicitly, if the retiree dies at age s after receiving the annuity payment ka_s the bequest would evolve according to $A_s = (1 + R_{s-1})A_{s-1} - ka_s$. We refer to this as the residual balance bequest and show the main effects in the fourth row of table 9.3.

The required value of k can be calculated by equating the actuarial present value of the regular life annuity ($\Sigma a_s p_{s|66}[1 + R]^{-(s-66)}$) to the sum of the actuarial present value of the reduced annuity ($\Sigma ka_s p_{s|66}[1 + R]^{-(s-66)}$) and the actuarial present value of the bequests ($\Sigma [p_{(s+1)|66} - p_{s|66}]A_s[1 + R]^{-(s-66)}$) where $p_{(s+1)|66} - p_{s|66}$ is the probability of dying at age s and $1 + R = E(e^{r(s)})$ is the expected return on the PRA balance. We find that $k = 0.71$, a 29 percent reduction in the potential annuity levels relative to providing only preretirement bequests.

Even with this reduction, the PRA program with a 6 percent saving rate would provide a mean annuity that is 1.83 times the benchmark Social Security benefit (column [2]). To maintain the "no postretirement bequest" probability distribution of annuity income while giving the "residual balance" bequest requires raising the saving rate from 6.0 percent to 8.5 percent (column [3]).

Turning from the annuities to the bequests, with the 6 percent saving rate the present value of bequests as of age sixty-seven is 2.49 times the mean wage in the year that the cohort reaches age sixty-seven, or $109,777 in 1998 prices. With the saving rate raised to 8.5 percent to maintain the original distribution of retirement annuities, the mean present value of the bequests rises to $154,745.

9.5 Bequests to Spouses and Double Life Annuities

Bequests to spouses are different from intergenerational transfers. Social Security provides additional benefits to surviving spouses whose own benefits are relatively low, and private pension plans in the United States are required to continue annuity payments to surviving spouses unless a spouse specifically relinquishes his or her right to a benefit.

There are a variety of possible arrangements for providing annuity benefits to a surviving spouse.[19] The simplest of these is a double life annuity.
This provides that the variable annuity continues to be generated in the
same way until both the retiree and the retiree's spouse have died. The cost
of providing such a double life annuity depends on the sex of the primary
beneficiary (the "retiree") and the difference in age between the retiree and
the spouse. For our calculations, we assume a male retiree who is two years
older than his wife.

With this assumption, the probability that the spouse is alive at the time
of the retiree's death decreases from 0.89 if the retiree dies at age sixty-
seven to 0.75 if the retiree dies at seventy-seven and 0.51 if the retiree dies
at eighty-seven. Our simulations imply that replacing a single life annuity
with a double life annuity reduces the annuity that can be financed with
our 60–40 stock-bond investment mix by 20 percent. Alternatively, maintaining the same annual payments if the single life annuity is replaced
with a double life annuity requires raising the saving rate by 25 percent,
increasing, for example, from 6.0 percent to 7.5 percent.

The double life annuity can also be extended to permit bequests to other
heirs after the retiree and the retiree's spouse have both died. Using the
residual balance method of calculating bequests means permitting other
heirs to receive the actuarial value of the remaining account balance. This
is equivalent to reducing the original account value at the time of retirement (A_{66}) by the sum of the annuities paid to the retiree and spouse and
supplementing it with the increases in the account values resulting from
the investment returns. If the "second to die" dies when the retiree would
have been age s, the bequest would be A_s, which evolves from A_{66} according
to $A_s = (1 + R_{s-1})A_{s-1} - ka_s$. Table 9.4 shows the probability of bequest
to nonspousal heirs, the mean bequest, and the standard deviations of the
bequests at each age as well as the overall mean and standard deviation of
the bequests. These bequests are shown as multiples of the mean earnings
of employees in each year. The projected mean earnings (in 1998 dollars)
in each year are shown for comparison. The analysis for bequests in all
years (shown in the last row of the table) converts the bequests into multiples of mean covered earnings in the year that the bequest is received.

The probability of a bequest shown in column (1) includes preretirement
as well as postretirement bequests. In both situations, the other heirs receive bequests only if both the husband and wife have died.

19. Recall that our basic analyses (e.g., Feldstein and Samwick 1998a; Feldstein and Ranguelova 1998) assume that benefits will be provided, as specified in current law, to spouses,
survivors, and the disabled as well as to retirees. The bequests that we study in this paper
would be supplementary to these additional benefits already provided in current law. Note
that, with a PRA saving rate of 6 percent, the benefits that we calculate are not of the amount
that must be set aside to pay the disability and survivor benefits called for in current law.
Operationally, a fraction of the 6 percent PRA saving could be set aside to purchase survivor
and disability insurance while still financing the retirement benefits cited in this paper.

The probability that an heir other than a spouse receives a benefit in any year is low until the primary retiree is quite old, because until then the probability that at least one spouse is alive is quite high. With the 6 percent saving rate assumed in these calculations, the mean bequests when they occur are quite substantial, rising from $126,000 (3.4 times average individual annual earnings) at age fifty to $324,000 (7.2 times average individual annual earnings) when the second member of the couple dies at the time that the primary annuitant would have been seventy years old. This amount is six times the annual individual earnings in the year of bequest. The final row of table 9.4 shows that the mean bequest is 5.1 times the average covered earnings in the year that the bequest is made.

The bequests described in table 9.4 assume a couple with only a single earner, an increasingly rare situation in the American economy. When both members of a couple work, a double life annuity with residual bequests offers more attractive prospects to other heirs. We analyze in table 9.5 the situation for a two-earner couple, both of whom have double life annuities. In this analysis, both members of the couple receive a PRA annuity while they are alive. When the first member of the couple dies, the remaining member of the couple receives both annuity payments. At the death of the remaining member, the other heirs receive the actuarial value of the remaining balances in both annuities.

The specific distribution of such residual balance bequests depends on the ages of the couple and on the amounts that each earns. As an example, we consider a couple in which both members earn the average wage and in which the wife is two years younger than her husband. We assume that the preretirement bequest that is paid to a surviving spouse is consumed

Table 9.4	Postretirement Bequests to Nonspousal Heirs with a Double Life Annuity			
Age	Probability of Bequest to Nonspousal Heirs (1)	Mean Bequest (2)	Standard Deviation of Bequest (3)	Mean Earnings ($000) (4)
30	0.000008	0.5	0.1	31
40	0.000032	1.5	0.6	34
50	0.000097	3.4	2.1	37
60	0.000550	6.9	5.8	41
70	0.004024	7.2	8.6	45
80	0.020680	6.3	10.1	50
90	0.075238	4.5	9.8	55
All		5.1	10.0	42

Notes: The PRA account earns a mean return of 5.5 percent with a standard deviation of 12.5 percent; see text for more details. The employee in these calculations is a male with a spouse who is two years younger. Bequests are stated as multiples of the mean earnings in the year of the bequest. Mean earnings, shown in column (5), are in constant 1998 dollars.

Table 9.5   **Postretirement Bequests to Nonspousal Heirs: Two-Earner Couples with a Double Life Annuity**

Age	Probability of Bequest to Nonspousal Heirs (1)	Mean Bequest (2)	Standard Deviation of Bequest (3)	Mean Earnings ($000) (4)
30	0.000015	0.5	0.1	31
40	0.000065	1.6	0.7	34
50	0.000218	3.6	2.2	37
60	0.001129	7.2	6.1	41
70	0.007612	9.6	11.4	45
80	0.036794	10.5	16.7	50
90	0.131211	7.7	16.6	55
All		7.1	15.5	42

Notes: The PRA account earns a mean return of 5.5 percent with a standard deviation of 12.5 percent; see text for more details. Husband and wife in these calculations both earn the mean age-specific covered earnings in each year. Bequests are stated as multiples of the mean earnings in the year of the bequest. Mean earnings, shown in column (4), are in constant 1998 dollars. The age refers to the age of the husband in the year of the bequest.

during his or her lifetime. Although we understand that additional amounts may be bequeathed, for the purpose of this analysis we count as a bequest to other heirs only the amounts that come directly from PRA accounts or annuities and not funds that were accumulated by the decedent from previous bequests received or in other ways. Table 9.5 shows, as a function of the age that the husband is or would have been, the probability of a bequest to nonspousal heirs, the mean and standard deviation of those bequests, and the average earnings in that year.

The probability of a residual balance bequest to other heirs during the preretirement years is higher in a two-earner couple than in a single-earner couple because a wife who is the second to die has a PRA balance to bequeath. In a single-earner couple, the other heirs receive a preretirement PRA bequest only if the husband is the second to die.[20] Similarly, a widow who dies in the postretirement years and who has had no labor earnings of her own has no PRA account if her husband died before age sixty-seven. She therefore leaves no PRA bequest. In contrast, a widow who had her own earnings history can leave her annuity to her nonspousal heirs even if her husband died before she died.

The expected value of the bequests is also higher in the two-earner case, because on the death of the second spouse the heirs can receive the residual balance of two accounts per couple if both spouses die after age sixty-six.

20. Recall the distinction introduced in the previous paragraph between PRA bequests and other bequests.

9.6   Macroeconomic Consequences of Bequests

An investment-based Social Security system in which the PRA deposits represent incremental saving also raises the national saving rate. An examination of the potential magnitude of the increased capital accumulation is presented by Feldstein and Samwick (1998a), who estimate the evolution of PRA assets in an economy in which population and wage earnings grow between the years 1995 and 2070 according to the projections of the Social Security actuaries. The Feldstein-Samwick analysis assumes that 2 percent of the covered wages of each employee are deposited in PRAs each year, that these assets earn a real nonstochastic 5.5 percent rate of return, and that individuals receive actuarially fair annuities beginning at age sixty-five. There are no bequests in either the preretirement or postretirement years. With these assumptions, the aggregate balance in the PRA accounts reaches 38 percent of gross domestic product (GDP) by the year 2030 and 79 percent of GDP by the year 2070.[21]

The extent to which this accumulation of PRA assets raises the nation's capital stock depends on the way in which other private and public saving responds to the introduction of investment-based Social Security. We ignore these issues here and focus only on the way in which the introduction of bequests would alter the accumulation of PRA assets.[22]

Although our framework of analysis in the current paper does not permit us to calculate the effects of bequests on aggregate PRA assets in each year, we can show the impact of bequests on PRA asset accumulation by comparing the mean PRA asset values for representative individuals of different ages under the different bequest assumptions. The figures in column (1) of table 9.6 are the cohort's aggregate PRA accumulations with no bequests. These figures, based on a saving rate of 6 percent, are in billions of 1998 dollars and are shown as a function of the age of the cohort members. The cohort's PRA assets rise from $54 billion at age thirty to $978 billion at age sixty before beginning a postretirement decline during the next decade. These aggregate accumulation values correspond to amounts per cohort member of approximately $16,000 at age thirty and $280,000 at age sixty.

The effect of preretirement bequests is shown in column (2). Each figure in this column shows the assets at the identified age as a percentage of the baseline assets shown in column (1). Most of the reduction in assets occurs at ages close to retirement. At age fifty, the mean PRA balance is 96.7

21. The analysis is partial equilibrium and ignores the effect of this calculation on the marginal product of capital, the level of wages, and the tax rates required to fund government purchases of goods and services. An updated version of this analysis, using Social Security projections of 1998, is presented in Feldstein and Samwick (1999).
22. The effect of bequests on national saving depends also on what the individual bequest recipients do with the received amount.

Table 9.6   **PRA Assets as a Percent of the No Bequest Baseline with Different Bequest Rules**

Age	No Bequests Baseline ($billion) (1)	Preretirement Bequests Only (2)	10-Year Certain (3)	20-Year Certain (4)	Residual Balance (5)
30	54	99.5	99.5	99.5	99.5
40	181	98.5	98.5	98.5	98.5
50	446	96.7	96.7	96.7	96.7
60	978	92.1	92.1	92.1	92.1
70	917	86.3	87.5	92.6	91.2
80	546	86.3	80.7	106.0	106.8
90	179	86.2	80.6	71.2	116.7

Notes: Baseline PRA Assets are based on a PRA plan with no bequests. Dollar amounts are in 1998 dollars. The other bequest options all assume the preretirement bequests. The postretirement bequests shown in columns (4) through (6) are based on single life annuities.

percent of the no-bequest baseline amount. This declines to 86.6 percent by the time of retirement and remains at that level because no further bequests are made. These figures imply that the net reduction in total PRA assets of all generations at a point in time is likely to be less than 10 percent.

A ten-year certain annuity (in combination with the preretirement bequests), shown in column (3), implies a decline in PRA assets at all ages. Until retirement age, the decline is the same as with the pure preretirement bequest, because the ten-year certain annuity is only available after retirement age. Between ages sixty-seven and seventy-seven the PRA assets decline more slowly because the annuity payout rate is reduced in order to finance the ten-year certain option. The difference, however, is not large. After age seventy-seven the assets are smaller than with only the preretirement bequests because of the larger average annuity payout between ages sixty-seven and seventy-seven and the corresponding reduced annuity to be financed after age seventy-seven.

With the twenty-year certain option, the PRA assets actually rise relative to the baseline amount during the early retirement years, because in those years the reduced level of the annuity outweighs the twenty-year certain payments made to the heirs of those who have died. By age eighty-seven, however, the annuity payments must be lower than in the ten-year certain case (to compensate for the greater number of years of guaranteed benefits), and therefore the assets that support those annuities must be lower.

Finally, the residual balance bequests imply higher assets at all ages because of the much more substantial reduction of the annuity payments. Unlike the ten-year certain and twenty-year certain annuities, in the residual balance case the assets do not decline in old age because the annuity benefits remain unchanged, and the expected value of the residual balance bequest increases as the assets accumulate.

In general, therefore, permitting bequests is likely to reduce PRA assets by relatively small amounts. Even these modest declines overstate the effect of bequests on total capital accumulation because they do not take into account the effect of bequests on non-PRA assets that are accumulated as a result of PRA bequests. Moreover, if the PRA saving rate is adjusted to stabilize the annuity levels, the net effects of bequests on asset accumulation would be positive.

9.7 Conclusions

Experience in private pension plans and recent policy discussions about Social Security suggest that some form of bequests is likely to be part of any enacted investment-based Social Security reform. This paper provides a first examination of the potential magnitudes of such bequests and of their effect on retirement annuities and asset accumulation.

Investment-based PRAs would accumulate substantial funds, some of which would be distributed as bequests. We analyze the effects of a 6 percent saving rate, a level that would provide a nearly 80 percent probability that the annuity payments at age sixty-seven are at least equal to the future benefits promised in current Social Security law. (Pure PAYGO financing would require a payroll tax rate of more than 18 percent to finance the same benefits.) With such a saving rate, the cohort reaching age twenty-one in 1998 would expect to accumulate more than $50 billion by age thirty and more than $900 billion by age sixty, all expressed in the prices of 1998. These amounts are about $16,000 per employee at age thirty and $300,000 at age sixty.

The most likely form of bequest is the preretirement bequest, made when employees die before retirement age. The alternative to such bequests would be a 100 percent tax at death on all accumulated PRA assets or an administratively complex system of mandatory annuitization of all savings as they accumulate. Providing such bequests reduces the funds available for postretirement annuities by about 16 percent or, equivalently, requires a one-sixth increase in the PRA saving rate (e.g., from 6 percent to 7 percent) to maintain the same level of postretirement annuities as would be possible with the mandatory annuitization of all savings.

We also analyze a variety of postretirement bequest options. The least costly option that we consider is adding a ten-year certain feature to the life annuity, thereby providing a bequest whenever the retiree dies before age seventy-seven. This would reduce annuities, relative to providing only preretirement bequests, by about 6 percent. The most costly option that we consider would provide a bequest equal to the remaining actuarial value of the PRA annuity at the time of death and would require reducing all annuities by about 29 percent. These reductions in the annuity levels could be avoided by increasing the PRA saving rate by a corresponding amount. The size of the bequests and the impact on asset accumulation are proportional to the PRA saving rate. The results in this paper are based on a PRA saving rate of 6 percent, a level of saving that could in principle eventually substitute completely for the PAYGO tax and finance all benefits with a margin of safety. The PRA saving rate required for the more realistic task of stabilizing the current 12.4 percent payroll tax rate, while maintaining the benefits projected under current law, would be about 2 percent. The pension and capital accumulation effects of such a mixed system would be about one-third of the amounts shown in this paper.

References

Bernheim, Douglas, and S. Severinov. 1999. Bequests as signals: An explanation for the equal division puzzle, unigeniture, and ricardian non-equivalence. Stanford University, Department of Economics. Mimeograph, April.

Bernheim, Douglas, A. Shleifer, and L. Summers. 1985. The strategic bequest motive. *Journal of Political Economy* 93 (6): 1045–76.

Brown, Jeffrey R., Olivia S. Mitchell, and James M. Poterba. 1999. The role of real annuities and indexed bonds in an individual accounts retirement program. In *Risk aspects of investment-based social security reform*, ed. John Campbell and Martin Feldstein, 321–60. Chicago: University of Chicago Press.

Feldstein, Martin, ed. 1998. *Privatizing social security*. Chicago: University of Chicago Press.

Feldstein, Martin, and E. Ranguelova. 1998. Individual risk and intergenerational risk sharing in an investment based social security system. NBER Working Paper no. 6893. Cambridge, Mass.: National Bureau of Economic Research.

Feldstein, Martin, E. Ranguelova, and A. Samwick. 1999. The transition to investment-based social security when portfolio returns and capital profitability are uncertain. In *Risk aspects of investment-based social security reform*, ed. John Campbell and Martin Feldstein, 41–81. Chicago: University of Chicago Press.

Feldstein, Martin, and A. Samwick. 1997. The economics of prefunding Social Security and Medicare benefits. In *NBER macroeconomics annual 1997*, 115–47. Cambridge, Mass.: MIT Press.

———. 1998a. Potential effects of two percent personal retirement accounts. *Tax Notes* 79 (5): 615–20.

———. 1998b. The transition path in privatizing social security. In *Privatizing Social Security*, ed. M. Feldstein, 215–60. Chicago: University of Chicago Press.

———. 1999. Maintaining Social Security benefits and tax rates through personal retirement accounts: An update based on the 1998 Social Security Trustees Report. NBER Working Paper no. 6540R. Cambridge, Mass.: National Bureau of Economic Research, March.

Kotlikoff, Laurence. 1996. Privatization of social security: How it works and why it matters. *Tax Policy and the Economy* 10:1–32.

———. 1998. Simulating the privatization of social security in general equilibrium. In *Privatizing Social Security,* ed. M. Feldstein, 265–310. Chicago: University of Chicago Press.
Rosen, Harvey, D. Holtz-Eakin, and D. Joulfaian. 1993. The Carnegie conjecture: Some empirical evidence. *Quarterly Journal of Economics* 108 (May): 413–35.
World Bank. 1994. *Averting the old age crisis.* Washington, D.C.: World Bank.

Comment   Jonathan Skinner

One positive influence of a privatized Social Security system is that contributors feel a proprietary interest in their accumulating accounts. This encourages greater responsibility for prudent investment choices and helps contributors to view Social Security payments as saving rather than a burdensome tax. Developing a proprietary interest, however, also raises the potential for resentment in the event of an early death—why, the contributor might think, should the government confiscate *my* investments? Under the current system, of course, there is little or no sense of ownership, so the idea that benefits cease at the time of death does not appear quite so unfair.

Feldstein and Ranguelova have anticipated this hurdle faced by a privatized Social Security system and have proposed a sensible and economically sound solution—that contributors be allowed to bequeath some of their accumulated benefits in the event of an early death. The purpose of the paper is to quantify how much a modest bequest package would cost, either in terms of increased payments into the Social Security system or in terms of reduced benefits. The major result is that the costs of setting up such a program are quite modest, often costing less than 1 percentage point of additional saving. The analysis is very carefully performed, and I have no reservations about the approach that they take or the parameter values they use to estimate the costs of bequests.

What I will argue in these comments is that Feldstein and Ranguelova are, if anything, too modest in presenting their case for bequests, or for some kind of lump-sum award near death. The potential tradeoff between annuities and a payoff near death holds for *any* Social Security system. That is, enrollees in the current Social Security system may be willing to give up modest levels of benefits, or pay slightly more in taxes or contributions, so as to enjoy the insurance value of lump-sum payments in the event of early death or other contingency. Indeed, there is a death benefit equal to $255 under the current Social Security system, apparently de-

Jonathan Skinner is the John French Professor of Economics at Dartmouth College and a research associate of the National Bureau of Economic Research.

signed to help with burial costs, but clearly not indexed to inflation! Although the Feldstein and Ranguelova results are clearly designed to dovetail with a more thoroughly developed Social Security plan (as in Feldstein and Samwick 1997; Feldstein, Ranguelova, and Samwick 2001; or Kotlikoff 1996), the striking results shown in their paper raise a more general issue about the optimal payout schedule for any annuitization program.

It is useful as a starting point to think about a simple life-cycle model wherein the only uncertainty is the time of death. Then the individual would prefer to annuitize all retirement wealth, and the optimal Social Security benefit should replicate the optimal postretirement consumption stream. If the optimal consumption path increases over time (for example, because the interest rate exceeds both the discount rate and the annual probability of dying), then the Social Security payment should increase over time, and conversely. In this idealized story, Social Security provides complete annuitization of retirement consumption, and it is smooth, without death benefits or any contingency payment. Even in the case in which Social Security provides incomplete annuitization, as is true for the vast majority of Social Security beneficiaries, the optimal Social Security payment could be a smooth consumption payment that might even increase over time in real terms to provide the maximum degree of insurance against living to an old age.

As Feldstein and Ranguelova and others have observed, the world is not simply a certainty life-cycle model. People do have preferences to leave bequests, whether through life insurance policies at younger years, or by choosing "ten-year certain annuities at retirement (through TIAA-CREF), which pay ten years of benefits, either to the primary enrollee or to the designated heir, following an early death.

It is useful to distinguish, as Feldstein and Ranguelova do, between bequests designed for younger decedents and bequests for older postretirement decedents. For younger contributors, grafting an actuarially fair term life insurance with low administrative costs onto a privatized Social Security system is not very expensive as long as the probability of death is low. The benefits could also be substantial, particularly if the decedent has not adequately provided for his or her spouse and children; Bernheim et al. (1999), for example, suggest that many households hold life insurance coverage that would prove inadequate should the principal earner die.

It is important to note that Social Security already has in place survivorship benefits that partially address this problem for younger decedents. In 1996, an average of $487 per month was paid to some 1.9 million dependent children of deceased enrollees, for a total of about $11 billion annually (U.S. House of Representatives 1998). Paying out an annuity may be more useful for supporting children, since a single lump-sum life insurance payment could be spent rapidly by a surviving parent or stepparent, leaving little or nothing for the child's support. On the other hand, their proposed insurance plan does not replace the dependent children program, but supplements it; the revenue projections in the Feldstein, Ranguelova, and Samwick (2001) proposal allow for full continued funding of the program for dependent children and spouses.

The issues surrounding bequests among postretirement elderly people are somewhat more complicated, as the cost of such a program can be quite large, given the much higher mortality rates in this population and hence the much higher costs of providing a death benefit.[1] Nor is there quite the same perceived need for bequests beyond spousal support, since the children of the decedents are typically either at their peak earning capacity or nearly retired themselves. Nevertheless, Feldstein and Ranguelova have touched upon a legitimate desire for retirees to leave bequests, and as long as they are willing to pay more in taxes, or reduce their annuitized benefits, it is reasonable to consider providing such an option.

Evidence from the 1995 Survey of Consumer Finances certainly appears to support the view that the demand for leaving a bequest is strong. Of a broad sample of individuals asked, more than half replied that they thought leaving a bequest is important or very important (Dynan, Skinner, and Zeldes 2000). If anything, the fraction desiring to leave a bequest was slightly higher among high school dropouts than among college graduates, so the interest exists across broad socioeconomic groups. Thus, it might appear that providing an option to leave a bequest provides exactly what contributors want.[2]

A somewhat different view, however, on the motives for saving comes from respondents to a question in the 1983–1989 Survey of Consumer Finances panel with respect to their motives for saving. Of retired households, 43 percent replied either "in case of illness" or "emergencies" as their most important reasons for saving, with less than 5 percent mentioning saving for their children. How can these two survey responses be reconciled? Dynan, Skinner, and Zeldes (2000) suggest a model in which saving while old serves a dual role of both guarding against future catastrophic or end-of-life expenses (with a small probability p) and the more likely function of providing a bequest for heirs (with a higher probability of $1 - p$).

The message from these survey questions, therefore, suggests a more complicated story than a simple bequest motive. If a Social Security sys-

---

1. It seems likely, however, that mortality for this age group will fall in coming years (Lee and Skinner 1999), making the bequest option that much less costly.
2. This raises a related question: Why don't enrollees simply save for a bequest on their own? The answer may be linked to the justification for a forced saving program such as Social Security; perhaps there is a problem with making intertemporal plans that are dynamically consistent among some households, as in Laibson (1997) or Akerlof (1991).

tem wanted to replicate, through forced saving, what people *said* they were saving for, then the nature of the benefits might be quite different from a bequest. Perhaps beneficiaries would prefer an option that allows them to spend down some of their bequest balances for nursing home care or medication should they be stricken with serious illness. Perhaps a program that protects them against inflationary erosion of bonds or other assets that they rely upon for retirement income would be another option. An elderly couple in which one person is battling Alzheimer's disease may prefer to access some of their cash balances instead of passing them along to their heirs.

Instituting such a program would raise all sorts of difficult questions in terms of who is and is not eligible to access the bequest balances and how to design the program to prevent abuses or fraud. Particularly for a privatized Social Security system with personal accounts, a simple bequest program might be most practical, particularly if private markets arise that allow beneficiaries to borrow against such payments. However, the general point remains that if the Social Security system, privatized or not, wishes to expand benefits beyond the standard option that provides for a smooth level of annuity payments, it should determine why people save, and design benefits that capture, as closely as possible, those motives for saving.

References

Akerlof, George A. 1991. Procrastination and obedience. *American Economic Review* 81 (2): 1–19.

Bernheim, B. Douglas, Lorenzo Forni, Jagadeesh Gokhale, and Laurence J. Kotlikoff. 1999. The adequacy of life insurance: Evidence from the health and retirement survey. NBER Working Paper no. 7372. Cambridge, Mass.: National Bureau of Economic Research, October.

Dynan, Karen, Jonathan Skinner, and Stephen Zeldes. 2000. Do the rich save more? Dartmouth College. Mimeograph.

Feldstein, Martin, Elaine Ranguelova, and Andrew Samwick. 2001. The transition to investment-based social security when portfolio returns and capital productivity are uncertain. In *Risk aspects of investment based social security reform,* ed. J. Campbell and Martin Feldstein, 41–87. Chicago: University of Chicago Press.

Feldstein, Martin, and Andrew Samwick. 1997. The economics of prefunding social security and Medicare benefits. *NBER Macroeconomics Annual 1997.* Cambridge, Mass.: MIT Press.

Kotlikoff, Laurence. 1996. Rescuing Social Security. *Challenge* 39 (6): 21–22.

Laibson, David. 1997. Golden eggs and hyperbolic discounting. *Quarterly Journal of Economics* (May): 443–77.

Lee, Ron, and Jonathan Skinner. 1999. Will aging baby boomers bust the federal budget? *Journal of Economic Perspectives* 13 (1): 117–40.

U.S. House of Representatives. Committee on Ways and Means. 1998. *1998 green book overview of entitlements programs.* Washington, D.C.: GPO.

Discussion Summary

Stephen C. Goss noted that, although Social Security does not provide a lump-sum bequest, it does provide child survivor benefits as well as benefits for a spouse caring for a child. The present value of these benefits to a twenty-seven-year-old with average earnings, a spouse, and two young children is between $250,000 and $300,000. These benefits are intended to replace lost income. If the twenty-seven-year-old had life insurance or other assets, these monthly Social Security survivor benefits would allow a family to maintain its existing assets. In this situation there is little difference between a lump sum benefit and an annuity.

Gary Burtless believed that there is not a very strong public policy case for bequests. Why should a labor tax be imposed on everybody to fund bequests? Why should old age and survivor benefits be linked to bequests to people that may not have any financial need for these bequests? Clearly, this is a very inefficient way to reduce the Gini coefficient for the financial wealth distribution. The authors responded that there are two reasons to study bequests. First, people seem to like bequests, because they do not want the wealth in their government-sponsored individual accounts to be taken away by the government when they die. Perhaps more importantly, there has been significant interest in bequests by the policy makers considering Social Security reform, so whether or not bequests are a good idea, it is important to understand how they would work. In particular, a senator may believe that increasing the individual account contribution rate from 6 percent to 7 percent is a reasonable price to pay for having a system with bequests, and providing policy makers with the information necessary to make those choices is valuable.

Stephen Zeldes worried about the availability of annuities in private markets. If the level of annuitization is reduced in the current system or a system with individual accounts, will people be able to purchase similar annuities from financial institutions? Is there a large adverse selection problem in the private sector? Mandatory annuities in the Social Security system may be actuarially more fair than annuities offered by insurance companies.

Jeffrey B. Brown found the residual balance annuity to be a somewhat puzzling design feature. If a retiree's estate receives the full remaining actuarial balance of the account after death, then the retiree's resources are no longer really annuitized. Instead, the retiree is simply amortizing the account balance at a variable rate over the maximum remaining life span. One implication of this amortization approach is that the choice of the maximum life span has a more important effect on the income that is available to retirees than true life annuities, the future payments of which are discounted by survival probabilities. In this paper, the account balance is amortized over thirty-three years, which may not be long enough, given that more and more people are living beyond age 100. A higher maximum life span would further reduce the income that is available from these residual balance annuities.

Eytan Sheshinski indicated that first-best efficiency could be achieved using life insurance markets. After retirement, when most of the uncertainty about income has unfolded, individuals want a bequest of a particular size. A ten-year certain (any year certain) annuity merely offers a random bequest, because the size of the bequest depends upon when the individual dies. Bundling Social Security and bequests seems to have problems. Why not allow people to choose the size of their bequest by purchasing life insurance with some percentage of their Social Security benefits? In addition, it could be interesting to examine simulations in which bequests before retirement are an increasing function of age. Such a program would definitely be more cost-effective and might be sensible if bequests become more important as people age.

Laurence J. Kotlikoff mentioned a reason to avoid committing to life insurance. Because income uncertainty is largely unresolved for a retired individual's children, the size of the bequest motive could be changing significantly over time. Since life insurance and annuity markets have adverse selection problems and administrative costs, many people might decide to share risk with their children and avoid the private sector completely.

Martin Feldstein emphasized a more basic problem that underlies all discussions of bequests. The standard models indicate that people will choose to buy some combination of life insurance and annuities. Clearly, the decision-making procedure is poorly understood because the actual behavior observed is quite different. People care about leaving something to the next generation, but they also care about how they make this bequest. For example, people might desire to bequeath wealth in the same way that it was bequeathed to them. The recent stock market rise has made universities, museums, and so on very rich, yet that has not stopped donors from contributing after these organizations met their goals for capital accumulation. People care about the process.

10

Differential Mortality and the Value of Individual Account Retirement Annuities

Jeffrey R. Brown

Numerous proposals have emerged for supplementing or partially replacing the current U.S. Social Security system with a system of individual savings accounts. These accounts are similar to defined contribution pension plans, in that each individual contributes a fraction of annual earnings so that, upon reaching retirement, the individual then has a potentially large stock of wealth from which to finance consumption in the remaining years of life. Under such a system, a retired individual faces the problem of choosing a consumption path financed by the assets accumulated in the individual account without incurring too great a risk of outliving available resources. One way to avoid this risk is to purchase a life annuity contract, which promises a stream of income for as long as the policyholder is alive.

This paper examines the distributional implications of alternative annuity options within a mandatory retirement savings system. Distributional considerations arise from heterogeneity in mortality risk across the population, as life annuities are structured to transfer unused resources of early decedents to longer-lived individuals. For purposes of this paper, transfers from shorter-lived to longer-lived individuals should not, in and of themselves, be considered "redistribution." If everyone experienced the same risk of dying at each age, then every individual would have an equal chance of being the survivor, and thus an annuity would not redistribute in expec-

Jeffrey R. Brown is an assistant professor of public policy at the John F. Kennedy School of Government, Harvard University, and a faculty research fellow of the National Bureau of Economic Research.

The author is grateful to Peter Diamond, Martin Feldstein, Estelle James, Jeff Liebman, Olivia Mitchell, Jim Poterba, Andrew Samwick, Dimitri Vittas, and NBER conference participants for helpful comments and discussions. He thanks Stephanie Plancich and Joshua Pollet for excellent research assistance, and the National Institute on Aging and the National Bureau of Economic Research for financial support.

tation. Rather, the ex post transfers that would occur would simply be carrying out the very function of an annuity market.

This paper focuses on the redistribution that arises from differences in the *expected* transfers between particular demographic groups in an individual accounts system as a result of mortality differences. Heterogeneity in mortality means that annuities that ignore individual or group characteristics will result in expected transfers away from high-mortality risk groups to low-mortality risk groups. The groups considered in this paper are differentiated by gender, race, Hispanic status, and level of education. Mortality rates differ substantially across these groups, leading to very different valuations of annuities. Calculations suggest that the size of the expected transfers is quite sensitive to the specific design of the annuity program.

The extent of redistribution depends on how both the accumulation phase and the payout phase are designed. In the accumulation phase, the key question is whether or not to allow preretirement bequests. The probability of a present twenty-two-year old's dying prior to retirement age and thus leaving a bequest were one permitted is very high for certain demographic groups. For example, while 20 percent of all men who are twenty-two years old in the year 2000 will die prior to reaching age sixty-seven, this probability is as high as 41.2 percent for black males with less than a high school education, and as low as 13.1 percent for college-educated white males. Therefore, even though lifetime earnings will be much lower for poorly educated black males, the expected discounted value of bequests for this group is 56 percent larger than it is for college-educated white males.

Assuming an individual survives to retirement age, there are numerous dimensions along which the payout phase can be designed, including the structure of the payment trajectory, the number of lives covered, and the survivor and bequest options that are included. Results indicate that the degree of redistribution that occurs within an individual accounts system is quite sensitive to the specific structure of this payout phase. Mandating the use of a single life, inflation-indexed annuity leads to very substantial transfers from men to women, from blacks to whites and Hispanics, and from lower education groups to higher ones. The size of these expected transfers can be significantly reduced through the use of joint and survivor annuities, period-certain or refund options, or "frontloading" in annuity payments. However, the mechanisms that lessen the extent of redistribution often do so at the expense of insurance provision, because the way to reduce the impact of mortality differentials is to lessen the importance of mortality in the calculation of benefits. Period-certain and refund options do this, but at the expense of providing a lower level of monthly income. In the extreme, one could completely eliminate redistribution by forgoing annuitization entirely. However, to do so would be to forgo the potentially large welfare gains that arise from access to annuitization.

This paper is organized as follows. Section 10.1 examines the impact of gender, race, and socioeconomic status on mortality risk. The relevant literature on differential mortality is reviewed, and then new estimates are presented that use the National Longitudinal Mortality Study. Section 10.2 discusses the accumulation phase of an annuity, with particular focus on how differential mortality affects the decision of whether to allow for preretirement bequests. Section 10.3 examines the "money's worth" of annuities for each demographic group under several different assumptions about how the payout phase is designed, including real annuities, nominal annuities, period-certain options, joint life products, and refund options. It also discusses implications for variable annuity design, as well as the impact of partial or delayed annuitization. Section 10.4 provides a brief discussion of how the results change if we loosen the constraint that all individuals face the same price. Section 10.5 concludes.

10.1   Mortality Differentials by Gender, Race, and Economic Status

10.1.1   Previous Literature on Differential Mortality

At least since the influential study by Kitagawa and Hauser (1973), it has been known that mortality differs across socioeconomic groups in the United States. In addition to documenting the significant differences in mortality across racial lines, Kitagawa and Hauser found differences along educational and income margins. One of their most-cited findings is that mortality varied inversely with the level of educational attainment. They found that for those aged twenty-five to sixty-four, this inverse and monotonic relationship between years of schooling and mortality existed for all race and sex classes.

In the years following this study, the literature on differential mortality has grown rapidly, and consequently I will not attempt to provide a comprehensive review of this literature.[1] Rather, I focus on what the literature has found with respect to the four factors—gender, race, ethnicity and measures of economic status—that form the basis for the analysis that follows.

Gender

It is well known that mortality rates of females are lower than those of males. This differential exists at all ages in the United States, leading to significant differences in life expectancy for men and women. The cohort

---

1. Readers interested in a more complete review of the literature should consult Feinstein (1993).

used in this paper, those turning age twenty-two in the year 2000, had a life expectancy at birth (in 1978) of 75.5 years for males and 82.1 years for females. To account for these differences in the analysis that follows, estimation of mortality rates will be performed separately for males and females.

Race and Hispanic Status

Racial and ethnic differences in mortality also exist, although there is controversy about the precise nature of these differences. It is generally agreed that mortality rates of blacks are higher than that of whites at all ages below seventy-five, for both men and women. However, a number of studies have reported that there exists a mortality "crossover" between blacks and whites at older ages, meaning that black mortality rates fall below those of whites at older ages (Sorlie et al. 1992). However, other authors have concluded that the racial crossover does not exist but, rather, is a result of "serious errors and inconsistencies in the data on which national estimates of African-American mortality at older ages are based" (Preston et al. 1996). The ages reported on death certificates appear to be systematically younger than those reported in the U.S. Census. As a result, when researchers correct for this misreporting bias, the racial crossover in mortality disappears. If the racial crossover exists before or shortly after retirement, it is potentially important for understanding how blacks fare relative to whites under alternative annuitization schemes. While resolving this conflict is beyond the scope of this paper, I find little evidence of racial crossover in the data and therefore make no corrections in the analysis that follows.

While research on the mortality experience of Hispanics is more limited, available evidence suggests that U.S. Hispanics have lower mortality rates than non-Hispanic whites, despite a greater proportion of Hispanics living in poverty, lacking health insurance, and having more limited access to health care (Sorlie et al. 1993). Hispanics tend to have lower rates of heart disease, cancer, and pulmonary disease, although these differences do not seem to be explained by the major known risk factors for these diseases, suggesting perhaps a genetic or biological explanation. However, there are several reasons to suspect that some of the observed difference is not real but, rather, due to sampling bias. For example, if sampling techniques tend to undersample less healthy Hispanics (e.g., migrant farm workers), this would bias mortality rates down. In addition, studies like the National Longitudinal Mortality Study (NLMS), which is used in this paper, obtain mortality information by linking to the National Death Index (NDI). This means that, because deaths outside of the United States are not recorded in the NDI, some individuals' deaths will therefore be missed. One research has labeled this effect the "Salmon bias," due to the "compulsion to die in one's birthplace," which leads to a bias in mortality rates (Pablos-

Mendez 1994). In the NLMS data, I find that mortality rates for Hispanic women are, in fact, lower than those for white women at most ages. For Hispanic men, the data indicate that mortality rates tend to be slightly higher than for white men through the late forties and then fall below that of white men until the late eighties.

It should also be noted that there is substantial heterogeneity within the Hispanic population. Of particular importance is the fact that foreign-born persons tend to have lower mortality risk than native-born persons (Sorlie et al. 1993). Because a large fraction of the U.S. Hispanic population is foreign born, this "healthy migrant effect" may partially explain the lower mortality rates among Hispanics. Projecting forward, if the native-born segment of the U.S. Hispanic population increases as a share of the total Hispanic population, these mortality differentials may decrease.

Economic Status

A third factor that is significantly correlated with mortality is an individual's economic status. The evidence suggests that individuals who are in a higher socioeconomic group tend to live longer. There is, however, no definitive way to measure these effects. Three measures of economic status are used in the literature, namely education, income, and wealth, and each is subject to its own limitations.[2]

A significant negative correlation between education and mortality is frequently found (Kitawaga and Hauser 1973; Deaton and Paxson 2001; Lantz et al. 1998). This could be due to the fact that education serves as a rough proxy for lifetime earnings, and hence reflects the fact that people with more resources tend to live longer. On the other hand, there could be a very direct effect of education on mortality if, for example, more highly educated individuals better understand the risks of certain behaviors and avoid them as a result. In this paper, I will use education as the only proxy for lifetime resources. This choice is driven in part by a belief that education is a better proxy for lifetime resources than other measures, and in part by necessity—the NLMS income data are of questionable value, and wealth data do not exist.

A second widely used indicator of economic status is a measure of individual or family current income. Again, a significant negative correlation between income and mortality is universally found (e.g., Kitawaga and Hauser 1973; Hadley and Osei 1982; Lantz et al. 1998; Kaplan et al. 1996; Deaton and Paxson 2001). In fact, many of these studies indicate that income and education have independent effects. However, current income is a poor measure of lifetime resources for several reasons. The most important criticism of this approach is the problem of simultaneous causa-

---

2. Smith (1999) provides an excellent discussion of the issues involved in understanding these relationships.

tion between income and health. Low-income individuals are more likely to suffer from health problems and thus experience higher mortality rates. However, it is also true that individuals in poor health may be unable to earn a high income, in which case the causality of the relationship is reversed. As a result, it is quite difficult to provide any causal interpretation to the coefficient in a simple regression of mortality rates on current income.

A third measure of economic status that is used in the literature is wealth. Attanasio and Hoynes (2001), Menchik (1993), and Palmer (1989) all provide compelling evidence that wealth and mortality are inversely correlated. The use of wealth partially addresses the simultaneity problem that arises when using current income, since presumably wealth accumulation is less affected by health problems. However, as noted by Attanasio and Hoynes (2001), wealth cannot be considered a purely exogenous variable, both because of correlation with health, and because wealth accumulation behavior of individuals with different life expectancies could be different.

10.1.2   Previous Literature on Social Security and Differential Mortality

The importance of differential mortality has not gone unnoticed in the economics literature, especially with regard to its impact on Social Security. It has long been recognized that high-income individuals might receive relatively higher benefits relative to taxes paid than low-income individuals if they have a higher life expectancy. A spate of recent studies (Liebman, chap. 1 in this volume; Gustman and Steinmeier 1999; Coronado, Fullerton, and Glass, chap. 5 in this volume; Panis and Lillard 1996; Duggan, Gillingham, and Greenlees 1995; Garrett 1995) have investigated the progressivity of the existing Social Security benefit system, making use of mortality differences by economic factors. These authors agree that there are significant correlations between measures of economic well-being and mortality. Several of these authors find that the mortality differences, when combined with other features of the U.S. Social Security benefit rules, are sufficient to eliminate the progressivity of the current system on a lifetime basis.

All of the aforementioned papers have focused primarily on the impact of differential mortality on the existing Social Security system. However, these have limited applicability in quantifying the distributional impact of an individual accounts system. There are at least three distinct factors that affect the progressivity of the current system: a regressive payroll tax, a progressive benefit formula, and differential mortality.[3] Many individual account proposals do not involve progressive benefit formulas, and so the potentially regressive effects of mandated annuitization may have a much

---

3. In addition to these three factors, there are other features of the U.S. Social Security system that affect system progressivity, including spousal benefits, survivor benefits, and disability insurance.

more direct effect in such a system.[4] This paper, along with recent work by Feldstein and Liebman (chap. 7 in this volume), is among the first papers to explore the implications of mortality differentials within the specific context of an individual accounts system.

10.1.3   Estimates of Differential Mortality Using the National Longitudinal Mortality Survey

Rather than piece together estimates of the impact of gender, race, and economic status on mortality from several disparate sources, this paper uses new estimates from the NLMS. The NLMS is a survey of individuals who were originally included in the Current Population Survey and/or the Census in the late 1970s and early 1980s. Throughout the 1980s, death certificate information from the NDI was merged back into the survey data, allowing researchers to compare the death rates of individuals on the basis of demographic characteristics at the time of the interview.

Age-specific mortality estimates from the NLMS are constructed based on gender, race, ethnicity, and educational attainment.[5] I first construct separate mortality rates for black, white, and Hispanic males and females, a total of six groups. I then further differentiate whites and blacks into three education groups, namely less than high school, high school plus up to three years of college, and college graduates. Due to small sample sizes, it is not possible to differentiate Hispanics along educational lines. While the NLMS data do include a measure of family income in 1980, I do not make use of this information, due to the problem of simultaneous causation.

Several steps are required in order to use the NLMS to construct complete cohort mortality tables for specific groups. The first step is to split the NLMS sample into separate groups based on the gender, race, ethnic and education categories. For each group g, the age-specific nonparametric (np) mortality rate, $q_{x,g}^{np}$, is calculated as the fraction of those individuals age x who die before attaining age $x + 1$. This procedure provides a simple, nonparametric estimate of the age-specific mortality rate for individuals with the characteristics of group g.

There are several reasons one does not want to stop here and simply use these nonparametric estimates. First, sample sizes are quite small in some groups (e.g., college-educated black men) at many ages, and therefore the point estimates are noisy and even nonmonotonic with age, which is clearly inconsistent with known actuarial experience. Second, even if the NLMS data perfectly represented the population alive in 1980, this approach would only provide a 1980 "period" mortality table, or the mortality expe-

---

4. There is no reason that individual accounts cannot themselves be made redistributive.

5. The mortality estimates used in this paper were constructed in joint work with Jeffrey Liebman and Joshua Pollet, and more detail can be found in the appendix to this volume (Brown, Liebman, and Pollet). These estimates continued to be refined over time, and thus the estimates in the data appendix differ slightly from those used in this paper.

rience of individuals alive in 1980. For purposes of this study, the table of interest is a "cohort" mortality table that represents the mortality experience of individuals born in a particular year. The difference between these two tables arises from the fact that mortality rates have historically improved over time. Thus, some method of conversion from a 1980 period table to a particular birth cohort table is required. Third, the NLMS study is not fully representative of the entire U.S. population, in part because it excludes the institutionalized population and thus understates overall mortality rates. Therefore, although the NLMS may contain valuable information about the relative mortality rates of various groups, it is unlikely to provide accurate information about the absolute levels of mortality for the population as a whole.

In order to address these concerns, several additional steps are required. In order to correct for nonmonotonicity, the nonparametric estimates, $q_{x,g}^{np}$, are treated as the independent variable in a nonlinear least squares regression on age x. The nonlinear regression is used to estimate three parameters of a Gompertz-Makeham survival function. As explained in Jordan (1991), with the proper choice of the three parameters, this formula can be applied from about age twenty almost to the end of life. The Gompertz-Makeham formula used is

(1)
$$l_x = ks^x g^{c^x}$$

$$\text{where } k = \frac{l_0}{g}$$

$$\text{and } q_x = \frac{l_{x+1} - l_x}{l_x} ,$$

where x is age, and g, c, and s are the parameters to be estimated. Note that if l_0 is set equal to 1, then l_x is simply the cumulative survival probability at age x. Using the regression estimates of g, c, and s, one then has a "Makeham formula" that gives mortality q_x as a function of x. Let us denote these fitted values of mortality for group g at age x as $q_{x,g}^{fit}$. An important feature of this approach is that fitted mortality rates are a monotonically increasing function of age x. Another feature is that it allows one to create out-of-sample estimates of mortality. Therefore, although only data from age twenty-five to eighty-four are used to fit the curve, the formula can provide estimates of mortality for ages outside of this range.

Once these predicted mortality rates are in hand, the next step is to convert them into cohort life tables for each group by making two related assumptions. The first is that the ratio of a group's age-specific mortality to that of the population as a whole ($q_{x,g}/q_x$) in the NLMS sample is an accurate portrayal of these ratios in the full population in 1980. The second assumption is that these ratios are constant over time. By invoking these two assumptions, it is possible to then construct a group-specific cohort life table for any year.

Specifically, let $q_{x,g}^{\text{fit}}$ be the fitted value of the mortality rate for an individual age x belonging to group g, and let q_x^{fit} be the mortality rate for an individual age x for the population as a whole, both from the fitted NLMS data. Let q_x^{SSA} be the age-specific mortality rate from the 1978 birth cohort table from the Social Security Administration, which represents individuals turning age twenty-two in the year 2000. Then the cohort, group-specific mortality rates that I will use are constructed as follows:

$$(2) \qquad q_{x,g}^{\text{SSA}} = q_x^{\text{SSA}} \frac{q_{x,g}^{\text{fit}}}{q_x^{\text{fit}}}$$

The one exception to this methodology is that in the case of college- and high school–educated black males and females, I assumed that the mortality ratio between education groups was the same for blacks as for whites. I then applied the white education ratio to the fitted q's for blacks in order to construct the estimates for higher-educated blacks, because the sample sizes at many ages were too small for these black education groups for the reliable construction of an independent estimate.

Table 10.1 reports how the age to which a twenty-two-year-old in the year 2000 can expect to live varies by the gender, race, ethnicity, and education as calculated using the above methods. The average twenty-two-year-old male can expect to live to age 77.4, while the average twenty-two-year-old woman can expect to live to age 83.4. However, these estimates vary widely by race. White, black, and Hispanic twenty-two-year-old males have life expectancies of 78.3, 71.8, and 77.7 years respectively, and white, black and Hispanic females have life expectancies of 84.0, 80.0, and 85.2 years respectively.

Life expectancy conditional on reaching age twenty-two also varies substantially by education level. Twenty-two-year-old white men with less than a high school education can expect to live to age 75.3, a full 5.2 years less than that of a white male with a college degree. Low-educated black males have by far the lowest conditional life expectancy of any group examined, at 68.1 years. The highest conditional life expectancy is college-educated white women, who can expect to live to age 87.8.

Two partially offsetting limitations of these mortality differentials should be noted. First, using education as a proxy for lifetime earnings may actually understate the extent to which mortality rates differ across socioeconomic groups. Deaton and Paxson (2001) suggest that, even after controlling for education, income differentials may continue to have an independent effect on mortality. Second, these results do not differentiate based on disability status. Disabled individuals experience higher mortality rates than the nondisabled. If the disabled population is insured by a

Table 10.1   Conditional Life Expectancy by Gender, Race, Hispanic Status, and Education

	At Age 22		At Age 67	
	Men (1)	Women (2)	Men (3)	Women (4)
All	77.4	83.4	83.5	87.2
All Whites	78.3	84.0	83.6	87.4
All Blacks	71.8	80.0	82.3	86.1
All Hispanics	77.7	85.2	84.8	88.3
Whites				
College+	80.5	85.1	84.4	87.8
HS+	77.8	83.9	83.4	87.3
< HS	75.3	82.1	82.3	86.5
Blacks				
College+	75.7	81.9	83.4	86.8
HS+	71.6	80.0	82.2	86.1
< HS	68.1	77.5	81.0	85.1

Source: Author's calculations, as described in text.

Notes: "Conditional Life Expectancy" describes the age to which an individual may expect to live, conditional on having attained age 22 or 67.

separate program (e.g., the disability insurance program in the United States), then their higher disability rates should not be included when calculating the intergroup transfers that result from the retirement portion of an individual accounts program. If it were possible to condition mortality on being nondisabled, the average mortality rates would decline for all groups, but more so for those groups that have higher disability rates. The net effect of this change would likely be to reduce the amount of redistribution that occurs through a mandatory annuity program.

Because a life annuity is a financial vehicle that pays income contingent on the individual's being alive, people with longer life expectancies generally expect to receive more annuity income than individuals with shorter life expectancies. These differences suggest that demographic groups with lower average life expectancies will fare poorly under an annuity rule that mandates the use of a single annuity conversion factor, or a single price, for all individuals of the same age. However, these differences can vary substantially based on the specific form that the annuity takes. Therefore, the next section discusses annuities in more detail.

10.2   The Accumulation Phase

In general, there are two phases to an individual accounts retirement system. The "accumulation phase" corresponds to an individual's working life, when he or she is contributing a portion of earnings to an account that is invested in a diversified portfolio of securities. Then, upon retirement, the individual stops contributing to the account and starts the "payout phase" in order to finance retirement consumption.[6] The design of each of these phases has potentially important distributional effects. This section discusses the issues involved in the accumulation phase of the account. Section 10.3 discusses payout options.

The central question in the accumulation phase from a distributional perspective is what happens to the balance of an individual account upon the preretirement death of a worker. There are two options. First, the account may be considered part of the decedent's estate and thus be made available to the individual's family or other beneficiaries. Second, the account could become the "property" of the Social Security system and redistributed to the remaining workers in the system. In this latter case, the contributions made by early decedents are used to increase the rate of return to other participants in the system.

Let q_x represent the annual mortality rate for an individual of age x, and let r be the rate of return on investments in an individual account. For simplicity, let us assume that r is fixed. Under the first option, whereby the account balance is bequeathable, the gross annual rate of return on the account is simply $1 + r$ for all participants. If an individual contributes \$1 at the beginning of the year and survives, he will have $1 + r$ dollars in his account at the end of the year. If he dies, his estate will have a value of $1 + r$ dollars at the end of the year. In the second case, in which the assets of deceased participants are redistributed to remaining participants, the gross annual rate of return on the account, which I will call $(1 + R)$, is as follows:

$$(3) \qquad 1 + R = \begin{cases} \dfrac{1 + r}{1 - q_x} & \text{if alive ,} \\[2mm] 0 & \text{otherwise} \end{cases}$$

The $(1 - q_x)$ factor in the denominator is the amount by which the return is increased to survivors. Thus, if the investment rate of return is 5 percent, and 1 percent of the population dies during the year, the account balance of survivors would increase by 6.06 percent in that year. Feldstein and Ranguelova (chap. 9 in this volume) have shown that over the course of a lifetime, the cumulative effect of allowing preretirement bequests as part of a "Personal Security Accounts" system is to decrease the mean accumulation of assets at retirement by 14 percent.

Therefore, the question of whether to allow bequests boils down to a choice between providing wealth to estate beneficiaries or providing higher rates of return to those who live a long time. In thinking about the relative

---

6. The accumulation and payout phases may overlap in some cases, such as when an individual begins a partial annuitization process prior to retirement. For an example of this, see Kotlikoff and Sachs (1998).

importance of bequests across groups, one must consider two factors, namely the relative size of accounts (the "income effect") and the probability of dying before retirement age (the "mortality effect"). Individuals with large account accumulations and with a high probability of dying before retirement will benefit the most from the bequest option. However, these two factors often work in different directions: Individuals with larger account balances are likely to have lower mortality rates, due to the inverse correlation between economic status and mortality.

In order to estimate the net effect of allowing bequests, I have constructed a measure of the expected discounted value of bequests for each of the racial, ethnic, and education groups as follows: Suppose an "average" male enters the labor force at age twenty-two, earning annual income I_{22}. Assume that annual income increases each year at a real rate of $1 + g$, so that

$$(4) \qquad I_a = I_{22} \cdot (1 + g)^{a-22}$$

where a represents the individual's age. Assume that α is the fraction of income that is saved in an individual account each year, and that the account earns a real rate of interest r. If q_a represents the mortality rate at age a, and P_a represents the cumulative probability of surviving from age twenty-two to age a, then the expected present discounted value (EPDV) of future bequests is

$$(5) \quad \text{EPDV of Bequest} = \alpha \cdot I_{22} \cdot \sum_{a=22}^{67} \frac{\left[P_{a-1} \cdot q_a \cdot \sum_{s=1}^{a-21} (1 + g)^{s-1}(1 + r)^{a-20-s} \right]}{(1 + r)^{a-21}}.$$

If we assume that α, g, and r are the same for all groups, then differences in the expected present discounted value of bequests will arise from differences in mortality rates (P_a and q_a) and differences in the level of income (I_{22}).

To parameterize the income effect—that is, differences in I_{22}—I use the Social Security earnings records from the restricted data supplement to the Health and Retirement Survey (HRS). Specifically, I take the ratio of the mean Average Indexed Monthly Earnings (AIME) for males in each socioeconomic group to the mean AIME for all males (using HRS population weights). These ratios are reported in column (1) of table 10.2. As these results indicate, there are substantial differences in the level of income earned by each group, with the average white male earning 6 percent more, the average black male earning 30 percent less, and the average Hispanic male earning 28 percent less than the average for all three groups combined.[7] For purposes of calculations in table 10.2, I will assume that

7. These numbers reflect the AIME as of the survey date, when most of these individuals were still between the ages of fifty-one and sixty-one and thus still in the labor force. Consequently, these figures should be considered only a "rough approximation," as they do not control for differences in the age composition of each demographic group.

Table 10.2   Expected Bequests by Gender, Race, Hispanic Status, and Education (men only)

| | Ratio of Mean AIME (1) | Cumulative Probability of Bequest, by Age | | | | | EPDV of Bequest ($) (7) | Ratio of EPDV of Bequests (8) |
		30 (2)	40 (3)	50 (4)	60 (5)	67 (6)		
All	1.000	0.012	0.035	0.064	0.120	0.200	8,306	1.000
All Whites	1.058	0.009	0.027	0.053	0.105	0.182	8,178	0.985
All Blacks	0.696	0.033	0.087	0.141	0.224	0.323	8,504	1.024
All Hispanics	0.714	0.027	0.066	0.098	0.140	0.192	6,752	0.813
Whites								
College+	1.111	0.007	0.021	0.037	0.073	0.131	6,197	0.746
HS+	1.066	0.009	0.029	0.056	0.112	0.193	8,776	1.057
< HS	0.965	0.011	0.037	0.075	0.149	0.249	10,205	1.229
Blacks								
College+	0.864	0.027	0.064	0.098	0.154	0.230	7,512	0.904
HS+	0.733	0.033	0.087	0.142	0.227	0.328	9,111	1.097
< HS	0.624	0.040	0.111	0.185	0.294	0.412	9,651	1.162

Source: Author's calculations, as described in text.

Notes: AIME Ratio is the ratio of the mean value of Average Indexed Monthly Earnings for men in each group to the mean AIME of the entire male population as calculated from the Health and Retirement Survey. Cumulative Probability of Bequest is the probability that an individual dies before the age shown, conditional on being alive at age 22. EPDV of bequest is the expected discounted value of bequests calculated using equation (5) in text. The discount rate is 3 percent ($r = 0.03$), individual accounts consist of 6 percent of earnings ($\alpha = 0.06$), annual earnings at age 22 (I_{22}) are \$30,000 times the AIME ratio, and earnings grow at an annual real rate of 1 percent ($g = 0.01$). Ratio of EPDV of Bequests is the ratio of the EPDV of bequests for each group to that of all men.

these differences in AIME are indicative of a constant difference in annual earnings throughout one's working life. In other words, I use these ratios to shift the entire income path up and down, and assume that the slope of the income path [g in equations (4) and (5) above] is the same for all groups.

Columns (2) through (6) of table 10.2 report the cumulative probability of leaving a bequest at ages thirty, forty, fifty, sixty, and sixty-seven. These figures provide some insight into the "mortality effect" on bequests, namely that, holding account size equal, the expected value of bequests will be higher for individuals with higher mortality rates. As these columns indicate, there is substantial heterogeneity in the cumulative probabilities at all ages.

Column (7) reports the EPDV of bequests using equation (5) above, setting $g = 0.01$, $r = 0.03$, $\alpha = 0.06$, and $I_{22} = \$30,000$. As can be seen, the EPDV of bequests for each group lies in between \$5,932 and \$10,205. These rather small expected present values mask that fact that, conditional on dying and leaving a bequest, the average bequest size can be substantial. For example, with a riskless real interest rate of only 3 percent, the account balance of an "average" male would grow to over \$200,000 before retirement. Feldstein and Ranguelova (chap. 9, this volume) show that an individual investing in a mixed portfolio of bonds and equities would have an expected account size at retirement of nearly \$500,000. However, when these large bequests are discounted and multiplied by the relatively small probability of dying at each age, the expected present value of the average bequest is only \$8,306.

The final column of table 10.2 provides a simple metric by which to compare the importance of bequests across groups, which is the ratio of the expected discounted value of bequests for each group to that of the average male. As a starting point for interpreting these results, let us begin by comparing whites and blacks, without differentiating by educational attainment. Looking at column (1), we again see that whites have higher earnings than blacks, and therefore will (holding α and r equal) have higher individual account balances to bequeath. However, the probability of a black male's dying and leaving a bequest is substantially higher than that of a white male. The net effect is that the expected present value of bequests is approximately 4 percent higher for black men than white men (\$8,504 versus \$8,178).

Looking down the last column provides insight into which groups stand to benefit the most from bequests. Bequests are larger for lower education groups for both blacks and whites. Black men with a high school education or less, and white men with less than a high school education, have an expected discounted value of bequest that is much higher than the average for all men. This is driven primarily by high mortality rates among these groups. Bequests are smallest relative to the average for white college-educated men and for Hispanics. White college-educated men have earnings that are 11 percent higher than average but have a relatively low expected discounted value of bequests due to very low mortality rates. The Hispanic result is driven largely by the fact that their earnings are quite low, with an AIME ratio of only 0.714, and the fact that their mortality rates are lower than for other groups with similarly low earnings, such as low-educated blacks. On the whole, it appears that allowing preretirement bequests is most beneficial to lower socioeconomic groups. This is because the mortality effect is, in most cases, more important than the relative income effect.

10.3   The Payout Phase

Assuming survival to retirement age, the individual then enters the payout phase, or decumulation phase, of the individual account. Perhaps the single most important design decision that must be made at this point is whether to require annuitization of the account balances at all. Then, assuming that some level of annuitization is required, there are many additional choices that must be made. How will the annuities be priced? Will the payout be fixed in real terms or nominal terms, or will it vary with some underlying portfolio? Will there be any provisions for bequests, such as guarantee periods or refund options? Will the annuity be written to cover one life or two? Will there be opportunities to take partial lump-sum withdrawals or to delay annuitization? Each of these choices has different implications for how different groups fare under the individual accounts system. Therefore, it is important to examine each of these issues separately.

10.3.1   To Annuitize or Not to Annuitize

The first issue that must be addressed is whether or not the individual accounts system mandates annuitization. If individuals are allowed to freely access their account balances upon retirement, there would be no implicit transfers across groups, because at retirement all individuals would have access to their own contributions plus accumulated interest. This approach would make the individual account little more than a traditional saving vehicle, albeit a required one.

One problem with this approach, of course, is that it fails to provide individuals with any longevity insurance. As a result, individuals facing an uncertain date of death would find it difficult to allocate wealth in a manner that does not "waste" resources in the event of an early death without placing the individual at risk of outliving their resources. The insurance aspect of an annuity is potentially quite valuable. As shown by Brown, Mitchell, and Poterba (2001), a sixty-five-year-old male life cycle consumer with log utility and no bequest motive would find the opportunity to participate in an actuarially fair, real annuity market equivalent to a 50 percent increase in nonannuitized wealth. While this measure probably overstates the value of annuitization due to the omission of precautionary saving motives, bequest motives, and pricing loads, it is nonetheless an indication that the longevity insurance benefits of annuities are quite valuable. Many proposals to reform the existing Social Security system, which currently provides a real annuity to retirees, recognize that some form of annuitization may be desirable for this reason.

If annuitization is deemed desirable, there are many reasons to consider mandating a minimum level. These reasons include the possibility that myopic consumers may fail to provide adequately for old-age consumption, as well as the possibility of actuarially unfair pricing that arises due to adverse selection and/or the correlation between income and mortality. In what follows, I proceed under the assumption that some level annuitization would be mandated in an individual accounts system, and focus on the implication of using different types of annuities. After reviewing the distributional implications of various annuity mandates, I consider whether partial or delayed annuitization can lessen the distributional impact.

10.3.2 Pricing Assumptions

The initial working assumption in this paper is that the entity that provides the annuity, be it the government or a private insurance firm, provides a "single price, zero profit" annuity to all individuals. "Single price" means that all individuals of the same age face the same price for a given stream of annuity income: That is, annuity prices are not differentiated on the basis of individual or group characteristics.[8] Prices would be permitted to vary based on the age of annuitization only. This assumption is made for two reasons. First, the existing OASI benefit formula does not differ along any gender, race, or educational guidelines. Two same-age individuals with the same AIME who claim benefits on the same day are entitled to identical monthly payments, regardless of any socioeconomic or demographic differences. Second, permitting such differences in the United States, particularly along racial lines, would likely be politically infeasible. While the private individual annuity market in the United States is permitted to use gender-specific pricing, job-based pension annuities are not permitted to provide different annuity prices based on sex.[9]

---

8. Sheshinksi (1999) has demonstrated the conditions under which a uniform pricing scheme may be optimal.

9. In *City of Los Angeles v. Manhart,* 435 U.S. 702 (1978), it was ruled that section 703(a)(1) of the Civil Rights Act of 1964 barred requiring women to contribute more than men to pensions to receive the same benefits. Five years later, *Arizona Governing Committee v. Norris,* 463 U.S. 1073 (1983) held that the same law barred giving men a higher monthly benefit than women.

The second assumption, that of "zero profit," simply means that the annuities are priced so that the system breaks even over the whole population. That is, the expected present discounted value of all future payouts is equal to the total of the premiums paid. The implicit assumption is that administrative costs of the program are zero. Another way of stating this is that the system is actuarially fair for the population as a whole, although not necessarily for any one individual. While this assumption is clearly inaccurate, given the likely existence of some level of administrative costs,[10] as long as these costs are apportioned as a fixed percentage of the account balance, this will reduce the money's worth ratio for everyone by the same amount. Therefore, the *relative* transfers that occur between groups would be unaffected.

10.3.3   Measures of Distribution: The "Money's Worth" Ratio

In order to evaluate the distributional consequences of a particular annuity structure, it is necessary to choose a metric. There are at least three measures of valuation that have been used in the literature on Social Security and annuities. These are (a) a money's worth ratio, (b) an internal rate of return, and (c) a utility-based measure of annuity valuation. Each of these measures provides a slightly different way of comparing annuity options.

The money's worth measure is defined as the EPDV of the stream of annuity payments, divided by the premium paid. Take the simple case of an individual who pays an up-front single premium to purchase an immediate life annuity that pays $\$A$ per month as long as the individual is alive. The money's worth, or MW, is defined as follows:

$$(6) \qquad \text{MW} = \frac{\sum_{j=1}^{T} \dfrac{A \cdot P_j}{(1 + r)^j}}{\text{premium}},$$

where P_j is the probability of living to period j, r is the interest rate, and T is the number of periods remaining to the end of the maximum possible life span.

The interpretation of the money's worth ratio is quite simple. If the MW is equal to 1, then the expected discounted value of the benefit flow is exactly equal to the premium paid and can be said to be "actuarially fair" for the individual. If the MW is less than 1, then the individual is expected to receive less back in payouts than he paid in the premium, and thus the system is placing a negative expected transfer, or expected tax, on this

---

10. Several chapters in Shoven (2000) explore the potential importance of administrative costs in an individual accounts system. Samwick (1999) also provides an excellent discussion of reasons why these issues may be of less concern in the context of U.S. Social Security reform.

person. If the MW is greater than 1, then the individual is expected to receive more in annuity payments than he or she paid into the system in premiums, and is therefore receiving a positive expected transfer.

The first thing to note about this setup is that as long as mortality risk differs across groups, providing life annuities under a single price constraint will generally lead to the MW measure's differing across individuals. That is, one can either have equal annuity payments per dollar premium for everyone, or one can have equal MWs for all individuals, but generally not both.[11] Only by completely eliminating the role of mortality risk in the valuation of annuities can we make the differences in MW across groups disappear.

The second method of measuring differences in annuity value is to use an internal rate of return, or IRR. This measure is really just a restatement of the MW measure, since the internal rate of return is, by definition, the value of r that makes MW in equation (6) equal to 1. Because the same information is contained in the MW measure and the IRR measure, little is gained by reporting both. Therefore, I will limit the results to the MW measure.

Both the MW and the IRR measure are purely financial measures that do not capture the utility gains or losses associated with changes in a particular income stream. Risk-averse individuals will value the longevity insurance provided by annuities. For example, Mitchell et al. (1999) show that the utility gains to single life-cycle individuals are large enough that an annuity with a MW of only 0.80 might still be welfare enhancing.

In the context of measuring distributional impacts across demographic groups, however, using financial measures is a natural starting point. The magnitude of the utility gain will be sensitive to the parameterization of the utility function, and utility functions may differ across the demographic groups being analyzed. For example, there is some evidence that risk aversion may differ between men and women (Eisenhower and Halek 1999). In addition, many annuity options involve payments to the estate of an insured individual after death. In order to value these payments, it would be necessary to have a precise way to parameterize the utility of bequest function. There is remarkably little consensus in the literature about how to model bequest motives, and virtually no consensus about the particular parameterization. Research by Bernheim (1991), Laitner and Juster (1996), and Wilhelm (1996) all point to the existence of operative bequest motives, while Hurd (1987, 1989) and Brown (2001a, 2001b)

11. While it is generally true that different survival curves lead to different EPDVs of a given annuity flow, there are special cases in which two individuals with different survival curves will have an equal EPDV. This requires a crossover in mortality rates (i.e., that one person have higher mortality at one age) and lower mortality at a different age. Similarly, it is possible that, with a nonzero discount rate, an individual with a longer life expectancy would nonetheless value an annuity less than an individual with a shorter life expectancy.

find little evidence in support of such a view. For these reasons, I focus on the financial measure of money's worth, keeping in mind that the utility consequences of a particular policy may differ from the distribution of MWs. In particular, an individual may find an annuity to be welfare enhancing even if its MW is less than 1. Extending this analysis to account for the utility implications is left for future research.

10.3.4 Individual Annuities: Real and Nominal

I first examine an annuity that closely mirrors the existing U.S. Social Security system for a single individual—an immediate real annuity written on a single life. With this form of annuity, individuals simply exchange their accumulated assets to the annuity provider (i.e., the government or the insurance company), and monthly payments to the individuals commence immediately. The monthly payout is received until the individuals die, at which time the annuity contract ends. If the nominal payments from the annuity are indexed to the rate of inflation (as with the current OASI system), then the real value of the annuity payments is constant for the remainder of one's life.

The monthly income that would derive from an actuarially fair real annuity is easily computed. Assuming that an individual converts $100,000 into such an annuity, the monthly annuity payment, A, to which the individual is entitled is found from the following equation:

$$(7) \qquad \$100,000 = A \cdot \sum_{j=1}^{T} \frac{P_j}{(1 + r)^j} \, ,$$

where r is the monthly real interest rate, P_j is the cumulative probability of surviving from the date of purchase of the annuity to date j, and T is the number of periods remaining until the individual reaches the assumed maximum life span. If the annuity were fixed in nominal dollars instead of being indexed to inflation, the monthly real interest rate r would be replaced by the monthly nominal interest rate.

Due to the "single price" constraint, the value of A is constrained to be the same for all individuals. This is accomplished by constructing P_j from a dollar-weighted average mortality of all participants in the individual accounts program. For purposes of this paper, the value of A is determined with a unisex version of the 1978 birth cohort table from the 1999 Social Security Administration Trustees' report. This represents the "average" mortality of the entire population that turns age twenty-two in the year 2000, including men and women of all races and economic groups. Assuming a 3 percent real interest rate, the value of A for a real single life annuity for a sixty-seven-year-old individual is $621.25 per month.

It should be noted that this method of constructing the monthly payout of an annuity may differ from the value of A that would be required to make the system break even. This is because the unisex table is weighted by the number of lives rather than the number of dollars in the accounts. It is not clear in which direction this may bias the value of A, because there are two offsetting effects. First, a unisex table places heavy weight on female mortality, especially at older ages, when the number of women in the population surpasses the number of men. If women, who have lower mortality rates, tend to accumulate lower account balances due to lower earnings and/or lower labor force participation, the use of a unisex table will understate average mortality. The second effect is that if individuals with larger account balances live longer, then using people-weights instead of dollar-weights will tend to overstate average mortality. Because these two effects work in offsetting directions, the net bias is unclear. Importantly, the effect of any such bias is to change the value of A for everyone, so while the absolute level of the MW may change, the difference in MW across groups will remain unaffected.

To compute the MW for each gender, race, and education group, the survival probabilities for that group are substituted into equation (6), so that

$$(8) \qquad MW_g = \frac{\left[\sum_{j=1}^{T} \frac{A \cdot P_{g,j}}{(1 + r)^j} \right]}{100,000}.$$

Note that if $P_{g,j}$ from equation (8) equals P_j from equation (6) (i.e., group mortality equals the mortality rates used in pricing the annuity), then the annuity is priced in an actuarially fair manner for that group, and the MW will equal 1.

Table 10.3 reports the MW values for the various demographic groups under three different assumptions. The first two columns report the MW for an individual real annuity when real rate of interest is 3 percent (column [1]) and 6 percent (column [2]). Column (3) reports the MW for a nominal annuity when the real rate of interest and the rate of inflation are both set equal to a fixed 3 percent. Note that a "nominal" annuity with a fixed inflation rate corresponds to a declining real annuity.

The first finding is that the use of a unisex pricing structure results in large expected transfers from men to women. Focusing first on the case of a real annuity with a 3 percent interest rate, we can see that because female mortality rates are lower than male mortality rates at all ages, the average MW for men is 0.920 while the average for women is 1.076. This means that the average male can expect to receive $0.92 in annuity income for every dollar used to purchase the annuity, while the average woman can expect to receive nearly $1.08 for every dollar contributed. In essence, this pricing structure results in a transfer from men to women equal to approximately 8 percent of the accumulated wealth. Importantly, one way to

Table 10.3   **Money's Worth of Real and Nominal Individual Annuities**

	Real Annuity ($r = 0.03$) (1)	Real Annuity ($r = 0.06$) (2)	Nominal Annuity ($r = \pi = 0.03$) (3)
Men			
All	0.920	0.937	0.938
All Whites	0.927	0.943	0.944
All Blacks	0.862	0.885	0.886
All Hispanics	0.988	0.998	0.998
Whites			
College+	0.967	0.979	0.980
HS+	0.916	0.933	0.934
< HS	0.865	0.888	0.889
Blacks			
College+	0.916	0.935	0.935
HS+	0.857	0.880	0.881
< HS	0.800	0.829	0.830
Women			
All	1.076	1.060	1.059
All Whites	1.084	1.067	1.067
All Blacks	1.022	1.011	1.011
All Hispanics	1.123	1.097	1.097
Whites			
College+	1.106	1.086	1.086
HS+	1.080	1.063	1.063
< HS	1.044	1.031	1.031
Blacks			
College+	1.055	1.041	1.041
HS+	1.022	1.012	1.011
< HS	0.976	0.970	0.970

Source: Author's calculations, as described in text.

"correct" for this transfer across genders, at least for the case of married individuals, is to require the purchase of a joint and survivor annuity, which will be discussed below.

Looking within gender groups, we also see large differences in the MW across racial or ethnic lines. Black men do particularly poorly under this individual real annuity, having an MW of only 0.862. This means that the average black male can expect to lose approximately 14 percent of his account balance due to his higher mortality risk. White and Hispanic men, on the other hand, have quite slightly more favorable MW ratios of 0.927 and 0.988 due to their low mortality rates. A similar pattern is found among women, although in all cases the MW ratios are higher than for men. Black women on average have an MW close to 1 (1.022), indicating that the mortality advantage of being female is largely offset by the mortality disadvantage of being black. White women have an MW of 1.084, while Hispanic women have a very high MW of 1.123. Thus, just as black men are at a 14 percent disadvantage, Hispanic women are at a 12 percent advantage when an individual real annuity is used.

Further segmenting the population by educational attainment shows even further diversity in the MW calculations. Across all racial and gender lines, there is a monotonic positive relationship between the level of education and the MW. Having at least a college education raises the MW to 0.967 for white men. It is also clear that low-educated black males are the most disadvantaged group, due to their poor mortality prospects. They can expect to receive only $0.80 on the dollar that is annuitized in a real annuity. The biggest "winners" are well-educated white women and Hispanic women, who have MW ratios of 1.106 and 1.123, respectively.

The next column in table 10.3 shows how the results for a real annuity differ if the interest rate is 6 percent instead of 3 percent. The central result is that a higher interest rate reduces the dispersion in MW ratios, raising the MW for groups with a low MW and lowering the MW for groups with a higher MW, although the reduction in dispersion is small. Increasing the interest rate from 3 percent to 6 percent increases the monthly payment from $621.25 to $805.14. In this case, individuals who die early will have already received a higher income in the early periods. Long-lived individuals also receive the higher benefit, and for longer, but these later payments are being discounted at a higher rate.

Column (3) of table 10.3 reports the MW results for a nominal annuity. Nominal annuities may be less attractive than inflation-indexed annuities, since the latter offer the advantage of providing a constant real consumption stream. Previous work by Brown, Mitchell, and Poterba (2001) indicates that real annuities offer utility gains in excess of those provided by annuities that are fixed in nominal terms, particularly in a world with uncertain inflation. However, the initial annuity payment is lower for real annuities. For example, if there were a constant inflation rate of 3 percent annually, the real annuity would have an initial payment of $621.25 per month, while the nominal annuity would have an initial payment of $808.86 per month. Due to inflation, however, the real value of the nominal annuity would decline over time at a rate of 3 percent per annum. Thus, the real value of a nominal annuity is "front loaded." For individuals facing higher-than-average mortality risk, front-loading annuities will increase their MW, since they are relatively more likely to be alive to receive these larger early payments.

Not surprisingly, the use of a nominal annuity has a similar effect to an increase in the real interest rate: Namely, it decreases the degree of dispersion in MW. This is simply because the shorter duration of the nominal annuity helps those with high mortality risk and hurts those with low mortality risk. Using a nominal annuity in a world with a fixed inflation rate of 3 percent reduces the largest negative transfer (from low-educated black men) to 17 percent of the account balance, as compared to 20 percent for a real annuity. It is again important to stress, however, that although providing a nominal annuity has the possibly beneficial effect of compressing the dispersion in MW ratios, it is possible that all groups could be made worse off by this choice. In a utility-maximizing framework, the benefit of nominal annuities to high–mortality risk individuals could be completely offset by the loss in utility from being subjected to an uncertain income stream.

It is important to recognize that the results so far may represent the worst-case scenario from a distributional perspective. This is because the use of survivor and bequest options can improve the MW for individuals who value money left to beneficiaries. It is to these types of policies that I now turn.

10.3.5 Period-Certain Options

Continuing to operate within the realm of single life annuities, there are several options available that can help to increase the MW for individuals who face poor mortality prospects. A period-certain option specifies a minimum number of years that the annuity payout will be made, regardless of the survival of the insured. Then, at the end of the guarantee period, the contract reverts to a straight life annuity, and payments continue if and only if the insured individual is alive. In the current market for single premium immediate annuities in the United States, insurance companies are willing to offer certainty periods of nearly any length, although ten and twenty years are most common.

With a period-certain option, even if an individual faces a high probability of death early in the payout phase, the beneficiaries of the individual's estate will continue to benefit from the annuity. The reason these options serve to compress the distribution of MW ratios toward 1 is that they lessen the importance of individual mortality risk in the MW calculation.

Period-certain options are quite common in private annuity markets in the United States. According to the Life Insurance Market Research Association (LIMRA), if one looks at individually purchased (nongroup) fixed individual annuities sold in the United States, 73 percent of individual life annuities and 64 percent of joint and survivor life annuities included a period-certain option (LIMRA 1998). TIAA-CREF also reports that 74 percent of male annuitants choose a period-certain option on their annuity (King 1996). It is unclear what motivates this choice. Bequests are certainly one reason, since it is the beneficiaries of the policy who stand to gain from this policy. However, it seems unusual that an individual should desire to leave a bequest only if he dies in the next ten years, but not thereafter. One natural alternative would be to leave a portion of wealth unannuitized and either gift it or bequeath it upon death. Discussions with

Table 10.4   Initial Monthly Income from Annuities

	Real Life Annuity ($) (1)	Real Annuity + 10 PC ($) (2)	Real Annuity + 20 PC ($) (3)
Real ($r = 0.03$)	621.25	586.11	503.35
Nominal ($r = 0.03, \pi = 0.03$)	808.86	759.92	669.29

Source: Author's calculations, as described in text.
Note: PC = period certain (see text).

individuals in the insurance industry indicate that the guarantee periods are often used more to overcome superstition or some form of ex ante regret that comes from the fear that one might turn over one's money to an insurance company and then die soon thereafter. A second alternative for leaving a bequest is for an individual to use a portion of the monthly annuity payment to pay the premium on a life insurance contract, thus off-setting a portion of any mandated annuitization (Bernheim 1991). In previous work, however, I have shown that elderly individuals do not appear to use life insurance to offset the annuity from the existing Social Security system (Brown 2001a).

The pricing of a "life annuity with C year certain" is a straightforward extension of equation (7) above. Again assuming a $100,000 initial premium, the annuity amount A_{PC}, is calculated as follows:

$$(9) \qquad \$100,000 = A_{PC}\left[\sum_{j=1}^{12*C} \frac{1}{(1+r)^j} + \sum_{j=12*C+1}^{T} \frac{P_j}{(1+r)^j}\right]$$

The difference from the formula for a straight life annuity is that for the first C years, payments are made regardless of the individual's survival. Therefore, the P_j term is excluded from the pricing equation for the first $12*C$ months.

Because the first C years of payments are not life contingent, the amount of the monthly payment A_{PC} is less than the monthly income that would be received under a straight life annuity A. Table 10.4 shows the monthly income that would be available to an individual who chooses a single life annuity, a life annuity with ten-year certain, and a life annuity with a twenty-year certain. Looking at the first row, for real annuities, and again using the assumption of a unisex population average mortality table and a real interest rate of 3 percent, we see that the monthly incomes for a sixty-seven-year-old annuitant are approximately $621, $586, and $503 respectively. Thus, a ten-year period-certain option reduces the income available to the insured by 6 percent, while a twenty-year option reduces monthly income by 19 percent. For a nominal annuity, the nominal monthly incomes from these three options are approximately $809, $760, and $669.

The fact that the survival probabilities for the first C years are irrelevant for the pricing of annuities with period-certain options means that mortality differentials across individuals are also irrelevant during the first C years. As a result, period-certain options offer an effective vehicle for bringing the MW ratios of various groups closer to 1 if an individual values benefits to survivors as much as benefits to himself. To think about the MW of a period-certain product, let us generalize the MW formula as follows:

$$(10) \qquad \text{MW} = \frac{A_{PC} \left[\sum_{j=1}^{12^*C} \frac{P_j + (1 - P_j)\mu}{(1 + r)^j} + \sum_{j=12^*C+1}^{T} \frac{P_j}{(1 + r)^j} \right]}{\$100,000},$$

where μ represents a measure of the value of a dollar left to beneficiaries to the value of a dollar consumed by the individual purchasing the annuity. If $\mu = 1$, we are back to purely a financial calculation, and assuming that a dollar to the insured individual's estate is equivalent to a dollar to the individual while alive. In this case, the individual fully values the first C years of payments, regardless of survival. If $\mu < 1$, then the individual values a dollar to his estate less than a dollar while alive. In the extreme case of $\mu = 0$, the individual does not value the period-certain benefits at all, and the formula collapses to equation (9). Now, however, because A_{PC} is less than A when there is no period-certain benefit, the MW will be much lower.

Table 10.5 reports results for real annuities with period-certain options, for the case of $r = 0.03$. The first column reports the MW for the real individual life annuity first reported in table 10.3. Columns (2) and (3) report the MW for a real annuity with a ten-year period-certain feature, under two different assumptions about μ (1 and 0). Columns (4) and (5) report results for a real annuity with a twenty-year period-certain feature, again for two values of μ.

Comparing columns (1) and (2), we see that if individuals fully value income to beneficiaries ($\mu = 1$), then the use of a ten-year period-certain option reduces dispersion by pushing most of the MW measures toward 1. The overall effect is modest, increasing the average male MW from 0.920 to 0.936 and decreasing the average female MW from 1.076 to 1.061. Usually, however, the more a group's mortality differs from that of the average, the greater the change in the MW as we move from straight life to period-certain annuities. Considering the effect on the "outliers," we see that the MW for low-educated black males increases by roughly 6 percent of wealth, from 0.800 to 0.861, and that for highly educated white women decreases from 1.106 to 1.080.

Column (3), however, shows that this reduction in the MW dispersion is clearly dependent on the assumption that $\mu = 1$. If $\mu = 0$, so that indi-

426   Jeffrey R. Brown

Table 10.5   **Money's Worth of Period Certain Annuity Products**

	Real Life Annuity (1)	Real Annuity + 10 PC		Real Annuity + 20 PC	
		$\mu = 1$ (2)	$\mu = 0$ (3)	$\mu = 1$ (4)	$\mu = 0$ (5)
Men					
All	0.920	0.936	0.868	0.972	0.745
All Whites	0.927	0.940	0.874	0.973	0.751
All Blacks	0.862	0.900	0.813	0.964	0.698
All Hispanics	0.988	0.979	0.932	0.980	0.800
Whites					
College+	0.967	0.965	0.912	0.978	0.783
HS+	0.916	0.934	0.864	0.973	0.742
< HS	0.865	0.900	0.816	0.964	0.701
Blacks					
College+	0.916	0.932	0.864	0.970	0.742
HS+	0.857	0.897	0.808	0.964	0.694
< HS	0.800	0.861	0.754	0.955	0.648
Women					
All	1.076	1.061	1.015	1.026	0.872
All Whites	1.084	1.066	1.023	1.027	0.879
All Blacks	1.022	1.025	0.964	1.018	0.828
All Hispanics	1.123	1.097	1.060	1.042	0.910
Whites					
College+	1.106	1.080	1.043	1.030	0.896
HS+	1.080	1.063	1.019	1.027	0.875
< HS	1.044	1.040	0.985	1.022	0.846
Blacks					
College+	1.055	1.046	0.995	1.023	0.855
HS+	1.022	1.025	0.964	1.018	0.828
< HS	0.976	0.996	0.920	1.011	0.790

Source: Author's calculations, as described in text.

Notes: μ represents the relative value of $1 in an estate relative to the value of $1 in income to the insured individual. *PC* = period certain (see text).

viduals place no value on money left behind in an estate, the MW falls below the level of a real annuity for everyone, and the level of dispersion is similar to the level in column (1). For example, the difference between the highest MW (Hispanic women) and the lowest MW (black men less than high school) is 0.323 for a life annuity and 0.306 for an annuity with a ten-year period-certain option that has no value ($\mu = 0$).

The final two columns of table 10.5 show results for the case of a twenty-year period-certain option. The effect on the MW of a twenty-year period-certain option is substantially greater than that of a ten-year, because mortality is rising rapidly between ages seventy-seven and eighty-seven (the second ten-year period for an individual annuitizing at age sixty-seven).

Assuming that survivor benefits are valued fully, all of the MWs are now much closer to 1. The largest negative transfer is now less than less than 5 percent, down from 20 percent with a straight life annuity. Thus, to the extent that annuitants fully value benefits to their beneficiaries, a twenty-year period-certain option substantially reduces the degree of redistribution. Once again, however, if benefits paid to beneficiaries are not fully valued, individuals can be made substantially worse off. In fact, with μ = 0, every single MW ratio is less than 1. Even college-educated white women have an MW of below 0.90. The reason is simple—a twenty-year period-certain option reduces monthly income by 19 percent. This 19 percent is a pure cost if the individual does not place any value on the benefits paid after death.

10.3.6   Refund Options

Annuity providers often provide "refund" options to annuitants as an alternative to a period-certain feature. Although there are many possible ways to structure a refund option, the most popular form in the U.S. market for immediate annuities is to offer a money back guarantee. The annuity company offers to provide a monthly payment A_r for as long as the individual lives. Upon death, the company agrees to return to the beneficiary the initial premium, minus any annuity payments made to date. For example, suppose an individual purchases an annuity with a $100,000 premium and receives $500 per month in income from a refund annuity. After ten years (120 months), the individual will have received $60,000 in (nominal) payments. If the insured dies at this point, his beneficiaries would receive $40,000. Note that the amount guaranteed is the *nominal* value of the original premium, and no consideration is given to issues of discounting.

A second popular refund option works in a similar manner. The difference is that, instead of providing a lump-sum payoff at death, it continues to provide monthly payments A_r to the beneficiary until such time that the nominal value of the premium has been paid out. In this case, the annuity is little more than a C-year period-certain product in disguise, where the guarantee period C is chosen so that $A_r(12C)$ = Premium. For example, with an interest rate of 3 percent and an inflation rate of 3 percent, an installment refund annuity sold to a sixty-seven-year old is identical to a life annuity with 11.4 year period certain. Calculations of the MW ratios for both of these options indicate that they lie between the rates for a straight life annuity and a life annuity with a twenty-year period-certain option, and so are not reported separately in the tables.

In theory, one could provide a refund option that ensures that the beneficiaries receive a death benefit that returns the full actuarial value of the annuity upon the death of the beneficiary. In fact, such a "residual balance annuity" is discussed in chapter 9 by Feldstein and Ranguelova for the case of a variable annuity product. In the case of a fixed annuity, this would result by definition in a MW equal to 1 for everyone. However, this product offers no mortality premium, and in fact no insurance market is even required. Individuals can replicate this residual balance annuity by amortizing the account balance in real terms over the maximum remaining years of life. For perspective, while a real annuity with no period certain offers a real monthly payment of $621, amortizing the $100,000 until age 100 results in a monthly income of only $389, a 37 percent reduction. In addition, this approach requires that the individual know the maximum possible age with certainty. If there is any chance that the individual would live past age 100, she would outlive her resources.

10.3.7   Joint and Survivor Annuities

According to the Census Bureau projections for the year 2000, 62.4 percent of individuals aged sixty-five to seventy-four will be married with a spouse present. Married individuals nearing retirement are concerned with the consumption opportunities of both spouses, and therefore a single life annuity may be inappropriate. Joint and survivor annuities, which provide a stream of income as long as either spouse is alive, provide a spouse with protection against a drop in living standard upon the death of the insured individual.

Another reason for considering joint life annuities is that they provide a mechanism for providing for nonworking spouses of insured individuals. While the labor force participation of women has been steadily increasing throughout the twentieth century, it is likely to continue to be the case that large numbers of married individuals (primarily women) will accumulate very little in an individual account. Mandating the use of joint and survivor annuities for married couples is one way to ensure some level of income for elderly widows.

As discussed in more detail in Brown and Poterba (2000), there are two primary types of joint annuity contracts. The first is a joint life annuity with a last survivor payout rule. This rule specifies a monthly payment that will be paid as long as both members of the couple are still alive, and also specifies a fraction of this payment, ϕ, that will be paid to the survivor after the death of one member of the couple. With the second type of contract, often called a joint and contingent survivor annuity, one member of the couple is specified as the primary annuitant. As long as the primary annuitant is alive, the annuity payment is fixed at A. However, upon the death of the primary annuitant, the payment to the secondary annuitant declines to a fraction θ of the original payment. If, on the other hand, the secondary annuitant dies first, the payment to the primary annuitant does not change.

This paper will restrict attention to joint and last survivor annuities, which treat the spouses symmetrically. The pricing of a joint and survivor

(J & S) annuity is again a simple extension of the pricing of a single life annuity.

$$(11) \quad \$100{,}000 = A_{J\&S}\sum_{j=1}^{T} \frac{P_{m,j}P_{f,j} + \phi[P_{m,j}(1 - P_{f,j}) + P_{f,j}(1 - P_{m,j})]}{(1 + r)^j}$$

In pension plans and in the individual annuity market, ϕ is usually set equal to 0.5, 0.67, or 1.0, although insurance companies are generally willing to provide annuities for any value of ϕ between 0 and 1. When ϕ takes the value of 1.0, these products are often called "joint and full survivor" annuities. In this case, the monthly annuity payment does not change upon the death of the first spouse. In order to compute the value of $A_{J\&S}$ above, one must decide which values of $P_{m,j}$ and $P_{f,j}$ to use for pricing the annuity. Rather than use a unisex table, in this case I choose to use average male mortality rates to compute $P_{m,j}$ and average female mortality rates to compute $P_{f,j}$.[12]

To compute the MW for different groups, it is now necessary to match up characteristics of husbands and wives. With seven different racial, ethnic, and education groups for each gender, this leads to forty-nine different possible "couples." Rather than examine every combination, I present results for the case in which matching occurs within groups. Therefore, white college-educated men are matched with white college-educated women. Table 10.6 reports results for real annuities, both for a 50 percent survivor benefit (top panel) as well as for a full survivor benefit (lower panel). In column (1), I report results for a J & S annuity with no period-certain option. In columns (2) through (5), I report the MW for J & S annuities with ten- and twenty-year period-certain options. In each of the period-certain cases, I show results for $\mu = 1$ (full valuation of beneficiary income) and $\mu = 0$ (zero valuation).

As the results indicate, the MW ratios are substantially closer to 1 than in the case of individual annuities. For example, even in the case of the lowest MW for a full survivor annuity, that of low-educated blacks, the MW for a joint and full survivor annuity is 0.932. The highest couple MW is 1.033, for Hispanic couples. While these implicit transfers are still large in magnitude, they are much smaller than those for individuals alone, for two reasons. First, even if two individuals with identical mortality purchase a J & S annuity, the MW will be closer to 1.0. This is because the annuity will continue to pay out as long as either of the two individuals is alive, and the probability that both individuals will die very early is less than the probability that either one of them will. For example, even if two individuals with the mortality characteristics of low-educated black males

---

12. I have also calculated the MW ratios for J&S annuities under the assumption that they are priced using the unisex table for both spouses. The results are nearly identical, with the MW calculated under these two methods never varying by more than 0.003.

Table 10.6   **Money's Worth of Joint and Survivor Annuities**

	Real Life Annuity (1)	Real Annuity + 10 PC		Real Annuity + 20 PC	
		$\mu = 1$ (2)	$\mu = 0$ (3)	$\mu = 1$ (4)	$\mu = 0$ (5)
100% Survivor Benefits					
All	1.000	1.000	0.994	1.000	0.944
All Whites	1.004	1.004	0.998	1.001	0.948
All Blacks	0.967	0.971	0.961	0.989	0.912
All Hispanics	1.036	1.033	1.029	1.016	0.976
Whites					
College+	1.019	1.016	1.012	1.005	0.961
HS+	1.001	1.001	0.995	1.001	0.945
< HS	0.975	0.978	0.969	0.992	0.920
Blacks					
College+	0.991	0.992	0.985	0.996	0.935
HS+	0.966	0.970	0.960	0.989	0.912
< HS	0.932	0.941	0.926	0.979	0.879
50% Survivor Benefits					
All	1.000	1.000	0.943	1.000	0.809
All Whites	1.008	1.008	0.950	1.001	0.815
All Blacks	0.944	0.964	0.890	0.992	0.764
All Hispanics	1.055	1.038	0.996	1.011	0.855
Whites					
College+	1.038	1.024	0.979	1.005	0.840
HS+	1.000	1.000	0.943	1.001	0.809
< HS	0.956	0.971	0.902	0.993	0.774
Blacks					
College+	0.987	0.991	0.931	0.997	0.799
HS+	0.941	0.963	0.888	0.992	0.762
< HS	0.889	0.930	0.839	0.984	0.720

Source: Author's calculations, as described in text.
Note: PC = period certain (see text).

were to purchase a joint and full survivor annuity, the MW would be 0.843, as opposed to an MW of 0.800 if each individual purchased a separate single life annuity. The second reason, which has an even greater effect on the results, is that one of the primary sources of variation in mortality rates is gender. Pooling together the mortality of a male and a female, and pricing accordingly, largely removes this source of dispersion in the MW ratio. Thus, even in the case of a couple consisting of a black male and a black female, both with less than a high school education, the MW ratio is 0.932. The lower panel of table 10.6 shows similar results for the case of a joint and 50 percent survivor annuity. Comparing the upper and lower panels, we see that higher survivor benefits tend to reduce MW dispersion by more.

The remaining columns in table 10.6 report results of combining a real J & S annuity with a period-certain option. As with the case of individuals, the inclusion of a period-certain option tends to decrease the dispersion of MW ratios if the benefits to beneficiaries are fully valued. In the case of a joint and full survivor annuity with a twenty-year period certain, the MW ratios are extremely close to 1. The largest negative transfer appears to be from low-educated blacks, but it represents only a 2.1 percent reduction in wealth. The largest positive transfer is to Hispanic couples, who receive a net surplus of 1.5 percent.

It must again be noted, however, that providing a J & S annuity with a twenty-year period-certain option has a cost. This cost is a decline in the monthly income that is made available to individuals when they annuitize. For example, whereas a real single life annuity provides $623 per month in income, a joint and full survivor annuity provides only $503 in income. Adding a twenty-year certain option to this annuity reduces the benefit further to $474 per month. As a result of this nearly 6 percent reduction in income from adding a twenty-year period-certain option to a joint and survivor annuity, the MW of the twenty-year period-certain feature is significantly lower if the couple does not value income to beneficiaries (i.e., if $\mu = 0$).

10.3.8 Variable Annuity Issues

Up until this point, the annuities discussed in this paper have been fixed nominal or fixed real annuities. The defining feature of these annuities is that, once the initial value of the annuity is determined, it remains constant in nominal or real terms for the duration of the annuity contract (excepting predetermined reductions upon one death in a J & S annuity). However, many proposals for an individual accounts system, such as that outlined by Feldstein, Ranguelova, and Samwick (2001), foresee a role for variable annuity products.

The general conclusions of the distributional analysis conducted for fixed annuities carry over for variable annuity products as well. With variable products, it will still be the case that, in expectation, resources are transferred from high–mortality risk individuals to low–mortality risk individuals. It also remains true that the use of joint life annuities, period-certain guarantees, and refunds reduces the extent of these transfers. However, there is one additional "choice variable" in constructing a variable annuity payout stream that deserves attention here—the "assumed interest rate," or AIR.

As discussed in Bodie and Pesando (1983) and Brown, Mitchell, and Poterba (2001), the amount of the initial variable annuity payment is a function of the AIR. To determine the initial value $A(0)$ of a single life variable annuity, the insurance company solves an equation such as

$$(12) \qquad\qquad 1 = \sum_{j=1}^{T} \frac{A(0) \cdot P_j}{(1 + R)^j} \,,$$

where R is the AIR. The annuity-updating rule depends on the return of the assets that back the annuity, which is denoted by z_t, according to

$$(13) \qquad\qquad A(t + 1) = A(t) \cdot \frac{(1 + z_t)}{(1 + R)} \,.$$

R is the key parameter in designing a variable annuity. Assuming a high value of R will enable the insurance company to offer a large initial premium, but the stream of future payouts is less likely to increase, or more likely to decline, as the assumed value of R rises.

For example, if R is set equal to the expected real return on the underlying portfolio, then the expected slope of the real consumption stream is flat. That is, if the portfolio return in each period was equal to its expectation, and thus equal to R, the real value of the annuity would be constant in real terms. In periods when the portfolio's real return fell short of its expectation, the real value of the annuity payment would fall. Similarly, when the portfolio outperformed expectations, the annuity value would rise in real terms. If R is set equal to 0, the initial value of the annuity, $A(0)$ is relatively low, but the income stream will rise and fall in exact proportion to the underlying portfolio. Therefore, the annuity payments will, on average, increase in value at a rate equal to the expected return of the underlying portfolio.

As was the case with fixed annuities, front-loading annuities has the effect of lessening the size of the expected transfers, since high–mortality risk individuals are more likely to receive a higher proportion of their premium back. Thus, setting a higher assumed interest rate will result in less redistribution from high mortality rate groups to lower mortality groups. This finding is directly analogous to the difference between real and nominal annuities discussed earlier—high–mortality risk individuals receive a higher MW out of nominal annuities because the real value of these payments is higher in the early periods.

10.3.9   Delayed Annuitization

As reported by Finkelstein and Poterba (1999), pensions in the United Kingdom since 1995 have offered an "income withdrawal option." This option allows an individual to delay the purchase of an annuity until age seventy-five, provided that he or she draws an income from the pension fund in the meantime that is between 35 and 100 percent of the amount that would otherwise be received from an annuity. If the pensioner dies prior to annuitization, the assets in the fund become part of the individual's estate.

From an expected bequest point of view, this option benefits the estate

Table 10.7   **Probability of Surviving from Age 67 to Age 77**

	Men (1)	Women (2)
All	0.744	0.828
All Whites	0.751	0.836
All Blacks	0.688	0.779
All Hispanics	0.812	0.857
Whites		
College+	0.791	0.856
HS+	0.739	0.832
< HS	0.693	0.799
Blacks		
College+	0.744	0.810
HS+	0.682	0.779
< HS	0.628	0.736

Source: Author's calculations, as described in text.

of individuals who have particularly high probabilities of dying between the ages of sixty-seven and seventy-seven. Table 10.7 reports the ten-year mortality probability of each group, conditional on reaching age sixty-seven. As the table indicates, large disparities in mortality rates continue at these older ages. Female mortality rates are still below those of men, blacks have higher mortality rates than whites and Hispanics, and lower-education groups have higher rates than high-education groups.

As with all bequest options, the difficulty with this approach is that it must reduce the income available to annuitants. I have already shown that a sixty-seven-year-old individual purchasing an annuity with $100,000 would be entitled to a monthly income of $621, assuming that annuities were priced on a unisex basis. Imagine that, instead of purchasing an annuity at age sixty-seven, the individual instead consumed $621 per month out of the individual account, and that the account continued to accrue interest at a rate of 3 percent per annum. After ten years, the individual would have an account balance of $47,759. If the individual annuitized the account balance at this point, the annuity would provide monthly income of approximately $419, or fully one-third less than the income that would have been provided if an annuity had been purchased ten years earlier. This is the fundamental trade-off: If the individual dies between ages sixty-seven and seventy-seven, the heirs receive at least $47,759 dollars, but if the individual survives, her income is 33 percent less for the rest of her life.

Alternatively, consider what would happen if the individual did not annuitize at all, but continued to consume $621 per month starting at age sixty-seven. The individual account would be depleted after seventeen years and two months, or at age eighty-four. Approximately 44 percent of all men and 61 percent of all women will still be alive at age eighty-four, the point at which they would exhaust their resources if they tried to "self-annuitize." This is quite obviously not the optimal consumption path in the absence of annuitization, but it illustrates the key point that delaying annuitization comes at a cost of future consumption for longer-lived individuals.

10.3.10   Partial Annuitization Revisited

Now that we have discussed numerous annuity payout options in more detail, it is instructive to revisit the issue of partial annuitization. All of the transfers noted above occur as a result of mortality differentials across groups. Any portion of an account that is not annuitized is therefore not subject to these redistributive effects. Put simply, if individuals are required to annuitize exactly 50 percent of their account balances, then the amount of redistribution would be cut in half, since the MW of the nonannuitized portion is equal to 1.0.

One possible partial annuitization policy would be to require a minimum amount of annuitization, where the minimum was chosen to be above some baseline level, such as the poverty line. In the United States, it would be important to set the baseline above the level of any other government income guarantee program, such as Supplemental Security Income (SSI) in order to ensure that individuals did not rapidly spend down their individual account assets and then become dependent on SSI.

The primary disadvantage of allowing for partial lump-sum withdrawals is that individuals lose part of the longevity insurance that an annuity is meant to provide. The individual is still faced with the problem of determining how to optimally allocate the nonannuitized wealth in the face of an uncertain lifetime. If one of the reasons for requiring a forced retirement saving program at all is that individuals are too myopic to save adequately for old age, then this myopia may lead them to squander the lump-sum portion of their savings in a suboptimal fashion.

Despite these disadvantages, allowing for some fraction of benefits to be left unannuitized has several potential benefits. First, as we have seen, it reduces the amount of redistribution in the annuity pricing system from long-lived to short-lived individuals. Second, it loosens the liquidity constraint on the elderly that an annuity imposes, which can be beneficial in cases in which the elderly are hit with large unplanned expenditures, such as unforeseen medical expenditures. Third, it provides individuals who have bequest motives with a natural way to provide gifts and/or bequests to their children that is not subject to the somewhat arbitrary timing constraints of the bequest that comes with period-certain or refund options on an annuity. Finally, it should be noted that the utility gains that come from annuitizing one's resources are a decreasing function of the amount of wealth already annuitized. In other words, the first dollar of annuitized wealth has a much larger utility impact than the last dollar. Therefore, annuitizing 50 percent of one's wealth captures significantly more than 50 percent of the utility gains from annuitization. Thus, the "cost" of the lump-sum option may not be as great as it seems at first glance.

The U.K. retirement system has a "partial annuitization" option in its personal pension schemes, as described in Finkelstein and Poterba (1999). In these personal pension plans, individuals are permitted to take up to 25 percent of their fund (up to a maximum amount) as a lump sum at retirement. It is important that this lump-sum option is an *option,* not a requirement, of the program. Allowing this as an option rather than as a requirement has two partially offsetting effects from a distributional perspective. If it is primarily lower socioeconomic groups (with higher mortality rates) that choose the lump-sum option, this places more resources into their hands prior to death, presumably making them better off. However, this selection process will also have the effect of making annuities more expensive, since the dollar-weighted mortality rates of the annuitized pool would be improved. This would reduce the MW of annuities to all participants, including those in the least well-off groups.

10.4   Alternative Pricing Assumptions

Nearly all of the numerical results of the last section were driven entirely be the "single price" assumption—the constraint that all individuals of the same age would receive the same monthly annuity income per dollar of premium paid, regardless of individual characteristics. This assumption is certainly not the only assumption that can be made, although it is arguably the most politically feasible. For example, private annuity markets in the United States currently price annuities separately for men and women. In addition, there is at least one U.S. company that offers a "smokers preferred" annuity contract, which offers higher monthly income for individuals who are smokers and thus have higher mortality risk.

It is in the interest of individuals who face high mortality risk to allow the annuity provider to use as much information as possible to price annuities. The reason is that a provider can offer a much higher level of monthly income to a high–mortality risk individual if it is allowed to base the price on this higher risk level. This leads to some results that are quite counter to our usual sense of political feasibility. For example, it would be very much in the interest of black men with less than a high school education to allow insurance companies to use race as a factor in the pricing of annuities.

For perspective, table 10.8 reports the monthly annuity payment that would be offered to individuals if annuity prices were set separately for each demographic group and were priced in an actuarially fair manner for each group. Recall that when individual real annuities were priced based

Table 10.8   **Monthly Income from $100,000 Policy if Price is Based on Group-Specific Mortality**

	Men ($) (1)	Women ($) (2)
All	675.36	577.36
All Whites	670.42	572.90
All Blacks	720.83	608.15
All Hispanics	629.12	553.08
Whites		
College+	642.73	561.83
HS+	678.25	575.13
< HS	718.40	595.19
Blacks		
College+	678.22	589.01
HS+	725.13	608.01
< HS	776.92	636.84

Source: Author's calculations, as described in text.

on a single unisex life table with a real interest rate of 3 percent, a $100,000 premium bought an individual a stream of payments of approximately $621 per month for a sixty-seven-year-old. Allowing for gender-specific pricing only, men would receive $675 per month, while women would receive $577 per month.

Allowing pricing based on gender and race would result in white, black, and Hispanic men receiving $670, $721, and $629 respectively per month. White, black, and Hispanic women would receive $573, $608, and $553 respectively. Further differentiation by educational status results in an even wider dispersion of monthly payments. Again looking at the extreme cases, a low-educated black male would receive $777 per month, fully $215 more per month than a college-educated white woman.

It is also important to note, however, that group mortality rates are only averages, and that there is a significant degree of dispersion around this average within each group. Thus, while it is true that college-educated white women on average live longer than black men with less than a high school education, it is not true that this holds for every individual in each group. Some white women will have mortality rates that more closely resemble that of black men, and vice versa. As a result, any pricing scheme that seeks to address mortality heterogeneity by pricing based on group characteristics will make some individuals even worse off. For example, if annuities are priced on a gender-specific basis, this will be especially harmful to women who have mortality rates that resemble those of men. Of course, it is now conceivable to think that, given the rapid rise in medical technology, companies in the future will be able to determine individual-specific mortality rates with a fairly high degree of precision.

Already there is debate about whether to allow insurance companies to use data from DNA tests to make insurance decisions. Unlike markets for health insurance and life insurance, in which unhealthy individuals would prefer that the insurance company not be permitted to use this information, in annuity markets the preferences are reversed. Individuals who can be identified as having a higher risk of dying should welcome the use of this information in the pricing of annuities, as it would lead to a higher benefit.

10.5 Summary and Future Directions

This paper has measured the magnitude of the expected transfers that would result under various annuity options in an individual accounts system. These expected transfers arise because mortality is significantly correlated with socioeconomic factors such as gender, race, and level of education. These transfers appear to be economically important in both the accumulation phase of the individual accounts and in the payout phase.

Allowing for preretirement bequests from individual accounts is relatively more important to groups with high mortality rates at younger ages. For example, estimates from this paper suggest that 41.2 percent of twenty-two-year-old black males with less than a high school education in the year 2000 will not survive to age sixty-seven. While these high–mortality rate groups tend to have below-average lifetime earnings, the net effect appears to be that these low-income groups tend to have higher expected bequests than do higher-income groups. Thus, allowing preretirement bequests may be an important element in reducing the extent of regressive redistribution.

During the payout phase of the annuity, mortality differences are also quite important. Assuming that the political system constrains annuity prices to be blind to socioeconomic mortality differences, the MW of retirement annuities can vary greatly across groups. The MW is lower for men than for women and for blacks than for whites, and increases in an individual's education level. For some annuity design options, such as an individual real life annuity, these transfers can be as large as 20 percent of wealth. Importantly, these expected transfers are generally regressive, in the sense that they are going from the economically worse-off individuals to better-off individuals.

The degree of dispersion in the MW ratios is very sensitive to the precise structure of the annuity program. Annuities that front load payments, or provide continued payments to an individual's estate after death, result in much less redistribution. The use of joint life annuities rather than single life annuities largely eliminates the transfers that occur across gender lines. The use of a J & S annuity with a twenty-year certain provision reduces the largest negative transfer to only 2 percent of wealth.

All of the options that reduce the implicit transfers do so at the cost of lowering the monthly income that can be provided to all annuitants. For example, moving from a real single life annuity with no bequest provision to a real joint and full survivor annuity with a twenty-year period-certain feature would reduce the monthly income from the annuity by nearly 24 percent. If a goal of an individual account system is to ensure a level of monthly income that is no lower than would be available under the current OASI system, as suggested by Feldstein, Ranguelova, and Samwick (2001), the use of a joint and full survivor annuity with a twenty-year certain option would require a 24 percent increase in the annual contribution rate over the rate required with a single life annuity.

There are at least two potentially useful avenues for further research. First, all of the above results are based upon purely financial considerations, namely the expected present value of payments received. Future work could focus on the effect of differential mortality on the utility gains associated with the longevity insurance component of annuities. Second, it would be useful to disentangle the effect of disability status on the mortality differentials across socioeconomic lines. This would be especially important if any future individual accounts system was to maintain a separate disability insurance program.

References

Attanasio, O. P., and H. W. Hoynes.2000. Differential mortality and wealth accumulation. *Journal of Human Resources* 35 (1): 1–29.

Bernheim, B. D. 1991. How strong are bequest motives? Evidence based on estimates of the demand for life insurance and annuities. *Journal of Political Economy* 99:899–927.

Bodie, Z., and J. Pesando. 1983. Retirement annuity design in an inflationary climate. In *Financial aspects of the U.S. pension system,* ed. Z. Bodie and J. Shoven, 291–316. Chicago: University of Chicago Press.

Brown, J. R. 2001a. Are the elderly really over-annuitized? New evidence on life insurance and bequests. In *themes in the economics of aging,* ed. D. Wise, 91–124. Chicago: University of Chicago Pressl

———. 2001b. Private pensions, mortality risk, and the decision to annuitize. *Journal of Public Economics* 82:29–62.

Brown, J. R., O. S. Mitchell, and J. M. Poterba. 2001. The role of real annuities and indexed bonds in an individual accounts retirement program. In *Risk aspects of social security reform,* ed. J. Campell and M. Feldstein, 321–60. Chicago: University of Chicago Press.

Brown, J. R., and J. M. Poterba. 2000. Joint life annuities and annuity demand by married couples. *Journal of Risk and Insurance* 67 (4): 527–53.

Deaton, A., and C. Paxson.2001. Mortality, education, income and inequality among American cohorts. In *Themes in the economics of aging,* ed. D. Wise, 129–65. Chicago: University of Chicago Press.

Duggan, J. E., R. Gillingham, and J. S. Greenlees. 1995. Progressive returns to social security? An answer from social security records. Research Paper no. 9501. Washington, D.C.: U.S. Department of the Treasury.

Eisenhower, J. G., and M. Halek. 1999. The demography of risk aversion. *Journal of Risk and Insurance,* forthcoming.

Feinstein, J. S. 1993. The relationship between socioeconomic status and health: A review of the literature. *Milbank Quarterly* 71 (2): 279–322.

Feldstein, M., E. Ranguelova, and A. Samwick. 2001. The transition to investment-based social security when portfolio returns and capital profitability are uncertain. In *Risk aspects of investment-based social security reform,* ed. J. Y. Campbell and M. Feldstein, 41–81. Chicago: University of Chicago Press.

Finkelstein, A., and J. M. Poterba. 1999. Selection effects in the market for individual annuities: New evidence from the United Kingdom. *Economic Journal,* forthcoming.

Garrett, D. M. 1995. The effects of differential mortality rates on the progressivity of social security. *Economic Inquiry* 33 (3): 457–75.

Gustman, A., and T. Steinmeier. 1999. How effective is redistribution under the social security benefit formula? *Journal of Public Economics* 82 (1):1–28.

Hadley, J., and A. Osei. 1982. Does income affect mortality? An analysis of the effects of different types of income on age/sex/race-specific mortality rates in the United States. *Medical Care* 20 (9): 901–14.

Hurd, M. D. 1987. Savings of the elderly and desired bequests. *American Economic Review* 77 (3): 298–312.

———. 1989. Mortality risk and bequests. *Econometrica* 57 (4): 779–813.

Jordan, C. W. 1991. *Life contingencies,* 2nd ed. Chicago: Society of Actuaries.

Kaplan, G. A., E. R. Pamuk, J. W. Lynch, R. D. Cohen, and J. L. Balfour. 1996. Inequality in income and mortality in the United States: Analysis of mortality and potential pathways," *BMJ* 312.

King, F. 1996. Trends in the selection of TIAA-CREF life annuity income options, 1978–1994. *TIAA-CREF Research Dialogues* 48.

Kitagawa, E. M., and P. M. Hauser. 1973. *Differential mortality in the United States: A study in socioeconomic epidemiology.* Boston: Harvard University Press.

Kotlikoff, L., and J. Sachs. 1998. The personal security system: A framework for reforming social security. *Review of the Federal Reserve Bank of St. Louis* 80 (2): 11–13.

Laitner, J., and T. Juster. 1996. New evidence on altruism: A study of TIAA-CREF retirees. *American Economic Review* 86:893–908.

Lantz, P. M., J. S. House, J. M. Lepkowski, D. R. Williams, R. P. Mero, and J. Chen. 1998. Socioeconomic factors, health behaviors, and mortality. *Journal of the American Medical Association* 279 (21).

Lillard, L. A., M. J. Brien, and C. W. A. Panis. 1993. The value of annuities at age 65: Race, marital status, wealth, health, and mortality. RAND Corporation. Mimeograph.

Menchik, P. L. 1993. Economic status as a determinant of mortality among black and white older men: Does poverty kill? *Population Studies* 47:427–36.

Mitchell, O. S., J. M. Poterba, M. J. Warshawsky, and J. R. Brown. 1999. New evidence on the money's worth of individual annuities. *American Economic Review,* 89 (5): 1299–1318.

Pablos-Mendez, A. 1994. To the Editor. *Journal of the American Medical Association* 271 (16).

Palmer, B. L. 1989. Implications of the changing male mortality. Ph.D. diss. MIT.

Panis, C., and L. Lillard. 1996. Socioeconomic differentials in the returns to social security. RAND Corporation. Mimeograph, February.

Preston, S. H., I. T. Elo, I. Rosenwaike, and M. Hill. 1996. African-American mortality at older ages: Results of a matching study. *Demography* 33 (2): 193–209.

Samwick, A. 1999. Social security reform in the United States. *National Tax Journal* 52 (4): 819–42.

Sheshinksi, E. 1999. A note on the optimum pricing of annuities. Unpublished Manuscript, Hebrew University, Jerusalem.

Shoven, J. 2000. *Administrative costs and social security privatization.* Chicago: University of Chicago Press.

Smith, J. P. 1999. Healthy bodies and thick wallets: The dual relation between health and economic status. *Journal of Economic Perspectives* 13 (2): 145–66.

Sorlie, P., E. Backlund, N. Johnson, and E. Rogot. 1993. Mortality by Hispanic status in the United States. *Journal of the American Medical Association* 270 (20): 2464–68.

Sorlie, P., E. Rogot, R. Anderson, N.J. Johnson, and E. Backlund. 1992. Black-white mortality differences by family income. *The Lancet* 340:346–50.

Wilhelm, M. 1996. Bequest behavior and the effect of heirs' earnings: Testing the altruistic model of bequests. *American Economic Review* 86:874–92.

Comment   Andrew A. Samwick

Ideally, all of the individuals covered by an insurance system would face the same probability of experiencing loss. They could each be charged the actuarially fair premium (based on that probability) and would then choose to insure themselves against the full amount of the loss. In practice, however, insurance systems cover individuals who face very different probabilities of experiencing the loss but who are nonetheless charged the same premium. Under these circumstances, individuals who have below-average probabilities of facing the loss may prefer incomplete insurance if insurance is only available at a premium that reflects the average risk.

In the design of any social security system, the loss is the probability of an individual living "too long," and the insurance offered is a real annuity for the full amount of the individual's benefit entitlement. A real annuity is the ideal payout method to transfer resources from short- to long-lived members of a group with the same expected longevity. The key problem is that it is well known that observable groups—distinguished by race, gender, and income—also differ in their average expected longevities. Annuities consequently appear to redistribute resources from short- to long-lived *groups* within the population. Depending on one's views on social welfare, this may or may not improve perceived equity within a society.

While the current paper discusses the implications of differential mortality for a system of individual accounts, there is nothing about the constraint of using a single mortality table that is particular to individual ac-

Andrew A. Samwick is professor of economics at Dartmouth College and a research associate of the National Bureau of Economic Research.

counts. The current pay-as-you-go, defined benefit system also suffers from the same unintended redistribution between observable groups. The chapter's results consequently apply more broadly than to the ongoing debate of Social Security privatization. They are just as relevant to any fundamental discussion of how to improve the equity and efficiency of the current system.

In that spirit, the chapter explores—without making the case for a policy change—the feasibility of offering partial annuitization of social insurance payouts. On the whole, the paper is thorough and clear, providing several illustrative calculations of transfers between groups as well as estimates of how those transfers might change under different annuitization schemes. I can offer a few brief comments on both the research design and its discussion.

The key analytical point is that front-loading the payments from the social insurance system to early ages after retirement lessens the scope for unintended redistribution across observable groups. It does so, of course, because it makes the total payments less sensitive to the beneficiary's mortality. The cost of avoiding unintended redistribution across observable groups with different mortality risks is therefore a reduction in intended redistribution within groups with the same mortality risks.

The chapter provides three mechanisms to achieve front-loading relative to a baseline real annuity. One is to offer nominal annuities rather than real annuities. With a nominal annuity, the real value of the payments decreases over time as the price level rises. If the concern in moving to a system of individual accounts is that private annuities are typically not protected against inflation, then the equity arguments inherent in differential mortality suggest that this is less of a concern than previously thought. Another mechanism is to offer period-certain annuities, in which payments are lower than a conventional annuity but are guaranteed for a minimum number of years even if the annuitant dies. These products are surprisingly popular in the private market; perhaps this would also be the case in a social insurance system. A final mechanism is to use a high rather than a low assumed interest rate (AIR) in variable annuities.

It is well known that women have higher average survival probabilities than do men—about six years at age twenty-two in table 10.1. Choosing the individual as the unit of observation, this seems to imply that the use of a single mortality table forces men to transfer resources to women. Table 10.3 shows that for a real annuity with an interest rate of 3 percent, men have an average money's worth of 0.920, compared to 1.076 for women. At the extremes, black men with less than a high school education have a money's worth that is 20 percent less than the population average, and white women with a college degree have a money's worth that is 10.6 percent more than the population average.

The most striking result in the chapter is the effect of considering couples rather than individuals. Since a couple is comprised of both a male and a female, the couple's longevity is an average of male and female longevities. This averaging reduces the differences across most groups in the population. As shown in table 10.6, with 50 percent survivor benefits, these disparities are cut in half. White couples with a college education have an average money's worth of 1.038, and black couples with less than a high school education have an average money's worth of 0.889. These discrepancies are cut nearly in half again with 100 percent survivor benefits. In effect, those huge transfers that a typical man makes to a typical woman are generally made to his wife. It is also worth noting that mortality differences across couples are maximized when couples include members of the same race and education groups. To the extent that husbands and wives have different races or education levels, the remaining differences in average mortality across couples will be less than what is suggested in table 10.6. Considering couples rather than individuals goes a long way toward smoothing out longevity differences across groups.

The chapter considers three groups across which unintended redistribution might occur—gender, race, and education—with education serving as a proxy for permanent income. I do not understand why the first two are relevant in policy discussions. If women tend to live longer than men, then women have a greater need for "insurance against outliving their means," and that is why they appear to have a higher money's worth than do men. The same argument can be made in comparing racial groups. If the goal is to redistribute based on longevity, then why do we care about observable but, in most cases, immutable characteristics that are correlated with longevity?

We might also not care about differences across income groups for the same reason, except for two differences between income and race or gender. The first is that income is under the control of the individual, and a low money's worth can discourage a person from earning income in the same way as any other redistributive tax. The second is that Social Security's tax and benefit formulas are explicitly based on income and cannot be based on race or gender. Presumably, the goal of policy makers is to make sure that the system is financed in a sufficiently progressive manner. Perhaps policy makers are unaware of the correlation between income and longevity, and, if they were made aware, they would prefer a benefit formula that was more progressive on paper. It would be very interesting to know how much more progressive the benefit formula needs to be in order to offset the impact of the income-longevity correlation on the present value of benefits (based on any reasonable estimate of average income by race, education, and gender groups). For example, what benefit formula with differential mortality has the same degree of progressivity as the current benefit formula under the assumption of uniform mortality?

I have two main criticisms of the way the analysis is presented. The first is that the chapter discusses only the variation in average longevity *between* groups, to the complete exclusion of variation in longevity *within* groups. There is no doubt that the differences across groups are statistically significant, but it is not clear that these groupings explain much of the total variation in longevity. This is analogous to running a regression of longevity on an indicator for race and getting a very high t-statistic and a very low R^2.

Focusing on average differences across groups tends to suggest that all members of a given group experience the average longevity of that group. This need not be the case. It would be useful to know the probability that individuals in each group have a money's worth less than 1 in addition to the average money's worth for the group as a whole. If mortality differences across groups do not account for a large proportion of total variation in longevity, then these probabilities will cluster near 50 percent despite the large average differences across groups. If the data used in this study do not permit such calculations, then clearly the role of within-group heterogeneity in longevity is an important direction for future research.

My second criticism pertains to the discussion, although ultimately not the use, of the money's worth rather than an expected utility measure. Two arguments are made for not relying on an expected utility calculation. First, the magnitude of the gains depends on the utility function, and the utility function differs across groups. Second, some schemes (such as a period-certain payout) might pay beneficiaries, rather than the annuitant, and these payments may differ in their utility from annuity payments. However, neither of these problems is avoided by assuming $U(W) = W$ and that bequests have either no value or full value. Of course, the choice of a utility function involves a degree of arbitrariness, but what (apart from transparency) justifies the assumption of risk neutrality? The money's worth is a natural starting point, but the analysis should be expanded to include reasonable choices for expected utility and the utility of bequests and to use measures of equivalent variation as the metrics for comparison.

The analysis in the chapter suggests that equity arguments associated with differential mortality across groups could rationalize incomplete annuitization if it is constrained to be done with a single life table. There are other factors that also make partial annuitization a more viable option than is commonly appreciated. The first is that there are diminishing returns to annuitization. Once there is a basic benefit that is guaranteed in every period of life, then, at the margin, failing to annuitize additional dollars reduces expected utility by very little. This is important because the benefits provided by Social Security are far more than are needed to simply keep pensioners out of poverty. The second is that individuals who have higher ex post longevity are, in the grand scheme of things, the lucky ones. Another year of life means another year of leisure. If the social welfare function that aggregates individual utilities is concave in total lifetime utility, then this suggests that failing to provide complete annuitization results in little loss of social welfare.

There is a perception in policy circles that a move to individual accounts would imply lower annuitization of retirement income, with some welfare costs. This chapter provides important evidence and insights that suggest that there may also be less desirable equity consequences of full annuitization. The presumed inability of a private annuity market to match the annuity currently provided by the Social Security system is less of an impediment to reform than is commonly believed. Further, although this analysis is presented in the context of Social Security reform, it is clear that the unintended redistribution across groups is relevant in any system that uses a single life table in paying benefits, especially a life table that is invariant to lifetime income. This chapter's analysis is therefore relevant even if the current pay-as-you-go system is not substantially reformed in the coming years.

Discussion Summary

Martin Feldstein said it was important to recognize that even though the discounted values of most bequests in this paper are between $6,200 and $10,200, these numbers are consistent with bequests of $51,000 for a forty-year-old and $193,000 for a fifty-five-year-old. Furthermore, Feldstein mentioned taxation of benefits as a potential factor in the redistribution between different education groups. *Jeffrey R. Brown* said that his aim was to examine a simple system in which a certain percentage of income is placed in an account and at retirement the balance of the account is annuitized. It is certainly true that taxes on benefits and subsidies for contributions could offset the mortality differences across different groups. He pointed out that if reducing the effect of differential mortality is an important goal, then this paper describes the magnitude of the problem that must be overcome by other features.

John B. Shoven believed that there is strong social interest in mandatory annuitization. A large percentage of expenses at the end of life have an ability-to-pay component such as Medicaid. Annuitized income is a better approximation of lifetime resources, and annuitization alleviates the moral hazard problem caused by depleting assets to purchase other goods while using Medicaid to cover medical expenses.

The effects of differential mortality are exacerbated by the correlation between income and differential mortality. *Jeffrey B. Liebman* stated that because people with higher incomes have longer life expectancies, the rate that balances the system is closer to the actuarially fair rate for the wealthy. He wondered whether the calculations in this paper take this factor into account and how much accounting for this would increase the difference between groups in the results.

Angus Deaton was concerned about the quality of the estimated mortality rates. Mortality experience has changed significantly since 1980; for example, the mortality for young white males has risen dramatically. Moreover, the results may be biased because part of the effect of socioeconomic status on mortality is caused by voluntary lifestyle choices such as smoking, drinking, and regular exercise. While the National Longitudinal Mortality Survey income measure is not ideal, it does have predictive power conditional on education. Consequently, the effect of lifetime income on mortality is underestimated. The author was open to any suggestions for eliminating these problems and acknowledged that mortality experiences change significantly over time. However, the absence of data capable of addressing these issues seems to be a major stumbling block.

Peter Orszag felt that the interpretation of the results for Hispanics is ambiguous. He noted that Jeffrey Liebman had said that there were important differences between the mortality experiences of foreign-born and U.S.-born Hispanics. To the extent that foreign-born Hispanics have longer life expectancies and are also less likely to be covered by the Social Security system, the interpretation of the results for Hispanics is unclear.

Courtney Coile suggested one possible remedy for groups hurt by mandatory annuitization. Offering people different annuity options might allow people to undo the transfers between groups that may be undesirable. While choice is a possibility, the author thought choice would lead to adverse selection within the system. For example, if individuals expect to die early, they might choose a period-certain annuity instead of a straight life annuity.

Steven C. Goss mentioned the relationship between disability and mortality as an important factor in the analysis. In studies that focus only on retirement benefits, it is important to use mortality estimates that exclude the disabled from the analysis. This should reduce the dispersion between groups.

Stephen Zeldes questioned the measure of redistribution between groups, positing one group that lives ten years and another group that lives for twenty years. If both groups have equal consumption in each year, then there will be redistribution from group 1 to group 2. However, neutral distribution would imply that the first group's consumption level would be approximately half the second group's consumption level. The author said that there were two ways to approach this: either to equate expected values or to equate incomes. He noted that if the correct measure of income redistribution is conditional on being alive, then the conclusions will be very different.

Eytan Sheshinski indicated that this problem is essentially the standard trade-off between ex post and ex ante efficiency. Using one annuity table for all risk classes (pooling) leads to ex post inefficiency. At the same time, pooling provides valuable ex ante insurance across risk classes. If everyone can only purchase one annuity, the fraction of wealth that a person will want to annuitize depends on the price of the annuity and the risk class of the individual.

Appendix
Estimating Life Tables That Reflect Socioeconomic Differences In Mortality

Jeffrey R. Brown, Jeffrey B. Liebman, and Joshua Pollet

Three of the papers in this volume (Brown, Feldstein-Liebman, and Liebman) make use of a new set of life tables that differentiate mortality experience by sex, race, and education level.[1] This appendix describes the methodology used to develop these life tables and presents the estimates themselves.

The underlying data for these life tables come from the National Longitudinal Mortality Survey (NLMS). The NLMS was created by matching individuals who were in the Current Population Survey (CPS) between 1979 and 1985 to death records from the National Death Index (NDI). This match occurred in 1989. The total sample population from the CPS data is 1,046,959, and by 1989 the NDI had death records for 69,385 of the individuals in the sample population. Since the earliest data are from 1979 and the match to mortality records occurred in 1989, each person in the sample was followed for a maximum of ten years (Rogot et al. 1992).

Because the CPS contains detailed demographic information for each sample member, this matched data set can be used to generate mortality estimates that take into account a wide variety of demographic characteristics. However, since the probability of death at a given age is small, especially at younger ages, we limited our categories to ones representing race,

Jeffrey R. Brown is an assistant professor of public policy at the John F. Kennedy School of Government, Harvard University, and a faculty research fellow at the National Bureau of Economic Research. Jeffrey B. Liebman is associate professor of public policy at the John F. Kennedy School of Government, Harvard University, and a faculty research fellow at the National Bureau of Economic Research. Joshua Pollet is a graduate student in the department of economics at Harvard University and a research assistant at the National Bureau of Economic Research.

1. Because we have continued to refine these mortality tables over time, the three papers use slightly different versions of these mortality tables.

ethnicity, sex, and education level. We chose these characteristics because, unlike household income or marital status, these are largely predetermined and invariant to change at the time an individual enters the labor force.[2,3] In particular, we divided the data into six race-ethnicity-gender categories: non-Hispanic white males, non-Hispanic black males, and Hispanic males (table A.1), and non-Hispanic white females, non-Hispanic black females, and Hispanic females (table A.2). The number of education groupings for which we could produce reliable estimates varied by race and ethnicity. For white males and females, we developed separate life tables for individuals who did not complete high school ("less than high school," or LTHS), who completed high school but did not complete a four-year college degree (HS+), and who completed four years of college (COL). For black males and females, we did not have a sufficient number of observations to reliably estimate separate life tables for individuals with a college degree. Therefore, the Feldstein-Liebman and Liebman papers (chapters 7 and 1, respectively) used two education subgroups for blacks: individuals who did not complete high school ("LTHS"); and high school graduates, including those who completed college ("HS+"). Brown (chapter 10) used a slightly different approach. For black high school graduates who did not complete college, he estimated a life table that corresponded to that population. Then, for black college graduates he assumed that the ratio of mortality between black college graduates and other blacks was the same as the ratio for whites. The Hispanics samples were not large enough to develop reliable estimates with any variation by education level. Thus, we generate a total of twelve different life tables (six for whites, four for blacks, and two for Hispanics).

The NLMS data file that is available to researchers outside of the U.S. government contains roughly half the observations in the full NLMS. This sample was not sufficient for us to produce precise estimates for all of our groups, so instead we used summary tabulations produced by a Census Bureau employee from the full NLMS that contained nonparametric mortality rates for each age-by-sex-by-ethnicity-by-education group cell from age twenty-five to eighty-four. For example, the nonparametric sample estimate for the mortality rate of sixty-five-year-old college-educated white males is the number of sixty-five-year-old college-educated white males in the NLMS matched to a death record from the NDI before age sixty-six,

---

2. In addition to the demographic variables, the NLMS includes a CPS-based measure of annual family income. While recent research by Deaton and Paxson (2001) has shown that income has an impact on mortality even when race and education are controlled for, we chose not to incorporate income into our analysis. It is difficult to establish causality when examining correlations between contemporaneous income and mortality, because of the possibility that negative health shocks affect both measures.

3. Some individuals do, of course, obtain additional education after age twenty-five, the initial age used in our analysis.

Table 10A.1   Relative Mortality Rates for Males Aged 25–100 by Race, Ethnicity, and Education: Ratio of Subgroup Male Mortality to General Population Male Mortality

	White			Black		Hispanic
Age	LTHS	HS+	COL	LTHS	HS+	All
25	1.038637	0.880302	0.719848	3.955698	1.655740	2.734350
26	1.056137	0.881084	0.707339	3.913315	1.673879	2.646963
27	1.073668	0.882054	0.694940	3.868796	1.691346	2.558439
28	1.091155	0.883218	0.682718	3.822210	1.708028	2.469093
29	1.108517	0.884582	0.670741	3.773642	1.723815	2.379255
30	1.125676	0.886149	0.659077	3.723197	1.738603	2.289268
31	1.142551	0.887921	0.647796	3.670994	1.752293	2.199477
32	1.159065	0.889897	0.636961	3.617167	1.764794	2.110232
33	1.175142	0.892075	0.626637	3.561860	1.776026	2.021876
34	1.190709	0.894452	0.616884	3.505232	1.785916	1.934746
35	1.205698	0.897022	0.607757	3.447445	1.794407	1.849165
36	1.220047	0.899778	0.599307	3.388671	1.801450	1.765438
37	1.233700	0.902711	0.591579	3.329082	1.807010	1.683851
38	1.246605	0.905811	0.584612	3.268853	1.811065	1.604665
39	1.258721	0.909067	0.578441	3.208154	1.813603	1.528113
40	1.270009	0.912466	0.573091	3.147154	1.814625	1.454403
41	1.280443	0.915995	0.568585	3.086016	1.814145	1.383712
42	1.290000	0.919640	0.564936	3.024894	1.812183	1.316186
43	1.298666	0.923387	0.562155	2.963932	1.808773	1.251945
44	1.306431	0.927220	0.560244	2.903267	1.803954	1.191078
45	1.313294	0.931124	0.559202	2.843021	1.797774	1.133645
46	1.319259	0.935084	0.559022	2.783308	1.790286	1.079683
47	1.324334	0.939085	0.559694	2.724226	1.781547	1.029204
48	1.328532	0.943113	0.561204	2.665864	1.771621	0.982198
49	1.331870	0.947151	0.563533	2.608297	1.760572	0.938636
50	1.334368	0.951187	0.566664	2.551589	1.748464	0.898471
51	1.336049	0.955206	0.570571	2.495793	1.735367	0.861644
52	1.336936	0.959194	0.575233	2.440950	1.721345	0.828080
53	1.337057	0.963139	0.580622	2.387094	1.706465	0.797696
54	1.336438	0.967026	0.586713	2.334248	1.690792	0.770403
55	1.335107	0.970844	0.593479	2.282425	1.674387	0.746102
56	1.333091	0.974580	0.600891	2.231633	1.657312	0.724694
57	1.330417	0.978223	0.608922	2.181873	1.639623	0.706073
58	1.327113	0.981759	0.617543	2.133139	1.621376	0.690137
59	1.323204	0.985179	0.626728	2.085421	1.602620	0.676780
60	1.318716	0.988471	0.636447	2.038704	1.583406	0.665899
61	1.313671	0.991622	0.646674	1.992969	1.563777	0.657391
62	1.308093	0.994622	0.657382	1.948194	1.543777	0.651157
63	1.302003	0.997459	0.668543	1.904357	1.523443	0.647102
64	1.295420	1.000122	0.680130	1.861430	1.502812	0.645132
65	1.288362	1.002599	0.692117	1.819387	1.481916	0.645157
66	1.280847	1.004878	0.704476	1.778200	1.460786	0.647093
67	1.272891	1.006948	0.717182	1.737841	1.439451	0.650857
68	1.264506	1.008797	0.730207	1.698282	1.417935	0.656370

(*continued*)

Table 10A.1   (continued)

Age	White			Black		Hispanic
	LTHS	HS+	COL	LTHS	HS+	All
69	1.255708	1.010413	0.743524	1.659495	1.396264	0.663559
70	1.246509	1.011784	0.757105	1.621453	1.374459	0.672350
71	1.236920	1.012898	0.770923	1.584131	1.352542	0.682675
72	1.226954	1.013745	0.784948	1.547505	1.330532	0.694468
73	1.216621	1.014312	0.799153	1.511553	1.308451	0.707664
74	1.205934	1.014589	0.813506	1.476254	1.286316	0.722201
75	1.194905	1.014568	0.827979	1.441593	1.264148	0.738019
76	1.183546	1.014240	0.842540	1.407556	1.241967	0.755056
77	1.171874	1.013599	0.857159	1.374131	1.219795	0.773252
78	1.159905	1.012640	0.871804	1.341313	1.197656	0.792549
79	1.147658	1.011361	0.886445	1.309099	1.175575	0.812886
80	1.135157	1.009765	0.901052	1.277492	1.153581	0.834201
81	1.122428	1.007857	0.915595	1.246500	1.131705	0.856433
82	1.109503	1.005646	0.930048	1.216136	1.109984	0.879519
83	1.096419	1.003150	0.944385	1.186421	1.088458	0.903395
84	1.083219	1.000391	0.958587	1.157381	1.067174	0.927993
85	1.069955	0.997400	0.972637	1.129050	1.046183	0.953247
86	1.056685	0.994215	0.986525	1.101471	1.025545	0.979089
87	1.043478	0.990886	1.000248	1.074694	1.005327	1.005450
88	1.030413	0.987474	1.013813	1.048778	0.985603	1.032261
89	1.017579	0.984053	1.027238	1.023793	0.966457	1.059453
90	1.005079	0.980710	1.040552	0.999819	0.947983	1.086959
91	0.993029	0.977549	1.053801	0.976945	0.930286	1.114714
92	0.981558	0.974689	1.067045	0.955273	0.913482	1.142657
93	0.970812	0.972269	1.080364	0.934917	0.897697	1.170727
94	0.960950	0.970445	1.093856	0.916000	0.883071	1.198870
95	0.952149	0.969394	1.107638	0.898660	0.869755	1.227032
96	0.944598	0.969307	1.121844	0.883042	0.857911	1.255159
97	0.938498	0.970394	1.136623	0.869302	0.847711	1.283189
98	0.934057	0.972871	1.152125	0.857596	0.839330	1.311045
99	0.931479	0.976952	1.168491	0.848078	0.832939	1.338615
100	0.930953	0.982838	1.185832	0.840889	0.828698	1.365729

Note: See text for explanation of abbreviations and makeup of education subgroups.

divided by the total number of sixty-five-year-old college-educated white males in the NLMS sample. These tabulations were generously provided to us by Hugh Richards and have been used previously in Richards and Barry (1998).

There are several reasons that we do not use these nonparametric estimates directly. First, the sample sizes for some cells are very small, and therefore some single year of age mortality probabilities have very large standard errors. Consequently, estimates are often not a monotonic function of age for a particular race-gender-education classification, suggesting that some smoothing would be desirable. Second, we needed to construct

Table 10A.2   Relative Mortality Rates for Females Aged 25–100 by Race, Ethnicity, and Education: Ratio of Subgroup Female Mortality to General Population Female Mortality

Age	White			Black		Hispanic
	LTHS	HS+	COL	LTHS	HS+	All
25	1.131830	1.042855	0.864270	2.649466	0.711158	1.185041
26	1.138879	1.033564	0.853033	2.681900	0.759445	1.166252
27	1.146161	1.024175	0.841630	2.713179	0.808499	1.146999
23	1.153650	1.014734	0.830117	2.743030	0.858107	1.127352
29	1.161315	1.005292	0.818552	2.771177	0.908037	1.107389
30	1.169120	0.995900	0.807000	2.797344	0.958041	1.087195
31	1.177026	0.986615	0.795528	2.821258	1.007857	1.066864
32	1.184991	0.977492	0.784209	2.842658	1.057211	1.046494
33	1.192969	0.968588	0.773113	2.861297	1.105824	1.026188
34	1.200911	0.959962	0.762316	2.876947	1.153415	1.006053
35	1.208766	0.951668	0.751889	2.889405	1.199706	0.986194
36	1.216484	0.943759	0.741903	2.898496	1.244427	0.966718
37	1.224014	0.936286	0.732426	2.904078	1.287320	0.947730
38	1.231305	0.929294	0.723523	2.906042	1.328144	0.929328
39	1.238307	0.922825	0.715251	2.904318	1.366680	0.911606
40	1.244973	0.916912	0.707664	2.898870	1.402733	0.894650
41	1.251260	0.911586	0.700807	2.889702	1.436135	0.878538
42	1.257127	0.906868	0.694717	2.876854	1.466749	0.863336
43	1.262538	0.902776	0.689426	2.860399	1.494467	0.849103
44	1.267460	0.899317	0.684956	2.840443	1.519212	0.835883
45	1.271865	0.896495	0.681321	2.817122	1.540938	0.823713
46	1.275732	0.894306	0.678527	2.790594	1.559631	0.812615
47	1.279043	0.892741	0.676576	2.761040	1.575300	0.802604
48	1.281783	0.891785	0.675459	2.728658	1.587985	0.793680
49	1.283944	0.891419	0.675163	2.693658	1.597746	0.785839
50	1.285521	0.891619	0.675669	2.656258	1.604664	0.779064
51	1.286514	0.892359	0.676953	2.616684	1.608839	0.773333
52	1.286924	0.893609	0.678987	2.575160	1.610383	0.768617
53	1.286758	0.895336	0.681741	2.531909	1.609422	0.764879
54	1.286022	0.897507	0.685181	2.487152	1.606090	0.762081
55	1.284729	0.900087	0.689271	2.441099	1.600527	0.760178
56	1.282888	0.903041	0.693974	2.393957	1.592875	0.759124
57	1.280515	0.906332	0.699253	2.345918	1.583281	0.758872
58	1.277623	0.909925	0.705068	2.297165	1.571888	0.759371
59	1.274228	0.913786	0.711383	2.247871	1.558841	0.760572
60	1.270345	0.917878	0.718159	2.198195	1.544278	0.762424
61	1.265990	0.922170	0.725359	2.148283	1.528335	0.764878
62	1.261180	0.926627	0.732947	2.098270	1.511143	0.767885
63	1.255929	0.931220	0.740887	2.048281	1.492826	0.771397
64	1.250253	0.935917	0.749147	1.998427	1.473503	0.775369
65	1.244169	0.940690	0.757692	1.948808	1.453286	0.779756
66	1.237690	0.945511	0.766492	1.899516	1.432281	0.784515
67	1.230832	0.950354	0.775515	1.850632	1.410588	0.789605
68	1.223608	0.955194	0.784734	1.802229	1.388299	0.794988

(*continued*)

Table 10A.2   (continued)

	White			Black		Hispanic
Age	LTHS	HS+	COL	LTHS	HS+	All
69	1.216033	0.960008	0.794121	1.754371	1.365503	0.800626
70	1.208121	0.964774	0.803648	1.707115	1.342281	0.806484
71	1.199884	0.969470	0.813292	1.660513	1.318708	0.812530
72	1.191338	0.974077	0.823027	1.614610	1.294857	0.818731
73	1.182495	0.978578	0.832833	1.569445	1.270794	0.825059
74	1.173370	0.982955	0.842686	1.525054	1.246581	0.831488
75	1.163978	0.987194	0.852568	1.481470	1.222277	0.837990
76	1.154333	0.991282	0.862458	1.438720	1.197938	0.844545
77	1.144453	0.995206	0.872340	1.396832	1.173615	0.851130
78	1.134354	0.998956	0.882198	1.355828	1.149360	0.857728
79	1.124055	1.002525	0.892016	1.315733	1.125221	0.864320
80	1.113577	1.005906	0.901782	1.276566	1.101244	0.870894
81	1.102942	1.009098	0.911485	1.238350	1.077476	0.877438
82	1.092175	1.012098	0.921115	1.201104	1.053961	0.883943
83	1.081303	1.014909	0.930667	1.164851	1.030744	0.890404
84	1.070359	1.017537	0.940135	1.129611	1.007872	0.896818
85	1.059375	1.019993	0.949520	1.095409	0.985389	0.903188
86	1.048391	1.022291	0.958823	1.062268	0.963344	0.909521
87	1.037452	1.024452	0.968053	1.030215	0.941787	0.915827
88	1.026606	1.026501	0.977222	0.999281	0.920770	0.922125
89	1.015911	1.028472	0.986350	0.969499	0.900349	0.928440
90	1.005432	1.030411	0.995464	0.940908	0.880586	0.934805
91	0.995245	1.032370	1.004602	0.913552	0.861547	0.941266
92	0.985438	1.034420	1.013814	0.887483	0.843308	0.947881
93	0.976114	1.036646	1.023168	0.862764	0.825954	0.954725
94	0.967396	1.039158	1.032753	0.839468	0.809585	0.961894
95	0.959433	1.042093	1.042685	0.817688	0.794317	0.969514
96	0.952405	1.045627	1.053121	0.797536	0.780291	0.977746
97	0.946537	1.049985	1.064264	0.779154	0.767676	0.986801
98	0.942108	1.055461	1.076390	0.762723	0.756685	0.996955
99	0.939474	1.062435	1.089863	0.748476	0.747586	1.008572
100	0.939091	1.071408	1.105174	0.736714	0.740721	1.022134

Note: See text for explanation of abbreviations and makeup of education subgroups.

out-of-sample estimates of age-specific mortality rates, because mortality estimates for people above age eighty-four are required for our analysis. Third, this methodology yields data for a period mortality table describing the mortality experience of people alive during the NLMS. In contrast, our research projects required cohort life tables representative of people born in a given year.

To smooth the data, we estimated a nonlinear model for age-specific mortality separately for each group. With the proper choice of three parameters, the Gompertz-Makeham survival function can be applied from age twenty-five almost to the end of life (Jordan 1991). The Gompertz-Makeham formula is usually written as

$$l_x = \frac{l_0}{g} s^x g^{c^x} \, ,$$

where x is age, l_x is the number of people in the population alive at age x, and l_0 is the number of people in the population alive at birth. The parameters to be estimated are c, g, and s. Note that if l_0 is normalized to 1, then l_x is the cumulative probability of survival at age x, and we can define q_x, the mortality rate at age x, as

$$q_x = \frac{l_x - l_{x+1}}{l_x} \, .$$

Then, rearranging the Gompertz-Makeham formula and solving for q_x yields the equation that we estimate using nonlinear least squares:

$$q_x = 1 - sg^{(c^{x+1} - c^x)} \, .$$

We estimate the parameters in this equation separately for each of our twelve groups described above. By substituting the nonlinear least squares estimates of c, g, and s into the equation above, fitted estimates of mortality rates for a particular group at age x are formed. This approach guarantees that the fitted mortality rates are a monotonic function of age. Figure A.1 shows the fitted mortality rates and original nonparametric estimates for two of our twelve groups. The fitted values track the original data quite closely.[4]

As we mentioned above, the estimates from the NLMS are period estimates. Our basic approach to producing cohort life tables is to assume that the ratio of age-specific mortality in our disaggregated groups to more aggregated age-specific mortality rates stays constant over time. Then, to generate disaggregated cohort life tables, we can simply apply a ratio of period mortality rates from our data to the more aggregated cohort life tables published by the Social Security Administration or Census Bureau. For example, the cohort age-specific mortality estimates for white female college graduates could be constructed as

$$q_{x, \text{ white female}}^{\text{cohort, college graduate}} = q_{x, \text{ female}}^{\text{cohort}} \left(\frac{q_{x, \text{ white female}}^{\text{fitted, college graduate}}}{q_{x, \text{ female}}^{\text{fitted}}} \right) \, .$$

---

4. This is true for the other ten groups as well.

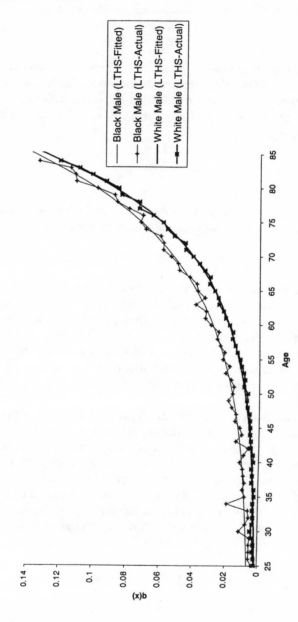

Fig. A.1 Comparison of fitted and nonparametric estimates of mortality rates

The assumption that relative mortality rates stay constant over time is clearly a strong one, though there is some evidence, for example, that differences in mortality rates between socioeconomic groups were not shrinking in the late twentieth century and may actually have been widening (Pappas et al. 1993; Preston and Taubman 1994). Moreover, even if relative mortality rates among demographic subgroups remain constant, changes in the share of the population within each demographic group could alter the relationship between a subgroup's mortality ratio and the aggregate ratio.

Because there has been such significant change in the educational attainment of Americans over the past century, we make one further adjustment to our data. Specifically, we produce aggregate mortality tables from our data weighting the various subgroups to represent the distribution of education rates (within sex-by-race cells) for thirty- to thirty-four-year-olds in the March 1999 CPS. Ratios of subgroup mortality to these aggregates will therefore be appropriate for use with aggregate cohort life tables for cohorts born in the late 1960s and for other cohorts with a similar distribution of educational attainment.[5]

Figure A.2 illustrates the impact of this adjustment for white males. The dashed line displays our unadjusted fitted estimates, which lie almost exactly on top of the published Vital Statistics period life table for white males in 1989–91. The dark line shows our estimate of aggregate white male mortality under the counterfactual assumption that the educational shares of the population had remained constant over time at rates like those for recent cohorts. Because recent cohorts have a larger share of individuals in the high-education (and therefore low-mortality) groups than the older cohorts in the NLMS did, this reweighted aggregate estimate shows lower mortality rates than the estimates based on the actual period data do.

Table A.1 contains the estimated ratios of subgroup age-specific mortality rates to aggregate mortality rates for males. Table A.2 contains the identical data for females.

One last issue requires discussion. Table A.2 indicates that mortality estimates for college-educated white males above age eighty-seven are higher than mortality rates for white males with less education at similar ages. A similar phenomenon appears at age ninety among white females. Because our summary tabulations from the NLMS do not contain data for ages above 84, the fitted estimates for ages 85 to 100 are heavily dependent on the relatively noisy raw data at slightly younger ages. Hence, it is possible that this crossover in the mortality estimates is simply the product

---

5. We used the late 1960s birth cohorts in creating our weights because they were the youngest for whom we could safely assume that nearly all members of the cohort had completed their educations.

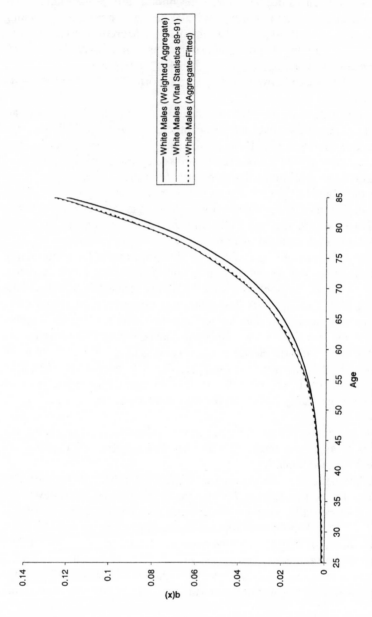

Legend:
White Males (Weighted Aggregate)
White Males (Vital Statistics 89-91)
White Males (Aggregate-Fitted)

Fig. A.2   The impact of adjusting mortality rates for changes in education shares

of measurement error in the NLMS data combined with the functional form assumptions implicit in the Gompertz-Makeham formula. However, it is also possible that the crossover is a real phenomenon. In particular, if it is assumed that there exists a maximum age of survival, then at some very high age we would necessarily observe a crossover.[6]

References

Deaton, Angus, and Cristina Paxson. 2001. Mortality, education, income and inequality among American cohorts. In *Themes in the economics of aging,* ed. David A. Wise, 129–70. Chicago: University of Chicago Press.

Jordan, C. W. 1991. *Life contingencies.* 2d. Chicago: Society of Actuaries.

Pappas, Gregory, Susan Queen, Wilbur Hadden, and Gail Fisher. 1993. The increasing disparity in mortality between socioeconomic groups in the United States: 1960 and 1986. *New England Journal of Medicine* 329 (2): 103–9.

Preston, Samuel H., Irma T. Elo, Ira Rosenwaike, and Mark Hill. 1996. African-American mortality at older ages: Results of a matching study. *Demography* 33 (2): 193–209.

Preston, Samuel, and Paul Taubman. 1994. Socioeconomic differences in adult mortality and health status. In *Demography of aging,* ed. Linda G. Martin and Samuel H. Preston, 279–318. Washington, D.C.: National Academy Press.

Richards, Hugh, and Ronald Barry. 1998. U.S. life tables for 1990 by sex, race, and education. *Journal of Forensic Economics* 11 (1): 9–26.

Rogot, Eugene, et al. 1992. *A mortality study of 1.3 million persons by demographic, social and economic factors: 1979–1985 follow-up.* Bethesda, Md.: National Institutes of Health and National Heart, Lung, and Blood Institute.

---

6. See Preston et al. (1996) for a discussion of the racial crossover in mortality.

Contributors

Jeffrey R. Brown
John F. Kennedy School of
  Government
Harvard University
79 John F. Kennedy Street
Cambridge, MA 02138

Gary Burtless
The Brookings Institution
1775 Massachusetts Avenue NW
Washington, DC 20036

Julia Lynn Coronado
Board of Governors of the Federal
  Reserve System
20th and Constitution Avenues NW
Washington, DC 20551

Angus Deaton
347 Wallace Hall
Woodrow Wilson School
Princeton University
Princeton, NJ 08544-1013

James E. Duggan
Office of Economic Policy
Department of the Treasury
1500 Pennsylvania Avenue NW
Washington, DC 20220

Martin Feldstein
National Bureau of Economic
  Research
1050 Massachusetts Avenue
Cambridge, MA 02138

Don Fullerton
Department of Economics
University of Texas
Austin, TX 78712-1173

Thomas Glass
Glass & Company
515 Congress Avenue
Suite 1900
Austin, TX 78701

Jagadeesh Gokhale
Research Department
Federal Reserve Bank of Cleveland
East 6th & Superior
Cleveland, OH 44116

Stephen C. Goss
Office of the Chief Actuary
Social Security Administration
Room 700 Altmeyer Building
6401 Security Boulevard
Baltimore, MD 21255

Pierre-Olivier Gourinchas
Department of Economics
331 Fisher Hall
Princeton University
Princeton, NJ 08544

R. Glenn Hubbard
Graduate School of Business
609 Uris Hall
Columbia University
3022 Broadway
New York, NY 10027

Laurence J. Kotlikoff
Department of Economics
Boston University
270 Bay State Road
Boston, MA 02215

Jeffrey B. Liebman
John F. Kennedy School of
    Government
Harvard University
79 JFK Street
Cambridge, MA 02138

Kathleen McGarry
Department of Economics
University of California, Los Angeles
405 Hilgard Avenue
Los Angeles, CA 90095-1477

Bruce D. Meyer
Department of Economics
Northwestern University
2003 Sheridan Road
Evanston, IL 60208

Christina Paxson
316 Wallace Hall
Woodrow Wilson School
Princeton University
Princeton, NJ 08544-1013

Joshua Pollet
National Bureau of Economic
    Research
1050 Massachusetts Avenue
Cambridge, MA 02138

James Poterba
Department of Economics, E52-350
Massachusetts Institute of Technology
50 Memorial Drive
Cambridge, MA 02142-1347

Elena Ranguelova
Lehman Brothers
3 World Financial Center
New York, NY 10285

Andrew A. Samwick
Department of Economics
Dartmouth College
6106 Rockefeller Hall
Hanover, NH 03755-3514

John B. Shoven
National Bureau of Economic
    Research
30 Alta Road
Stanford, CA 94305-8715

Jonathan Skinner
Department of Economics
6160 Rockefeller Hall
Dartmouth College
Hanover, NH 03755

Kent Smetters
The Wharton School
University of Pennsylvania
3641 Locust Walk, CPC-302
Philadelphia, PA 19104-6218

Jan Walliser
Fiscal Affairs Department
International Monetary Fund
700 19th Street NW
Washington, DC 20431

David W. Wilcox
Assistant Secretary, Economic Policy
Department of the Treasury,
    Room 3454
1500 Pennsylvania Avenue NW
Washington, DC 20220

David A. Wise
National Bureau of Economic
    Research
1050 Massachusetts Avenue
Cambridge, MA 02138

Author Index

Subject Index

rity on, 145; factors reducing and increasing, 144–45; in life-cycle model without bequests, 6; under permanent income hypothesis, 117–25; preretirement increase in, 145; programs reducing, 144

Inequality of wealth: annuitization and Social Security increases, 111–12; role of inheritance and Social Security in, 104–6, 111

Internal rates of return: under alternative OASI policies, 243–445; calculation for individuals, 292; comparison of mixed plan and PAYGO Social Security, 300, 305; comparison of PRAs and PAYGO Social Security, 293–96; as income redistribution, 19–21, 24, 26–28; paid by OASI, 224–25t, 230–31, 243; of PRAs with lower return compared to Social Security, 307, 310–11

Investment: model of uncertain returns to, 375–77; risks in proposed PAYGO plus investment-based system, 306–16

Life expectancy: conditional, 409–10; indifferences for men and women in United States, 21, 403; of higher-income individuals, 16; relation to educational levels, 215

Lifetime net tax rates: by benefit quintiles, 222–23t, 229–30; under existing OASI system, 229–30; under OASI alternative policies, 242–43

Mortality: differences across socioeconoic groups, 18, 403–6, 437; indifferential, 407–10; impact on redistribution from Social Security, 30–31; offset to effects on redistribution, 38; race and ethnic differences in rates of, 404; rates among Hispanics, 404–5; rates for females compared to males, 403

Mortality rates: assumptions in extension of tables, 190; factors influencing, 212–18; income-differentiated, 157–59; for males and females by race, ethnicity, and education, 447–51

Moynihan reform proposals, 165t, 170–82, 202–3

National Commission on Retirement Policy (NCRP) reform proposal, 165–68, 173–76, 202–5

National Longitudinal Mortality Survey (NLMS), 18, 404–5, 407–10, 447–48

Net present values: comparison between PRAs and PAYGO Social Security system, 293–96; comparison of mixed plan and PAYGO Social Security, 300, 305; of PRAs with lower return compared to Social Security, 307, 310–11

Normal retirement age (NRA): under proposed OASI alternative policy, 233, 240, 249, 251; when disabled worker reaches, 200

Old-Age, Survivors' and Disability Insurance (OASDI): insurance components financed by OASDI tax, 42; predicted rise in payroll tax, 1–2, 4–5; treatment of postwar Americans, 221–31

Old-Age and Survivors' Insurance (OASI): aids poor postwar Americans, 229; effect of choice of discount rate on projections for, 241–42; financial dilemma, 231–33; impact of reforms on average benefits, 249–51; impact of reforms on lifetime net tax rates, 235–41; impact of reforms on wealth tax rates, 245–49; as insurance policy, 207, 228; internal rates of return paid by, 224–25, 230–31; 224–25t, 230–31; lifetime net tax rates, 222–23, 229–30; present value imbalance of, 231–32; wealth tax rates levied by, 226–27, 231

Old-Age and Survivors' Insurance (OASI) alternative policies: accelerated increase in NRA (3), 235, 240, 245, 249; CPI as nominal wage index (4), 233, 249, 251; current benefit formula with growth of PIA bend points (7), 234, 240, 251; under current PAYGO system, 208; cuts in OASDI benefits (2), 233, 245, 249; different impacts on lifetime net tax rates, 235–41; effect on internal rates of return, 243; elimination of ceiling on taxable earnings (8), 234, 240, 251; implicit wealth tax rates under, 245–49; increased years used to computed AIME (10), 234, 241, 251; maintenance of current benefit formula (5), 234, 251; OASI payroll tax increase (1), 233, 242, 245, 249; stabilize real per capita benefits (6), 234, 240, 242, 243, 245, 251; tax collection without earnings ceiling (9), 234, 240, 242–45, 249